GOLIATH

ALSO BY THE AUTHOR

Republican Gomorrah

GOLIATH

Life and Loathing in Greater Israel

MAX BLUMENTHAL

NATION
BOOKS
New York

Published by
Nation Books, A Member of the Perseus Books Group
116 East 16th Street, 8th Floor
New York, NY 10003

Nation Books is a co-publishing venture of the Nation Institute and the Perseus
Books Group.

Books published by Nation Books are available at special discounts for
bulk purchases in the United States by corporations, institutions, and other
organizations. For more information, please contact the Special Markets
Department at the Perseus Books Group, 2300 Chestnut Street, Suite 200,
Philadelphia, PA 19103, or call (800) 255-1514, or e-mail special.markets@
perseusbooks.com.

Editorial production by Lori Hobkirk at the Book Factory.
Designed by Timm Bryson.

The Israeli-Palestine map was created by Mike Morgenfeld. The map of
depopulated Palestine towns and villages of 1948 is a simplified version of one
compiled by Dr. Salman Abu Sitta, founder and president of Palestine Land
Society, in London; permission has been granted for use. The map of the West
Bank is a simplified version of one created by B'Tselem. Permission has been
granted for use, and they can be found at http://www.btselem.org. The Gaza
Strip map was created by Mike Morgenfeld. Several names throughout the text
have been changed.

Library of Congress Cataloging-in-Publication Data

Blumenthal, Max, 1977- author.
  Goliath : life and loathing in greater Israel / Max Blumenthal.
    pages cm
  Includes bibliographical references and index.
  ISBN 978-1-56858-634-2 (hardback)
    1. Arab-Israeli conflict—1993- 2. Israel—Politics and government—1993- 3.
Palestinian Arabs—Government policy—Israel. 4. Blumenthal, Max—Travel—
Israel. I. Title.
  DS119.76.B58 2013
  956.9405'4—dc23
                            2013026422
E-Book ISBN: 978-1-56859-972-5

10 9 8 7 6 5 4 3 2 1

In memory of Akiva Orr
(1931–2013)

"The people don't like to be conquered, sir, and so they will not be. Free men cannot start a war, but once it is started, they can fight on in defeat. Herd men, followers of a leader, cannot do that, and so it is always the herd men who win battles and the free men who win wars. You will find that is so."

—MAYOR ORDEN, FROM *THE MOON IS DOWN,*
BY JOHN STEINBECK

"Israel is a normal country that is not normal."

—ISRAELI SUPREME COURT JUSTICE
ELYAKIM RUBINSTEIN

CONTENTS

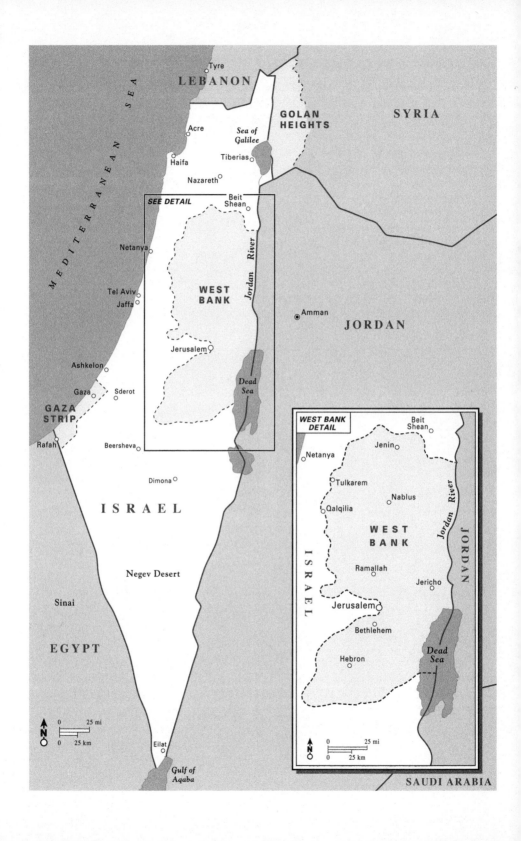

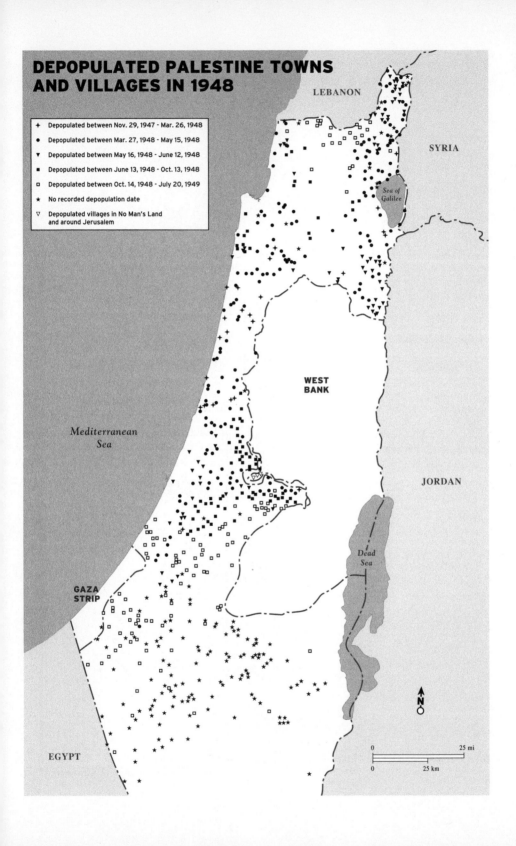

DEPOPULATED PALESTINE TOWNS AND VILLAGES IN 1948

LEBANON

SYRIA

+ Depopulated between Nov. 29, 1947 - Mar. 26, 1948
● Depopulated between Mar. 27, 1948 - May 15, 1948
▼ Depopulated between May 16, 1948 - June 12, 1948
■ Depopulated between June 13, 1948 - Oct. 13, 1948
□ Depopulated between Oct. 14, 1948 - July 20, 1949
★ No recorded depopulation date
▽ Depopulated villages in No Man's Land and around Jerusalem

Sea of Galilee

WEST BANK

Mediterranean Sea

JORDAN

Dead Sea

GAZA STRIP

N

EGYPT

0   25 mi

0   25 km

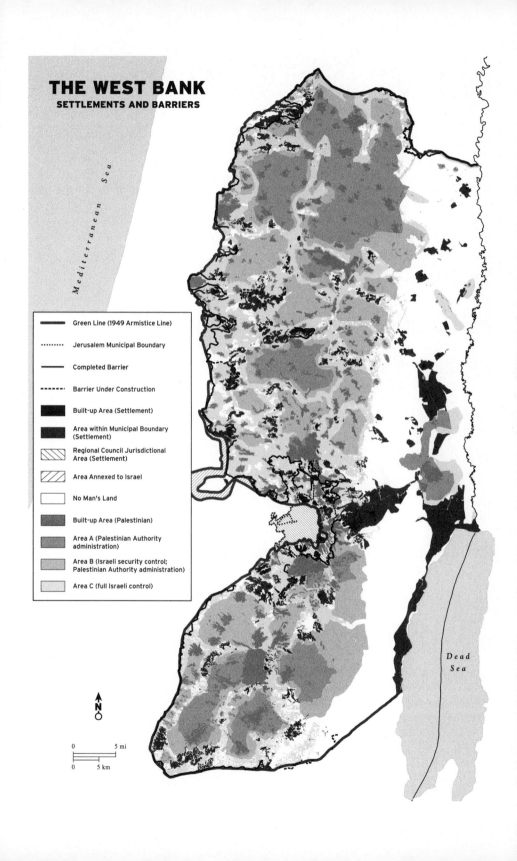

THE WEST BANK
SETTLEMENTS AND BARRIERS

Mediterranean Sea

Legend	
——	Green Line (1949 Armistice Line)
··········	Jerusalem Municipal Boundary
——	Completed Barrier
– – –	Barrier Under Construction
■	Built-up Area (Settlement)
■	Area within Municipal Boundary (Settlement)
▨	Regional Council Jurisdictional Area (Settlement)
▨	Area Annexed to Israel
☐	No Man's Land
■	Built-up Area (Palestinian)
■	Area A (Palestinian Authority administration)
■	Area B (Israeli security control; Palestinian Authority administration)
☐	Area C (full Israeli control)

N

0   5 mi

0   5 km

Dead Sea

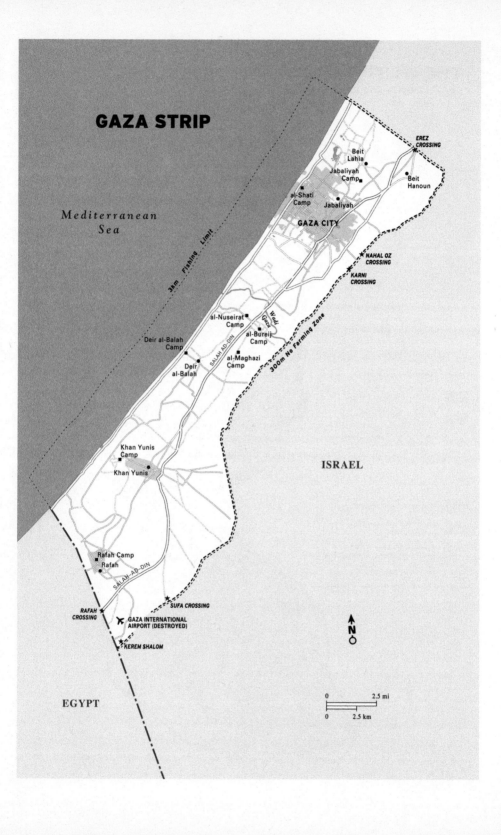

PREFACE: COVERING "GOLIATH"

In pursuing this reporting project, I have relied on the same journalistic methods that I employed in writing my last book, *Republican Gomorrah: Inside the Movement That Shattered the Party*. Just as before, when I journeyed into the American far right and documented its takeover of the Republican Party, I immersed myself in the atmosphere of my subject and cultivated intimate access to those who defined its unique sensibility. This time, my subject is the State of Israel during a period of deepening political and societal crisis. Most Americans know far less about this situation than they do about the political polarization in their own country, but it is an issue on which they have opinions—and an issue of paramount significance to US national security and relevance to their own professed values of democracy, equality, and decency. And it is Americans' tax dollars and political support that are crucial in sustaining the present state of affairs. I want to show what they are paying for, the facts as they really are today, in unadorned and unsanitized form, without sentimentality or nostalgia.

I began working on this book in May 2009, almost as soon as I completed the book tour of *Republican Gomorrah*, and I have conducted uninterrupted research for four years, through early 2013. When I began, Israelis had just elected the most right-wing government in their history in an election conducted during Operation Cast Lead, a three-week-long military assault on the Gaza Strip that left much of the besieged coastal enclave in ruins. A transitional period that began with the collapse of the Camp David negotiations in 2000 was accelerating, with extreme nationalist elements consolidating control over the key institutions of Israeli society, from the Knesset to the courts to the educational system and the army. Through my reporting, I attempted to illuminate the impact of this momentous transition on the people themselves—both Jews and Palestinians—charting its progression through the 2012 Israeli national elections, and against the historical backdrop of the cataclysmic events of 1948 that haunt the Holy Land to this day.

Thanks to my US passport and Jewish heritage, I have been able to report from the frontiers of Israel-Palestine with relative ease, receiving favorable treatment from ethnic profiling experts at Ben Gurion International Airport, passing effortlessly through checkpoints, and cruising from the West Bank to Tel Aviv on highways made off limits to most Palestinians. I spent months living in Ajami, a rapidly gentrifying Palestinian ghetto just south of Tel Aviv; in central Jerusalem, an increasingly frenetic hotbed of Jewish religious nationalism; and in Ramallah, the occupied, seemingly prosperous capital of a Palestinian state that may never be. I have interviewed leaders of Israeli political parties and leaders of Palestinian protests. And I have done my best to explore everywhere in between and speak with as many people as I could.

The stories that make up this book unfolded all around me, in the cities and towns throughout Israel-Palestine, in the streets outside my rented flats, and inside their walls through the lives of my roommates, friends, and journalistic colleagues. These are the stories of people living under a regime of separation, grappling with the consequences of ethnic division in a land with no defined borders.

Readers may not agree with all of my conclusions, but I hope they will carefully consider the facts that appear on these pages. They are, after all, the facts on the ground.

—*Max Blumenthal*

PART

THE CAMPAIGNS

To the Slaughter

B y the end of 2008, the 1.5 million residents of the Gaza Strip had been left to fend for themselves. Gaza was surrounded on all sides by Israeli sniper towers, electrified fences, concrete walls, and a naval blockade that prevented fishermen from trawling waters more than 3 kilometers from shore. Weaponized drones hovered overhead night and day, humming an incessant single note dirge that served as a constant reminder of Israeli control. Heeding Israeli government pledges to push Gaza's economy "to the brink of collapse," army bureaucrats in Tel Aviv developed complex mathematical formulas to regulate the caloric intake of each person trapped inside the coastal strip. Gazans were forbidden from exporting products and prevented from importing cardamom, potato chips, seeds and nuts, cement, fruit preserves, ginger, fishing nets, notebooks, musical instruments, size A4 paper, and toys.

"It's like an appointment with a dietician," Dov Weissglass, an Israeli government aide, joked during a meeting of top military and intelligence officials. "The Palestinians will get a lot thinner but won't die."

With the blockade tightening, a student at the Islamic University of Gaza named Yousef Aljamal watched helplessly as his younger sister was denied a permit to leave Gaza for a basic surgery on her gall bladder. Denied entry on the grounds that she was a "security threat," she died days later.

"During the time of the siege," Aljamal wrote in his diary, "Gaza was turned into an open air prison, walls were built to prevent the shine of the sun, tanks were on the borders prepared to shell, and soldiers observed the hungry and sick people inside but still prevented them from getting their food and medicine, much in the same way they prevented them from getting their freedom."

For a few hundred Gazan police cadets, December 27, 2008, held the promise of a short relief from the suffocating climate of the siege. That morning in Gaza City, the cadets assembled to celebrate their graduation from Hamas's new police academies. They stood as a symbol of the order that finally presided over Gaza after years of gangland-style corruption and repression by the Fatah-controlled Palestinian Authority (PA). After winning what the US Congressional Research Service called a "free and fair election," then fending off a US-backed Fatah coup attempt, Hamas, the Islamist political party, sought to consolidate its control over Gaza, faithfully observing a ceasefire with Israel. In November, Hamas's armed wing, the Al Qassam Brigades, al-Quds Brigades (from the Palestinian Islamic Jihad), and the Popular Front for the Liberation of Palestine (PFLP) fired dozens of rockets at Israeli military

bases and towns in the western Negev Desert in retaliation for an Israeli army operation that killed six Hamas members in Gaza. The Israeli raid occurred on November
5, violating the ceasefire one day before the US election, when the Western media
was almost entirely focused on the outcome of the presidential election. The Hamas
rocket attacks caused consternation but did not kill any Israelis.

A brass band assembled as the police cadets prepared to march before their commander, Major General Tawfiq Jaber. Many of the cadets' parents hurriedly made
their way to the ceremony from across Gaza. Just as the band struck up a martial tune,
an Israeli F-16 roared across the sky, launching a laser-guided missile into the center
of the ceremonial procession. When the choking plumes of thick smoke cleared, a
scene of terrible carnage came into view. At least forty police officers, including General Jaber, lay dead on the concrete. Survivors squirmed around helplessly, writhing
in pain, their uniforms stained with the flesh and blood of their comrades.

Sixty more Israeli F-16s were now in the air, on their way to target police stations
and civilian installations across the Gaza Strip. Within a matter of minutes, Israeli
forces killed 240 Palestinians, including scores of children while they were leaving
school. The initial volley of precision-guided weapons was aimed at civilian targets,
from universities to factories to family homes. Earlier in the year, Israeli Minister of
Defense Matan Vilnai warned the people of Gaza that they "will bring upon themselves a bigger Holocaust because we will use all our might to defend ourselves."

In Bethlehem, just over the Israeli separation wall in the occupied West Bank, a
twenty-seven-year-old Texas transplant named George Hale lit his customary morning cigarette and hustled through the brisk mountain air to his job at Ma'an News
Agency, a Palestinian wire service. Two days earlier the city center had been lit up
with Christmas decorations. Thousands of local Christian worshippers and international pilgrims had descended upon the Church of Nativity, fully restored from the
destruction wreaked by Israeli troops that had besieged it during the Second Intifada. Now the streets were nearly empty. Hale wandered into the modest office, hung
over from drinking late with a few of his ex-pat coworkers. He sank into his chair,
expecting to spend another day curating reports about ordinary Israeli violence and
intra-Palestinian spats. Suddenly, his e-mail in-box began to fill with panicked messages from Ma'an's Gaza bureau. The first e-mail read, "Israel attacking. Hundreds
dead." Hale blurted out in disbelief, "Hundreds? Bullshit!"

With Hale's outburst, the office flew into chaos. Editors grabbed their phones and
dialed up Ma'an's Gaza contacts, seeking details about the horror taking place. It was
worse than they had heard: Israel was pounding the Gaza Strip with the full capacity
of its navy and air force. A land invasion was likely on the way. "Hardly anyone outside Palestine read our website," Hale said. "Then, on the first day, our traffic lit up
like we'd never seen before. It almost crashed our server. All of a sudden, the whole
world was watching, which basically meant all eyes were on Gaza."

As reports of atrocities in Gaza spread throughout the Fatah-controlled Palestinian Authority in the West Bank, Palestinians rushed to organize protests, demanding
an end to the rivalry between Fatah and Hamas. Mahmoud Abbas had taken to the

local media to howl about the "massacre and act of criminal aggression" by the Israelis. But the conduct of his security forces, which had been trained by the US General Keith Dayton and coordinated with the Israeli army, belied his militant histrionics. As crowds of Palestinians gathered in downtown Nablus, Hebron, and in Ramallah's Manara Square, the epicenter of Mahmoud Abbas's mini-fiefdom, Palestinian Authority forces swarmed the protesters, arresting them in droves, attacking some with pepper spray, and even killing one demonstrator. Elsewhere in the West Bank, Israeli troops dispersed stone-throwing youths with rubber bullets and teargas. Calls for the Palestine Liberation Organization (the umbrella group known as the PLO) to break diplomatic ties with Israel were virtually absent from the Palestinian news agency, Wafa, the official media organ of the PA, which instead projected an image of widespread protests to Arabic language audiences. In fact, Israel's Defense Ministry had given Abbas advance notice of the assault on Gaza, beseeching him to take control of the coastal strip after it vanquished Hamas. Though Abbas refused, he kept the governors of Gaza in the dark about the coming onslaught.

With the West Bank quieted by a blanket of internal repression, and the Gaza Strip transformed into a theater of human despair, Israeli society was witnessing some remarkable developments.

The Peace Camp

The day after Israeli forces slaughtered the Hamas police cadets, Haim Oron was awakened at 2:30 a.m. by the sound of knocking at his door. The chairman of the Meretz Party threw open the door, allowing a gust of cold Negev Desert air to sweep into his home in Kibbutz Lahav. A stranger standing in the doorway handed him a secure mobile telephone. On the line was Oron's good friend, Prime Minister Ehud Olmert. Olmert relayed a brief but consequential message: The Israeli military had initiated a major attack on the Gaza Strip. After the prime minister described the first day of operations, he said goodnight.

As the chairman of Meretz—the party founded in 1992 to push for a two-state solution and liberal social policies—Oron was one of the Israeli peace camp's most visible figures. The day that the assault on Gaza began, he issued a public statement announcing his full support for the attack, just as he had done at the onset of Israel's assault on Southern Lebanon in 2006. The Meretz press release read, "The time has come to act without compromises and without political compromises to defend the residents of the Gaza perimeter and [Southern Israeli city] Sderot."

Having endorsed Israel's brutal and bungled bombardment of Southern Lebanon in 2006 before withdrawing his support, Oron knew full well that a military operation could spiral out of control. But even with two sons serving as officers in the Israeli Air Force, Oron lined up once again with the army. "I am living with the constant tension of clashing truths," he later explained to the Israeli newspaper *Ha'aretz*.

Major icons of the Israeli peace camp echoed Oron's support for the escalating bombing campaign. Chief among them was Oron's friend, the liberal Zionist literary lion Amos Oz. Less than one week into Operation Cast Lead, however, at the eightieth birthday celebration for Meretz Party founder and peace camp icon Shulamit Aloni, Oz criticized the assault as "disproportionate." Then, two months later, he reversed himself again, calling the operation "understandable and acceptable." A. B. Yehoshua, the prize-winning Israeli author invariably described as a "peacenik" and "dovish" in the international media, immediately chided Oz, insisting that the operation "needed to be done." And David Grossman, the celebrated Israeli author often portrayed in the West as "Israel's anguished conscience," called for a ceasefire in the *New York Times*, but on purely strategic grounds—he said not a word about civilian casualties.

Just two days after announcing his backing for Operation Cast Lead, and with national elections approaching, Oron changed his mind. "Even though we supported initiating the operation after Hamas broke the cease fire, now we are saying enough," he said, incorrectly blaming Hamas for initiating the hostilities. But by the time Oron changed his mind, it was too late. Disgusted left-wing voters defected from Meretz to Hadash, the non-Zionist, Jewish-Arab communist party. Other left-of-center voters began organizing a tactical vote for the Kadima Party, a supposedly centrist umbrella faction that brought together defectors from the once hegemonic but now rapidly crumbling Labor Party and right-of-center elements from the Likud Party that had supported Ariel Sharon's Gaza withdrawal in 2005 against the will of Likud's rightist leader, Benjamin Netanyahu. Liberal Zionists hoped that by supporting Kadima and its candidate, the telegenic, Western-friendly Foreign Minister Tzipi Livni, they could head off a victory by the bellicose Netanyahu, who sought to rally his base within the ideological Jewish settlements of the West Bank.

For more than a week, as the Israeli army escalated its operation against the "cancer" in Gaza, only small bands of Israeli radical leftists took to the squares of Tel Aviv and Jerusalem to protest the attacks. Meretz and Peace Now, the liberal Zionist group that had organized major demonstrations in favor of the peace process and the evacuation of Israeli settlements, waited a full two weeks before sending their members into the streets.

On the seventh day of the assault, the Israeli army's Givati Brigade invaded the densely populated Zeitoun neighborhood in Gaza City, attempting to transform the homes of local residents into a base of operations and cut the city off from the rest of the strip. At dawn on January 4, Givati troops burst into the home of a man named Ateya al-Samouni with their faces blackened for night combat, and tossed a percussion grenade into the center of his salon. When Samouni approached the soldiers with his arms up, waving an Israeli driver's license and his ID, declaring that he was the owner and was unarmed, they shot him and left him to bleed to death while they opened fire on twenty members of his family, badly wounding a four-year-old child. Next, the soldiers corralled about one hundred more people—all members of the Samouni family and mostly women and children—into a nearby storehouse, forbidding them from fleeing to Gaza City. The soldiers even sent back an ambulance the family had summoned for its wounded. After verifying that the Samounis were unarmed civilians, a soldier barked at them, "You are bad Arabs!"

The following day, when a few older Samouni men attempted to gather firewood and water for those trapped in the house, the army attacked them with heavy ammunition. As soon as survivors of the barrage rushed back to the storehouse for safety, Givati Brigade Commander Ilan Malka ordered airstrikes. Inside the house, the trapped family listened with horror as an American-made Apache helicopter hovered overhead then launched a fusillade of missiles into the house, reducing it to rubble. Nineteen members of the Samouni clan died immediately, and several others lay bleeding heavily.

For days, the Israeli army prevented ambulances from reaching the dead and wounded. When a group of Samouni men attempted to evacuate hurt family members who were on the verge of death, Israeli soldiers fired on them. "Go back unto death!" a soldier shouted at them in classical Arabic. "Fine," Salah Samouni responded defiantly, determined to carry as many as possible to safety. "Then we will die on the road." After four days of agony, rescue crews finally reached the Samouni family, discovering two children buried beneath the rubble and dead bodies but miraculously still breathing.

"My father, mother, wife, and six-month-old son were killed. I had been married for a year and a half. My entire life was destroyed," Helmi Samouni told the journalist Jared Malsin, who visited the family in the aftermath of the massacre.

"After everything that happened," Salah Samouni told Malsin, "we still want to know why. We are civilians. There was no resistance in this area. . . . Give a reason."

When Palestinian rescue crews finally cleared the rubble of the Samouni homes, they found a total of forty-eight corpses. Family members returning to the few houses left standing discovered another unpleasant reminder of Israel's incursion: The Givati soldiers had scrawled racist graffiti all over their walls. Some of the messages left for the Samounis read, "ARabs need 2 die," "Arabs are pieces of shit," and "1 is DOWN 999,999 TO GO." After defacing the homes of Gaza, the young men of the Givati brigade returned to their homes only minutes away inside Israel and in the settlements of the West Bank. They were not only soldiers but citizens of the "Jewish and democratic state." As voters, their mood would define the tone of the national elections underway in Israel.

Blood for Votes

With Israeli society's nationalistic impulses summoned to the fore in December 2008 and January 2009, leading politicians struggled to outdo one another in a competition for the most convincing exaltation of violence against the Arab evildoers. Subtle suggestions by Livni's opponents that her gender made her unfit to lead a macho, militaristic country nestled in the heart of a "tough neighborhood" prompted Kadima to produce an ad featuring a blurry-faced male candidate with many impressive achievements who surprisingly morphed into Livni at the end. Who could believe a woman could accomplish such wonders? During press conferences, Livni overcompensated for her gender liability. "Hamas now understands if you fire on Israel's citizens, it responds by going wild—and this is a good thing," she proclaimed.

Meanwhile, Netanyahu stumped through the fever swamps of "Judea and Samaria," the biblically inspired Israeli term for the occupied West Bank, warning radical settlers of the catastrophic consequences of a Livni victory. Giving the Palestinians a state of their own, as Livni claimed she would do, "will simply implant a new Hamas terror base here, stacked by Iran with Iranian missiles that would fire on Tel Aviv," Netanyahu told a crowd of settlers. His campaign ads amounted to a collection of his most apocalyptic warnings about the looming specter of Arab terror, presenting him as a prophet of doom whom his rivals copied but only after it was too late. Netanyahu's knack for leveraging the fear and trauma of the Jewish public into votes earned him a new nickname among the Israeli press corps: "Scaremonger-in-Chief."

Ehud Barak, the defense minister, leader of the dying left-of-center Labor Party, and the most decorated military veteran in Israel's history, boasted on a special election broadcast intended for Russian citizens of Israel, "As you people say, [Arab terrorists] should be whacked when they're on the toilet." With the crude populist appeal, Barak deliberately channeled Russian strongman Vladimir Putin's famous boast that he would shoot Muslim terrorists, even when they were going to the bathroom. Lily Galili, a veteran Israeli journalist who had covered Israel's Russian sector for more than a decade, reported at the time that Barak was mounting an aggressive campaign to "Putinize" his image—a makeover that spoke volumes about the state of the Israeli electorate. In his role as defense minister, Barak fueled his political ambitions by attempting to run up the body count in Gaza. As Galili wrote, "Barak hopes that the fighting in Gaza will change the tide and restore him as a player in Russian speakers' eyes."

Barak's makeover was a conscious attempt to outflank the man who stood to gain the most from the belligerent atmosphere that had overtaken Israeli society. He was Avigdor Lieberman, a gruff former bouncer and airport baggage handler from Moldova who founded the far-right Yisrael Beiteinu Party in 1999 as a vehicle for Israel's secular Russian population. Each election cycle, Lieberman's party escalated its campaign against Israel's Arab citizens. And each election cycle, it gained at least two new Knesset seats.

Earlier in the year, Lieberman previewed some talking points for his upcoming bid for prime minister. At a press conference announcing his departure from the Kadima-led governing coalition in protest of Prime Minister Ehud Olmert's resumption of negotiations with the Palestinian Authority, Lieberman singled out two Palestinian-Israeli members of the Knesset, Mohammed Barakeh and Ahmed Tibi. "The present negotiations with the Palestinians will not lead anywhere," Lieberman thundered. "Whoever thinks that the reason for the dispute is land and settlements is deluding himself and others. . . . Our problem is not Judea and Samaria [the West Bank], but the extreme fundamentalist leadership that is in the Knesset. . . . Our problem is Ahmad Tibi and Barakeh—they are more dangerous than [Hamas president] Khaled Meshal and [Hezbollah spiritual leader Hassan] Nasrallah. They work from the inside; they operate methodically to destroy the State of Israel as a Jewish State."

As soon as the election campaign began, Yisrael Beiteinu blanketed Israeli airwaves with ads, hammering on the theme of Arab treachery, reminding Israeli voters that Lieberman—and only Lieberman—would purge the country of its "fifth column." One ad featured mug shots of current and former Arab members of Knesset flashing on the screen, one after another. After a baritone narrator read out supposedly anti-Israeli statements by each politician, images of Palestinian-Israeli students demonstrating against the attack on Gaza at an Israeli university appeared. "We won't forget that when the military operation in Gaza had just begun, there were those among us who supported Hamas," the narrator intoned. The ad closed with Lieberman's two campaign slogans: "No loyalty, no citizenship" and "Lieberman: I believe him." Livni, for her part, sought to channel Lieberman's transferist appeal into her own candidacy, declaring in a campaign speech that Arab citizens of Israel should seek their "national aspirations" in a future Palestinian state.

The Hill of Shame

Parash Hill is a scenic overlook near Sderot, which is one of the underserviced development towns originally constructed in Southern Israel to accommodate some of the hundreds of thousands of Jews who arrived to Israel from Arab nations during the 1950s, often as impoverished victims of government-led campaigns on expulsion. Parash Hill offers sweeping views of the Gaza Strip, and beyond it is the Mediterranean Sea. Here, hundreds of Israelis gathered at the vista to revel in the violence. For them, the hill offered mezzanine seats for the bombing; they cheered or stared with silent satisfaction while the hometown team exacted blood vengeance on the Enemy. "Of course I'm happy," a twenty-six-year-old Orthodox Jew told a reporter from the UK's *Sunday Times* as he watched Israeli jets bombard the strip. "It would be better if innocent civilians weren't hurt, but the ones who cooperate with Hamas—that's their problem."

A secular, middle-aged woman pointed to Gaza and calmly explained to Ulla Terkelsen, a Danish TV reporter, "They should just wipe the whole thing off the map." With a dramatic wave of her hand, she added, "Yeah, I'm a little bit fascist." A twenty-seven-year-old student surveyed the scene of picnicking Israelis and lamented, "People in Israel are addicted to violence."

Resentment had been simmering among Israelis since the homemade rockets began falling on Southern Israel following the Gaza withdrawal in 2005. The humiliating defeat Israeli forces suffered at the hands of Hezbollah in Southern Lebanon in 2006 only added to the sense of frustration and anger. By the 2008, Israelis were ready for a redemptive war that would reestablish their national morale.

During the first week of the assault on Gaza, support for the bombing among Israeli Jews was nearly unanimous, with 90 percent of respondents expressing their approval. When ground forces entered Gaza several days later, the percentage dropped to 65 percent, though not because Israelis were outraged by the suffering of Gaza's besieged population. As Ronen Shoval, a right-wing student activist, explained in an editorial for the mainstream Israeli daily paper *Yedioth Ahronoth*, Israelis saw soldiers as "their children"—the loss of a single one was occasion for a national outpouring of grief. According to Shoval, Israel expressed its moral imperatives not by concerning itself with the lives of the Palestinians, which were immaterial, but by using as much force as it needed to guard the Jewish "children" from harm. An Israeli soldier identifying himself as Lt. Col. Amir articulated the mentality on Israeli TV during the attack on Gaza, declaring, "We are very violent. We are not shying away from any method of preventing casualties among our troops."

Members of Jewish Israeli society who opposed the assault on Gaza in purely moral terms were few and far between, but they made their presence felt by protesting in front of the Defense Ministry in Tel Aviv and in public squares around the city. Rebecca Vilkomerson, a Jewish-American social justice activist, was living in Israel at the time with her Israeli husband. When she joined the Tel Aviv demonstrations, she found that she and the leftist protesters were often outnumbered by nationalist mobs that gathered to jeer and attack them. "We had to travel in large groups to the demonstrations just to be safe," Vilkomerson recalled. "Then when we got there, we were put behind police barriers to keep the right-wing mobs away. Normal looking people, businessmen in suits, would see and all of a sudden literally try to hurl themselves over the barrier to attack. They would spit at us, throw rotten eggs at us; there was this sense of nationalism, like, 'How dare you criticize our war?'"

During the three-week-long military offensive, Israeli police detained 832 protesters, holding almost all Arab protesters—including minors—until the end of their criminal proceedings while quickly releasing most Jews, though not before subjecting some to interrogations by the Shin Bet General Security Service or seeking guarantees that they would not protest again. With police designating the protests in the most ironic terms possible—as "a disruption of the peace"—state prosecutors called for "deterring the protesters with force and detaining them until the end of the proceedings in order to convey a message to the public that such behavior is unforgivable." The repression of anti-war protests was systemic and calculated at an official level, while nationalist counterdemonstrators were given free reign.

At Haifa University, where 20 percent of the student body was Arab—the highest percentage at any Israeli university—school administrators summoned mounted riot police onto campus to disperse peaceful demonstrations. At the same time, the administration took out advertisements in local media and issued announcements supporting the offensive. "As a show of solidarity with IDF soldiers fighting in Gaza and residents of the south," one such announcement read, "the University of Haifa has made its central tower into a national flag . . . the university is not an ivory tower and is inseparably connected to the community. With this symbolic act, it expresses its great appreciation for the residents of the south and its support for the IDF's soldiers."

The Israeli General Press Office—the official government bureau in charge of handling the foreign press—and the military forbade the international press from entering Gaza, forcing them to observe the war with the Israeli revelers on Parash Hill. Frustrated with the heavy-handed attempts at censorship and information control by the Israeli authorities, a few reporters renamed the lookout point "The Hill of Shame." As they milled around the hilltop, interviewing slick Israeli government flacks, tales of unspeakable horror flooded out of Gaza. All of them would be confirmed in the days ahead.

Unarmed civilians were torn to pieces with flechette darts sprayed from tank shells; several other children covered in burns from white phosphorous chemical weapon rounds were taken to hospitals; a few were found dead with bizarre wounds after being hit with experimental Dense Inert Metal Explosive (DIME) bombs designed to dissolve into the body and rapidly erode internal soft tissue. A group of women were shot to death while waving a white flag; another family was destroyed by a missile while eating lunch; and Israeli soldiers killed Ibrahim Awajah, an eight-year-old child. His mother, Wafaa, told the documentary filmmaker Jen Marlowe that soldiers used his corpse for target practice. Numerous crimes like these were documented across the Gaza Strip.

"The orders were clear," a tank commander named Ohad told the Israeli filmmaker Nurit Kedar. "If a car came within two hundred meters of me, I could simply shoot—shoot a shell at it. . . . We needed to cleanse the neighborhoods, the buildings, the area of the neighborhood. It sounds really terrible to say 'cleanse,' but those were the orders. I don't want to make a mistake with the words. . . . I don't remember if it was the squadron or the battalion commander, but with a laser he simply marked for the line of homes that were to be shelled, and he said clearly, 'Every house gets a shell.'"

Ohad added, "I feel good. I'm proud about what I did."

Ha'aretz's Gideon Levy, one of perhaps two or three major Israeli columnists who expressed opposition to Operation Cast Lead, noted that the horrors emanating from Gaza were reported in passing, cumulatively, and without detail, on the back pages of the daily newspapers *Yedioth Ahronoth* and *Maariv*. "All of these reports came after numerous articles on the postponement of bar mitzvah parties in Sderot, a honeymoon that went on despite the war, pizza deliveries to Israel Defense Forces soldiers, and folk dancing in a bomb shelter in Kibbutz Yad Mordechai," Levy reflected. Indeed, if the mainstream Israeli media focused at all on the toll of the assault on Gaza, it did so primarily to highlight the inconveniences experienced by the Jewish public.

Toward the end of the operation, Israelis were finally confronted with a harrowingly intimate description of the straightforward slaughter their army was carrying out. It was delivered during a prime time news broadcast by Izeldeen Abuelaish, a fertility doctor and widower raising eight children on his own in Gaza's Jabaliyah refugee camp. The Harvard-trained Abuelaish had spent years working as a researcher at a hospital in Southern Israel, earning a staff position by helping Jewish Israelis have children. Each day during the assault on Gaza, Abuelaish—a fluent Hebrew speaker—delivered a dispatch to Israel's Channel 10, one of the country's major broadcast outlets.

On January 16, Abuelaish appeared on Israeli TV, sobbing uncontrollably as he struggled to describe to Israeli viewers how an Israeli tank crew had just lobbed a shell into his living room, decapitating two of his daughters and leaving two more of his children shredded to pieces. "My daughters! Oh God! Oh Allah!" the doctor screamed. "I want to save them but they are dead, they are dead. They were hit in the head. What have we done to them, oh God? My daughters, they killed them!" The visibly shaken Channel 10 anchor Shlomi Eldar interrupted Abuelaish to order ambulances to the scene of his home before quietly removing himself from the studio.

A day later, Abuelaish received a large delegation of reporters at Israel's Sheba Medical Center, where his surviving daughters lay in an intensive care unit. "They participated in peace camps everywhere," he told the reporters of his dead children. "Were they armed when they were killed? They were not armed with weapons, but rather, with love; love for others. They planned to travel to Canada; I got a job in Canada, and they wanted to come with me."

As Abuelaish spoke, an Israeli woman named Levana Stern charged through the press gaggle and lunged wildly in his direction. "My son is in the paratroopers! Who knows what you had inside your home, nobody is talking about that!" she shrieked, pointing accusingly at Abuelaish. "Nobody is talking. Who knows what kind of weapons were in your house! So what if he's a doctor? The soldiers knew exactly. They had weapons inside the home; you should be ashamed. I have three soldiers, why are they firing at them?" Stern turned to the members of media and shouted, "All of you should be ashamed!"

Abuelaish held his head in dismay. "They don't want to see the other side," he murmured to himself. "They only want to see one side. They don't want to see the others."

Hooligans

With the attack on Gaza approaching its peak, the election drew to a close. Lieberman had staged a dramatic surge into third place, bringing him within a hair's breadth of Livni and Netanyahu—and moving him decisively ahead of Barak, the standard bearer of the Labor Party. Lieberman's message resonated well beyond his Russian Israeli base, especially among Israeli youth. When older Yisrael Beiteinu activists gathered at their party's national convention in Nazareth Illit—a Jewish city overlooking the historic Arab city of Nazareth that had served as a staging point for anti-Arab riots during the Second Intifada—they were greeted by crowds of cheering high school students who were chanting, "Death to Arabs" and "No Loyalty, No Citizenship."

"This country has needed a dictatorship for a long time already. But I'm not talking about an extreme dictatorship. We need someone who can put things in order. Lieberman is the only one who speaks the truth," an eighteen-year-old student, Edan Ivanov, told *Ha'aretz* reporter Yotam Feldman. "We've had enough here with the 'leftist democracy'—and I put that term in quotes, don't get me wrong. People have put the dictator label on Lieberman because of the things he says. But the truth is that in Israel there can't be a full democracy when there are Arabs here who oppose it."

"Someone who doesn't declare his loyalty to the state, who has no patriotism, should have his citizenship taken away," said an eleventh-grader named Nicole Parnasa. "Anyone who's against the operation in Gaza, for example—that's a kind of disloyalty. Anyone who burns the flag, that's disloyalty. The military operation was for the sake of the country, after we kept quiet for eight years, so now they don't support it?"

Leading up to the attack on Gaza and the national elections, Israeli youth had assaulted Arabs in the Israeli mixed city of Acre, badly beaten two Arab youths on the eve of Holocaust Remembrance Day, and formed a club-wielding mob to chase more Arab youths down the boardwalk in the northern city of Tiberias. As they prepared for the army, Israel's most revered institution, where many would follow orders to commit far more lethal acts of violence against Arabs, the youth of Israel—or some of them at least—engaged in vigilante attacks as a form of play acting. Supporting Lieberman, one high school senior named Sergei Leibliyanich said, was a natural extension of the phenomenon: "It gives motivation against the Arabs. You want to enlist in the army so you can stick it to them. The preparation gives you the motivation to stick it to the Arabs, and we want to elect someone who'll do that. I like Lieberman's thinking about the Arabs. Bibi [Benjamin Netanyahu] doesn't want to go as far."

In mock elections conducted at ten high schools across Israel during the attack on Gaza, Yisrael Beiteinu triumphed over all other parties. Meretz finished last, and not a single vote was cast for an Arab party, a reflection of Israel's officially segregated education system. At Tel Aviv University—a reputed bastion of liberalism—a sample poll showed Yisrael Beiteinu doubling its support, while other polls revealed the party as the third most popular among the general population of Israeli college students. "Loyalty is the most burning issue for the youth. They're about to go in the army, and therefore national honor is important to them," explained Alex Miller, the twenty-eight-year-old Yisrael Beiteinu youth outreach coordinator who was the youngest person ever to serve in the Knesset.

When Miller appeared before a crowd of wildly supportive students at a Tel Aviv high school, he promised to punish anti-war protesters by stripping them of their citizenship rights. A veteran civics teacher named Moshe Slansky watched with anguish as the students hung on Miller's every word. Finally, Slansky seized the microphone from Miller. "If anyone repeats the undemocratic things said here by Miller on my exams, I will deduct points from his grade," Slansky admonished his audience. According to the *Ha'aretz* reporter Feldman, the teacher was met with a hail of boos. "After they booed, I realized I didn't have a chance there," Slansky moaned.

On January 10, the date of national decision, Yisrael Beiteinu's list won third place, increasing its number of Knesset seats to fifteen and ensuring Lieberman a decisive role in the governing coalition. The biggest winner, the right-wing Likud Party, gained fifteen Knesset seats from its previous total, virtually ensuring that Netanyahu would be Israel's next prime minister. Meretz and Labor—the two standard bearers of the old Ashkenazi establishment—saw their worst returns in history, with Meretz reduced to a piddling three Knesset seats and Labor losing six seats, putting it in fourth place. For the next four weeks, indecision reigned, as Kadima and Labor seemed unlikely to join both Netanyahu and Lieberman in a coalition government.

Meanwhile, the operation in Gaza entered its final week, with Israeli soldiers initiating a comprehensive slash and burn operation, destroying 80 percent of all arable farmland in the coastal strip, bombing the strip's largest flour mill, leveling seven concrete factories, shelling a major cheese factory, and shooting up a chicken farm, killing thirty-one thousand chickens. "For a few days we were shooting at chicken coops," an Israeli tank gunner named Yegev told the filmmaker Kedar. "I thought it was idiotic. Yeah, yeah, at chickens. Deterrent fire, they called it. Every hour we had to shoot a few rounds from a machine gun at the chicken coops. To deter people or to deter chickens? I don't know!"

Tzipi Livni, the foreign minister and prime ministerial hopeful, claimed personal responsibility for the indiscriminate violence in Gaza, remarking, "Israel demonstrated real hooliganism during the course of the recent operation, which I demanded."

By the end of Israel's assault, around 400 women and children had been killed; the total death toll was 1,400—mostly civilians and noncombatant members of Hamas, which put up minimal resistance to the Israeli invasion. Israel suffered 15 casualties, including four from fratricidal accidents.

Pawns in the Game

One month after the end of Operation Cast Lead, Kadima leader Livni declared her intention to lead the opposition, but not after she made efforts to form a governing coalition that would have included Yisrael Beiteinu. The Labor Party, led by Ehud Barak, vowed "never to sit with Yisrael Beiteinu in the same government." Days later, Barak pushed Labor to join the coalition, after receiving guarantees from his longtime friend and former army buddy, Benjamin Netanyahu—the Likud leader placed in charge of forming the new government.

Netanyahu invited Yisrael Beiteinu to join the coalition despite—or perhaps because of—Lieberman's declaration that he would join "only if practical steps are taken for Israel to 'finish the job' of annihilating Hamas. . . . In addition," Lieberman continued, "we demand a new citizenship law that will ensure what we said repeatedly during the campaign: 'No loyalty, no citizenship.'" If there was any public outrage in Israeli society about Labor and Likud's accession to Lieberman's brazenly anti-democratic demands, it was muted and marginal.

With Barak and Lieberman by his side and Kadima in the opposition, Netanyahu formed what Livni accurately described as "the most right-wing government in Israel's history." Sixty-eight of the eighty-one Knesset members serving in the coalition were members of extreme right-wing parties. Out of the 120 seats in the Knesset, at least 75 were filled by right-wing ideologues. Oren Yiftachel, a human rights activist and professor of public policy at Ben Gurion University, wrote that the "main trend" of the election results was "the return of openly declared Jewish colonialist goals and the intensification of apartheid-like measures as popular political agendas."

Indeed, while Israel had always discriminated against its Palestinian minority as a matter of national policy, the ascent of Lieberman and a rightist-dominated Likud faction signaled a collective vote in favor of stripping away whatever remained of the country's democratic patina, from its human rights NGO's to the social sciences departments of its universities to the Supreme Court, all in order to consolidate a system of open apartheid. The parliament's political makeup was not an aberration, but rather the reflection of an authoritarian trend that had gained momentum with each electoral contest since the collapse of the so-called peace process in 2000. The hunger for an iron-fisted strongman who could "finish the job" was reflected in opinion polls, exposing the attitudes of a deeply traumatized, heavily indoctrinated society with little patience left for the complications of democracy.

Daniel Bar-Tal, a world-renowned political psychologist from Tel Aviv University, conducted a groundbreaking survey of Jewish Israeli attitudes after Operation Cast Lead. Summarizing Bar-Tal's findings, journalist Akiva Eldar wrote, "Israeli Jews' consciousness is characterized by a sense of victimization, a siege mentality, blind patriotism, belligerence, self-righteousness, dehumanization of the Palestinians, and insensitivity to their suffering. The fighting in Gaza dashed the little hope Bar-Tal had left—that this public would exchange the drums of war for the cooing of doves."

"There was almost unanimous support of the war [on Gaza] and very few members of this society . . . expressed any type of misgivings about the way that this was handled when so many were killed," Bar-Tal told me in an interview about his study. "There is no doubt these attitudes were the product of indoctrination. The narrative of the war was all constructed and well prepared, and information was heavily controlled."

Bar-Tal's study reinforced the findings of a 2006 poll by the Center for the Struggle Against Racism, an Israeli NGO, which revealed that 68 percent of Israeli Jews would refuse to live in the same building as an Arab. Nearly half of those polled would not even allow an Arab into their home, while 63 percent agreed with the statement, "Arabs are a security and demographic threat to the state." Meanwhile, 40 percent expressed support for encouraging Palestinian citizens of Israel to leave.

The racist trend was driven as much by Israel's policy of demographic separation as it was by a national identity crisis emerging from the ethnically stratified, conflict-driven atmosphere that increasingly defined Israel's immigrant society. Those occupying the lowest social strata—working-class Russians and the Jews of Arab descent known as Mizrahim—were encouraged to demonstrate their Israeliness before the wealthy and politically dominant Ashkenazi elite by acting out against Arabs in exaggerated displays of violence and racism. Their attitudes mirrored the crude bigotry that poor whites living under the boot of an agrarian oligarchic class displayed toward poor blacks in the Jim Crow South. And like in the American South, polls of Israeli Jewish opinions demonstrated that racism rose in inverse proportion to levels of wealth and secularism. As Bob Dylan wrote of impoverished white racists, denizens of the Israeli Jewish underclass were only pawns in the game.

In post-Oslo Israel, the exclusively Mizrahi Shas Party had emerged as one of the country's most ferocious vehicles of anti-Arab racism. The longtime head of Shas, Aryeh Deri, a Tammany Hall–style wheeler and dealer, had served as the key representative of Mizrahi Jews throughout the Oslo era, providing crucial support to the Labor-led peace process. But in 2000, Deri was sentenced to prison after being convicted of taking $155,000 in bribes, turning leadership of the party over to Eli Yishai, a crude racist and xenophobe who exploited his role as Israel's interior minister to fund the construction of cheap settlement housing in East Jerusalem and the West Bank for his constituents. His hardline politics compounded longstanding frictions between the Palestinians and Mizrahim while eroding the domestic stability of the Israeli general public. Only Ovadiah Yosef exceeded Yishai in his extremism, the Shas Party spiritual leader and Israeli chief Rabbi, who peppered his weekly radio sermons with genocidal rants. "It is forbidden to be merciful to [Arabs]," Yosef proclaimed in a typical screed. "You must send missiles to them and annihilate them. They are evil and damnable."

Like the Mizrahim, the Russian population of Israel witnessed a changing of its political guard at the onset of the new government. Natan Sharansky, a former Soviet dissident who spent ten years in a Soviet gulag for his Zionist ideals, arrived in Israel as an internationally renowned hero. The centrist, nearly apolitical platform of Sharansky's Yisrael Ba'Aliyah Party promised to address problems specific to the Russian-Israeli public, whose members faced daily discrimination, professional marginalization, and mockery for not speaking Hebrew well enough. But Sharansky's particularist politics carried little national appeal. Avigdor Lieberman, a clever political operator who helped Sharansky establish his platform, exploited the void Sharansky created, hammering on secular lower-class resentment of Israel's Arab minority and non-Zionist, ultra-Orthodox population. He immediately surpassed Sharansky, mobilizing ethnic tension and class envy to establish a national party with a Russian base that would soon challenge Likud as the face of Israel's right wing.

The Ashkenazi elite of Israel's central coast heaped scorn on Lieberman, branding him fairly accurately as a proto-fascist thug—David Grossman called him "a political pyromaniac." But the liberal scorn only emboldened Lieberman. During each election, he watched with glee as his party gained seats while the old left-wing Zionist establishment slid further into irrelevancy. Lieberman and his growing band of hard-right henchmen gave expression to the authentically authoritarian attitudes that radiated from the heart of Jewish Israeli society, while Meretz and Labor seemed mired in the faded illusions of the peace process. Once a lowly baggage handler at Ben Gurion Airport, Lieberman's moment had finally arrived.

This Man Is Clean

On a sunny day in 1999, a hulking, bear-like man with a close-cropped, salt-and-pepper beard that outlined a pudgy face and beady, darting eyes lumbered through the quiet residential streets of Nokdim, a Jewish settlement in the occupied West Bank. The man was hunting for a twelve-year-old boy who had punched his young son. When he found the boy huddling in terror inside a trailer, he lifted him off his feet and slammed his wiry frame into a wall, leaving him with a painful head wound. The fearsome man then grabbed the injured kid by the collar and dragged him back to his parents' home in the nearby settlement of Tekoah, warning him that if he ever returned to Nokdim, he would clobber him again.

The man was Avigdor Lieberman, the nightclub bouncer from Moldova who had just won a seat in the Knesset. Lieberman was promptly placed on trial for assaulting a minor. But thanks to the help of a well-connected legal fixer with access to the highest levels of the Israeli government, Dov Weissglass, Lieberman got off with a fine and no jail time. Thus he continued his political ascent, exciting his growing base of supporters with bombastic rhetoric that rivaled the most sinister of James Bond villains.

Lieberman's appeal stemmed not from his speaking style, which was blunt and truculent, or his capacity for charming crowds, which was nonexistent. Though he claimed to be a playwright with scripts in production in Hollywood, and compared his enemies to the fascistic rhinoceroses from the famous Eugene Ionesco play—a supremely ironic insult—he was anything but erudite. He was not religious, either. Unlike David Ben Gurion and countless secular Israeli political figures who infused their rhetoric with a strain of theocratic messianism, Lieberman did not even feign interest in the Torah or the "3,000 year old dream." For him, serving in the army was enough to "earn" the rights and benefits that came with citizenship in the Jewish state—he was content to allow the army to define who was a Jew. Lieberman's politics melded authoritarian populism with a distinctly anti-clerical strain, appealing to anyone who loathed the presence of Muslims, radical leftists, and the ultra-Orthodox. And there was no shortage of citizens in Israel who held this sentiment.

"In a world of polished, Westernized Israeli politicians such as Prime Minister Ehud Olmert and Netanyahu, the forty-eight-year-old Lieberman stands out. Any American notions of political correctness are absent from his vocabulary," wrote Lily Galili, the reporter who had covered Lieberman and his Yisrael Beiteinu Party for more than a decade.

Lieberman's rejection of the cultural and political norms that defined the leadership of the traditional Ashkenazi elites of Labor and Likud earned the adulation of voters exhausted by years of conflict and fruitless negotiations, particularly the new post-Soviet class of Russian immigrants who arrived in Israel with at best a tenuous connection to the Jewish religion, little understanding of the country's history and no warning that over a million indigenous Palestinians also lived as citizens in their new country.

When Lieberman returned to his home in Nokdim, passing through a checkpoint the soldiers informally referred to as "Checkpoint Yvette"—after the nickname bestowed on him by his adoring Russian supporters—he pulled up in a shiny black Mercedes Benz SUV, clad in a dark, impeccably tailored, broad-shouldered suit, often chomping on an expensive cigar. Lieberman's business dealings were part of his gangster image. He owned two foreign import-export companies, Mountain View and Mayflower, which served as slush funds for a coterie of wealthy businessmen from Russia, Cyprus, and the Virgin Islands seeking to buy access and favors inside Israel. One particularly infamous Jewish-Russian oligarch, Michael Cherney, told police investigators he initiated daily communications with Lieberman as soon as Lieberman was appointed to serve under Netanyahu. Accused of paying Lieberman nearly $500,000 through a Cypriot firm he owned, Cherney was widely suspected of ties to criminal gangs in Russia. In leaked diplomatic cables, US officials described Cherney as "a notorious crime figure" and a "Russian mobster."

Cherney took Israeli citizenship in 1994 after fearing that he had become the subject of a criminal investigation in Russia. Cherney had been a central figure in Russia's "aluminum war" during the 1990s, during which scores of people were killed, from top government officials to reporters to company executives, in a battle for control of the country's lucrative non-ferro US metal market. But even in Israel, where authorities resisted the extradition of criminal citizens more staunchly than most countries in the world, Cherney could not elude the air of suspicion that surrounded him. In 2004, Israel's then–interior minister Avram Poraz informed the oligarch, "According to information that has been received by the police of Israel, you are responsible for murder and attempted murder, which was undertaken upon your orders or by your commission in a period of the war for the aluminum market."

Cherney vehemently denied mob links. "The State of Israel raises charges of suspicion that I am involved in the murder of dozens of people," he moaned. "I was charged with everything except the crucifixion of Christ." Meanwhile, posters appeared throughout Israel mocking Lieberman as "the Russian mafia's poodle." Unbowed by the derision, Lieberman rose to his friend's defense. "This man is clean," he said of Cherney. "And I believe his decency and honesty more than the decency of all heads of investigative authorities put together."

Another prolific financial angel of Lieberman's was the Austrian businessman Martin Schlaff, who, with his close ties to the Stasi, became one of Europe's richest men by supplying the German Democratic Republic with goods embargoed by the West, often with the help of a KGB agent named Vladimir Putin, who worked out of his Dresden office. In 2003, Schlaff allegedly paid a $3 million bribe to the sons of Ariel Sharon in order to gain permission to build a casino in the occupied Palestinian city of Jericho, a scheme that apparently also involved substantial payments to the easily plied Palestinian Authority. A day after Israeli police raided Schlaff's apartment, discovering evidence of the pay-off, Sharon fell into a comatose state from which he would never emerge, saving him from the scandal.

After the raid, Schlaff stepped up his payments to Lieberman, who had reentered politics and whose party, Yisrael Beiteinu, stood to gain a new base of support in the wake of Sharon's departure from the scene. At the time, Lieberman was receiving several million dollars a year, thanks to mysterious foreign payments funneled through a company run by his twenty-one-year-old daughter. A subsequent police investigation of Lieberman's alleged money laundering and fraudulent schemes seemed to place his career in jeopardy. However, he continued to gather new constituents and Knesset seats at a steady clip. By 2006, after seven years in and out of the Knesset, Lieberman's Yisrael Beiteinu Party was a force to be reckoned with, gathering 11 seats (out of a total of 120) and critical leverage over Prime Minister Ehud Olmert's faltering government, which was forced to create a phony cabinet position for Lieberman called "Minister of Strategic Threats."

"What need is there for a new ministry run by a man who has no experience in security affairs, unless you count his rumored links to the Russian mafia, and is not distinguished by his penetrating strategic thought?" wrote Azmi Bishara, the Palestinian-Israeli politician whom Lieberman constantly antagonized and threatened. "This is a ministry for incitement, mobilization, and conspiracy mongering. It is a ministry made to win popularity in the Israeli street by beating the war drums against 'the enemy.'"

While Lieberman inveighed against Arabs and Muslims from his new post—he called Bishara a Nazi collaborator who deserved to be executed—he simultaneously recruited a coterie of unknown but colorful right-wing apparatchiks, mostly from the Russian sector, to do his bidding in the Knesset. Among them was Esterina Tartman, the Yisrael Beiteinu party chair who called the appointment of an Arab to a cabinet post "a lethal blow to Zionism." Lieberman was forced to withdraw Tartman's nomination for tourism minister when it was revealed she had faked her master's degree in economics from Hebrew University and received $350,000 in disability payments for claiming that a car accident left her with permanent physical disability that limited her to work four hours a day and severely impaired her concentration—an injury that might have excused her erratic behavior in the Knesset.

Another top Yisrael Beiteinu recruit poached by Lieberman from the ranks of Likud, Anastasia Michaeli, based her reputation on her career as a Russian model crowned Miss St. Petersburg in 1996. After marrying a former Israeli boxing champion, she converted to Judaism and moved to Israel where she became a TV celebrity among the country's Russian immigrants. Her signature show, *The Pleasures of Life*, was a Russian version of America's *Lifestyles of the Rich and Famous*, flaunting a gaudy Eastern European fantasy of extreme wealth that virtually none of her viewers could afford or would ever experience.

Michaeli's decadent image was exceeded only by her crude racism. In 2007, while serving on a panel to select Israel's representative for the Eurovision song contest, Michaeli objected to a Mizrahi contestant because he "looks Arab." "I am looking at this competition from a Zionist point of view," she was quoted as saying at the time. During a debate in the Knesset, she interrupted Ghaleb Majadele, an Arab member of the Labor Party, shouting, "You take steps against the country!" When Majadele demanded that a Yisrael Beiteinu colleague on the Knesset committee "shut her up," Michaeli stood and threw a glass of water on his face, then stormed out of the chamber. "Mr. Chairman, this sums it up," Majadele said with a smile. "It's a shame she's in your party. I'm sure you won't tolerate this kind of wild, impudent, fascist behavior. But I'll tell you, I'm not even shaken up. It was expected."

Michaeli's outbursts infuriated Israel's mostly Ashkenazi liberal class, who viewed her as the symbol of everything that alienated them about the new generation of Russian immigrants. She not only seemed to revile Arabs, but also homosexuals, exposing an embarrassingly retrograde current that increasingly dominated elements of the country's cultural and political mainstream. But while those the eminent Israeli Supreme Court chief justice described as the Enlightened Public—the secular, liberal, coastal middle class—moaned about the flood of Russians that had washed up on the shores of their civilized fortress, they were reluctant to acknowledge the degree to which the great Russian influx had fulfilled a top strategic imperative of the state's ethnocratic nature. Indeed, to offset the growth of the Palestinian and ultra-Orthodox populations inside Israel, the state had expended enormous stores of resources corralling post–Soviet Russia's Jewish community into the Zionist project, using them as human fodder to fill the ranks of the army and the major settlement blocs.

From demographic assets to objects of derision among an element mourning its rapid loss of control over the affairs of the state, the Russians of Israel forged ahead, determined to secure the privileges promised to them by the Jewish state. With the rise of Perestroika in the 1980s, Israel's Jewish Agency was able to entice one million Soviet Jews to immigrate to Israel with the promise of handsome social and economic benefits. It was the largest single influx of Jewish immigrants to Israel in the country's history, enlarging the Jewish majority by 20 percent—a temporary triumph in Israel's war against the perceived Arab demographic threat. However, more than 300,000 of the new immigrants were not kosher according to rabbinical *halakhic* law, which mandated that a child have a matrilineal Jewish heritage in order to be considered an authentic Jew. Indeed, though they quickly adopted a hardline Zionist viewpoint, very few of the Russian immigrants had any connection to Jewish religion and culture. Anastasia Michaeli channeled this sensibility when she declared, "Judaism is at the basis of why we have this country to begin with. It's not just a religion."

While Lieberman appealed to narrow Russian Israeli concerns with calls for legalizing civil marriage, his belligerent politics and strongman style resonated strongly with his rapidly expanding base. A 2009 poll taken by the Israel Democracy Institute found that 77 percent of immigrants from the Soviet Union supported forcibly transferring the Palestinian population out of Israeli-controlled territory. Though Lieberman drew his support almost exclusively from the Russian-Israeli sector, there was no shortage of support for transfer among the broader Israeli public. Indeed, according to the poll, a narrow majority of Jewish Israelis supported transfer. An Israeli poll taken in 2004 found authoritarian attitudes to be widespread among Jewish Israeli youth, with only 17 percent listing democracy as a "subject of national preference."

The Russian siege mentality evolved under Stalin and flourished until the end of the Soviet system, as one leader after another cultivated a state of constant emergency against a continually morphing great Enemy (under Stalin, Lieberman's father was taken captive by German troops before being imprisoned in a gulag for seven years). In Israel, the authoritarian trend intensified with the death of the Oslo era, providing a prime political climate for a strong-arm figure like Lieberman. As Israeli-American journalist Liel Liebovitz wrote, "It takes a very small leap of imagination to see how perfectly this [post-Soviet] mentality translates into Hebrew: In Israel, aspiring politicians born in the former Soviet Union found that talk of trenches and enemies made for stellar political currency."

Like Vladimir Putin, Lieberman believed he was called by history to restore the honor and morale of a traumatized, economically ravaged population. Both men demanded total compliance to the system of crony capitalism and social repression they sought to impose, exploiting every regulatory and bureaucratic mechanism at their disposal to neuter civil society, especially the pesky human rights NGOs that produced embarrassing English-language human rights reports every now and again. Most significant, perhaps, was the terrifying street-level atmosphere Putin and Lieberman cultivated in their respective societies. While Putin oversaw Nashi, a proto-fascistic and occasionally violent youth group that provided his authoritarian regime with the veneer of grassroots appeal, Lieberman's base included freelance gangs of aimless Russian immigrant youth who amused themselves by preying on African refugees and Arabs across the drab development towns and blue collar neighborhoods of Israel (Netanyahu's Likud kept close ties to the right-wing Im Tirtzu youth group, which menaced Arab students on college campuses and lobbied for McCarthyite investigations of "post-Zionist professors" and which is profiled later in this book).

As the home of the world's largest population of racist skinheads, Russia exported its neo-Nazi plague to the Jewish state. Starting in 2007, mobs of Russian teens who received automatic citizenship under Israel's Law of Return began spray-painting swastikas on synagogue walls and attacking Holocaust survivors, reportedly screaming, "Heil Hitler!" during several attacks. "There are groups in many towns," said Zalman Gilichenski, a Russian immigrant teacher who ran a hotline for victims of neo-Nazi attacks in Israel. "They distribute cassettes and written material. They began with graffiti and then graduated to beatings."

But Lieberman's open advocacy of state-sponsored ethnic cleansing set him apart from Putin, rendering him more extreme than even right-wing European populists like Jean-Marie Le Pen or Jorg Haider. As *Ha'aretz*'s Akiva Eldar wrote, "Haider is far from being a righteous man, but even in his most fascist days, he never called on Austria to rid itself of citizens who'd been living in the country for generations."

According to the details of "Plan Lieberman"—Lieberman's blueprint for ending the conflict—Israel would unilaterally establish permanent borders along demographic lines, bringing the major settlement blocs into "Israel proper" while leaving remote settlements out. Lieberman said he was willing to evacuate his own house in Nokdim to bring the plan to fruition, a vow that distinguished him from the Greater Israel types who comprised Likud and the religious nationalist parties.

The desire to consolidate demographic separation led Lieberman to propose leaving the Arab population cluster known as the "Little Triangle" in the Galilee outside of Israel's borders. In turn, at least twenty-five thousand Arabs would be stripped of their citizenship and transferred into the hands of the Palestinian Authority. Then, Lieberman would unilaterally establish a demilitarized, cantonized Palestinian entity in densely populated parts of the West Bank, permanently relieving Israel of the demographic burden of two million non-Jews under its control. While Plan Lieberman was widely derided and dismissed by Lieberman's opponents as a "Soviet" document reflecting an exogenous, totalitarian ideology, it was in fact a crudely articulated blueprint of the mainstream Israeli vision for a future "settlement" with the Palestinians. Indeed, Lieberman's plan was well in line with previous US peace process proposals advanced in secret by Labor and Kadima. As Azmi Bishara wrote, Lieberman "shares with the [Zionist] left a concern with 'the demographic issue' and the need to get rid of the Palestinians in the framework of an agreement in which they give up all their historic demands with the exception of a political entity, which just happens to be an Israeli demand as well."

As the longtime leader of Israel's "centrist" opposition party, Kadima, Tzipi Livni bridged the divide between Lieberman and the Zionist left. And unlike the Moldovan hard man, she was friendly enough to Western liberal sensibilities to advance his most controversial ambitions with the consent of international diplomats and to some degree, even the Palestinian Authority. During the so-called Annapolis track of peace process negotiations that lasted from 2007 to late 2008, Livni—who was then foreign minister—attempted to transform the negotiations into a forum for salvaging the Jewish demographic majority through transfer. Livni demanded that the Palestinian Authority allow Israel to transfer a series of impoverished Arab towns in northern Israel located near the Green Line—and all their non-Jewish residents—into its hands. The residents of these cities and neighborhoods would then have to choose between accepting citizenship in an impoverished, occupied territory ruled by a Western-imposed autocracy, or giving up their land and property in order to relocate to "Israel proper." Though they were technically citizens in the Middle East's "only democracy," Israel's Palestinian residents would have no say over which country they had a right to live in.

In a 2008 meeting with then–secretary of state Condoleezza Rice, Livni emphasized Israel's rejection of the Palestinian refugees' right to return to their confiscated land and property inside Israel on the grounds that the refugees threatened Israel's Jewish character. Rice, an African-American raised in the Jim Crow American South by a pro–civil rights Baptist preacher, shuddered at the implications of Livni's statement. "I must admit that though I understood the argument intellectually," Rice reflected, "it struck me as a harsh defense of the ethnic purity of the Israeli state when Tzipi said it. It was one of those conversations that shocked my sensibilities as an American. After all, the very concept of 'American' rejects ethnic or religious definitions of citizenship. Moreover, there were Arab citizens of Israel. Where did they fit in?"

But Rice's personal obligation to the legacy of racial justice was superseded by her loyalty to her boss, President George W. Bush. She was committed first and foremost to his messianic "war on terror," which she had compared in a speech to the American Civil War and the emancipation of the country's slaves. Like Bush, Rice was prone to conflating Israel's predicament with America's—both were employing military shock and awe to induce the "birth pangs of a new Middle East," as she said. "I took a deep breath and tried to understand, and slowly I came to see what she meant," Rice reflected after considering Livni's demand. Silencing her initial doubts, she proceeded to insert language into White House position papers, insisting the refugees return to the future Palestinian state in the West Bank or Gaza. "That would allow the democratic State of Israel to be 'Jewish,'" Rice wrote.

In cooperation with Livni, Rice then proposed to the Palestinian Authority's negotiating team that the refugees be airlifted en masse to Chile and Argentina, where they would begin a new life in permanent exile. "Bad things happen to people all around the world all the time," she told the Palestinians. "You need to look forward."

Lieberman learned of Livni's attempts to transfer the "demographic threat" into the hands of the Palestinian Authority as most Israelis did: through Al Jazeera's report on the so-called Palestine Papers. Leaked by a disgruntled Palestinian negotiator named Ziad Clot, the papers represented thousands of classified documents containing minute-by-minute accounts of the meetings between Israel and the Palestinian Authority. ("Far from enabling a negotiated and fair end to the conflict, the pursuit of the Oslo process deepened Israeli segregationist policies and justified the tightening of the security control imposed on the Palestinian population, as well as its geographical fragmentation," Clot later wrote). Lieberman was positively delighted by the revelations.

He promptly ordered Yisrael Beiteinu's chairman, Robert Ilatov, to invite Livni to the party's weekly faction meeting to present her plan for transfer. "Livni's proposal is consistent with the program of Yisrael Beiteinu so we will be happy to hear the full details from her," Ilatov stated in a tongue-in-cheek press release crafted to humiliate and embarrass the image-obsessed, Western-oriented Livni. Gilad Erdan, a close Netanyahu ally from Likud, piled on, announcing with unconcealed delight from the Knesset podium, "Thanks to Al Jazeera, we know that Livni's views are not far from those of Yisrael Beiteinu."

Lieberman's mockery tainted the moderate image Livni sought to project to Jewish American liberals, while on the domestic front, Livni was increasingly seen as feckless, insincere, and at the helm of a party that seemed like a randomly assembled collection of characters.

With roots in Likud, she struggled to find a coherent base anywhere else in Israeli politics. The dissolution of her party was almost inevitable, though her career seemed likely to linger on as marginalized Israeli liberals struggled for a viable alternative to the right-wingers who dominated the government. In the meantime, though she was insulated against the stain of direct collaboration with Lieberman, Livni's myriad challenges left her paralyzed in the face of the right's onslaught in the Knesset, prompting her to look the other way as one anti-democratic proposal after another came up for floor debates.

With Lieberman's party serving as the linchpin of this right-wing coalition government, and with Likud's old guard overwhelmed by younger zealots, Prime Minister Benjamin Netanyahu came down firmly on the side of the party's hardline future. By leaning on his right-wing base as nationalistic sentiment deepened throughout Israeli society, the slick-talking, basso profundo ideologue hoped to consolidate himself as the King of Israel, the country's first genuinely right-wing prime minister.

The Salesman

Well before Israel's Russian sector developed its own affinity politics, Avigdor Lieberman rose through the ranks of Likud under the stewardship of Benjamin Netanyahu. When Netanyahu was appointed Likud chairman in 1992, he tapped Lieberman as party manager, using him as his liaison to the Russian public. Even as the head of Yisrael Beiteinu, Lieberman remained open to merging his party with Likud in a dominant electoral coalition that would keep the center-left in permanent isolation. But even before the 2009 elections approached, Netanyahu envisioned the dawn of a one-party state, with himself at the helm. With the humiliation of diplomatic concessions etched in his memory, from his patron Yitzhak Shamir backing down to President George H. W. Bush to his own retreat under pressure from President Bill Clinton, Netanyahu saw his new term as a mandate to restore himself the guarantor of Greater Israel.

Raised in suburban Philadelphia and educated in business management at MIT in Cambridge, Massachusetts, Netanyahu pitched himself to Israelis as the man best able to explain Israel's supposedly unique situation to the world, and especially to its chief benefactor in Washington. During the Gulf War of 1991, when Netanyahu served as deputy foreign minister, he emerged as a familiar face on CNN, the first twenty-four-hour American news channel. Following a successful Likud-inspired campaign the previous year to oust CNN's chief Jerusalem correspondents, branding them as "self-hating Jews" with the help of Jewish American establishment groups, Netanyahu was able to single-handedly turn CNN into what one PLO official called "a propagandist for the Israelis."

For his extended televised diatribes branding the PLO as a front organization for Saddam Hussein, the *Washington Times* recommended Netanyahu for an Emmy Award, the honor bestowed on American daytime TV actors. Well before Netanyahu was an internationally recognized figure, veteran Middle East analyst Leon Hadar labeled him, "The Joe Isuzu of the Middle East Wars," referring to the fictional pitchman who amused American audiences with outrageously false claims about Isuzu cars—"Hi, I'm Joe Isuzu, and I used my new Isuzu pickup truck to carry a two-thousand-pound cheeseburger." With a straight face and a tone of total conviction, Netanyahu marketed a lemon to American consumers, and arguably faced fewer challenges than most used car salesmen.

By emphasizing the essential role of government public relations years before *hasbara*—the Hebrew term for the societal obligation to "explain" Israel's predicament to the world—became a national focus, and leveraging his success in the frenetic American media environment, Netanyahu improved his position himself on the domestic stage. He campaigned as much more than a politician: he was an American-accented marketing agent, so slick he could sell a dirty diaper to a garbage can—the Joe Isuzu of the Jewish state. He was the self-proclaimed master of *hasbara*, the explainer extraordinaire who could obliterate inconvenient truths about occupation and war crimes with emotionally potent talking points. As Netanyahu told a conference of Likud activists, "It doesn't matter if justice is on your side. You have to depict your position as just."

Netanyahu believed that if Israel was ever portrayed abroad as a strong-armed oppressor, it was because of a national failure to generate clever *hasbara*, not because of the state-practiced apartheid toward Palestinians. "Contrary to conventional wisdom, the issue here is not just what kinds of pictures will flicker across the television screen . . ." Netanyahu wrote in his 1993 manifesto, *A Durable Peace*. "I have found over the years . . . that occasionally one word can be worth a thousand pictures, rather than vice versa. For example, the word *occupation* [italics in original], or the expression *homeless people*. Or *Arab land*. Or *land for peace*. In countless newspaper pieces, journal articles, and books, the Arabs have devoted untold intellectual resources to framing the argument in such a way that it frames Israel. Israel will have to devote an even greater intellectual effort to extricating itself from the trap into which it has so readily entered."

When he entered the prime minister's office in 2009, Netanyahu immediately set himself to what he did best: spinning the herd of clueless American reporters and columnists who parachuted into Jerusalem and Tel Aviv each week. In August 2010, following the bloody Israeli raid on the Gaza Freedom Flotilla, the conservative American columnist George Will flew to Israel to meet with the prime minister. Will returned with an error-laden ode to Netanyahu, rehashing a tall tale that the prime minister first told at the annual American Israel Public Affairs Council's annual conference in Washington. "Nevertheless, a display case in Netanyahu's office could teach the Obama administration something about this leader," the awestruck Will wrote. "It contains a small signet stone that was part of a ring found near the Western Wall. It is about 2,800 years old—200 years younger than Jerusalem's role as the Jewish people's capital. The ring was the seal of a Jewish official, whose name is inscribed on it: Netanyahu."

What was Netanyahu's connection to the ring, and by extension, to the ancient land of Israel? There was none. Netanyahu's grandfather, Nathan Milikovsky, had merely changed his name to Netanyahu after he emigrated from Lithuania to Palestine. Thus Netanyahu had a much closer relation to the former Alaskan governor and vice presidential hopeful Sarah Palin, whose Lithuanian maternal grandfather was rumored to be a Jew, than to any late Bronze Age "Jewish official" from the Middle East. Intended to assert his legitimacy to rule over the Land of Israel, Netanyahu's magical ring tale rested on the same logical fallacy as my own dubious assertion to a historical mandate to rule over Mexico because my grandfather, Hymie Blumenthal, had changed his name to Hymie Quetzalcoatl. Despite his reliance on childlike myths that recalled the plot of the J. R. R. Tolkien *The Lord of the Rings* fantasy trilogy, or perhaps because of it, Netanyahu was able to inject his *hasbara* into the mainstream American media without the slightest difficulty.

As his term as prime minister wore on, Netanyahu extended more access to easily duped American reporters than to Israeli journalists who might be inclined toward skepticism. Instead of interacting candidly with the Israeli press, the prime minister's office briefed Israeli reporters with American reports that portrayed him in positive terms. Netanayahu achieved perhaps his greatest media coup in May 2012, when *Time* magazine managing editor Richard Stengel arrived at his doorstep eager to relay a heavy dose of Bibi-think to the American public. The result of the interview, carefully managed by Netanyahu and his American-born advisers, was a fawning profile in which Stengel compared the prime minister to Moses, imagined him arguing with God, and dubbed him, "King Bibi." "He's conquered Israel. But will Netanyahu now make peace—or war?" the cover read. Sixteen years prior, *Time* published a nearly identical cover, juxtaposing a triumphant Netanyahu with the question, "Can He Make Peace?"

Having convinced one of the American media's most influential figures to market him as a potential peacemaker, even as he rattled off violent threats against Iran and authorized thousands of new settlement units in the West Bank, Netanyahu and his inner circle celebrated the sensational public relations score. At a press conference in Prague with his Czech counterpart, the prime minister reveled in his coronation by *Time* as King of the Jews. "We are [engaging] in a *hasbara* effort and every opportunity to explain Israel's position is something that I welcome," Netanyahu declared.

The PR victory would not have been possible without the help of Netanyahu's American fixer, the Florida-born Ron Dermer. The son of a wealthy trial lawyer and brother of the former mayor of Miami Beach, a Democrat who helped elect Republican George W. Bush, Dermer enjoyed more proximity to Netanyahu than perhaps any other adviser. His principal role was to finesse the network of neoconservative think tanks, Israel lobbying organizations, and assorted Beltway influentials, leveraging them against an Obama administration that Netanyahu viewed with outright hostility. Dermer's apparent success in stymieing pressure from the White House confirmed a remark Netanyahu made to a family of bereaved settlers in 2001: "I know what America is," he said. "America is a thing you can move very easily, move it in the right direction. They won't get in the way."

The selection of Michael Oren, an American-born neoconservative and intellectual, as Israel's ambassador to the United States, was consistent with Netanyahu's obsession with shaping the American media's meta-narrative. Having reportedly named the *New York Times* one of Israel's "main enemies," then angrily denied even making such a statement, Netanyahu dispatched Oren as both his emissary to the thoughtful precincts of the political class and attack dog, siccing him and Dermer on the newspaper after a series of critical editorials and articles accusing him of interfering in the American political process in an effort to damage President Obama. In the tumultuous Netanyahu era, Oren was kept constantly busy.

When the ambassador learned that *60 Minutes*, the popular American news program, was planning a segment on the plight of Palestinian Christians living under occupation, he placed a panicked phone call to *CBS News* chief Jeff Fager, demanding that Fager pull the segment before it aired. Instead of acceding to Oren's demand, however, CBS correspondent Bob Simon grilled the ambassador about the phone call during the broadcast. Unaccustomed to hard questioning by American reporters, Oren was flustered, issuing a contorted, barely coherent response. "When I heard that you were going to do a story about Christians in the Holy Land," he stuttered, "and my assum . . . and . . . and had, I believe, information about the nature of it . . . and it's been confirmed by this interview today."

When confronting questions of occupation, or of anything related to the Palestinians, Netanyahu and his American-accented PR cadre seemed to recognize that they were not likely to win much international sympathy. Thus Netanyahu rehashed the public relations strategy he introduced during the early 1990s, when he openly urged the United States to invade Iraq and remove Saddam Hussein from power, warning that the consequence of inaction was a nuclear holocaust. This time, the Hitlerian enemy was the Islamic Republic of Iran, which had initiated a nuclear program with murky goals, and which provided sponsorship to Hezbollah and to a decreasing degree, to Hamas in the Gaza Strip. Shifting away from the traditional Israeli emphasis on shared values of democracy and liberalism, Netanyahu sought to recalibrate the Israeli's "special relationship" through the framework of the Islamophobic clash of civilizations narrative, in which the freedom-loving West waged an existential global fight against what Netanyahu called "the insatiable crocodile of militant Islam." In the battle for the heart of American opinion, Netanyahu assiduously cultivated Israel's image as a Fort Apache on the frontlines against the Muslim menace—and the United States as a larger Fort Apache that could learn from the Israeli model.

As Netanyahu ramped up the pressure for an American military strike on Iranian nuclear facilities, interviewers scarcely asked him questions about Palestinians, settlement expansion, or other disturbing issues. Speaking at the 2012 AIPAC policy conference in Washington before an audience of thousands of Jewish American supporters of Israel and the national press corps, Netanyahu did not use the word "Palestine" or "Palestinians" once. Instead, he delivered a surreal rant about the Iranian "nuclear duck," demanding that "the world start calling a duck a duck." As his stemwinder drew to a close, Netanyahu grew increasingly apocalyptic, suggesting that an American refusal to bomb Iran's nuclear facilities—or to authorize a unilateral Israeli strike—would repeat the Allied Forces' failure to attack Auschwitz during World War Two. Finally, the prime minister raised the Jewish holiday of Purim by reminding the crowd that "some twenty-five hundred years ago, a Persian anti-Semite tried to annihilate the Jewish people."

Aluf Benn, the editor-in-chief of *Ha'aretz*, worried that by invoking the Holocaust in such a spectacular fashion, Netanyahu had essentially committed himself to military action against Iran in some form in the near future. But Benn underestimated the prime minister's cynical gamesmanship. In the year following Netanyahu's address, while his hysterical rhetoric persisted, the Obama administration made it clear to him that it had no intention of attacking Iran and would continue to pursue sanctions and its diplomatic track. Netanyahu's nuclear show went on, allowing him to achieve another strategic goal. Behind the curtain Israel gained a free hand to act against the Palestinians as it pleased, sustaining the siege of Gaza. Slowly but surely, Netanyahu was realizing the fruits of a long-term plan for setting final borders on the exclusive terms of Greater Israel.

Like every Israeli prime minister before him, Netayahu's strategy depended on increasing the number of Jews living on Israeli-controlled territory and reducing the number of Palestinians. In November 1989, while he served as a junior minister in Shamir's government, Netanyahu spoke at Bar Ilan University, the academic mecca of religious nationalism in Israel. "Israel should have taken advantage of the suppression of the demonstrations in China [Tiananmen Square], when the world's attention was focused on what was happening in that country, to carry out mass expulsions among the Arabs of the Territories," Netanyahu told his audience. "However, to my regret, they did not support that policy that I proposed, and which I still propose should be implemented."

By all accounts, Netanyahu has remained a transferist—a term that has gained currency within Israel to describe a politician in favor of expelling Palestinians one way or another. By the time he reentered the prime minister's office in 2009, he seemed aware of the unfeasibility of mass expulsions, both politically and morally. It was only under the cover of two wars that Israel was able to force more than one million Palestinians outside the frontiers it controlled. Unless an attack on Iran triggered a prolonged regional conflict, such an opportunity was unlikely to arise again, at least, not in the foreseeable future. Though the Palestinians presented an existential challenge to Israel's demographic imperatives, Netanyahu believed that through careful but audacious planning, persistent low-intensity military operations, and aggressive public relations or hasbara, he could secure his vision of Greater Israel.

To consolidate Israel's control over the West Bank, Netanyahu sought massive land annexations in Area C, the vast portion of land placed under Israeli control by the Oslo Accords. He would then extend the corridors of major settlement blocs deep into Palestinian territory, strategically severing the Palestinian population clusters from one another while permanently encircling East Jerusalem, where massive settlement activity was already forcing Palestinians from their homes in droves. Toward the Gaza Strip, where Netanyahu had vowed to "crush the rule of Hamas," the Israeli military would "mow the lawn," an expression used to describe periodic assaults on the enclave's civilian and military infrastructure, hoping to whittle away at Hamas's deterrence capacity while battering the besieged population into submission. In the Negev Desert and the Galilee, the Israeli government ramped up its strategy of "Judaization," planting new, exclusively Jewish communities around, and sometimes in place of, ghettoized Arab towns. Judaization also formed the basis of Israel's approach to the mixed cities in the interior, creating unbearable pressure on

Arab city dwellers to move. On Netanyahu's watch, evidence of a clear and comprehensive plan to control all space—and the lives of all people—between the river and the sea was clearer than ever.

In the Likud-dominated Knesset, the plan took the form of legislation aimed at strengthening the "Jewish" character of the state at the expense of its purported democratic charter. Immediately after the new Knesset was sworn into office, bills aimed at limiting the speech rights of Palestinian citizens of Israel, imposing harsh penalties on human rights activists and separating Palestinian families became the order of the day. The anti-democratic legislative agenda proceeded with cooperation from Kadima, the loyal opposition party, and general acquiescence from a marginalized Labor Party. With Avigdor Lieberman by his side and a party full of far-right upstarts, Netanyahu would preside over the rapid deterioration of Israel's democratic veneer, prompting him to redouble his efforts against the international public relations threat he now called "delegitimization."

In his first book, *A Durable Peace*, Netanyahu hinted at the goals he would seek to fulfill if he ever managed to gain the title of "King Bibi." Mocking the culture of social justice he had witnessed among American Jews, Netanyahu rejected what he called "the relentless Jewish desire to see an end to struggle." To him and an increasing number of Israelis, the status quo of low intensity warfare was perfectly acceptable, while a one-way peace in which Israel enjoyed relative tranquility as it periodically decimated Palestinian urban centers was ideal. And the Israeli public that put him into office seemed to agree. Thus Netanyahu called on Israelis to steel themselves for "an ongoing national exertion and the possibility of periodic bouts of international confrontation." This single line neatly summarized the colonial logic animating his approach to the Palestinians and rationalizing it to the outside world.

In May 2009, months after Netanyahu, Lieberman, and the most right-wing government in Israel's history came to power, I landed at Ben Gurion International Airport, arriving for the first of many prolonged stays in the Holy Land.

PART II
LAWS OF
THE LAND

Number 1

n July 1948, the Israeli Haganah militia's armor columns rumbled into the twin cities of Lydda and Ramle, leaving in their wake a trail of captured and destroyed Palestinian villages near the coast, and bearing down on hundreds of thousands of refugees who had fled for the cities in Palestine's interior. Many refugees had sought shelter in Lydda and Ramle. Through Operation Danny, General Yigal Allon of the Haganah's elite Palmach strike force and General Yitzhak Rabin sought to dislodge them while placing the strategically located city in Israeli hands. Once Rabin and Allon initiated their assault on the city, they beseeched the Haganah commander-in-chief and prime minister David Ben Gurion for instructions. The commanders were particularly concerned with the tens of thousands of Palestinian Arabs huddled in the cities. What should we do with them? Rabin asked. With a wave of his hand, Ben Gurion gestured to expel the besieged refugee population. "Drive them out!" he exclaimed, according to an account by Rabin.

And so they did, sending nearly fifty-five thousand indigenous inhabitants on a forced march eastward to Ramallah in which hundreds died of exhaustion—the so-called "Lydda Death March." One young doctor trapped during an Israeli-imposed curfew in the Lydda hospital was overcome with horror at the carnage he had witnessed: His own sister died before his eyes, but he was unable to bury her because of the curfew. He was forced to dig a grave with his bare hands in the yard of her home. The young doctor was named George Habash, and would go on to found the Popular Front for the Liberation of Palestine, a leftist political faction that led the armed struggle against Israel for several decades, including through several notorious hijackings of international airliners.

Riding into Lydda in an armored car he dubbed "The Terrible Tiger," at the helm of the 89th Commando Battalion, was a little-known career soldier named Moshe Dayan. After Dayan's blitz into the city, an embedded reporter from the *New York Herald Tribune* surveyed the damage: "the corpses of Arab men, women, and even children strewn about in the wake of the ruthlessly brilliant charge." "Practically everything in their way died," a *Chicago Sun-Times* reporter wrote of the Israeli forces, describing Operation Dani as a "Blitzkreig." More than 170 Palestinian Arabs instructed to take shelter in the Dahmash mosque near Ramle were slaughtered by forces under Rabin and Allon's direct command, then left to rot in the July heat. About twenty to fifty more Palestinian men sent into the mosque by Israeli forces to extract the corpses and bury them were shot dead in the graves they had just dug.

Some soldiers robbed fleeing Palestinians of their gold jewelry. Others, according to Amos Kenan, a famous Israeli writer and bon vivant who participated in the conquest of Lydda, took further liberties. "At night," Kenan casually recalled in a 1989 article for the *Nation*, "those of us who couldn't restrain ourselves would go into the prison compounds to fuck Arab women." A few soldiers caught up in the orgy of violence succumbed to psychological trauma. As Rabin later recalled, "Prolonged propaganda activities were required after the action . . . to explain why we were obliged to undertake such a harsh and cruel action."

By the end of Operation Dani, Israeli forces had captured more than thirty Palestinian communities, including the cities of Lydda and Ramle. Most of the captured villages were bulldozed to the ground or destroyed with high explosives, expanding the territorial basis for the Jewish state that was soon to be founded. Having expelled all but a few hundred of Lydda Ramle's Palestinian residents, the Israelis cleared an open path for transportation between Tel Aviv and newly captured areas of West Jerusalem. Almost as importantly, they had taken control of Al-Lydda Airport, a major airfield formerly administered by the British colonial authorities. "We had a great time," Kenan wrote of the days he spent at the newly captured airport. "After morning parade and breakfast, we would chew the fat until lunchtime." As with the city of Lydda, the conquerors Hebraicized the name of the airport, renaming it Lod Airport.

Today, Lod Airport is named for the man whose stern wave of the hand brought it under Israeli control—it is Ben Gurion International Airport. Ben Gurion International is a cavernous, modern, glass-and-steel edifice that seems from an exterior glance like any other airport in a major Western capital. Once inside, however, the terminal's unique qualities come into immediate focus. As soon as they land or seek to depart from Israel, passengers are subjected to a rigorous process of ethnic categorization and psychoanalysis designed to vet the suitability of their presence inside Israeli-controlled frontiers. Masquerading as security measures, the vetting procedures are reflections of the discriminatory policies that govern the relationship between Israeli Jews, Palestinians, and the outside world. With an atmosphere crackling with the neurotic mood of ethnic suspicion and its hyper-securitized, high-tech gleam, Ben Gurion International is a microcosm of the modern Jewish state.

After landing at the airport in May 2009, I strolled past the exhibit of vintage Jewish National Fund posters—"Conquering the Wilderness," one of them read—and the newly posted signs urging Israelis to be "good ambassadors" when they traveled outside the country. In the weeks before my trip, several prominent left-wing international political figures had been denied entry to areas controlled by Israel. They included the Spanish clown Ivan Prado, who arrived at Ben Gurion International two months before me with the intention of organizing a clown festival in the occupied Palestinian city of Ramallah. Prado was detained for six hours and deported because the Shin Bet (Israel's general security service) claimed he had "links to Palestinian terror organizations." And there was Professor Noam Chomsky, the iconic left-wing intellectual, who was detained and interrogated at Israel's border for five hours by the Shin Bet on his way to speak at Bir Zeit University in the West Bank and finally deported to Jordan. Though Chomsky had been a withering critic of Israeli policy for decades, Israeli officials were unable to explain why they barred his entry.

Before traveling to Israel in May 2009, I met in New York City with Jared Malsin, then a twenty-seven-year-old Jewish-American correspondent for Ma'an News, who was back in the city after a long stint reporting from the occupied West Bank. He is clean cut, bespectacled, soft spoken, and reserved, hardly the kind of person a security officer might identify as a threat. However, when he returned to Israel from a trip to Prague with his girlfriend, Malsin told me Shin Bet officers had immediately escorted him to a holding cell. In the small room, an unidentified female Shin Bet officer interrogated Malsin about articles he had published on Israeli army abuses of civilians in the West Bank. After seizing Malsin's cellphone and belongings, the officer coldly informed him, "In this office, you have no rights." For eight days, Malsin was held in virtual solitary confinement with one pair of clothes, no opportunity to shower, no toothbrush, and for most of the time, no reading material. "I could have tried to hold out while my lawyer appealed my case, but without any books or any way to write anything down, I felt like I was slowly beginning to go crazy," he said. After over a week in detention, and separated from his girlfriend, whom he was unable to communicate with, Malsin decided to accept his deportation.

Chronicles of harsh interrogations and the arbitrary deportation of journalists, international human rights activists, and dissidents at Ben Gurion Airport are legion. But their treatment pales in comparison to the abuse meted out by Shin Bet officers to Palestinians, Palestinian citizens of Israel, and Arabs in general. Any Arab flying out of Ben Gurion must arrive at least five hours in advance for what one friend described as the "mandatory proctology exam" at the hands of security officers. "This phenomenon is so widespread that it is hard to find any Arab citizen who travels abroad by air and who has not experienced a discriminatory security check at least once," the Arab Association for Human Rights and the Centre Against Racism concluded in 2006.

EL AL Airlines, the national airline of Israel, coordinates closely with the country's intelligence services. The airline has been accused of allowing Mossad officers to pose as EL AL staffers to collect information on non-Jewish passengers in foreign airports. In 2010, EL AL was forced to pay $8,000 to two Arab citizens of Israel who were humiliated by a female security officer who stood over them for an entire flight, ordering them not to speak or use the bathroom without her escort—and after they had passed every airport security check. Another Arab citizen of Israel, the journalist Yara Mashour, said she was forced to switch airlines after EL AL agents refused to relent in an interrogation process that seemed aimed more at denigration than investigation. "I felt like they were raping me in many senses," Mashour said afterward. Another Arab journalist from Israel, Ali Waked, who wrote for the major Israeli daily *Yedioth Ahronoth*, was banned from flying to Egypt in 2004 with Israel's then–foreign minister Silvan Shalom without any explanation.

No Arabs are exempt from discrimination at Ben Gurion International, not even the six-month-old Arab baby who was separated from her parents and strip-searched by airport security agents. The discrimination against Arabs at Ben Gurion Airport is so systematic the Israeli authorities make little attempt to conceal it; in 2006, the Shin Bet and Israeli Ministry of Transportation ordered a local airline to block any Arabs from flying until a temporary glitch in X-ray machines was repaired. Jewish passengers, meanwhile, were not even subjected to extra searches.

In August 2010, former Clinton cabinet secretary of Health and Human Services Donna Shalala traveled to Israel on a delegation organized by American Jewish Committee. Shalala, who was serving at the time as the president of the University of Miami, met with top Israeli officials, including Shimon Peres, during her visit to coordinate strategies to battle Palestinian solidarity activism on American college campuses. However, when Shalala arrived at Ben Gurion, a security officer noticed her Arab-sounding last name—Shalala was born to Lebanese immigrant parents—and took her to the "Arab room" for a two and a half hour interrogation procedure that nearly caused her to miss her flight.

Israeli security services claim to operate under a complex behavior detection system that focuses on "micro-expressions" evincing nervousness or malicious intent. A keen observer who has traveled through Ben Gurion on multiple occasions might conclude, however, that the Shin Bet's screening system is based on a model of racial profiling. Even before entering the airport, drivers must pass through a checkpoint where an armed security officer peers into the vehicle, looking for Arabs and other "threats." On almost every occasion in which I have taken an airport shuttle from Jerusalem, an Arab or a dark-skinned non-Jew was taken off the bus for questioning. Inside the terminal, the moment a passenger enters the security queue, an officer approaches to initiate an "interview." The officers, who are usually young, well mannered, and educated Israelis trained in the practice of "psychotechnics," immediately conduct an "accent check" to determine the flyer's ethnicity and nationality.

The accent check occurs during an "interview," which invariably begins with questions about the flyer's ethnic and religious origins. At the conclusion of the interview, the security officer classifies the passenger with a number between one and six. One is reserved for Jewish Israelis and most international Jews, who are allowed to forgo an intensive and invasive hand check of their luggage before they check in. Three and four are reserved for non-Jews, especially Arabs and foreign people of color, who are often escorted to what is commonly known as "the Arab room" for demeaning and time-consuming interrogations. Those who receive a six—the greatest "security threat"—are either Arabs or "hostile" leftist solidarity activists, usually those who had the misfortune to wind up on a Shin Bet blacklist. While Palestinians are detained for an extended period and sometimes blocked from flying, activists are generally deported and banned from Israel for a period of ten years. Palestinians who pass through security procedures receive a special sticker on their passport reading, "Did you pack a bomb by mistake?"

In 2012, the Israel Airports Administration created what it called a "unit entrusted with liaising with the population of members of minorities in Israel." The new unit began issuing a special "Ethnic Minorities Form" to Arab families planning to fly from Ben Gurion. The form requires Arabs to list the names and all passport numbers of their family members, as well as the names of whoever authorized their trip, thus assuming that Arabs do not travel abroad for leisure or business trips. "I would be thankful for any assistance you can extend at the airport," the form reads, suggesting that Arabs should express gratitude for being discriminated against. Dimi Reider, the Israeli journalist who revealed the new forms, commented, "More than anything else, this is a clear and stark example of normalization of apartheid: when both parties accept an ethnically discriminative practice as a given, and just seek to make it a little more palatable."

In July 2011, hundreds of international solidarity activists organized a protest of discriminatory practices at Ben Gurion informally known as the "flytilla." They planned to land at the airport on flights from around the world in a coordinated fashion, then unapologetically inform airport security agents of their intention to volunteer for human rights and aid organizations in refugee camps in the West Bank (even the slightest hint that a tourist plans to travel into occupied territory can lead to immediate deportation). On July 8, when the demonstrators converged at Ben Gurion, chanting "Free Palestine!" upon arrival, they were set upon by mobs of angry Jewish Israeli travelers. Men charged at the demonstrators, who consisted mostly of middle-aged European women, shouting, "Sons of bitches!" and "Garbage!" Israeli police waiting at the scene for the protest to forcibly herd the demonstrators away into holding cells, instead saved them from a possible mob assault.

When Larry Derfner, an Israeli journalist who had arrived to cover the incident, was mistaken for a protester, an old woman began screaming at him, "Get out of here!" prompting police to throw him into a van and attempt to haul him to prison until he displayed his government-approved press credentials. "Watching my enraged countrymen at Ben-Gurion, I imagined the daily headlines having been distilled into a kind of political methadrine and mainlined into their veins . . . in their insistence that protesters like these be silenced because their words are acts of violence, acts of war, of terrorism, they represent the majority," Derfner wrote afterward. "They are an authentic expression of the national will."

Justifying the mass arrest of peaceful demonstrators seeking to volunteer in the West Bank, Benjamin Netanyahu declared, "Every country has the right to prevent the entry of provocateurs and troublemakers into its territory. That is how all countries behave, and that is how Israel will act. We must prevent the disruption of normal life for Israeli citizens."

Before any trip to Israel-Palestine, I receive a dizzying array of advice from journalist and activist friends on how to pass through Israeli security with minimal harassment. A Jewish-American writer for a Palestinian diaspora publication told me she always wore blue-and-white clothing—the colors of the Israeli flag—and a gold Star of David necklace, and flirted openly with security officers of the opposite sex. A left-wing Israeli activist advised me to behave in an irritable, churlish fashion, blurting out terse responses to questions from security officers to avoid creating the perception that I was overcompensating for any "anti-Israel" intentions. Other journalist friends warned me to erase any and all Arab contacts from my phone, and to delete any material I had published about the Israel-Palestine conflict from my computer hard drive. They reminded me about Lily Sussman, the twenty-one-year-old Jewish American college student detained in December 2009 by the Shin Bet at Israel's border with Egypt because she was carrying suspicious items, such as an Arabic phrasebook. After two hours of intense interrogation, a baby-faced Shin Bet officer appeared to inform Sussman, "I'm sorry, but we had to blow up your laptop." He then handed her a MacBook riddled with bullet holes. Luckily for Sussman, the bullets missed her hard drive.

After deciding that I was too lazy to purge my computer and cellphone of Arab contacts, I concluded that I had nothing to hide and that the Israeli intelligence services could not possibly be foolish enough to treat me as a security threat. I then reminded myself that I was an Ashkenazi Jew who would be automatically afforded special rights according to the designs of Zionism.

My Jewish privilege would be borne out during many trips in and out of Ben Gurion Airport. Whenever a security officer greeted me with the requisite opening question, "Are you Jeweesh?" I have learned to casually respond, "Of course." If I were ever asked if I had any Israeli family, I would tell them about all my imaginary cousins in Tel Aviv or about my imaginary Israeli girlfriend. "Are you thinking of marrying your girlfriend," a young female security officer asked me once. "I sure am!" I said with a bashful smile, bringing a satisfied grin to the face of the officer. Because the maintenance of a Jewish demographic majority is Israel's national priority, the production of Jewish babies is a key national priority. With my promise to inject top-grade Ashkenazi Jewish sperm into the ovum of a young Jewish Israeli woman, I was marked with a level-one security classification.

Each time I reach the kiosk at passport control on my way into Israel-Palestine, I do my best to appear calm, and even a little bit bored, while the officer examines my documents. With bated breath I wait for the loud thump of the metal visa stamp when it meets the pages of my passport. Only with that noise will I know that I have gained admission through the fortified frontiers controlled by Israel. As a sense of relief washes across my body, a single thought enters my mind that is constantly reaffirmed throughout my time inside Israel-Palestine: I am a lucky Jew.

Settling in the Hearts

When I arrived in Israel-Palestine in July 2010 for an extended reporting trip, I stayed in Jaffa, an impoverished traditionally Arab city that formed Tel Aviv's southern ghetto and the next frontier of its yuppie high-tech class. I rented a room in a dilapidated two-story house on the border of Ajami that from the outside vaguely resembled a Wild West saloon. The house stood on "Doctor Paul Erlich Street," a two-lane boulevard of crumbling homes named after a fin de siecle Austrian Jewish medical pioneer who never set foot in Palestine. Prior to 1948, before the state's Naming Committee Hebraicized street names across Israel, the road was named for Doctor Fouad Dajani, an early leader of the Palestinian national movement who dedicated his life to maintaining a first-class hospital he founded in Jaffa.

During the 1947–1948 campaign of expulsions and ethnic cleansing that Palestinians refer to as the Nakba, or "the catastrophe," Dajani's former hospital, which I would pass by every day on my way into Tel Aviv, was seized by the State of Israel. After being expropriated, the hospital was promptly renamed "Zahalon Geriatric Center" in honor of Jacob Zahalon, a rabbi and physician from seventeenth-century Italy who was about as familiar to Arab residents of Jaffa as an ice skating rink.

Situated in the center of Israel's coastline, and sprawled out against the Mediterranean Sea, Jaffa is one of the oldest continually inhabited places in the world. Before the fateful years of 1947 and '48, the city was known as "The Bride of the Sea," a cosmopolitan hub boasting over a dozen newspapers and magazines, a bustling port, renowned schools and hospitals, and a roaring citrus export industry. Arabs from Lebanon, Iraq, and Egypt flocked to Jaffa to toil in the port, build wooden crates for oranges, and join crews on fishing trawlers. The Palestinian entrepreneurs who oversaw the port's operations took pride in their position of economic preeminence in the Arab world.

Jaffa's orchards and port also served as incubators of Jewish-Arab cooperation and coexistence. The Palestine Citrus Board, overseen by the British colonial authorities in the 1930s and early '40s, mandated a mutually beneficial arrangement in which Arabs worked for Jewish orchard owners and vice versa. A local cooperative called Pardes relied on both Jewish and Arab labor to ship Jaffa's oranges to Western Europe. "We lived among the Arabs, or within the Arabs, they lived around," Gideon Makoff, the Israeli general secretary of the Pardes cooperative, remarked in Eyal Sivan's 2010 documentary, *Jaffa: The Orange's Clockwork*. A Pardes promotional document emphasized the importance of economic cooperation between Arabs and Jews:

"This is the first time a committee has been formed in Jaffa to organize fruit shipping. Its work has been fruitful and we may hope that all orange producers regardless of race, religion, will unite to form a body dedicated to organizing all mutual interests."

But the cooperative spirit of Pardes rankled the emerging Labor Zionist establishment, which preached a strict doctrine of *Avodah Ivrit*, or Hebrew labor, and *Kibush Ha'avodah*, or the strict enforcement of Jewish-only labor. As the vanguard of the Zionist movement, the Labor movement hewed closely to socialist ideology and a statist doctrine as the best means of establishing the infrastructure for a Jewish state in Palestine. Unlike other socialists around the world, the Labor Zionists fused ethnic exclusivism with their vision of worker solidarity. Like the state they sought to found, their socialism was for Jews only.

"We were considered the right wing, in a distinction the [Zionist] left cared to make. But we weren't for total separation, we didn't think we couldn't live together," Makoff of the Pardes Cooperative told Sivan. Throughout Palestine, the Labor Zionists organized boycotts of Jewish businesses that employed Arabs, and attacked merchants who sold Arab goods.

In a speech before the Mapai secretariat, the left-wing Israeli politician David Hacohen recalled his discomfort as he defended the prestate Zionist "conquest of labor" against criticism from a group of socialist comrades from around the world. "I had to fight my friends on the issue of Jewish socialism, to defend the fact that I would not accept Arabs in my trade union, the Histadrut," Hacohen remarked, "to defend preaching to housewives that they not buy at Arab stores; to defend the fact that we stood guard at orchards to prevent Arab workers from getting jobs there. . . . To pour kerosene on Arab tomatoes; to attack Jewish housewives in the markets and smash the Arab eggs they had bought. . . . And despite the fact that we did it—maybe we had no choice—I wasn't happy about it."

In 1936, David Ben Gurion, then the leader of the Histadrut labor union that organized the boycotts, declared, "The destruction of Jaffa, the city, and the port will happen, and it will be for the best. This city, which grew fat on Jewish immigration and settlement, is asking for destruction when it swings a hatchet over the heads of its builders and benefactors. When Jaffa falls into hell, I will not be among the mourners."

On May 13, 1948, two days before Israel declared its "independence" from Great Britain, Ben Gurion's wish came true. Zionist militias attacked Jaffa in full force, with up to 5,000 troops invading the city in waves, raining artillery shells down on the civilian population. By the end of the siege, many of the over 50,000 Arab Jaffans forced from their homes had been literally driven into the sea—forced to flee by boat to Gaza and Lebanon with whatever they could carry, and never to return. Others marched off to Ramle-Lydda, only to be chased off to Nablus and other West Bank cities by the advancing Haganah forces.

Among the refugees driven from Jaffa was Ghassan Kanafani, who would become the famed Palestinian poet and author who was blown up by a car bomb in Beirut by the Israeli Mossad in 1972, allegedly in retaliation to the Japanese Red Army's terrorist attack on Lod Airport. Kanafani recalled the harrowing journey his family took into Lebanon, and the pangs of sorrow they felt at the first sight of oranges, the symbol of the lives they had been forced to leave behind. "As the women walked back with the oranges, the sound of their sobs reached us," he wrote. "Only then did oranges seem to me something dear, that each of these big, clean fruits was something to be cherished. Your father alighted from beside the driver, took an orange, gazed at it silently, then began to weep like a helpless child."

Once Israel conquered Jaffa, its new government ordered the bulldozing of 75 percent of the city's Arab section. Under the auspices of the new Absentee Property Law, the state placed all remaining Arab property in the hands of the Custodian of Absentee Property, which promptly redistributed it into Jewish hands under a law passed in 1953 called the Land Acquisition Law. The legislation cruised through the Knesset despite vehement opposition by Palestinian citizens of Israel and a few Jewish Israelis.

Among the dissidents was Israeli writer Moshe Keren, who denounced the law as "wholesale robbery with a legal coating." Simon Shereshevsky, who cofounded the binationalist Ihud Party with Judah Magnes, condemned the discriminatory logic behind the law. "They are agricultural people, like you, citizens like you," he proclaimed before his fellow Israelis. "There exists only one difference between them and you: they are Arabs and you are a Jew." But Shereshevsky's pleadings fell on deaf ears.

According to the details of both laws, the State of Israel was authorized to expropriate the property of anyone who fled their home or land at any time between the dates of November 29, 1947 and September 1, 1948. Given that these were the dates between which the UN ratified the plan to partition Israel and Palestine and when the hostilities ended, the laws clearly singled out Palestinians without explicitly mentioning them. Between 1948 and 1953, 95 percent of new Jewish communities were established on "absentee" Palestinian land. As former Israeli prime minister Menachem Begin's adviser on Arab affairs said, "If we needed this land, we confiscated it from the Arabs. We had to create a Jewish state in this country, and we did."

Some of the most valuable "absentee property" lay in Jaffa's vast and profitable orange groves. Immediately after the Israeli conquest of Jaffa, the fields were surrounded with barbed wire and signs that read "State Property: Entrance Forbidden." They were among the two hundred thousand dunams of active farmland seized from their Arab owners by the new State of Israel. In Jaffa, a few former Palestinian orange grove owners returned to the land they had once owned to toil as field hands in the hot sun for their new Jewish owners. By 1951, the expropriated orange groves accounted for 10 percent of Israel's export earnings, while olive produce from seized Arab land served as the third-largest source of the country's exports in 1949. With sustained marketing campaigns, the Jaffan orange became one of the most widely identified symbols of Israel in the West—and one of the few that carried no military association.

From 1948 to 1966, the remaining Palestinian residents of Jaffa were confined to the ghetto of Ajami under emergency military regulations imposed by the state's purportedly socialist leadership. Their freedom of movement was severely restricted by guard dogs and barbed wire for the first two years of military rule. "Before Zionism came to us, we didn't even know what a ghetto was," remarked Sami Shehadeh, director of the Popular Committee for the Defense of Jaffa's Homes.

Following the imposition of martial law, the new State of Israel sent its army to conduct ruthless hunts for "infiltrators" inside Arab communities. Any refugee who managed to slip back into their old town or city to reunite with their family members was violently rooted out. Carried out under the pretext of security precautions, the operations were in fact designed to preserve the fragile Jewish demographic majority.

In 1954, Ben Gurion authorized a new law passed by the Knesset that legalized the mass deportation of refugees attempting to return home. Called the "Prevention of Infiltration Law," the bill designated anyone a criminal who had entered Israel after November 29, 1947—the fateful date of partition—and who was not Jewish. Moshe Dayan, who was then the head of the Israeli army's Southern Command, declared at the time, "I hope that there will perhaps be another opportunity in the future to transfer these Arabs from the Land of Israel, and as long as such a possibility exists, we must do nothing to foreclose the option."

By the 1980s, Jaffa had degenerated into an impoverished suburb of Tel Aviv, plagued by substance abuse, crime, and the ongoing trauma of a Nakba that continued at a slow, inexorable pace. After the Tel Aviv municipality destroyed three thousand apartment units near Jaffa's beach in 1985 while failing to clear the rubble away, the beach became known as the "Mountain of Trash." Tel Aviv's authorities agreed to remove the heap of decaying waste in the 1990s only when rubbish began to explode from the rotting piles at random, creating dangerous fires. Around this time, the Tel Aviv municipality bulldozed the orange groves that had once served as the symbol of Jaffa, using the open fields to make way for new Jewish residential areas. No new residential areas were created for Arab inhabitants, however.

In 1986, the Israeli producer-director Menahem Golan (he was born Menahem Globus in an act of patriotic fervor) chose Jaffa's Ajami slums as the set for *Delta Force*, a classic piece of anti-communist kitsch, starring hardboiled action heroes Chuck Norris and Lee Marvin. The plot was set in civil war–era Beirut, where Norris and Marvin heroically mowed down teams of Arab terrorists played by Jewish Israeli actors. With Ajami chronically neglected, de-developed, and impoverished since it was conquered by Israel, it was virtually indistinguishable from the most war-torn areas of Lebanon. It was therefore an ideal site to shoot a film like *Delta Force*.

After the catastrophe of 1948, the four thousand remaining Arabs of Jaffa saw their homes placed in the hands of a state-run holding company called Amidar. In 2007, Amidar began issuing demolition orders on 497 Jaffan houses, threatening to make more than five thousand local Palestinians homeless. The holding company justified the mass evictions on the basis that the residents had made renovations without attaining proper permission. But Sami Shehadeh explained to me, "The Tel Aviv municipality has made attaining a permit for making any kind of renovation virtually impossible. These houses are all crumbling and are in dangerous condition, but nothing can be done without risking eviction. So it's clear that the municipality has an agenda, which is to make way for people from Tel Aviv to move in after the local Palestinian community is moved out."

Blocks away from my house, on Hatzadef Street, wealthy developers from Tel Aviv had taken advantage of the eviction orders to build gaudy, multimillion-dollar developments for wealthy Jews and international diplomats. "The whole neighborhood is one big construction site," Shehadeh complained. On the corner of the street was a spacious three-level home that, according to Shehadeh, recently sold for around $3 million. After the home's original residents vacated the property, Ilan Pivko, a famed Israeli architect known as the "new hedonist representative," completely gutted it, installing a luxurious interior while only slightly retouching the rustic Arabesque façade, maintaining the prized property's "authentic" character—but without its authentically Arab inhabitants. Across a narrow lane and overlooking the glimmering Mediterranean Sea was a new multi-million dollar home just put on the market by its former owner, the Danish ambassador to Israel. Behind a wall and thick hedges of elegantly landscaped desert foliage was a swimming pool that seemed to hover at the same level as the horizon of the sea. Ostentatious homes like these were sprouting up across Ajami's coastline, driving the cost of living to impossibly high levels for longtime Palestinian residents.

Hatzadef led straight into Jaffa's old city, a conglomerate of charming restaurants, craft shops, and art studios. In 1968, the area was transformed into an artist's colony, enabling the state to expropriate Arab homes from their expelled original residents under the guise of bohemian cultural progress. In the center of the old city was a large metal sign guiding foreigners through the history of Jaffa—or at least the Zionist version of it. According to the sign's English timeline, Jaffa was "liberated" in 1948.

The old city was also home to Israel's only S&M bondage club. Called "Dungeon," the dingy restaurant-club occupied what was once a three-hundred-year-old Palestinian mosque. Israelis from across the country flocked to Dungeon for its assorted theme parties, from chocolate fetish night, where participants bathed one another in chocolate milk, to medical fetish night, where male bondage enthusiasts enjoyed having the remainder of their circumcised foreskin sewn over the tip of their penis. "Outside everything is abnormal, and if you want to make people feel normal inside you need people that are a little bit weird," Dungeon's owner, Amos Levy, mused to a visiting journalist.

Just north of the old city lay Andromeda Hills, a colossal gated community of faux Arabesque, luxury condominiums rising high over the Mediterranean coast. In 2010, the Jewish residents of Andromeda Hills began bombarding the Tel Aviv municipality with noise complaints, demanding an ending to the tolling of bells by St. George Church, an Orthodox church built in 1870. They also called for a halt to the muezzin's call to prayer that emanated from the Siksik and Jabaliya mosques, which were both built well before the establishment of the State of Israel.

"The noise is simply intolerable," said a lawyer for the Andromeda Hills residents. Suspicions among local Arabs that the noise complaints were part of an ulterior long-term agenda aimed at driving them away from Jaffa were reinforced when Yisrael Beiteinu's ultranationalist exmodel Anastasia Michaeli introduced a bill in the Knesset proposing to illegalize the use of loudspeakers to broadcast the call of the muezzin from mosques. In December 2011, Prime Minister Benjamin Netanyahu endorsed the bill, declaring that such a ban "is legitimate in Belgium; it's legitimate in France. Why isn't it legitimate here? We don't need to be more liberal than Europe."

While Jaffa's pockets of Jewish wealth constantly expanded, young Palestinian couples struggled desperately to find housing. When they have children and begin searching for a larger apartment, local real estate agents often redirect them to housing in depressed, dilapidated sections of Lod or Bat Yam, a working class, mostly Russian city to Jaffa's immediate south. Though it pointedly refused to authorize new housing for local Arabs, the Israeli government initiated a program to offer new apartments in Jaffa to reserve soldiers of the Israeli army at a 15 percent discount.

With a lack of economic opportunity among the local Palestinian population, the black market is often the only option for earning a viable income. But with crime on the rise, police violence has become an epidemic in the area. The Oscar-nominated film *Ajami* provided a vivid portrayal of the violence that punctuated daily life in Jaffa's imperiled Arab ghetto. Just days before the 2010 Academy Awards, the brother of *Ajami*'s Palestinian-Israeli codirector Scandar Copti was assaulted by Israeli police when he attempted to prevent them from arresting a group of children allegedly burying a dead dog—the police thought they were hiding drugs. Enraged by the incident, Copti refused to appear on Israel's behalf at the awards ceremony, declaring, "I don't represent Israel. I cannot represent a country that does not represent me."

But it was not just common criminals the police were searching for; demographic threats were roaming the streets in plain view. There were many nights when I witnessed Border Police officers stalking the neighborhood for "infiltrators," or Palestinians from the West Bank who had sneaked through the separation wall. On a few occasions, I witnessed the police administering a flying checkpoint on Yefet Street, a two-lane thoroughfare in the center of Jaffa, stopping olive-skinned drivers to demand their identification cards. The ad hoc checkpoints in my neighborhood reminded me distinctly of the occupied West Bank, but without the obtuse militarization.

At the southern tip of Ajami was the gleaming headquarters of the Peres Center for Peace, a multimillion dollar outfit dedicated to promoting Jewish-Arab coexistence and dialogue. The center is named for Shimon Peres, a politician regarded in the West as a dovish Nobel Peace Prize–winner, but known by Palestinians and Lebanese citizens for his role as the architect of countless brutal military operations like 1996's Operation Grapes of Wrath, which culminated with artillery strikes that killed 102 Lebanese women and children while they huddled in a UN bomb shelter at Qana. His outfit in Jaffa was a central cog in an effort to leverage the hundreds of millions of dollars that poured into Israel from Europe and the US after the Oslo Accords into institutionalizing the structure of the peace process. In recent years, the Peres Center focused its efforts on organizing joint Palestinian-Israeli soccer matches in European cities, particularly where activist efforts to divest from Israeli companies were gaining steam.

In the view of Sami Shehadeh, a leading local activist and one of only a handful of Arab doctorate-level students at Tel Aviv University, the Peres Center's efforts were aimed at muting resistance to the state's discriminatory policies. "Rich people from abroad are pumping money into these groups to promote coexistence. But the problem here is not coexistence," Sami Shehadeh remarked to me. "The problem is *equal* coexistence. I mean, blacks and whites coexisted in the Jim Crow South, didn't they?"

Designed by the renowned Italian architect Massimiliano Fuksas, the Peres Center was built atop the entrance to a historic Muslim graveyard, and over vehement local opposition. Set beside the crumbling graves and amid rows of dilapidated homes, the futuristic, parallelepiped building seemed completely alien to its environment, as though it had been dropped in the heart of the crumbling Mediterranean ghetto by a spaceship from Planet Zargon. On the wall of a crumbling house across the street from the Peres Center, someone had spray-painted an arrow pointing north toward Tel Aviv. Below the arrow, the graffiti read, "Europe, 2 KM."

When *Ha'aretz* published a negative review of the Peres Center's design, criticizing the building as "foreign to its surroundings," two readers wrote to the paper in protest. "This is a completely minor foreignness," they countered, "as the entire area is radically changing and from a typical Arab, Mediterranean neighborhood; it is now becoming a well-tended neighborhood with a Western character and a well-designed beach, paved walkways, and new buildings that are slowly pushing out the ancient Arab ones." Thus the concerned readers reassured their fellow Jewish Israelis that the ongoing colonial process was proceeding smoothly. The Palestinian outclass would be gradually swept away once again, and an exclusively Jewish, European-style utopia would soon prevail.

"Israelis want to recreate a kind of European reality here," Shehadeh remarked. "Their whole society is directed toward Europe. What they don't understand is that we love the Arab world. It's who we are. We are Palestinians, not Israeli Arabs with separate identities."

Shehadeh went on: "Do you know what my dream is? It's to have lunch in Beirut and dinner in Damascus. My grandfather used to take a taxi to Beirut from Jaffa. Because I am a Palestinian in Israel, that is only a dream."

While the process of gentrification kept tensions at a constantly elevated state in Jaffa, a reverse migration of fundamentalist settlers to Israel's coastal heart threatened to set the neighborhood of Ajami alight. In 2010, the Israeli Supreme Court authorized a group of religious nationalist Jewish settlers from the West Bank to build a Jews-only settlement in the heart of Ajami, on a plot of land originally promised by the state to the local Arab population to help ameliorate its housing crisis. The new settlement was a central cog in the radical right's "building in the hearts" campaign, which aimed to create a bloc of settlements in the center of mixed Arab-Jewish cities that would be impossible to dislodge, and to use them as citadels for the incitement of ethnic conflict. Rabbi Eliyahu Mali, a West Bank rabbi who planned to lead the Jaffa settlement's yeshiva, said that if settlers "would send one-tenth of their residents to large cities . . . this one-tenth of people imbued with faith will establish a community, a yeshiva, and a center amid the Jewish populace, which will create a different reality than we know today." In the event of a two-state "solution" requiring the evacuation of ideological settlements in the West Bank, many of the most hardline settlers planned to relocate to mixed cities like Jaffa and Acre.

Following the rightists' victory before the High Court, the ultranationalist settler Baruch Marzel began leading provocative anti-Arab marches through the center of Jaffa and other mixed cities on the central coast. Groups of young Jewish fundamentalists followed the trail Marzel had blazed, storming through Jaffa to carry out miniature pogroms. In May 2010, a group of young men waving Israeli flags burst into the yard of Zeinab Rechayel, a local Palestinian woman, and began chanting, "This is our land!" "Yafo is just for Jews," one of them told her, using the Hebrew translation of Jaffa. "Get out of Yafo!" he shouted. The following January, a similar group attacked the Al Nozha Mosque with rocks, chanting "Death to Arabs!" while police stood by passively, intervening only to prevent a fight between the settlers and men who had been praying inside.

In November 2010, the Tel Aviv District Court rejected a petition filed by Jaffa residents that challenged the construction of the Jews-only housing development planned in the heart of their city. The court ruled that B'Emuna, the right-wing construction company that planned to build the development, and which had already constructed several ideological settlements in the West Bank, had the right to discriminate as it saw fit because it had outbid everyone else when the land in Jaffa was auctioned. "Our ideology is not to enter an Arab neighborhood," said B'Emuna director Israel Zeira, after winning the decision, "but to go to Jaffa in order to bolster Jewish identity."

On January 29, 2011, following the attacks on local mosques, hundreds of Jaffans gathered to stage a rare protest march through the heart of their city. It was in fact the first time in recent memory that the Tel Aviv municipality had granted Jaffa's Arab community a protest permit. The local merchants who earned their keep by serving hummus and sandwiches to Jewish Israelis on beach trips and late night post-party excursions were uneasy about organized displays of Arab indignation. They feared a return to the early days of the Second Intifada, when Jaffan demonstrations in solidarity with the revolt by occupied Palestinians provoked a Jewish boycott of local restaurants, with Tel Aviv companies even refusing to deliver milk to shops in Jaffa, according to Shehadeh. "Most of us work in restaurants serving Jews from Tel Aviv," Shehadeh said, "so they know they can control economically by boycotting when we fail to hold up their expectations." But the anger had boiled over again, creating a rare consensus for protesting.

It was a blustery, gray afternoon when demonstrators assembled next to the Peres Center. While the protest crowd grew, I spotted Nadia Hilou, a Palestinian Christian who had served in the Knesset as a member of the Labor Party until 2009. Over lunch during the previous summer at Jaffa Café, a bookstore and restaurant that served as a gathering point for local activists, Hilou told me how she decided to join Labor to give Jaffa's Arab community a stronger voice from inside the system. I asked her how she was able to remain a member of the party while its leader, Ehud Barak, directed the assault on the Gaza Strip. Hilou told me she voiced her opposition to the attack from the Knesset floor, but with a look of discomfort and irritation quickly changed the subject to local issues. Upon our second meeting at the protest, her attitude seemed to have shifted. When I asked her if she had spoken to Barak or anyone in Labor about the deteriorating situation in Jaffa, she waved her hand dismissively. "I don't talk to any of those people," she said emphatically. "I'm through with them."

Standing next to Hilou was Sheikh Sliman Satel, the imam of the Alnozha mosque that Jewish fundamentalists had recently attacked. "For years we had enjoyed good relations with the local Jewish community," Satel told me. "But now I'm afraid about the future because these [settler] groups have the backing of the government. The government gives them the ability to come here and hurt people at will. If we did the same thing in Tel Aviv they would surely stop us."

At twilight, the march began. Hundreds of young Jaffans proceeded slowly towards Yefet Street in the center of Ajami, chanting boisterously behind a line of Arab legislators and community leaders linking arms. Some of the demonstrators held Egyptian flags as a show of solidarity with the Egyptian revolutionaries who had just filled Cairo's Tahrir Square demanding the overthrow of the dictatorship that had ruled their lives for decades. "The people want to overthrow the regime!" the youth of Jaffa chanted, reprising a slogan that had become common in Tahrir. About fifty Jewish radical leftists brought up the rear of the protest, banging drums and chanting in Hebrew, "Fascism will not pass!" The march ended at the Jews-only development that B'Emuna established as a beachhead for the campaign to Judaize Jaffa. Ahmad Tibi, an Arab member of Knesset, bellowed from the protest stage, "The settlers in the heart of Hebron are a cancerous growth, and this is the same for those in the Arab neighborhoods of Jaffa."

Two months later, the Hebron-based settler Baruch Marzel led another series of "Jaffa For Jews" marches into the heart of the area. In October, right-wing youths slipped into the city's Arab neighborhood under the cover of darkness to attack the old Muslim cemetery next to the Peres Center, spray-painting "Death to Arabs" on the gravestones. Soon afterward the youths firebombed Abu el-Abed, an Arab-owned local restaurant where I often invited friends from Tel Aviv to eat Mediterranean branzini and drink San Miguel beer. After the attack, Tel Aviv mayor Ron Huldai demanded draconian punishment. "I expect the hands of those who do such things to be cut off," he proclaimed. A week later, right-wing vandals attacked the memorial to Yitzhak Rabin in north Tel Aviv. Again, Huldai swore that the perpetrators would face medieval consequences: "We should cut off the hands that allow themselves to harm what is sacred and important to the people of Israel." Even while condemning racism, the rhetoric of Israeli leaders was suffused with violence and biblical vengeance.

Huldai was a high-ranking former fighter pilot who made his name as the headmaster of a prestigious Tel Aviv–area high school. During the 2009 elections, Huldai held off an insurgent challenge from Dov Khenin, a hardworking social justice activist from the communist Hadash Party. Khenin aimed to unite Tel Aviv's most marginalized groups in a coalition with the city's base of progressive, worldly twenty-something residents calling his campaign "A City For All." Against all expectations, Khenin succeeded in mobilizing droves of voters from North Tel Aviv's liberal Ashkenazi elite, energized radical leftists and young progressives, and poor *Mizrahim* from the city's hardscrabble Hatikvah Quarter who faced mass evictions in order to make way for the construction of luxury condos. But his coalition was not enough to stop the corporate juggernaut that was the Huldai campaign. In the end, Huldai won in a landslide with sizeable contributions from powerful real estate and commercial interests seeking a foothold in Hatikvah and Jaffa.

Huldai's Tel Aviv was the liberal cultural bubble that Israel promoted to the outside world, a mish-mash of quirky cafés, rollicking bars and nightclubs, and almost year-round beachfront fun. Its eclectic restaurant scene, where chef experiments resulted in wildly exotic fusion dishes, had garnered rave reviews in international culinary magazines. The skyscrapers rising up around Tel Aviv lent it the feeling of any other thriving center of capital, but there was something about the city that was truly distinct from anywhere else. For all its trappings of cosmopolitanism, Tel Aviv was intentionally planned to be one of the most ethnically exclusive mega-cities in the world. It may have been situated in the heart of the Middle East, yet Tel Aviv had far fewer Arab residents than Chicago, the largest city in the American Midwest.

And Huldai was determined to keep it that way, not only in a demographic sense by, for instance, supporting the construction of the separation wall that obstructed Palestinian workers from reaching Tel Aviv from the West Bank, but in a symbolic sense as well. When city council members introduced a motion to include the name of Tel Aviv–Jaffa in a small Arabic font beneath the official Hebrew language logo, Huldai vehemently rejected their proposal.

"The city has an overwhelming Jewish majority, more than 90 percent compared with 4 percent Arabs," Huldai declared. "There is no reason to add the caption. Nowhere in Israel or indeed the world has this been undertaken in similar circumstances."

During my time in Jaffa, I often would jog from the crumbling center of Ajami toward Tel Aviv. I ran at night, through thick, sweltering humidity, past the golden glow of old Jaffa and toward the office towers and condominium high rises that shadowed Neve Tzedek. As I grew closer, jogging along a boardwalk that was filled with young couples and teenage revelers, I passed by a park named for the wealthy Jewish financier Charles Clore. Lining the rocky Mediterranean beachside, the area was a long stretch of grassy dunes that provided Arabs from Jaffa and Tel Aviv Israelis with an open space for barbeques and nighttime picnicking. Iconic turn of the century photos of Zionist "pioneers" drawing straws on the dunes outside Tel Aviv for plots of land suggested this place was a *tabla rasa* when they arrived from Europe. If only that were true, my jogs would have been so much more pleasant.

At the front of the park was the stone foundation of a once-grand Arab home. The only remaining remnant of the neighborhood of Manshiyya, it had been converted into a state-funded museum honoring the Irgun, the right-wing Zionist terror outfit commanded by future Herut Party leader and prime minister Menachem Begin. The Irgun joined with the militant Stern Gang in committing the mass execution of Palestinians at Deir Yassin, one of several massacres committed by Zionist forces in 1948, and also played a critical role in the expulsion of thousands of Palestinians from Jaffa. Beneath the dunes of Charles Clore Park were the ruins of Manshiyya— homes, business, and the history of a people buried beneath well-tended grass lawns and a mountain of lies. The original inhabitants of Manshiyya and hundreds of other Palestinian neighborhoods were gone now, scattered like dried leaves in the wind. But their ghosts loomed over Israeli society, haunting those who replaced them and reminding them of the precarious nature of a colonial existence. Even as the official Zionist narrative still denied their historical presence, the new Israeli government was taking extraordinary actions to ensure their absence, struggling to keep them out of sight and out of mind.

Banning Books

In central Jerusalem, just east of Jaffa Road, was a small, insignificant plot of pavement known as Davidka Square. At the center of the square was a stone memorial with a Hebrew inscription above an enlarged replica of a vintage mortar launcher. The inscription was a verse from the Book of Kings: "I will defend this city, to save it." And the mortar was the Davidka, a weapon created by Israeli engineers during the 1948 war solely for the purpose of driving masses of Palestinian Arabs from their villages in terror.

According to the Palestinian historian Walid Khalidi, the Davidka was a homemade mortar launcher deployed in "crowded built-up civilian quarters where the noise and blast maddened women and children into a frenzy of fear and panic." Its designers traded accuracy for a maximum fear factor, welding metal tubes to the mortars so that they emitted high-pitched shrieks as they tumbled to the ground. Though the Davidka's 88-pound shells did negligible damage to infrastructure, they generated an explosive sound so frightening they were able to chase tens of thousands of Palestinians away from their cities and villages. The weapon was used to drive out the Palestinians of Haifa, Jaffa, Ayn Zeitun, Biddu, and Safed, where local residents had become convinced that Zionist forces possessed the atomic bomb. Primitive in design but devastating in its effect, the Davidka was the Excalibur of ethnic cleansing.

By memorializing the weapon, Israel encourages its citizens to celebrate the mass expulsion of the Palestinian Arab outclass as a climactic moment in the history of the Jewish people—as a collective liberation. At the same time, the state has reacted with ham-fisted violence and legal suppression to quash attempts by its Palestinian citizens to observe the events of 1948 as a catastrophe. Indeed, public ceremonies marking the occasion of the Nakba are treated as an insult, at best, and at worst, as a grave threat to the state's Jewish character.

Each year, on Independence Day, the Israeli organization known as Zochrot ("Memory") organizes a public commemoration of the Nakba in order to educate Israelis about the Palestinian catastrophe and of the cost of maintaining an ethnically exclusive Jewish state. On April 25, 2012, the sixty-fourth birthday of the State of Israel, Zochrot activists gathered inside their central Tel Aviv offices to organize their action, which would consist of laying placards on the sidewalk listing the names of Palestinian villages destroyed in 1947 and '48. But before the activists could even leave the offices, an Israeli police riot squad surrounded them and attempted to barricade them inside.

The police informed Zochrot director Eitan Bronstein that he and the other activists would be arrested if they attempted any interaction with the crowds in the streets enjoying the fireworks and festivities celebrating Israel's birth. "We will not allow you to enter the celebrations with your pictures or your fliers," a cop told Bronstein. "We will not allow this form of protest. It might disturb the peace so we won't allow it." Another police officer told Bronstein his placards represented "inciting material."

As heavy-handed as the police might have seemed, there was considerable reason to believe the Zochrot activists could have encountered harsh violence if they had been allowed to proceed with their action. Even while they stood behind metal gates erected by the police to isolate them from the Israeli revelers, passersby surrounded the activists and let loose with a torrent of abuse and invective. "You're lucky the police are here. You should thank them," said a bald, beefy man, threatening to attack the dozen or so Zochrot activists until police led him away.

Another hulking character identifying himself as a member of Unit 51 from the Israeli army's Golani Brigade paratrooper corps barked at the activists, "The only thing you are is a bunch of traitors! Every day people here are fighting. . . . This is unbelievable. You are traitors, and if we had the chance we would shoot you one by one. One by one we would shoot you . . ."

When a middle-aged woman approached Bronstein to ask what his demonstration was about, he explained, "Almost a million people were expelled before Israel was created."

"They can go fuck themselves in the ass!" she snapped in Russian-accented Hebrew.

"Every palace made of gold has its toilet," a man told the Zochrot activists. "We have a palace of gold, and you are its toilet."

Finally, one of the demonstrators broke out of the metal police barricade and stood amid the crowds on the street. Holding a small book in one hand, he began reading out the names of Palestinian neighborhoods and villages. "These are the towns that stood on the lands of the Tel Aviv–Jaffa before the Nakba," he shouted. "You are currently preventing people from learning and commemorating the history of their city."

While a procession of settlers from Hebron marched down the center of the street, bellowing religious nationalist anthems, the police dragged the man away, arresting him along with two other demonstrators.

The police repression on Nakba Day reflected a longstanding institutional hostility to virtually any expression of the Palestinian version of 1948. Since the foundation of the State of Israel, Palestinian students in the country's segregated Arab schools have been forbidden from learning about the Nakba. Though textbooks in Arab schools are replete with Holocaust history, references to the Nakba have been completely omitted. Applications to work in the Arab sector's school system are vetted by a Shin Bet officer working inside the Ministry of Education, and teachers face the threat of stern punishment for contradicting the official Zionist narrative. To ensure total compliance with the state's educational agenda, the Shin Bet operates a network of collaborators and informants in Arab schools, just as it does throughout Palestinian Israeli society.

In 2007, the battle over the teaching of the Nakba came to a head when Israel's education minister, a relatively liberal member of the Labor Party named Yuli Tamir, attempted to introduce a mild reform to the Arab curriculum. "The Arab public deserves to be allowed to express its feelings," she explained. A grade school textbook authorized by Tamir, *Living Together in Israel: Textbook for Homeland, Society and Citizenship*, featured one line acknowledging the Nakba as an important and painful chapter in the history of Palestinian citizens of Israel. It read, "Some of the Arab residents were forced to leave their homes and some were expelled, and they became refugees in the neighboring Arab countries. Some of them became refugees and were forced to move to other Arab communities in the State of Israel, because their villages were destroyed during and after the war."

That single line, written for the consumption of Arab third graders, set off a national firestorm of outrage and indignation at the highest levels of Israeli society. Benjamin Netanyahu, then leading the opposition as the chairman of the Likud Party, cast the textbook revision as an unprecedented calamity for the Jewish people. "I can't remember a greater absurdity than this in a decision made by an education minister in the State of Israel," Netanyahu proclaimed. Back when Likud controlled the Education Ministry, all references and allusions to the Nakba were stripped from the state's curriculum. "We sent out a clear message to textbook publishers that we would not tolerate a Palestinian narrative in our books," said a hardline Likud official, Yaakov Katz. But now that the Palestinian narrative was back, Zevulon Orlev, a religious nationalist member of Knesset from the National Religious Party, despaired, "The day the education minister made the decision is the Nakba day of the Israeli education system." Limor Livnat, the rightist former education minister who excised Nakba references from Israeli textbooks, warned that if Israeli children learned about the mass expulsion of Palestinians, they were likely to turn against the state.

Almost as soon as Netanyahu returned to the prime minister's office, he and his education minister, Gideon Sa'ar, dispatched government apparatchiks to bookstores around Israel with orders to confiscate all copies of a high school textbook called, *Nationalism: Building a State in the Middle East*. According to Sa'ar, the textbook threatened to subvert the mission of the Jewish state. At issue was a short section citing Walid Khalidi, the renowned Palestinian historian, about the Nakba. The textbook informed students that Palestinians "contended" the expulsions of 1948 were a form of ethnic cleansing. This mildly worded disclosure was too much for the draconian Sa'ar, who demanded a total ban on the use of the term "Nakba" in Israeli textbooks. "There is no reason that the official curriculum of the State of Israel should present the establishment of the state as a 'Holocaust' or 'catastrophe,'" he said.

The government's effort to purge the Palestinian narrative from Israel's educational system flowed effortlessly into the legislative push to criminalize public observation of the Nakba, a campaign of government organized censorship designed to accelerate the mounting political assault on Palestinian civic activism inside Israel. It would be orchestrated from the floor of the Knesset, the living symbol of the "Jewish and democratic" state.

The Fortress of Democracy

On January 14, 1948, as violence intensified around Jerusalem, the Haganah (the main Zionist military force) ordered the residents of Sheikh Badr, a Palestinian suburb-village in the Jerusalem municipality, to evacuate their homes. Expecting to return after the fighting subsided, some residents handed their keys over to Jewish neighbors. But they never came back. Instead, goon squads from the lower-class neighborhood of Nahla'ot descended on Sheikh Badr to loot and vandalize the homes. After being briefly driven away by Haganah troops, the vandals returned to steal and torch whatever remained of the empty village.

From his office in nearby Mount Scopus, Hebrew University Rector Judah Magnes watched the looting in Sheikh Badr with horror. Born in San Francisco and educated at the University of Cincinnati and Berlin University, Magnes began his career as a Reform rabbi in New York City. He cofounded the American Jewish Committee and was the guiding force during World War I behind the creation of the American Jewish Joint Distribution Committee, the chief international Jewish welfare agency. In 1922, he emigrated with his family to Palestine to cofound Hebrew University with Chaim Weizmann and Albert Einstein—and was instrumental in the revival of Hebrew as a language. Erudite, charismatic, and idealistic to a fault, Magnes emerged as the leader along with Henrietta Szold, founder of the Hadassah Women's Organization, of Ihud, a political party that agitated for the creation of an Arab-Jewish binational state called "The United States of Palestine." Magnes beseeched leaders of the Zionist *Yishuv* to negotiate with leaders of Palestine's emerging Arab nationalist movement before it was too late. He warned them that establishing an exclusive Jewish state would doom its inhabitants to endless bloodshed and war. "A Jewish home in Palestine built on bayonets and oppression is not worth having," Magnes said, predicting that a partition would create a Jewish "Balkan state." His pleas fell on deaf ears, however. Ihud members were roundly assailed by *Yishuv* leaders as ghetto-minded traitors, while Magnes became the target of regular death threats.

Now, as he watched Jewish residents of Jerusalem pillaging neighborhoods like Sheikh Badr and, in some cases, murdering their residents, Magnes begged them to stop. As in the past, his pleas were ignored. On April 12, following the massacre by right-wing Zionist militias of over one hundred Arab civilians in Deir Yassin, Magnes wrote in his diary: "For more than a generation I have been pleading for peace, conciliation, understanding. How can I not and stand before the world and say: 'Friends, stop the bloodshed. Understanding is possible.' This is the moment I have been preparing for all these years." The following day, thirty-four members of his staff at Hebrew University were killed in an Arab reprisal attack on Mount Scopus.

In one last desperate maneuver, Magnes set off for Washington to lobby Secretary of State George Marshall and President Harry Truman to put Palestine under an American trusteeship that would hold Jewish and Arab provinces together in a federal union. He urged the United States to immediately impose military sanctions to stymie what he called "the Jewish war machine." Once again, his efforts to secure peace failed. By October, a disgusted Magnes had withdrawn his affiliation from the American Jewish Joint Distribution Committee in protest of its refusal to assist the Palestinian refugees driven into exile by Zionist militias. "How can I continue to be officially associated with an aid organization which apparently so easily can ignore such a huge and acute refugee problem?" he asked. Just days later, he died.

In 1958, with a generous 1.25 million pound donation from the financier Lord James de Rothschild, a team of architects laid the cornerstone for the new Knesset on the ashes of Sheikh Badr, which the Jerusalem municipality had renamed Givat Ram. By 1966, the building was completed, providing a permanent home for lawmakers who had previously gathered in ad hoc locations around the city. At the first session in the Knesset's plenum hall, Prime Minister Levi Eshkol congratulated the legislators assembled before him. "I wish for the Knesset that the new premises will provide contentment and between its walls Israeli democracy will take shape, parliamentary endeavor will expand and national unity will increase," he said.

Three years later, the legendary Jewish artist Marc Chagall installed a series of large, wildly colorful tapestries in the heart of the Knesset, in what is now known as Chagall State Hall. Through the tapestries, Chagall attempted to evoke the Zionist narrative, an unbroken tale of tragedy from the Jewish exodus from Egypt to the Holocaust, symbolized by a burning village. The Jewish people are finally delivered with the founding of Israel. Nearby, in the lobby of the Government Room, where the prime minister meets with cabinet ministers, Knesset designers installed a giant oil painting by Joseph Kuzkovsky called *The Last Way—Baba Yar*. The painting depicts a procession of meek, defenseless Jewish peasants being marched out of their village in the Russian Pale of Settlement to be massacred by Nazi SS soldiers—"like sheep to the slaughter," in the words of Abba Kovner, a Jewish partisan fighter and Zionist activist who hatched an abortive postwar plan to poison the drinking water of six million Germans in revenge for the Holocaust.

By adorning the halls of Israel's deliberative body with representations of the European Jewish genocide (while ignoring the rich and varied history of Jewish life in the Arab world), the building's decorators and designers deliberately enveloped Israel's center of decision making with the insecurity of diaspora Jewish life. Thus the Knesset was presented as a living symbol of Jewish power and self-determination, the ultimate redemption from 3,000 years of "exile." But more than 60 years after driving Palestinians from the future site of the Knesset, the lawmakers who filled its halls had not shed the sense of insecurity that colored the actions of Israel's founding generation. Consecrated as the symbolic happy ending to the historical oppression of "the Jewish people," the Knesset became the nerve center of a campaign to erase another people's tragedy from official memory.

The campaign to silence the Palestinian narrative centered on a bill conceived by Yisrael Beiteinu, the party of Avigdor Lieberman. Known as the Nakba Law, the bill was presented as the fulfillment of Lieberman's campaign slogan: "No loyalty, no citizenship." According to the initial version of the bill, anyone who participated in Nakba Day commemorations on Israel's Independence Day could face criminal fines and imprisonment for up to three years. The bill's author, Alex Miller, was a thirty-four-year-old Yisrael Beiteinu apparatchik who immigrated to Israel from Moscow in 1992. He spoke Hebrew with a pronounced Russian accent and not as fluently as Arab legislators like Dr. Ahmad Tibi and Jamal Zehalka, both born in Israel and educated at Hebrew University. Hammering on the urgency of his bill's passage, Miller fumed, "It is inconceivable for a sovereign nation to allow people to organize rallies in which they call for the state's destruction and denounce our very existence."

In the legal canon of enlightened Western-style democracies around the world, there were few precedents for legislation like the Nakba Law. In the present day, the only putatively democratic country with anything on the books like the Nakba Law was Turkey. Article 301, an article of the Turkish penal code that forbade insulting Turkey, the Turkish ethnicity, or Turkish government institutions, bore a striking resemblance to the Nakba Law, and the countless other anti-democratic proposals that followed it. Under Article 301, public figures could be prosecuted for accusing Turkey of committing genocide against Armenians during World War I. Though Turkey's authoritarian provision became the subject of strident and sustained criticism from diplomatic representatives of the European Union and the United States, the EU and US were curiously reticent about the Nakba Law and other Israeli proposals targeting the citizenship rights of the Arab minority.

In June 2009, a few days after arriving in Jerusalem from the West Bank, and a month after the Nakba Law hit the Knesset floor, I made an appointment to visit Miller in his office in the Knesset. I arrived at the Knesset in the early morning, just as a dry heat began to sweep in through the mountain winds. I was immediately struck by the building's imposing appearance. Set back several hundred yards from the street, sealed in by high metal gates and barbed wire, and patrolled by armed guards in dark shades, the Knesset looked more like an ugly neoclassical bunker than any other parliament building I had ever seen. It was a fortress within the fortress.

When I arrived at Miller's office, a friendly, exuberant young aide named Tsah welcomed me into the compact, spartan space. Inside, Miller sat in a leather chair at his desk busying himself with a round of Minesweeper. With the exception of a framed portrait of Lieberman hanging on his wall and beaming down like Yisrael Beiteinu's Dear Leader, Miller's office was threadbare. Clad in a neatly tailored dark pinstripe suit, the baby-faced immigrant from Moscow stared into his computer and dragged slowly on a cigarette. He did not acknowledge me for a long, uncomfortable two minutes. Finally, when Tsah sat on a couch at the back of the office, Miller looked up and offered me a curt greeting.

To my opening question about his motivation for introducing such an extreme measure, Miller explained in a dispassionate, near-mumble why the legislation was urgently needed. "No country in the world allows large minority groups to protest against their independence day," he claimed. "But a year ago we had a violent protest at Tel Aviv University against our Independence Day. This law was the response. These violent protests are organized by leaders who have a cynical message of opposition to Israel as a Jewish state." Miller injected an appeal to my American patriotism: "Imagine that on July Fourth people got up and rallied against America's celebration of Independence Day."

(Of course, Frederick Douglass, in one of his most famous speeches, declared at an Independence Day celebration in 1852: "What, to the American slave, is your Fourth of July? I answer; a day that reveals to him, more than all other days in the year, the gross injustice and cruelty to which he is the constant victim. To him, your celebration is a sham; your boasted liberty, an unholy license; your national greatness, swelling vanity; your sounds of rejoicing are empty and heartless; your denunciation of tyrants, brass fronted impudence; your shouts of liberty and equality, hollow mockery; your prayers and hymns, your sermons and thanksgivings, with all your religious parade and solemnity, are, to Him, mere bombast, fraud, deception, impiety, and hypocrisy—a thin veil to cover up crimes, which would disgrace a nation of savages. There is not a nation on the earth guilty of practices more shocking and bloody than are the people of the United States, at this very hour.")

I countered that burning the American flag was technically legal in the United States, and that while few did it, some Native Americans have held mourning ceremonies on July 4 and Thanksgiving. Miller did not flinch. "Israel already has a law prohibiting any damage to Israel's symbols—with a penalty of up to one year," he stated. Suddenly, Tsah rushed across the room with a note for his boss. Miller read the note back to me almost verbatim: "It is important to note that the Islamic leadership uses the right to protest to incite hatred. Most participants at these protests are young and being preached hatred that passes on from generation to generation."

I asked Miller if Yisrael Beiteinu was a fascist party, as even some of its mainstream Israeli critics have claimed. I wondered if this question might shake Miller out of his stoicism. But his expressionless gaze remained set in stone. "I'm not a media analyst, but it is clear from our election campaign that our country must ensure that citizens do not conduct massive protests opposing the existence of the state," Miller said. "The Israeli public believes in loyalty. Duties must be equivalent to rights."

He proclaimed with a confident tone: "Israel sees Lieberman as a leader who knows how to implement what he believes in. The party believes rights should be given in accordance with obligations, such as serving in the army."

Once again, Tsah rushed to Miller's side. "Or national service," he whispered. Miller now added, "We support Arab citizens serving country through national service, but their leaders are doing everything possible to discourage Arab citizens from doing national service."

I proposed to Miller that broad sectors of the American liberal elite who had traditionally supported Israel were growing alienated by Lieberman's anti-democratic

agenda. Did he think the Nakba law would damage the US-Israeli special relationship? "This law only strengthens Israel's national honor and its desire to develop
further," Miller replied. "Israeli citizens should contribute to the strengthening of the
country and not to negating its existence."

For the third time, Tsah hurried across the room to Miller. In Hebrew, he whispered into his boss's ear: "Our connection to the US is strong."

Miller looked directly at me and proclaimed, "Our connection to the US is strong."

It was difficult to discern any clear sign of left-brain activity from Miller. He
refused to stray from the talking points that had won him a fervent following. Miller
therefore acted with the confidence that his party and its authoritarian agenda represented the wave of the future. A Friedrich Ebert Foundation poll of Jewish Israeli
youth attitudes published in 2011—the most comprehensive poll of its kind with
data compiled through twelve years of research—showed that 60 percent of Israeli
Jews between fifteen and eighteen years old preferred "strong leaders" to the rule of
law. In cases where security conflicted with democratic values, 70 percent said security came first. Right-wing opinions had spiked by 14 percent over the past twelve
years while support for left-wing parties had fallen to a measly 12 percent among
Israeli youth. The poll was confirmation of Yisrael Beiteinu's authentic appeal and
suggested expanding power in future electoral contests.

"I don't have to believe Yisrael Beiteinu will grow in strength," Miller told me. "I
can see it. Since the founding of the party we have grown in strength. We have never
changed our platform, and we are seeing increasing support from the public."

I left Miller's office and walked down a narrow, carpeted corridor that reminded
me of a haphazardly renovated hotel somewhere in the generic suburbs of Chicago.
After a few wrong turns, I realized I was lost in the bowels of the Knesset. I wandered
into a spacious hallway near the committee hearing rooms and noticed a display of
photographs installed along the walls. They depicted Israel's political legends delib-
erating and kibitzing with one another: A stoic-looking Golda Meir stood in the back
of the Knesset puffing on a cigarette while she observed a debate; Shulamit Aloni, the
fierce stalwart of the old Zionist left, spoke passionately from the parliament floor;
Toufiq Toubi, the country's first Arab member of Knesset, an early member of the
Jewish-Arab communist party, whispered in the ear of a *kippa*-wearing colleague;
right-wing former prime minister Yitzhak Shamir pored over confidential files in
the Knesset gallery; and Ahmad Tibi, a veteran Arab legislator, laughed jovially with
a Jewish lawmaker.

Judging from the photo display, women, Arabs, and Jews felt at ease serving
together in Israel's great deliberative body. Any rancor that might have naturally
risen up amid so much diversity seemed to have dissolved in the collegial culture
of the Middle East's "only democracy." Sure, the Jewish state had its flaws, but what
other country in the Middle East afforded its minorities so much freedom? As Benjamin Netanyahu boasted to the US Congress in 2011, "Of the 300 million Arabs in
the Middle East and North Africa, only Israel's Arab citizens enjoy real democratic
rights. . . . Of those 300 million Arabs, less than one-half of 1 percent are truly free
and they're all citizens of Israel."

In reality, Arab representatives in the Knesset were denied any chance to influence national policy or assert national rights, and none had ever served in an Israeli governing coalition. As Ariel Sharon proclaimed before the Knesset in 2002, Palestinian citizens of Israel (or those he called "Israeli Arabs") had "rights *in* the land," but "all rights over the Land of Israel are Jewish rights." Each time an Arab party attempted to challenge the Jewish majority's unlimited control over state land policy and laws, they could expect to be met with sustained harassment, legal persecution, and official suppression. For Israel's Palestinians, challenging Jewish legal and political privilege was considered a form of high treason.

When I wandered into the Knesset cafeteria, I spotted Ahmad Tibi reaching below a buffet table sneeze guard for a biscuit. Having appeared on Israeli TV news and on the cover of the nation's papers on a regular basis for at least the past five years, often in heated confrontations with right-wing legislators worked into a petulant frenzy, the chubby, mustachioed career politician was easy to recognize. Tibi emerged from the ranks of Balad to found a party, United Arab List-Taal, that had become a vehicle for his political ambitions, allowing him to hold his Knesset seat for over decade. Over the years, Tibi earned headlines with pithy one-liners and rhetorical bursts that infuriated and stymied his antagonists across the Zionist spectrum. Tibi was so reviled within mainstream Jewish society that an Arab man was once refused entry to a club in Haifa merely for keeping a photo of him inside his ID card.

Dan Schueftan, an influential political scientist who served as the deputy director of Haifa University's National Security Studies Center, had grown obsessed with Tibi. Schueftan was credited with selling Ehud Barak and Ariel Sharon on the wisdom of *hafrada*, or the unilateral demographic separation that led to the construction of the West Bank separation wall and the Gaza disengagement. Having fulfilled the goals of *hafrada*, which Schueftan designed to "disconnect the radical trends of the Arabs in Israel from the hinterland supporting their struggle in the territories," he turned to the problems that lurked inside the Jewish state. He spent years collecting transcripts of Tibi's speeches and writings, filing them away as research for his forthcoming 844-page tome, *Palestinians in Israel—The Arab Minority's Struggle Against the Jewish State.*

Written for the consumption of Israel's political and military elites, Schueftan hoped to sway his readers to take urgent action against Tibi and other leaders of the Arab sector—those he accused of seeking to "demolish the Jewish national project and establish their own entity on the ruins of the Jewish state." Among the measures he recommended for weakening and suppressing Arab political aspirations inside Israel was legislating Hebrew as the official language of Israel at the expense of Arabic. Schueftan's book was reviewed favorably by all of Israel's major newspapers. And, as in the past, it was received as a blueprint by many of the country's top lawmakers. "If this book has an effect similar to my previous book, I'll be delighted," Schueftan remarked.

Having banned Tibi's party in 2009 (the Supreme Court overturned the ban), members of Knesset were preparing plans to do the same as soon as the next national elections rolled around. Tibi's service as a liaison to PLO Chairman Yasser Arafat during Oslo era negotiations could have been seen as a boon to Israeli diplomacy, but instead, it only heightened the scorn of the Israeli public. And as with Azmi Bishara, it was Tibi's advocacy for Israel as a state of all its citizens that invited the most resentment from Jewish Israeli society. Some of the comments left by Israelis on Tibi's Facebook page (and published under their actual identities) included, "You will die soon," "You and all ravagers will meet your end in Gaza," and, "It is much better for you to leave and run away because they will kill you soon."

I sidled up beside Tibi and introduced myself, asking if he had any time for an interview. Without a moment's hesitation, Tibi invited me to join him at a small, square table a few feet away. I asked him about Miller's claim that the Nakba Law would strengthen Israel's democracy. "The question is: Is Israel a weak democracy? Yes, it is a weak democracy," he responded. "Yisrael Beitaynu is the Israeli Jewish fascist party and it seems that Alex Miller and his party are not confident about the Israeli Jewish narrative of Zionism."

Tibi explained why Palestinian citizens of Israel mourned the country's foundation: "We are victims of Zionism and have a different story of events about 1948. How do you expect our people to celebrate their agony and disaster? These are basic human feelings for a people to mourn destruction. I can understand that the Jewish people want to commemorate the Holocaust. But to have Jewish victims of Nazi racism impose their Independence Day celebration on another people's tragedy—that is horrible for us."

I asked Tibi if the Nakba Laws and other proposals like it threatened to consolidate a system of apartheid inside Israel. "In Israel you have three systems of laws," he said. "One is democracy for 80 percent of the population. It is democracy for Jews. I call it an ethnocracy or you could call it a Judocracy. The second is racial discrimination for 20 percent of the population, the Israeli Arabs. The third is apartheid for the population in the West Bank and Gaza. This includes two sets of governments, one for the Palestinians and one for the settlers. Inside Israel there is not yet apartheid but we are being pushed there with these new laws."

"Right now I would say Israel *is* a Jewish and democratic state," Tibi quipped with a wry grin. "It is democratic toward Jews and Jewish toward the Arabs."

The Nakba Law was only one among a constantly expanding battery of racist and anti-democratic proposals pouring from the legislative offices onto the floor of the Knesset. By 2012, the Association for Civil Rights in Israel (ACRI) had documented forty-six anti-democratic bills that had either passed, were close to passing, or which had been introduced but had either failed or were still up for deliberation. The laws were so popular with the general Israeli public that a few legislators from the "centrist" Kadima Party jumped on the bandwagon. Among the bills introduced by Kadima was one that proposed to outlaw any Israeli nonprofit associations that gave information to foreign authorities conducting investigations of Israeli politicians or military officers for war crimes. Kadima's leader, Tzipi Livni, maintained a strange silence about her party's sponsorship of the anti-democratic laws.

"Livni cannot say that her hands are clean," *Ha'aretz* declared in an editorial. "She is responsible for the anarchy that has spread to Kadima's Knesset members. It is inconceivable that such dangerous and extreme bills could be proposed from within the ranks of the supposedly centrist party that she leads without the party, and its leader, noticing."

Jamal Zehalka, a Balad Party leader who filled the exiled Azmi Bishara's seat in the Knesset, told me he promised a friend he would host an elaborate celebration if a week went by without the proposal of an anti-democratic law. "Until now, we have not had the party," Zehalka said. "I told him he is going to have to wait a long time."

Cut Off from the Tribe

By June 2010, increasingly draconian proposals were filling the Knesset agenda by the day, including at least five bills designed to limit the power of the Supreme Court, if not completely neuter it altogether. I wanted to gain more access to the lawmakers behind the Knesset's anti-democratic agenda. I set a goal of interviewing at least a dozen of them, hoping to gain an understanding of the sensibility that united the Knesset's populists behind the larger campaign to strip away whatever existed of Israel's democratic veneer.

But for a number of reasons, I needed help. First, I did not speak conversational Hebrew—I knew only enough to travel around the country, give commands, and order food (two journalistic colleagues translated my interview with Alex Miller). More importantly, I had no media credentials any Israeli official would recognize. My only institutional affiliation at the time was with a small left-wing think tank in New York City, the Nation Institute, which was associated with the *Nation* magazine and the publisher of this book. What I needed, I decided, was an Israeli journalist to help me gain access to the Knesset.

On a humid, sweltering night in June, I sat inches from a fan in my room in Jaffa and browsed through my e-mail. I noticed a cryptic message that had arrived through my personal Facebook page from someone who appeared to be operating under an alias. After a few exchanges, the person told me he was working as a Hebrew-to-English translator for *Ha'aretz*'s website. His name was David Sheen. He told me he was a fan of my journalism and requested to meet me to discuss a project he wanted to collaborate on, but he gave no details. I decided that this character, if he was for real, represented my best chance for getting back into the Knesset. He spoke Hebrew and had a *Ha'aretz* e-mail address. As long as he was not insane—and the Holy Land, it seemed, was a magnet for the mentally deranged—or a Shin Bet agent, I figured he could be a major asset.

Three days later, I met Sheen in front of a McDonald's on the first floor of Tel Aviv's chaotic and vast central bus station. He was tall, lanky, completely bald, and dressed in baggy camo pants and a loose, black T-shirt—the uniform of Israeli anarchists, but uncrinkled and much cleaner than the other *enrages* of the left. (This guy seemed like a kept man, I thought.) If Sheen had had a full head of hair, he might have looked like a radical leftist Keanu Reeves. He asked me to follow him up an escalator and into an Ethiopian hair salon. As he guided me toward the back of the salon, the hairdressers received him warmly, greeting him with big smiles. I told him I didn't have enough hair to do cornrows, wondering where he was leading me.

Sheen walked over to a young black woman sitting on a short stool while an older woman meticulously braided her hair. The young woman smiled and shook my hand but said nothing. Sheen introduced her as his wife, Anne. While the hairdresser tended to Anne, Sheen pulled out his iPhone to show me some viral videos he had produced to dramatize the crisis in Israel.

The first video featured animated images Sheen appropriated from the artist Yossi Even-Kama, whose recent exhibition at Ramat Gan's Shenkar College of Art and Design portrayed a dystopian Israel under the control of a Judeo-fascist government, earning unironic admiration from some right-wing settlers. "I would use different colors," one religious rightist said of the exhibition, "but this is basically what I believe." In Even-Kam's exhibition, it was the year 2020, and after the signing of a final status peace deal with the Palestinian Authority, rightist forces staged a coup, overwhelming the country's decadent, apathetic, liberal elite and founding the State of Judea on the ashes of Israel. In Sheen's flawlessly edited video, a ragged cartoon figure wandered helplessly through an imposing, gray cityscape, beaming with dismay at the symbols of the Judeo-fascist regime. The scene reminded me of a line from Alan Ginsberg's poem "Howl": "Mollock, whose buildings are judgment!" Even-Kama's mock propaganda posters hung on building walls around each corner the character turned. "Crush the democratic menace," one sign read. An image of a jackboot preparing to stomp a cockroach to death hovered above the Hebrew slogan. Sheen's video concluded with a single line against a black screen: "Fight the fascism."

Palestinian intellectuals had for decades likened the exclusive ideology undergirding Israel's national policies to fascism, but now, in the wake of the 2009 election results, even well-established liberal Zionists were beginning to discuss in unflinching terms the presence of fascism in Israeli life. Amnon Dankner, the former editor of *Maariv*, one of Israel's major newspapers, was moved to condemn what he saw as "neo-Nazi expressions in the Knesset" and "entire parties whose tenor and tone arouse feelings of horror and terrifying memories." David Landau, the former editor-in-chief of *Ha'aretz*, echoed Dankner, calling on Israelis to boycott the Knesset "to stand against the wave of fascism that has engulfed the Zionist project." And Uri Avnery, the famed Israeli journalist, politician, and *sabra,* warned, "Israel's very existence is threatened by fascism." If these august figures from the old Zionist left were to be believed, Sheen's video could have been viewed not as a dystopian fantasy but as a depiction of the current reality.

Once Anne's braids were in place, I redirected our meeting to a Chinese restaurant located next to the bus station near the Hatikva neighborhood. The area was the overcrowded, choking center of migrant life in the city, where the cheap labor of North Tel Aviv lived in ramshackle housing, sleeping sometimes five to a room. The migrants had come from Thailand, the Philippines, Sudan, Eritrea, Congo—from poverty-stricken and war-torn regions across Asia and Africa to fill the low wage jobs that Palestinians from the Occupied Territories used to occupy before Gaza and the West Bank were physically separated from "Israel proper." They were the invisible glue that held Tel Aviv together, enabling hundreds of thousands of Jewish Israelis to enjoy a first world, Europeanized standard of living. Though many of the migrants were asylum seekers with refugee status, the Jewish state viewed them, like Palestinians, as a demographic threat that necessitated swift action. "The goal is to ensure Israel's Jewish and democratic nature," Prime Minister Benjamin Netanyahu said of the migrants. "We will not let thousands of foreign workers flood the country."

Over a plate of surprisingly decent bean curd in black bean sauce at the Chinese restaurant—one of only a handful I knew of in the city—Sheen recalled how he arrived in Israel in 1999 from a solidly middle class, ultra-Zionist family from Toronto, Canada. At age twenty-five, he was brimming with excitement about the earthy communal dream that awaited him: "I saw Israel entirely through the frame of a Zionist education. I grew up in a very heavily Jewish environment, in a Jewish neighborhood, a Jewish school, synagogue—everything. The school was Zionist, and I was heavily immersed in the idea that we need Israel so there won't be another Holocaust, and that Israel needs us because it needs to be built up—it's surrounded with enemies so it needs our help to build itself. So when I first arrived in Israel I was thinking about the collective, and the concept of the Jewish people represented the strongest collective."

Though Sheen was heavily immersed in the tribalistic culture of Zionism, he had also cultivated strong leftist views through his participation in anti-globalization protests in Toronto. "With every other issue besides Israel, I was on the left side of the spectrum," he said. "I was a PEP—a Progressive Except for Palestine." Within a month of arriving in Israel, that began to change. He realized that everything he had known about Israelis and Palestinians was a fantasy cultivated through years of heavy indoctrination. His view of the occupation as a necessary, albeit unpleasant, security measure was shattered after he spent long hours chatting with Palestinian workers who woke up at 4 a.m. each morning to slip into Israel from Nablus to work construction jobs for meager pay. "Once I saw how the occupation created a permanent underclass and that it existed to promote exploitation—just by realizing that I broke with the PEP mentality."

Sheen's contact with actual Israelis undermined his idealized vision of the Zionist collective. "Israelis were not exactly trying to pull together in the name of the Jewish people like I thought," he said. "It's a dog-eat-dog shark pool where you've got to swim to survive, and nobody has any idea of what civility means. People are manipulative and exploitative without any moral compunction or sense that there's anything wrong with that. They're not embarrassed about taking advantage of other people."

Alienated by the aggressive capitalism that was consuming urban life in Israel, Sheen retreated to a kibbutz in the Negev Desert called Kibbutz Samar. At first he thought he had finally found the slow-paced, communal lifestyle he had been seeking. But then he peered beneath the kibbutz's socialist veneer. "What broke me was they got workers from Thailand to work on the kibbutz for next to nothing," Sheen recounted. "I realized it wasn't really socialism they were practicing. It was socialism for Jews only. I grew up in multicultural Toronto, where diversity was a positive thing.

So it went against my values, and I tried to convince the kibbutz not to do this, to let the Thai workers live in normal apartments like everyone else—don't stick six of them in a fucking closet. Treat them like normal humans. Very few people even saw it as an issue worth discussing, let alone dealing with. They didn't see them as deserving of basic standards of living. They said, 'They're making more here than they would back in their country.' So that makes it okay? I wanted to get away from capitalism and away from exploitation, but I saw that kibbutz life was just that—it was segregationist Zionism. So I left."

In 2006, Israeli forces simultaneously carpet-bombed the Gaza Strip and Southern Lebanon. Israel blanketed the Gaza Strip with more than six thousand artillery shells and missiles, deliberately destroyed Gaza's main power plant, then bombed the access roads to prevent the plant from being repaired. Within the span of about two months, the army had killed at least 202 civilians including 44 children in an operation billed to Israelis as a search for the captured Israeli soldier Gilad Shalit. In Southern Lebanon, Israeli bombing turned 800,000 Lebanese citizens—over a quarter of the country's population—into refugees while killing more than 1,100 civilians, including at least 300 children. Summarizing the views of the Israeli military leadership at the time, columnist Yaron London, one of the most prominent television journalists in the country, wrote, "There is no longer any need for complicated distinctions. . . . In practical terms, the Palestinians in Gaza are all [Hamas leader] Khaled Meshal, the Lebanese are all [Hezbollah leader Hassan] Nasrallah, and the Iranians are all [President Mahmoud] Ahmadinejad."

Indignant at the disproportionate violence Israel had unleashed against civilians, Sheen joined up with the small but feisty bands of Israeli radical leftists who had dedicated themselves to direct action against their country's militaristic policies. During a gay pride rally in Tel Aviv called "Queeruption," Sheen and a group of friends held signs reading, "Stop the bombing." They were immediately set upon by riot police who beat them with billyclubs before dragging them away.

"I was shocked," Sheen remarked. "Nowadays everyone knows the police are brutal, but at the time I still couldn't believe that Israeli police would attack other Jews—and for simply holding signs." At another anti-war protest in Tel Aviv, a prim-looking waitress burst through the door of a nearby restaurant and hurled a glass at the protesters. "I watched that glass hit the ground and shatter. I can still hear the sound. It was when I realized that even in the heart of liberal Tel Aviv there is a seething hatred for anyone with humanistic values," Sheen said.

At the time, Sheen was living on a *moshav* (a collective farm) near the Gaza border. From his home, he listened to the thundering sound of bombs falling on Gaza all day and all night. "The ground was literally shaking underneath my feet," he recalled. Sheen ventured into town filled with revulsion at the shelling of Gaza. "When I told people at the supermarket what I thought of the bombing, they would all say, 'What do you care? It's not going to hit you, it's hitting *them*.' I said back, 'It's hitting actual people. Doesn't that matter to you?' And they would get enraged and say, 'What are you, a fucking leftist? You don't care about the Jews.' That's when I realized that in Israel, you're either in favor of any level of violence unleashed on *those people*, no matter who they were, or if you're against it, you're with the terrorists. I was shocked that that attitude was so mainstream."

Sheen went on: "To come out against these wars on civilians—you were cut off. You were not part of the tribe. You were not part of the Jewish people. You were alone. Once you have a personal experience like that, it etches those beliefs into your soul."

Sheen's struggle to reconcile his values with life inside Israel was complicated when his wife, Anne, whom he had met in Canada in 2009, joined him in Tel Aviv. Because Anne is not Jewish, the Interior Ministry erected what seemed like an endless array of bureaucratic hurdles against her application for permanent residency. One government document informed her that as someone from "outside the community"—a bearer of non-Jewish blood—her children could not receive health insurance in Israel.

In her daily life in Tel Aviv, Anne said she occasionally encountered the same sort of verbal abuse that African migrants and Ethiopians routinely receive. "I've had people call me 'Kunte Kente,' or *goya*—female goy," Anne told me. "I've never dealt with so much open racism in my whole life. For a while I didn't leave the house; I just didn't want to deal with the negativity that I got in the street, so I just stayed in my bubble. But now I've learned not to internalize the way people react to me—it's their problem. A lot of times they think I'm Ethiopian so they think I will be timid and not stand up for myself. So if I stare at them back with a hard look they are taken aback, and they eventually stop."

Sheen's tale of transformation was not unusual. Many Israelis I knew who had transitioned from a Zionist upbringing into radical left activity, especially those who had emigrated from Western countries where multiculturalism was celebrated, had snapped almost as soon as they were forced to reckon with the militaristic culture of their new country. In numerous cases, however, those who made the dramatic break with Zionism found sanctuary within a hermetic anarchist subculture where veganism, communal living, and a rejection of consumer culture were *de rigeur*. They had formed a tiny tribe within the tribe, mobilizing for a constant series of direct actions against the state while doing very little to inform the non-Hebrew-speaking outside world about what they were doing. Indeed, only a handful of the radical leftists I encountered were savvy with English language social media. Even fewer sought to cultivate a journalistic following. But the handful who were like Sheen were capable of making an enormous impact.

When I told Sheen about my intention to interview the Knesset members behind the new battery of anti-democratic laws, his eyes lit up. He had yet to produce any copy for *Ha'aretz*—his duties were limited to translating articles for the English website—but he recognized my proposed project as a chance to gather essential journalistic reporting. By the end of the week, Sheen had arranged five interviews with Knesset members from Kadima, Likud, and Yisrael Beiteinu.

The Robbed Cossack

Many of the most egregiously discriminatory, anti-democratic bills bore the name of one figure as either the key sponsor or principal author—David Rotem, a senior member of Yisrael Beiteinu and one of Avigdor Lieberman's closest friends.

On a clear day in West Jerusalem, David Sheen and I set out in a small, rented car to meet Rotem at his home in the West Bank settlement of Efrat. We passed smoothly through a series of tunnels and bypass roads constructed for the almost exclusive use of Israeli Jews. Concrete blast walls installed to protect the settlers during the Second Intifada remained along parts of the road. For much of the ride, we remained inside the separation wall, which had been routed near the perimeter of Efrat to effectively annex as much land as possible around the settlement into "Israel proper."

The streets of Efrat were nearly deserted except for a few Orthodox women pushing prams down sidewalks. As we drove cautiously through the placid streets, inching past stuccoed, Mission-style homes with neatly tended grass lawns, I began to wonder whether I was in the West Bank or the exurbs of San Diego. After a wrong turn, we asked a man watering his lawn for directions. In perfect, American-accented English, he directed us to Rotem's house (many of the nine thousand residents of Efrat spoke English as a first language, and some struggled to communicate in Hebrew). It was in places like this where the occupation was recast as an utterly benign endeavor that enabled its Jewish beneficiaries to drape themselves in a mantle of normality.

Built on a series of hills and slicing through Palestinian land like a snake, Efrat was an outgrowth of the original "Etzion bloc" of ideological settlements established by the religious nationalist Gush Emunim movement. The Gush Emunim secured its initial foothold in the West Bank thanks to the blessings of the Labor Party government of Yitzhak Rabin and Shimon Peres, who had sought to placate the settlers, as Peres said, "for reasons that reach into the very soul of the nation."

In April 1977, after the Rabin government approved the establishment of another settlement in the so-called Etzion bloc, a Gush Emunim leader named Meir Harnoy announced, "Here, at this place and at this hour, the first stake of the revolution in the perception of settlement in Israel was driven in. . . . Here, the stake was also driven in for the political change that occurred in 1977, when the Likud came into power, for the first time since the establishment of the state." Harnoy was right: in one of a protracted series of self-destructive moves, the Labor elite unwittingly authorized the death of their party. In the case of Rabin, who would be shot dead nearly two decades later by a right-wing fanatic inspired by the Gush Emunim's radical ideology, this was almost literally true.

While serving as agriculture minister in the Likud government of Prime Minister Menachem Begin during the late 1970s and early '80s, Ariel Sharon focused with single-minded determination on sprinkling settlements across the West Bank. Through the strategic planting of the colonies, Sharon said he planned to turn the Palestinian territories into a "pastrami sandwich"—in other words, a series of non-contiguous Bantustans. Efrat was among a group of major colonies he approved in 1982 with the goal of severing East Jerusalem from the West Bank. But the settlements were hardly a right-wing project. During the height of the Oslo era, the Israeli political consensus supported annexing Efrat and much of the Etzion Bloc in a future deal with the Palestinians.

"There is no meaning to our identity and everything that we are here for without the connection to Shiloh and Tekoa, Beit El and Efrat. These are the realms of our culture's childhood," Ehud Barak declared in 1996 as a Knesset representative of the Labor Party. "I am closer to these people," Barak said of the Etzion Bloc settlers, "than to the people of the Left."

Far from an accident or a wrong turn on Israel's democratic path, David Rotem's home in Efrat represented the organic product of popular will. In the settlers of "Judea and Samaria," the country's leaders believed they had realized a seamless continuation of the spirit of the original "pioneers" who ventured to Palestine to "redeem the land." Settler-colonialism was part of the country's ethos—of "everything that we are here for," as Barak said. It was only natural, then, for the Jewish majority to elect politicians who pledged to move the expansionist project into its next stage, even if it seemed to Western outsiders like an obstacle to Israel's long-term national interests.

Rotem took heart in the fact that the major settlements had become fully entrenched in both a physical and psychological sense, watching with contentment as new outposts sprouted up on hilltops across the West Bank almost every week. However, when he looked back across the Green Line, he saw a country in deep turmoil. Arabs were abusing their citizenship by protesting not only against infringements on their rights, he alleged, but also against the very foundation of the Jewish state. "Arab members of Knesset do not represent the Arab citizens," Rotem thundered from the Knesset floor. "They represent terror organizations in Gaza." And Jewish leftists were right behind them, exploiting foreign NGO funding to "lie, tattle, provide false information, and cause damage to the State of Israel," he complained. Rotem was convinced that the Jewish state was being destroyed from within, and that most Jewish Israelis agreed with him.

When we arrived at Rotem's home, he escorted us onto his patio to interview him in the shade. He was sixty-two years old, but the slow, limping gait he developed after a bout with polio, his close-cropped gray beard, darkened spectacles and gravelly voice made him seem more worn down by the vicissitudes of time.

Unlike Alex Miller and the other Russians recruited as Avigdor Lieberman's foot soldiers, Rotem was born and raised in Israel. And though he appeared to be a typical rightist settler, he did not resort to religious or messianic justifications for his political machinations. Instead, Rotem explained his ideological motives in terms more familiar to secular Israeli society. The demons of the Holocaust were at the base of his commitment to the Zionist cause, and it seemed to inform just about everything he did in the Knesset.

Rotem came of age during the early 1960s, right when the Israeli government made a calculated decision to feature the Holocaust at the heart of the Zionist narrative. After years of looking upon the European genocide as a shameful episode of Jewish impotence, the Zionist leadership decided to appropriate an emerging narrative of victimhood and redemption to counteract a potentially massive Jewish exodus to the diaspora and general sense of malaise that had overtaken the new country.

The trial of Adolph Eichmann, a top Nazi functionary captured by the Mossad in Argentina and dragged to a courtroom in Jerusalem, took center stage. "When I was fourteen years of age, or fifteen years of age, the Eichmann trial took place, and I read every sentence in the evidence," Rotem said with a wistful smile. "*Every* sentence. It was funny because the prime minister's office gave out later the books of the evidence and the judgments, and I used to buy it as presents for my friends for their Bar Mitzvah. And people said to me that I am a nutcase. And I told them, 'No—if you don't know what your history is you will never have a future.'"

Like many Israelis subjected to a lifetime of seeing the Holocaust lurking behind current events, Rotem conflated the Holocaust with Arab resistance to Zionism. In his view, Israel was an innocent lamb surrounded by hordes of olive-skinned Nazis braying for Jewish blood. On the massacre at Deir Yassin, where more than one hundred Palestinian villagers were massacred in 1948, he remarked, "Deir Yassin was a fight. They were asked to surrender. They didn't want to surrender. . . . It's not a massacre. It's not coming into Tel Aviv and planting a bomb in a bus."

On the Palestinian refugees: "They were leaving because they were promised that they would leave now, that they would come back in three months, and then they would be able to rape our daughters and our wives."

And on the 1973 Yom Kippur War, when Egypt and Syria attacked Israel to recover land Israel had occupied: "We didn't have anything to do with Egypt or Syria, and were attacked again."

To Rotem, Israel was a perpetual victim with no responsibility for the cycles of violence and tragedy.

Rotem met Lieberman while serving as a legal adviser to the Gush Emunim during their first foray into the West Bank in the late 1970s. After helping Lieberman establish the settlement of Nokdim just over the hills from Efrat, Rotem set up a law office to assist the waves of religious nationalist settlers seeking a foothold in Greater Israel. In 2005, as the conflict between the state and the Arab sector mounted, Rotem got back in touch with Lieberman. "I decided that it's about time to do a change in the State of Israel, so I connected with him and he offered to let me join [Yisrael Beiteinu]," Rotem explained. "So I joined."

As soon as he entered the Knesset, Rotem became a one-man legislative machine, cranking out bill after bill to advance his party's aim to consolidate the Jewish majority's total control over state and society. The Acceptance to Communities Bill, which would allow small communities to officially segregate on an ethnic basis, was Rotem's brainchild. Two Declaration of Allegiance bills, requiring both members of Knesset and citizens of Israel to swear allegiance to the "Jewish and democratic state, its laws, symbols, and anthem" as a condition of maintaining their citizenship, also bore his sponsorship. Another bill Rotem proposed, and which was subsequently passed, revoked the citizenship of anyone found guilty of treason or terrorism, though not Jewish fanatics like Yigal Amir, who was serving a life sentence for murdering Yitzhak Rabin—the bill exclusively targeted Palestinian citizens of Israel. Two more bills he introduced would strip the Supreme Court of most of its power to overturn anti-democratic laws validated by the Knesset, especially those pertaining to the rights of Israeli citizens.

Minority rights advocates and civil libertarians decried his proposals as a recipe for authoritarianism, but Rotem saw his work as a form of altruism. "I think that it is important to propose laws and to pass them," he commented. "But it's much more important to help people. I'm getting about 200 or something, near to 200 e-mails every day from people that are seeking help. I'm answering everyone. I'm opening the e-mails to myself. I get to the Knesset at seven o'clock, I open my e-mails by myself, and I answer by myself. I don't want anyone—not even my assistant to deal with it because I feel that my duty is to help people, and I'm trying to do it in the best way."

If Rotem was dedicated to helping Jews, Sheen asked him, why did he devote so much of his energy to fretting about the activities of non-Jewish citizens of Israel? In a calm and confident tone, the lawmaker insisted that "the Jewish part and the democratic part of the state are the same. Therefore everyone, even if he is not Jewish, has got a right to live here, has got a right to citizenship, has got a right to vote. But he has to be loyal to the state that he wants to be a citizen in. By the way, in the United States if I would like to become an American citizen, I will have to take an oath of loyalty."

I informed Rotem that the United States does not ask its new citizens to take an oath upholding the ethnic dominance of the white, Christian majority, and that Thomas Jefferson might have condemned his legislative proposals as efforts to consolidate the tyranny of the majority. "Yes, yes," Rotem said with a dismissive wave of the hand. "But the tyranny of the majority is the heart of democracy. Democracy *is* the rule of the majority. . . . And it's not a tyranny if you decide in your policies to go against the minorities."

Rotem's blunt language might have startled some Western outsiders, but within the Israeli establishment, the distinction between his approach towards Palestinian citizens of Israel and the attitude expressed by prominent Israeli liberals was not so sharp. Benny Morris, professor at Ben Gurion University, once regarded as the doyen of the Israeli revisionist historians who shattered the state's founding mythology in his book *The Birth of the Palestinian Refugee Problem, 1947–1949*, expressed an increasingly common opinion when he remarked in 2003, "The Israeli Arabs are a time bomb. Their slide into complete Palestinization has made them an emissary of the enemy that is among us. They are a potential Fifth Column."

Nothing exemplified the Zionist establishment's willingness to cast off its constantly professed democratic aspirations in favor of the kind of ethnocratic imperatives Rotem advanced better than its support for the Citizenship and Entry Into Israel Law. Passed in 2003, the bill represented one of the most nakedly discriminatory laws the state had ever placed on the books. It not only banned West Bank Palestinians from obtaining citizenship if they married Israeli citizens, but it also blocked them from receiving temporary residency. The bill's author, Avraham Poraz from the centrist and now-defunct Shinui Party, presented the proposal as a "defensive measure" against the Arab demographic threat. Amnon Rubinstein, a former Israeli government minister, echoed Poraz by condemning those who "claim that human rights demand Israel commit national suicide." An overwhelming majority of the Knesset agreed—only twenty-five legislators voted against it. Ignoring the protestations of Arab members of Knesset, the Supreme Court temporarily approved the law on the basis of guarding the state's Jewish character.

"This law actually means that the state sees every Palestinian and every Arab as a threat to the security of the State of Israel only because he is an Arab, therefore it is completely racist. Such a law does not exist in any other democratic state in the world," Sawsan Zaher, a lawyer for Adalah, a Palestinian-Israeli legal rights organization, declared.

The Israeli mainstream welcomed the law, with the *Jerusalem Post* editorial page hailing Israel's political leadership for dropping all the disingenuous justifications about preventing "terrorism." "The government must be congratulated for having summoned the courage—even if belatedly—to cease citing immediate security concerns as its reason for making it more difficult for Palestinians and other Arabs to obtain Israeli citizenship," the editors wrote. Dan Margalit, one of the most prominent columnists and TV pundits in Israel, claimed the law saved Israel from a "well-planned invasion."

In January 2012, the Supreme Court permanently approved the Citizenship and Entry Law, with most judges basing their ruling on at least implicitly demographic grounds. As the legal scholar Yoram Rabin noted in *Ha'aretz*, "It is quite clear that at least some of the judges in the majority opinion 'talked security' while 'thinking demographics.'" The ruling not only shredded whatever remained of the myth of Israel's liberal Supreme Court, it demonstrated the extent to which demographic panic superseded democratic rights. Indeed, liberal, and centrist Zionists—Israel's "Enlightened Public"—might have condemned the treachery of right-wing settlers and some of the anti-democratic bills pouring out of the Knesset, but they remained committed to the engineering and maintenance of a politically dominant Jewish demographic majority. Like Rotem, they were implacably opposed to the very concept of a heterogeneous society.

Asa Kasher, an influential professor of philosophy at Tel Aviv University who authored the code of ethics that guided the Israeli army during Operation Cast Lead was a member of the Enlightened Public in good standing. His opinions underlined the ethnocratic sensibility that guided national policy. "I want a decisive Jewish majority which enjoys national, political, and social freedom . . . by being the ruler in all unorganized aspects of the social life of the state," he told an interviewer. "Every-thing is conditioned on being a decisive majority, not just a majority." Yossi Beilin, a veteran politician from the left-wing Meretz Party and a stalwart of Israel's peace camp, echoed Kasher when he remarked, "If this country is not the Jewish State, and has no Jewish majority, it doesn't interest me."

In the battle between Israel's right- and left-wing parties, the principal disagree-ment lay in how to best to maintain the country's Jewish demographic majority, and then in how to preserve its political dominance over Palestinians. While many right-wingers argued for open methods of ethnic cleansing like transfer, members of the Zionist left responded with calls for a separation wall or "land swaps" amounting to a population transfer through negotiations. Neither side considered the notion of equal rights for all Palestinians living under Israeli control to be anything short of a recipe for the destruction of Zionism. Thus both the Israeli right and left collabo-rated in the limiting of Palestinian rights and opportunities behind the smokescreen of a heated political rivalry. In a society where maintaining the tyranny of the ethnic majority formed the underpinnings of national policy, there could be little wonder that an unapologetically supremacist party like Yisrael Beiteinu was able to consoli-date a mainstream foothold in such a rapid fashion.

By the time Sheen and I interviewed Rotem, Avigdor Lieberman had installed him as chairman of the Knesset's Constitution, Law, and Justice Committee. Thus Rotem held the gavel in the Knesset committee responsible for piecing together the nation's political structure in lieu of a formal constitution, a weighty responsibility that afforded him vast political powers. In November 2011, Rotem asserted his power by tossing five opposition members of Knesset out of a committee debate over his bill to alter the composition of the Judicial Selection Committee in order to further neuter the Supreme Court. "Get out of here!" he barked at Zehava Gal-On of the Meretz Party, when she protested his heavy-handed maneuver. "You're not even an animal."

A week later, Rotem rushed a vote on the so-called Grunis Bill, a law that would allow the Knesset to vote to appoint the right-wing ideologue Asher Grunis—a key supporter of the Citizenship and Entry Law—as Chief Justice of the Supreme Court. By holding the vote in a mere three minutes, Rotem was able to secure the bill's pas-sage without any debate and before any of the opposition legislators even entered the room. The law was originally conceived by Yaakov Neeman, a religious nationalist ideologue appointed by Netanyahu as Israel's attorney general. By clearing the path for Grunis's ascent, the hard right's agenda could proceed virtually unabated. As a former Supreme Court justice told Ha'aretz, "It is no secret that Grunis holds rigidly to the idea of reducing the powers of the Supreme Court, and that is why wild weeds on the right want him as president. He is their favorite son."

The Grunis Bill also enabled the appointment of the first resident of an illegal settlement to ever serve on the Supreme Court. He was Noam Sohlberg, a fifty-year-old rightist ideologue who defined his judicial career presiding over the Jerusalem district court with rulings advancing the transfer of Palestinians from Jerusalem and the stripping of citizenship of Israeli expats who refused to perform army service. In his most notorious ruling, Sohlberg awarded an army officer known only as "Captain R." a whopping $100,000 in a libel case against the veteran investigative journalist Ilana Dayan.

Dayan's crime? She had reported that Captain R. murdered a thirteen-year-old Palestinian girl, Iman Al-Hams, in cold blood during a patrol in Gaza, shooting her twice in the head before emptying his entire clip into her lifeless body. In a radio transmission to his subordinates broadcast by Dayan on Israel's Channel 2, Captain R. declared, "This is commander. Anything that's mobile, that moves in the zone, even if it's a three-year-old, needs to be killed. Over." (Captain R. was acquitted of all charges by an Israeli court.)

The libel ruling was later cancelled by the Supreme Court, but with Sohlberg sitting on the bench, decisions guarding the freedom of the press against the military were far less likely in the future. The outgoing chief justice, Dorit Beinisch, was one of the last remaining judicial activists who had given the court its liberal veneer. Even as she applied a stamp of legitimacy on the occupation, defending the building of Israelis-only highways in the occupied West Bank as a necessary security measure, she faced a mounting chorus of attacks from right-wingers who saw the Supreme Court as the key obstacle to the untrammeled will of the Jewish majority. Chief among Beinisch's antagonists was Rotem, who had attempted to establish an alternative judicial authority that was incapable of overriding Knesset votes or military edicts.

In her farewell speech, Beinisch lamented the success of a "campaign to damage the court, a campaign of delegitimization." Referring indirectly to Rotem and his allies, she proclaimed, "Like the robbed Cossack, they loudly declare that the public has no faith in the court and the judicial system. This is a campaign of deception by its very nature, and its character is earthshaking and poisonous. . . . " Finally, Beinisch conceded defeat, predicting doom for the court and danger for Israeli society. "The writing was on the wall," she said. "The warning was heard, but no one rose up."

Following Beinisch's impassioned jeremiad, *Ha'aretz* asked a "close associate" of the outgoing judge to elaborate on her gloomy mood. Beinisch, said the associate, decided to "defend the judges with her own body, because she thinks a red line has been crossed. This is a very slippery slope that could lead to Germany of the 1930s, when the majority rode roughshod over the rights of minorities."

While Rotem and his allies whittled away at the power of the Supreme Court, they prepared the groundwork for barring Palestinian citizens from serving in the Knesset. They did so by stacking the Central Elections Commission with the kind of hardline nationalists who increasingly occupied the political mainstream. Yet Rotem denied his intention was to purge the Knesset of all Arabs. "No way, because I am not asking to disqualify Arab members of parliament," he claimed to me. "I am asking to disqualify every member of parliament—and I don't care if he is Jewish, Muslim, or Christian—if he's not loyal to the job that he's being elected, if he's not loyal to the state, if he wants to sit in the parliament and work against this parliament."

But only Palestinian citizens were likely to refuse to take loyalty oaths to the Jewish state and its Zionist symbols. I told Rotem his proposals seemed like thinly disguised mechanisms to strip Palestinian Israelis of their citizenship rights, if not expel them from Israeli society altogether. He replied that total homogeneity was the only recourse. "If we have a 100 percent Jewish state and a 100 percent Arab state, we might find a solution," he said. But until then, the Jews could not give an inch: "This is my land and I haven't got another state. I haven't got an American passport; I don't have a German passport. I don't want to have it. I'm very happy with my Israeli passport, and therefore if I am an occupier, well okay, I am an occupier, but I am still having my state, and I am happy with it, and I will stay here."

Rotem brought our conversation to a close by harkening back to the dark days of Europe. It was a Shabbat morning in Berlin and his grandfather was strolling home from the synagogue. On the way he encountered dozens of Jewish friends in varying states of despondency and fear. They were doctors, lawyers, shopkeepers, and most of all, German patriots, who had just been thrown out of their professions upon the passage of the Nuremberg Laws. All over town, racist mobs forced Jewish shopkeepers to shutter their stores.

"On the same night, he had to leave, and he left," Rotem said. "I got older and understood that we need to have a strong State of Israel, which is showing the world that Jew's blood is not nothing. There is an importance to Jewish blood. It will never happen again as long as there will be a strong Israel that a Jewish baby should be blown up or should be thrown up in the air and shot. Never again! Now we have to fulfill this oath, because the Jews, when they went to Auschwitz, they wrote on the trains and in the chambers—'take revenge.' Now, I am not going to take revenge by killing somebody, I am going to take revenge by having a strong Jewish state that no one will be able to attack, that no one will be able to threaten."

"Why, when we try to ask you about all the bills you have introduced, and about Yisrael Beiteinu's agenda, do you keep bringing up the Holocaust?" I asked him.

"I will bring it up fifty times," Rotem announced. "I have got a chip on my shoulder and a click in my head, and it's called the Holocaust."

"Correct me if I'm wrong," I interjected, "but it seems like you are openly admitting that you are psychologically consumed by this terrible historical trauma. Are you sure you are thinking rationally—and do you think it's a good idea?"

"I am completely rational. I am *completely* rational," Rotem insisted, repeating himself with a confident tone. "It is because of the Holocaust that I know how to prevent another Holocaust."

To avenge the humiliation of the Nuremberg Laws, a suite of discriminatory measures that stripped Jews of the right to work or participate in the affairs of German state, Rotem was introducing a battery of measures intended to do more or less the same to Israel's Palestinian minority. But the cruel irony of Rotem's actions was completely lost on him. To him, the ghosts of Europe cried out for revenge, while Palestinians inside Israel continued Hitler's work in spirit. By proposing bill after bill that stripped away the minority's citizenship rights in the Jewish state, he believed he was preventing what could be another great historical injustice.

After our interview, I watched Rotem limp toward his front door, swinging his crippled leg like a club to advance forward. The ravages of disease must have presented an enormous burden to such an intensely committed man, I thought. But Rotem never allowed his physical handicap to circumscribe his ambitions. His wounds defined him, especially the unseen ones inflicted on him by a history of genocide, the demons that seemed to preoccupy his thoughts each day. The chip on his shoulder and the tic in his brain helped elucidate his far-reaching goals, propelling him resolutely toward their fulfillment.

Rotem's legislative agenda could not have succeeded so resoundingly without significant help from outside his party—and especially from lawmakers to his political left. "Plenty of my laws are being signed by parties from both sides," Rotem said. "Zionists are not only on the right hand side; there are some Zionists on the left side too. Not too much and not enough. But some of them are still on the left."

On one of his signature bills, the Communities Acceptance Law, which would allow the small, exclusively Jewish towns planted across Israel's Galilee region to formally reject applicants for residency on the grounds of "suitability to the community's fundamental outlook," Rotem found eager cosponsors from the centrist Kadima Party, including a veteran kibbutz leader. Introduced in the spirit of the state's longstanding policy of "Judaization," which aimed to disperse the Jewish population into majority Arab areas, interrupting and confining Palestinian communities with Jews-only towns, the law was certain to pass.

While presiding over a debate on the law in the Constitution, Law, and Justice Committee, Rotem responded to allegations of exclusionary racism with a casually racist quip. "In my opinion, every Jewish town needs at least one Arab," he joked. "What would happen if my refrigerator stopped working on a Saturday?"

Judaization

On March 11, 1976, the Israeli authorities announced a fresh round of confiscations in Arab areas of the Galilee for what it said were "security and settlement purposes." Three Arab villages that had already lost hundreds of acres when the state expropriated their land to create a national water project now faced the loss of thousands more acres of their best agricultural land, and the prospect of permanent impoverishment. The confiscations were part of a larger plan initiated a year before designed to expand Jewish towns in the area while preventing the natural growth of those populated by Arabs.

In Nazareth, the largest Arab city in the Galilee, a charismatic poet-politician named Tawfiq Zayyad had scored a dramatic victory as mayor, shocking Israeli government officials, who never expected a Palestinian nationalist to garner so much cachet. With the confiscations in the works, Zayyad immediately called for a general strike. In response, the military government ordered a curfew for all residents of the villages slated to lose their lands, threatening to fire all schoolteachers who led their students into the streets in protest. Despite official intimidation, popular enthusiasm for the strike swelled in the villages. The protest was known simply as "Land Day," a mass demonstration against the discriminatory national laws that intentionally kept state land out of non-Jewish hands, and against the regime that was determined to "Judaize" the Galilee through mass expropriations and settlement construction.

Perhaps the most nakedly discriminatory of Israel's land regulations was the so-called Jewish National Fund (JNF) law enacted in 1960,which effectively placed control of 70 percent of Israel's public land in the hands of JNF, a quasi-governmental entity created to advance Jewish settlement. A subsequent law that stated that the JNF existed "for the purpose of settling Jews on such lands and properties," made the organization's discriminatory mission explicit. The rules officially blocked Arabs from leasing land from the state or from expanding their villages, while facilitating the practice of "Judaization," which aimed to divide and control areas densely populated with Palestinian residents by strategically encircling them with Jews-only communities. The verdant hills of the Galilee, home to hundreds of thousands of Arabs, became ground zero for the JNF's Judaization campaign in the 1960s and '70s. As the government planted exclusively Jewish communities between and around Arab population clusters in order to interrupt their demographic continuity, tensions in the Galilee rose to a boiling point.

Zayyad, an accomplished translator whose poetry was familiar even to illiterate farmers, channeled the rising anger of the agrarian people fighting the latest wave of dispossession in the North. With Land Day approaching, Zayyad published his masterpiece, a poem that expressed the sensibility of *sumud*, or steadfastness, a single word that captured the entire spirit of Palestinian resistance. He called it, "Here We Shall Stay."

> *As though we were twenty impossibilities*
> *In Lydda, Ramla, and Galilee*
> *Here ... Like a brick wall upon your breast*
> *And in your throat*
> *Like a splinter of glass, like spiky cactus*
> *And in your eyes*
> *A chaos of fire*
>
> *Here we shall stay*
> *A hard Wall on your breast*
> *We hunger ...*
> *We defy ...*
> *Sweep the sick streets with our angry dances*
> *Saturate the prisons with dignity and pride*
> *Keep on making children*
> *One revolutionary generation*
> *After another*
> *As though we were twenty impossibilities*
> *In Lydda, Ramla, and Galilee!*

As Land Day drew close that March, a group of activists from the Mapai Party—the quasi-socialist founding party of Israel that would soon be known as the Labor Party—produced a confidential memorandum offering strategies for reducing the political influence and number of Arab citizens in the Galilee. The document's primary author, Yisrael Koenig, was the Northern District Commissioner of the Ministry of the Interior—essentially the governor of the Galilee. His paper, which would become known as the "Koenig Memo," provided both a perfect reflection of the establishment's attitude towards the country's Palestinian minority and a semi-official blueprint for the state's campaign of Judaization. And at times, he verged on advocating racial eugenics to assuage Israel's demographic fears.

Koenig opened the memo with a warning about the "Arabization" of the Galilee: "There is ground for serious apprehensions that within the next decade an Arab political and demographic takeover of the Acre and Nazareth areas will occur." To remedy the problem, he first recommended that Israel "expand and deepen Jewish settlement in areas where the contiguity of the Arab population is prominent and where they number considerably more than the Jewish population." Further, he urged his superiors to "examine the possibility of diluting existing Arab population concentrations," cautioning them against acting in good faith toward "the superficial and Levantinistic Arab character whose imagination tends to exceed rationality."

The increasing popularity of Rakah, the communist political faction Zayyad represented, filled Koenig with panic. He warned that the party could win as many as 10 seats in the coming round of Knesset elections, a far-flung scenario that was consistent with the paranoid tone of the entire document. Koenig recommended the creation of an Arab collaborationist party comprised of "figures who are equitable and charismatic" and who would demonstrate a more submissive posture before the Jewish authorities. Next, he called for a campaign of dirty tricks to unravel Rakah's leadership. "Special teams should be appointed to examine the personal habits of Rakah leaders and other negative people and this information should be made available to the electorate," Koenig wrote.

Koenig complained that the "jet sets" of Israel's Arab minority were attempting to upgrade the Palestinian struggle with the sophistication and militancy they cultivated in institutions of higher learning. He demanded that the state impose strict testing standards on Arab students in order to "produce a natural selection and . . . considerably reduce the number of Arab students." For Arabs seeking acceptance into universities, Koenig proposed that they be systematically categorized on the criteria of potential political troublemaking. "Encourage the channeling of students into technical professions, to physical and natural sciences," he urged. "These studies leave less time for dabbling in nationalism and the dropout rate is higher." Those who could not be dissuaded from studying the humanities should be coerced into leaving forever, Koenig wrote. "Make trips abroad for studies easier, while making the return and employment more difficult—this policy is apt to encourage their emigration."

Finally, Koenig proposed an array of aggressive measures aimed at the Palestinian citizens of Israel in general. "Neutralize and encumber Arab [shopkeepers] . . . in order to avoid dependence of the Jewish population on those agents," Koenig wrote. He continued: "Neutralize the payment of 'big family grants' to the Arab population . . . so that the grant is paid to Jews only." Then, in a statement that perfectly encapsulated its prejudice, Koenig issued one final recommendation: "Endeavor to have central institutions pay more attention in giving preferential treatment to Jewish groups or individuals rather than Arabs."

Though the Koenig memo is virtually forgotten today, it stands as one of the most important exhibits of official discrimination against Palestinian citizens of Israel. It can read as the answer to Zayyad's "Here We Stay." As such, it could have been entitled, "You Must Go." With its open call for a concerted government campaign to produce an Arab-free state, the document was more stridently racist than the most demagogic campaign propaganda produced by Yisrael Beiteinu. And unlike Avigdor Lieberman's race-baiting ads, which merely suggested what the candidate wished to do once in office, the Koenig memo recommended a formal state policy in concrete terms.

Just a month after the final section of the Koenig memo was completed, Israeli authorities attempted to crush the Land Day demonstration with brute force, dispatching four thousand police officers, army units equipped with tanks, armored vehicles, and a helicopter tactical unit against the protesters, who were all Israeli citizens. A riot quickly ensued during which the Israeli army and riot police shot six unarmed demonstrators to death.

Hatim Kanaaneh, a Palestinian-Israeli medical provider who operated a public health clinic in the impoverished village where the Land Day demonstrations took place, Arrabeh, recalled the aftermath of the Land Day massacre in his memoir, *A Doctor In Galilee*. "In nearby Sakhnin," Kanaaneh wrote, "a few dozen Golani crack troopers linked arms in a circle and danced the Hora to their own chants of 'A'am Yisrael hai—The people of Israel lives!' on the very spot where they had shot dead two young villagers."

In September 1976, six months after the Land Day massacre, the Israeli newspaper *Al-Hamishmar* leaked the contents of the Koenig memorandum to the public. Not one government official repudiated its contents. Instead, they either condemned the document's release or, like Yosef Burg, the Israeli interior minister, proclaimed their complete faith in Koenig. For his part, Koenig remained in his post for twenty-six years without ever having to renounce the views he articulated in his notorious memo. In 2002, after retiring from public life, Koenig defended his legacy, telling an interviewer from *Ha'aretz* that the Arabs inside Israel "want to suck the best out of us." He went on to recount how he convinced a "rich Christian friend from Nazareth" to immigrate to Canada. He remembered telling his friend, "Your children will never have it good here."

When the right-wing Likud Party came into power in 1977, the new minister of agriculture, Ariel Sharon, began transforming Koenig's recommendations into facts on the ground with characteristic ruthlessness. In 1978, Sharon ordered construction to begin on a new round of Jews-only settlements, reviving the dormant campaign of Judaizing the Galilee. Though these small communities operated without any official discriminatory rules, they each contained a "welcome committee" devoted to excluding the Arab undesirables (and oftentimes, homosexuals, Mizrahim, and single people) from settling inside their confines. In 1991, Sharon introduced his "Seven Stars" plan, planting settlements along the Green Line in order to establish a Jewish demographic barrier—a human wall—between the Palestinian citizens of Israel and occupied residents of the West Bank.

To provide a local base for the Judaization campaign in the North, the Israeli government established the Misgav Regional Council. The Misgav council's mission was to distribute land generously to the Jewish settlements while denying building permits in almost all cases to longtime residents of Arab villages, including when permits were sought to build on land they already owned. Land confiscated from villages such as Sakhnin years before also fell into the hands of Misgav. "Misgav's real reasoning is not too difficult to discern. It is not a disinterested party after all," wrote Jonathan Cook, a veteran journalist who resides in Nazareth. "It was created as part of the government's Judaization policy, the drive to take land from Palestinian citizens and pass it to Jewish citizens."

The new Jews-only settlements Sharon established were known as *mitzpim*, or "watchtower" towns: small communities inhabited by young Jewish families and upwardly mobile professionals strategically placed above Arab towns, just like the

Jewish settlements in the occupied West Bank would be. Every *mitzpe* resident, from the shopkeeper to the teacher, was expected to serve as a kind of spy, reporting to the authorities each "illegal" building attempt by the Arabs below.

By the dawn of the twenty-first century, Sakhnin was flanked on all sides by military installations and Jews-only *mitzpim*. The town's double-digit unemployment rate reflected decades of aggressive dispossession. Sakhnin controlled only the land inside its town limits—10,000 acres for 25,000 people—while the 15,000 Jewish residents of Misgav had the rights to 180,000 acres. Much of the land Misgav had gained was confiscated by the state from the farmers of Sakhnin, who had become mired in poverty. As a Sakhnin resident told Cook, "We must be imprisoned in our ghetto towns so the Jews have the freedom to take our land."

In the year 2000, not a single Arab lived in one of the twenty-nine communities comprising the Misgav council—all applicants who applied were rejected, and generally on the basis of "lack of suitability" (six other towns in the Misgav are segregated Bedouin townships that often suffer from substandard conditions.) However, a slight crack appeared in the unspoken policy of segregation of the Galilee's *mitzpim*. In 1995, a young, middle-class Arab couple, Adel and Iman Qa'dan, had attempted to purchase a plot in Katzir, a community constructed on confiscated Palestinian land to advance the Judaization of the Galilee. The parcel they sought was owned by the Jewish Agency, an organization, which, like the Jewish National Fund, distributed land exclusively to Jews. The Association for Civil Rights (ACRI) in Israel took up the Qa'dans' case, demanding the Supreme Court resolve the dispute in their favor. But first, the Qa'dans had to tacitly agree to express loyalty to the "Jewish People." ACRI stressed to the court that the Qa'dans would not alter the Zionist character of Katzir through their residency.

For four years, the court dragged its feet, begging the local authorities to quietly resolve the issue. Finally, in 1999, the court president Aharon Barak grudgingly agreed to accept the case. Barak was a towering figure in the history of Israel whose legacy was as pivotal as any of the country's prime ministers. While he imposed his liberal politics on the state by establishing a series of "basic laws" in place of the formal constitution Israel was never able to write, Barak quietly rubber-stamped many of the occupation's most unsavory aspects, from targeted assassination to settlement construction. (Elena Kagan, a liberal-leaning judge serving on the US Supreme Court, described Barak during her confirmation hearings in 2010 as her "judicial hero"—the legal mind who "best advanced the values of democracy and human rights.")

Confronted with the Qa'dan case, a potential challenge to the state's campaign of Judaization, Barak confessed that "the problem which arises here is the most difficult one I had come across as a judge." Though he ultimately ruled in favor of the Qa'dans, Barak made certain not to challenge the segregationist land and residency policies at the core of Zionism. Along with his fellow judges, Barak hailed the work of the Jewish Agency, praising it for its efforts at Judaization and "the realization of the Zionist vision . . . to disperse the [Jewish] population and thus strengthen the security of the state." What's more, the court majority explicitly refused to extend its decision to apply to other communities—*kibbutzim, moshavim,* and *mitzpim*—throughout Israel that maintained admissions committees to exclude unsuitable (read: Arab) applicants. According to the court, the Qa'dans' victory would not impact areas that upheld "Zionist aims."

Despite the deliberately limited scope of the decision, leading lights from across the Zionist intelligentsia predicted doom. Joel Golovensky and Ariel Gilboa, directors of the right-leaning Institute for Zionist Strategies think tank, complained that the Qa'dan decision placed "the very essence of the effort to settle Jews on land within the boundaries of the State of Israel in question—judicially, politically, and morally," and threatened to "put Zionism itself on trial." They argued, "The aspiration to equality, however compelling it may be, must sometimes . . . abide by the principle of majority rule."

Ruth Gavison, a law professor and Israeli liberal who had once served as the president of the Association of Civil Rights in Israel—the group that brought the Qa'dan case before the Supreme Court—agreed with right-wingers who condemned the decision as a mortal threat to the exclusive essence of Zionism. While asserting that "blatant discrimination against Arabs" in housing "cannot be justified," Gavison went on to contend, "In the context of the ongoing conflict, Israel is justified in establishing Jewish towns with the express purpose of preventing the contiguity of Arab settlement both within Israel and with the Arab states across the border." She added that while she "welcomed" the court's decision, "I do not accept the ruling's further implication that there is no basis for permitting the creation of separate communities for Jews and Arabs."

For several years, the Supreme Court did little to nothing to enforce the execution of its decision, forcing the Qa'dans to wait until 2007 to receive their hard-won plot of land. The admission of a single Arab couple to a previously homogenous community had shaken the Israeli establishment to its core. The despair and anxiety of Israel's political elite was apparent in the pages of an influential 2008 paper by Arnon Sofer, the Haifa University demographer nicknamed "The Arab Counter" by his colleagues. Entitled "Israel: Demography and Density 2007–2020," Sofer's paper was distributed to leading Jewish American organizations, top Israeli policymakers, and American diplomats, who said nothing in public against its disturbing undertones.

In the paper, Sofer summarized the recommendations he had issued after the collapse of the so-called peace process in 2000—namely the West Bank separation wall and the Gaza withdrawal—claiming credit for influencing their implementation by the now-comatose former prime minister Ariel Sharon. But the battle was far from over. In an apocalyptic tone suffused with ethnocentric panic, Sofer warned that no diplomatic initiative would save Israel from the terrible reckoning it faced. "The demographic clock is ticking against the Jews of Israel at great speed, yet surprisingly, in Israeli society no serious discussion of this issue has been held for many years," he wrote. "The truth is that most of the world (including Europe) is waiting to see the end of Israel, and only an American veto saves it every few weeks."

According to Sofer, by 2020, Palestinian population growth and rising nationalism threatened to reduce Israel to a post-Zionist, cosmopolitan "Tel Aviv state," a "doomsday scenario" that he said "is liable to turn [Israel] into 'Masada.'" With Israeli Jews cramped into a dystopian urban Alamo, the encircling Arab horde would by then comprise 30 percent of the population, enough to qualify Israel as a binational state that could no longer call itself "Jewish," according to assessments by Sofer and major Israeli public figures like Benjamin Netanyahu. To remedy the dire situation, Sofer proposed redoubling state efforts at "aggressive population dispersal" in Arab areas inside Israel, or "Judaization."

He saw this as an essential complement to the unilateral separation from as much of the West Bank and Gaza Strip as possible. Settler evacuations would be followed by the construction of separation walls, which he described not as security measures but as an essential "part of the implementation of demographic policy in Israel." Sofer claimed his recommendations represented the only hope for preserving Israel as "an isolated island of Western-ness in this tempestuous and crazy part of the world."

Back in the Galilee, the Misgav council was taking increasingly desperate measures to prevent more Arabs from moving in. In 2009, when another Arab couple filed a court petition demanding the right to build a home on Misgav-controlled land, three towns in the Misgav council established bylaws requiring applicants to swear loyalty to "Zionism, Jewish heritage, and settlement of the land" as a condition of admission. (The Arab couple was initially rejected on the grounds that the husband lacked "knowledge of sophisticated interpersonal relations.") "The council's position is that it is appropriate to strengthen the character of the community—a community in which Zionist values and Jewish heritage stand at the heart of its way of life. We don't see this as racism in any way," said Misgav mayor Ron Shani, who was elected by the largely secular, liberal-minded community residents on the basis of his progressive image.

Though only an insignificant scintilla of the Misgav council's residents had voted for Avigdor Lieberman during his run for prime minister, it was Lieberman and Yisrael Beiteinu who took decisive measures to protect the townships from integration. Acting as Lieberman's point man in the Knesset, David Rotem introduced the Acceptance to Communities Law to officially sanction ethnic segregation in the small Jewish towns planted across the Galilee and Negev Desert. Just when Rotem's bill was proclaimed a non-starter, two members of the Kadima Party stepped forward to move the proposal toward mainstream acceptance. They were Shai Hermesh, a kibbutz leader with close ties to the Jewish Agency, and Israel Hasson, a former Shin Bet deputy director who lives in the Misgav Regional Council. The trio had apparently taken heed of Sofer's dire warnings, uniting behind the mission to stave off the rise of the dystopian, Arab-encircled "Tel Aviv State."

In July 2010, just after the Acceptance to Communities Bill passed its first reading in the Knesset, David Sheen secured appointments to interview Hermesh and Hasson. Despite a sustained attack from the marginalized left-wing and Arab parties on the proposal, or perhaps because of it, the two men were eager to take credit for their efforts in the Israeli media. Their initiative stood to make them folk heroes in their communities, where droves of terrified, middle-class families sought legal protection from the menace of integration.

Homogeneity

On a typically hot and dry June afternoon in Jerusalem, with the sun beaming down through a cloudless sky, David Sheen and I ducked inside a dark, musty café in the Crowne Plaza Hotel to meet a legislator named Israel Hasson. Hasson was a compact, mustachioed fifty-five-year-old man with a leathery visage and close-cropped salt-and-pepper hair. Born in Syria and fluent in Arabic (he learned Hebrew during early adulthood), he had risen rapidly through the ranks of the Shin Bet, serving four prime ministers as an emissary to Western-backed Arab autocrats across the region. The friendly relations he forged with then-Egyptian president Hosni Mubarak prompted him to resign from Yisrael Beiteinu in protest when Avigdor Lieberman lashed out at the dictator for refusing to visit Israel. In 2009, Hasson joined Kadima, running for Knesset at the bottom of the party's list, and barely squeaking through. His name rarely surfaced in the media until he attached it to the Acceptance to Communities Law.

Hasson's last-minute interest in the legislative push proved to be fortuitous. Just when Rotem's version of the bill seemed certain to fail, Hasson mounted a fervent, nationwide lobbying effort, securing support for the bill from the heads of all thirty-two of the regional councils that governed Israel's small, almost exclusively Jewish communities. "These small communities that are far from the center of the country, they are on the periphery, where people's dependence on one another is much greater, where the quality of life is dependent on the social make-up of the population," he said. Hasson's own town, which belonged to the segregationist Misgav Regional Council, served as the spearhead in the campaign to Judaize the Galilee. In a separate interview, he said his signature law "reflects the Knesset's commitment to work to preserve the . . . Zionist dream in practice in Israel" through "population dispersal."

Despite the colonial agenda behind the bill, Hasson denied harboring any malice toward the Palestinians of the Galilee. Instead, he claimed that by promoting separateness inside Israel, he was preventing the rise of dangerous social friction. "This is not about homogeneity," Hasson maintained, "but the ability to coexist in a slightly larger space. For the Druze [a Shia offshoot community based in Syria, Lebanon, and Israel] to live wherever he wants to according to his values, he doesn't have to see my daughter walking around in a bikini, just like I don't have to respect that his wife is covered up from head to toe. Fine, different cultures, that is legitimate. I don't want his son to hit on my daughter, I don't think it's right; it's not right for him, and it's not right for her. The minute things can be different, by all means, there is no problem."

When we spoke to the bill's other cosponsor, Shai Hermesh, also of the "centrist" Kadima Party, he undercut Hasson, revealing his desire to prevent unwanted residency applicants from "undermin[ing] the unified homogeneity of these small communities." Hermesh explained, "To live in a small community means that the group should have a kind of common culture, they should be able to find a common language. If someone decides to join the community, they should accept the culture and the atmosphere and the values, in addition to what is expected from a regular citizen in Tel Aviv."

We met Hermesh in his office inside the massive headquarters of the Jewish Agency in downtown Tel Aviv. He was a longtime resident of Kfar Aza, an exclusively Jewish kibbutz on the Gaza border. While boasting of spearheading the Knesset's initiative to fund the construction of a concrete wall around the Gaza Strip that would seal in the natives once and for all, he simultaneously presented himself as an ardent supporter of Peace Now, the vanguard liberal Zionist organization advancing the concept of a two-state solution. He might have been cosponsoring one of Yisrael Beiteinu's key initiatives, but he could not have been further from Avigdor Lieberman's racist line of thinking—or so he liked to tell interviewers.

A slender man in his fifties with a shock of gray hair and a narrow, angular face, Hermesh initially presented himself with a self-effacing, affected sense of humility, joking about his English while offering a choice of cookies. As the interview progressed, however, he physically trembled as his anxiety rose. Finally, when Sheen directly challenged him to amend the bill to specifically state that acceptance committees could not discriminate on the basis of race or religion, marital status or sexual orientation, Hermesh exploded.

"I don't apologize! Never!" he shouted, startling the young female secretary who had been snacking on Bomba while she observed the interview with a bored, distant gaze. "I should state that I won't discriminate against Arabs? I should state that I won't discriminate against homosexuals? I should state that I won't discriminate against single mothers, that I'm not going to discriminate against the handicapped?!" Hermesh thundered. "Not at all! Because *I don't discriminate.*"

However personally tolerant Hermesh might have been, he and his cosponsors had tucked special caveats into the body of the Acceptance to Communities Bill to ensure that community leaders seeking to deny residency to "unsuitable" candidates would face minimal legal scrutiny. When I asked him if those who felt they were rejected on the basis of their race, religion, or sexuality could challenge a regional council's decision before the Supreme Court, Hermesh opened up a binder containing the draft language of the law. According to the new rules, he said, no one could contest a residency rejection before the Supreme Court. Instead, they could appeal to a committee comprised of representatives from two government ministries and the kibbutz and moshav authorities.

"So instead of relying on legal precedent you will be placing the decision in the hands of a group of political agents acting on ideology," I said.

"Right! Right!" Hermesh responded in an annoyed tone.

I noticed that Hermesh had kicked off one of his sandals and was using his toes to scratch at the other. With his nervous energy threatening to boil over into open anger, I wondered if he had not been subjected to such critical questioning by other reporters. Finally, when I described his proposed appeals committee somewhat inelegantly as a real estate cartel, he immediately gathered his files and stormed out of the room, harrumphing and calling me a *chutzpon* on the way out. Sheen chased him and his assistant down the hallway, begging them to return to the office, but to no avail.

In contrast to Hermesh, Hasson was unfailingly calm. "He managed to keep his sandals on for the whole interview," Sheen joked to me afterward. Hasson explained his motives in the clinical language particular to a veteran intelligence man: Israelis and Palestinians represented irreconcilable national movements, he said, and therefore required as much separation as possible, even inside Israel. And unlike Rotem, he was not inclined to invoke the Holocaust to justify a segregationist proposal like the Acceptance to Communities Bill. In his view, the law was simply a practical means of maintaining the Jewish demographic majority, a measure that any Shin Bet assessment would support.

Throughout the interview, a bald, stocky, and square-jawed character dressed in black paced around the café impatiently, listening in on the interview with a look of mild concern. As soon as we concluded, the man approached Sheen, whom he had apparently identified as a *Ha'aretz* employee. "May I add something to the discussion?" he rumbled in Hebrew. "Every time you say the word 'Muslim extremist' or 'anti-Israel activity' or 'anti-Zionist,' you should replace that with '*Ha'aretz* newspaper.' In my opinion, I would like to give to the Hezbollah the exact coordinates of your newspaper's offices." As the bald man stomped toward the exit with his friend Hasson, he turned back to and said, "I'm only joking." Then he punched his finger at us and warned, "You better not be recording this."

The regional councils that demanded swift passage of the Acceptance to Communities laws represented a near consensus of small Jewish periphery communities, *moshavim*, and *kibbutzim*. One village that both Rotem and Hasson pointed to as a shining example of cultural homogeneity was Amirim, where applicants were vetted on the basis of their commitment to the vegetarian lifestyle. Nathan Onh-Bar, the village council chief, explained to David Sheen, who visited the little hamlet, "The fact that no one around me will barbeque is great. I can't stand the smell of barbecues. It's a great environment for us."

But Amirim, with its crunchy, seemingly anodyne criteria for admission, was an anomaly within the larger constellation of Jewish towns seeking the government's approval to segregate. And this was precisely why Rotem and Hasson mentioned it—to insulate themselves against accusations of racism. However, most other small Jewish communities planted in the Negev Desert or the Galilee existed as part of an ongoing plan to limit Arab growth by physically confining the demographic threat to compressed spaces. For Israel to remain a "Jewish state," ethnic homogeneity was a strategic imperative that could not be compromised.

Besides the *mitzpim* in the North, there were southern communities like Kerem Shalom and Kfar Aza, kibbutzim planted directly on the border of the Gaza Strip. They were the frontline of the Eshkol Regional Council, one of the thirty-two town conglomerates that signed on to Yisrael Hasson's version of the Acceptance to Communities Bill. In these communities, maintaining ideological and ethnic homogeneity was not simply a cultural preference—it was seen as central to the survival of the Jewish state. Indeed, the kibbutz and its affiliates in the Eshkol Council were strategically planted at the border of Gaza like pillboxes in a demographic trench war. As they battled to hold back the restive natives amassed on the other side of the wall, their homogeneity served as the mortar that bonded them together.

At the Heavy Gates of Gaza

The Jewish Agency established the Eshkol Regional Council in 1951 (at the time, it was called Hevel Ma'on), uniting twenty-nine Jewish communities on the border of Gaza together as "strategic outposts, cast in a supporting role to the IDF in the defense of the Southern Front," according to the Agency's website. Just three years before, the Israeli army had ethnically cleansed the southern area of the country, driving hundreds of thousands of Palestinian Arabs off their land. An overwhelming number wound up in tent camps in Gaza. Yitzhak Pundek was a top commander during Operation Yoav, the decisive Israeli military thrust into the Negev Desert. He recalled the euphoria he felt as thousands of Palestinian Arabs fled for their lives toward Gaza. "My heart is singing," he wrote in a 2005 memoir excerpted in *Ha'aretz's* Hebrew edition. "There were two hundred Palestinian villages here and they are no more. It was necessary to destroy them. Otherwise there would have been here another million Arabs among us. After two thousand years of exile, one cannot create a state by using silk gloves."

But the state's work was far from complete. In the years after the Nakba, Palestinian shepherds still slipped across the open border to tend flocks they were forced to leave behind, while others returned to search for family members separated from them during the great dispersal. Hoping to root out those they designated as criminal "infiltrators," the Israeli army staged a string of violent roundups in Arab villages. Pasha John Glubb, the famous latter-day Lawrence of Arabia who had trained Jordan's British Legion army, witnessed the aftermath of a particularly brutal anti-infiltration raid with horror. "The Jews want them all to emigrate," Glubb wrote. "They therefore try to persuade them with rubber coshes and by tearing off their fingernails whenever they get the chance. . . . I do not know whether this is the policy of the Israel cabinet, but it must certainly be known and winked at on a ministerial level. . . . The brutality is too general to be due only to the sadism of ordinary soldiers."

From their base in the refugee camps of Gaza, Palestinian *fedayeen* supported by Egyptian president Gemal Abdel Nasser mounted periodic guerilla attacks on the kibbutzim, hoping to prevent the establishment of more Jewish settlements on land they still saw as their rightful property. Tensions along the border erupted on April 29, 1956, when Roi Rotberg, the security coordinator for a kibbutz called Nahal Oz, spotted a group of shepherds heading toward the kibbutz fields. He mounted a horse and galloped toward the men, demanding they return to Gaza. Instead of obeying

Rotberg's orders, the shepherds shot him dead, tore his eyes out, and left his body hanging like a limp rag on the barbed-wire fence that marked the border.

Moshe Dayan, the eye-patched southern commander of the Israeli army, whose reputation for ruthlessness preceded him, had just spent the afternoon with Rotberg and his pregnant wife. They received him warmly at their small home while Nahal Oz planned for a wedding the next day of four couples, a joyous occasion in a tiny community burdened with conflict. The killing shook Dayan in a way few others had. Forty-five minutes before Rotberg's funeral, Dayan shut himself inside a small room and scrawled down a short eulogy for the fallen security guard. He would transform the ceremony into a national clarion call, using the occasion to impel Israel's founding generation forward during a period of turmoil in which their survival in an ethnically exclusive Jewish state was far from inevitable.

When it was broadcast on Israeli National Radio the next morning, Dayan's speech took on historic proportions, attaining the status of "a keystone Israeli text," as *Ha'aretz* editor-in-chief Aluf Benn said. In just 238 words, Dayan distilled the essence of his country's settler-colonial mission. No other Israeli figure of his stature had spoken so honestly about the cruel task that lay ahead, and few, if any, would ever do so again.

Dayan opened the eulogy with a frank acknowledgment that the motives behind Palestinian resistance and rage were justified: "Who are we that we should bewail their mighty hatred of us?" he declared. "For eight years they have been sitting in refugee camps in Gaza, and before their eyes we have been transforming the lands and the villages, where they and their fathers dwelt, into our estate." The remarkable statement came with an underlying suggestion that if the refugees were ever allowed to return to the land, they would surely exact a terrible revenge.

Conscious that his real audience was the thousands of city dwellers living far from the periphery, Dayan sought to remind Tel Aviv, Haifa, and Jerusalem that the "destiny of our generation" lay in the southern kibbutzim that held the line against the Arab outclass: "Did we forget that this group of young men and women, which dwells in Nahal Oz, bear on their shoulders the heavy gates of Gaza," he said, "gates on the other side of which are crowded together with hundreds of thousands of eyes and hands that pray for our weakness, that it may come, so that they may rip us to shreds—have we forgotten this?"

Dayan freely conceded that the Zionist project was colonial in nature, but urged his countrymen not to shrink from their responsibility to participate in its most unpleasant aspects. "In order that the hope to destroy should die we have to be armed and ready, morning and night. We are a generation of settlement, and without a steel helmet and the barrel of a cannon we cannot plant a tree and build a house," the veteran *kibbutznik* and commander explained. "Our children will not live if we do not build shelters, and without a barbed-wire fence and a machine gun we cannot pave a road and channel water."

In Dayan's view, though the Palestinians were justifiably aggrieved, the logic of Zionism offered no choice but to fight with total ruthlessness—*ein breira*, or, "there's no choice," as the common Israeli expression went. Six months after Rotberg's burial,

Dayan ordered Israeli troops into Gaza to occupy the coastal strip as the bungled tripartite Israeli-British-French assault on Egypt unraveled. Hoping to permanently wipe out the *fedayeen* harassing Israel's border communities, Dayan commanded his troops to conduct widespread "screening operations." In the refugee camps of Khan Younis and Rafah, Israeli soldiers rounded up all men aged fifteen to fifty-five, herded them into open lots, beating many along the way with wooden clubs, then lined them up against concrete walls and executed them by the dozens. Israeli forces killed as many as 275 unarmed civilians in Khan Younis; days later in Rafah, the army massacred 111 more.

The streets of the refugee camps were left lined with long rows of dead bodies bearing bullet wounds in the back of their heads. During the massacre, a Khan Younis resident named Abdel Aziz al-Rantissi witnessed the execution of his uncle. Rantissi was just nine years old at the time. "It left a wound in my heart that can never heal," he said. "I'm telling you a story, and I am almost crying. . . . They planted hatred in our hearts." When Rantissi came of age, he helped found Hamas, the Islamist military and political faction that currently rules the Gaza Strip.

On April 17, 2004, Rantissi was blown to pieces by an Israeli missile strike during the punishing campaign of demolitions, raids and assassinations Israel waged to suppress the Second Intifada in the occupied Palestinian territories. In 2005, once the Intifada was subdued, Israel withdrew its last settlers from the Gaza Strip. The disengagement signaled what Israel's military-intelligence apparatus hoped would be the final break from Gaza. With the settlers out, the state could close the gates of Gaza once and for all, transforming the densely populated strip into a quarantined ghetto that military administrators could keep "on the brink of collapse," and where surplus humanity would be indefinitely warehoused. With Gaza besieged from the outside, the Israeli military-intelligence apparatus saw its principal challenge as managing a Palestinian population the Israeli-American scholar Martin Kramer described as "economically superfluous young men."

Though the withdrawal of settlers required lucrative payoffs and violent police coercion, Israel received an infusion of thousands of Jews who could be resettled either in the hearts of mixed Jewish-Arab cities or in one of the mega-settlements that encircled East Jerusalem, shoring up the human wall severing the Palestinians of the West Bank from the city they had once dreamed of as their future capital. As with everything that guided Israel's national policy, demographics were an overriding factor. "Unilateral separation doesn't guarantee 'peace,'" Arnon Sofer, the so-called Arab Counter who helped devise the Gaza separation, remarked in 2004. "It guarantees a Zionist-Jewish state with an overwhelming majority of Jews."

Echoing the stark forecast Dayan presented at Nahal Oz almost five decades before, Sofer spelled out the implications of the withdrawal: "When 2.5 million people live in a closed-off Gaza, it's going to be a human catastrophe. Those people will become even bigger animals than they are today, with the aid of an insane fundamentalist Islam. The pressure at the border will be awful. It's going to be a terrible war. So, if we want to remain alive, we will have to kill and kill and kill. All day, every day. . . . If we don't kill, we will cease to exist."

Beethoven for Gaza

n June 2006, two weeks after Israeli gunboats bombarded picnicking families on a Gaza beach, scattering body parts into the water and killing seven members of a single clan, a team of Hamas-affiliated fighters set out on a daring mission. They tunneled carefully beneath the walls sealing off the Gaza Strip, emerging in the dead of night to attack an observation post on the border under the cover of mortar fire. During the melee, the fighters captured a nineteen-year-old soldier named Gilad Shalit who served in a tank unit that helped enforce the siege of Gaza. The incident embarrassed Israel's military-intelligence establishment, which had sold the separation with Gaza to the public as a security panacea. And it shocked a population of citizen-soldiers whose greatest fear was to be left behind by their government to languish in Arab hands. Almost overnight, a nationwide campaign mobilized to demand the government negotiate a landmark prisoner exchange to secure Shalit's release. The shy, bookish conscript became a symbol of Israel's citizen-soldier culture—he was the "national son."

Four years after Shalit's capture, his father, Noam, was leading a national movement to demand that the Israeli government negotiate with Hamas for his release. I would often see the stoic-looking Noam Shalit milling around outside Prime Minister Benjamin Netanyahu's office in Jerusalem, preparing for the weekly demonstration to begin. Conducted within the parameters of Israel's militaristic ethos, which made full citizenship rights contingent on performing army service, the campaign for Shalit's freedom was the only socially acceptable anti-government protest movement in the country. And even as it urged negotiations with Hamas, the Free Gilad movement also provided unlimited political space for Israeli military assaults on the Gaza Strip, which Noam Shalit occasionally blessed. As a captive soldier's father and a member of the liberal "Enlightened Public" with roots in France, Noam Shalit was among the few figures in Israel capable of touching the national conscience across the political and religious-secular divide.

In July 2010, Zubin Mehta, the dashing, world famous conductor led the Israeli Philharmonic Orchestra through a classical concert in a field near Kfar Aza, an Eshkol Council kibbutz planted hard against the gates of Gaza. The occasion was a forum for amplifying the calls for Netanyahu to negotiate for Shalit's release, but held explicitly to impel the Hamas government to allow the Red Cross to visit the captive soldier. On stage before a crowd of thousands of mostly secular, middle class Israelis, including many recent immigrants who felt a special Francophone connection to the

French-Israeli Shalits, Mehta stood in a flowing white tunic beside Shlomo Artzi, the famous Israeli pop-rock singer, who also graced the crowd with his voice. In a chair by the side of the stage was Noam Shalit. And over the orchestra bandshell hung a massive photo of his son in captivity, looking gaunt and vulnerable.

Mehta addressed the crowd in his Indian-accented English. "We are playing for Gilad, but at the same time, I, who am not an Israeli, but who grew up one of you, since fifty years—please don't applaud!" he admonished the crowd, preparing them for an unexpected plea. "I cannot help but think of also hundreds of Palestinian mothers who, although their sons are not in the same position, their sons are also in jail, and I also have to think of them too." Mehta's appeal to basic human compassion was met with polite applause and a smattering of jeers.

Next, Mehta explained that the evening's music would be directed at the people living on the other side of the wall, in the Gaza Strip. "We hope and we pray that tonight's music will inspire people on the other side to open their hearts and be sincere in saying that he is being well taken care of," Mehta proclaimed, "that they will not mind if the Red Cross visits him. And I hope this will happen really from tomorrow."

Now, the orchestra sounded the dramatic opening chords of the first movement of Beethoven's *Fifth Symphony*. Mehta positioned himself before the violin section, waving his conductor's wand fluidly at first, then slashing it through the air with increasingly furious sweeps as he gathered intensity, driving the orchestra forward with surges of effusion, guiding its lilting strings towards Gaza, guiding the pure light of European civilization into the heart of darkness. Surely if Beethoven could reach the uncultivated ears of the natives, they would turn back on barbarism and allow the helpless Shalit a visit with the international medical teams to which they themselves were often denied access.

After the performance, I spoke with some of the Israelis who had descended on the southern kibbutz in buses and minivans to display solidarity with Shalit. Each of them expressed a familial connection to the young soldier. "My brother is gonna be in the army," a twenty-year-old social worker told me. "If that situation [captivity] goes to my brother, it's the same. So Gilad is my brother."

"All the Jews of Israel are our sons," said a sunburned middle-aged woman with a thick French accent, dyed-blonde hair and imitation Gucci sunglasses. "Gilad is our blood. He is defending our country. Our people. Our religion. He is the symbol of the defense of Israel."

The woman told me she had immigrated to Israel because of "the French misinformation." "In France, now, Israel is the symbol of the devil. We are the devil. When you think of Israel—the devil! The devil!" she exclaimed.

Standing with a group of fellow French immigrants who repeated again and again to me that Hamas were "animals," the woman said, "You know who were here? Arabs were here! You haven't seen them? Go see them!"

In fact, Salam Ruzian, an accommodationist Bedouin sheikh from the Negev development town of Rahat, built by Israel to "concentrate" the Bedouins of the Negev, had attended the concert as a guest of honor. When the woman spotted

Sheikh Ruzian pacing out of the concert in traditional Bedouin garb, she grew excited. "Wait, there are Arabs here! There!" she chirped, pointing at Ruzian.

"They have no problems circulating here," she assured me. "Go to the Galilee—no problems! We have Palestinians who are Israeli!"

"So because you don't kill them you are good people?" I asked.

"Do you feel like Israeli behave like Nazi?" a bald guy in a tank top said to me.

"Why would I feel like that?"

"Just a question," he explained. "Because I heard it."

The woman with the knock-off Gucci glasses interjected: "I *really* hope they [the Arabs] have listened to the music because there were no war songs. Soft music! Did you see any violence here?"

"We are not a people of warriors," the bald man reassured me.

Next, I met Orna Dar, an Israeli woman in her late thirties whose three pre-adolescent sons were being raised in the United States. Like the French immigrants, they viewed Gilad Shalit as a surrogate son who simultaneously protected them from harm while demanding to be rescued from his Arab captors. He was the embodiment of Israel in the eyes of the Jewish diaspora. Strangely, while Dar was eager to appear on camera, she deferred to her young sons on all questions.

"Are you going to join the army when you're older?" I asked her son, a thirteen-year-old with short, curly hair and braces who had arrived in Israel to celebrate his Bar Mitzvah.

"Yeah, we're gonna join the army," he nodded, pointing at his two younger brothers.

"But aren't you too young to really understand the situation?" I asked.

"I kind of know what's going on," the kid said. "The, like, suicide bombers, we have to kind of like, stop 'em. We have to solve the problem."

I asked his mother if she was comfortable about sending her sons into the army, into a situation where they could potentially be taken captive like Shalit.

"If you are soldiers," she told me, "you consider all the dangers when you are gonna to go the army, so it's okay—yes." She added, as Israeli mothers I had spoken to so often did, "But I hope there's gonna be peace."

"So it's good to die for your country?" I asked her. The expression, supposedly uttered by the right-wing Zionist activist Joseph Trumpeldor during his dying breaths while defending the settlement of Tel Hai in 1920, had become the motto of Israeli nationalism, providing an easy answer for skeptical youth concerned about their impending conscription in an army unit.

"It *is* good to die for your country," Dar stated emphatically. "I mean, I don't want him to die, of course, but if we want to support and defend Israel, that's the price that we have to pay."

I turned to her son and asked him, "Are you willing to die for Israel?"

Without a moment's hesitation, he nodded and said, "Yeah." His mother clapped joyfully and congratulated him with a big slap on the back.

"Yaaaaaaay!" she exclaimed with a big smile.

The Zionist

Almost exactly four years after Gilad Shalit's capture, I was led to the site of the incident by Jay Carney-Haddas, the security coordinator of Kerem Shalom, a tiny kibbutz a few kilometers south of Kfar Aza, and planted directly against the wall separating Gaza from Israel. A barrel-chested, goateed, middle-aged man with a mane of yellow hair and short, bulging arms decorated with tattoos, Carney-Haddas fashioned himself as the modern incarnation of the martyred Roi Rotberg. With his sidearm and walkie-talkie, he was proud to have assumed the heavy responsibility of bearing the gates of Gaza on his shoulders, even if the siege policy had lifted the burden to a substantial degree.

An hour after Shalit was taken, Carney-Haddas rushed out into the barren field separating Kerem Shalom from the Gaza border and attempted to sort through the chaos with the bewildered soldiers arriving on the scene. "It took an hour to realize that someone had been kidnapped," he told me. "Only when we realized Shalit wasn't in his tank did we understand that he was gone." He added, "For some strange reason, the commander had ordered his crew out of the tank." I imagined the terror the fresh-faced conscripts must have felt at being exposed at close quarters for the first time to a guerilla force they were used to shelling from inside the comfort of an air-conditioned tank.

The incident prompted an upgrade of Kerem Shalom's already elaborate system of barriers. Among the new defensive mechanisms added to the kibbutz exterior was a long row of red flags planted in the middle of the field. According to Carney-Haddas, the flags were anchored by sophisticated weights that would be triggered by tunneling, dropping to signal suspicious subterranean activity. High concrete blast walls had been installed around the kibbutz to prevent sniper fire. As we headed down a single lane road lined on the other side by a barbed wire fence, another series of barriers came into view.

A red, white, and black flag fluttering in the wind signaled Israel's border with Egypt, where young revolutionaries were quietly plotting to topple the dictatorship that had ruled them for decades. Over another imposing wall lay the ruins of the Yasser Arafat International Airport in Gaza, whose runway was cut to pieces by Israeli bulldozers in 2001. During the summer of my visit to Kerem Shalom, thousands of Palestinian scavengers seeking material to rebuild the thousands of structures the Israeli army destroyed during Operation Cast Lead began digging up the tarmac and carting it away in small pieces. From their little fortress inside the big fortress, the people of Kerem Shalom were kept oblivious to the struggles and aspirations of the Arabs living just meters away. If they encountered someone from the other side, he was likely a "terrorist" seeking to harm those innocent souls, who, as Dayan said of Rotberg, were simply "yearning for peace."

Unable to see even a glint of horizon beyond the walls, I asked Carney-Haddas about the recently imposed "no-go" rule on the Gaza border. According to Israeli military policy, anyone who came within 300 meters of the border fence would be shot. With 30 percent of arable land located inside the "buffer zone," Palestinian farmers were forced to harvest wheat under heavy gunfire, or simply watched their fields turn fallow. "It's not a kill zone," Carney-Haddas said. "The policy is to shoot high, to shoot over their heads. But if they have a weapon, yeah, it's a kill zone." Without any prompting, his tone turned somber. "You don't want to kill a man," he said in a low, grumble, stroking a semi-automatic Czech-made pistol as he spoke. "Trust me. It's something that sticks with you and never goes away." Apparently he had some experience in the "kill zone."

I asked Carney-Haddas if he was not the least bit troubled by the fact that he lived steps away from a caged population that was digging up an abandoned runway to forage for building material. Did he think there were legitimate grievances on the other side? He responded gruffly, "My philosophy is, you stay on your side of the fence, and I stay on mine. Okay?" This was clearly a delicate subject he did not want to entertain or reflect upon.

Carney-Haddas escorted me back inside the residential confines of Kerem Shalom. The kibbutz was a walled-in hamlet comprised of about fifty people living in drab, austere-looking, single-story dwellings. A small swimming pool and a basketball court were the only amenities I could identify. In 1995, Kerem Shalom collapsed when its members staged an exodus for better living conditions. But in 2001 the community managed to reconstitute. Since then, its members have held together through a sense of shared responsibility to each other and the needs of the state. However, their kibbutz still teetered at the brink of collapse. Like kibbutzim around the country, Kerem Shalom was being supported for reasons of political sentimentalism, while the state directed the bulk of its subsidies to the settlement enterprise in the West Bank. Since the separation from Gaza, hardly anyone in Israel wanted to lend a presence to a frontier outpost widely known as the site of Shalit's capture and which directly abutted a ghetto most Israelis considered the embodiment of evil.

The residents of Kerem Shalom faced a state deadline of about one year to increase their population to eighty. If they failed, they stood to lose substantial funding and benefits. In a desperate bid to attract new members, kibbutz residents invested around $35,000 into a public relations campaign to lure Israelis to join their community. New members were promised a spacious apartment and free academic studies for their children—but only on the condition that they upheld a firmly Zionist ideology. Ilan Regev, the community manager of Kerem Shalom, marketed the kibbutz on the basis of its strategic importance, describing it as "collective, secular, and Zionist" and located "in an area that in effect determines the borders of the state."

I continued my conversation with Carney-Haddas in the kibbutz cafeteria, a sparsely decorated room with linoleum tile floors that reminded me of summer camp. I asked him if the kibbutz acceptance committee would be willing to welcome non-Jews. "We had a long debate about that issue," he told me, "and we decided that we will declare our kibbutz to be secular, Jewish, Israeli, and Zionist. Our mentality is, we will not turn anybody away—you will turn yourself away."

"In that case you would have to reject virtually any Arab who applied for membership," I said.

"If you as an Arab can live here with celebrating Jewish and Zionist holidays, then fine," Carney-Haddas replied.

"But how can you define yourselves as secular and still maintain Jewishness as a criteria for admission?" I asked him.

"It's the same as a Christian who celebrates Christmas but doesn't go to church," he explained. "So what does it mean to be secular and Jewish? It means on *shabbos* we go to the pool and crank up the music and drink beer."

Carney-Haddas's faint Scottish accent made me wonder about his background. I asked him about the significance of the tattoos that lined his arms and upper chest. He pointed to a boar drawn above his pectoral in a Celtic tribal style. "The boar never gives up or turns his back," he said. Then a tattooed dog: "He is a loyal protector." And finally, two medieval shields: "These assure me reincarnation," he explained with a dead serious expression on his face.

Despite professing his deeply held commitment to the Zionist cause, Carney-Haddas seemed more committed to pagan lore familiar in medieval action kitsch like Mel Gibson's *Braveheart* than anything remotely related to the Jewish religion or culture. I was not even sure if he was actually Jewish in any traditional sense. He told me he was born to Scottish parents and spent much of his adulthood in a suburb of Washington, DC, then immigrated to Israel, attempting to find acceptance on a kibbutz. Kerem Shalom welcomed him into its small community. And now that he was in, he ardently defended the narrow, exclusive criteria the community applied to keep others out. He was a pure Zionist now.

While escorting me out of Kerem Shalom, Carney-Haddas stopped to show me a small memorial listing the names of the troops killed along the border of Gaza. In January 2002, an attack near Kerem Shalom by Palestinian militants killed four soldiers from a Bedouin tracker unit. They had enlisted with the hope that they would receive state benefits otherwise denied to Arab citizens of Israel. Now their names were chiseled into a rock at the gates of a Jews-only kibbutz. "Only when a tragic incident occurs do they remember," a Bedouin army veteran, Mohammad Sawayyid, told a reporter after the incident.

Carney-Haddas pointed at the memorial and turned to me. "You asked me what we mean when we say we are Zionist?" he proclaimed in a stentorian voice rising with an affected tone of pride. "It means we will remember the soldiers who were not from our kibbutz, but who died on the kibbutz ground—that is what we mean."

Six months before my visit to Kerem Shalom, on the day before the secular New Year, a group of Israeli and Jewish American schoolchildren marched from Sderot to a lookout over the Gaza border. In their hands were Israeli flags, signs with slogans like "Sderot wants peace" and "Students against extremism"; and bunches of white balloons bearing "messages of hope" written by fourth- and fifth-graders from Sderot for the children in Gaza. From the lookout point, a few participants shouted across to Gaza, "Israel is a peaceful country!" The march was organized by Yuli Edelstein, a right-wing settler from Russia who served as the Israeli minister of Public Diplomacy and Diaspora Affairs—the government's official propaganda director. "I think that the powerful message carried from children is sometimes better than the cunning negotiations for this or that Palestinian negotiator," Edelstein told reporters. "They are probably talking peace but at the same time making war."

As the children who marched from Sderot arrived at the Gaza lookout point, hundreds of international protesters assembled on the other side of the wall to demonstrate their solidarity with the Palestinians living under the blockade. At the same time, in capitals around the world, a sophisticated network of activists organized a flotilla of civilian boats that would attempt to penetrate the Israeli naval blockade of Gaza. With unprecedented resources and tacit endorsement from the Turkish government, they were confident that even if they failed to break through, they could draw the world's attention to the cruelty of Israel's siege.

Finally, the Israeli child marchers let the balloons loose, releasing their "messages of hope" toward the border with Gaza. A breeze lifted the balloons high in the air, briefly guiding them towards the border. Suddenly, a swirling gust of wind blew them backwards, sending them over the heads of the marchers and toward a grassy hillside where they quickly sagged to the ground. When the marchers filed back along a dirt path toward their cars, past the litter of deflated balloons and undelivered letters, they clapped and sang Hebrew songs, though they had failed to make any contact with the people on the other side of the buffer zone.

PART III
PIRATES OF THE MEDITERRANEAN

Dark Forces

May 26, 2010, began like so many other days in the Gaza Strip. That morning, jets from the Israeli air force soared across the sky, bombed the ruins of the Yasser Arafat International Airport in southern Gaza and a Hamas training camp in the north of the coastal strip, and left twenty-two civilians wounded. The same morning, Israel's then-Government Press Office director Danny Seaman blasted out a sarcastic e-mail to virtually every credentialed foreign press correspondent working inside Israel-Palestine. The e-mail subject read, "GPO Recommended Restaurant in Gaza." In the body of the e-mail, Seaman provided a menu of the Roots Club and Restaurant in Gaza. "We have been told the beef stroganoff and cream of spinach soup are highly recommended," Seaman wrote. "There is also the possibility of an enjoyable evening on the Greens Terrace Garden Cafe, which serves 'eclectic food and fresh cocktails.'"

Thanks to the Israeli siege of Gaza, around 80 percent of the coastal strip's residents subsisted off United Nations–supplied food aid while the overwhelming majority struggled with "food insecurity." The blockade had spawned a black market economy that enriched a tiny minority that controlled the business of importing goods through the smuggling tunnels from Rafah, Egypt. Without the tunnels, the Roots Club and Restaurant would have had little food to serve its customers. But in the era of *hasbara*, none of these facts mattered to Seaman. With his press release, he mocked both organizers of the Gaza Freedom Flotilla sailing from a Turkish port toward Gaza with five ships full of humanitarian aid and those for whom their aid was intended—the caged Morlocks forced to take "an appointment with a dietician," as Israeli former government aide Dov Weissglass put it. But Seaman's e-mail backfired. Members of the international press corps instantly leaked it, generating a wave of derisive and indignant blog posts from observers of the crisis.

On the day of Seaman's e-mail, the Israeli government leaked details of its preparation to deploy lethal force against the oncoming flotilla. Israeli army officials discussed the plan exclusively with Hebrew language media, essentially concealing it from the foreign press and ensuring an audience consisting entirely of Jewish Israelis. The army's intention appeared to be instilling in the Israeli public the fear of a terrorist naval onslaught, thus preparing them for a violent confrontation at sea and a potentially rancorous aftermath. *Maariv*, one of the four major Israeli newspapers, first reported the details in an article titled, "On the way to violence; one of the boats is on its way."

"We are afraid that there will be a terror attack by the boats," an officer described as "high ranking" told *Maariv*. "If terrorists have gotten on the boats or if there is an intention to use hot weapons [guns] against our forces, we will use full seriousness and caution. We want to avoid using force but as soon as there will be danger to the life of our forces we will be forced to use live fire as a last resort." The raid strategy, according to *Maariv*, had been approved by Prime Minister Benjamin Netanyahu, Minister of Defense Ehud Barak, and the commander of the Israeli Navy, Admiral Eliezer Marom.

An aid ship piloted by Palestine solidarity activists had successfully skirted Israel's siege of the Gaza Strip in August 2008, causing no repercussions beyond the jubilant celebration of nearly ten thousand of Gaza's desperately impoverished residents who were waiting on shore for the ship's arrival. In 2009, the Israeli Navy intercepted aid ships at sea without any resistance, and the international media yawned. But this time, the Israelis were confronted with a flotilla comprised of five ships. The lead ship—an old cruise boat called the *Mavi Marmara*—was led by the Islamist Turkish aid organization, IHH, which was closely linked to the Justice and Development party of Turkish prime minister Recep Tayyip Erdogan. Israel's relations with its only ally in the Muslim world, a diplomatic connection that David Ben Gurion spent untold stores of energy to establish and nurture, hung in the balance.

The *Mavi Marmara* was loaded to the gills with hundreds of activists from around the world, including political leaders of the Palestinian citizens of Israel, who wanted to demonstrate their solidarity with those quarantined inside Gaza. Passengers on other boats included the famed Swedish novelist Henning Mankell, members of the German Bundestag and British parliament, the eighty-five-year-old Melkite Greek Catholic archbishop of Jerusalem, a one-year-old child, and a Nobel Peace Prize–winner, Mairead Corrigan-Maguire.

The evening of May 30 began in serenity for the activists onboard the flotilla. As the *Mavi Marmara* chugged ahead on calm seas, some of its passengers argued politics on the bottom deck while others laid out prayer carpets and performed the Muslim *salaat*. Everyone seemed to be enjoying the balmy Mediterranean evening. But the passengers' pacific mood was tinged with nervous anticipation. At 10 p.m., an Israeli naval commander called to inquire about the route of the ship. "Gaza," the captain informed them. An hour later, according to Sumeyye Ertekin, a Turkish television correspondent, the captain and crew decided to reverse course, turning the ship away from Israel. But even as they retreated, the silhouettes of destroyer boats appeared on the horizon. By 4 a.m., fourteen warships surrounded the *Mavi Marmara*—"they followed and approached gradually," Ertekin recounted. At the time, the ship was in international waters more than ninety miles from the shores of Israel. Just minutes after the morning call to prayer began for the ship's Muslim passengers, the Israelis began their attack, attempting to storm the ship from Zodiac attack dinghies.

In February, before "flotilla" became a household word, I spoke to Huwaida Arraf, a key organizer of the Gaza Freedom Flotilla, about her expectations. Arraf was an Israeli citizen, a Palestinian Christian, educated at the Hebrew University, the

University of Michigan and American University's School of Law, and had served as program coordinator for Seeds of Peace, the US non-profit to bring together young Israelis and Palestinians, endorsed by President Clinton. She was confident that the Israelis would back down and allow the boats through the blockade rather than attempt a potentially catastrophic raid. Ertekin said the *Mavi Marmara* passengers felt the same way: "They thought that Israel could not do anything to such a large fleet, composed of people from fifty different countries. According to them, Israel would eventually let us through to Gaza." They had assumed that Israel, despite its record of leveling disproportionate violence against unarmed civilians, would behave rationally, and not treat a few rusty boats as an existential threat to its national security. Now masked commandoes from the elite Shayetet 13 unit were rappelling onto the top deck of the *Mavi Marmara* from Blackhawk helicopters hovering overhead. As activists gathered on the deck, the Shayetet commandoes sprayed them at random with beanbag rounds and live bullets.

Early in the day of the Israeli raid on the *Mavi Marmara*, some members of IHH's leadership gathered with a large group of passengers to discuss plans to resist any possible attempts by the Israeli Navy to board the ship. They decided that if the moment arrived, they would defend the ship at any cost. As soon the Zodiac boats filled with commandoes came within yards of the ship, passengers pelted them with bottles, forcing the boats to retreat. While pulling away from the ship, the commandoes fired live bullets at the passengers—the first volleys of the attack. Blackhawk transport helicopters were approaching as well, filled with more members of the Shahayet 13. Now groups of men on the *Mavi Marmara* scrambled to the top deck with homemade weapons, from chains to iron bars, waiting for the soldiers to descend. From the helicopters, soldiers fired potentially lethal beanbag rounds and live bullets at the crowds below, hitting several activists, including one who died when a beanbag shattered his skull. When the commandoes scaled down to the ship from ropes, they opened fire almost at random, immediately killing two men, including one at point blank range with a shot through the head.

Some of the activists rushed to the top level of the ship with clubs they had fashioned from the ship's railings, using them to batter the commandoes as they rappelled onto the deck. Once they managed to disarm the soldiers, the activists took them inside the ship for medical treatment. Photos smuggled out by a reporter from the Turkish daily *Hurriyet* revealed the expressions of sheer panic that had washed over the faces of the captured commandoes when unarmed activists led them into the bottom of the ship. Though the commandoes were stunned, none were seriously harmed. In fact, those who were injured in the clash received immediate attention from medics on the ship. But the soldiers' captivity exacerbated the violence, prompting other members of Shayatet 13 to accelerate the shooting spree they had begun.

As the melee intensified on the top deck, a nineteen-year-old Turkish student with American citizenship, Furkan Dogan, sat alone in a room in the galley. Listening intently to the sound of combat, to gunfire popping, to the pounding of feet sprinting across the top deck, and to the guttural groans associated with unbearable pain,

Dogan agonized about his next move. Should he join the other men on the top deck, he wondered, even if it meant his death? Would he be killed anyway, even if he stayed in the galley? Dogan opened his diary and wrote what would be his final entry:

"I think there is not much time left for that moment of martyrdom. Is there anything more honorable? If there is, it should be my mother. I am not sure of that either. Which one's better? My mother's compassion or dying for a noble cause? Everyone has left the room now. I can see a serious expression on everyone's face, so serious that I have never seen anything like this before."

With distress sirens blaring across the halls of the ship, the teenager made his way onto the upper deck, armed not with an iron bar or an oar but a small video camera. He found himself in the middle of the fracas, with commandoes spraying a fusillade of bullets at the activists assembled on the deck. Bullets immediately struck Dogan in his leg, left foot, and his back, causing him to crumple to the ground in pain. He lay there for several minutes on his back, in a pool of his own blood, dazed but conscious, while a massacre unfolded before him. At some point, an Israeli commando advanced toward Dogan, placed the barrel of his gun against the youth's face, and fired four times, killing him execution style.

"It was a bloodbath," recalled Sumeyye Ertekin, a Turkish journalist who traveled on the *Marmara*. "The floors were like a slaughterhouse. I saw people whose internal organs were out."

Ibrahim Bilgen, a sixty-one-year-old Turkish electrical engineer and politician, met a similar fate. Immobilized by bullets fired from an Israeli helicopter, Bilgen was executed by a commando, who fired a single shot at point-blank range to his head. Three other crewmembers were killed by gunshot wounds to the head, including Cevdet Kiliclar, a Turkish photographer who had jury-rigged an elaborate system allowing journalists to broadcast from the ship despite sustained Israeli electronic warfare. Kiliclar was killed while taking pictures; then the ship's online livestream broadcast went dark.

The killing continued even after crewmembers announced through the ship's loudspeaker that resistance had ended. "Blood was pouring out of the bodies, from their heads," Lubna Masarwa, a Palestinian-Israeli community organizer, recounted. "An old man was brought in who been shot in the head. He was lying on the floor, dying. There was nothing we could do for him except hold his hand."

Hoping to slow the soldiers' killing frenzy, Hanin Zoabi, a Palestinian member of Israel's Knesset, fashioned a sign reading in Hebrew, "We have surrendered. We are unarmed. We have critically injured people. Please come and take them. We will not attack." When she displayed it before a group of commandoes, they pointed laser-guided assault rifles at her head and ordered her to vacate the area. By the time the shooting finally subsided, nine activists lay dead and dozens were seriously wounded.

Meanwhile, on the *Sophia*, a rusty old cargo ship accompanying the *Marmara* as part of the Gaza Freedom Flotilla, the commandoes attempted to herd passengers to the bottom deck as rapidly as possible. "Someone who is going too slowly immediately gets a stun device fired into his arm," Henning Mankell, a passenger on the

Sophia who was also an internationally famous novelist, wrote in his diary. "Another man who is not moving fast enough is shot with a rubber bullet. . . . People who have done nothing are being driven like animals, being punished for their slowness."

As soon as the Israelis gained control of the *Marmara*, they rushed to the ship's kitchen and gathered up all of the knives they could find. Then they laid them out beside *keffiyehs*, Qurans, and any object that might convince the average Western news consumer that the flotilla was in fact a covert terrorist convoy. As the soldiers followed apparent orders to prepare the groundwork for a massive propaganda campaign, Masarwa noticed that "letters written by hundreds of children to children in Gaza were on the floor, under the soldiers' boots. I realized that we must not be human in the eyes of the Israeli soldiers when I saw them joking with each other—one of them was petting his dog—after they had just killed innocent people in cold blood."

Seven hours later, passengers were taken as prisoners to the Israeli port city of Ashdod, where they were interrogated and jailed. "We are taken ashore and forced to run the gauntlet of rows of soldiers while military TV films us," Mankell wrote. "Right beside me a man refuses to have his fingerprints taken. He accepts being photographed. But fingerprints? He doesn't consider he has done anything wrong. He resists and is beaten to the ground. They drag him off. I don't know where."

Having stockaded the flotilla activists, the Israelis proceeded to the next phase of their mission, robbing passengers—including credentialed journalists—of their cameras, laptops, and recording equipment. Credit cards and other valuables were taken from many passengers, including Mankell. The Israelis intended to exploit the footage they had seized in order to establish a narrative that portrayed themselves as the true victims. SD cards and videotapes containing footage shot by passengers, including scenes Dogan and Kiliclar may have recorded of their own killings, were thrown in a giant junk heap, ensuring that the most damning and disturbing records of the attack would never see the light of day.

Back in Tel Aviv, some soldiers used the credit cards they had stolen to cover the tab for beery nights on the town, while an IDF officer was arrested for selling as many as six stolen laptops to lower-ranking soldiers. An army spokesman took to the media to denounce the scofflaws as "soldiers who don't know what their uniforms represent." They would be the only Israelis prosecuted for their role in what a United Nations investigation would later label the "arbitrary and summary executions" on the deck of the *Mavi Marmara*. As the world turned its attention to Israel's massacre on the high seas, and the Israeli government threw its *hasbara* machine into high gear, I boarded a flight from the United States for Ben Gurion International Airport in Lod.

After enduring the standard procedures at Ben Gurion, in which young security officers prompted me to declare which Hebrew school I attended, where it was located, who my rabbi was, how many of my grandparents were Jewish, and how many Israeli relatives I had (this time, I invented two cousins), I flopped into a taxi and rode to Jaffa.

My friend Woody, a law school graduate from New York, had rented out the place in Jaffa a few months before my arrival. I met him during my first reporting trip to

Israel-Palestine in the spring and summer of 2009, just after he had moved to Tel Aviv after a yearlong stint living in a Palestinian refugee camp in the West Bank monitoring Israeli human rights abuses for the International Solidarity Movement (ISM), cofounded by Huwaida Arraf. ISMers took on pseudonyms to avoid army raids and Shin Bet dragnets, so Woody's friends dubbed him with the first name of the film director Woody Allen, who shared his hysterical wit, nervous energy, and nebbishy appearance. One difference between Woody the film director and Woody the activist was that the latter was not a Jew. He was a Christian. When I first met him, he was already struggling with the social climate in Israel, as renting apartments, finding employment, and interacting with Israelis on a daily basis yielded the inevitable question: "Are you Jew-eesh?" Oftentimes, "no" was not an acceptable answer.

In an e-mail one month before my arrival, Woody explained to me his mounting frustration with life in Israel, especially the restrictions on his relationship with his Israeli girlfriend, Netta. "I live in Israel as a perpetual visitor only because I have a relationship with a Jew that is approved to the satisfaction of the Ministry of the Interior—*Misrad Hapanim*—of the Jewish State," he said. "Part of this satisfaction involves providing evidence that the Jewish parents of my partner approve of the relationship of a Jew to a Goy. I don't receive benefits here, as I am not a Jew. I am asked when renting apartments or applying for jobs: 'Are you a Jew?' People choose to disassociate with me based on my goyishness. Objectively, the main economic forces and entire political structure are ruled by Jews implementing both civil Jewish regulations as well as religious Jewish regulations, which include a ban on being able to marry my girlfriend, as I am not a Jew."

A bill proposed by Prime Minister Benjamin Netanyahu that would have forced any non-Jewish foreign partner of an Israeli who had lived in the country for more than three years without obtaining permanent residency to leave the country for a ten-year "cooling-off period" placed Woody's relationship in jeopardy. "I might be expelled for ten years for attempting to prove my relationship? Insane!" he stated.

Woody became my initial liaison to Tel Aviv's radical left, introducing me to a loose-knit band of a few hundred anarchists, disillusioned ex-soldiers, disaffected children of ultra-Zionists, queers, academics, and generally idealistic and disillusioned young people who came of age during the Second Intifada when the liberal Zionist "peace camp" closed ranks with the militaristic right wing. This tiny band of social deviants comprised the only grouping of people I met who sincerely embraced multiculturalism and who took concrete action against the discriminatory foundations of their country's political apparatus. Right-wingers and many Jewish Israelis who considered themselves part of the social mainstream referred to members of the radical left as *smolinim*, which simply means "leftists," but the word carried a deeply insulting connotation of an unacceptable caste, an Other. As branded social outcasts, inflexible in their principles, disdainful of ordinary politics, and brazen in their racial liberalism they resembled nothing so much as the pre–Civil War abolitionists.

Woody's girlfriend, Netta, appeared to be his primary reason for remaining in the country. In 2009, she and nine other Israeli high school seniors who called themselves the *Shministim* released a letter explaining their rejection of military service.

It read: "Our refusal comes first and foremost as a protest on the separation, control, oppression, and killing policy held by the State of Israel in the Occupied Territories, as we understand that this oppression, killing, and routing of hatred will never lead to peace, and they are all contradictory to the basic values a society that pretends to be democratic should have." The letter was only the third of its kind in Israeli history.

Like the rest of the *Shministim,* Netta spent a month in prison, where she was forced wear a surplus American army uniform and stand watch for suicide-prone inmates who were in solitary confinement—despite her refusal to perform army service, she had nonetheless been corralled into a form of national service. "Much harder than going to jail was accepting the fact that we had become outsiders," Netta said. "You know that when you go out the first question you will get is, 'What did you do in the army?' And having to go through this process again and again of explaining to them why I didn't go, and dealing with their reaction, which is usually negative, it's a very hard experience." Because employers in Israel generally require applicants to list the highest rank they achieved in the military, Netta's job opportunities were severely limited as well.

Like Netta, most of the radical leftists I met in Israel had arrived at their political awakening only after accepting that they could not adjust to the militaristic, ethnically exclusive society they were born into. Their first step on their way to "the other side" usually began with a single question. "Nobody in Israel asks why they're going into the army," Netta told me. "It's just what you are expected to do. But at a very early stage I began to ask why. And I decided dominating people I had never met wasn't what I wanted to do."

When I arrived in Jaffa, Netta was working at the African Refugee Development Center, an NGO that attempted to secure political asylum for African refugees who had migrated to Israel. The group was the target of a sustained right-wing campaign to deprive it of funding that the prime minister's office had largely endorsed. Netta told me that in the past year her organization had attempted to secure asylum for thousands of refugees from war-stricken areas of Africa. "Do you know how many the government approved?" she asked me. "Three! Just three!"

When Woody pulled open the creaky iron door that led into the flat, I could tell I was not about to enter the happiest place in the Holy Land. His face was gaunt, and behind his wire-rimmed glasses his eyes seemed to have sunk beneath dark bags of accumulated stress. While in the past he would accompany me into the field to shoot video, these days he mostly wanted to be left alone. Just a few years in Israel had clearly taken its toll.

For now, Woody showed me to my room, which had just been vacated by Yusuf, an openly gay, twenty-three-year-old Palestinian citizen of Israel who had just moved to Nazareth to diffuse tension with his parents, who were not terribly thrilled to say the least about his lifestyle. The room was a ten-by-twelve-foot box with an old mattress on the floor, a tattered, slanted table in the corner, and a note from Yusuf wishing me well. My roommate, Noa, had to walk through my room in order to exit hers. Though I heard her shuffle in and out of the room every morning, she almost never spoke to me—I rarely heard her voice unless her boyfriend, Diaz, an immigrant from Sudan who had mysteriously secured residency in Israel, was spending the night. After a few hours of restless sleep, a family living in an apartment just a few meters across the alley from my window was awake and bustling. "Alaaaaaaaaa!" the mother screamed at her son again and again. Children began to cry and would not stop. This would be my office for the next two months. Though I rarely got a good night's sleep here or a moment of privacy in the house in Jaffa, I gained an intimate connection to a group that existed at Israel's fringe, but which was always present at the crucial friction points of the country's crisis.

The flat, which was owned by a local gangster named Johnny who showed up on rare occasions to collect rent and threatened to bludgeon Yusuf for demanding a few basic repairs, was like so many other radical leftist houses I had visited in and around Tel Aviv. The living area was appointed with tattered furniture rummaged from the street; dirty cups, overfull ashtrays, and history and literary tracts were strewn across the room; the kitchen was a virtual biohazard area with an oven that required a series of magic tricks to operate; the walls were covered with maps detailing illegal settlement activity across the West Bank and posters commemorating the joint campaigns of the Israeli left and besieged Palestinian farmers—especially the latest actions in the East Jerusalem neighborhood of Sheikh Jarrah, where Palestinian families were thrown out of their homes in the middle of the night, then watched as religious nationalist settlers moved in literally fifteen minutes later under police guard.

That afternoon, I turned on the battered TV set standing on a cardboard box in the corner of the flat, hoping to catch an opening round World Cup match. While flipping through channels, I found Brigadier General Avi Benayahu, the portly spokesman for the Israeli Defense Forces, seated in his custom-size uniform at a table across from Dana Weiss, the perky host of Israel's version of *Meet the Press*. A five-second clip of commandoes being battered by activists while descending onto the deck of the *Mavi Marmara* played in a loop while Benayahu spoke. He declared confidently, "It was a lynch. It was an ambush." Weiss did not challenge any of Benayahu's contentions despite what *Ha'aretz* called his "knack for manipulation." The media seemed to be solidly behind the army as it spun a version of the flotilla raid that bore little resemblance to passenger testimonies.

"It's taken four days for our videos to start moving on Youtube," Benayahu said. "The Hamas spokesman has been issuing false declarations, and no one was going to sue him, but I have to always be correct. It's really important for me to be reliable and credible."

The five-second clip of what Israelis came to refer to simply as "The Lynch" was culled from the trove of footage the IDF had stolen from the flotilla activists and journalists. Heavily edited over the course of two days, the clip was the only piece of footage that seemed to support the army's line. It was broadcast around the clock on the country's three main news channels, branding into the Israeli public's mind a sense that the commandoes who stormed the *Mavi Marmara* had been unfairly and savagely abused by a band of terrorists and were forced to open fire just to survive. To complement this clip, the IDF Spokesperson's Unit pumped out buckshot of unsourced press releases to the national press corps insinuating that the flotilla was in fact an al-Qaeda-linked armada captained by anti-Semites. In almost every case, reputable military correspondents and network anchors diligently reproduced the press releases as news with only the most minor alterations.

The day the Israeli army opened its *hasbara* front, I met my fourth roommate, Lia Tarachansky, a twenty-five-year-old video journalist working as the Israel-Palestine correspondent for a left-wing online news outlet called The Real News. Though we had never spoken in person, I had become an avid follower of her journalistic work, which focused not just on the injustices of the occupation, but on the psychological, economic, and historical motives of the occupier. Having spent her youth in the West Bank mega-settlement of Ariel, where she was raised by right-wing parents who had emigrated from the former Soviet Union during *perestroika*, Lia had firsthand experience in the occupation.

"The first years of my life in Israel were hell because we were Russians," Lia recalled to me. "But then, growing up in Ariel, I suddenly felt accepted, like I had a community. I didn't know what we were fighting against or why we were on the frontlines, but I got a sense of unity with my neighbors from it. It was such a euphoric feeling to be bound together against an outside enemy. The brotherhood and sisterhood was amazing, and we had just the right amount of blinders to ignore the reality of our surroundings."

Like the rest of her friends growing up in Ariel, and like most other Jewish Israelis, Lia was indoctrinated into the country's militaristic culture from a young age. "I was never taught in school that we should ethnically cleanse the Arabs or kill them all," she said, "but what I finished school with was a sense that, of course, it would be better if they just weren't here. So when we started studying Arabic, I said to the teacher, 'Why do we need this? We live in a Jewish settlement.' And she said, 'You need to know Arabic in case you get kidnapped by a terrorist and you need to explain to him that you're a good soldier.'"

Lia recalled another startling episode in which a soldier visited her ninth-grade class to teach the students Krav Maga, a hyper-aggressive Israeli brand of hand-to-hand combat that focuses on neutralizing an opponent as quickly as possible by targeting the most vulnerable parts of their body—by gouging their eyeballs, smashing their genitals, or "fish hooking" their mouth. The soldier emphasized the importance of breaking out of chokeholds, though not to prevent rapes or street attacks. "The scenario was you're in a shopping mall, there's a terrorist with a bomb, and he's grabbing you by the arm or trying to choke you to kill everyone, so this was how we were told we'd get out. And this was part of a larger narrative designed to prepare us to be soldiers by the time we were finished with middle school," Lia recalled. "The idea wasn't to make us into good citizens with democratic values—it was all about preparing us to be good soldiers fighting the Palestinians."

Lia turned sixteen in 2000, just as the Second Intifada started. Instead of enlisting in the army like many of her friends, she went away to college in Southern Ontario, Canada. It was there, during a week of events organized on campus in protest against Israel's invasion of the West Bank, that she had her first actual conversation with a

Palestinian. "I had been living in a settlement my whole life and never had the chance to meet anyone who thought differently from me," she said. "And all of a sudden I'm talking to a Palestinian who isn't a terrorist, who doesn't want to kill me. And everything I was taught and all that was drilled into my head just collapsed. Now I was overcome with curiosity about who these people were."

Before I arrived in Jaffa, Lia was working tirelessly to complete a self-produced documentary about the illusions and mythology surrounding the foundation of the State of Israel. During shooting, she returned to Ariel to record a segment on a hilltop two hundred meters from the home she was raised in. Just as she began to narrate into the camera, she heard the Muslim call to prayer blaring from a mosque in one of the six Palestinian villages surrounding the settlement. The sound sent a jolt through her body. "I had lived surrounded by Palestinian villages until I was eighteen, and it was the first time in my life I had actually heard the call to prayer," Lia told me. "I still don't know how to explain it. It took me a whole decade to make Palestinian friends, to humanize them in my own mind, to turn anti-Zionist, for me to actually notice the Palestinian presence that had always existed all around me. And I realized me and my friends had been taught to erase Palestinians from our conscience by people who had in many cases actually physically erased them—our teachers, our parents, our army commanders, our media."

Now that I had arrived and announced my determination to poke holes in the propaganda barrage that had just begun, Lia stepped away from her editing deck to help me monitor the Army Spokesperson's Unit's claims. In between heated phone arguments with her mother, who had eagerly accepted the government line—that the flotilla activists were a Trojan horse for al-Qaeda and other nefarious terror groups—Lia would call the Israeli desk to interview spokespeople in Hebrew. Meanwhile I called the army's North American and Latin American desks, asking questions in English. From the cluttered, smoky salon of our crumbling flat in Ajami, we were able to force the Army Spokesperson's Unit to issue several public retractions and clarifications on key allegations, putting a dent in the army's well-honed public relations strategy. Though we may have done little to shake the self-confidence of the public relations apparatus, we were able to provide forensic evidence of military and media collusion, demonstrating how army officials and seemingly professional military correspondents worked together to implant a factually inaccurate and distorted version of events in the public's mind.

The first official retraction came on June 2, when the Israeli Army Spokesperson's Unit disseminated a press release to reporters entitled, "Attackers of the IDF found to be al-Qaeda mercenaries." The accusation was not accompanied by any conclusive evidence—the army simply reported that *Mavi Marmara* passengers were equipped with night-vision goggles, as though this would suffice as proof of their links to the international network of Osama bin Laden. Ron Ben-Yishai, a veteran military correspondent from the large daily newspaper *Yedioth Ahronoth* who was embedded with the Navy commandos, took the baseless charge and improvised. Citing an "interrogation" of *Marmara* passengers—"lynchers," he called them—Ben-Yishai wrote the same day, "Some among the [flotilla passengers] are believed to have ties with World Jihad groups, mainly al-Qaeda." The article made no reference to any efforts on part of Ben Yishai to investigate this claim, nor did he seem to think to ask why the IDF was about to release dangerous operatives of al-Qaeda—presumably they would attack again, wouldn't they?

When Lia and I called the Israeli Army Spokesperson's Unit's Israel and North American desks, we received identical responses: "We don't have any evidence," army spokespeople told us. "The press release was based on information from the National Security Council." Hours later, the IDF retracted its claim, quietly changing the title of its press release to, "Attackers of IDF Soldiers Found Without Identification Papers." Despite the official retraction, Ben-Yishai's article remained uncorrected, as did similar reports aired on Israeli television news, which played the now infamous "lynch" clip over and over.

Two days later, the Spokesperson's Unit released an audio clip purporting to consist of transmissions between the *Mavi Marmara* and a naval warship. "Go back to Auschwitz!" a *Marmara* passenger shouted to the Israeli naval captain, according to the IDF. YNet and *Ha'aretz* reported on and reproduced the audio clip without investigating its authenticity. Not only did the anti-Semitic slur sound like a mentally disturbed teenager making a prank call, but had reporters performed a cursory search of the IDF Spokesperson's Unit website they would have found a longer clip released on May 31 that featured a dramatically different exchange between the Israeli Navy and the *Mavi Marmara* with no mention of Auschwitz. Further, the voice of flotilla organizer Huwaida Arraf was featured in the "Auschwitz" clip, yet Arraf was not aboard the *Marmara* (she was on the *Challenger 1*). It seemed the army had fabricated the clip in order to inject the Holocaust into coverage of the flotilla raid, thereby inflaming the Israeli public with the notion that the whole world was indeed against them—and through no fault of their government.

On my blog, I pointed out the discrepancies in the IDF's footage and raised the question of doctoring. The next day, the IDF conceded that it had, in fact, doctored the footage, releasing a "clarification" and a new clip claiming to consist of the "full" exchange between the navy and the flotilla. Unfortunately, the authenticity of the new clip was impossible to verify. Despite the IDF's admission, YNet and *Ha'aretz* never corrected their original reports, though *Ha'aretz* altered its headline.

On June 6, *Ha'aretz*'s top military correspondent, Anshel Pfeffer, reported on an IDF press release claiming without evidence that five flotilla passengers had links to international terrorist groups. The press release was filled with highly implausible claims, including that Ken O'Keefe, a *Mavi Marmara* passenger who ran an aid organization with Tony Blair's sister-in-law, Lauren Booth, was planning to train a Hamas commando unit in the Gaza Strip. When I called the Army Spokesperson's Unit, I learned that once again, no evidence was available to support their press release. "There is very limited intelligence we can give in this specific case," Sgt. Chen Arad told me. "Obviously, I'm unable to give you more information." I wondered why Pfeffer had not demanded more evidence, and if he did, why he published unsubstantiated spin as fact.

A week earlier, Pfeffer teamed up with fellow military correspondents Avi Issacha-roff and Amos Harel to channel another daytime deception by the IDF. The three reporters produced an article based exclusively on testimony from naval comman-dos—the flotilla passengers' side of the story was ignored—claiming they had faced live gunfire and lynching attempts from *Marmara* passengers. Since the story was published, the IDF has produced scant evidence to support either accusation. The article was accompanied by a suspicious photo from the IDF Spokesperson's Unit depicting a bearded Muslim man brandishing a knife and surrounded by photojour-nalists. Daylight beamed in from a window behind the man. *Ha'aretz*'s caption, which was sourced to the IDF, asserted that the photo was taken "after" the commandos had boarded the *Marmara*. However, the commandos raided the ship at night, while the photo was taken during the day. Once again, the IDF's story seemed like a fabrication and should have warranted skepticism.

As I did with the "Auschwitz clip," I called Sgt. Arad to investigate. He told me he had no evidence to support the photo's questionable caption. Soon after our phone conversation, *Ha'aretz* quietly altered the caption, removing its claim that the photo was taken "after" the commando raid. For nearly a week, the false photo caption had remained intact. Why did *Ha'aretz* suddenly change it? The most plausible explana-tion was that the paper received a tip from the Army Spokesperson's Unit. If true, the tip-off suggested a scandalous level of coordination between the Israeli military and the country's media. In any case, the subject of the photo turned out to be a Yemeni lawmaker named Mohammad al-Hazmi, who was showing off his ceremonial dagger (known as a *jambiya*), which is carried by men in Yemen and is an essential part of the traditional Yemeni dress.

Members of the Israeli press corps were not any more unscrupulous than any other country's media, nor were they any lazier. Some Israeli reporters served in the army reserves, trading in their press badge for a month each year for an M-16, while many more had received their journalistic training at Army Radio. And many vet-eran reporters watched with pride as their children enlisted for military service, then returned home for supper after days at the base, or a routine patrol in the West Bank. In a society that treated politicians with suspicion, if not outright contempt, the army was the only institution that remained above reproach. This attitude extended to Israeli military correspondents, who were more psychologically and emotion-ally invested in their country's military than most Western outsiders understood. In partnership with the IDF Spokesperson's Unit, some of Israel's most widely dissem-inated journalists helped form a sophisticated military-media complex fighting on the frontlines of the country's public relations battle.

The career trajectory of the Army Spokesperson's Unit's director, Avi Benayahu, provided a perfect example of the form and function of the military-media com-plex. A former reporter for Army Radio, Benayahu quickly worked his way up the ranks of a top paper, *Maariv*, where he was eventually promoted to lead military correspondent, a vaunted post in a country stuck in a permanent state of warfare. Now Benayahu had direct access to the generals who held sway over Israel's political class, enabling him to build an unparalleled portfolio of connections. He leveraged his contacts into high-profile jobs, serving as a communications aide and political adviser to former prime ministers Yitzhak Rabin and Shimon Peres, as well as former transportation minister Yitzhak Mordechai, whom he energetically defended against sexual abuse charges, trumpeting the accused ex-general's long record of military heroism. (Mordechai ultimately received an eighteen-month suspended sentence for sexual harassment and two counts of sexual assault.) In 2007, Benayahu returned home to the army to head the Spokesperson's Unit.

"In the morning, [Benayahu] briefs reporters, and in the evening he sits down in front of the TV to hear how they recite his texts," wrote Yossi Klein of *Ha'aretz*. "There are some journalists who actually like it. Laziness isn't exactly foreign in the profession, and competition is for the diligent."

"Avi Benayahu has really done the job. He enables his client to quietly carry out that which he is supposed to do," said Yinon Magal, a news anchor for Israel's Channel 1 and a former correspondent for Army Radio. Magal added, "I'm not just a journalist. I'm a citizen, and as such, it's important to me to see the IDF win."

On June 2, 2010, Netanyahu emerged from hours of tense meetings with his kitchen cabinet of national security advisers to deliver a defiant address before the international media. He began by defending Israel's right to besiege the Gaza Strip, where he flatly denied that any humanitarian crisis existed. Next, Netanyahu presented the Gaza Freedom Flotilla as an Iranian Trojan horse that threatened Israel with imminent doom. "Israel cannot permit Iran to establish a Mediterranean port a few dozen kilometers from Tel Aviv and from Jerusalem," the prime minster thundered. "And I would go beyond that, too. I say to the responsible leaders of all the nations: the international community cannot afford an Iranian port in the Mediterranean."

Though all ships involved in the flotilla had undergone inspection at their ports of disembarkation, Netanyahu insisted the raid was intended as necessary inspection measure. Without any evidence beyond a few video clips that showed a few Turkish activists pacing the deck of the *Mavi Marmara* with metal bars in their hand, he claimed the flotilla was filled with some of the world's most dangerous terrorists. "It is very clear to us that the attackers had prepared their violent action in advance," the prime minister confidently proclaimed. "They were members of an extremist group that has supported international terrorist organizations and today support the terrorist organization called Hamas. They brought with them in advance knives, steel rods, other weapons. They chanted battle cries against the Jews. You can hear this on the tapes that have been released."

Netanyahu concluded, "This was not a love boat. This was a hate boat. These weren't pacifists. These weren't peace activists. These were violent supporters of terrorism."

But with the massacre on the *Mavi Marmara* and Netanyahu's bellicose remarks, Israel's strategic partnership with Turkey, nurtured for decades by David Ben Gurion and his Labor Party acolytes as a key avenue of regional trade and military cooperation, swiftly collapsed. Back in Ankara, Prime Minister Recep Tayyip Erdogan reacted with unbridled fury. "Israel cannot clean the blood off its hands through any excuse," Erdogan rumbled. "It is no longer possible to cover up or ignore Israel's lawlessness. This bloody massacre by Israel on ships that were taking humanitarian aid to Gaza deserves every kind of curse." As the prime minister and leader of the Islamic-inspired Justice and Development Party, Erdogan was a longtime critic of the special relationship his country's military rulers forged with Israel, claiming it compromised the country's reputation in the Arab and wider Muslim world. Yet after Erdogan entered office in 2003, ousting the military junta from power, he stressed his commitment to the alliance, though on a more conditional basis than his predecessors.

Six months later, after the fallout from the *Mavi Marmara* massacre, Erdogan was basking in the admiration of the Arab and Muslim world while quietly strengthening his country's military and diplomatic cooperation with NATO. Israel's deputy foreign minister Danny Ayalon retaliated by summoning his Turkish counterpart, Oguz Celikkol to his office to dress him down over a popular Turkish TV drama that portrayed Israeli soldiers as indiscriminate killers. As soon as Celikkol arrived, Ayalon seated him in a humiliating position on a customized couch that placed the Turk literally at the knees of then glowering Israelis. Then, Ayalon turned to the gallery of photographers he had invited for the stunt and boasted that he had deliberately forced Celikkol into that position and made certain no Turkish flag would be on display for the meeting. When photos of the meeting surfaced in Turkish and Israeli media, Ayalon's office was bombarded with frantic calls from both Turkey's Foreign Ministry and senior members of Israel's Labor Party demanding he apologize. But Ayalon doubled down. "It's the Turks who need to apologize," he defiantly proclaimed.

Next, Netanyahu dispatched lobbyists from the Washington, DC–based American Israel Public Affairs Committee (AIPAC) to warn Turkish diplomats that after years of officially denying the Armenian genocide and supporting efforts to suppress it, pro-Israel groups would reverse course, supporting a congressional resolution to acknowledge Turkey's atrocities—unless Turkey reverted its formerly conciliatory posture. Back in the Knesset, as lawmakers advanced a bill to criminalize public observance of the Nakba, Knesset Speaker Reuven Rivlin of Likud prepared plans to formally recognize the Armenian genocide, reversing decades of official Israeli denial.

A decade before tensions erupted between Israel and Turkey, when the left-leaning politician Yossi Sarid served as Israel's education minister, he visited an Armenian church in Jerusalem to declare that he would do everything in his power to correct the historical injustice committed against them by the Turks. His remarks infuriated then–prime minister Ehud Barak and Shimon Peres, who publicly scolded him. "These events," Peres told Sarid, "should be left to historians and not to politicians." But now that relations with Turkey had deteriorated, the government was eager to exploit the Armenian genocide for political leverage. "The Israelis no longer favor the Turks and are willing even to give up the charms and temptations of Antalya; that's how angry they are," Sarid wrote sardonically. "Now we will demonstrate to you what happens to a country that Israel no longer favors—we will sit it in the low chair as revenge against the gentiles. Now we'll show them who's boss."

Netanyahu packaged the fraying of international relations as a whole new threat that must be met by a concerted campaign of *hasbara*—the "delegitimization" threat. During a June 14 meeting with top ministers from his ruling Likud Party, the prime minister explained the danger. "We find ourselves in the midst of a difficult and continuous battle against the State of Israel," he informed his rightist comrades. "Dark forces from the Middle Ages are raging against us," Netanyahu rumbled. "I have received calls from concerned officials in the Balkans and Eastern Europe who are very worried about these developments."

In March 2013, after expending endless stores of energy to paint the Mavi Marmara passengers as terrorists with intimate links to al Qaeda and other violent Islamic extremist organizations, Netanyahu acceded to pressure from President Barack Obama to apologize for the lethal raid and to pay compensation to the victims' families. Had Israeli commandos killed actual terrorists with a sincere intent to harm Israelis, as Netanyahu, his allies, and the Israeli media insisted, the prime minister would have treated any demand to apologize as a terrible insult. With his conciliatory gesture, all the bluster about a "hate boat" bringing "Global Jihad" to Israel's shores was exposed as just that: a bunch of bluster. Israel moved to normalize relations with Turkey, but the damage had been done, not only to those who had lost family and friends aboard the flotilla, but to the majority of Israelis who never questioned their government's campaign of paranoid *hasbara*.

The People, United

When I ventured out into the streets of Tel Aviv in the days after the raid of the *Mavi Marmara*, I was able to witness the extent to which the barrage of propaganda orchestrated by the prime minister's office and the military-media complex had worked the Israeli public into a hysterical lather. On June 5, as I approached the Israeli Ministry of Defense on the way to an annual protest against the occupation organized by a coalition of liberal Zionist groups—the faded remnants of the old "peace camp"—and the non-Zionist communist Hadash Party, I noticed a small group of counterprotesters assembling nearby. In a plaza outside the Defense Ministry, I listened to then–Meretz Party leader Haim Oron call the flotilla raid an example of the right-wing government's "idiocy," but none of the speakers condemned the siege of Gaza. The occupation was bad for Israel and Israelis—that was the dominant theme. Peace Now activists filled the protest with Israeli flags with the word "Shalom" inserted in place of the Star of David.

The right-wing counterprotesters, who now numbered in the hundreds, saw the demonstrators as nothing short of traitors. After a military-grade smoke grenade exploded in the middle of the protest, part of an unsuccessful attempt to provoke havoc and mass trampling, protesters poured out of the plaza by the thousands, marching directly by the right-wing rally, which had been organized by the government-linked student group Im Tirtzu. As a booming chant rang out from the left-wing crowd—"Fascism will not pass!"—mounted riot police rode into the demonstrators, attempting to separate them. In between shouting taunts and insults—terrorist lovers, Nazis, or just *smolinim* (leftists), perhaps the worst insult of all—the young counterprotesters chanted for the release of Gilad Shalit, an involuntary reflex of Israeli nationalists seeking to demonstrate their identification with the army. When I began to film the right-wingers, one of them charged at me with an Israeli flag and began screaming, "Do you see this flag?! Do you see this flag?!" When he attempted to drape it over my camera, I tried to calmly inform him that I couldn't see anything anymore.

An hour later, the right-wing students poured out into the streets of liberal North Tel Aviv, marching by the cafés and bars that flanked Rabin Square, and taunting patrons as "stinking Tel Avivians" who had retreated from their duty to the Jewish state into a bubble of apathy and decadence. I followed them as they waved large flags and stomped through the streets singing "*Am Yisrael Chai*" ("The People of Israel Live"), the unofficial anthem of Israeli ultra-nationalists. A group of Im Tirtzu supporters spotted Uri Avnery who was attempting to leave the anti-occupation protest. Avnery, a peace camp icon, who was a teenaged member of the right-wing Irgun terrorist gang against the British, and later a member of the Knesset, began publishing widely read anti-establishment polemics in the 1950s, and was still vigorous at age eighty-six. When the right-wing students set themselves on him, attempting to drag him out of a taxi, Avnery was able to fend them off with help from police arriving on the scene in the nick of time. This was not the first time Avnery had to defend himself against nationalist thugs: In 1975, after founding the Israeli Council for Israeli-Palestinian Peace to initiate relations with the PLO, he was stabbed and assaulted on multiple occasions.

"The violence of the rightists is a direct result of the brainwashing, which has been going on throughout the last week," Avnery said after the attempted assault. "A huge propaganda machine has incited the public in order to cover up the terrible mistakes made by our political and military leadership, mistakes which are becoming worse from day to day."

The intra-Jewish conflict on display outside the Defense Ministry—"Jew against Jew," *Yedioth Ahronoth* called it—hardly represented the dynamic that characterized Israeli society after the flotilla raid. As during most outbreaks of war, the majority of the public was solidly united behind the army, and against whatever external force the government had designated as enemy number one, from Hezbollah to Hamas to a bunch of aging European peace activists. A poll of Israeli post-flotilla attitudes showed that not only 46 percent of Jewish Israelis believed the army used the "right amount of force" against the flotilla, but that 39 percent felt that the commandoes did not use enough force—nine dead activists was too few, apparently. A whopping majority supported the siege of Gaza, believed Israel should take no steps to moderate its policies in the face of international criticism, and rejected the creation of an international committee to investigate the raid. Though President Obama refused to condemn the massacre aboard the *Mavi Marmara*, casting it as a "tragic" incident that highlighted Israel's "legitimate security concerns," his disapproval rating among Israelis rose to 71 percent.

On June 1, at least two thousand Israelis assembled spontaneously outside the Turkish Embassy in Tel Aviv to vent their rage at their country's newest foe, which also happened to have been one of its oldest and most valuable allies. The rally was organized through Facebook groups without a formal endorsement or support from any political party or organization. It attracted a broad sampling of Israeli citizens, young and old, from across the spectrum of opinion. When I arrived on the scene with Lia Tarachansky, it was clear how deeply the sustained campaign of propaganda disseminated through Israel's military-media complex had influenced the public's understanding of the flotilla incident. Beneath a canopy of Israeli flags—it seemed that nearly everyone was waving one—the demonstrators held handmade signs reading "Erdogan Islamic Fascist" and "Turkey = Hamas." In the middle of the swelling crowd, a man held an enlarged photograph of Mohammad al-Hazmi, the Yemeni legislator whom the Army Spokesperson's Unit falsely portrayed as a knife-wielding terrorist.

A chubby teenager holding a sign that portrayed Erdogan with a Hitler moustache painted on his face rushed up to me and exclaimed excitedly, "Turkiya is Hamas! Hamas is Iran! Turkiya is Iran! Hamas is Iran!"

The notion that the flotilla was a covert terror convoy determined to destroy Israel was absolutely unanimous, while the commandoes were viewed as innocent victims. "What happened here was totally justified by Israel because a group of people who came under the disguise of peacekeepers coming to Gaza to break a siege that doesn't exist," a plain-looking man in his early twenties remarked to me.

"If we put our weapons down, everyone will kill us. If the Arabs put their weapons away, there will be peace. This is the difference," a clean-cut thirty-something guy in a polo shirt, told me. I asked him if most Israelis he knew shared this mentality. He told me he was an apolitical "common civilian," just like everyone else at the rally. "We truly believe this. We're a peaceful nation. We want peace."

The longer I spoke with the demonstrators, the more likely they were to merge their nightmare visions of the flotilla activists as hardcore agents of the Islamic Republic of Iran and al-Qaeda with Holocaust demons. "Everything is against the Jews, and we have the right to defend ourselves," the guy in the polo shirt complained to me. He went on: "Sixty to seventy years ago, everyone wanted us dead. They killed six million of us, and this reminds us of these days."

"So this really reminds you of the Holocaust?"

"Yes, it reminds us of the Holocaust," he stated without hesitation. "No matter what we do, everything is against us—*everybody*. And we know we're right."

An older man with messy silver hair and glasses interjected: "When our soldiers went on the ship, you know what those Turkish terrorists shouted on them? 'We will bring you to Auschwitz.'" He was alluding to the "Go back to Auschwitz" audio recording apparently fabricated by the Army Spokesperson's Unit and introduced to the public through the eagerly cooperative Israeli media.

I asked where he had learned about the incident. "I read it from the soldiers. I believe *every* word our soldiers say. *Every word!*"

As darkness fell on the rally, young hooligans associated with the rightist Beitar Jerusalem football club poured in by the dozens, injecting a frenzy into the crowd. A pack of about one hundred young men started the chant that erupts from the Beitar crowd practically every time their team scores a goal: "Death to Arabs!" While the chant spread throughout the crowd along with plumes of smoke wafting from a flaming Turkish flag, a tall, stocky man with an Israeli flag draped over his shoulders pulled Lia aside. Describing himself as a "left-winger," he attempted to present a more moderate image of the demonstration.

"We don't want those [Palestinian] territories," he assured Lia in a carefully measured voice. "We will withdraw from all of it the first day that the Arabs will acknowledge our state. If they will acknowledge our state, there will be no more war. I tell you one more thing. . . . " Suddenly, a teenage boy with a "Kahane Was Right" sticker applied to his shirt leapt in front of the man and shouted into Lia's camera, "Death to Arabs! Death to Arabs!" (Meir Kahane was an icon of extremism: an American-Israeli settler rabbi notorious for calling for the forced transfer of all

Palestinians to another Arab country, who urged all American Jews to emigrate to avoid a "second Holocaust" in the United States, and was assassinated in 1990 by a lone Egyptian-American gunman.)

A look of embarrassment washed over the man's face. "Stop it, dude!" he shouted at the teen.

Turning back to Lia, he attempted to explain why a "peacenik" like him wound up united alongside Kahanists at the rally: "What happened this time unites the left-wing Israelis and our extremists because we don't know how to perceive what happened."

The undercurrent of excitement that coursed through the crowd reflected the sense that the outpouring of international condemnation against Israel was a blessing in disguise. "Erdogan, the Turkish anti-Semite and Jew hater and terrorist—he made a great service to us because I never seen such unity and I lived here for sixty years," the older man with messy silver hair remarked to me.

A man in his thirties with closely cropped hair leaned against a parked car and told me with a wistful look in his eyes, "I'm very happy about what happened because it united the country. And everything now, all the Israelis, all the Jewish, everybody's united for a cause. Now the world can see we're a brave nation, we don't do the things that Hamas do in the country, we all want peace." He added, "It's the first time that we don't have to kiss anybody's ass; not the United States, not the United Nations. We are on our own, we did it about sixty years ago, and we can do it again. And I don't care."

Nearby, Lia had positioned her tripod on the median strip of the road. In front of her camera stood a cherubic boy who could not have been older than five. Like many of the adults at the rally, he had donned an Israeli flag as a cape, like a football fanatic at the World Cup or a super hero. And like his elders, the little boy was able to recite the official government version of the flotilla raid without missing a beat.

"The Turkish, in the night, two days, came with boats and with metal sticks, and we came and took control of their ship," the boy explained to Lia in Hebrew.

"Why are you here?" she asked him.

"To support those who battled the Turkish."

"When you'll be eighteen, will you be in the army too?"

"Yes."

"What role?"

"The navy."

"Is there anything else you'd like to say?"

The little boy closed his eyes momentarily to concentrate. When he opened them, a smile broadened across his cheeks. He announced with pride, "My brother is a commander."

The spectacle outside the Turkish Embassy in Tel Aviv was a bit terrifying, but there was also something absurd about it. Worked into a petulant frenzy by their prime minister, Knesset members and the military-media complex, the workaday Israelis howling at the walls of an empty office building sincerely believed that a small convoy of rusty old vessels filled with Turkish Muslims and graying antiwar activists transporting a shipment of hearing aids to the besieged people of Gaza posed an existential threat to their lives. Behind the *Mavi Marmara* they saw the Turkish Islamist Recep Tayyip Erdogan, and behind him Iran and al-Qaeda and a grotesque gallery of Islamic evildoers were dead set on throwing the Jews into the sea. And behind all the fearsome Islamic beardies was the man with the moustache: Adolf Hitler, whom these Israelis discussed as through his brain had been preserved in a cryogenics lab somewhere in the jungles of South America and was emanating magnetic rays.

I had not spent time in Israel for any prolonged period before 2009, but it was not hard to believe that the political atmosphere had ever been more closed or suffused with paranoia. "Fascism" was a word the leftists used almost invariably as they told me about having their homes defaced with graffiti death threats by right-wing thugs or about being summoned to interrogations by a Shin Bet agent named "Rona," then finding out that the police had been monitoring their every move for years. On the bus ride back to Jaffa, the "F" word came up again as Lia gave me her impressions of the rally we had just covered. I challenged her to define what she meant by the term. How could she claim fascism was in the air when anti-Zionists like her were still allowed to conduct their journalism and activism without being jailed or simply eliminated? Wasn't Israel at least a semi-open society?

"To explain the fascism in Israel, it's not that easy," Lia said, "because honestly I don't let myself think about it that much. It's so depressing and so terrifying that I usually repress my thoughts about it. But if you really want me to define it, then I'd tell you that it's not just the anti-democratic laws, it's not the consensus for occupation, it's not the massive right-wing coalition government, it's not watching the people who ask questions and think critically being interrogated by the *Shabak* [Shin Bet]. What it really is, is a feeling that you have sitting on a bus being afraid to speak Arabic with your Palestinian friends. It's a feeling when you are sitting there having dinner—what you feel when you're alive here. It's the essence of what this society is. And the closer we get to the brink—and everyone is feeling that we're getting to the breaking point—the worse it gets."

A young woman in a pink cotton dress with streaks of red dye in her hair and a face caked with makeup had turned around and tuned in on our conversation from two rows ahead. We made eye contact momentarily. "Who are you for? Israel or Turkiya?" she asked, looking at me with a raised eyebrow. Her tone was not accusatory, at least, not in an aggressive way. She seemed genuinely curious, but I also detected suspicion in her voice.

"I'm just an American. You know, a tourist," I said, hoping to deflect a question that seemed to have only one right answer. Now a few others on the bus were paying attention. Their craggy faces shone with layers of half-dried perspiration; most likely they were returning from jobs in affluent North Tel Aviv to their homes in Bat Yam, a working-class Russian suburb south of Jaffa.

"You are American? You with us, yes?" the woman said, this time more forcefully. "You with Israel or Turkiya?"

Someone had signaled for a stop, and the back door of the bus suddenly flung open. Without considering where I was, I darted toward the door and out into the humid night, shrugging at the woman on my way. As the doors closed, I caught a glance of her staring at me. Now Lia and I were standing on a corner of Yerushalayim Boulevard, almost a kilometer from home. I worried that she would be upset with my abrupt exit, but instead she offered empathy. "You can kind of see what I mean," she said. I nodded sheepishly and we started walking home.

The Enemies

A few decrepit cargo vessels were not the only things driving the Israeli public into full panic mode. In the days after the flotilla raid, a petite, bespectacled Arab woman with short hair and a small, mousy voice managed to shake the Jewish state to its core. She was Hanin Zoabi, a member of Knesset from Azmi Bishara's Balad, the party that advocated transforming Israel into a "state of all its citizens" in which Palestinians and Jews both enjoyed the same rights. Zoabi had traveled aboard the *Mavi Marmara*, manning the loudspeaker system and using her Hebrew to convince the Israeli commandoes to stop firing on unarmed passengers. Afterward, with several other political leaders of Palestinian Israeli society still in jail, Zoabi returned to the Knesset determined to confront the majority of lawmakers who cheered on the raid, and to demand her peers' release.

When Zoabi approached the Knesset podium on June 2, 2010, to address her colleagues, Anastasia Michaeli, the six-foot-tall ex-Russian model-turned-dominatrix of the Yisrael Beiteinu party, charged from her seat and rushed her. Screaming hysterically and waving an unidentified document, Michaeli came within inches of attacking Zoabi before the security guards assigned to Zoabi could hold her back. A melee erupted around the podium, as more members of the Knesset rushed forward to heckle Zoabi. "Terrorist!" one shouted. "Go to Gaza!" screamed another. Finally, Reuven Rivlin, the Knesset speaker, arrived to attempt to restore the order his acting replacement could not.

Rivlin was an eighth generation Israeli sabra whose father had translated the Quran into Hebrew. Though he held a leading position in the right-wing Likud Party, embodying its pro-settler, Greater Israel philosophy, his instincts seemed far more liberal than many members of Kadima and even the supposedly left-of-center Labor Party. While Rivlin was absolutely opposed to dividing Israel and the West Bank into two states, he called Arabs "an inseparable part of this country" and "integral to Israeli society." Rivlin derived some of his political tendencies from Ze'ev Jabotinsky, the Zionist ideologue who expressed a schizophrenic blend of Italian-style fascism and Enlightenment-era concepts of democratic pluralism. He also took inspiration from Menachem Begin, the rightist former Israeli prime minister, a Jabotinsky protégé, who had opposed David Ben Gurion's plans to impose martial law on Israel's Arab citizens. As for the new generation of thirty- and forty-something Likudniks who made up much of the Knesset, Rivlin reeled in disgust. "The new Likud is not committed to the ethic of liberty, to the values of Jabotinsky and [former prime minister] Begin," he said. The fiasco in the Knesset highlighted Rivlin's waning role in Israeli politics as the fanatics of his party took control.

Zoabi opened her speech by calling the raid on the *Mavi Marmara* an illegal "pirate military operation" that merited an international investigation. When she asked why the Israeli government opposed such an investigation and why it had destroyed all recordings of the raid by passengers on the ship, a chorus of furious legislators leapt up from their chairs in the gallery with insulting taunts, attempting to drown Zoabi with their heckling. "Go to Gaza, traitor!" shouted Miri Regev, a telegenic female lawmaker, who had formerly served as the Israeli army's chief spokesperson and who perfectly represented the "new Likud" Rivlin abhorred. Before the speech, Regev had called Zoabi a "Trojan horse," remarking, "The sail to Gaza was a sail of terror. Zoabi must be punished."

Next, Yohanan Plesner, the director general of the opposition Kadima Party then led by self-proclaimed feminist Tzipi Livni, homed in on Zoabi's gender. "I just wish you would go to Gaza for at least a week, and then we'll see how you talk about women's rights and civil rights," Plesner barked at her. "Just one week, and we'll see what happens. One week in Gaza as a thirty-eight-year-old single woman, and we'll see how they treat you! You are the last person capable of preaching morals to us."

Among Zoabi's few defenders was Mohammed Barakeh, an Arab lawmaker from the Hadash Party facing prosecution at the time on charges of assaulting a police officer at an anti-occupation protest, even though videotape of the incident showed the opposite—Barakeh was attempting to intervene between angry demonstrators and the police officers who were violently attacking them. When Barakeh rose to speak in the Knesset, cries of "Enemies! Enemies!" rang out from the gallery. David Rotem stood up, garbled a series of inaudible insults at Zoabi and continued shouting while Knesset guards led him limping out of the hall. Next, it was the turn of Rotem's Yisrael Beiteinu comrade, Moshe Mutz Matalon, to heckle Zoabi. "Nice work," he barked. "In one day you've managed to accomplish what the treacherous people around you have been trying to do for years. Unfortunately, the [commandos] acted with too much restraint. They left only nine floating voters."

Rivlin banged his gavel furiously and invoked his seniority over and over, attempting to silence the braying mob that was determined to silence Zoabi. "Gentlemen, please allow her to finish her words," he appealed to the gallery. "Does your strength lie within what she might say? What do you care?" But Rivlin's pleading was useless. In Israel, shouting down Arab lawmakers had become a form of electioneering. Each legislator, from the "centrist" Kadima to the far-right Yisrael Beiteinu, scored points with voters by hectoring Zoabi and her Arab colleagues. As one after another sprung up like kangaroos to confront her, they formed a competition for the most demeaning insult and extreme rhetoric. The prize was enhanced popularity with an Israeli mainstream overcome with anti-Arab eliminationism.

Though Rivlin had promised Zoabi five minutes to speak, he ordered her to leave the podium after only a minute and a half, a time period consumed almost entirely by heckling and interruptions. As she passed through the Knesset gallery, legislators lunged at her again, one by one, shouting, "Where is your knife?" and calling her a "terrorist." Finally, a female security guard lifted Zoabi off her feet and attempted to carry her out of the main hall. But when she reached the door, Zoabi broke free from the guard, stomped back into the hall, took a seat in her chair, and crossed her arms in a defiant pose while the red-faced screamers surrounded her, their violent fury restrained only by a wall of security guards and a few of Zoabi's colleagues from Balad. Many Israeli liberals were shocked by the spectacle, but the scenes were nothing new in Israel's Knesset.

By Right and Not Grace

During the early 1950s, Israeli forces were engaged in a campaign of deportation sweeps in the Galilee, searching for "infiltrators" who were in fact indigenous Palestinians driven from their homes in 1947 and '48. When Arab legislators began to protest the sweeps, sometimes showing up during raids to block the path of military vehicles with their own bodies, Rehavam Amir, the Israeli governor of the Western Galilee, called for a "psychological war against the Arab public" to break their political will. Paranoia about Arab subversion peaked in October 1956, when Israel joined an ill-fated plot with Britain and France to attack Egypt in a bid to retake control of the Suez Canal. (President Dwight Eisenhower, infuriated at the neocolonial invasion, told Britain and France to withdraw—and the adventure collapsed.) Under the cover of war, Israeli military authorities initiated Operation Hafarferet, a top-secret blueprint for the expulsion of thousands of Palestinian citizens from the so-called Little Triangle, a concentration of Arab towns in the Galilee. During the initial stage of the abortive plan, a curfew was imposed in the area while many of the villagers were still working in their fields.

Unaware that they were violating any rules, the villagers of Kafr Kassem attempted to return home in the evening as they normally did. On the road leading toward their villages, they met Israeli armored vehicles and troops that immediately opened fire at close range with automatic weapons, massacring 47 innocent people including over 20 children in the course of an hour. "I don't want any sentimentality," unit commander Yiska Shadmi had said when a commander asked what to do with the villagers. "*Allah Yirhamu*," he added—Arabic for "may God have mercy on their souls." Shadmi would be fined one piaster—the equivalent of a penny—for his role in the massacre. Despite his conviction for killing forty-three villagers in Kafr Kassem in one hour, Lieutenant Gavriel Dahan was appointed "officer responsible for Arab affairs" in Ramle, a mixed city with a substantial Arab population. Other key participants were given plum appointments in the state bureaucracy, including at the top-secret nuclear reactor at Dimona.

In a stormy meeting with his cabinet, Ben Gurion said he wanted to hang the culpable officers in Kafr Kassem's town square. But instead of going to the public, the prime minister ordered a media blackout on the massacre, cordoning off the village for several months to keep reporters away. News of the killings leaked out only because of Latif Dori, an Arabic-speaking Israeli journalist who reported for the official news outlet of Mapam, which was then in a coalition with Ben Gurion's

Labor Party. After sneaking into Kfar Kassem, Dori heard from villagers of the terror they endured and how they were convinced that the massacre was part of a wider campaign to drive them over the border to Jordan, which lay only ten kilometers from their village—a suspicion that was confirmed only decades later.

When Dori lobbied Knesset members from his party to lift the curtain of silence, they rebuked him. He was forced to turn for help to Toufiq Toubi, the Knesset's first Arab representative and, like Hanin Zoabi, its most hated member. Dori also found support from Meir Vilner, the outspoken leader of the Israeli Communist party and survivor of the European genocide. "What we wanted to escape in Vilna [Lithuania] we found here [in Israel]," he said. "There, hatred was directed against Jews, here against Arabs." Both Toubi and Vilner had issued lengthy Knesset speeches denouncing the atrocities in Kafr Kassem, and each watched with frustration as their comments were immediately stricken from the Knesset record. With Dori's help, Toubi and Vilner managed to slip through a heavy police guard at a hospital in Petah Tikvah to interview wounded survivors. The two went next to Ben Gurion to demand he establish an independent investigative panel.

When Ben Gurion finally appeared before the Knesset to brief members on the massacre, he rejected the call for an investigation. The prime minister's attitude infuriated Toubi, who accused the prime minister of whitewashing atrocities and allegedly shouted at him and his fellow Mapai members in the Knesset, "Murderers!" Jewish Knesset members formed an angry mob and nearly set themselves on Toubi—just as they did with Zoabi—calling him a traitor and a Trojan horse for Arab nationalism. They were outraged that an Arab would have the chutzpah to criticize Jewish authorities, and especially the universally revered army. He should have been grateful to be allowed to participate in Israel's magnificent democracy, they shouted at him. Ben Gurion, for his part, tried and failed to convince the Knesset to sanction Toubi for his outburst. "Is it possible that this, by a Knesset member who is nothing but an enemy of Israel and a traitor to the state as a member of the Communist faction, will be permitted and go unpunished?' Ben Gurion boomed before the assembly.

For several years, Toubi warned that Israeli society was approaching a political tipping point. "A fascist movement has emerged in Israel," he declared. "We are witnessing the growing fascistization of the right-wing." While a crude populist element grew within Menachem Begin's Herut Party, which would later morph into Likud, Toubi complained that "Every week Ben Gurion's government opens a new page of racist provocation and national oppression." After his latest dust-up with the prime minister, who had made a point of refusing to meet with non-collaborationist Arab members of Knesset throughout his entire tenure as prime minister, Toubi braced himself for a possibly career-ending political backlash.

Remarkably, one of Ben Gurion's closest confidants, Nathan Alterman, a writer known at the time as Israel's national poet, stepped out of his customary role as a courtier to chastise the country's leadership. Toubi served in the Knesset "by right and not by grace," Alterman wrote. "His presence is legal and authorized; it is a basic freedom. . . . This is the essence of democracy. If it is not instinctively understood, then we have no inkling of what it is about." With Alterman's backing, Toubi's position was secure in the young parliament, even if he remained an object of scorn and resentment by many of his colleagues.

In the days after the mob attack on Zoabi in the summer of 2010, no Nathan Alterman emerged. Indeed, the incident in the Knesset was on the front page of every Israeli newspaper and broadcast at the top of the evening news, but with the exception of Amnon Levy, a columnist for the center-right *Yedioth Ahronoth* newspaper, almost no one with any standing expended a scintilla of energy in condemning it. Even Tzipi Livni, the opposition leader who once told of a personal feminist awakening in which she realized, "I'm part of a wider system, and that some of my struggles are because I'm a woman," said nothing about the nearly all-male mob that bullied Zoabi, taunting her over her status as a single Arab woman. Meanwhile, the Knesset prepared a series of motions to strip Zoabi of her parliamentary privileges, paving a legal path for driving her and her party out of the political system altogether. As the Knesset deliberated Zoabi's fate, David Sheen and I traveled to the development town of Askhelon to meet one of the many centrist lawmakers disgusted by the mob scene that had developed days before, a self-proclaimed feminist, confidant of Livni, and friend of Zoabi's who nonetheless had done nothing to counter her public abuse.

The Silence of the Lambs

Before the foundation of the State of Israel, the city of Ashkelon was a Palestinian Arab enclave known as Majdal Asqalan. Though Israeli commander Yigal Allon ordered his forces to drive the town's Arabs away, Majdal's community of Palestinians managed to slip back in and gradually reconstituted. For two years, the Israeli government kept the indigenous residents—"infiltrators," they now called them—confined in a small ghetto surrounded by barbed wire, until Army Southern Commander Moshe Dayan, in 1950, following consultation with the government's "Committee for the Transferring of Arabs," had his forces load the unwanted Palestinians into trucks and dump them in the Gaza Strip, where they would be permanently confined.

Just prior to the expulsion, Naeim Giladi, a former member of the Iraqi Zionist underground who had immigrated to Israel, waited anxiously with other Iraqi Jews in a squalid transit camp administered by the Jewish Agency. "Be patient," Giladi recalled a Jewish Agency director telling him. "Soon we shall expel the Arabs out of Majdal, and you will be able to have their homes." The promise did not sit well with Giladi, who still identified as an Arab and refused to internalize the prejudices of Israel's Ashkenazi establishment. Soon afterward, he and a few friends slipped through the barbed wire surrounding Majdal and met with its inhabitants, speaking to them in their native tongue. "Talking to them, we discovered that they were very peaceful people, very hospitably disposed toward us, and ready to behave as loyal citizens of the state that has just been founded," Giladi recounted. "And it was those people they wanted to drive out to settle in their houses!"

Today, Askhelon is a working-class development town populated by the offspring of the Arab Jews who once languished in transit camps. Their numbers were supplemented by thousands of Russian Jews who were brought to Israel after the collapse of the Soviet Union. The presence of Majdal's Palestinians can be felt only through their absence and perhaps also by the occasional Grad rocket launched from the Gaza Strip into the city's general vicinity.

Sheen and I arrived in the city to meet with Marina Solodkin, a local resident serving her fifth term in the Knesset as the Kadima Party's top Russian representative. A Muscovite who immigrated to Israel in 1991 after years of Zionist underground activity in the Soviet Union, Solodkin emerged as a popular politician in Israel's Russian sector and an accomplished Russian-language academic author. In the new Knesset, Solodkin had sought to establish herself by proposing a bill banning women from wearing the *niqab*, or from otherwise covering their faces for religious reasons. Because only a tiny handful of Arab women inside Israel veiled their faces, the bill appeared to be another populist ploy to leverage anti-Arab resentment into political momentum.

Solodkin received us warmly when we entered her modest-sized condo, providing a spread of tea and cookies. She then introduced us to the collection of Crusader-era artifacts she had gathered from her yard and surrounding environs. She was a stout, cheerful fifty-eight-year-old woman who related to us like a Jewish mother, telling us fondly about her own children who were studying hard for their master's degrees.

When we finally reached the topic of her so-called burqa ban, Solodkin insisted she had proposed it in the spirit of liberalism—the same spirit that France embodied in its own burqa ban and which the Soviets had brought to Afghanistan when they invaded and occupied the country. She read to us from an op-ed published in a Russian-language Israeli paper. The column praised her bill by recounting a scene from a Russian war film depicting a Soviet commander "liberating" the women of Afghanistan by ordering them to "open your face." "It is a blow to the freedom and respect of individuals to hide your face," Solodkin told us. "That's why for me it's purely from liberal and equality reasons that I put this law forward."

The law ultimately failed to pass a first reading, but only because it was seen as addressing a problem that did not exist. Jamal Zehalka, an Arab legislator who served alongside Hanin Zoabi in the Balad Party, said that Solodkin's proposal revealed the arrogance of the recent immigrants who had arrived in Israel from Russia, thanks to the country's Jews-only "Law of Return." "There is a difference between laws like this in Europe, and here. In Europe, you are speaking about immigrants. I am against these laws there, as well!—but there you are speaking about immigrants. They came to France, they came to a secular state," Zehalka remarked to Sheen and me. "But here, Mrs. Solodkin came to us. We were living here. We didn't come to the State of Israel, the State of Israel came to us. So it's going too far to make laws like this here."

Despite having offended Arab lawmakers with her proposal, Solodkin told us that she had forged a warm relationship with Zoabi and that she sometimes ate breakfast with her in hotels near the Knesset. The two had even discussed plans to cosponsor a bill providing special loans for female entrepreneurs. Following the mob scene in the Knesset, Solodkin conferred privately with Tzipi Livni, the chairperson of her party and one of her closest political confidants. Both women were upset by the intimidation and insults directed against Zoabi, even though they recoiled at her participation in the Free Gaza Flotilla. They were particularly displeased with the conduct of their party mate Yohanan Plesner, who had decided that her status as an unmarried thirty-eight-year-old woman was fair game. "It's not Russian for one hundred to gang up on one," Solodkin said. In her view, the appropriate response would have been to stage a mass walkout, just as many Jewish Israeli legislators did during the Second Intifada when members of Knesset Ahmad Tibi read out documentations of Israeli atrocities in the Occupied Territories.

But now the question was how Livni should respond. In the end, the two women decided that condemning the treatment of Zoabi would be politically suicidal.

"Because my community [Russian Israelis] thinks it was horrible what Hanin did, I was not capable [of mustering a response] because I have to respect them," Solodkin claimed. "I don't want to get 150 letters and e-mails in big volume and the phones ringing." Fearing a terrible backlash from her constituents, she advised Livni to act just as she did during the debates over various anti-democratic laws, from the Nakba Law to the Acceptance to Communities Bill: to keep silent and worry about the consequences later.

Less than two weeks after Zoabi was shouted down, the Knesset House Committee voted to strip her of her parliamentary privileges. The vote was initiated through a measure submitted by Michael Ben-Ari, a former henchman of Meir Kahane. During the debate, which had the feeling of a Soviet kangaroo court, committee chairman Yariv Levin of the ruling Likud Party bandied around "evidence" of Zoabi's treachery he had collected from the Balad Party's website, including photos of an official visit she and other Arab members of Knesset had made to Libya. The only committee member who voted against the measure, Ilan Ghilon of Meretz—one of the few liberals in the room—made sure to qualify his opposition to the proceeding by first suggesting his loyalty to the imperatives of the Jewish state, declaring, "I can't stand MK Zoabi's opinions on anything."

In a vote conducted by the full Knesset the next week, the assembly voted overwhelmingly to punish Zoabi, even though she had broken no laws. She was summarily stripped of her diplomatic passport and her right to be compensated for legal fees if taken to trial. Levin, who had presided over the earlier proceedings, denounced Zoabi in the most scathing language he could summon. "You have no place in the Israeli Knesset, you are unworthy of holding an Israeli ID, and you embarrass the citizens of Israel, the Knesset, the Arab population, and your family," the Likud legislator proclaimed.

Finally, the Yisrael Beiteinu diva Anastasia Michaeli handed Zoabi a mock passport from the Islamic Republic of Iran she had produced for the special purpose of her public humiliation. "Ms. Zoabi, I take your loyalty to Iran seriously and I suggest you contact [Iranian President Mahmoud] Ahmadinejad and ask him to give you an Iranian diplomatic passport that will assist you with all your diplomatic incitement tours, because your Israeli passport will be revoked this evening," Michaeli exclaimed before being ushered out of the Knesset chamber by a team of guards. Michaeli was not punished for her histrionics. But a year later, the Knesset barred Zoabi from addressing the assembly or participating in committee votes for a full parliamentary season.

Behind the scenes, Zevulon Orlev, a religious nationalist politician known as the most prolific author of anti-Arab legislation in the Knesset, was preparing a new law targeting Zoabi and her Palestinian colleagues. Honored as the "champion of lawmakers" for his success in passing laws—twenty-one had been enacted during his tenure—Orlev topped the right-wing Institute for Zionist Strategies' "Zionist Legislation Scale." He was the force behind the libel law that multiplied by a factor of six the fine journalists would have to pay the politicians wounded by their criticism. And his anti-boycott law threatened to punish those calling for economic sanctions on Israeli companies operating in the occupied territories with unlimited lawsuits from Jewish settlers.

But his most reactionary bill, which he proposed in part as a means of clamping down on Zoabi's speech, was the Anti-Incitement act, which promised to criminalize any peaceful act, even speech that suggested that Israel could not be "Jewish and democratic." Seated behind his desk in his cluttered Knesset office, Orlev, a portly, clean-shaven settler with an eerie resemblance to Dick Cheney, flipped through a binder and told David Sheen and me that any Israeli who even convinced a fellow citizen to behave in a "disloyal" fashion would face a year-long prison term. He called speech like Zoabi's "verbal terror." But when we asked him what sort of speech constituted "negating the Jewish character of the state," he could not say, telling us that the issue would be decided later on in a Knesset committee.

Thus he suggested that the bill was just another means of turning up the heat on Palestinian legislators in the Knesset, intimidating them into silence. "If this bill passes," Orlev told us, "I think Zoabi is going to have some big problems."

For several days after the fiasco in the Knesset, Zoabi did not appear in public without a security detail. An Israeli grocer offered on Facebook free groceries for life to anyone who assassinated Zoabi, while a Facebook page spontaneously appeared entitled, "Execute Zoabi." Featuring an image of Zoabi's face behind sniper crosshairs, the site quickly garnered hundreds of enthusiastic Israeli supporters. Sami Shehadeh, the Balad activist who led Jaffa's popular committee, made a frantic call to Jamal Zehalka, the most senior member of Balad, urging him to hire guards for himself. But Zehalka refused, casually dismissing the incitement as a fact of life in Israel.

By the time I visited Zoabi at her office in Nazareth, her guards were gone. Unlike her antagonists, she showed little sign of fear.

Defensive Democracy

The city of Nazareth had survived as a center of Palestinian Christian cultural and political life, thanks in large part to a Canadian named Benjamin Dunkelman. A veteran of the D-Day landing at Normandy during World War Two, Dunkelman volunteered to assist the Israeli army during the fighting in 1948, providing crucial assistance to its inexperienced officer corps. In July 1948, Dunkelman's 7th Brigade easily captured Nazareth, whose local inhabitants put up only the lightest resistance. He quickly signed a pact with the city's local leadership, who agreed to surrender and cooperate with the Jewish authorities on the condition that they would not be expelled. Soon afterward, when Dunkelman received an order from the Israeli General Chaim Laskov to forcibly evacuate the city's Arabs, he angrily refused, remarking that he was "shocked and horrified" that he would be commanded to renege on the agreement he had just signed.

Laskov went back to his superiors, demanding they override Dunkelman. David Ben Gurion, the prime minister and commander-in-chief of Israel's armed forces, had just ordered the ethnic cleansing of Ramle and Lydda with the wave of his hand, thus avoiding leaving a written record of the high-level decision. When asked to provide a formally recorded order to evacuate Nazareth, Ben Gurion was forced to refuse. Thus the city's population was saved from the terrible fate that more than seven hundred thousand other Palestinian Arabs suffered. After the war, Dunkelman promptly returned to his hometown of Toronto, where he spent the rest of his life.

During the 1960s and '70s, Hanin Zoabi's cousins, Abd-El-Aziz El-Zoubi, Sayf al-Din al-Zoubi, and Abd El-Rahman Zuabi were appointed by the Labor Zionist establishment to prominent roles in the political leadership in and around Nazareth. Prior to the foundation of Israel, Sayf al-Din had worked with the Jewish National Fund in arranging the sale of vast tracts of Arab land, receiving a sizable plot of coveted land in return. In the years after, he was considered a key asset by the Shin Bet, which used him to neutralize "negative" influences like the communist Rakah Party. He soon became the state-supported mayor of Nazareth for more than a decade before being rewarded for his loyalty with appointment as deputy speaker of the Knesset. Aziz El-Zoubi became Israel's first Arab minister, appointed as the deputy health minister in Yitzhak Rabin's first government in 1971. In 1999, Abd El-Rahman Zuabi was the first Arab to serve on Israel's Supreme Court, though only for a temporary term of nine months.

As the Jewish state's so-called good Arabs, the Zoubi patriarchs helped inspire the Palestinian Israeli politician and author Emile Habibi's classic book, *The Secret Life of Saeed: The Pessoptimist*, which told the tale of a hapless Arab collaborator who was repaid for his exaggerated displays of loyalty with harsh punishment and betrayal, and whose son turned toward violent resistance in the wake of the 1967 war. In real life Israel, however, the true stories of collaborators were often more absurd than fiction, and certainly as tragic. Abd al-Hamid, an Arab collaborator who worked for the Israeli army in 1948 and was conscripted into an intelligence unit in the Gaza Strip at the end of the 1956 Sinai Campaign (which culminated with the Israeli massacres in Rafah and Khan Younes), demanded medals for the valorous services he had performed for the Jewish state. Denied on the grounds that he was never officially inducted into the army, the humiliated al-Hamid purchased a few army service pins in a Jerusalem shop with some loose change. Seen strutting around town with the surplus medals affixed to his jacket, Israeli police immediately arrested him for impersonating a soldier.

During the early years of the state, those Arabs who attempted to agitate for equality outside the established Zionist political framework were marginalized and swiftly punished. The fate of a small Arab party called Al-Ard, or "The Land," starkly illustrated the intolerance of the Israeli government. Founded in 1959 by Palestinian intellectuals living inside Israel, Al-Ard advocated for the creation of a secular, democratic state in which Jews and Arabs enjoyed equal rights and freedom of religion. It encouraged both Palestinian refugees and Arab citizens of Israel to agitate for their rights under international law, while calling for Israel to honor the refugees' right of return and to follow the guidelines of the UN Resolution 181—the Partition Plan that it had violated—in order to establish a just solution to the conflict. The party's genesis signaled one of the first cohesive surges of Palestinian political resistance inside Israel since 1948.

Though the party's program represented a direct and deliberate challenge to the exclusive nature of the Jewish state, its activities were entirely nonviolent, conducted in the open and in full keeping with Israeli laws. Israeli officials nonetheless saw the tiny, fledgling organization as a dangerous challenge to a status quo that confined Arab political activity to left-wing Zionist parties and the Arab-Jewish Communist Party. Israel's adviser for Arab affairs warned his superiors that Al-Ard could become "a natural home for most of the Arab citizens in the country" if it was not swiftly crushed. He called for an immediate government crackdown on its operations. In short order, the state banned Al-Ard's newspaper, arrested its publishers, and put them all on trial. It was the first time in Israeli history that anyone faced felony charges for the crime of publishing a newspaper.

Blocked from operating inside the "Jewish and democratic" state, Al-Ard sent a letter to the United Nations outlining in meticulous detail the repressive legal and political measures Israel imposed on its Arab minority. The authors appealed for UN protection against a state they saw as determined to sweep them and all Arab citizens of Israel away into refugee camps. Widely reported in Israeli media, the release of the document pushed tensions to a breaking point. Now convinced that Al-Ard was possessed with a "poisonous nationalist character," Israeli minister of defense Moshe Dayan banned the movement altogether. The outlawing of Al-Ard was validated by the Supreme Court, which justified its ruling on the basis of "defensive democracy." "I did what the people wanted," boasted Justice Agranat, who delivered the majority decision. As soon as Al-Ard was driven underground, its leaders were arrested, imprisoned, and released only after the imposition of severe restrictions on their freedom of movement.

By the 1980s, in the shadow of the transformative trauma of the Land Day massacre, much of the Arab public inside Israel embarked on a process of Palestinianization, replacing the Labor Party's cast of collaborators with more assertive figures like Nazareth's new mayor, Toufiq Zayyad, who were determined to act in concert with their brethren who lived under occupation and in refugee camps around the Arab world. Then, as the Oslo era dawned on Israeli in the mid-1990s, some Palestinians in Israel streamed back into the left-wing Zionist parties; a few Palestinian residents of Nazareth were seen hoisting the Israeli flag on "Independence Day," a day that for most Palestinians symbolizes their dispossession. Creating a complaisant "Israeli Arab" community disconnected from Palestinians and the broader Arab world had always been a goal of the Zionist establishment. With the ratification of the Oslo Accords, it suddenly seemed within reach.

One of the few prominent Palestinian Israeli figures to oppose Oslo and the attendant Israelification of the Arab sector was the founder of the Balad party, Azmi Bishara. Bishara had organized Balad around the goal of transforming Israel into a "state of all its citizens" in which no group enjoyed privilege over any other on the basis of ethnic identity—a negation of Zionism's exclusive essence. "I say that a nation should include all its citizens with all the national differences," Bishara explained. "True, nations establish states, but after the state is established, a nation of citizens should arise, even if it's made up of different nationalities and religions. Ultimately, the element that will reinstate the concept of a nation, that will secularize it, won't be a religious concept; it will be citizenship."

Throughout Bishara's adult life, he found himself at the center of the conflict between Israel's Palestinian minority, a group that he led, and the leadership of its Jewish majority, which loathed him and sought by any and all means to drive him into exile. A stout, effusive philosopher-politician with a bushy moustache and a thick mane of jet black hair, Bishara peppered his speeches with elaborate musings rich with metaphors and references to figures ranging from Immanuel Kant to Mahmoud Darwish to Ahad Ha'am, the father of "spiritual Zionism" who fiercely opposed Herzl's messianic ambitions. With his philosophy Ph.D. and fluency in advanced political theory, Bishara projected his intellect defiantly against a state that insisted on viewing Palestinians as culturally retrograde—"hewers of wood and drawers of water" for the Chosen People, as former Labor Party operative Uri Lubrani said. Bishara's ideas shook the foundations of Israel's political and security establishment, which viewed them as a call for Israel's destruction.

Raised in Nazareth by a family from the Galilee town of Tarshisha, whose land was forcibly expropriated by the Jews-only Kibbutz Cabri, Bishara devoted himself to academic pursuits at an early age. While in high school in 1973, he was chosen for a Hebrew University camp for youth who excelled in math and science. It was there, on a bus trip to the West Bank, that he experienced Jewish Israeli racism for the first time. "We went to Hebron," he told the filmmaker and academic Ariella Azoulay, "and I saw how [the Jewish youth] perceived the Occupied Territories. And I heard their racist remarks about Arabs. I lasted through eight days of the three-week program and then told them, 'I can't take any more.'" A teacher scolded Bishara, accusing him of "isolating himself."

That day, Bishara retreated to East Jerusalem, strolling aimlessly down Sultan Suleiman Road, a long, bustling street lined with Arab vendors and restaurants. "I felt like myself finally," he recalled. "I wanted to make amends with my surroundings. I was the only Arab boy among Jews from around the world getting the most intensive Zionist education possible when I was just becoming aware of my national identity." Arabs attending Israeli high schools (especially the segregated schools in the "Arab sector") shared Bishara's sense of frustration. "The curriculum drove us crazy," Bishara recalled. "When they taught singular and plural, we had to say, 'A Jewish teacher, Jewish teachers. An Arab shepherd, Arab shepherds.' . . . The amount of Zionism we learned—we learned the history of this country with the most mainstream Zionist narrative. There was no mention of people existing here before '48. It was just too provocative, too alienating. Too much denial."

In high school, Bishara organized Arab students against the curriculum, forming the first nationwide Arab youth group in Israel's history. When the Israeli army killed two female Arab high school students as they left school for a demonstration—they were shot to death in their pin-striped uniforms—Bishara distributed their photos to Arab high schools around the country, galvanizing the activist spirit of his generation. A few years later, while at Hebrew University, he led protests after a group of Border Policemen stormed onto campus in search of Arabs to abuse, and wound up strapping an Arab student to the front of a jeep, then drove after his friend while he fled in terror.

In 1996, Bishara was elected to Knesset on the list of the party he founded, the National Democratic Assembly–Balad. As his prominence increased, so did the amount of incitement directed against him. In September 2000, at the dawn of the Second Intifada, and on the eve of Yom Kippur, the holiest of Jewish holidays, a nationalistic delirium overtook many residents of Nazareth Illit, the Jewish development town built above Nazareth to limit the city's natural growth. Young men from the town descended on the Palestinian neighborhoods of Nazareth, waving Israeli flags while they assaulted Arab demonstrators and chanted, "Death to Arabs!" Amid the violence, a local radio host put out a call to torch Bishara's home. While Bishara huddled inside with his pregnant wife, a mob vandalized the house's exterior walls. "Imagine if Arabs had attacked the house of a Jewish member of parliament," Bishara said. "They would have shot them. At my house, the police were just trying to persuade the mob nicely to go home."

The campaign against Balad intensified during the next national elections in 2003, when the Israeli Central Elections Committee deemed it a traitorous front group for the enemies of the Jewish state. Through a Knesset vote, Balad and another Arab party, the United Arab List-Taal, were officially banned. The Supreme Court overturned the decision, frustrating and angering the populists in the Knesset. Avigdor Lieberman, the leader of the far-right Yisrael Beiteinu Party, called for Bishara's execution while demanding that Israel's entire Arab minority "take [their] bundles and get lost."

To the delight of Lieberman and much of Israel's political establishment, by April 2007, Bishara had fled Israel for good. Following the humiliation of Israel's defeat in the Second Lebanon war, the Shin Bet prepared charges against Bishara, accusing him of helping Hezbollah direct missile attacks against Israeli targets. "Hezbollah . . . has independently gathered more security information about Israel than any Arab Knesset member could possibly provide," Bishara wrote in an editorial. "What's more, unlike those in Israel's parliament who have been involved in acts of violence, I have never used violence or participated in wars. My instruments of persuasion, in contrast, are simply words in books, articles, and speeches." Rather than submitting himself to a highly politicized prosecution based on secret Shin Bet evidence, or standing trial in an Israeli courtroom where Arab citizens were convicted at a dramatically higher rate than Jews, Bishara went into exile, eventually becoming the general director of the Arab Center for Research and Policy Studies in Doha, where he was eventually credited with convincing the Qatari Emir to back the Syrian popular revolt against the regime of Bashar Al-Assad. He was stripped of his pension as a Knesset member. The state had ejected possibly the most forceful advocate of secular democracy ever to hold Israeli citizenship, but it was not done yet.

A month after vanquishing Bishara, the Shin Bet's then-director Yuval Diskin sent a chilling letter to Adalah, a Palestinian Israeli legal rights group that had recently filed a public complaint against the Shin Bet's harassment of editors of the Balad Party's journal. Diskin informed Adalah's lawyers in no uncertain terms that his agency reserved the right to spy on anyone it deemed to be "conducting subversive activity against the Jewish identity of the state." Diskin warned that the Shin Bet would not hesitate to crack down on groups like Balad that conducted activities within a legal, democratic framework, adding, "the [Shin Bet] believes that subversion may also include working toward changing the basic values of the state by obviating its democratic or Jewish character, as a form of subversion against the processes of the democratic regime and its institutions."

The Israeli Declaration of Independence had defined Israel as a Jewish *and* democratic state. But according to Diskin, the state was "Jewish *or* democratic." In such a system, his intelligence service was the last line of defense against democratic challenges to Jewish political and legal dominance. Israel's then–attorney general Yehuda Weinstein attached his endorsement to Diskin's letter, expressing the consensus opinion of the elected government of Israel. Meanwhile, Diskin fretted about Balad in a private meeting with then-ambassador to Israel Richard Jones, complaining that the Palestinians inside Israel "take their rights too far."

During the fateful 2009 national elections, when the Israeli right consolidated its total dominance over the political field, the Knesset voted to ban Balad and United Arab List-Taal for the second time. And this time, the Labor Party endorsed the decision. "Balad just went a bit too far in its positions against Israel," a Labor spokesman explained. Tzipi Livni's Kadima also supported the vote. Though the Supreme Court overturned the decision, the calls for permanently ousting Arab parties were gaining momentum and support from inside the Israeli mainstream. Already, the state was preparing its case. "The Shabak [Shin Bet] has opened files on every one of Balad's top figures," Sami Shehadeh, Balad's leading representative in Jaffa, told me. "Our entire leadership is under investigation. But we don't tell our members because we don't want to frighten them."

Hanin Zoabi was among the Balad leaders who were certain they were being monitored, though she did not seem frightened. While she prepared instant coffee and a spread of biscuits for me at her neatly appointed office in downtown Nazareth, Zoabi told me how a Palestinian journalist who had interviewed her hours before had just called to inform her laptop was seized during her detention at an Israeli checkpoint near the West Bank city of Nablus.

I asked Zoabi if she ever feared for her personal safety. "This is a dangerous time, and it is dangerous for Jamal [Zehalka] and others in Balad," she said. "I'm worried, but what worries me more is not the personal threats but the long-term political effect of this campaign because it represents a delegitimization of our party and our political platform." The day when authentic representatives of Israel's Palestinian community would be barred once and for all from the Knesset seemed to be rapidly approaching.

Zoabi grew active in Balad during the late 1990s after becoming captivated by Bishara's stem-winding lectures about the crisis of citizenship in Israel. At the time, she was a Hebrew University media studies PhD who advanced a radical feminist critique of Jewish-Arab relations inside Israel-Palestine. Zoabi told me her interest in feminism preceded her advocacy for Palestinian rights, partly in reaction against a domineering father whose accomplishments as a lawyer and translator always seemed to overshadow those of her mother, a local high school teacher. In 2009, Zoabi was elected to the Knesset on the party's parliamentary list, which mandated at least one woman for every three members who received seats (Balad is the only party in Israel with a female quota). For more than a year, she remained virtually unknown to the Israeli public. All that changed with her post-flotilla appearance in the Knesset.

"I was not so surprised," Zoabi told me of the vitriolic reception from her colleagues. "I expected to be called traitor, to be asked, 'Where are your knives?' Or to be told, 'You are the one who killed them!' But they shouted at me without any political argument and such shallowness. I thought, this couldn't be a parliament, these are just gangsters. If I gave them guns, they would shoot me. I said the soldiers on the flotilla treated me more respectfully than them. At least after the soldiers killed nine people they tried to ask me for help."

What shocked Zoabi the most was the muted reaction to her treatment by the Jewish Israeli public, and especially from its traditionally liberal elements. "Hardly anyone spoke up for me. Jamal [Zehalka, the veteran Balad legislator] said the

Knesset is the worst we've ever had," she remarked. "The guards and the workers who've been around the Knesset for thirty years told me it's never been this racist before. I think when you have a government led by the likes of Avigdor Lieberman it means that the extremists are not the margins of the Knesset; they are the mainstream. Those who shouted at me were from Kadima, not from the extreme right. Even Meretz is becoming very center. And because of this it has lost power."

She continued, "[Knesset Speaker] Rivlin was more afraid of hurting the image of the Knesset than of my rights being violated. There are no limits anymore and the famous slogan of Lieberman is now the slogan of everyone: 'Citizenship depends on loyalty.' He of course means loyalty in a fascist sense. Even when [Interior Minister] Eli Yishai asked to revoke my citizenship, there was only one article in the Israeli media saying that this was crazy. What kind of state is this? I read just one article about this!"

Zoabi explained that while Israel's reaction to the Gaza Freedom Flotilla might have been the "beginning of a new historical moment" that spotlighted the state's treatment of its Palestinian citizens for the first time before a global audience, the clash between Israel's Palestinian political leadership and its Jewish majority had begun years ago during the Second Intifada. "This [Intifada] was a clear message for Israelis that the state had failed to create the model of the new 'Israeli Arab.' This is what the state was trying to do, trying to create an Israeli Arab, someone who was not 100 percent Israeli because we were not Jews but of course not 100 percent Arab, either," she commented. "We were told we could preserve our language and our culture but not our historical memory, our culture, or our identity except on an emotional, romantic level. Essentially we couldn't be Palestinian. The Second Intifada told Israel that it might control the schools, our history, and the media, but they couldn't stop us from asserting our identity."

By the time I visited Zoabi, her cousin, the former Israeli Supreme Court judge El-Rahman Zuabi, had lost his patience. He would no longer allow his name to be used to promote the illusion of Israeli democracy, especially after Netanyahu's approval of a new law requiring non-Jews to swear loyalty to the "Jewish and democratic" state as a condition of obtaining citizenship. El-Rahman told Israel Radio, "There will be two countries in the world that in my opinion are racist: Iran, which is an Islamic state, and Israel, which is the Jewish state."

Two years after I met Zoabi, the campaign to expel her from public life continued without interruption. In 2012, the Israeli police authorized a permit to extreme right-wing legislator Michael Ben-Ari for a march through the middle of the Nazareth. According to Ben-Ari, the theme of the march was, "Expel Zoabi from the Knesset."

The same year, Alex Gedalkin, a local Nazareth Illit official from Yisrael Beiteinu, announced a private initiative to pay $10,000 to every local Arab family that would agree to sell its home "and leave town forever." Gedalkin explained that his intention was to "maintain the Jewish character of Nazareth Illit." Shimon Gaspo, the mayor of the mostly Jewish *mitzpe* town located just north of Nazareth proper, praised the initiative, explaining that he was "all for a democratic Upper Nazareth, but first of all a Jewish one."

Gaspo claimed his inspiration derived from the State of Israel's founding fathers. "Just as [David] Ben-Gurion and [Shimon] Peres said in the 1950s that the Galilee must be Jewish, we say the same about Nazareth Illit [Upper Nazereth]," he wrote in a message posted on the city's official website. "The primary goal is to put the brakes on the demographic deterioration."

For her part, Zoabi saw the conflict inside Israel approaching a final breaking point. "The state is pushing to a crisis," she said. "If they disqualify Balad then no Arab party would enter the Knesset, and this would provoke a huge crisis. Arabs without a parliamentary role would result in a different kind of relationship between us and the state. This would be the end of democracy. But we know this is what a Jewish state will lead to—the end of democracy is an inevitable outcome."

Caliber 3: "The Values of Zionism"

When I left Zoabi's office and tried to find a minibus out of town, it was already dusk. And it was Shabbat, the Jewish weekly day of rest that turned vast sections of Israel into virtual ghost towns. Even in this mostly Arab city, there was virtually no public transportation that would take me back to my next destination, the coastal city of Haifa. My only option was to take a taxi to the town of Hadera, a minibus to Tel Aviv, and another one back up the coast to Haifa. It would be a tortuous journey, but I had interviews in Haifa I could not miss.

As soon as I boarded the bus from Hadera to Tel Aviv, a frumpy, middle-aged American man with thinning hair and sweat-stained, white-collared shirt stumbled in, bumping his head on the roof as he looked for a seat. "Is this going to Tel Aviv?" he shouted as he slumped into the chair directly beside me. "Tel Aviv? Tel Aviv?" he said in a tinny voice, craning his head around for a response. I did not want to get into a conversation with him, but I needed to put a halt to his incessant questions, so I told him yes. "You're from the US?" he immediately asked me. I tried to hide my grimace. I was exhausted and wanted to take a nap, but without any prompting, the man started into his story. He was a doctor from Long Island, New York, who had been working with a team of heart surgeons at a hospital in Jerusalem. With a few days off from his assignment, he decided to see some of the Holy Land.

As our minibus blasted down Israel's central coast toward Tel Aviv, we passed Jewish *mitzpim* built high on the hills to our left, and the remains of "abandoned" Arab homes on the coastal dunes to our right. The doctor peered out the window and nudged me with his elbow. "It's amazing what they've built, isn't it?" I was tempted to reply that it was almost as remarkable as what they had destroyed, but I had no appetite for antagonizing such a seemingly well-meaning, bumbling character. He was just another American Jew on the trip of his life to Eretz Israel, seeing what he wanted and projecting his dreams onto everything else.

Out of the blue, a skinny Russian teenager with wraparound shades and a gelled up fauxhawk demanded my attention from a few seats away. "Hey! Israel good?" he said, flashing a thumbs-up sign at me. "Israel good, yeah?" I pretended I couldn't hear him.

After a few minutes of conversation with the doctor, it became clear he had no idea where he was. He told me he had just visited a kibbutz in Gush Etzion, but it was no kibbutz—it was an illegal settlement in the West Bank. He extracted a T-shirt from his duffel bag and presented it to me with pride. It was emblazoned with a logo of a giant bullet inscribed with the name "Caliber 3." "On the kibbutz I went to a shooting range and did an antiterror training session with some special forces guys," the doctor told me. "These guys were elite soldiers, you know, they had been on missions in Lebanon, Gaza, everywhere. They did a drill for us and wow, you should have seen them knock down the targets, one terrorist after one another."

"Israel is good? Number one!" the Russian guy with the wraparounds muttered at me again.

I decided that if I answered in the affirmative, he might shut up. "Yeah Israel is good. Real good," I said in a flat tone. "It's the best country in the world. It made the desert bloom and invented the cherry tomato and the disk-on-key and nuclear ambiguity. You happy?" I flashed him a big, all-American thumbs up sign.

"Yaaaaa!" the Russian kid exclaimed, pumping his fist. He did not understand a word I was saying, but he seemed satisfied.

The doctor, for his part, had continued talking as though nothing had happened: "When we were on the shooting range, a few of the special forces guys told me the Hezbollah fighters, you know, the terrorists, are so wacked out on cocaine and PCP that they have to shoot them, like, forty times before they go down."

The scene he had conjured of pious Shia Muslims crowded around a glass table in the Dahiya District blowing rails of dusty roads before rushing headlong into a hail of machine-gun fire by a squad of Jewish Rambos was so absurd it could only have been lifted from the outtakes of an Orientalist exploitation film like *Delta Force*. But I did not dare ruin the doctor's action-revenge fantasy by making light of his experience. He reminded me of one of my distant relatives from the American Midwest, and I felt a faint sense of pity for him. And besides, the thrill of shooting swarthy "terrorists" with burly Israel commandos lurking over their shoulder is what droves of Jewish-American tourists flocked to the Caliber 3 for. The more tall antiterror tales they heard, the more their lurid fantasies were satiated. According to Caliber 3's promotional website, "At our program we combine together the values of Zionism with the excitement and enjoyment of shooting, which makes the activity more meaningful."

As soon as the tourists arrive at the Caliber 3 range, they are treated to a fifteen-minute "antiterror" demonstration that features a small team of crack soldiers rushing through a gauntlet of targets, knocking down one after another in a lightning-quick hail of bullets. Each target depicts a different Arab, though not necessarily the kind clad in a baklava that totes an AK-47 or bears any other identifiable "terrorist" trappings. Some look like average 1970s-era Palestinian men, with bushy moustaches, sideburns, dark sunglasses, and tight button-down shirts. A few are smiling. This might seem dangerously irresponsible to outsiders, but in fact, it reflects the genuine culture of an army that has seldom regarded distinctions between combatants and civilians as a top priority. "Twelve [years old] and up, you are allowed to shoot. That's what they tell us," an Israeli sniper told *Ha'aretz* correspondent Amira Hass in 2004, during the height of the Second Intifada. "This is according to what the IDF says to its soldiers. I do not know if this is what the IDF says to the media."

After observing the drill, tourists turn from spectators to participants, firing on Arab targets with the guidance of their commando instructors. "Your mommy won't be here to protect you, so stand up like a man," an instructor shouted at a fourteen-year-old American teen after handing him an automatic rifle. "Are you ready to take out a terrorist?"

"Yes I am," the boy proclaimed.

According to a profile of Caliber 3 published in *Yedioth Ahronoth*, a forty-year-old Miami banker named Michael Brown brought his entire family to the shooting range to "teach them values." *Yedioth* reported:

> Upon entering the range, his five-year-old daughter, Tamara, bursts into tears. A half hour later, she is holding a gun and shooting clay bullets like a pro.
>
> "This is part of their education," Michael says as he proudly watches his daughter. "They should know where they come from and also feel some action."

Halfway through the minibus ride down the coast, the doctor from Long Island trailed off, allowing me to sink into a deep slumber. I awoke with the side of my face pasted to the grease-stained window of the *sherut*. We were parked at the base of Tel Aviv's noisy central bus station, and the van was empty except for me. I stumbled toward the bus station entrance, opening my bag for the mandatory, slipshod search by a disheveled-looking private security guard posted at the gate. Then I headed into the bustling, soot-caked terminal, up the concrete reinforced staircase leading to the nuclear fallout shelter, to get a "toast" at one of the food kiosks on the sixth floor. The toasted cardboard-like sandwiches, filled with varieties of canned meat, salad vegetables, and processed cheese had become the staple of my diet inside Israel, where I rarely had time to sit down for a proper meal.

My next stop was Haifa, a picturesque city on Israel's northern coast that was home to about 260,000 Jews and 30,000 Palestinian Israelis. It was a "mixed" city known as a redoubt from the enforced cultural homogeneity that presided over much of the country. With its long history of socialist labor organizing and laid back, beachfront atmosphere, Haifa felt a bit freer than the demographically homogenous Tel Aviv. However, the deeper I explored Haifa's Arab community, the more I was forced to conclude that there was no sanctuary.

PART IV

OUTCASTS

A Lesson in Israeli Democracy

Just a short walk away from Haifa's Hof HaKarmel train terminal stands a warren of crumbling stone homes with windows filled with cement. They are "absentee properties," the once grand houses of upper-middle class Palestinians driven from the city by Zionist militias during 1947 and '48, now left empty by the state, which holds them in perpetuity for refugees whose return it will never allow, and which has placed some on the real estate market in violation of international law. The abandoned homes can be found all over Haifa—along the beach and on the hills overlooking the city's municipal courthouse, itself constructed on confiscated Palestinian land. And only those who managed to maintain total ignorance to Haifa's past and present could avoid seeing the remnants of the Nakba that fester like open sores on the city's scenic landscape.

When Zionist militias descended on Haifa in early 1948, the traditional coexistence between Jews and Arabs still presided. But Mordechai Maklef, the commander of the Carmeli Brigade charged with ethnically cleansing the city, was determined to change all that. His soldiers blared orders through loud speakers for the Arab population to evacuate, then he instructed them, "Kill any Arab you encounter, torch all inflammable objects, and force doors open with explosives." The orders came to fruition in February 1948 (months before Israel declared its "independence"), when Zionist militias rolled barrels of explosives from Haifa's Jewish neighborhood down on the city's Al 'Abasyah Arab neighborhood, forcing its residents to flee in terror.

Two months later, the Carmeli Brigade shelled Haifa's central marketplace, sending the rest of the Palestinian population rushing toward the shore. There, as they frantically boarded boats to Lebanon, Gaza, and Acre—now an Israeli city renamed "Akko" where many would be expelled again just weeks later—they were literally thrown into the sea. According to an eyewitness chronicle of the scene, "Men stepped on their friends, and women on their own children. The boats in the port were soon filled with living cargo. The overcrowding in them was horrible. Many turned over and sank with all their passengers."

When I first arrived in Haifa in June 2010, the port hosted a ship that served as a powerful reminder that the Nakba was an ongoing process—that the past was not even past, as William Faulkner had said of the American South. It was the rickety Turkish cruise liner raided by Israeli naval commandos and towed back to Haifa— the *Mavi Marmara*—where the blood of its dead and wounded passengers was promptly hosed off of the top deck. While the Israeli government turned a deaf ear to Turkey's requests to return the ship, Haifa mayor Yonah Yahav introduced a novel, if not remarkably macabre, idea: "If Israel decides to confiscate the Turkish ship, I ask for it to be given to the city of Haifa to turn it into a floating hotel opposite the city's shore," Yahav wrote in a letter to Defense Minister Ehud Barak. Without any apparent sense of irony, the mayor added, "I feel that Haifa, a symbol of coexistence and cooperation between all religions, would be the appropriate home for this ship, which will turn into an international symbol of reconciliation and hope."

While the Israeli government struggled to clean up the mess it made on the *Mavi Marmara*, Haifa's Arab community reeled from the disappearance of one of its most forceful political leaders: Ameer Makhoul, a human rights activist who had emerged as one of the effective operators in Palestinian-Israeli civil society. Early in the morning on May 6, Makhoul's wife, Janan Abdu, heard a hard knock at the door. Fifteen men and one woman stood in the shadows demanding entry. Most were masked members of the *Yassam*—heavily armed Israeli riot police—while the rest were grim-looking Shin Bet agents. As soon as Abdu opened the door, the cops rushed inside, opening drawers and cabinets, tossed belongings on the floor, and rushed out with the laptops and cellphones, including those belonging to Makhoul's two adolescent daughters.

Still clothed in her pajamas, Abdu confronted a Shin Bet agent, demanding to see a court order giving them permission for such an invasive search. "Who is the man of the house? Where is your husband?" he bellowed.

Makhoul stepped forward and clasped onto Abdu's hand. "We both are," he answered. "This is *our* house."

"Sit down," the agent commanded Abdu, pointing to the family's couch. "We are arresting your husband."

As the police led Makhoul away in handcuffs, Abdu admonished the Shin Bet agent, "This is a great lesson for my daughters in their citizenship. What my daughters see of your hatred toward us, I will never be able to erase. This is a great lesson in racism and unfairness. And you will never be able to bullshit them later when you try to teach them about citizenship and Israeli democracy."

Abdu welcomed me into the salon of her modest apartment in Haifa's Wadi Nisnas neighborhood in late June 2010, just weeks after the traumatic incident. She was slender and strikingly pretty, with high, angular cheekbones and straight, naturally light brown hair. While we sat in her living room and talked, her daughters, both adolescents who shared her sandy brown hair and her husband's greenish eyes, scampered in and out of the house, seemingly impervious to the presence of yet another journalist. Abdu was still shaken by the Shin Bet's invasion of her home. She trembled with anger when she recounted the nightmarish incident that seemed at the center of her thoughts, as though she relived it several times a day.

Abdu had recently learned that Makhoul's arrest warrant was issued on April 22 while he was attempting to help a group of Bedouins fight Israel's plan to destroy their village in the southern Negev Desert. "They had two weeks to come to his office or to get him at home at a normal hour if they wanted," she told me. "So it wasn't by accident that they chose to come at 3 a.m.—it was to terrify us and to take him away while he's worried about his family and what's going on. They used his concern about his family when they interrogated him. It was all about humiliation."

Only a week before I met Abdu, both her parents died—her father from cancer and her mother from an asthma attack compounded by grief. At almost the same time, she had to attend her oldest daughter's high school graduation ceremony without her husband. It was an emotionally wrenching time. "My daughters are filled with anger now," Abdu confided. "When we wait at Gilboa prison, which is an hour away, for two hours in the hot sun and a bad situation, they stare at the jailers sitting inside with air-conditioning and burn with anger. Sometimes it's so humiliating it becomes too much."

Abdu said since her husband's case made national news, she received an outpouring of support from people across the country who considered the arrest a grave escalation of the state's authoritarian measures. She had also received a pile of hate mail, including several letters marked with swastikas. The case had begun to complicate her part-time job at a shelter for battered women and sexually abused children. "Now part of the trauma that affected me because of my husband makes it impossible for me to deal with others going through trauma," Abdu told me. "I can't bear the emotional effort anymore. We serve a mixed group of Arabs and Jews, and I'm not able to be in a place anymore where some of the women I work with can threaten me in a racist way for refusing to be her therapist. I just can't take it."

Like many of the more assertive Palestinian political activists inside Israel, Makhoul and Abdu knew they were being watched, but didn't know to what degree. Makhoul's arrest exposed the state's spying as an aggressive, hell-bent operation that had recorded thousands of his phone calls—as many as thirteen thousand—over the last decade. Once he was jailed, he had to endure what was perhaps the cruelest violation of privacy: all communications with his wife, from letters to phone calls to the "non-contact" visits he was limited to, would be monitored and recorded by the Shin Bet.

The state had hounded Makhoul since at least 2001, when he served as president of the Arab delegation at the United Nations Durban Conference Against Racism. It was there that he initiated the campaign to indict the State of Israel for the crime of apartheid, an effort that has since emerged as a central plank in the growing international movement to boycott, sanction, and divest from Israel, known as BDS. As the years went on, Makhoul amplified his calls for a single democratic state between the river and the sea in which all enjoyed equal rights and representations. He did so not as the chairman of any political party, but as the leader of Itijah, the most prominent civil society umbrella group campaigning for Palestinian rights inside Israel. At the grassroots level, he was arguably more influential than any Arab member of Knesset.

In 2000, Makhoul's brother Issam, then a member of Knesset, went public with Israel's worst-kept secret: its nuclear weapons program. In a Knesset debate in 2000, Issam Makhoul warned that the production of nuclear warheads had turned the country into "a poisonous nuclear waste bin" that threatened the lives of all its residents. With most right-wing legislators absent, the accusation of treason fell to leaders of the Zionist left like the Labor Party's Ophir Pines-Paz, who denounced him for "committing a crime against Israeli Arabs today." Three years later, Issam Makhoul narrowly survived an assassination attempt when a small, sophisticated bomb exploded beneath his car as he pulled out of his driveway. "I know your game. You eat Jews. People like you shouldn't stay in this country!" a rightist former Knesset member barked at him during a debate on a popular radio talk show two weeks after the bombing. The Jewish terrorist who was later convicted of attempting to assasinate Issam Makhoul, Alexander Rabinovitch, received a prison term of just four years.

Ameer Makhoul's prosecution marked the latest phase in the state's campaign against the Palestinian-Israeli political leadership, which had already claimed the career of Azmi Bishara. Like Bishara, Makhoul was accused of spying for Hezbollah—"assisting an enemy in war"—a crime that carried a penalty of lifetime imprisonment. Just weeks before Makhoul's arrest, Omar Said, a leading Balad Party activist, was arrested at the Jordanian border and eventually charged with meeting the same Hezbollah official. According to the Shin Bet's indictment, which was revealed despite a media gag order, Said met the official at a conference he attended in Egypt and rejected his request to spy for Hezbollah.

As details of the case seeped out, the Shin Bet's "evidence" appeared increasingly absurd. The alleged Hezbollah official who was said to have attempted to hire Said and Makhoul turned out to be Hassan Jaja, a landscape contractor from Jordan who operated an NGO in Lebanon dedicated to repairing the environmental damage caused by Israeli airstrikes during its 2006 bombing campaign. Makhoul, a committed environmentalist, was said to have met Jaja, possibly to discuss his rebuilding projects. Unfortunately for Makhoul, Jaja had become the Shin Bet's all-purpose "Hezbollah agent" whose name could be used to implicate virtually any Palestinian activist they deemed a threat to state security.

Jamal Juma, a leading Palestinian activist known for his coordination of nonviolent protests in the West Bank against the Israeli separation wall, was arrested and held incommunicado for weeks in an Israeli military prison, after being accused of meeting with Jaja. Curiously, Juma was released without being charged. For Makhoul's part, he was accused of a grave breach of national security for his alleged coffee date with Jaja, who happened to be an avid grower of herbs and a practitioner of traditional Arabic medicine with no known record of Hezbollah involvement.

In Abdu's view, her husband's prosecution was a ploy to discourage Palestinian citizens of Israel from forging bonds of solidarity with the wider Arab world. "Ameer always said the Arab world is not our enemy—it's our natural community," Abdu remarked. "Now, if I meet someone abroad I'm supposed to be afraid that he's an Arab and ask him if he's from Hezbollah. It's ironic that if I meet a French or Italian person at a conference, I don't have to ask him if he's from an illegal group, but if I meet an Arab, I am not only supposed to ask him, I'm supposed to tell the Shin Bet I met him as soon as I come back to Israel."

Orna Kohn, a Jewish Israeli member of Makhoul's defense team who worked on the staff at the Palestinian-Israeli legal rights group Adalah, told me Makhoul's indictment was simply part of an ongoing campaign to crush the new generation of Arab political leadership inside Israel. "The arrests are all related to the fear of these figures refusing to accept the Jewishness of the State of Israel. Once accepting Israel as a 'Jewish state' became the central demand of negotiations under [former prime minister] Ehud Olmert, it put intense pressure on the Palestinians living inside Israel. Forcing the Palestinians to accept the Jewishness of the state, which is like giving blacks the right to vote in South Africa only on the condition that they accept apartheid—that is the key issue now. Because of their refusal to give up their identity, the Palestinian citizens of Israel have become the biggest obstacle to the Zionist dream."

In days after Makhoul's arrest, while Abdu and her allies sought for his whereabouts, the Shin Bet held him incommunicado, apparently torturing him during long interrogations designed to coerce him into confessing his "crime." Finally, after twelve days, an Israeli judge allowed Makhoul to meet for ten minutes with Abdu and a team of lawyers who had assembled to defend him. "Ameer was not able to make eye contact with us," Abdu recalled. "The lawyers were shocked—he was exhausted, with bruises all over his arms, between his fingers, and with yellow welts across his face."

Makhoul described to them the torture he had just endured, telling the lawyers how Shin Bet agents tied him in a low chair bolted to the ground, binding his arms and legs so each time he moved, it intensified the amount of strain on his joints. He was not allowed to sleep for a full day and denied the chance to bathe. Then he was left for almost two weeks in a tiny cell only two meters wide without a mattress or blankets. According to Abdu, the Shin Bet manipulated the temperature in the room in order to keep him in a constant state of discomfort, but without allowing him to develop hypothermia.

In a country that had not lifted its state of emergency since its foundation, and which instead extended the emergency regulations to allow the state unfettered control over everything from land seizures to ice cream production, just about anything could be justified on the grounds of national security. As Supreme Court Justice Elyakim Rubinstein attempted to explain in a decision affirming the continuation of emergency law, "Israel is a normal country that is not normal."

By cultivating an atmosphere of perpetual siege, the state was able to classify citizen activists like Makhoul as "security prisoners," depriving them of basic civil rights protections, including the right to attorney-client privilege, without risking a substantial public outcry. "We can't talk to Ameer without the phone taping system and a glass wall," Kohn told me at the time. "We are not even allowed to talk through the glass without a phone. So we can't discuss our defense. How do you prepare a defense when you can't talk to your client about the most important factors without the Shabak [Shin Bet] recording everything for the prosecution?"

After arresting Makhoul, the Shin Bet imposed a blanket gag order on the Israeli media, threatening to strip any Israeli news outlet of its press license for revealing details of the arrest. The clampdown on press freedom might have enraged members of the Israeli media, but none dared to risk the wrath of the dreaded Shin Bet. And so, for several days, the Israeli print and broadcast media faithfully observed the gag order. On May 10, when tens of thousands of Palestinian Israelis gathered for a spontaneous rally to protest Makhoul's arrest—"steps reminiscent of dark dictatorships," according to the emergency announcement—*Ha'aretz* reported the massive protest in a small item on page ten, next to the obituary section, without specifying why the demonstrators had mobilized. Until the following day, when the gag order was lifted, no Israeli news outlet even dared allude to Makhoul's detention.

The role of publicizing Makhoul's arrest fell to a small, defiant band of left-wing Israeli bloggers. Besides Rechavia Berman and Yossi Gurvitz, the online writers included Idan Landau, a Ben Gurion University linguistics professor and protégé of Noam Chomsky who was denied part of his university salary and sentenced to prison for refusing to perform mandatory army reserve duty. And Richard Silverstein, a Seattle-based Jewish-American blogger who often broke Israeli gag orders on security-related stories, brought the disappearance of Makhoul to a worldwide audience by translating the bloggers' reports into English. He then formed a "Free Ameer Makhoul" Facebook group that became a clearinghouse for commentary about Makhoul. "Media outlets in Israel won't violate a gag order for fear of losing their press license, or they're just cowardly," Silverstein told me. "So this is where I came into the picture."

Silverstein broke his first Shin Bet gag order in March 2010, when he became the first person to publish details of the arrest of Anat Kamm, a twenty-four-year-old Israeli journalist who had been serving at the time as a clerk in the office of Israeli army Central Command director Major Yair Naveh. For two months, news of Kamm's arrest was suppressed by a Shin Bet gag order, and by the complicity of the Israeli media. Kamm was accused of leaking thousands of secret Israeli army documents to reporters, including the intrepid *Ha'aretz* military correspondent Uri Blau, revealing the army's willful disregard for a Supreme Court ruling requiring soldiers to avoid assassinating Palestinian militants who complied with arrest orders. According to the documents Kamm supplied Blau, which he later revealed on the pages of *Ha'aretz*, the army was given explicit approval to execute unarmed militant leaders, even if they consented to arrest—a liberty they took in several cases.

Kamm was initially charged with endangering national security, a crime that carried a penalty of life in prison. But unlike Makhoul, who was held for a time in solitary confinement and kept under lock and key, Kamm was allowed to remain under house arrest. In fact, a journalist friend in Tel Aviv told me during the summer of 2010 that Kamm was seeking a roommate who was willing to fetch her groceries and tolerate her chain smoking.

Perhaps the principal difference between Kamm and Makhoul—besides the fact that she was Jewish and he was not—was that she was clearly guilty of the crime of exposing army lawlessness, while the charges against Makhoul were dubious at best. The bloggers' coverage of Kamm's case prompted an article in widely read online American publication, the Daily Beast, by Judith Miller, the former *New York Times* reporter. (Miller gained notoriety for her reports that Iraq possessed weapons of mass destruction, and went to jail to protect her conversations with Scooter Libby, Vice President Cheney's chief of staff, who was indicted and eventually convicted of perjury and obstruction of justice in a case stemming from the White House campaign to defame former ambassador Joseph Wilson, who at the CIA's behest reported that one of the George W. Bush administration accounts related to Saddam Hussein's weapons of mass destruction was bogus, and reveal the identity of his wife, covert CIA officer Valerie Plame.) The Miller article on Kamm led to a burst of coverage by major news outlets, embarrassing the Israeli government and possibly complicating its case against Kamm. But Makhoul received no such interest among mainstream American reporters.

"Judy Miller was willing to do the Kamm story probably because she saw a nice Jewish girl in trouble, and the gag order was an attack on press freedom," Silverstein commented to me. "But with Makhoul, there was no Judy Miller to tell the world about his persecution. If only some celebrity journalist had written about the case, it would have made a huge difference." According to Abdu, "The Israeli media—most of it—made [Makhoul] appear guilty. Instead of referring to him as "the suspected spy," they called him, 'the spy.' And as soon as he was charged, they all disappeared."

Since 1967, the State of Israel has detained at least 750,000 Palestinians in its prisons, including 10,000 women. According to the Palestinian prisoner rights group, Adameer, Israel currently holds over 4,500 political prisoners, including more than 200 children and 322 people jailed without charges—those it has labeled "administrative detainees." In its prosecutions of so-called security prisoners like Makhoul, the state boasts a 99.74 percent conviction rate. Many of the magistrate judges who rule in such cases gained their initial legal experience presiding over the military justice system that rules the occupied West Bank, learning through a day-to-day routine of show trials to accept Shin Bet and army's arguments as gospel.

A perfect exhibit of the seamless nexus between Israel's judicial system and the military was Einat Ron, the magistrate judge who approved the gag order in Anat Kamm's case. For much of her career, Ron served as the army's chief military prosecutor, advising the army to lie to human rights groups to cover up the killing of an eleven-year-old Palestinian boy, Khalil al Mughrabi, by a group of soldiers in 2003. Even after Ron's deceit made the pages of the international media, she was promoted to serve in Israel's civilian court system. With her record of complete deference to the army and the security services, perhaps she was the perfect judge to rule on a case like Kamm's. In the end, Kamm received four and a half years in jail for exposing the army's illegal killings, a conviction that revealed the power the occupation exerted over Israel's legal system and the whole of society. Uri Blau, the reporter who relied on Kamm's documents to publicize the killings, was prosecuted and sentenced to four months in prison for possession of classified information without intent to harm state security.

Like so many other Palestinian "security prisoners," Makhoul was presented with a stark option: go to trial and face an almost certain conviction, leading to a possible lifetime sentence, or sign a plea bargain granting him a lighter sentence in exchange for an admission of guilt. The plea deal would validate the Shin Bet's bogus indictment, but it would allow him to reunite with his wife and daughters in a few years.

On his lawyers' advice, he accepted it, receiving a sentence of nine years in the Gilboa prison for a lesser charge than "aiding an enemy in war." (Omar Said also took a plea deal, resulting in a seven-month sentence). There, he would share facilities with Palestinians arrested in the Occupied Territories, helping coordinate and report on the landmark hunger strikes that they planned in the near future, and which weakened the impact of repressive Shin Bet measures such as administrative detention and solitary confinement.

Left at home without her husband, Abdu redoubled her efforts to publicize his case, and despite the lingering trauma of his disappearance, delved into human rights activism with renewed intensity. "I have no choice but to campaign for my rights," she told me. "It's not enough to just live. This is about how to live. It's not enough to eat and drink and be able to say, 'I'm alive.' You have to have the right to be proud of who you are and to hold on to your dignity, to preserve your rights as a human being and be part of a community. So for me, the choice is between two things: to be or not to be."

Just Being a Guy

An hour after I left Janan Abdu's home, I was sitting on a plastic chair in the garden at Youssef's, a local *sheesha* spot that served as one of the few gathering places for Haifa's young Arab men. Seated across from me and sharing a *hookah* were Ala and Amir, both Haifa University graduates in their mid-twenties. Though neither was involved in any form of activism, the Shin Bet had called each in for an interrogation during the past year, a bewildering experience that neither could fully explain. Fearing more Shin Bet harassment, they asked me not to use their last names in anything I published. I had not expected anything beyond a leisurely chat, but as soon as we sat down, Ala and Amir made it clear they wanted to tell me all about their situation. They were not particularly political, but life in Israel was becoming unbearable for them and their community. And instead of joining the struggle, they were among those seeking an exit strategy.

With designer jeans and a polo shirt, Ala could have passed for a young professional in any city in the world. He had sandy brown hair with a tuft that hung over his forehead, accentuating his boyish features. Amir arrived wearing a T-shirt and shorts. He was heavyset and jocular, laughing heartily at the sarcastic asides I used to break up the mood when I sensed the discussion was becoming excessively gloomy. The two were at the top of the Palestinian totem pole, with Israeli ID's that allowed them the freedom to travel everywhere except "enemy" Arab states. When we met, Ala and Amir were preparing for a trip to Switzerland, a choice summer destination for young Western backpackers seeking rugged outdoor fun.

The two earned a good living in Haifa's booming tech sector, a conglomerate of start-up companies and multinational corporations drawing largely from the talent cultivated at the city's Technion University, known as Israel's version of MIT. Haifa's tech "miracle" inspired the title of a best-selling book *Start-Up Nation*, coauthored by Dan Senor, an adviser to Mitt Romney in his presidential campaign and a former public relations official in the Coalition Provisional Authority that governed Iraq after the invasion. The book had become a key vehicle for Israeli *hasbara,* with innovative start-ups serving as a counterweight against charges of human rights violations. Jerusalem-based writer David Hazony hailed the publication of *Start-Up Nation* as one of the three biggest *hasbara* triumphs of 2010, gushing, "Singer and Senor succeeded in changing the subject and constructing a positive image of Israel that is not all war."

Because Israel's tech sector was intimately intertwined with its military apparatus—Technion was a key idea factory for the army's robotic warfare projects—it
was virtually free of Palestinians. Indeed, Ala and Amir were among the only 2.8
percent of Arabs who had found places in Israel's *Start-Up Nation*. The exclusive
environment was largely the byproduct of the influence of Israeli army's Unit 8200,
a hyper-secretive cyber-warfare division that trained soldiers in the dark arts of
surveillance and hacking before sending them off into the job market. As Tobias
Buck reported in *Financial Times*, "One important reason for the ubiquity of 8200
alumni in the high-tech sector is personal connections. Many Israeli start-ups are
founded by men and women who worked together in the unit. When hiring new
engineers and programmers, [start-up founders] typically turn to their former unit
[Unit 8200], safe in the knowledge that the military has invested heavily in selecting
and training its recruits."

Few start-up companies reported receiving so few applications from qualified
Arabs in Israel, while many of those who managed to find jobs in the industry found
the social climate unbearable. For Ala, the hostility began at the Technion, where
one of his professors changed the username on his computer to "Terrorist." Hired
to work on nanotechnology at a local firm, Ala fell out of favor with his coworkers
during Operation Cast Lead.

"I work in a small firm so everyone is like family," he told me. "And during the
attack, all the Israelis I worked with were watching their news channels reporting
from the outside, showing a little puff of smoke and then announcing, 'We're winning!' I was watching Al Jazeera, and I saw the suffering inside Gaza. One day, five
of them cornered me and began shouting all the propaganda at me that they were
hearing on the news. I realized that if I wanted to keep my job I had to stop arguing,
but that only added to my stress."

Ala had lost a close friend during the October 2000 riots, during which young
Palestinians demonstrated in solidarity with the West Bank and Gaza, and were
mowed down by Border Police gunfire. "I told them that you have the green light for
any action necessary to bring about the rule of law," Ehud Barak, then the prime minister, said of his instructions to the security chiefs he gathered in his living room for
a meeting about suppressing the demonstrations. When the smoke cleared, thirteen
unarmed civilians—all young Palestinian citizens of Israel from the cities of Nazareth, Haifa, and Umm al-Fahm—lay dead. Scores more were badly injured by the
fusillade of rubber bullets the Border Police sprayed into crowds of demonstrators.
After the killings, Ala watched with dismay as the Israeli government ignored the
findings of the Or Commission, a badly flawed government inquiry into the police
shooting of rioters that nonetheless admonished the state to "work to wipe out the
stain of discrimination against its Arab citizens, in its various forms and expressions."

The October 2001 killings were a transformative event for the Oslo generation of
Arab youth inside Israel. "The Palestinian minority in Israel is more vocal and more
aware in struggling for the rights it was denied during the Oslo era in the nineties,"
Orna Kohn, the lawyer from the Adalah Center for Legal Rights, told me. "They are

thinking about more than what they have and what benefits they can receive, and instead about their rights as citizens. And since they have been told over and over that they live in a democracy, not a tyranny, the ongoing discrimination made it inevitable that the struggle would get more serious. Then, of course, there was also those who just gave up and want to leave for a better life somewhere else."

Ala's views neatly encapsulated the sensibility of the post-Oslo generation of Palestinian youth inside Israel. "All we are asking for is equality," he said, "for better schools, for new parks, and urbanization policies, but from their point of view, this would lead to social disorder. So they keep our villages in the old way—they reinforce the patriarchy, the family feuds, all to keep distracted from our rights."

"What gets to me the most is that we are still called a demographic threat," Amir added. "A state in the twenty-first century where major government officials use the term, 'demographic bomb'? Never mind that the birthrate is going down so much that this isn't even an issue. It's just so insulting."

According to Ala, though he had access to employment and opportunities for economic advancement, the gap between him and less-educated Arabs in Israel was yawning. Besides the fact that Arab schools were badly overcrowded and under-resourced—his younger sister was struggling to learn in a classroom with forty other students—the Judaization policies in the Galilee had deliberately stifled development in Arab towns. "You can't break out of the patriarchal structure, and you're just stuck there," he said. "Whether it's the lack of health clinics or good schools, the whole program is systematic."

Ala pointed me to a report in *Ha'aretz* dated February 13, 2008, that he said "drove him crazy." It opened:

> The Interior Ministry plans to submit to the government a proposal this year to build a new Arab city, Interior Minister Meir Sheetrit (Kadima) announced yesterday. If the plan goes through, it will be the first time such a city is built in Israel, aside from towns meant to absorb the Bedouin.
>
> "The aim is a modern city that any young couple will be able to buy a house in and live there, as in any other modern city in the world," Sheetrit said.

To Ala's chagrin, just as soon as the new Arab city was proposed—the first of its kind since Israel's foundation—the plan was withdrawn following indignant protests by legislators such as David Rotem. "The government has lost its Zionism entirely," Rotem howled. This left Haifa as one of the only escapes from the state-engineered stagnation of village life. "There is limited parking and no parks in our neighborhoods here," Amir commented, "but Haifa is still attractive for Arabs. It has a more liberal setting than other cities. You can feel unbound from tradition here."

But even in the big city, Arabs experienced sustained pressure to participate in the Jewish state's security sector. "We overheard five guys talking the other day about how they wanted to be a security guard at a coffee shop or a hospital," Ala recalled. "You can't really be friends with most people here or talk to them about serious things. It's hard to blame them because they have no motivation to do anything out-side the box. But then you start to feel alone when you only have four or five friends."

The pressure was so extreme it played out in everyday conversations. "Every Arab here has made an active decision on whether they want to use the Arabic pronun-ciation of the letter 'r' or the Jewish way when they speak Hebrew," Ala remarked.

"A psychologist told me the Arabs who use the Jewish 'r' are trying to show the Jews that they are the Good Arabs," Amir added. "Or they roll their 'r's the Arabic way to show they're not inferior. There are no institutions in this country to promote multicultural values so everyone has to figure out their own way to deal with the situation."

While typing Ala and Amir's comments in my laptop, I thought about my friend Yasmina (name changed to protect identity), a twenty-four-year-old Arab woman who had left Nazareth, where she was raised by a prominent Muslim family, for the hipster scene of Tel Aviv. She had dated Jewish men, including a soldier, partied at bohemian bars, vacationed in Berlin—a favorite summer getaway spot for young Israelis—and maintained a vegan lifestyle that annoyed her father, who was the quintessential meat-eating, conservative patriarch. If I accompanied Yasmina any-where near Tel Aviv's trendy Rothschild Boulevard, there was hardly a place we could go without a few Ashkenazi hipsters rushing forward to greet her. In fact, she hosted her own semi-satirical Facebook fan club with more than forty members—mostly Jewish Israeli guys who hung around the local bohemian and activist scene.

Yasmina could speak Hebrew with a flawless Jewish Israeli accent. She claimed this helped her insinuate herself into the homogenously Jewish cultural framework of Tel Aviv. Her linguistic skills came in handy when she dropped me off at Ben Gurion International Airport in June 2009. At a checkpoint outside the airport where Arabs were frequently taken out of their vehicles for lengthy searches, she passed through with ease. "The soldier thought I was Jewish," Yasmina told me with a con-tented grin. "With my Hebrew, I can convince most Israelis that I'm a Jewish girl, maybe from Iraq or Yemen."

Though she had easily assimilated into a mostly Jewish, Europeanized social set-ting, Yasmina could hardly be called a "sellout" or even a "Good Arab." Only a few of her Jewish friends knew that she had named her bicycle "Toufiq" after Toufiq Zayyad, the Palestinian Israeli poet and politician who helped organize the first Land Day protests. She made no secret of her rejection of Zionism, and few of her Tel Aviv friends seemed threatened by it. "The Israeli flag will never represent me, and I will never feel at home in this place as long as it waves over my head," she confided to me once. No one could have questioned her desire for equal rights, however; when faced with a choice between the suffocating environment of village life, the activ-ist path of unending, rancorous struggle, and the individualistic, cloistered cultural bubble of Tel Aviv life, with its Western European escape valve, the last option was the most appealing. For her and for many other educated, cosmopolitan Arabs, even the fleeting illusion of normality was better than the destiny assigned to them by the Jewish state.

Ala and Amir told me they understood Yasmina's choice, even if they chose to handle the same predicament in a different way. I asked them if they ever thought about leaving Israel for good. "Only a few of us have the opportunity to leave, so there is not that much guilt around the issue," Ala said. "But everyone who does have the opportunity—especially Arab Christians—they are at least thinking about it."

He added, "In this place, sometimes you want to stop being an Arab and just start being a guy."

Leaving Haifa

Whenever I was in Haifa, I often arranged to rendezvous with my friends and contacts at Fatoush, a Palestinian restaurant that used to serve as a wine cellar for the German Templars during the Crusades. This area, now known as the German Colony, is in a particularly touristy section of Haifa. The restaurant is located on Ben Gurion Avenue, a long promenade that leads west toward the spectacular Bahai Gardens atop Mount Carmel, where the administrative heart of the world's Bahai religious community is located. While seated at a long table in Fatoush's outdoor garden, listening to a mélange of English, Arabic, and Hebrew amid a crowd of Palestinians, Jews, and internationals, it is sometimes possible to imagine the kind of place Israel could be if it ever managed to shed its settler-colonial armor. However, the atmosphere of easy coexistence that sometimes blossomed inside the gardens of Fatoush did not develop because of the prevailing culture of Haifa, but in spite of it.

Throughout the day, small groups of young soldiers can be seen milling around Ben Gurion Avenue. Some wear uniforms, while some just wear shorts and a T-shirt. But the automatic rifle slung over the shoulder seems to be a requisite piece of fashion. Many of the soldiers are on leave, staying at a hotel-style barracks on the street. Others are stationed at the nearby naval cadet school. They are the pride of Israeli society, members of its most respected institution—an army that most Jewish citizens believe protects them from imminent destruction. But to local Palestinian Arabs, the uniforms and weapons represent an omnipresent symbol of hostility and aggression. "To them, they are serving their country," Ala commented. "But to me, their presence is an attack on me and who I am." Amir added, "I can't stand seeing their guns every time I walk out on the street. I hate what it reminds me of."

By chance, on the night after I met Ala and Amir, I encountered a young woman who dared to challenge Haifa's militaristic environment, and whose symbolic act of defiance led to her expulsion from Israeli society.

After I left Youssef's café, my friend Fadi (name changed), a twenty-five-year-old videographer I had met while he was studying at New York University, picked me up in a car filled with two twenty-something Palestinian women. We drove to an apartment in the hills of Haifa, high above the harbor, and gathered in a salon with a bottle of arak, a cheap, highly alcoholic anise-based aperitif. As Fadi, who was ubiquitous at leftist cultural happenings from Tel Aviv to Jenin, busied himself with the younger woman, I fell into conversation with the other, who spoke better English. She was a club promoter and bartender named Fidaa Kiwan. With a nose ring, a leather armband, and a brash demeanor, she reminded me of a prettier, Levantine version of Janis Joplin. Fidaa had heard from Fadi that I was a journalist and was now eager to tell me about her year from hell.

More than a year ago, Fidaa and a business partner opened a café in Haifa called Azad, or "Free People." With its easygoing, bohemian atmosphere and constantly flowing supply of Tayybeh, a local Palestinian beer, Azad became a favorite of young people and creative class types from around the country, both Arabs and Jews. To cultivate the café as a sanctuary of equal coexistence, its owners insisted on enforcing a policy that defied Israeli society's culture of militarism: "No uniforms allowed" read the sign on its door. The policy applied not just to soldiers, but also to boy scouts and security personnel—to anyone identified with the state's exclusive institutions.

"It was our café, and we wanted to keep it clear of any barriers to an open dialogue," she told me while I threw back another glass of arak. "We thought we would stand up for local values and that meant that our identity as Palestinians had to be respected. So why should we allow people to bring guns inside and wear uniforms that we identify with our own oppression?"

In February 2010, an army sergeant named Raviv Roth stomped into the café in his uniform with a gun slung over his shoulder and demanded service. "I told him we have a policy against uniforms, so if he comes back in civilian clothes I will be happy to serve him and I'll give him the best service he's ever had," Fidaa recalled. Instead of returning without his olive drab, the young man called his father, a well-connected local politician, who promptly called the police, demanding they shut down the café. But when the police arrived, they told the angry young man there was nothing they could do: Azad had the right to refuse service to customers just as other private businesses in Israel did. "The guy was used to being treated like he ran the show," Fidaa said. "I didn't break any laws at all, but he and his father believed there was a higher law I had to follow."

Within hours, reports of Fidaa's policy and the insult it caused to the golden sons and daughters of Eretz Israel were broadcast on the Israeli national news to an audience of millions. As the national outrage mounted, one Israeli citizen took the initiative, forming a Facebook group called "Boycott Azad." Thousands of Israelis joined almost overnight, filling the page with vitriolic commentary about Fidaa, her café, and Palestinians in general. "What really set me over the edge," recalled Ala, "was seeing hundreds and hundreds of people posting all those racist talkbacks and threats on the Boycott Azad Facebook page, and doing it under their own names, next to their pictures, like they were proud to think this way."

In March, a mob of Israeli students and soldiers, including members of the Likud-linked Im Tirtzu student group, rallied outside the café, waving flags and holding signs that read "Don't discriminate against soldiers" and "Soldiers keep us safe." After a raucous rendition of the Israeli national anthem, protesters climbed atop the roof of Azad and draped Israeli flags over the café's sign, while blocking the view of the patrons inside with an even larger Israeli flag. A few police officers stood by and watched without doing a thing. Images of the scene recalled images from Shuhada Street in Hebron, where violent Jewish settlers living under the protection of Israeli soldiers have forced hundreds of Palestinian shops to close, marking the triumph of each store driven out of business by spray-painting a Star of David on its front door, or by planting an Israeli flag on its roof.

The episode shook the local Palestinian community. At the leftist bars located near Azad on Haifa's Masada Street, the attacks were discussed in terms of a decisive social rupture. "What happened with Azad was a terrible sign. We're just waiting for the next escalation now," a local theater director told me.

To young Palestinian Arabs like Fadi, the episode smacked of hypocrisy. "I can't get into half the nightclubs in Tel Aviv," Fadi remarked to me, "because the bouncers will stand outside asking everyone for proof of military service. It's the same for jobs: whenever I apply, more and more companies ask for proof that I did army. I see more and more want ads in the papers saying, 'Army service required.' This is just another way of saying, no Arabs allowed, because we don't serve in the army. We are discriminated against all the time, but does the whole country stop to protest for one of us? Of course not."

In March, the Haifa municipality officially sanctioned the mob campaign against Azad, issuing an order to shut down the café. But when Adalah, the local Arab minority legal rights center, challenged the order in the Haifa Court for Local Affairs, a judge struck it down, noting in her decision, "The alleged discrimination [against Sgt. Roth] was not supported by even a shred of evidence when the motion was submitted to the court."

Frustrated by the restrictions imposed on him by the law, Sgt. Roth, the aggrieved soldier, filed a civil lawsuit against Azad. On June 30, 2010, Haifa's Magistrate Court Judge Shimon Sher ruled that the owners of Azad had to pay Roth $4,373 in punitive damages and around $600 to cover the legal costs they incurred when he sued them. Though they had broken no laws, Judge Sher placed the blame squarely on the owners for all the troubles they had caused the good people of Haifa. "The action taken by the restaurant owner only increased tensions and led to a situation where his attempt to bring about equality created inequality—which I am certain neither side desires," Sher declared in his ruling.

Weeks after the ruling, Azad closed down for good. "Now I'm stuck with the legal bills, and I'm thousands of shekels in debt because I can't pay back the fucking loan. All because one soldier decided he was the victim, and because the army turned out to be the real owner of my restaurant—because of that I am fucked," Fidaa complained to me.

She had gone from investing her money and energy into a space that encouraged "open dialogue" to gathering her bundles and preparing to relocate to Ramallah, the seat of the Palestinian Authority's occupied Bantustan. I asked her if by leaving Israel for the West Bank she was essentially self-transferring.

"It's complete shit to live under occupation, for sure, but at least it's honest," she responded. "At least all the people know they are up against the Israeli occupation and don't pretend otherwise. Here we are still occupied, all our lives are controlled; everything we do is subject to the power of the Jewish state. But we can't be honest about it. Look," she continued, "it's not easy being a woman in the West Bank. It's a double occupation, you know—we have to deal with the Israelis *and* the fucked-up sexist attitudes. But I'd rather live with people who recognize the reality of the occupation than be here where the occupation is hidden behind all these layers of fake democracy."

The following morning, as the sun rose above the Mediterranean sky, sending a shimmering glow across Haifa's port that illuminated the outlines of the Lebanese coast to the north, I wandered out into the road for a coffee at one of the cafés on Masada Street.

I realized that I was only blocks away from Azad, which lay empty on Hillel Street. Out of curiosity, I decided to pass by the shuttered restaurant. There, I found the café's front windows shattered by vandals, who left the ground covered in shards of glass. Later in the day, when I described the scene to Fadi, he muttered, "They did it again?"

PART V

WHAT LIES BENEATH THE FOREST

The Days of '48 Have Come Again

In the eyes of Palestinians, there are few symbols of Israel's occupation more recognizable than the Caterpillar D-9 bulldozer. Custom fitted with explosive-resistant armor, the forty-nine-ton tractor was the instrument responsible for Rachel Corrie's death and the demolition of more than fifteen hundred civilian homes in Rafah between the years of 2000 and 2005. Since the dawn of the occupation in 1967, according to the Israeli Committee Against House Demolitions (ICAHD), the State of Israel has destroyed well over twenty-six thousand Palestinian homes. Most of these demolitions occurred in and around occupied East Jerusalem and in the Gaza Strip, but also in places such as the Jenin Refugee Camp, where a drunken bulldozer pilot nicknamed "Kurdi Bear" reduced densely populated neighborhoods to a canyon of doom, boasting that he "left [Jenin's] residents with a football stadium so they could play."

As the state stepped up its campaign of "Judaization" under the watch of Prime Minister Benjamin Netanyahu, Palestinian neighborhoods in mixed Israeli cities were becoming acquainted with the US-manufactured Caterpillar D-9 as well. Fifteen minutes east of Tel Aviv, in the Lod ghetto, where Palestinian citizens lived surrounded by lower-class Jewish communities, I visited a de facto refugee camp filled with the residents of an entire neighborhood that had been leveled to the ground the night before.

On December 13, 2010, seventeen-year-old Hamza Abu Eid was taken out of class at his high school in Lod and summoned to the principal's office. "The Israelis are destroying your house right now," the principal told him. "It is best that you remain here. The last thing we want is for you to have a confrontation with a police officer."

But Abu Eid could not stay. He rushed to his family's house, hoping to salvage whatever belongings he could before the bulldozers from the Israeli Lands Administration (ILA) rumbled through. When he arrived, it was too late. The bulldozers had destroyed virtually everything—all seven homes belonging to the Abu Eid family were reduced to rubble. A black-masked Israeli riot police officer grabbed Hamza, restraining him while the bulldozers finished their work and preventing him from attempting to save his belongings. Three refrigerators and a TV set were among the appliances that Hamza's family lost in the destruction.

In the end, 74 people were left homeless—including 54 children—and were forced to sleep under the open sky during the coldest period of the year. No government social workers arrived with assistance, nor did the state offer any temporary aid. The families gathered whatever belongings they could, pitching tents like so many Palestinian refugees have done in the past, and placing a sign over their land plot. It read, "Abu Eid Refugee Camp."

When I arrived at the encampment, the area looked like Rafah after Israeli operations during the Second Intifada, or the Khan Younis refugee camp in Gaza after Operation Cast Lead. Unlike these occupied areas, however, the Abu Eid camp was located only 15 kilometers from Tel Aviv in the Abu Toq neighborhood of Lod. All of Lod's Palestinian residents are citizens of Israel, but they are treated by the state like foreign aliens, or worse, as an existential threat to the survival of Zionism.

For years, the Abu Eid family applied for permits to allow them to renovate their homes to accommodate their growing family. But the state zoned their neighborhood as agricultural land and refused their requests (applications for renovation and building permits are almost always denied to the Arabs inside Israel). Finally, the state ordered them to seek residency elsewhere because their homes were slated for demolition.

Directly beside the Abu Eid refugee camp, building has begun on a *yeshiva* directed by an Orthodox rabbi from the United States named Yaakov Saban. And plans were authorized to build a road directly through center of the neighborhood. Pressure on the Palestinian Israelis of Lod to leave intensified day by day, thanks to the far-right takeover of the city.

Widespread corruption had prompted the collapse of the elected municipality, enabling the Israeli Ministry of the Interior to install an emergency government consisting of hand-picked military officials. With the Ministry of the Interior under the control of Eli Yishai, who led the right-wing religious Shas Party, the new municipality became a means for meting out the wrath of anti-Arab populists against the local Arab population. "They are poor in culture, poor in behavior. No ambition," the mayor of Ramle, a neighboring city, said of the Palestinians of Lod.

By the time the Abu Eid family's homes were demolished, as many as 30 demolition orders hovered over the Arab residents of Lod, and 42,000 such orders had been issued across Israel against other Arabs. After the homes were leveled, Yishai pledged to settle thousands of Orthodox Jews inside Lod. The Arabs of Lod were not only denied the right to renovate their own houses, they also claimed they were forbidden as Arabs from living in a giant, new public housing complex built in the heart of the city. Thus they were confined to an overcrowded ghetto doomed by state plans that prioritized Judaization.

I arrived at the Abu Eid camp on January 25, 2010, to observe a protest by Sheikh Jarrah Solidarity, a national movement that grew out of the protests against East Jerusalem evictions of Palestinian families, and which was establishing a presence in mixed cities around Israel, as well as in the most threatened areas of the West Bank. Amiel Vardi, a veteran activist, explained to me, "For years I've been trying to say, 'Don't think the occupation will stop at the Green Line.' Now we see it's not stopping. They're using the same methods with the settlements, with the courts, and with the Shabak [Shin Bet] on both sides of the Green Line. Go to the Abu Eid camp in Lod or to Al Arakib [a repeatedly demolished Bedouin village in the Negev], and there's absolutely no difference from what I see in the Hebron Hills."

I entered the remains of the Abu Eid family dwellings at the end of Lod's Helen Keller Boulevard, finding small groups of grizzled men seated around open fires and sipping tea, while small children clambered in and out of tents erected beside piles of rubble, debris, and shattered home appliances. A forlorn-looking middle-aged man named Riyah Abu Eid met me at the entrance and took me into the makeshift camp.

"This place was here before 1948," he said. "They destroyed it because they said we had no permit. But we can't get permits because we are '48 Arabs. We asked many times and were denied every time. They say we are terrorists. But look around—this is the real terror. Throwing children into the street on the coldest day of the year—that is terror."

According to Riyadh Abu Eid, many children from camp were unable to attend school because they could not concentrate. A nine-year-old girl who was especially traumatized had refused to leave her bed for days. Riyadh did not try to conceal his desperation. "We do not feel safe here," he said. "We want to ask the United Nations and Obama for international protection from a fascist government that has proven capable of massacring the unarmed." He added, "The days of 1948 have come again."

Only a kilometer away from the Abu Eid camp was Dahmash, an unrecognized Palestinian village tucked behind railroad tracks and a garbage dump, hidden from a Jewish neighborhood by a concrete separation wall, and cut off from the surrounding city after the Lod municipality ordered most of its entrances sealed. In Dahmash, the family of Ali and Farida Sha'aban had defended their home for two years from a demolition order. When I met them encamped in a tent outside their home in July 2010, awaiting the bulldozer that could come at any time, Ali Sha'aban told me, "If there is a democracy in Israel, then why are we forbidden from living here?"

Faridah Sha'aban chimed in: "We are not much better off than the people of Gaza. Here they portray us as well off, but we have nothing. Our situation is worse than that of the people in Gaza. We witness injustice and demolitions on a daily basis while in Gaza there is publicity, and they show the whole world what is happening there. Here they don't show anybody what they are doing to us."

On January 22, the Lod police violently arrested Ali and Farida Sha'aban and five members of their family, accusing them of harboring illegal workers. Video of the arrests portraying the police kicking the Sha'abans while shouting, "Go to Gaza!" was shown during the court hearing. The family's detention in the city jail was unknown until days later, when they were finally allowed to see a lawyer. A judge extended their imprisonment until the following week on the grounds of secret evidence the Sha'aban family's lawyer was not allowed to view—a tactic familiar to Israel's system of martial law in the occupied West Bank.

On the night that I visited the Abu Eid camp, the Sheikh Jarrah Solidarity movement planned a demonstration to demand the release of the Sha'abans, who were still locked in a local prison. Joining the activists were members of the Palestinian rap trio, DAM ("eternity" in Arabic and "blood" in Hebrew). Influenced by conscious

American hip-hop artists like Public Enemy and KRS-One, the group's politically charged lyrics had elevated them to the status of cultural spokesmen for the post-Oslo generation of Palestinians raised inside Israel.

In the 2006 anthem, "Born Here," DAM's Tamer Naffar rapped in Hebrew:

> *I broke the law? No, the law broke me!*
> *Enough, enough, gentlemen*
> *I was born here, my grandparents too,*
> *You will not sever me from my roots*
> *Even if I believed in this phony regime*
> *You'd forbid me a porch to proclaim it from*

In a large tent in front of the Abu Eid family encampment, activists and locals gathered for an impromptu open mic. Teenage guys from Lod took hold of the microphone, one after another, and recited rap lyrics they had composed about the situation in their city. Then, a small boy who could not have been more than six years old stood before the audience and began to recite DAM's most popular protest anthem, "Min Irhabi" ("Who's the Terrorist"). He had memorized it word for word. With a few members of the crowd singing along, the little boy rapped:

> *I'm not against peace,*
> *Peace is against me.*
> *It's going to destroy me,*
> *Erase my culture*
> *You don't listen to our voices*
> *You silence and degrade . . .*
> *Who's the terrorist?*
> *I'm the terrorist?*
> *How am I the terrorist when you've taken my land?!*

Following the open mic, the crowd marched to a one-story Lod police station a few blocks away to demand the Sha'aban family's release. At the front of the crowd, bellowing anti-occupation slogans into a megaphone was Michael Solsberry, a burly Jerusalem-based activist with jet-black hair and the word *Emet*, or truth, tattooed across his forearm. Solsberry was raised by right-wing Jewish nationalists from Pisgat Ze'ev, a settlement in East Jerusalem, but spent much of his youth in the ghettoes of Lod and Ramle, forging close friendships with impoverished Palestinians caught up in the city's underworld of petty crime.

Transformed through his experiences, Solsberry emerged as one of the most visible figures in the movement fighting the evictions of Palestinian families in the East Jerusalem neighborhood of Sheikh Jarrah. In March 2010, during a crackdown on the marches in Sheikh Jarrah, Israeli police raided the settlement home of Solsberry's family while they were holding a Shabbat dinner. "Get the hell out of my house!" Solsberry's father shouted at the police as they led his son away in handcuffs. "You threw us out of Gaza," he screamed at the cops, referring to the settlers of Gush Katif, "and now you raid our homes on Shabbat?"

At the demonstration, Solsberry told me he was recently fired from his job at a construction company when his boss learned that he was under investigation by the Shin Bet. "It's almost impossible for me to find work these days," he said. "Everyone knows I'm doing this kind of activism, that I've gone to jail for it, so it's not that easy to find any opportunities anymore."

As the demonstration concluded, a few activists slapped stickers on the bumpers of the police cars outside, mocking Israel's claim to be "Jewish and democratic." Composed in blue-and-white Hebrew script, they read, "*Yahudit V'Gezanit*," or "Jewish and racist."

Back in the Abu Eid camp, Solsberry took me behind the tents, into a warren of homes where some of the children made homeless by the demolitions were staying. There, we found Hamza Abu Eid, the seventeen-year-old high school student, seated on a plastic chair outside his grandmother's home and chatting with a few friends. I asked him what his life has been like since his home was destroyed.

"I get distracted when I'm in class now," he told me. "Sometimes when I think about the aggressive way the police treated the women—one of them kicked my brother's pregnant wife—I get so angry I can't focus."

Hamza said his family plans to buy trailers to live in until the state delivers them "a solution." He said, "For now, we have no solution. I expect that I will stay in this life and it will keep going on. The government has done nothing for me but destroy my house. As a citizen, I have no rights."

He paused, staring at the ground, and then said, "I see a future full of darkness."

Despite being homeless and traumatized, Hamza said he was excelling in school. He told me had just received 92 out of 100 on a chemistry exam, and that he scored near-perfect marks in biology. When he finished high school, Hamza said he planned to pursue a career in economics or medicine.

"I know there is a hope," he said. "I just don't know what it is."

At the other end of Israel, more than 100 kilometers away, in the heart of the Negev Desert, a larger but undeniably related campaign of ethnic cleansing was beginning to unfold. This one was directed at the highest levels of the Israeli government, designed to remove the majority of Bedouin Arabs from their ancestral lands to make way for the construction of Jews-only communities and a massive forestation project that would "make the desert bloom." The destruction focused on Al Araqib, a village inhabited by Bedouin citizens of Israel whose presence predated the arrival of Zionist settlers to Palestine, and who stood in the way of the next phase of state-planned "Judaization."

On July 27, 2010, bulldozers leveled every structure in Al Araqib, marking the first of at least forty-five times at the time of this writing that the State of Israel would attempt to wipe the village off the map.

The Blueprint

At 1 a.m. on August 10, 2010, a dozen Israeli activists gathered in a parking lot in Jerusalem's Independence Park received text messages informing them of the danger that awaited Al Araqib. They were told that police helicopters were buzzing above the village and bulldozers were parked nearby ready to destroy the village for the third time. Israeli Border Police had slipped into the area the night before and nabbed four activists staying with local families to document the demolitions. Having already witnessed the razing of their homes twice in the past two weeks, the residents of Al-Araqib expected the third round of demolitions to arrive tonight on the eve of Ramadan. During Ramadan, when the villagers fasted all day, the police and the ILA reasoned they would be too weakened to rebuild—it was prime time for destruction.

I joined the activists as they filed into a small van and barreled south into the desert, taking turns peering through the back window of the van in search of any police vehicle that might have been tailing. Seated to my left was Tali Shapiro, a rail-thin writer and activist who could have passed for any other glamorous Tel Aviv bohemian if her name did not appear so routinely in smear pieces by right-wing Israeli bloggers. Shapiro told me she began to question the imperatives of the state during the Second Intifada, when she was holed up as a soldier in an army base in Northern Gaza. "There were thousands of us in this heavily fortified base," she recalled, "and every day our commanders told us we were going to be overrun. They had to indoctrinate us to believe that we were the victims, that we were in constant danger of being thrown in the sea, when in fact we were the ones in full control of the lives of everyone in the Gaza Strip."

"They call me a *yafeh nefesh* now," she said. "That means a beautiful soul or a do-gooder. It is one of the biggest insults in Israel."

Shapiro pulled out her Israeli ID card and pointed to the section labeled "nationality," where she was classified as Jewish. "There is no such thing as an Israeli nationality," she explained to me. "According to the Interior Ministry, you are either Jewish or Arab. Your citizenship is defined here by the ethnicity, and your privileges are afforded to you accordingly. That's the basis of apartheid. And what I want is to be able to choose my own identity instead of letting the state define it for me."

As a Jew born in the "Jewish and democratic" State of Israel, Shapiro inherited Type A citizenship. Her democratic rights were secure, and no matter how many times she was arrested, she was guaranteed due process. For the Bedouins we were about to meet, being born in Israel as non-Jews relegated them not to "second-class status," but to something like Type D citizenship, if not in letter, then in practice. Though many of them served with distinction in the army as elite trackers who helped regular units through densely populated areas of the Gaza Strip, engendering widespread resentment from Palestinians in the process, the state has always treated them as criminal invaders who had no property rights on their own land.

Nearly half of the 170,000 Bedouins in Israel live in a series of forty-five "unrecognized villages" in the Negev, where they are often denied access to public health clinics and permits to engage in their traditional lifestyle of subsistence farming— something residents of Jews-only *kibbutzim* have taken for granted. In fact, though the unrecognized village of Wadi al Na'am was located directly next to electricity grids and central water arteries, its residents have never been allowed to connect to them, something the village sheikh called "a criminal act of discrimination."

As early as 1950, the Knesset enacted discriminatory laws that prevented the Bedouins from grazing their goatherds on their ancestral lands, threatening to completely extinguish their agricultural traditions. Three years later, the state forcibly moved the Bedouins to a corner of the Negev known as the *Siyag*, or the enclosure zone, where they lived under martial law and were unable to leave without special permits issued by the army. Those clans not immediately expelled to the Gaza Strip saw much of their land expropriated for the construction of army bases, firing ranges, and exclusively Jewish *kibbutzim* and *moshavim*. The subsequent construction of nuclear power plants and dumping of petrochemical waste near the Bedouin villages caused elevated cancer rates, while state campaigns of crop destruction and goat eradication carried out by a paramilitary "Green Patrol" claiming ecological motives have left the Bedouins in desperate economic shape.

Throughout the history of Israel, the Bedouins have been treated as a demographic threat that demanded neutralization. As Moshe Dayan said in 1963, "Without coercion but with governmental direction . . . this phenomenon of the Bedouins will disappear." Dayan proposed transforming the Bedouin tribes into an "urban proletariat" that would benefit the state by performing manual labor for the Jewish middle class. By the 1980s, the state managed to transfer nearly half of the Bedouin population into reservation-like communities built for the express purpose of fulfilling Dayan's vision. Plagued by crime and drug addiction previously unknown in Bedouin circles, the ramshackle municipalities happen to be the only new Arab towns authorized by Israel since 1948. The towns are overseen by the Or Movement, a para-governmental division of the Jewish National Fund (JNF) run by former West Bank settlers on a mission to plant new Jewish towns in the Negev. According to the Or Movement's website, "Rahat [the largest of the Bedouin municipalities] is one of the seven Negev towns planned to concentrate the Bedouin population."

The removal and "concentration" of the Bedouin tribes—a practice first employed by the fascist regime of Italy during its campaign to colonize Libya—represented the first step toward the utopian dream of Jewish redemption hatched in the exceptionally active imagination of Israel's first prime minister, David Ben Gurion. In 1953, Ben Gurion (original name: David Gryn) moved to Sde Boker, a small, windswept kibbutz in the Negev. A self-described messianist who rejected the existence of God while simultaneously describing the Torah as his political guidebook, Ben Gurion saw the Negev as a blank slate for realizing his revolutionary dreams. In his memoirs, he fantasized about evacuating Tel Aviv and settling five million Jews in small settlements throughout the Negev, where they would be weaned off the rootless cosmopolitanism they inherited from life in the diaspora. Just as he disdained the worldly spirit of Tel Aviv's urbanists, Ben Gurion was repelled by the sight of the open desert, describing it as "a reproach to mankind," "a criminal waste," and "occupied territory"—from his standpoint, the Arabs were the occupiers. In the place of sand dunes, he imagined a Jewish replica of Northern Europe.

"When I look out of my window and see a tree standing [in the Negev]," Ben Gurion wrote, "that tree gives me a greater sense of beauty and personal delight than all the vast forests I have seen in Switzerland or Scandinavia. . . . Not only because I helped to grow them, but because they constitute a gift of man to Nature, and a gift of the Jews to the cradle of their culture."

With the ethnocentric Ashkenazi outlook characteristic of early Labor Zionism, Ben Gurion held the Arab world in total contempt, even to the degree that he refused to carry the standard Israeli ID card because it featured Arabic writing, forcing the government to print a unique, Hebrew-only card especially for his use. He wrote, "In all the centuries of their existence on this earth, the Palestinian Arabs remained at the most rudimentary levels of human existence." In his public writings about the Negev, Ben Gurion did not mention the tens of thousands of Arab Bedouins whose villages abutted his kibbutz, nor would he acknowledge the legitimacy of their presence. They were a non-people he viewed as intruders, even though they had tended the land of Palestine for centuries while his ancestors languished in the frostbitten *shtetls* of Lithuania.

In private, Ben Gurion was unalterably committed to replacing the Bedouins with masses of Jews. Well before the United Nations approved the partition of Palestine, Ben Gurion had vowed to colonize the Negev through military might. In a letter to his son, Amos, written on October 5, 1937, Ben Gurion wrote, "We can no longer tolerate that vast territories capable of absorbing tens of thousands of Jews should remain vacant, and that Jews cannot return to their homeland because the Arabs prefer that the place [the Negev] remains neither ours nor theirs. We must expel Arabs and take their place. Up to now, all our aspirations have been based on an assumption—one that has been vindicated throughout our activities in the country—that there is enough room in the land for the Arabs and ourselves. But if we are compelled to use force—not in order to dispossess the Arabs of the Negev or Transjordan, but in order to guarantee our right to settle there—our force will enable us to do so."

Over seventy years later, the Israeli government remained stubbornly committed to fulfilling Ben Gurion's mission. However, the Jewish middle-class essentially turned its back on the Negev, refusing to budge from its Europeanized, urban enclave on the central coast. Their interest in the early Zionist dream of "redeeming the wilderness" was negligible at best. "If we don't work fast, we might find ourselves in a situation, which is on the verge of catastrophe, with 80 percent of our land which is not disputed today," fretted Dany Gliksberg, the founder of Ayalim, a group that aims to encourage young Israelis to settle in Jews-only communities in the Negev.

But the Bedouins have held fast to their unrecognized villages, refusing to submit to the state's plan to "concentrate" them in development towns. And their population grew apace, making them one of the fastest growing demographic groups in the world. Naturally, this fact disturbed the state's strategic planners, who saw the maintenance of the Jewish demographic majority as the key to Israel's survival. In 2003, before entering the Knesset to cosponsor the Acceptance to Communities Bill, Shai Hermesh served as the director of the Jewish Agency's effort to engineer a "Zionist majority" in the Negev. "The trouble with the Bedouin is they're still on the edge between tradition and civilization," Hermesh told the *Guardian* at the time. "A big part of the Bedouin don't want to live in cities. They say their mothers and grandmothers want to live with the sheep around them. It is not in Israel's interest to have more Palestinians in the Negev."

The Israeli government's in-house "Arab Counter," Arnon Sofer, echoed Hermesh's despairing assessment in his influential report, *Israel: Demography and Density 2007–2020*. Sofer identified the Bedouin of the Northern Negev Desert as a key "strategic threat" to the state's survival, warning, "At present the Bedouins form a bridge between Egypt and the West Bank, between Egypt and Jordan, between Gaza and Jordan and the West Bank (a connection that could be fatal!)." Sofer claimed that if Bedouin population growth rates continued, "Tel Aviv will become Masada"—an encircled, suicidal fortress of Jewish fanaticism—by 2020. To stave off the nightmare, Sofer recommended the Israeli government implement a steep reduction in child allowances to Bedouin communities, initiate construction of "a wedge of Jewish settlements intervening between the Gaza Strip and the Bedouins in the south," and move Israeli army bases from the center of the country to the south to interrupt Bedouin communities—all demographic fixes that he confessed "will not sound sweet to those who forever show concern for the rights of the other man."

The demographic warnings were translated into concrete action through the Jewish National Fund's "Blueprint Negev," a $600 million Judaization project funded in part by the billionaire Republican Party donor and cosmetics baron Ron Lauder, a close friend and longtime benefactor of Benjamin Netanyahu. Lauder promoted the Judaization of the Negev as the modern incarnation of early American settler-colonialism, remarking, "The United States had its Manifest Destiny in the West. . . . For Israel, that land is the Negev." Russell Robinson, the president of the Jewish National Fund's wing, saw the project as a defensive maneuver that would consolidate the Negev as exclusively Jewish domain. "This land is ours," Robinson said. "There is no controversy, no argument, no discussion. But if we don't take care of it, it can become desert; it can be taken from us."

Formally introduced in 2005, Blueprint Negev aimed to establish a conglomerate of twenty-five Jews-only colonies surrounded by a lush landscape implanted on top of the former "wasteland." President Shimon Peres marketed the colonies to American Jews as ideal communities for those "who want to make *aliyah* and live in style," promising them golf courses, Olympic-sized swimming pools, and elegant homes with central air-conditioning. An article in *B'nai B'rith* magazine attempted to highlight the Negev's diaspora appeal: "Central Israel is already developed, West Bank settlement is politicized and socially divisive, and Zionism is in short supply among the cosmopolitan, post-Zionist yuppies of metro Tel Aviv. In southern Israel, far from the strip malls of Tel Aviv's suburbs, the Negev is the closest thing to the tabula rasa many of Israel's pre-state pioneers found when they first came to the Holy Land." Among those who signed up to live in one of the new colonies was Rabbi Asher Lopatin, a Chicago-based Modern Orthodox synagogue leader whose congregation included some of the city's most influential political elites. "Pure Zionism" is how Lopatin described Blueprint Negev.

But five years after its inception, almost none of the gleaming American expat communities had come to fruition. According to the writer Rebecca Manski, the apathetic American response and delayed Israeli construction revealed Blueprint Negev as "less a concrete development plan than a public relations and fundraising campaign seeking to inspire American Jewish investment in Jewish settlement of the Negev."

By 2010, only one colony from the proposed demographic beachhead had taken root. Called Givot Bar, the small community was legally authorized to discriminate against non-Jewish residential applicants by the newly passed Acceptance to Communities Bill. As it grew under the auspices of the Jewish National Fund, the town demanded land claimed by the Bedouin village of Al Araqib. And so the ILA, a government agency controlled by the JNF, resolved to wipe the obstinate Bedouin town off the map.

The planned demolition and mass expulsion hardly raised an eyebrow among mainstream Israelis. While Israel's liberal Enlightened Public kept up a curious silence, as they so often did about human rights abuses that occurred behind the Green Line, a few dozen scraggly radical leftists stood up against the plan, throwing their bodies against waves of burly riot cops and bulldozers in a futile bid to slow the inexorable pace of ethnic cleansing.

As the activists' van arrived in Al Araqib at 3 a.m., a Bedouin couple welcomed them to the side of their trailer, then hauled out foam mattresses and blankets and poured small cups of coffee. They were waiting for the next round of destruction, which they planned to endure as they had before, with *sumud*—the Bedouins of Al Araqib had adopted the Palestinian culture of steadfastness.

"I've had enough of sleeping," the man grumbled as he reclined next to his wife. He seemed grateful to have company. I stared at the stars glimmering across the desert sky, listening as he described the experience of watching his neighbors' homes crumple under the teeth of bulldozers again and again. As he trailed off, I heard a low droning sound in the distance. Were they here already? I looked around at the others. No one registered the slightest sign of concern. After a few minutes, I slipped into a light slumber.

Two hours later I was torn from my sleep. "They're here!" someone shouted in Hebrew. I scrambled up a dune until I reached the center of the village. A phalanx of one hundred *Yassam* (riot cops) stood in a tight formation. They were bristling with assault weapons and Plexiglas centurion shields. Flanked by Caterpillar D-9 bulldozers and demolition equipment, the police quickly ringed the activists and journalists, who numbered about two dozen, and began forcing them away from the site of the demolitions, sending a short Israeli woman tumbling off her feet when she attempted to make a stand in front of one of the homes. "Just give him five minutes! Five minutes!" screamed Ashley, a young woman who had come from Brooklyn to stay in Al Araqib and guard it from destruction. She, too, was tossed away like an empty crate, leaving her host family's home exposed to destruction.

As the bulldozers trundled around the village, tearing tarps from plywood pylons, crushing tin roofs, and dragging the shattered structures into hulking piles, the people of Al Araqib watched with resignation. A girl wiped a few tears from her eyes, grimacing at the sight before her. She was seated on her bed in the middle of the naked desert. On a nearby hill, a man quizzed his daughter on *surahs* from the Quran before sending her to collect mattresses from beneath the dusty waste of what used to be their sleeping quarters. An old woman stood impassively by a flock of birds perched on the collapsed remains of her house. It was only one among more than twenty-six thousand Arab homes the State of Israel has demolished since 1967. The plague of homelessness known by so many of Palestinians had arrived in Al Araqib, courtesy of the Jewish National Fund and Israel's Green Patrol.

Having completed their demolition, the riot police squad assembled in a neat triple-file line and marched out of the village, escorting the vehicles out toward the main highway. At the end of the convoy, a truck towed away Al Araqib's lone water cistern as well. Only minutes after the wrecking crew left, the people of Al Araqib began piecing together the rubble of their community with help from the activists. Within days they would have their village rebuilt, or at least some semblance of it, without the trees and crops that were uprooted during the first demolition. And then, the bulldozers marked with Jewish National Fund insignia would come to destroy it all over again. The cycle of destruction and rebuilding likely cost the state more than it would have if it had allowed Al Araqib to connect to the public electric and water supply, or to provide its residents with public schooling and a health clinic. But according to *Yediot Ahronoth*, "[Israeli] Land Administration official Shlomo Zeiser said the state was seeking a permanent solution to the al-Arakib issue."

The Summer Camp of Destruction

Though there are few experiences as jarring as witnessing the demolition of an entire village while its inhabitants helplessly stand by and watch, I had only begun to discover the perversity of Israel's activities in the Negev. A week before I watched Al Araqib be razed to the ground, I visited the village with a delegation from Ta'ayush, a joint Israeli-Palestinian initiative that began by staging direct action protests against settler activity in the south Hebron Hills of the occupied West Bank, but which had begun devoting an increasing amount of energy to abuses occurring back inside the Green Line. Upon their arrival, they gathered on the floor of an open-air tent to hear about the first time the bulldozers rampaged through the community.

Jillian Kestler-D'Amours, an independent journalist who had stayed in the village for over a month, told me the children had begun to suffer from nightmares, chronic bedwetting, and the inability to complete their schoolwork. Nearby, a local resident named Ata Abu Madyam led the visitors on a tour of the land around Al Araqib. He pointed out the vast plot that the all-Jewish town of Givot Bar sought to expropriate. "They are offering massive benefits to the families of former soldiers to settle here," he said. "And if there is a two state solution, this is where they will move the settlers. They want to make peace on top of my head."

I asked Abu Madyam about a report I had read in CNN. According to the article, the hundreds of Israeli riot police who stormed the village were accompanied by "busloads of cheering civilians." Who were these civilians? And why didn't CNN or any outlet investigate further? I asked him. Abu Madyam happened to be a journalist who published a local Arabic language newspaper called *Arab Negev News*. The cover of the paper's latest issue featured a photo of Palestinians being expelled to Jordan in 1948 juxtaposed with a photo of a family fleeing Al Araqib one week before. The headline read "Nakba 2010." For the Bedouins of the Negev, as for the Palestinians of Gaza, the West Bank, and across the Holy Land, the Nakba was a continuous, ongoing process of dispossession.

In response to my question, Abu Madyam whipped out his cellphone and displayed for me a series of shocking photographs. In one image after another, I saw Jewish Israeli youth volunteers participating in the destruction of his village. "What we learned from this summer camp of destruction," Abu Madyam told me, "is that Israeli youth are not being educated on democracy, they are being raised on racism."

I studied the photographs closely. One showed a group of teens inside a local home; they had apparently amused themselves by smashing mirrors and littering the floor with family photographs. Another depicted the youth emptying the homes of furniture in advance of the demolition. And another showed the teens posing on couches and chairs in the open desert. They looked proud, with a sense of swagger, their arms folded and heads cocked like rappers in an album cover photo shoot. According to Abu Madyam, when the bulldozers moved in, belching up smoke while they smashed down house after house, the youth stood on a hill singing, "*Am Yisrael Chai!*"—the people of Israel live.

Who were these teenage boys? Most appeared to be *mizrahi*, with olive skin and strikingly similar features to those of the people whose homes they had vandalized. The rest looked like Ethiopian Jews or Russians. They were the kind of kids that affluent Ashkenazim elites from North Tel Aviv denigrated as *arsim*, or brown trash. Ben Gurion once demeaned Jews who had immigrated to Israel from Arab countries as "savage" and as "a primitive community" that revered pimps and thieves. Stuck at the bottom of the totem pole in a militaristic settler society, the lower-class Jews of the periphery remain consigned to carrying out Israel's ugliest projects, as low-wage ushers for the Green Patrol and perhaps when they came of age, as Border Police grunts. To the frontlines of ethnic cleansing they marched to secure their status from the Ashkenazi elite who issued them with their orders.

After showing the disturbing photos to several Israeli friends and examining the insignia on the work vests the teenagers wore, we were able to determine that they had probably been employed by a private security company in Kiryat Gat. Named for the ancient Philistine city of Gath, which actually existed 13 kilometers away, Kiryat Gat is a run-down Jewish development town that sits on the ruins of al-Faluja, a Palestinian village ethnically cleansed by Israeli forces in 1949, months after Israel signed its armistice with Egypt. Today, the city is home to the Intel Corporation's microchip plant, which mostly employs upwardly mobile commuters from Tel Aviv while many residents of Kiryat Gat subsist on state welfare, comprising one of the highest unemployment rates in Israel. One of the few afterschool centers in the city is operated by the International Fellowship of Christians and Jews, a US-based group funded by Christian Zionists who believe Israel is the future site of the Rapture. Indeed, there is little to prevent youth from the city from joining a gang or seeking a living on the black market.

With its proximity to the Negev, the enforced culture of separation between Jews and Bedouins has occasionally broken down, even if only in a marginal sense. In several cases, this has resulted in romantic relationships, usually between young Bedouin men and Jewish women. But in a generally segregated society like Israel, relationships like these can easily turn sour, and even abusive.

Rather than encouraging a culture of coexistence, Kiryat Gat's municipal welfare department did all it could to maintain the structure of ethnic separation. The department's youth education program included the screening of a short video for local high school students called "Sleeping with the Enemy." In the film, the local police department chief, Haim Shalom, declares, "The girls, in their innocence, go with the exploitative Arab." At a subsequent "emergency" anti-miscegenation conference in Kiryat Gat, a local police spokesman warned participants that the Bedouins' "goal is to take advantage of the girls. There is no element of love or an innocent-friendly relationship here."

Unlike more affluent teens from Tel Aviv who attended summer camp in the verdant north of the country, or who headed off to Europe with their families, a low-paying job as the member of a village demolition advance team was probably among the few summertime activities open to the youth of Kiryat Gat. And in an environment where racism against the Bedouins and other non-Jews is officially sanctioned, and where youth are encouraged to confirm their Jewish identity through conflict with the "exploitative Arab," participating in an operation to drive away the Bedouin might have guaranteed serious bragging rights back home.

Of course, the kids were just pawns in a much larger operation of ethnic cleansing and colonization. Behind the curtains of Al Araqib's theater of destruction a little-known but internationally influential South African televangelist who was the project's most flamboyant backer.

Preparing the Land for Jesus

A s the Blueprint Negev project progressed, an unlikely and virtually unknown character injected the plan with his titanic fundraising prowess and seemingly unlimited messianic zeal. He was Rory Alec, the founder and owner of GOD-TV, a Jerusalem-based cable television network that claimed to reach half a billion people around the world with programming blending New World Order conspiracism with Greater-Israeli zealotry. Alec's wife, Wendy, is the author of a series of books called *Chronicle of Brothers* that depict a race of humans blessed with God's DNA doing battle with Black Magi, the Dread Warlocks of Ishtar, Demon Witches of Babylon, and other Satanic villains. According to Rachel Tabachnik, an expert researcher on the international Christian Right, "The narrative parallels widespread New World Order conspiracy theories."

Alec's role in the activities around Al Araqib was first exposed by activists from the Alternative Information Center in Jerusalem, who noticed a large sign posted on the highway near the village marked with the emblem of the Jewish National Fund but which read as follows:

GOD TV FOREST

A GENEROUS DONATION BY GOD-TV

MADE 1,000,000 SAPLINGS AVAILABLE TO BE PLANTED

IN THE LAND OF ISRAEL AND ALSO PROVIDED THE CREATION

OF WATER PROJECTS THROUGHOUT THE NEGEV

When I investigated further, I found that Alec was funneling millions to the JNF to plant a non-native forest on what would be the former site of Al Araqib. In a promotional page on GOD-TV's website, Alec solicited donations for the project from his rapture-ready flock. "GOD TV is planting over ONE MILLION TREES across the Holy Land as a miraculous sign to Israel and to the world that Jesus is coming soon," the page informed visitors. "This is a unique opportunity to make your mark on the land of Israel."

A video accompanied the donation drive depicting Alec, a stocky, potbellied man with a 1970s-era mod rock mullet, standing less than one kilometer from Al Araqib among a field of saplings planted by the JNF. "He's coming back, and the Lord's saying to us, 'Prepare the land, and this is the land that He's preparing,'" Alec excitedly declares into the camera, extending his arms to frame the Negev Desert in the background. At the conclusion of the video, Alec is seen with Sigal Moran, the mayor of Givot Bar, the Jews-only colony that has claimed Al Araqib's land as its own, and whose handful of residents the JNF describes as "twenty-first-century pioneers making the desert bloom." Alec hands over a check for $170,000 to the visibly grateful Moran, who seems to have no reservation about accepting the beneficence of a figure who openly declares his interest in preparing Israel for the End Times.

Countless evangelical Christian leaders have adopted Christian Zionism as a central article of faith, linking their international ministries to the cause of Israel while sending millions to West Bank settlements and various Israeli charities, all in expectation of a glorious rapture in which the non-Christians would suffer, their "bodies bursting open from head to toe at every word that proceeded out of the mouth of the Lord," according to Tim LaHaye's best-selling End Times pulp fiction novel *Left Behind*. LaHaye, a key player in the American radical right who joined the Christian Zionist cause in the 1980s, has led a "Where Jesus Walked Tour" tour through the Jezreel Valley, where his followers measure the river of blood that will flow from the two and a half billion impure non-Christians who are due to be ritually slaughtered during the Rapture.

During the 1980s, the government of Menachem Begin sought to expand Israel's base of support in the United States by cultivating Christian right leaders such as Pat Robertson and Jerry Falwell to promote Zionism among their multimillion-member TV flocks. (Falwell arrived for the first time in Israel on a private jet supplied by Begin.) Robertson, Falwell, and others like them were active supporters of Israel's allies among the right-wing military juntas of Central America and the apartheid government of South Africa. Perhaps for them, joining the pro-Israel fray was just a logical progression. Benjamin Netanyahu cemented the evangelical alliance when he first entered the prime minister's office, keynoting a massive 1997 rally convened by Falwell against then-president Bill Clinton's attempts to pressure Israel to withdraw from small slivers of the West Bank as gestures toward a final status peace agreement.

When Netanyahu returned to power in 2009, he had a massive army of Christian soldiers at his disposal, ready to lobby for an all-out push to consolidate full Israeli ownership of "Judea and Samaria." The product of long-term collaboration with the American Israel Public Affairs Committee (AIPAC), the official arm of the Israel lobby, they called themselves Christians United For Israel (CUFI). At the helm of the organization was an influential Texas mega-church pastor named John Hagee, who had described the Holocaust as divine providence and publicly predicted that the anti-Christ would be homosexual and "half-Jewish, as was Adolf Hitler." In July 2009, Prime Minister Benjamin Netanyahu welcomed the leading Christian Zionist pastor John Hagee and hundreds of members of his Texas congregation as VIP guests at a rally the night before Vice President Joe Biden arrived in Jerusalem to demand a freeze on Israel's settlement activity. "Israel loves you, and the Jewish people love you," Netanyahu told the cheering crowd, with a host of top government officials seated by his side. Against the threat of "delegimization," the new fear that consumed the prime minister, the Israeli government did not seem to think it had the luxury of picking and choosing its friends, even if they happened to hold views that many Jews might find peculiar if not highly disturbing.

While Christian Zionists pumped their money into Israeli settlements, even volunteering to pick grapes for wine companies based in the West Bank, the involvement of GOD-TV's Alec in Blueprint Negev represented the Christian right's most direct role in Israeli human rights abuses to date. With help from a handful of writers and activists, I publicized GOD-TV's participation in the destruction of Al Araqib in a series of widely distributed blog posts and articles, which led to coverage in *Ha'aretz*. The wave of reporting compelled Alec to issue a defensively worded statement on GOD-TV's website: "It has come to our attention that reports have been posted on the Internet. These reports mislead readers to believe that GOD TV may be responsible for displacement of Bedouin people in the Negev Desert in Israel. These claims are false." Placing the blame squarely on the Israeli government, GOD-TV pleaded, "We do not want to become involved in political debate."

The JNF was also feeling the heat from its role in destroying Al Araqib. Its March 2011 newsletter included a strident diatribe by the organization's CEO Russell Robinson against the critics of Blueprint Negev. "I can tell you one simple thing," Robinson wrote. "No other organization is doing anywhere near as much as the Jewish National Fund is to help enhance the quality of life for this [Bedouin] population."

Despite having been fully apprised of the human cost of their activities in the Negev Desert, neither Alec nor the JNF curtailed their destructive activities. The demolitions continued apace, with Israeli police unleashing teargas and rubber bullets against the families who dared to resist. A year after the demolitions began—after the ILA had leveled the Al Araqib twenty-seven times—the State of Israel filed a formal lawsuit against the residents of Al Araqib, seeking $480,000 from the defendants, demanding that they foot the bill for the State's repeated bulldozing of their homes and villages. According to the lawsuit, thirty-four residents of Al Araqib were accused of a "permanent illegal invasion" of Israel state lands.

Nuri el-Okbi was not named in the lawsuit, but he had also suffered at the hands of the state for attempting to live on his land in Al Araqib. El-Okbi, a tireless activist who founded the Association for the Protection of Bedouins in Israel, had saved his family's deed to their plot in Al Araqib in a halvah tin. He even carried aerial photos from 1947 proving that his family's home and agricultural fields existed before the foundation of Israel. But, according to el-Okbi, the state's records clerks deliberately refused to accept Bedouin land ownership claims from 1973 to 2005, hoping that all the witnesses would die of old age so that the documents would simply disappear. But el-Okbi persisted, becoming a major annoyance to a state determined to deny property rights to all non-Jews under its control.

"We had been sitting on this land for generations," el-Okbi told an interviewer. "We have houses on this land, stone structures built in the Turkish era. We have waterholes. We have vineyards. We never did anything against the state, against the Jews. We accepted the State of Israel, but despite everything, they forced us off our lands."

In 1951, the Israeli army forcibly removed el-Okbi's family and all other Bedouins living around the Al Araqib area, promising them they would be allowed to return after the military carried out a series of training exercises. Years passed, but the el-Okbi clan was never allowed to return. Instead, like hundreds of thousands of Arabs displaced by the Israeli army, they became "present absentees"—internal refugees who lived inside Israel, but were legally forbidden from returning to their homes and property, which had been placed in the hands of Jewish colonists through the Absentee Property Law and various other discriminatory ordinances. For el-Okbi's part, his family's land had been seized by the ILA, which authorized the JNF to carry out its stated mission of developing it "on behalf of its owners—Jewish people everywhere."

Since the inception of Blueprint Negev, el-Okbi began camping on his family's privately owned land. Each time he appeared near Al Araqib, he was forcibly removed by private security guards hired by the JNF, who often found themselves physically restraining him from blocking the advancing bulldozers. After his fortieth attempt to return to the land of his childhood, an Israeli court slapped el-Okbi with a restraining order that forbid him from setting foot anywhere near the area. Shlomo Sizar, an official from the ILA who has overseen the destruction of Al Araqib, remarked, "Every year, [the Bedouins] invade, and we remove them. They invade, and we remove them. We're not going to let this land be invaded."

Severed from his family's land, el-Okbi was relegated to operating a garage in Ramle, the rough twin city of Lod, located in the center of Israel. Though he was hundreds of kilometers from Al Araqib, el-Okbi was not safe from the vindictive designs of the state. In December 2010, after applying for a license to operate his garage with the local municipality and being repeatedly denied, el-Okbi was summoned to a Ramle courtroom and sentenced to seven months in prison and a $13,000 fine. In meting out the draconian penalty, the judge drew a clear connection between el-Okbi's unlicensed garage and his human rights activism, proclaiming that a lenient sentence "would constitute a negative message to the public, and especially to the Bedouins." El-Okbi, who was sixty-eight years old at the time, collapsed upon the reading of his verdict and was taken to a hospital, where he lay handcuffed to a bed.

Just days later, after a Tel Aviv district court convicted former Israeli president Moshe Katsav of raping one female subordinate while sexually assaulting two more, Katsav's successor, Shimon Peres, trumpeted the decision as proof of his country's vibrant democracy. "There are no two states of Israel, just one state," Peres declared. "There are no two kinds of citizens here; citizens of only one kind exist in Israel—and all are equal in the eyes of the law."

That same month, as the JNF's bulldozers sought to clear the northern Negev of the Bedouins to make way for the GOD-TV Forest, a spark caught some tinder at the base one of the first forests the JNF ever planted in Israel. With a gust of wind, the flames quickly grew into a massive wildfire that consumed large swaths of the Carmel forest in northern Israel. As the fire overwhelmed towns and bore down on Haifa, it laid bare a terrible history concealed by layers of mythology, officially sanctioned political repression and piles of fallen pine needles.

There Are No Facts

On December 2, 2010, a burning tree trunk fell into a bus full of Israeli Prison Service cadets on their way to Damon Prison, a detention center described by female Palestinian inmates as "the worst jail ever." Forty of the cadets were immediately killed by the felled tree, marking the opening chapter of a rapidly unfolding national tragedy that generated an outpouring of anti-government rage that had rarely been seen in Israel. Within four days, hundreds of thousands of trees planted along the Carmel Mountains had been turned to ash, while the outskirts of Haifa were engulfed in smoke. More than 12,300 acres were burned in the Mount Carmel area, a devastating swath of destruction in a country the size of New Jersey.

In characteristically apocalyptic language, Prime Minister Benjamin Netanyahu described the fire as "a catastrophe the likes of which we have never known." A prison guard who visited the site of the bus accident collapsed in his friend's arms. "It's worse than a terrorist attack in Gaza," he cried. "They just laid there on the floor, dozens of people, and there was nothing to do."

But once Israelis progressed beyond grief, they quickly turned their anger on their leaders. At a memorial for the prison guards, Netanyahu was heckled by dozens of infuriated mourners, who interrupted him with insults so many times he was unable to finish his eulogy. At one point, the prime minister's bodyguards were forced to shield him when the mourners surged forward, threatening to attack him. The partner of Ahuva Tomer, the Haifa police chief who died in the fire, stood before the vigil and demanded that Interior Minister Eli Yishai immediately leave. As mourners stormed out in anger, the ceremony was only able to proceed once the crowd was informed that Yishai had left.

Netanyahu's government had confronted the fire with complete passivity. The day after the conflagration began to spread, he informed the country, "We do not have what it takes to put out the fire, but help is on the way." Having prioritized the procurement of advanced military gear and occupation maintenance over the country's infrastructure, Netanyahu was powerless in the face of natural disaster.

Forced into a corner, Netanyahu begged for assistance from his counterpart in Turkey, Prime Minister Recep Tayyip Erdogan, the man he had accused during the flotilla imbroglio of collaborating with al-Qaeda and Hamas in Israel's destruction. Next, Netanyahu beseeched the Palestinian Authority, another entity he frequently demonized, for firefighting assistance. Having spent years carping about the whole world being against Israel, Netanyahu found that even those he had labeled as murderous terrorists were willing to help. And his government repaid them with humiliation and disrespect. After the PA sent its most able team to help snuff the blaze, most of its firefighters were refused entry to Israel to attend a ceremony organized to honor their contributions, forcing Israeli officials to cancel the ceremony altogether. In the words of Arab member of Knesset Ahmed Tibi, the incident was "not just a march of folly or a theater of the absurd but stupidity and the normative lordly attitude of the occupation regime."

The bulk of Israeli public anger focused on Yishai, the Shas leader who headed the Interior Ministry. It was up to Yishai to ensure the viability and preparedness of Israel's firefighting corps, however, he seemed far more interested in diverting public money into the settlements, especially those that were home to his religious Mizrahi constituents. As he declared in June 2009, "I promise to use my ministry, all the resources at my disposal, and the ministry's impact on local authorities for the good of expanding settlements." With his near-criminal negligence exposed and his cabinet post in grave danger, Yishai claimed he was the victim of anti-Mizrahi prejudice, moaning, "What is happening here is a lynching." Adding insult to injury, the spiritual leader of Yishai's Shas Party, former Chief Israeli Rabbi Ovadiah Yosef, blamed the fire on the sins of its victims, proclaiming in his weekly sermon, "Fires only happen in a place where Shabbat is desecrated. Homes were ruined, entire neighborhoods wiped out, and it is not arbitrary. It is all divine providence."

As the circular political firing squad unloaded in the wake of the disaster, with one minister blaming another for a failure that indicted the government as a whole, the Carmel fire inadvertently exposed an open wound at the heart of the country's character and identity as a Jewish state. The pine trees that had burned so easily across the Carmel mountains were originally intended as instruments of concealment, strategically planted by the JNF atop the sites of the hundreds of Palestinian villages the Israeli military evacuated and destroyed in 1948 and '67. With forests sprouting up where towns once stood, those who had been expelled would have nothing to come back to. And that was exactly what the JNF intended.

The JNF's showcase forest, Canada Park, is built on the ruins of the Palestinian villages that once stood in Latrun—Imwas, Yalu, and Beit Nuba. Having failed to remove the villages in 1948, the 82nd Regiment of the Israeli army returned to Latrun in 1967 to finish the job. Besides the desire for revenge after the punishing loss at Latrun in '48, the state considered the villages an obstruction to building a direct highway from Jerusalem to Tel Aviv. At nine in the morning, the soldiers gathered the eight thousand residents in an open area and, with direct orders from General Yitzhak Rabin, ordered them at gunpoint to march to Ramallah. Hours later, bulldozers arrived to destroy the villagers' homes.

"The chickens and the doves were buried under the ruins," the regiment commander, Amos Kenan, later recalled. "The fields turned desolate before our very eyes, and children walked down the road sobbing. That was how we lost our victory that day."

Though some of the enlisted soldiers cried as they witnessed the pathetic scene unfolding before them, none disobeyed their orders to guard the bulldozers. Moshe Dayan reassured Israeli skeptics that the expulsions were conducted "with Zionist intentions."

During the 1970s, the JNF constructed Canada Park with generous donations from the Canadian government, planting thousands of non-indigenous pine trees on the rubble of Imwas, Yalu, and Beit Nuba. Today the park is an idyllic setting for cyclists, hikers, and families who spend Israel's Independence Day picnicking in the sun. However, those who venture too deeply into the forest may risk stumbling over the still-intact spring and water wells belonging to the scattered refugees of Yalu, or the rubble of a church where the Christians of Imwas worshipped each Sunday until the Israeli bulldozers sent it crashing to the ground. Though few Israelis realize it, when they stroll in the shade of Canada Park's pines, they are actually inside a section of the West Bank captured from the Palestinians—that the JNF trees mask the occupation.

Until 2006, the JNF omitted the history of the Palestinian villages from the explanatory signs it posted around the park, instead presenting details of life in the Second Temple, Hellenic, and Roman periods, adhering to a strictly Eurocentric narrative. When Zochrot, an Israeli non-profit dedicated to preserving the memory of the Nakba, petitioned the Supreme Court to amend the signs to include the history of Arab habitation, the JNF first attempted to deflect all responsibility onto the Israeli government before it finally conceded to the demand. But almost as soon as the revised signs were posted, one mysteriously disappeared, while vandals meticulously blacked out the section mentioning Palestinian villages on another.

The JNF was intimately involved in the Nakba, with its then-director Yosef Weitz establishing the Transfer Committee, where a pantheon of leaders orchestrated the final and most brutal stages of ethnic cleansing, which they called Plan Dalet. Described by the Israeli revisionist historian Ilan Pappe as "the quintessential colonialist," Weitz personally guided the expulsions with a deliberate, calculated hand, dispatching his staff to identify Palestinian villages to destroy—a practice David Ben Gurion called, "cleaning up." "It must be clear that there is no room in the country for both peoples," Weitz declared at the time. "If the Arabs leave it, the country will become wide and spacious for us. . . . The only solution is a Land of Israel . . . without Arabs. . . . There is no way but to transfer the Arabs from here to the neighboring countries, to transfer all of them, save perhaps for [the Palestinian Arabs of] Bethlehem, Nazareth, and the old Jerusalem. Not one village must be left, not one tribe."

In the ethnically pure Israel of Weitz and Ben Gurion's dreams, a distinctly European, alpine landscape would be able to flourish atop the "wilderness" the Palestinians had supposedly failed to cultivate. Having fulfilled most of the goals of Plan Dalet, namely, expelling as many Arabs as possible and replacing them with new Jewish immigrants, the JNF planted hundreds of thousands of trees over the freshly destroyed Palestinian villages. In establishing the Carmel National Park in northern Israel, the JNF strategically concealed the ruins of al-Tira, a once-populous and picturesque town that joined the hundreds erased from the map. As the trees matured and developed into a full-fledged forest, an area on the south slope of Mount Carmel came to resemble the landscape of the Swiss Alps so closely that Israelis nicknamed it "Little Switzerland."

But the nonindigenous trees of the JNF were poorly suited to the dry Mediterranean climate of Palestine. Most of the saplings the JNF plants at a site near Jerusalem die soon after taking root, requiring constant replanting. Elsewhere, needles from the pine trees have killed native plant species and wreaked havoc on the ecosystem. And when the wildfires swept through the Carmel Mountains, "Little Switzerland" quickly went up in smoke.

Among the towns evacuated during the Carmel fires was Ein Hod, a bohemian artists' colony nestled in the hills to the north and east of Haifa. During the great conflagration, residents of the village came pouring out in search of escape, with some seeking shelter in nearby Arab villages. It was not the first time Ein Hod was evacuated. The first time was in 1948, when the town's original Palestinian inhabitants were driven from their homes.

Before the establishment of Israel, Ein Hod was called Ayn Hawd. The town had been continuously populated since the twelfth century, after Arabs from Iraq settled the area. During the Nakba, Israeli troops expelled most of Ein Hod's residents to refugee camps in Jordan, Syria, and Jenin in the West Bank. But a small and exceptionally resilient clan fled to the nearby hills, set up a makeshift camp, and watched as Jewish foreigners moved into their empty homes.

In 1953, when the army authorized plans to bulldoze the town, a Romanian Dadaist sculptor named Marcel Janco successfully lobbied them against it. Janco was not acting out of humanitarian concern but self-interest: in place of the Arab village, he proposed establishing an all-Jewish art commune to generate tourism and contribute to the culture of Zionism, which he claimed would benefit from the modernist traditions he had brought over from Europe.

Thanks to Janco, the rustic stone homes that once belonged to Palestinians contain quaint artist studios and a large museum dedicated to his paintings. Janco drew his scenes of Arab life in typically Orientalist fashion, depicting the indigenous residents of the Galilee as a faceless, agrarian mass or as cartoonish stereotypes. The mosque that once served Ayn Hawd's Muslim population has been converted into an airy bar called Bonanza, where Goldstar beer flows from the tap and pizza bakes in a woodburning oven. Visitors to the town are greeted at the entrance by Benjamin Levy's *The Modest Couple in a Sardine Can*, a sculpture depicting a nude woman and a suited gentleman in a sardine can, which was unveiled at a ceremony led by President Peres in 2001.

Having survived the catastrophe of 1948, the al-Hija clan of Ayn Hawd set up a new village three kilometers away from what is today known as Eid Hod. They thus joined the eighty thousand Palestinians classified by Israel as "present absentees," or refugees who had been permanently driven from their homes but not outside the borders of the country. In the decades that followed, the villagers resisted state attempts at removal. Unable to dislodge the al-Hija clan, the state surrounded them with a fence to prevent them from expanding their unrecognized village. In 2005, after decades of deliberate official neglect and a sustained campaign to highlight their plight, the residents of Ayn Hawd won official recognition—a stunning rarity for an unrecognized Arab village. For the first time, they were able to receive public services like trash removal and electricity.

I visited Ein Hod in June 2010. The village was charmingly quaint, and if I had not arrived with the intention of investigating its history, I might have felt welcome enough to spend a night or two at the local bed and breakfast. But Ein Hod's residents had apparently been conditioned to treat the overly curious outsider poking around for details about the ghosts that still haunt them with extreme wariness. When I pulled out my video camera and began to ask the local artists about their studios, I was met with a mixture of suspicion and outright hostility. "I know what you're doing!" a silver-haired woman sneered at me, insisting that I not film her.

Inside the Bonanza bar, I asked patrons if the place was in fact a converted mosque. "Yeah, but that's how all of Israel is," a talkative young woman from a nearby kibbutz told me as she sipped on a beer. "This whole country is built on top of Arab villages. So maybe it's best to let bygones be bygones."

Near a cluster of stone homes, I joined a group of aging Israeli tourists with waistpacks and big, floppy hats as a professional guide led them around Ein Hod. Speaking in Hebrew, the guide took them through the studios, informing them that they were inside "third generation houses," deceiving them into believing that Israeli Jews were the original owners. While browsing the studios, I noticed that much of the art being produced was Judaica kitsch for sale to foreign tourists—generic *shtetl* scenes from the long lost world immortalized in Yiddish scribe Sholom Aleichem's *Tevye and His Daughters*, a play that concluded with a tragic scene of Russians expelling the Jews from their *shtetl*.

Later, before taking her group to the town's Hurdy Gurdy museum, a rustic workshop dedicated to the restoration and preservation of medieval European instruments, the guide mentioned a "welcoming committee" that vetted potential residents. This was apparently one device the residents of Ein Hod used to keep the Arabs down the road from returning home. Then there was the Absentee Property Law of 1950, which placed all "abandoned" Arab property in the hands of the JNF and the ILA, consolidating the state-sanctioned theft committed during the Nakba through democratically approved legislation.

During a break in the tour, the guide pulled me aside and demanded to know who I was. Introducing herself as Shuli Linda Yarkon, a PhD candidate at Tel Aviv University, the tour guide told me with great modesty that she was the leading authority on Ein Hod. She insisted that I allow her to review all the footage I planned to shoot, claiming that this would ensure that I not mistranslate words she used like *kibbush*, a Hebrew term that means "conquest" but is commonly used to refer to the occupation of Palestine.

"So what about the conquest you mentioned?" I asked her. "Why didn't you tell the tourists who lived in the houses before 1948?" Visibly irritated, Yarkon resorted to the dreary vocabulary of post-structuralism to justify her revisionism. "I've concluded after years of research that there are really no facts when you discuss this issue," she stated coldly. "There are only narratives."

She assured me that Ein Hod's Jewish population maintained excellent relations with the expelled residents: "Go ask them. They will tell you how they feel."

So I did. After following a winding dirt road around a hillside for several kilometers, I was inside Ayn Hawd, the Arab village. There was no installation art here, just a collection of mostly ramshackle houses, dirt roads, a mosque with a tall minaret, and crowds of scruffy kids playing in the streets. Almost immediately some of the town's residents appeared from their homes to greet me. Among them was Abu Moein al-Hija, a village council member and schoolteacher who invited me to spend the rest of the afternoon with his family on a patio beside his home, which appeared newer and more stately than those of his neighbors.

Al-Hija told me his ancestors arrived in the village more than seven hundred years ago from what is now Iraq. Those members of his family who were expelled to Jenin in 1948 never returned home, even to visit. They told him they would be too angry to even lay eyes their former homes with the new Israeli occupants inside. When I mentioned the bar built into the old mosque, al-Hija shook his head in disgust. "It's very bad. It's an insult," he said.

Al-Hija took me inside his home for a tour, showing me the spacious, immaculately clean parlor and the picture window with a sweeping view of the valley below. He had built the whole place, he said with pride. Down a hall, his thirteen-year-old daughter, Ansam, was reclining on the floor of her room reading John Knowles's novel of American prep school boys, *A Separate Peace*. She leapt to attention when I entered and spent the next ten minutes showing me her library.

With night setting in, Moein and his family took me back on the patio. There, he unfurled the map of Mandate-era Palestine that so many Palestinian families I have visited kept in their homes. It was maps like these, which highlighted the hundreds of towns disappeared by the State of Israel, that Uri Avnery called "more dangerous than any bomb." Al-Hija ran his fingers over the names of scores of villages destroyed on the coast between Jaffa and Haifa by Zionist forces in 1948, pointing to Kafr Saba, Qaqun, al-Tira, and Tantura, the site of a massacre of unarmed Palestinian prisoners on the beach just one month after the Deir Yassin massacre. Moein was a history teacher, but the state had forbidden him from discussing these events in his classroom and was in the process of criminalizing their public observance.

As darkness blanketed the hills, I realized that I had lost track of time. I told al-Hija that I needed to get back to Tel Aviv. With that, his wife rushed into the house and gathered a bunch of grapes she had picked from a tree in the family's garden, handing them over to me in a Tupperware bowl. On the drive down the coast, as I breezed by the dunes and sandy flats where the heart of Palestine once pulsed with life, I thought of a quote by the seventeenth-century Jewish mystic Baal Shem Tov inscribed on a wall at Yad Vashem, the Israeli Holocaust memorial museum. "Forgetfulness leads to exile," it read, "while remembrance is the secret of redemption."

In his 1963 short fiction story "Facing the Forests," the Israeli author A. B. Yehoshua portrayed a mute Palestinian forest watchman taking revenge by burning down a JNF forest to reveal the hidden ruins of his former village. Imagining that the fictional tale had come to life, right-wing Israelis began demanding a search for the Arab who must have sparked the blaze on the Carmel Mountains, which the Israeli police described as a deliberate act. While *Yedioth Ahronoth* blared without evidence, "Hezbollah Overjoyed by Fire," Michael Ben-Ari, a extremist member of Knesset from the National Union Party, called for "the whole Shin Bet" to be mobilized to investigate what the settler media outlet Arutz Sheva said "may turn out to be the worst terror attack in Israel's history." After the damage was done, an official investigation determined the fire to be the result of simple negligence.

PART VI

THE YEAR OF DEMOCRACY

These Things That
Were Done to Us

I n the early afternoon on December 27, 2010, at Yad Vashem, a museum and research
institute that describes itself as "the Jewish people's living memorial to the Holocaust," fourteen Palestinian women arrived to learn about the Jewish genocide in
Europe as part of a program organized by the Israeli Bereaved Families Forum, which
promotes dialogue and understanding between Jewish Israelis and Palestinians who
have lost family members in the conflict. The women received special passes to travel
from the occupied city of Nablus through the separation wall to Jerusalem, a place
that is off limits to most West Bank Palestinians except under special circumstances.

Accompanied by a group of Jewish Israeli women who planned to visit a Palestinian village destroyed in the Nakba the following week, the women from Nablus
had hoped to achieve a cultural breakthrough. Despite all they and their families
had suffered under Israel's occupation, they were willing to expose themselves to the
historical trauma that had impacted the psyche of their neighbors living on the other
side of the wall. But instead of the hearty welcome they expected, they earned curses
from a mob of preadolescent Jewish children.

"*Sharmouta!*" the children shouted at the women, using the Arabic word for
"whore." "*Zonot!*" the kids continued, this time employing the Hebrew for "hookers."

For the Palestinian women on the tour, the behavior of the Israeli children was
completely foreign. "In Palestinian culture, older women are most honored, and they
could not believe their ears," said Siham Abu Awwad, a Palestinian coordinator of
the tour. "We never talk like this to older women. The Palestinians, who were all
grandmothers, were very shocked and offended."

The Jewish women on the tour were just as horrified, attempting to mitigate
the damage the children had caused with profuse apologies on their behalf. But as
mothers and educators, they understood the roots of the racist outburst were firmly
implanted in the foundations of Israeli society. Tamara Rabinovich, an Israeli facilitator of the trip, remarked to a reporter from the Hebrew news site Walla!, "For these
children, it doesn't matter where they are, even at Yad Vashem. They have been taught
to see the Palestinians as enemies, so that's how they behave."

In the cultivation of the Israeli psyche, there is no more important historical episode
than the Holocaust. A two-minute-long siren sounds across Israel on Yom Hashoah,

or Holocaust Memorial Day, bringing all traffic to a standstill and marking the emotional zenith of the springtime holiday season in Israel, which spans a highly compressed period from Passover to Independence Day, showcasing the foundation of Israel as the salvation of the Jews around the world from thousands of years of endless anti-Semitism.

Throughout Israel's history, the state's leaders have justified the country's seemingly permanent state of siege by invoking the immediate prospect of a second Holocaust. In 1982, when Prime Minister Menachem Begin attempted to rally the Israeli public behind the army's invasion of Lebanon, he declared, "The alternative [to war] is Treblinka, and we have decided there will be no more Treblinkas." Five years later, in a speech at Israel's Holocaust Memorial ceremony, as the First Intifada was approaching its crescendo, then minister of defense Yitzhak Rabin proclaimed, "In every generation they rise up to destroy us, and we must remember that this could happen to us in the future. We must therefore, as a state, be prepared for this."

With the onset of the Second Intifada and the deepening of Israel's regime of separation, an all-consuming sense of doom and despair began to pervade Israeli society. A study by the Israeli political scientist Uriel Abulof showed that in the six years after 2001, the number of articles in *Ha'aretz* focusing on existential threats to the country increased by 65 percent from six years before—244 a year compared to 147. The narrative of existential doom has intensified even further thanks in large part to Prime Minister Benjamin Netanyahu, the "Fearmonger-in-Chief" who has repeatedly identified Iranian President Mahmoud Ahmadinejad, a figure with no control over his country's military, as a "new Hitler," while comparing its nascent nuclear facilities to Auschwitz, the engines of Jewish annihilation.

"Netanyahu is well entrenched through the socialization process to be a typical representative of a Jew who views the world through the prism of Jewish persecution," the Tel Aviv University political psychology professor Daniel Bar-Tal told me. "When he talks about Iran being a Nazi country or Ahmadinejad being Hitler, he really believes it. But it also falls on a really fertile soil. When he speaks in these terms, many Israelis believe what he's saying. It falls on very open ears, this kind of rhetoric, with people who are used to the trauma of Hitler and the Holocaust."

The Holocaust is a focus of history classes and Jewish education in Israeli public schools and is relentlessly invoked in Israeli media, with Palestinian militants often portrayed as "Nazis" while Jews are presented as victims requiring heroic rescue from brave Israeli soldiers. In 1960, well before Netanyahu's time, and before the Eichmann trial forced the Holocaust into the Israeli national ethos, *Yedioth Ahronoth* columnist Eliahu Amikam justified the massacre at Deir Yassin in 1948 by claiming that Nazi storm troopers were found among the Palestinians slaughtered in the village. "In Deir-Yassin there were soldiers of regular foreign armies, including Nazis with swastika emblems," Amikam wrote. "Among the corpses there were Iraqis, Syrians, and Yugoslavs lying in their military uniform. Swastika ribbons were torn off their sleeves."

Giulio Meotti, a neoconservative Italian commentator who maintained a column for *Yedioth Ahronoth* until he was dismissed for chronic plagiarism, channeled Amikam's moral exceptionalism when he wrote in 2012, "Because of the Holocaust, Menachem Begin ordered the destruction of the nuclear bomb plant built by Saddam

Hussein on the outskirts of Baghdad. Because of the Holocaust, Golda Meir ordered Mossad operatives to kill Palestinian terrorists who slaughtered Jewish athletes at the 1972 Olympic Games in Munich. Because of the Holocaust, Israel raided Tunisia to kill Abu Jihad, Yasser Arafat's terrorist chief." By Meotti's reasoning, which expressed the mindset upheld by Israeli prime ministers from Ben Gurion to Netanyahu, because of the Holocaust Israel had the exclusive moral right to inaugurate a nuclear weapons program of its own and to conceal it from International Atomic Energy Agency (IAEA) inspectors. And under that logic, Israel was justified in raining shells containing an experimental, mint-smelling poison gas down on Gaza's Khan Younis refugee camp that caused hysteria and "thrashing of limbs" among its victims.

The lessons of the Holocaust have been imparted across the world to promote greater tolerance for minorities and marginalized social groups. But in Israel, they are routinely exploited to advance narrow nationalistic goals. "In Israel, people relive the Holocaust every day," Gal Harmat, a thirty-five-year-old peace education professor at Tel Aviv's Kibbutzim Teachers College, told me. "People are trained to think that the Arabs are going to unite with the Nazis and come and kill us. This chip was planted in my brain at a very young age. In kindergarten, our teacher told how they made soap out of Jews and described it to kids in very graphic terms. So every night as a five-year-old, I had nightmares about being made into soap. Then in first grade, they took to us the Yad Vashem, but only to the children's house. When the siren blew that year on Yom Ha'Shoah (Holocaust Memorial Day), I smiled a little for some reason. For smiling, I was publicly humiliated in front of the whole class. The teacher shouted, 'You disrespected the Holocaust victims who died for you, Gal!' The fears I developed from all this made me want a strong and capable boy to protect me. I wanted a pilot in the Air Force because we were told they were the strongest."

While living in Austria as a young adult, Harmat encountered a teenage neo-Nazi on a train from Salzburg to Vienna. "I asked him why would he wear a swastika on his jacket. And he told me he truly believed in white supremacy, in fascism, and these kind of ideas," she recalled. "From this short conversation I had with this teenager, it made me want to leave everything behind and come home to strengthen Israel. There was a chip planted in me that made me think every racist incident or misbehavior was a reason for me to strengthen the Jewish nation."

Daniel Bar-Tal has produced some of the most comprehensive research to date on the impact of the Holocaust on the Jewish Israeli psyche. In a 2000 survey Bar-Tal conducted with Israeli university students, Bar-Tal found that those who experienced the Holocaust personally or through family members were actually less resentful toward Palestinians than those without direct experience with loss. Bar-Tal also found that people who had formed their opinions of the Israel-Palestine conflict through direct contact with Palestinians were more likely to express tolerance and empathy toward the other. In stark contrast, test subjects who had experienced the Holocaust or interacted with Palestinians only through "collective experiences"—the Israeli education system, the media, and mass Holocaust observances—were most likely to fall captive to the kind of anti-Arab outlook that bolstered Israel's militaristic objectives. A prime example of the kind of person who embodied the latter phenomenon, according to Bar-Tal, was Benjamin Netanyahu.

"People like Netanyahu did not live through the Holocaust, but you have to understand what the Holocaust plays in the life of youngsters in this nation," Bar-Tal explained to me. "It is through memorials through trips taken during the adolescent period, the Holocaust is a central feature of the Israeli identity. So it doesn't matter at the moment whether you came directly from the Holocaust or you came from an Arab country that didn't experience it, or you are fourth generation. It is a kind of lever that can be pulled to bring everyone into the Israeli experience. It unites people."

In recent years, more than 25 percent of Israeli eleventh-graders have been flown to Poland to tour Auschwitz and other extermination centers—always one year before they begin army service. A 2011 study by the Education Ministry found that most participants had experienced a dramatic surge of positive feelings for the army and the Jewish state after completing the trip. "The army was less important to me before I saw the soldiers at Majdanek. Now I have more motivation," one participant remarked after witnessing a brigade of Israeli troops march through a concentration camp. The trips were so successful that in 2011, the Education Ministry began requiring all students to participate in initial preparations for the journey, even if they would not be traveling to Poland. To support the new policy, the ministry increased funding for the school trips from one million to six million shekels—a symbolic figure that seemed likely not to have been chosen arbitrarily.

In his 2009 documentary *Defamation*, a biting commentary on the exploitation of anti-Semitism, Israeli filmmaker Yoav Shamir embedded himself with a group of Israeli eleventh-graders on a class trip to Auschwitz, Poland, filming them as they participated in the annual "March of the Living" Holocaust commemoration. Shamir began recording the students during their preliminary preparations, depicting a briefing in which a school counselor warned the kids, "Israel was founded as a result of the Holocaust, but anti-Semitism still exists. . . . You as Jews, as the next generation who are about to join the army, you will also have to face this aspect of our life."

The students seemed primed for indoctrination. A girl named Adi told Shamir before embarking on the trip, "'We were raised in this spirit, that we know we are hated."

"Everybody knows Jews are hated," added her classmate, Notar. "We were raised in that way."

And so the students flew to Poland along with a Shin Bet officer assigned by the state to prevent the kids from interacting with the Polish locals—people "who do not like us," according to the school counselor. After sundown the students were ordered by the Shin Bet agent to stay in their rooms. Neo-Nazis were lurking in the streets, waiting to kill the Jews, or so they were told.

Yet even after days of visits to dank showers and dark crematoria where Jews were turned into fertilizer, and even after being subjected to graphic tales from the tour guide about "Bloodthirsty Brigitte," a notorious camp commander who tortured women with a barbed-wire whip, the students appeared to maintain a degree of critical detachment. "I wonder if our threshold might be too high," one participant confessed to Shamir. "When we see an Arab home demolished by the army on the news, we might say it's not too bad. We faced worse."

The trip concluded with an intense candlelit ceremony in a dank basement in which each student was compelled to take on the persona of an actual teenage

Holocaust victim. It was there that the kids were broken, and one after another, they fell to the floor in tears.

Following the ceremony, one of the girls who had complained to her counselor a day earlier about lacking any emotional connection to the Holocaust remarked to Shamir, "Would I like to kill? All of them . . . the Nazis. Our enemies who did this."

When Shamir informed her that the Nazis were dead, she snapped back, "They have heirs. They may be different, but they're there."

Only one member of the tour group seemed to have remained skeptical until the end. He was the class teacher, Assaf. Seated on a bench, the teacher confided to Shamir, "The Germans started it all, and we are perpetuating it. I thought a lot about it. Whether this March of the Living is good or bad, this death industry. . . . We perpetuate death, and that's why we will never become a normal people, because we emphasize death and what happened. We live too much in it, and it's preventing us from being a normal people." (An Israeli tour guide interrupted the teacher to admonish him for sitting on the bench: "Excuse me, please don't sit there," the guide said. "More than twenty people died here in this spot.")

The misgivings that the intense Holocaust tour stirred inside the teacher were also common among combat veterans who had served in the Occupied Territories. Indeed, a staggering number of Israeli army officers who participated in government-sponsored trips to the death camps of Poland have returned home with lingering doubts about Jewish nationalism. A 2012 Israeli army study revealed that the program, "Witnesses in Uniform," which sent three thousand career officers a year to Auschwitz in order to promote nationalistic values, wound up producing the opposite of its intended effect. According to a summary of the study published in *Ha'aretz*, after the soldiers participated in the trip, "the researchers found a drop in commitment to all values related to Jewish identity, including the importance of the Land of Israel for the Jewish people, the importance of the IDF's existence, feelings of national pride in being Israeli, and a sense of a shared Jewish fate." While the trips also produced a steep decline in the officers' commitment to the Jewish state and the army, the participants experienced a stunning rise in their commitment to universal democratic values.

The Israeli army's in-house researchers were befuddled by the findings. Why did the Holocaust trips to Poland promote a surge in nationalistic feelings among the eleventh-grade students while provoking an existential crisis among veteran army officers? Perhaps the answer lay in the fact that the high schoolers had yet to experience the realities of army service, while the officers were intimately familiar with the harsh duties of occupying and controlling an immiserated, demonized, indigenous population confined in ghettoes, behind checkpoints and concrete walls. Could the emotional intensity of the tour have provoked an outpouring of reflectiveness among the army officers? Had they suddenly come to see themselves perpetuating what the Germans started, as the class teacher, Assaf, told Shamir?

An anonymous testimony by a female officer to the non-profit, Breaking the Silence, which collects confessions from soldiers who committed abuses while maintaining Israel's occupation, offers a possible insight into the soldiers' crisis of conscience:

I recall once, this was after we moved to Mevo Dotan, to the base there, some Palestinian was sitting on a chair, and I passed by several times. Once I thought: Okay, why is he sitting here for an hour? I feel like spitting at him, at this Arab. And they tell me, go on, spit at him. I don't recall whether anyone did this before I did, but I remember spitting at him and feeling really, like at first I felt, wow, good for me, I just spat at some terrorist—that's how I'd call them. And then I recall that afterward I felt something here was not right.

Why?

Not too human. I mean, it sounds cool and all, but no, it's not right.

You thought about later, or during the act?

Later. At the time you felt real cool.

Even when everyone was watching, you felt real cool?

Yes, and then sometimes you get to thinking, especially say on Holocaust Memorial Day, suddenly you're thinking, hey, these things were done to us, it's a human being after all. Eventually as things turned out he was no terrorist anyway, it was a kid who'd hung around too long near the base, so he was caught or something.

A child?

An adolescent.

Slaps?

Yes.

Blindfolded and all?

Yes. I think that at some point no one even stood watch over him.

Consistent with the Israeli army's culture of *Yorim u'Vochim*, or shooting and crying, the soldier did not express her misgivings about the abuse of the Palestinian child until well after the incident occurred. Similarly, during a March 2002 Israeli army raid of the Tulkarm refugee camp, no soldier disobeyed his orders to inscribe in ink identification numbers on the forearms and foreheads of the blindfolded Palestinian prisoners they had yanked from homes and detained. Only afterward did anyone complain, with a spokesman for then–prime minister Ariel Sharon agreeing to halt the practice, but only on the ground that "it conflicts with the desire to convey a public relations message."

And when a few soldiers manning a checkpoint outside Nablus ordered a local Palestinian man named Wissam Tayem, to remove his violin and "play a sad song," no soldiers intervened to stop the humiliation. Instead, they gathered around Tayem and mocked him while he played. Thanks to Machson Watch, an organization of mostly middle-aged Jewish Israeli women who monitor and videotape checkpoint abuses, Tayem's humiliation was one of the rare incidents of cruelty that penetrated the Israeli army's information cordon. Yoram Kaniuk, a famous Israeli author who had published a book about a Jewish violinist forced to play for a concentration camp commander, wrote that the soldiers who abused Tayem should be punished "not for abusing Arabs, but for disgracing the Holocaust." He explained, "Our entire existence in this Arab region was justified, and is still justified, by our suffering; by Jewish violinists in the camps."

The Forbidden Tour

I n April 2009, a tour guide at Yad Vashem risked his job to challenge the nationalistic perspective the museum administration and its state-level overseers were attempting to promote. While most guides took tourists from the darkened halls of the museum toward the giant cattle car installed on its grounds that seems to hang in the air, pointing toward Jerusalem, the spiritual center of the Jewish state, Itamar Shapira, a former combat soldier turned human rights activist, led his group in a different direction. In an interview one month after the incident, Shapira told me that when he guided the visitors out of the museum, he ushered them to the hillside and pointed them to the ruins of a village clearly visible in the valley below.

Before the visitors was Deir Yassin, the site of the massacre of over one hundred Palestinian civilians during the 1948 war by the Stern Gang, a right-wing Zionist militia. Today it is home to the Kfar Shaul Medical Health Center, an Israeli mental institution where tourists who suffer from the religious delusions known as Jerusalem Syndrome are treated. Surrounding the mental hospital are the crumbling homes that once belonged to Deir Yassin's families, who now live in refugee camps across the Arab world.

"By the end of the official tour," Shapira told me, "Yad Vashem leads you in an impressive manipulation, maybe an emotional climax. You go down into the ground, until you get to the lowest place, Auschwitz, then you go up; the museum goes up from the ground and you are looking over the battlefields of our Independence War. And it doesn't say specifically before you go out, you pass through David Ben Gurion declaring independence. It has connotations to people saying this is our independence, this is our place, thanks to the establishment of the state."

In Shapira's alternative tour, visitors were forced to acknowledge the toll Israel's foundation took on the indigenous Palestinian population. "I was saying to them that from this war, many of the Israelis who participated in it, were coming from the Holocaust with no families, fighting the Palestinians—many of them did not know where it was, where they were, and they just had nothing to lose," he explained. "This was their shelter, they thought. On the other hand, I was saying that on these same battlefields massacres happened of Jews massacring Arabs, and this was the root of the refugee problem of the Palestinians."

Shapira added, "I thought this was the best way to end a tour of Yad Vashem, to say we have passed through our suffering, and now we have to acknowledge that in this place there are other sufferings, and if we don't understand them we will have no political means of resolving them. This was the best way: What do we remember about the Holocaust, and how do we apply it later?"

Unfortunately for Shapira, right-wing members of a group from the Jewish settlement of Efrat overheard his presentation and complained to Yad Vashem administrators. "They said, 'How can you say this?!' No one cared that I talked about Arabs besieging Jerusalem, fighting for our independence," he recalled. "The last sentence about the refugee problem, this was when they protested. How can you justify the violence of the Palestinians? People think acknowledging their suffering supports their violence!"

Shapira was summoned to a hearing, where he was instructed by the museum's directors to excise any mention of Palestinian suffering from his tour. When he refused, they fired him, accusing him of politicizing the Holocaust by likening it to other historical events. "Yad Vashem would have acted unprofessionally had Itamar Shapira continued his educational work for the institute," a museum spokesperson told *Ha'aretz* at the time.

After losing his job, Shapira became more aware of the rising climate of repression in Israeli society. The anti-democratic laws pouring out of the Knesset filled him with visions of a frightening authoritarian future. "This is an acceleration process of violence and support of violence because of fear and then legalizing this kind of violence," Shapira calmly remarked. "This is what happened in Gaza despite the strong will of the people to protest. Now, when laws like that are passing, in order to finish the Gaza massacre, you make it also illegal to say something against it.

"And this is the path we're going on. For me, thirteen hundred dead people in three weeks is already frightening. We've already passed the limit. The next cycle of violence will be more, and there will be less Israelis saying anything against it, not because they don't want to, but because they fear the laws and breaking with the Knesset."

Bleeding Over the Party

S oon after meeting Itamar Shapira, I became friendly with his older brother, Yonatan. Born to an Air Force squadron commander who fought in the 1973 Yom Kippur War, Yonatan Shapira was reared to continue his family's distinguished military legacy. During his adolescence and early adulthood, he was shaped to be the virile but sensitive scholar who wrote poetry and played guitar after landing his helicopter on a verdant hillside—the quintessential enlightened Israeli alpha male. So while he was weaned on humanistic, liberal values, Yonatan prepared to enter an elite unit of the Israeli Air Force. During the raid on the Gaza Freedom Flotilla's *Mavi Marmara*, it was Yonatan's Blackhawk helicopter transport and rescue unit that lowered the Shayatet 13 commandos onto the ship's upper deck. But Yonatan was not in the pilot's seat anymore. Instead, he was on his way to Poland to meet coordinators of the international, Palestinian-led movement to boycott Israel.

In late June 2010, Yonatan joined Ewa Jasiewicz, a Polish human rights activist who had just sailed on the Gaza Freedom Flotilla, for a special event near the Warsaw Ghetto, at the outer wall of what had once been the cramped, disease-ridden, Nazi-administered hellhole where the city's Jews were held until the Final Solution turned most of them to ash. The ghetto was also the site of the fiercest Jewish armed rebellion of World War II, when scores of ragtag partisans took up arms against the Nazis in a futile but ferocious fight for dignity. On a wall across the street from the symbolic site of armed resistance against transfer and genocide, Yonatan, the grandson of Polish Holocaust victims, spray-painted a slogan in Hebrew: "Liberate All Ghettoes." Then, another in English: "Free Gaza and Palestine." Finally, he and Jasiewicz hoisted a Palestinian flag over the crumbling cement wall.

"When I walk in what was left from the Warsaw Ghetto, I can't stop thinking about the people of Gaza who are not only locked in an open air prison, but are also being bombarded by fighter jets, attack helicopters, and drones flown by people whom I used to serve with before my refusal in 2003," Yonatan declared after the event. "I am also thinking about the delegations of young Israelis that are coming to see the history of our people but also are subjected to militaristic and nationalistic brainwashing on a daily basis. Maybe if they see what we wrote here today they will remember that oppression is oppression, occupation is occupation, and crimes against humanity are crimes against humanity, whether they have been committed here in Warsaw or in Gaza."

As soon as Yonatan returned to Israel, news of his provocative action was reverberating across the country, generating visceral anger and befuddlement. Israel's deputy minister for Pensioner Affairs, Leah Nass, demanded swift and stern punishment. "This vile act demonstrates how imperative commemoration is these days, in order to prevent Holocaust denial," Nass proclaimed. "I plan to contact the authorities in Poland to prosecute the law-breakers and anarchists." In the meantime, the Israeli embassy in Poland urged local authorities to paint over the slogans as soon as possible.

I met Yonatan just days after the event in Warsaw, and hours after he appeared on Israeli National Radio, where a lieutenant colonel from the army accused him of being mentally ill, then said he should be punished with a caning like scofflaws in Singapore. Yonatan responded, "The International Criminal Court should decide whether I'm the criminal or those who bomb civilians in Gaza."

When Yonatan was training in Israel's Air Force Academy, he and his fellow cadets constructed a giant cardboard diamond and placed it in the courtyard of their base in the Negev Desert. The mock sculpture referred to a humorous Israeli saying: "When you become a pilot in the Air Force, you get a diamond on the tip of your dick." Toward the end of the training course, a commander gathered the cadets for a pep talk. He told them that Israel was a large country with millions of people. Within Israeli society was the military, he explained, which was comprised of its best people. Inside the military was the Air Force, which consisted of the best of the best. And inside the Air Force were the pilots who were the best of the best of the best. "We felt like the *ubermenschen* of Israel," Yonatan recalled. "We might not have liked the fascist mechanisms of the state, but we wanted to be the best of the best. And if you are sure that you're the best, you can't possibly commit war crimes! How can the best of Israel be war criminals?"

Yonatan saw his first action during the most violent phase of the Second Intifada. On June 20, 2002, he was sent on a rescue mission in Itamar, a northern West Bank settlement whose extremist residents had a long record of violent attacks on Palestinian farmers in the area. A group of Palestinian militants had attacked the settlement, killing a mother and three of her children in cold blood, while badly wounding two other kids. After the militants holed themselves up in a house full of settlers, the army attacked, seeking to free the trapped hostages. Though the soldiers managed to kill the two militants, eight more children were wounded in the fighting. Yonatan's job was to load the children in his Blackhawk helicopter and ferry them to a hospital in Ramat Gan, a suburb of Tel Aviv, before they bled to death.

While swooping into Ramat Gan, Yonatan said he briefly hovered over a wedding party. The scene captivated him. "I was carrying these kids in the back, who were bleeding badly, and I didn't know if they were going to live, and there was this giant party, with everyone dancing and drinking right below me," he said.

An hour later, Yonatan returned to Itamar to load more bleeding kids in the back of his Blackhawk. When he returned to Tel Aviv, the wedding party was still rocking.

"It began to dawn on me," he recalled, "that the people in Tel Aviv had no idea about the violence in the West Bank, that they were not connected to reality."

Back at the base, Yonatan became consumed with questions about the psychological disconnectedness of Israeli society and doubts about the objectives of the military's means of crushing the Second Intifada. He was encouraged to air his criticism publicly, to challenge his superior officers, to vent so that he could return to duty with a clear conscience. "We were like a family," he explained, "and even though you are just a lieutenant, you could criticize the general when you flew together because we believed were all equal when it came to the actual operations. They planted the idea in our heads that the system would only improve and become progressive through internal, collective criticism. So the notion that things could go very wrong, with war crimes and abuses of power or rape and sexual harassment on the base—that was out of the question. We developed a sense of cognitive dissonance that allowed us to push away all the bad thoughts."

In one of the most glaring instances of Israel's disregard for civilian life during the Second Intifada, then–Air Force commander Dan Halutz and Shin Bet chief Avi Dichter authorized the assassination of a top-ranking Hamas military commander, Salah Shehadeh, while he slept with his family in a crowded apartment bloc in downtown Gaza City. That night, an Israel F-16 combat jet dropped a one-ton bomb on Shehadeh's building, killing him and fourteen civilians, including at least six children, the youngest of whom was eighteen months old. Halutz remarked afterward that he was "militarily and morally" comfortable with the assassination. "If you nevertheless want to know what I feel when I release a bomb, I will tell you," he remarked in an interview with *Ha'aretz* about the incident. "I feel a light bump to the plane as a result of the bomb's release. A second later, it's gone, and that's all. That is what I feel." (In 2010, an Israeli military court completely cleared Halutz of all responsibility for the civilian deaths.)

The killing destroyed Yonatan's lingering faith in the integrity of the Israeli army, and thrust him into a personal crisis that would unfold over the coming years. "I realized that I was the one who was the most detached from reality," he said. "In the Air Force, I was disconnected from the kids who were being blown to pieces. The pilots don't meet the people who are suffering. They are invisible or just dots on a screen. And now I could not go on with things as they were."

In September 2003, Yonatan organized twenty-seven active-duty and veteran Air Force pilots to sign on to a letter he had drafted declaring their refusal to fly any mission that endangered civilians in the West Bank or Gaza Strip. Among the original signatories was Yiftah Spector, a high-ranking Six Day War veteran who was involved in the *USS Liberty* incident, in which Israeli aircraft and torpedo boats attacked an American warship in the Mediterranean Sea, killing thirty-four sailors. Other refusers included a member of a coordinating unit who walked through a Lebanese marketplace that had just been bombed in a major harbor city and smelled the aroma of freshly charred flesh. "Everyone who refused had a specific story of a direct encounter with death," Yonatan said.

The pilots' letter of refusal read: "We, veteran pilots and active pilots alike . . . are opposed to carrying out illegal and immoral attacks, of the type carried out by Israel in the territories. We, who have been educated to love the State of Israel, refuse to take part in air force attacks in civilian population centers. We refuse to continue harming innocent civilians."

At the time, Yonatan believed that the act of protest would shock the army into compliance with normal rules of war, and that its commanders might cease the relentless attacks on Palestinian civilian centers. However, Defense Minister Shaul Mofaz immediately lashed out at the refuseniks, accusing them of handing "a propaganda weapon to the enemy." "A soldier has no right to refuse a legal order, and the IDF issues only legal orders," Mofaz declared, announcing that the refuseniks would have to publicly apologize or face stern punishment within the military. Next, Minister of Education Limor Livnat banned the pilots from speaking before public school students, while Israel's National Student Union announced a boycott of the two hundred left-wing professors who had written their own letter supporting the refuseniks.

"For those of who decided to refuse, we found out our whole family was rotten," Yonatan reflected. "We were forced to break away from the collective."

When he attempted to expand the refusenik movement's ranks within the Air Force, Yonatan ran up against an iron wall of denial. In 2006, many of Yonatan's friends attended a Roger Waters concert in Neve Shalom, the Jewish-Arab community dedicated to peace and dialogue. The day after his buddies sang along to "The Wall"—"We don't need no education, we don't need no thought control"—and chanted for peace, he said they embarked on deadly bombing missions over the refugee camps of the Gaza Strip. He realized that those who fashioned themselves as the biggest peaceniks in their civilian lives could be the most efficient killing machines as soon as they received their orders from above.

"I tried to convince my friends and I failed," he recalled. "I began grieving the loss of their humanity. This failure forced me to conclude that arguing and philosophizing would not lead to any big changes. I had discovered that the whole narrative I grew up on was false—I had been lied to and became extremely angry."

After leaving the army, Yonatan went to work as a commercial pilot for a foreign company that conducted maintenance work for an electric utility inside Israel. His boss, a former commander of a helicopter division in the army, treated his activism with hostility, firing him soon after he took time off to attend an academic summer course in Europe. When Yonatan demanded a letter of dismissal so he could file a lawsuit, the CEO told him, "If you want a letter, get one from Arafat."

Just as Yonatan's employment situation collapsed, a former classmate from the Rimon School of Jazz and Contemporary Music, the Israeli folk-pop singer Aya Korem, released a musical tribute entitled "Yonatan Shapira." The song, which featured Korem humorously proclaiming her desire to marry Yonatan and have his baby, became a smash hit inside Israel. While one commercial flight company after another boycotted Yonatan, he simultaneously witnessed young Israelis blithely singing along to Korem's lyrics, ignorant of who he was or what he had been through. By the time I met Yonatan, he had been forced to travel to the hinterlands of Northern California and the rural American South to find work.

Yonatan's close friend, Gal Harmat, the peace education professor at Kibbutzim Teachers College, told me that like Yonatan, many of her coworkers had been forced out of the country for their activism. She said her apartment had been broken into twice, but nothing was taken. More recently, she was interrogated at the airport and had her laptop seized. "They don't have to put us in camps," she remarked. "Yonatan has been pushed out, and almost everyone I've worked with is gone now. They are all living in Berlin or other European capitols. Those of my friends who stayed, they are getting strange phone calls warning them not to go to protests in the West Bank, or they are having their computers seized. Honestly, I don't know how much longer I'm going to be able to live here."

A Date with the Devil

A t the start of my meeting with Yonatan, he took the battery out of his cellphone and placed it on the table. He learned in the Air Force that this was the surest way to stifle spies. Several other Israeli activists did the same when I met them. They were all concerned about monitoring by the Shin Bet, which had begun to scrutinize activists with unprecedented ferocity, monitoring their movements and calling them in for interrogations, one by one.

One afternoon in July, about two weeks after my first meeting with Yonatan, he called me with an urgent request to meet him in North Tel Aviv. The Shin Bet had just called, demanding he come in for an "interview." Yonatan insisted he be allowed to bring a journalist to the interrogation, so he selected me.

On the cab ride from Jaffa to Tel Aviv, I started to entertain second thoughts. What would happen if I confronted the Shin Bet face to face, I wondered. I called up an Israeli lawyer I knew who spent most of his days defending Palestinian political prisoners, including children, who had been detained without charges by Israeli forces for participating in unarmed protests against the occupation. The lawyer was alarmed when I told him what I was about to do. "You are not an Israeli citizen, okay?" he told me in a stern voice. "You are messing with Shin Bet—the big devil—and you will pay for it. They will put you on a blacklist, and when you leave the country you will be interrogated and deported, banned for ten years at least. Do not go." The lawyer added that even publishing information about the interrogation before it became public knowledge would place me at serious risk.

I hated to disappoint Yonatan, and more importantly, I did not want to let what I considered a major story fall into some other reporter's hands. But when I met Yonatan on the corner of Ben Gurion Street and Dizengoff to explain my predicament, he agreed that I should not take the risk. So he walked alone to a nearby police station to meet "Rona," the pretty, bespectacled, Shin Bet agent in her early thirties whose job was to interrogate Jewish Israeli leftists and intimidate them against continuing their acts of public dissent.

As soon as Yonatan entered the police station, he was subjected to a full body search to ensure that he was not recording the interrogation. Then he was led into a small room where Rona seated herself across from him and demanded that he not discuss any details of their conversation. "I promise you I will publish every single word that you say to me," he responded. Rona grew agitated and argued for a moment before realizing her protests were futile.

Rona said she was puzzled by Yonatan's graffiti on the wall of the Warsaw ghetto, asking him to explain his motives: "Did you understand that you hurt the feelings of the general public? You know you really crossed a line with the graffiti." Rona repeated this over and over, attempting to draw Yonatan into a political discussion. "Who do you work with?" she asked. "Who is this BDS [boycott, divestment, and sanctions] group you work with?" She asked if he would be attending the anti-occupation rally at Bank Hapaolim or the one meeting at Aza Park in Jaffa—the Shin Bet knew exactly where both protests were and at what time they began.

Yonatan held his ground throughout the interrogation, refusing to take her bait. "Everything I do is public and nonviolent, and I have nothing to add," he said multiple times. "I give lectures with the people I work with and explain everything there. If you want, you can bring the whole Shin Bet to my next talk."

But he wondered, "How do you know so much about me? Are you listening to my phone calls?"

"You won't talk about BDS. So why should I tell you?" Rona responded.

Rona went on to explain that the Shin Bet considered Yonatan one of the most widely recognized Palestine solidarity activists inside Israel and therefore believed he merited monitoring. In recent months, the Shin Bet detected an uptick in his activism and protest activity. The graffiti in Warsaw triggered a general intelligence alert that led to the interrogation.

Then came a chilling disclosure: Rona said a new law had been proposed in the Knesset that was certain to pass in some form. When it was first introduced, the bill promised to criminalize supporting the BDS movement, or even promoting the boycott of settlement goods, inside Israel. Israeli citizens participating in BDS-related activity would face fines and possible jail time. And international activists would be deported for supporting BDS in their home countries. "We are just waiting for the law to pass," Rona said. "But you should be aware of the consequences you face since you are so involved in this kind of activity."

Later, when Yonatan debriefed me about the interrogation, he remarked, "I was just questioned about a crime I might commit in the future after my actions become illegal. It is like I'm in a science fiction movie about a future crimes unit or something."

The interrogation of Yonatan Shapira read like a short story by Franz Kafka: a young man summoned for police questioning for writing on a wall in a foreign country, but not for any crime, and threatened about any future thoughts he might have. Or perhaps the incident was like something from the Oscar-winning film *The Lives of Others*, about the constant monitoring of the relationships and conversations of people in totalitarian East German by the Stasi secret police. Or perhaps Shapira had entered the science fiction universe of Philip K. Dick, who in his short story, "The Minority Report," predicted a system that would arrest people for "precrime."

Delegitimization

Throughout its history, Israel's deterrence strategy focused on military threats, from terrorist hijackers from the Popular Front for the Liberation of Palestine (PFLP) to guerilla fighters from the Palestine Liberation Organization (PLO) to entire Syrian and Egyptian tank divisions. Its military-intelligence apparatus had honed smashmouth tactics to neutralize these dangers while its diplomatic elements easily leveraged violent incidents to brand Israel as a plucky underdog surrounded by a mass of fanatical Arabs hell-bent on its genocidal destruction. In the years after the Second Intifada, a time when armed Palestinian resistance had ebbed to the point that it was barely a nuisance, the BDS movement caught the Israeli government off guard.

The BDS movement took form in 2005 in the wake of the International Court of Justice's ruling that the Israeli separation wall constituted a grave breach of international law. Instead of taking action to enforce the ruling, the Palestinian Authority sent troops trained by General Keith Dayton and the private security contractor DynCorp to arrest uncompliant Palestinians and political rivals in droves, often sending them to dark chambers where they were subjected to abuse.

One hundred seventy Palestinian civil society groups, including refugee rights organizations, political parties, feminist NGOs, and trade unions, converged into the Palestinian BDS National Committee. The ad hoc group organized around the BDS call, a strategy inspired by the global boycott that helped end apartheid rule in South Africa. The call demanded various means of creative grassroots pressure and boycotts until Israel met three key obligations under international law:

1. Ending its occupation and colonization of all Arab lands occupied in June 1967 and dismantling the wall;
2. Recognizing the fundamental rights of the Arab-Palestinian citizens of Israel to full equality; and
3. Respecting, protecting, and promoting the rights of Palestinian refugees to return to their homes and properties as stipulated in UN Resolution 194.

During its embryonic phase, the BDS call generated little attention inside Israel-Palestine while gathering momentum at a slow pace across the West. Then came Operation Cast Lead, the assault on the Gaza Strip of December 2008 that killed nearly fourteen hundred Palestinians, most of them civilians. The wave of protest that ensued propelled a new crop of activists into the ranks of the BDS movement, breathing life into the moribund Palestinian struggle. For the first time, there existed a nonviolent strategy of international scope.

Among the new generation of campus activists was Sara Shihadah, a University of Pennsylvania student whose parents immigrated to the US from the Gaza Strip. Shihadah had little interest in Palestine solidarity activism until her first trip to the West Bank in 2010. At the Israeli occupied frontier on the border of Jordan, she was subjected to a humiliating interrogation. She recalled: "They kept me for six hours and said things that weren't true about my family." Shihadah's entry into the Palestine solidarity movement typified the experience of the mostly first and second generation corps of Arab-Americans asserting their cultural identity on campus against fervent opposition from pro-Israel administrators, powerful outside political interests and in many cases, from their own immigrant parents.

When she returned to UPenn's notoriously apolitical campus, Shihadah assumed the presidency of the newfangled group, Penn for Palestine, which joined the scores of Palestine solidarity groups sprouting up each year on campuses across the United States. Then, in February 2012, she and a diverse group of UPenn students organized the first National BDS Conference on campus. Even before the conference began, the Jewish Federation of Philadelphia hastily arranged a counterevent that featured David L. Cohen, a top Democratic Party donor and vice president of the broadcasting giant, Comcast, reading a letter of support from UPenn president Amy Gutman. With nine hundred deeply concerned, mostly affluent Jewish Federations supporters gathered in the auditorium, Alan Dershowitz, the Harvard Law School professor and high-profile attorney in controversial cases, who has thrown himself into the forefront of Israeli government *hasbara* advocacy, appeared onstage to rail against BDS.

In November 2010 at the Jewish Federation's General Assembly in New Orleans—the largest annual gathering of Jewish American groups—a small group of youthful Jewish Americans arrived at the conference determined to make their voices heard. With backing from Jewish Voice for Peace, an emerging national group that promoted targeted boycotts of companies involved in Israel's occupation, they called themselves Young, Jewish, and Proud. Among them was Rachel Roberts, at the time a thirty-three-year-old civil rights attorney from Los Angeles, California.

Roberts was upset that an all–African American conference security crew was given badges reading "*Bitachon*"—Hebrew for "security"—as though they were guarding a shopping mall in Israel or manning a checkpoint in the West Bank. While browsing through the convention's exhibition hall, Roberts and a few friends came across a particularly striking display table run by the Canadian Jewish Public Affairs, a pro-Israel public relations outfit. At the table were promotional materials for a *hasbara* campaign specifically designed to combat the BDS movement. Called "Size Doesn't Matter," the campaign invoked a slogan most commonly identified with insecure men to brand Israel as a tiny but potent bastion of biotech innovation and cultural enlightenment. The campaign revolved around a fifty-five-second advertisement rolled out at the Jewish Federation's conference that depicted an attractive young couple lying in bed together. Here is the complete transcription of the ad:

[Close-up of woman gazing at crotch area of shirtless man]

Man: What?

Woman: Don't be mad, but it's, uh, small.

Man [with wounded expression]: Small?!

Woman: I don't know if I can go there.

Man [looking toward his crotch area]: I consider this a spot of worship. It may be small, but it's brought the driest places to life. Baby, this is paradise.

[Camera pans out with a wide-angle shot revealing tour guides covering the man's groin area. The camera quickly zooms in on a map of Greater Israel, showing no delineation of occupied Palestinian territory.]

Woman: Okay. But—if I go down there for you, you have to promise you go down south for me next winter.

[Final card flashes onscreen: Size Doesn't Matter: Israel, Small Country, Big Paradise.]

While Roberts watched the ad in astonishment, an ultra-Orthodox man stomped up to the booth to berate staffers from the Canadian Jewish Public Affairs group, accusing them of corrupting conference attendees with immoral, pornographic smut.

Later in the day, at a panel on "delegitimization," a group of lobbyists introduced the Israel Action Network, a $6 million fund to battle BDS in the United States. "It was pretty obvious why they chose the six-million-dollar figure," said Roberts, who attended the session. "They were playing on the fears of a second Holocaust, which just fed the paranoia of many of the older people there." The panel featured an appearance from a top Israeli Foreign Ministry official, D. J. Schneeweiss, who had become the Israeli government's de facto "delegitimization" liaison to the Jewish American establishment.

While the PR professionals honed their tactics, the activists from Young, Jewish, and Proud launched their planned action. During a speech by Israeli prime minister Benjamin Netanyahu at the conference's closing ceremony, the activists rose from their seats, one by one, to interrupt him with a cleverly crafted message. "Young Jews say the settlements delegitimize Israel!" one protester shouted in the middle of Netanyahu's speech before being gang tackled. "Young Jews say the loyalty oath delegitimizes Israel!" screamed another before she was throttled by a group of middle-aged men who had been enjoying their catered dinner just moments before. Finally, when a protester attempted to hoist a banner reading, "The Occupation Delegitimizes Israel," Rabbi David Eliezrie, a member of the messianic Chabad sect, snatched it away and ripped it into two with his teeth, provoking wild applause from the crowd.

Roberts reflected on the feelings that prompted her to join the protest: "What I felt in that conference hall was just complete disappointment in the older generation of Jews, in the way their stewardship of the community has so badly betrayed the wonderful things that came before. The decision to deny and block out the other side of the argument and mute the Palestinians has just resulted in a betrayal of our generations, which is why I participated in the action. I feel like what's going on in Israel-Palestine is going to change the face of what it means to be Jewish throughout the world, so it's up to people like me to pick up the mess we've inherited and hopefully turn it into something that could be healing."

In New York City, the local Palestine solidarity group Adalah-NY held annual Christmas carol protests outside the jewelry stores owned by Lev Leviev, a Bukharian Russian-Israeli billionaire diamond baron whose construction firm, Africa-Israel, has built thousands of homes in major settlements in the West Bank, from Ariel to Har Homa to Modiin Illit. In 2010, while lobbying New York–based human rights groups and the United Nations, Adalah-NY activists contacted celebrity endorsers of Leviev's jewelry products, including the actresses Halle Berry and Drew Barrymore, and informed them about Leviev's company record of human rights abuses in the West Bank and Africa, where his diamond mining operations have been accused of widespread labor violations.

By the end of the year, most of the celebrities cut ties with Leviev's company, forcing his staff to remove their photos from his promotional website. Then, in November 2010, as the embarrassment mounted, Leviev's Africa-Israel announced that he would quit building settlements in the West Bank.* The *Yedioth Ahronoth* article about the BDS movement's success was hyperbolically headlined, "Anti-Israel boycotters increasingly successful in strangling economy of Jewish state."

Internationally acclaimed recording artists from Elvis Costello to the Pixies to Carlos Santana have pulled out of Israeli tour dates after BDS activists, including Israelis like Yonatan Shapira, beseeched them to heed the Palestinian boycott call. Roger Waters, the former Pink Floyd front man who performed a major "peace concert" in Israel in 2006, the largest of its kind in the country, pledged not to return to the country until the separation wall is fully dismantled. Noting that his 1980 anti-authority anthem, "Another Brick in the Wall Part 2" was banned by the apartheid government of South Africa, Waters wrote, "Artists were right to refuse to play in South Africa's Sun City resort until apartheid fell and white people and black people enjoyed equal rights. And we are right to refuse to play in Israel until the day comes—and it surely will come—when the wall of occupation falls and Palestinians live alongside Israelis in the peace, freedom, justice, and dignity that they all deserve."

The gathering momentum of the cultural boycott sent Israel's wealthiest and most prominent concert promoter, Shuki Weiss, into a sputtering panic. After the famous alternative rock band, the Pixies, canceled a June 2010 gig in Tel Aviv, Weiss lashed out at the BDS movement, calling it a form of "cultural terrorism." Then, at a February 2011 Knesset hearing on combating BDS, he pleaded for high-level government action to compel reluctant recording artists to perform in Israel. "The state must intervene," he demanded.

Ronit Tirosh, a legislator from the Kadima Party, proposed compensating concert promoters like Weiss for the financial damages they incurred from boycotts with some form of government insurance or state compensation. But in lieu of a taxpayer-funded program in place to cover the losses of rich bon vivants like Weiss,

---

* Africa-Israel may have started building new settlements in 2013.

Tirosh conceded that all the government could do was pump more resources into *hasbara*.

The Reut Institute, a Tel Aviv–based think tank led by the former Ehud Barak adviser Gidi Grinstein, rose to the occasion. In the first of a series of white papers, Reut warned, "The wave of cancellations by international artists and the increasing calls to boycott Israel are being led by the BDS movement, which under the disguise of a progressive liberal movement is in practice promoting delegitimization." Reut presented the paper, "The Delegitimization Challenge: Creating a Political Firewall," to the 2010 Herzliya Conference on Israeli national security, then offered its findings to a special session convened by the Israeli National Security Council.

Reut's recommendations blamed Israel's problems on an international "delegitimization network" centered in cities throughout the West. The white paper avoided any discussion of the occupation or institutional discrimination against Palestinians in Israel. In one section of the report and in subsequent statements by its staff, the Reut Institute recommended summoning Israeli "intelligence agencies to focus" on infiltrating and undermining the BDS movement by "sabotag[ing] network catalysts."

But a prominent figure soon suggested that the whole "delegitimization" campaign was misguided. Britain's ambassador to Israel, Matthew Gould, appeared in 2012 on Israel's Channel 10 to speak frankly. The first English Jew to serve in his position, Gould was especially attuned to views of Israel both among the cultural elites of London, which the Reut Institute had identified as a key "hub of delegitimization," and in parliament.

Asked by his interviewer about perceived "British media bias" against Israel, Gould dismissed the question, replying that "Israel is now seen as the Goliath and it's the Palestinians who are seen as the David." He acknowledged that the BDS movement had begun to gain mainstream traction. "Support for Israel is starting to erode, and that's not about these people on the fringe who are shouting loudly and calling for boycotts and all the rest of it," Gould said. "The interesting category are those members of parliament in the middle, and in that group I see a shift."

The ambassador continued: "The British public may not be expert, but they are not stupid, and they see a stream of announcements about new building in settlements, they read stories about what's going on in the West Bank, they read about restrictions in Gaza. The substance of what's going wrong is really what's driving this."

Finally, he delivered perhaps the most painful truth of all to his Israeli audience: "The problem is not *hasbara*." The problem was not public relations; it was the occupation. "The substance of what is going on is really what is driving this."

The Explainers

With government's concern about the supposed "delegitimization" of Israel rising to urgent levels, the language of *hasbara* took on unprecedented importance. The literal Hebrew meaning of the word *hasbara* is "explanation," but when put into practice most informed observers recognize it as propaganda. The more the State of Israel relied on force to manage the occupation, the more compelled it was to deploy *hasbara*. And the more Western media consumers encountered *hasbara*, the more likely they became to measure Israel's grandiose talking points against the routine and petty violence, shocking acts of humiliation, and repression that defined its relationship with the Palestinians.

Under the leadership of Prime Minister Benjamin Netanyahu, a professional explainer who spent the early years of his political career as a frequent guest on prime time American news programs perfecting the slickness of the Beltway pundit class, the Israeli government invested unprecedented resources into *hasbara*. Once the sole responsibility of the Israeli foreign ministry, the task of disseminating *hasbara* fell to a special Ministry of Public Diplomacy led by Yuli Edelstein, a rightist settler and government minister who called Arabs a "despicable nation."

Edelstein's ministry boasted an advanced "situation room," a paid media team, and coordination of a volunteer force that claimed to include thousands of volunteer bloggers, tweeters, and Facebook commenters fed with talking points and who flood social media with *hasbara* in five languages. The exploits of the propaganda soldiers conscripted into Israel's online army have helped give rise to the phenomenon of the "*hasbara* troll," an often faceless, shrill and relentless nuisance deployed on Twitter and Facebook to harass public figures who expressed skepticism of official Israeli policy or sympathy for the Palestinians. These efforts have been complemented by the office of the prime minister, the IDF Spokesperson's Unit, and the Ministry of Tourism and Culture, each of which hosted newly created *hasbara* units. Even the Jewish Agency, a state-funded para-governmental agency primarily engaged in absorbing and settling new Jewish immigrants, employed a full-time social media operative named Avi Mayer, who spent his days on Twitter, attacking Palestine solidarity activists with usually baseless claims of anti-Semitism and deception.

Whether they liked it or not, every Jewish Israeli citizen was a potential recruit for the national *hasbara* brigade. While Tel Aviv University sent *hasbara* delegations to campuses across Europe and the United States, the National Union of Israeli Students offered Israeli college students $2,000 to spread propaganda "from the comfort of home." EL AL Airlines deployed its stewards and stewardesses into American cities to make the case for Israel during specially allotted paid vacation days. Meanwhile, back at Ben Gurion International Airport, large billboards posted by the Ministry of Hasbara instructed Israelis to "be good diplomats" when they travel abroad. By corralling an entire population into promoting Israel as "the only democracy in the Middle East," the state unconsciously cultivated a culture that treated dissent and critical inquiry with instinctive hostility.

In 2005, the American reality TV program *The Apprentice* reappeared in Israel as *The Ambassador*, a hit reality show featuring hundreds of Israeli citizens engaging in heated *hasbara* competitions before a captive national audience and panel of judges that included top army generals and journalists. At stake were cash prizes, a chance to speak in international parliaments and the adulation of their countrymen. At a 2010 conference of liberal intellectuals in Herzliya sponsored by the Heinrich Böll Foundation, the think tank of the German Green Party, I encountered the winner of the second season of *The Ambassador*. She was pretty in a classically telegenic way, slender, and extremely poised. The thirty-year-old woman in a gray pantsuit was Melody Sucharewicz, but to many Israelis who saw her as a celebrity, she was simply known as "Melody." Since her reality show victory, Sucharewicz has spoken about Israel's "quest for peace" at the United Nations and secured a plum position at the Peres Center for Peace.

During a question-and-answer session at the conference, Sucharewicz leapt to defend Israel against even mild criticism from various US panelists, including the renowned Israeli historian Tom Segev. For the next five minutes, she delivered a breathless but at best semi-coherent rant, as though she were in a contest to spin as many currents events in Israel's favor as possible. Finally, the moderator asked Sucharewicz to conclude her remarks with a question. "Of course you want me to stop talking," she snapped at him. "You will never let a woman speak long enough to express herself." Having shamed the moderator into submission, Sucharewicz plowed ahead for five more minutes of *hasbara*.

When I interviewed her in the hallway afterward, I found her unflappable. To my question about the wave of anti-democratic laws flooding the Knesset, she responded, "Israel is not perfect. They can only strive to be more perfect. . . . I wouldn't go as far as saying there is pure discrimination." On issues ranging from civilian casualties in Operation Cast Lead to the bulldozing of Bedouin villages, Sucharewicz always returned to one point: Israel was not perfect, but it was constantly improving.

The same year that *The Diplomat* hit Israeli airwaves, the government focused on rebranding Israel as a cosmopolitan, technologically advanced, party playpen for Western visitors, especially sex-hungry, upwardly mobile men between the ages of eighteen and thirty-five. A series of edgy commercials promoting tourism to Tel Aviv highlighted the new Brand Israel campaign. The first of the ads, released in 2006, depicted two randy young men sitting shirtless on the Tel Aviv beach while a parade of scantily clad Israeli women appear before them:

> Man #1, staring at a nubile young woman rubbing lotion on her thighs: Holy shit, man!

Man #2: Holy fuck!

Man #1, glancing at the bouncing breasts of a bikini-clad blonde jogging in his direction: Holy Jesus! Oh! Come to papa!

[A brunette bikini model drops a paddleball near the men and gives them a sultry look]

Man #1, overcome with passion: Oooooh!

[Slogan appears on screen: "Israel: No Wonder They Call It the Holy Land]

With $90 million from the Tel Aviv municipality to promote the city as a gay paradise and free trips provided by the Tourism Ministry for gay Israelis willing to "conduct public diplomacy activities abroad," the Brand Israel campaign increasingly centered around what many international gay activists called "pinkwashing," or using the country's relatively progressive gay rights record to conceal its human rights abuses. The campaign included sending openly gay Israeli soldiers to speak on college campuses, screening pro-Israel films at gay rights festivals, and even sending a bizarre float into the 2011 San Francisco Gay Pride parade featuring a blow up doll of Iranian president Mahmoud Ahmadinejad being sodomized by a nuclear missile.

Among the most aggressive promoters of Israel's supposedly queer-friendly culture was Michael Lucas, one of the wealthiest gay porn producers in the world. A fervent supporter of Israeli airstrikes on Iran and a vehement Islamophobe ("I hate Muslims absolutely"), Lucas leveraged his fortune to found a company promoting gay tourism to Israel. "I find it absolutely maddening that gay people, who are the number one target of Islam, are so ignorant of the facts," he told an interviewer from the far-right US *FrontPageMag*. "They are romanticizing the same Palestinians that hang gay people on cranes, but demonizing Israel, which is a safe haven for gay people." Lucas's most heavily promoted porno film, *Men of Israel*, which became a vehicle for his gay tours, featured two actors having sex inside a Palestinian village that was ethnically cleansed by Zionist militias in 1947.

Incorrectly claiming that the village had been depopulated hundreds of years before, Lucas wrote in a press release, "We went to an abandoned village just north of Jerusalem. It was a beautiful, ancient township that had been deserted centuries ago . . . however, that did not stop our guys from mounting each other and trying to repopulate it. Biology may not be the lesson of the day, but these men shot their seeds all over the village." After the filming concluded in the "abandoned" home, Lucas and his cast were received by a news crew from Israel's Channel 1, which covered their pornographic project as a boon to Israeli public relations.

In June 2011, when activists around the world convened in Greece for the attempted launch of the second Gaza Freedom Flotilla, the Israeli government released a YouTube video designed to tar the flotilla organizers as homophobes. The video depicted a gay activist who called himself "Marc3Pax" who testified into a camera how flotilla organizers had refused to allow him on board because of concerns expressed by their supposed partners among the anti-gay Hamas. Marc3Pax closed the video by warning gay viewers that joining the Palestine solidarity movement meant "getting in bed" with bearded jihadis who hate homosexuals.

Sensing that the video was a deceptive hoax, US-based writers Ali Abunimah and Benjamin Doherty of the Palestinian news and opinion website Electronic Intifada quickly unmasked the star of the video as an Israeli actor and nightclub promoter named Omer Gershon. When I investigated the video's origins, I learned that the first person to promote the video on Twitter was a character named "Guy Seeman." At first, I could not believe that an actual person named Guy Seeman was disseminating a gay hoax video. I soon discovered that Guy Seeman was not only real, but that he was a low-level political operative working in the office of Prime Minister Netanyahu.

The Marc3Pax hoax was followed by another dunderheaded and downright weird video designed to undermine the Gaza Freedom Flotilla. Produced by a Tel Aviv-based production company with links to the prime minister's office, the video was entitled, *Sex with the Psychiatrist*. It featured an attractive and extremely bothered young woman reacting to Rorshach inkblots displayed by a leering, gray-haired psychiatrist. As the woman descended into varying stages of agitation, shots of her thighs flashed on the screen. "All you want to do is live in peace," she complained in South African–accented English, "but you keep trying to embarrass her and attack her and harass her." Her words were interrupted by jarring montages of knives and clashes on the deck of the *Mavi Marmara*. "Doctor why are you showing me these pictures?" she protested. "Stop telling me lies and presenting me only one side of the story. . . . Leave her alone, stop provoking her! . . . What do you want? For her to disappear off the map?"

The woman was apparently a metaphorical representation of the State of Israel as it wished to be seen: peaceful, cosmopolitan, and erotic, but also traumatized, vulnerable, and driven to neurosis by marauding terrorists and Jew-hating activists—an innocent victim in need of rescue. At the video's end, the woman stormed out of the psychiatrist's office and a message appeared on the screen: "Don't support another violent flotilla."

The lurid *hasbara* of Brand Israel was directly inspired by corporate public relations, which refined its techniques throughout thousands of high stakes damage-control campaigns. No single figure has devoted more time or effort to refining the vocabulary of corporate PR than Frank Luntz. Luntz earned acclaim—and notoriety—in 1994 when he crafted a memo for the new Republican Speaker of the House, Newt Gingrich, called "Language: A Key Mechanism of Control." The memo advised Gingrich to promote the Republican agenda with positive words like "moral," "lead," and "prosperity," while hammering the Democratic opposition with terms like "abuse of power," "corrupt," and "intolerant." Luntz went on to garner lucrative contracts for corporate raiders such as Enron, the anti-green energy oil company ExxonMobil, and most recently, the financial industry, which hired him to help undermine the Occupy Wall Street movement. Luntz's best-selling vocabulary guide, *Words That Work*, was originally entitled *Killer Words*.

Given his history of helping corporate crooks talk their way out of crises, perhaps it was appropriate that Luntz was contracted by The Israel Project, an international pro-Israel activism outfit with ties to Israel's Foreign Ministry, to craft its official *hasbara* handbook. In the 116-page guide, fine-tuned for the sensibilities of an audience that is high on passion and low on information, Luntz outlined strategies, arguments, and tactics for promoting Israel in the media and on campus. Throughout the document, Luntz urged pro-Israel activists to lead attacks on their adversaries by "start[ing] with empathy for *both* sides first." He advised Israel advocates to pantomime humility and concern for Palestinian children before opening up a relentless focus on the "Iran-backed Hezbollah, Hamas, and Islamic Jihad."

In an unusual—and probably unintentional—moment of candor, Luntz warned that if Israel remains in a perpetual state of war with no plan to resolve its crisis "Americans will not want their government to spend tax dollars or their president's clout on helping Israel." To hold off the storm looming on the horizon, Luntz advised Israel's supporters to "remind people—again and again—that Israel wants peace." For him and professional hasbarists like Sucharewicz, the word "peace" was nothing more than a rhetorical device.

While the Israeli government deployed a constant barrage of artifice, sophistry, and diversionary tactics to guard its image, the country's military-intelligence apparatus resorted increasingly to repressive measures to silence its internal critics. Besides interrogating Yonatan Shapira, in September 2009, Israeli authorities detained the Palestinian activist Mohammed Othman when he returned from a trip to Norway, where he had lobbied Norwegian officials to support BDS campaigns. Othman was released months later only following a sustained campaign by Amnesty International to publicize his status as a political prisoner. Two months later, Israel detained Jamal Juma, a leading member of the Palestinian BDS National Committee, designating him as a dangerous "security prisoner" before releasing him without charges weeks later.

The Shin Bet quickly expanded its anti-BDS dragnets into Jewish Israeli society. Among the dozens of Israeli activists caught in the Shin Bet's dragnet was Leehee Rothschild, a twenty-nine-year-old human rights activist who was a constant presence at unarmed Palestinian demonstrations against the occupation in the West Bank, and who had recently joined a small group of pro-BDS Israeli activists and academics called Boycott Within. In March 2012, a year after police raided her apartment and rummaged through her belongings, Rothschild was detained by the Shin Bet while returning home from a trip to Europe during which she had participated in a series of educational BDS events. At Ben Gurion International Airport, Rothschild was interrogated by "Shavit," the director of the Shin Bet's "extreme left and right department," who suggested that his agency was listening to her phone calls, reading her e-mails, and had bugged her apartment. Once she was released, Rothschild wrote, "[Shavit] said that for now, I've stayed within the law, but once I broke it, I'd better remember that they are watching me, and that they view me as a leader, so I could be held responsible for leading other people into illegal acts."

The mounting panic over BDS fed directly into a Knesset effort to criminalize the boycotting of Israeli products. On March 2011, a bill introduced by the Likud Party's Ze'ev Elkin, a right-wing populist from the party's cadre of thirty- and forty-something upstarts, passed a committee vote, sending it toward the Knesset floor for a final vote. The bill represented a streamlined version of a previous proposal that would have punished boycotters with actual jail time while deporting any non-citizen who called for boycotts of Israel in their own country. In its new, diluted form, the bill explicitly punished speech considered harmful to the Jewish state, allowing any Israeli who felt his or her business was damaged by another Israeli's call for a boycott—no evidence required—to sue the perpetrator in a civil court. The bill read: "It is forbidden to initiate a boycott against the State of Israel, to encourage participation in it or to provide assistance or information in order to promote it."

Anat Mattar was one of the first Israeli citizens to publicly promote a boycott. A professor of sociology at Tel Aviv University and the mother of the prominent left-wing journalist Hagai Mattar, Anat Mattar quickly became a hate figure for right-wingers in the Knesset, who demanded she be ousted from her tenured academic post. In a speech before Tel Aviv University's 2010 graduation ceremony, the super-*hasbara* super-lawyer Alan Dershowitz accused Mattar and two other pro-BDS Israeli academics of "impos[ing] their ideology on students," urging "patriotic" students and faculty members to "stand up to propagandizing professors . . . in appropriate forums outside of the classroom where different rules govern." Mattar told me that 250 of her academic colleagues were inspired by Dershowitz to sign a public letter condemning her in vitriolic terms.

Despite the mounting intimidation, Mattar told me she was not the real target of the anti-boycott legislation. "If the [anti-boycott] law passes," she said, "it's not only me who gets hurt, and if I'm fired, that's actually the least important thing. The most important is what will happen with the NGO's like Adalah [the legal center for Arab minority rights], with [the occupation monitoring group] Yes Din, with B'tselem. If I'm fired it's a personal inconvenience, but if that happens, it's much more than a sweeping attack on a lunatic from academia, I really don't know what's going to happen, and I don't see any way out of this."

The Real Government

●

By late July 2010, David Sheen and I were back in the Knesset, this time to meet Ze'ev Elkin, the primary author of the anti-boycott law promising harsh punishments to left-wing activists who participated in any form of BDS. Before we could interview Elkin, we sat through a hearing of the Knesset's Constitution, Law and Justice Committee where a fiery debate took place over another bill Elkin introduced, this one to compel Israeli human rights NGOs to publicly reveal their international donors, thereby pegging them as traitorous agents of a foreign, European agenda. There, we watched Dov Khenin, a leader of the leftist Hadash Party, complain furiously about an anonymous billboard campaign that suggested the New Israel Fund, a key Israeli human rights umbrella organization, was a Trojan horse for Arab nationalism. While Khenin demanded to know who funded the poisonous billboard campaign, Elkin sat at the end of the Knesset panel with a self-satisfied grin. His bill was likely to pass, and behind it were a raft of even more draconian proposals, including one from Yisrael Beiteinu's Fania Kirschenbaum, which called for McCarthy-style commissions of inquiry into left-wing organizations.

At the center of the panel, David Rotem embarrassed a legislator from Kadima who warned that the law hurt Israel's image abroad, reminding him that his party leader, Tzipi Livni, supported it before she suddenly turned against it. "And now you talk of democracy?" Rotem barked at the Kadima representative. The National Union Party's Michael Ben-Ari, a card-carrying Kahanist who had sponsored the bill to block state funding to filmmakers who refuse to take loyalty oaths, declared that "anti-Semitism is now anti-Zionism." He pledged his party's full, undivided support for the law, which he viewed as the continuation of the legacy of Rabbi Meir Kahane.

Throughout the hearing, a who's who of Israeli NGO representatives piped up from the long witness table to offer passionate but ultimately futile arguments against the bill. Hagai El-Ad, the youthful director of the Association for Civil Rights in Israel (ACRI), met me in the hall after the hearing adjourned. "The government is directing an all-out assault on the foundations of democracy," El-Ad told me. "The freedom of human rights organizations to operate is just the latest target."

A few minutes later, Sheen and I met Elkin inside the Likud faction's committee room inside the Knesset, a narrow conference room where Likud parliamentarians confer at a long table that often features Prime Minister Benjamin Netanyahu at the head. Elkin was a short man with a *kippa* sitting on top of close-cropped black hair. He looked slightly withdrawn and almost petulant as he spoke to us in better-than-average Hebrew with a slight Russian accent. In 1990, Elkin arrived in Israel from the Ukraine, where he suffered as a Zionist activist under the former Soviet regime. After a stint as the token Russian settler in Kadima, which had a dire need for such a figure, Elkin moved to his natural home in Likud in 2006, emerging as one of the party's most aggressive and extreme junior members. In more recent years, he began keynoting the annual Ramle conference, a gathering dedicated to discussing plans for the mass expulsion of Israel's Arab population, and spoke in favor of annexing most of the West Bank at a settler gathering called the "Application of Israeli Sovereignty over Judea and Samaria." While he casually labeled Arabs and leftists as traitors, Elkin provided logistical information to radical Jewish settlers who wished to prevent the evacuation of a settlement outpost by attacking Israeli army bases in the West Bank.

The so-called boycott bill was Elkin's signature proposal. As he told the pro-settlement news website Arutz Sheva, "I hope the [legislators] will understand that this is a battle between Zionism and the new left." If the law passed, Elkin stood to consolidate his position as one of the settlement movement's most effective advocates in the Knesset. His popularity among mainstream Israelis bombarded with constant warnings about "delegitimization" was likely to increase as well. When he first conceived the bill, Elkin was confident of its passage, but not certain. It was only when Dalia Itzik, the leader of the centrist Kadima Party's Knesset faction, stepped forward as the bill's cosponsor, that Elkin could make plans to celebrate.

Sheen and I seated ourselves across from Elkin and Meir. A young, bespectacled aide who had just completed graduate school at Hebrew University, Elkin made clear that his law was intended to protect Israeli companies based in the occupied West Bank, which existed only thanks to the protection of the Israeli army, but which he considered an integral part of the Jewish state. He named Ahava, the Dead Sea cosmetics manufacturer based in the illegal settlement of Mitzpe Shalem, as one of the companies he was determined to insulate against the impact of targeted boycotts. "The company is located there [in the settlement], not because it has a political opinion one way or the other," he tried to explain. "The area is under Israeli control, and under Israeli law they can operate there, and therefore, whoever acts against this company only because they are located there geographically—again, not asking the owners of the company about their political opinions, or what party they vote for in Israel—I think that this is an illegitimate act, an economic boycott that is directed against the State of Israel, and therefore doesn't matter if a company is located in the Galilee or in the area of the Dead Sea."

When Sheen presented Elkin with accusations that the anti-BDS law was anti-democratic, and that it called Israel's claim to be the only democracy in the Middle East into question, Elkin responded that the law was in fact modeled after a similar law on the books in the United States. "Today, if an American citizen or an American company participates in a boycott of Israel, they can expect very heavy fines; economic fines and even jail sentences of several years," Elkin claimed. It's a very far-reaching law, and it is an active law," he claimed.

But this was false—there was no law in the United States threatening these boy-cotters of Israel with any form of punishment. The only American legal provision remotely similar to Elkin's bill was an obsolete, Cold War–era rule that suspended tax breaks to companies that observed the Arab League's old boycott of Israel—and which had never been applied in any case. When I pointed this out to Elkin, asking that he provide an example of an American who was punished for organizing a cam-paign to boycott Israel for the occupation policy, he insisted—falsely again—that no American had ever done such a thing, so the law had never been applied.

Suddenly, Elkin's aide, a bespectacled, exceptionally aggressive twenty-something named Meir, piped up. "You can't tell me it's a law if it's never been applied!" he snapped at me.

"It's never been applied," I said.

"It doesn't matter. I don't care if it's never been applied," he replied, flashing a smug smile, as though I had been naïve to quibble with him.

"If it doesn't matter, then you are just citing this American law to present your own law in a democratic context," I countered.

Up until this point, Meir had been staring into his computer, researching the details of the law. Now he turned and faced me directly. "I think we are more demo-cratic than the [United] States," he proclaimed calmly, but confidently. Seated in the corner across from Sheen, Elkin was silent. Meir continued, "Israel is not putting two to three percent of its population in jail at any given moment. I think we treat our minorities better than the States. I think we have no immigration laws that let them mistreat everyone in the streets just because they look Latino. It's only a moral thing that other countries do—and [the anti-boycott law is] something that we have to do for our citizens. And it's not even a big punishment. Even in the biggest democracies, you have to put a price on hurting someone's business."

Next, Meir challenged me to name one instance in which another country's cit-izens had called for a boycott of its governing institutions or companies. I told him about the boycott by Latino human rights groups of Arizona, which had authorized the anti-immigrant laws Meir cited, and Martin Luther King Jr.'s famous boycott of the Birmingham Alabama public buses, which had forced African-Americans to ride near the back of the bus.

"What did the American people do when Martin Luther King called for his boy-cott?" Meir wondered.

"[MLK] was successful, he integrated the bus lines," I told him. "But first he was jailed by Southern racists."

"I remember, he wrote a book about it, and he wrote a letter to the Christian lead-ers. And then he got shot," Meir said in a dismissive tone. "It's not the point. Boycott is maybe a powerful tool, and that's why it has to be regulated. . . . But boycotts, the way they're used in Israel, they're just terror. There is nothing between bombing a factory and boycotting a factory. When people use methods of terror against civilians more than anything, just because of their political ideas, I think it's a problem."

"So why do you think there are growing numbers of Israelis calling for a boycott from within?"

Meir explained that they were bribed. "There are people in Israel that get a lot of money from the European Union just to make Israel weaker. And it's a problem that all the world is looking on Israel. . . . I don't know why the EU is looking on Israel so much."

I reminded him that the United States and the European Union were Israel's guarantors, that they supplied his country with the bulk of its most advanced weapons and that loans to Israel accounted for the majority of America's foreign aid, and much of the aid doled out by Western European nations like Germany.

"At least half of the States is built on settlements," he stated, seeming to assume that I was unfamiliar with the history of Native Americans. "The States is built on settlements and the US is the biggest settlement in the world."

"So two wrongs make a right?"

"No," Meir said, "but if you did wrong, don't teach me how to do right. Are you coming to teach me how to settle? I think that all of Israel is ours. It's not just the Bible—it's ours. No Arab can prove that he has any right to Shomron [the West Bank]; it was Jordan before and it was never Palestinian territory. Never before in the history of the world was [the West Bank]—just show me one minute that a Palestinian got [the West Bank]. . . . They gave up their right, I think thirty-five years ago. So right now there is no proof that anybody had a right over this land and we hold it. So it's even better than the States holding land over countries like California and all that."

On July 13, 2011, Elkin's boycott bill passed on a 47–38 vote. At least thirty-five members of Knesset did not vote on the bill, most of them out of fear of political repercussions from the all-powerful settler movement and the general mood of the Israeli public. Upon the bill's passage, the Likud's new generation of hardliners rushed to Elkin, wrapping their arms around him in elation. *Ha'aretz* reported, "If this had been the Teddy Stadium [Jerusalem's football arena], they would have hoisted Elkin onto their shoulders and carried him in a victory procession." Now Elkin rivaled David Rotem as the most popular lawmaker from the Etzion Bloc. His position near the top of Likud's list in the next national election was virtually guaranteed. *Ha'aretz* headlined Elkin's triumph: "The settlers are the real government of Israel."

As soon as Elkin's bill reached the Knesset floor for a full vote, one lawmaker after another rushed for the exits to avoid having to explain their "no" vote. Not one single member of Defense Minister Ehud Barak's "mainstream Zionist" Atzmaut Party, a centrist offshoot of the Labor Party, dared to vote on the bill. Though she abstained from voting, Einat Wilf, a senior member of Atzmaut and one of Barak's closest partisans, remarked in a floor speech that the bill had "admirable objectives."

With seven members of Kadima absent from the vote, only one, Yohanan Plessner, took an active role in opposing the bill. Tzipi Livni, the Kadima leader perceived by many Western liberals as a champion of democracy, said and did nothing about the bill until the day before the vote. "It was only on Monday, when she saw what was going on, that she remembered she was against it," Elkin gloated. For his part, Prime Minister Benjamin Netanyahu opted to stay home once he received word that the bill was certain to pass.

Soon after the fateful vote, Netanyahu appeared at the podium before the Knesset to issue a vehement endorsement of Elkin's bill. "Don't get confused," the prime minister declared. "I approved the law, and if I hadn't approved it, it wouldn't have passed. I am against boycotts targeting Israel."

Beating back criticism from Livni, who accused him of "leading Israel into an abyss," Netanyahu mocked the Kadima Party for its capricious behavior. "You initiated the bill. Central members of Kadima—the faction chairwoman supported the law," the prime minister reminded Livni's party. "Why did Kadima MKs who originally supported the bill decide to oppose the final draft? Because there was pressure, and you gave in to that pressure."

Finally, Netanyahu singled out the Israeli right's favorite punching bag, Hanin Zoabi, turning to her and booming, "You're lucky that you are a member of the Israeli parliament and not the Syrian parliament, for example."

"Go ahead, put me on trial! Put me on trial, like your soldiers should be put on trial!" Zoabi snapped back.

As Zoabi was set on by security guards and dragged from the Knesset gallery, Nissim Zeev, a right-wing member of the Shas Party, barked at her, "You are garbage!"

While Netanyahu continued his speech, cellphones belonging to members of Likud's central committee lit up with a text message: "Toward a revolution in the Supreme Court—the transparency law for appointment of justices, sponsored by MK Yariv Levin. The whole Likud is mobilizing!" The text referred to a bill Levin had just introduced with Elkin that would enable the Knesset to nullify Supreme Court decisions and disqualify judicial nominees. It would be debated the following week alongside another proposal to establish McCarthy-style panels of inquiry for left-wing organizations.

Back on the Knesset podium, Netanyahu reminded his audience, "Israeli democracy is excellent and will always remain so."

It Is No Dream

On the evening of February 1, 2010, hundreds of young Israeli demonstrators arrived at the home of Naomi Chazan dressed in Palestinian *keffiyehs*, holding Muslim prayer beads, and throwing up two-fingered peace signs pretending to be leftist-Islamist "terrorists." From her front lawn, they waved signs depicting the grandmotherly Chazan in classically anti-Semitic fashion, as a satanic villain with a hooked nose and horn jutting out of her forehead. "Thank you, New Israel Fund!" the mock-militant protesters sarcastically chanted.

Having doled out more than \$200 million to more than thirty-two human rights and pro-democracy groups in Israel over the past thirty years, the New Israel Fund (NIF) was the country's largest human rights umbrella group. Chazan, the NIF's chairperson, a longtime activist for women's and minority rights who had always remained solidly within the liberal Zionist orbit, earning herself influence in successive Knessets and within the Jewish establishment of the United States and Europe. By targeting such a well-respected figure of the old left-wing Zionist establishment as a traitor to the Jewish state, the protesters launched the opening salvo in a well-coordinated, heavily funded campaign to extend the hard right's grasp of Israel's institutions.

When I met Chazan in June 2009 in her office at Tel Aviv-Jaffa College, she warned me that the right's campaign had only begun to gather momentum. "Yisrael Beiteinu ran on a position of questioning the civil rights of 20 percent of the population of Israel. And because they won that position has been legitimized," she told me. "And it's time to wake up, because as soon as you start doubting [citizens'] rights—one day its the Arabs, the next day it's the secular people, and the next day it's the women, and you know where it starts, but you have no idea where it ends."

The demonstrators who appeared on Chazan's doorstep represented a relatively new and surprisingly influential right-wing youth group called Im Tirtzu—"If You Will It"—which derived its name from Theodore Herzl's famous statement, "If you will it, it is no dream." Presenting themselves as a mainstream "extra-parliamentary group that works to strengthen and advance the values of Zionism in Israel," the group functioned as a street-level expression of the Yisrael Beiteinu and Likud Party's political crackdown on left-wing NGOs, Palestinian Israeli civil society, and academia. With far-reaching plans to permanently marginalize Israel's already weak democratic camp, Im Tirtzu introduced itself to the country with a full-bore assault on Israeli human rights NGOs, especially those that documented army abuses in the occupied West Bank and Gaza.

The day before Im Tirtzu's mob appeared in front of Chazan's home, the organization published an ad in major Israeli newspapers featuring the image of Chazan with a hooknose and horn marked "N.I.F." The same image appeared draped over bridges in Tel Aviv and Jerusalem, as well as on billboards across Israeli highways. "Fact!" the text of the ad read. "Without the New Israel Fund, there would be no Goldstone Report, and Israel would not be facing accusations of war crimes."

Along with the ad blitz, Im Tirtzu released a detailed and factually flawed report to the Knesset, major Jewish organizations, and the media claiming that the NIF had funded the human rights groups responsible for 90 percent of the documentation in the United Nations *Goldstone Report*, which found Israeli forces culpable for war crimes against civilians in the Gaza Strip during Operation Cast Lead. The NIF grantees targeted by Im Tirtzu represented a who's who of human rights groups in Israel, from Adalah, the center for Arab legal rights in Israel, to B'tselem, a leading documenter of army abuse in the Occupied West Bank and Gaza.

Days after Im Tirtzu lauched its campaign against the NIF, it began to bear fruit. Ben Caspit, one of the most widely read columnists in Israel, published a glowing article about the Im Tirtzu "report" in *Maariv*, providing the campaign against Chazan with the veneer of mainstream respectability. David Horovitz, editor-in-chief of the right-leaning paper, the *Jerusalem Post*, where Chazan had served as the token liberal columnist for fourteen years, e-mailed Chazan to inform her that she was no longer welcome to contribute her opinions. Within a year, the NIF would replace her with Brian Lurie, a liberal American Jew who demanded an assurance from Adalah, the legal center for Arab rights inside Israel, that it would not "push" for BDS or call for Israel as a "state of all its citizens."

Following the attack on NIF, a top legislative cadre of Avigdor Lieberman and Im Tirtzu supporter named Fania Kirschenbaum demanded the creation of a Knesset panel to investigate human rights groups funded by the NIF. In short order, a bill found its way onto the Knesset floor proposing an investigation of NGOs, with punishments ranging from a 45 percent tax on foreign-based donations to a $20,000 cap on grants from abroad. The bill mirrored a law introduced in Russia by President Vladimir Putin forcing NGOs engaged in internationally funded "political activity" to register as "foreign agents" and file reports with the government four times a year.

By February 2010, the Knesset approved the creation of the investigative committees by a 40–34 margin. As had become the custom, dozens of "centrist" lawmakers skipped out on the contentious vote. Defending the measure against criticism that it recalled Senator Joseph McCarthy's witch hunts during the 1950s, Ofir Akunis, the Likud deputy speaker of the Knesset, and a sponsor of the anti-NGO inquisition, offered his opinion on a prime time talk show that McCarthy "was right in every word he said."

After passing a final vote in the Knesset, the bill seemed certain to become law. It was due only to unusual last-minute pressure from the European Union and government abuse that the prime minister's office finally felt forced to stop the law before enactment. Shaken after a stern warning from EU diplomats that the bill would cause a crisis in Israel's relationship with the international community, Netanyahu froze the bill indefinitely, demonstrating the Israeli government's extreme sensitivity to its image in the eyes of the West. But a suite of anti-democratic bills was due for a full vote, and this time, the prime minister intended to grant his stamp of approval.

At 2:42 a.m. on March 23 2011, a month after voting to enact a parliamentary inquisition against Israeli human rights NGOs, the Knesset rushed through the segregationist Acceptance to Communities Act, which would legally authorize towns to reject Palestinian Israelis as residents on the basis of "social suitability," and the Nakba Law, fining any municipality, including Palestinian Israeli ones, for any commemoration of Palestinian expulsion. As usual, only 55 of the Knesset's 120 members bothered to appear to vote on the bills, which both passed by wide margins. And only three members of Livni's Kadima Party bothered to show up, with two of them—Shai Hermesh and Yisrael Hasson—voting as sponsors of the Acceptance to Communities Bill. Having promised that Kadima would not be a "passive participant" in the anti-democratic agenda, Livni was nowhere to be found. Like so many others, she seemed to fear the backlash from her constituents for following up on her pledge.

Im Tirtzu founder Ronen Shoval hailed the movement he had helped ignite with an editorial for *Ha'aretz*, pronouncing 2011 "The year of democracy."

PART VII
FEELING THE HATE

Riding the Ass

Ronen Shoval was thirty-one years old, clean-cut, and absolutely secular, from the affluent North Tel Aviv suburb of Ramat HaSharon. In contrast to unapologetic demagogues like Avigdor Lieberman, Shoval attempted to present the severe charges he leveled against human rights groups and left-wing professors in the language of liberal democracy and post-modern academic discourse. Moreover, he carefully avoided taking a position on the project of Greater Israel, obscuring his role as a committed right-wing cadre. Indeed, if his talking points were slick, it was because Shoval was the product of a sophisticated, well-funded, professional public relations campaign—one that originated in the far shores of the right with the goal of capturing the Israeli mainstream.

Before founding Im Tirtzu in 2006, Shoval was the leader of the shadowy "Orange Cell," a radical right-wing student organization that battled the withdrawal of ideological settlers from the Gaza Strip in 2005. Shoval's right-hand man in the Orange Cell, Erez Tadmor, was the son of the only secular family in the fanatical Jewish settlement of Kiryat Arba, located inside the occupied Palestinian city of Hebron.

During Operation Cast Lead, Tadmor orchestrated a series of violent confrontations between Im Tirtzu activists and Palestinian Israeli students at Hebrew University. An Im Tirtzu banner warned the Arab students, "We will burn your villages and see you during our reserve duty." Tadmor was accused of physically attacking female students who called him a Nazi. The riots sparked by Tadmor and Im Tirtzu were quelled only when university administrators demanded the deployment of Border Police and special *Yassam* forces on camp.

In an interview with *Maariv*, Tadmor admitted to stealing small-scale explosives and ammunition magazines from the army during his service. Despite insisting that he needed the weapons for "personal security," he was stripped of his rank and slapped with a forty-five-day prison sentence for "breaking the trust" of the army. Having been expelled from Israel's most revered institution, Tadmor set about defending its honor against the human rights NGOs, hoping to restore his own tattered reputation in the process.

After graduating from Hebrew University in 2006, Shoval and Tadmor entered a special training program for young activists operated by the Institute for Zionist Strategies (IZS), a right-wing think tank funded by the neoconservative Washington-based Hudson Institute. The IZS had long embraced a stealth strategy, issuing press releases and statements in a seemingly secular language, even though its chairman, Israel Harel, was a founder of the Gush Emunim movement, the original ultra-nationalist settlers who coerced the Israeli government into allowing them to establish the Etzion Bloc after the 1967 war. Clean-shaven and erudite, he was more comfortable holding forth on stuffy think-tank panels than he was *davening* in settlement *yeshivas*. In a public exchange with *Ha'aretz* editor-in-chief Amos Schocken, who, in classic liberal Zionist fashion, blamed the Gush Emunim for corrupting the burnished democracy established by the secular Labor Zionists, Harel cast the settlement movement as the natural successors to the secular Labor Zionists, whom he described as "more zealous than religious Zionism." According to Harel, "Gush Emunim adopted these [messianic] roots and tried, with its own additions, to proceed in their light."

Harel's vision of the settlers as culturally superior heirs to the obsolete secular Zionists was consistent with the philosophy of Rabbi Zvi Yehuda Kook, the spiritual godfather of the Gush Emunim. Kook told his disciples that they represented the modern incarnation of the Jewish Messiah. In order to bring about the "final redemption," he instructed them to exploit the achievements of the secular Zionists, who had performed the necessary work of colonizing "Israel proper" in 1948 and conquering the West Bank in 1967. Just as the Messiah appeared riding an ass in biblical prophecy, Kook presented the secular public as an ass that the religious nationalists could ride all the way to dominion.

According to Kook's teachings, as soon as the Labor Zionist camp that colonized Israel became politically irrelevant, the religious nationalists would be free to institutionalize his vision of untrammeled religious supremacy into law. As Rabbi Aviner, an early Kook disciple wrote, Israel was called "to be holy, not moral, and the general principles of morality, customary for all mankind, do not bind the people of Israel, because it has been chosen to be above them." Many Kook acolytes proposed to guarantee the ethnic purity of Israel and some openly discussed "death camps" for non-Jews—the biblical "Amalekites."

After completing their IZS training, Shoval and Tadmor united with Moshe Klughaft, a twenty-eight-year-old public relations wunderkind named by Forbes magazine as the second most influential media consultant in Israel and one of the country's three hundred most influential adults. While taking up clients among hardline elements in Likud and Yisrael Beiteinu, Klughaft managed to conceal his radical agenda through appointments to establishment positions like the presidency of Israel's National Student Union. With Shoval and Tadmor as media savvy front men, he conceived the sophisticated, Kook-inspired, stealth campaign that would project the Greater Israel agenda into the Israeli mainstream—that would ride the secular "ass."

"I think I will always want to stay behind the scenes. I think that's where I have the greatest influence," Klughaft told an interviewer from Israel's Channel 7. "When everyone else is busily thinking about what to say on stage, I'm busily building the stage, [deciding] who actually listens to you. After they start listening, then we can talk about what we'll say."

When Shoval and Tadmor held the microphone at raucous camp rallies that more than often turned into ugly mob scenes, Klughaft served as their behind-the-scenes strategic consultant, calibrating each action to generate as much controversy as possible. "For religious Zionism and the right, in general, even to penetrate the public, they must move into the colorful, secular rhetoric of the playing field they are in," Klughaft explained. "What you think and how you see the world is nice, but when you get to this specific playing field of politics, of public action, you have to play by the rules that suit the place you are in."

To promote the campaign against human rights NGOs, Klughaft recruited one of Israel's most famous pop singers, the Mizrahi crooner Amir Benayoun, to record an Im Tirtzu theme song. Like Tadmor, Benayoun was an army reject, having been refused entry into the ranks of the military due to his long history of petty crime and drug use. Under the guidance of Chabad-Lubavitch, a Hasidic group that has become an extremist, pro-settler Jewish cult, and that considered the late Rabbi Menachem Scheerson, who died at the age of ninety-two in 1994, to be the Messiah, Benayoun was "born-again," emerging from the ashes of his debauched former existence.

Benayoun's Im Tirtzu anthem, delivered in an overdone, maudlin style against a backdrop of lilting violins, strangely rehashed the classical theme of the *Dolschtoss*, or the "stabbed in the back myth," which held that Germany lost World War I because civilians at home—Jews, "cultural Bolsheviks," and anti-Monarchists weakened the national resolve. Despite having never donned an army uniform, Benayoun sang from the perspective of an Israeli soldier returning home from duty, only to be spat upon by self-hating Jews:

> *After they failed to kill me from the outside*
> *you come and kill me from inside*
> *I haven't seen my mother in a month*
> *neither my son nor my house nor my wife*
> *I always charge forward*
> *with my back to you*
> *[but] you sharpen the knife*
> *more than anything, this thought burns my soul*
> *and you, how come you still don't understand . . .*

Shoval lent his hand to Im Tirtzu's growing body of propaganda with, "Im Tirtzu—A Manifesto for a Renewed Zionism," a tract intended as a Little Red Book for college-educated, post-army Israeli nationalists. Through the polemic, Shoval sought to mainstream the concept of "neo-Zionism," a rightist ideology that tracked closely with the typically fascist narrative of decline, cultural despair and internal subversion. According to Shoval's telling, the once-glorious project of Zionism had been eroded from within by a Fifth Column of foreign-backed human rights organizations, "post-Zionist" professors, and the traitorous Palestinian Israeli civil society. Israel's deliverance would arrive only through a secular version of Kook's "final redemption," with the Jewish state purified of its unholy elements. He termed this rapturous event, "The second Zionist revolution."

Once Israel arrived at the rendezvous of victory, the unhindered political dominance of the Jewish majority would be secure, providing the army with a free hand to act without limits against the Palestinians. The settlers, for their part, would never again fear the prospect of evacuation from "Judea and Samaria," their permanent heartland. As for the Arabs, if they wanted equal rights inside the frontiers of neo-Zionist Israel, they were free to become religious Jews. "Everyone can choose to be Jewish through the conversion process," Shoval wrote, "so anyone can enjoy all the rights and obligations involved in the Jewish people."

Despite Shoval's rhetoric, Im Tirtzu garnered enthusiastic endorsements from Prime Minister Benjamin Netanyahu and an array of top Likud officials, from Education Minister Gideon Sa'ar to Minister of Public Diplomacy Yuli Edelstein. Among the Likud's rising stars in the Knesset was one of Ronen Shoval's former lieutenants, the telegenic, far-right upstart Tzipi Hotovely, who said, "The feeling Ronen and I had was that our generation does not truly feel a commitment to be here and that our connection and commitment to the Zionist idea are diminishing."

As soon as she entered the Knesset, Hotovely began an effort to push Im Tirtzu's agenda, founding a Knesset lobby for promoting neo-Zionism on Israel's college campuses. In honor of the Knesset's "Jewish Identity Day," Hotovely convened hearings on the danger of Jewish women marrying Arab men. "We must confront the fact that the country has not valued education, which is the only way to prevent Jewish women from forging life connections with non-Jews," she declared, urging a nationwide "struggle against assimilation." Her crusade for separation between Jews and the *goyim* underscored her constant imprecations against Arab members of Knesset.

"I am in favor of removing Knesset members like you from their positions," she informed Hanin Zoabi during a televised debate. "The Balad Party should be outlawed."

"So the right-wing should run the state?" Zoabi asked.

"I have news for you," Hotovely shot back. "The majority of Israel is right-wing." She continued: "We can change the rules of the game. Until now, people like [Zoabi] have been taking advantage of the democracy."

While lawmakers like Hotovely as sponsors, the Institute for Zionist Strategies spearheaded the legislative agenda that would "change the rules of the game." Besides the anti-NGO bill, the Institute authored a proposed Basic Law that would formally define Israel as "the Nation State of the Jewish People," promising to subordinate Israel's supposedly democratic charter to its professed Jewish character, stripping Arabic from its list of official languages, and removing the illusion of minority rights promised in the country's Declaration of Independence. The law's sponsor, Avi Dichter, a hard-boiled former Shin Bet chief recruited by Livni to join Kadima, said, "With the Basic Law we can finally denote Israel as the nation-state of the Jewish people and not need the Palestinians' favors and recognition of us as a Jewish state."

Behind the scenes, Im Tirtzu had accepted a $100,000 cash infusion from a far right foreign donor: Christians United for Israel founder John Hagee, the apocalyptic mega-church pastor from San Antonio, Texas, who prophesied that the anti-Christ would return as a homosexual half-Jew, "as was Adolf Hitler." Flush with cash from Hagee and an assortment of Israeli oligarchs, Im Tirtzu expanded its list of soft targets. Though a few isolated leftists protested the organization's hypocrisy on foreign funding, the issue hardly registered.

On Nakba Day 2011, Im Tirzu distributed a short pamphlet entitled "Nakba Bull-shit," claiming that the Nakba was "a lie that threatens to drown us like a tsunami." Outside the offices of the United Nations Relief Works Agency, the international body responsible for the welfare of the millions of stateless Palestinians, the student activists chanted, "They were expelled! They attacked! They lost!" The same month, Im Tirtzu demanded that the Israeli attorney general investigate and punish a group of older Israeli women from the group Machson Watch, who had traveled to a village in the West Bank to help prevent settler vigilante attacks on local Palestinian farmers.

When a few Israeli leftists created a Facebook group that dubbed Im Tirtzu as a fascist organization, Shoval hired a team of lawyers to slap the activists with a $600,000 libel lawsuit. During the trial, the court heard testimony from Zeev Stern-hell, one of the world's leading experts on fascism and the former chair of the department of political science at Hebrew University. Three years before he testified, Sternhell was wounded when a fanatical settler named Jack Teitel mailed a pipe bomb to his home. Sternhell declared that he had examined Shoval's manifesto and the group's activities in careful detail, and had come to a disturbing conclusion.

"If we take into account that Im Tirtzu is just beginning and is operating in a society where rejection of the fundamentals of liberalism is perceived to be a sin," Sternhell said, "then it is showing early and troubling signs of fascist potential."

44

The Revolutionaries

resh off its success against the New Israel Fund, countless damaging personal attacks against leftists and professors condemned as insufficiently Zionist, and hearty endorsements from the heads of state, Im Tirtzu's top cadres gathered for a night of booze-filled celebration on August 3, 2010. The venue was "Theodore," a swanky bar in the wealthy Tel Aviv suburb of Herzilya, named for the man Im Tirtzu claimed as its inspiration for the "Second Zionist Revolution"—Theodore Herzl. The evening was dedicated to firing up the troops for the upcoming boycott targeting Ben Gurion University's faculty, where Im Tirtzu had identified nine out of twelve professors in the political science department as "anti-Zionists."

I traveled to the event with Joseph Dana, an Israeli-American journalist. Dana and I had learned about Im Tirtzu's party from a friend at Hebrew University, but when we told her we were interested in attending, she suddenly grew agitated. "If they find out who you guys are there, they will take you outside and lynch you," she said. With her warning in mind, we took the precautionary measure of introducing ourselves as clueless Jewish-American tourists.

At the door of "Theodore," we met a glowering young man munching on a slice of pizza. He was Erez Tadmor, Im Tirtzu's director of media relations. When Tadmor asked who we were, we said we were just two Jewish American guys passing through Herzliya on a tour of Israel. "We just heard there was some kind of party here," Joseph said.

Without prompting, Tadmor launched into a monologue about how he was unable to show his face at Hebrew University anymore after all the trouble he caused for its "anti-Israel, anti-Zionist professors trying to defend our Zionist values against what they're doing."

Tadmor told me he was confident of Im Tirtzu's coming victory, explaining that Israel's elites only represented the 3 percent of the population who were radical leftists. But Im Tirtzu had 70 to 80 percent on their side, he declared.

After listening to Tadmor's boasting, two Im Tirtzu activists approached to discuss campus politics in the United States. One of them, a chubby, slouching young man with a crew cut, asked, "Have you ever read *The Professors* by David Horowitz? Horowitz was a former leftist so he knows the truth about the left in your country." With his "Academic Bill of Rights" campaign, which would have allowed conservative students to sue their professors, and the Muslim annual extravaganza he organized on campuses around the country, "Islamofascism Awareness Week," the neoconservative, former Communist Horowitz had become the conservative movement's campus point man, reaping millions in donations from right-wing American plutocrats like the Koch brothers in the process. He seemed like a natural role model for Im Tirtzu's activists.

One of the Im Tirtzu members we met by the bar was Tamir Kafri, a bespectacled, chipper Ben Gurion University student with a long ponytail and newly budding facial hair. I asked him about the inspiration Im Tirtzu took from the American conservative movement. Kafri mentioned another popular right-wing tract from the United States. "You should read the book, *Liberal Fascism*," he said, referring to conservative writer Jonah Goldberg's screed conflating American liberalism to European fascism and Nazism. "I'm not saying all liberals are fascists," Kafri added, "but on campus here in Israel, the liberal professors really are."

Kafri led us up to the bar and perched himself next to us. As dozens of his comrades filed in, he ordered a pony-size Goldstar beer and entertained with his opinions on everything from Palestinians ("You know, the idea of the Palestinians was invented in the 1970s?") to women's rights ("If a woman hits me, I'll hit her back just as hard. That's feminism!").

On campus politics, Kafri commented, "[The Israeli communist party] Hadash is a bunch of pro-Palestinian radicals. But we've worked with Meretz. We even have some members of Meretz in our movement. They are the sensible left. They're Zionists, not radicals."

When we asked Kafri about the hundreds of thousands of donations pumped into Im Tirtzu's coffers each year by the apocalyptic Christian Zionist preacher Hagee, he spun the scandal as a fundraising coup. "Who cares about who takes the money?" Tamir said. "People should focus on the donors and not on us. He's the idiot! He's giving all his money to a bunch of Zionist Jews in Israel!"

While Kafri riffed on politics beneath a thumping soundtrack of seventies disco hits, we looked around the room and noticed an almost total absence of women. Indeed, the bartender seemed to be the only female interacting with the dozens of Im Tirtzu activists hunched over the bar. "Were any women invited your party?" we asked our new friend.

Kafri craned his head around nervously, then explained, "People show up late in Israel because we have no last call."

Twenty minutes later, a woman finally appeared. She turned out to be the wife of Kafri's pal, a short, bookish-looking character, whom he greeted with a hearty bear hug. "This guy acted with me in the *Rocky Horror Picture Show*," Kafri said, referring to the seventies-era British drag show that has become popular across Israel.

"I actually had to borrow a corset from my wife for the show!" the friend told us with a giggle of delight.

Kafri's friend was a genetic engineer at the Weissman Institute who boasted to us that he and a team of researchers were on the verge of curing cancer. He said he became enraged when he saw an art exhibition in the city of Holon that depicted Israeli army helicopters bombing civilians and soldiers humiliating Palestinians at checkpoints. He immediately called Im Tirtzu founder Ronen Shoval to complain. The next day, he was manning the barricades for the Second Zionist Revolution. "If the army did this sort of thing, it would be okay, because the art would have been factual," Kafri's friend remarked. "But the army doesn't do that! I was in the infantry, so I know."

Kafri and his friend were intent on regaling us with tales from the *Rocky Horror Picture Show* production he and Tamir starred in. "You know what the play really was?" he said to Tamir. "It was a hook-up scene for geeks!"

At this moment, as we glanced around the room full of twenty-something guys huddled around on couches, fiddling with their cellphones and exchanging jocular backslaps, we gained a new understanding of Im Tirtzu's cultural utility. The movement was not only a street-level proxy for rightist forces in the government. It also served as a social sanctuary for aimless young men unable to locate productive outlets for their pent-up post-army aggressions. Long sessions of PlayStation and back issues of *Maxim* were simply not enough for these rejects and reservists of Israel's warrior class. Through Im Tirtzu, fascism appeared not in medallioned uniforms and motorcycle processions, but in designer jeans, polo shirts, and gelled hair.

In the casual setting of "Theodore," Im Tirtzu might have appeared to be a benign dork squad, but unlike the students recruited by the American conservative movement to harass liberal professors, Im Tirtzu's activists were armed and blessed with the support of the prime minister.

With the party drawing to a close, Im Tirtzu's leader, Ronen Shoval, stood to deliver a speech announcing the coming onslaught against Ben Gurion University. "My grandmother was so proud to see us on the front page of *Ha'aretz!*" he announced to cheers from the dozens of admiring young men assembled in a semi-circle around him. "We have all the chapters from around the country ready for this campaign. We are going to go all the way."

As Shoval worked his troops into a frenzy, Joseph and I noticed two young women downing shots of liquor across the bar. They were two of the only females we had seen all night, so we approached them out of curiosity.

"Are you guys with Im Tirtzu?" we asked.

"You mean the disgusting fascists?" one of them snapped.

"We hate them!" the other one growled.

After a long interview process that included the examination of our ID cards, they established that we were not among "the fascists." The women eventually apologized for vetting us, explaining that an Im Tirtzu member seated beside them at the bar had attempted to chat them up earlier in the evening.

One of them told us she grabbed the Im Tirtzu activist's arm and shouted at him, "Are you ready to stop being a narrow-minded racist? Then you can talk to us."

45

Zion Square

By August 2010, I had left my apartment in Jaffa after accepting Joseph Dana's invitation to move in with him and his roommates in central Jerusalem. My new flat was a cramped, five-bedroom, one-bathroom compound on the top floor of a vast, gray apartment bloc located on Dorot Rishonim Street, just around the corner from the bustling Ben Yehuda Street pedestrian mall and a few blocks from Zion Square. It was an ideal perch to observe the frontline of Israeli internal opposition to the occupation and racist street violence. Draped over the covered porch overlooking the promenade was a ragged banner reading "Free Gaza—End the Siege." One month before my arrival, the Israeli immigration police force known as the Oz Unit had appeared at the door of the flat hunting for a foreign Palestine solidarity activist whom they would later arrest during a dragnet in Ramallah, the city where the Palestinian Authority supposedly exercised autonomy. The quasi-raid was part of a Shin Bet roundup of international activists aimed at winnowing out the ranks of protesters who demonstrated against the separation wall in the West Bank. If the Shin Bet was seeking subversives to monitor, it had come to the right place: my new flat was a mecca for Jerusalem's tiny activist community.

On most nights during the week, our porch would become a smoke-filled situation room, as my roommates and I gathered on the tattered secondhand couches with friends and local activists, drinking cheap arak and discussing local happenings, from the expulsions in the nearby, occupied neighborhood of Sheik Jarrah to the night arrests in the West Bank village of Bil'in. The wall on the porch was a constantly expanding rogues' gallery, decorated with photos of Defense Minister Ehud Barak, Interior Minister Eli Yishai, and Jerualem mayor Nir Barkat, who was overseeing the planned demolition of eighty-eight Palestinian homes in the occupied East Jerusalem neighborhood of Silwan in order to build a biblical theme park called "The City of David."

Directly below the flat were crowds of gun-toting Orthodox settlers and soldiers shopping for discount clothing and gorging themselves on pizza and frozen yogurt. The flat was cluttered, often choking with cigarette fumes, a virtual flophouse for scraggled activists and visiting European couch-surfers. At times, it was virtually uninhabitable. But it was one of the most fascinating vantage points in Jerusalem and a rare sanctuary from a climate of suffocating hyper-nationalism.

My flatmates were a motley collection of Jerusalemites, mostly in their early twenties, and all with life experiences that had turned them against the conventional Israeli

political thinking in one way or another. Besides Joseph, there was Yossi, an easygoing Hebrew University graduate student who had abandoned his ultra-Orthodox
family and the extremist *yeshiva* they raised him in; Tomer, another Hebrew U. student who balanced his obsession with death metal—a protest anthem he recorded
repeated the word "Nakba" for two minutes without a pause—with an immersion
in Jewish studies, regaling his roommates with bawdy Talmudic stories as though it
were *The Canterbury Tales*; Masha, a Russian immigrant who protested against the
Sheikh Jarrah evictions with a clown troupe, dressed in a mock army uniform, and
was arrested for the crime of blowing bubbles near a group of riot policemen. After
Masha was compelled to put on a real army uniform under threat of more jail time,
conscripted into a teachers' unit in faraway Dimona, her room was filled by Galia,
an anarchist whose non-Jewish mother had rendered her ineligible for many of the
benefits her family had been promised when the Jewish Agency coerced them into
immigrating to Israel from post–Soviet Russia.

Unlike the rest of my flatmates, Joseph did not grow up in Israel. He was a Jewish
American kid from the kind of affluent, liberal family in which Zionism was taken
for granted. With a master's degree from Hebrew University in Jewish Studies, he
could have easily risen through the ranks of academia. And with his journalistic
inclination and an ear to the ground, he had wound up in this flat, using it as a point
of disembarkation to report almost daily from West Bank village demonstrations
that were invariably crushed by the Israeli army.

When Joseph's younger brother graduated from a Jewish day school in San Diego,
he and his classmates were given a mock five-foot-high walking stick—the kind
Moses supposedly used to lead the Hebrews toward the Promised Land—and a copy
of Alan Dershowitz's *The Case for Israel*. They were instructed to take the two items
to college and fight for Israel on campus. But after a trip through the West Bank with
a Lebanese friend, his brother rebelled. By this time, Joseph was enthralled by the idea
of Israel, by the beaches, the effusive, physical culture, the mythical concept of Jewish
redemption, the Zionist dream as marketed to American youth. His brother tried to
warn him about what he had seen in Ramallah and Nablus, but it was useless. The
State of Israel was offering to pay for Joseph to pursue his master's at Hebrew University on the grounds that he make *aliyah*. In 2006, at age twenty-five, he emigrated, high
on Jewish nationalism and oblivious to the grinding day-to-day reality awaiting him.

"There is something among American Jews—and I reflected this tendency—
that Israel represents an escapist society where you can project yourself and who
you want to be onto a sunny, beachside environment with hot people all around
you," Joseph explained. "As a young adult, there's an idea that you can go by yourself,
be surrounded by Jews, and reinvent yourself as you wish here. As a male in my
mid-twenties it was an escapist decision that was fortified by lofty ideals that I could
tap into: I'm a Jew in the modern world, and I'm doing something great by contrib-
uting to Israeli society as a Jew. Like Alan Dershowitz and thousands of other Jews
who fetishize Israel but never want to leave the US, Israel was my object of desire."

The rigors of daily life began to chip away at Joseph's image of the Jewish state. "I
saw none of the essential aspects of the society precisely because I was an American

Jew, because I was an honorary member of their society," he said. "I was included in society but excluded from the actual debate. And as an American, getting basic things done—going to the post office, traveling from Tel Aviv to Jerusalem—was incredibly tedious and opened me up to whole series of disturbing experiences I never would have seen as a tourist. At first, it wasn't that I had a political awakening as much as an awakening to the very unpleasant reality of daily life in Israel."

"Having finally insinuated myself into the heart of the society, I started to get it—I started to be aware of what this country was about, and to see it against the backdrop of this explicit racism against Palestinians. It was always that the Palestinians are the horrible ones—the classic Bibi Netanyahu dismissal of Israeli responsibility based on the racist claim that the Arabs are culturally incurable barbarians."

I had met Joseph in May 2009 in an olive grove in the southern West Bank farming village of Safa, which was located at the base of the radical hilltop settlement of Bat Ayin, once the home of a Jewish terrorist underground that plotted the bombing a Palestinian girls' school in Jerusalem. Joseph had invited me to participate in an action aimed at protecting the farmers from the settlers, who had attacked them with axe handles a week before and had begun chanting, "Death to Arabs!" from the hilltop as soon as we arrived. A new wave of settler terror was just beginning, with attacks on Palestinians and their property rising at a 150 percent rate across the West Bank since 2009.

Ezra Nawi, a bald, olive-skinned Israeli with a straw hat and a long walking stick, led us through the parched fields of sagebrush into the valley below. The young activists regarded him with reverence, describing him to me as a mentor and an indispensible guide. During the 1980s Nawi was convicted of living illegally with a West Bank Palestinian man who happened to be his lover. The experience galvanized his activist spirit, leading him to donate the money he earned as a plumber to activism against the occupation. With the fluent Arabic his Iraqi parents spoke before him, Nawi had won the trust of the besieged Palestinian communities in the South Hebron Hills, forming an essential bridge for Israel's mostly Ashkenazi activist elements. However, as a Mizrahi who was also openly gay, Nawi became a natural target for soldiers who viewed him as both a race traitor and sexual deviant.

"Sometimes the prejudice is so deep and subconscious because there are very few activists from my background. Most of the police are from my background so they can't understand how I cross the line. It disrupts the order they like to see," Nawi told me. "There is no mercy here. I always say that if I would catch on fire the soldiers would not even piss on me to put it out." Also a constant target of settler hatred, Nawi added, "The soldiers say to me all the time, 'You are not Jewish.' I look around and the religious settlers are running around beating people, beating women, destroying my car, screaming curses. So according to the soldiers, that is what a Jew is—people who think they are entitled to rule other people."

When I met Nawi, he was facing three years in prison on trumped-up charges of assaulting a soldier while attempting to block a bulldozer from demolishing a group of Palestinian Bedouin homes. Videotape of the incident showed soldiers mocking

Nawi for attempting to help the Palestinian families. "I was also a soldier, but I didn't demolish houses!" he screamed back at them. "The only thing that will be left here is hatred." After a long legal spectacle during which a judge ordered a Hebrew translator appointed for Nawi, as though he were a Palestinian, and after an outpouring of support from international intellectuals, Nawi was sentenced to a month in prison— far less than the two-year term he expected.

Just a few minutes after we arrived in Safa, the settlers called a platoon of soldiers to remove us from the olive groves. The platoon commander immediately issued a closed military zone order, a standard procedure aimed at providing the settlers with free reign. A thin, middle-aged classics professor at Hebrew University named Amiel Vardi rushed forward with legal documents, arguing that a Supreme Court ruling gave us the right to remain on the scene. Vardi argued with the commander until he was red in the face, and for a moment it appeared he had persuaded him. A veteran campaigner for Palestinian rights, Vardi was shot by a settler in 2006 (the settler who shot him was freed without charges) and had seen his Jerusalem home spray-painted with death threats by right-wing activists. Vardi's nineteen-year-old daughter, Sahar, was jailed for refusing to serve in the army, and counseled other youth considering refusal.

Three weeks after we visited Safa, settlers from Bat Ayin chopped down the village's fruit trees by the dozens and torched the farmers' fields.

It was June 3, 2009, the night before President Barack Obama delivered his promised speech to the Arab world in Cairo, Egypt. The planned address and the new diplomatic posture it represented sent a wave of indignation through the ranks of the Israeli right. Prime Minister Benjamin Netanyahu, who had reportedly called Obama's Jewish chief of staff Rahm Emanuel a "self-hating Jew," planned to issue a "Zionist response" to Obama, as though he were countering a sworn enemy and not Israel's major patron. The old liberal Zionist "peace camp" was brimming with a mood of excitement it had not experienced since the Oslo era. Many among the faded movement had convinced themselves that Obama was The One who would finally force both sides to the table and generate a historic agreement, or who would at least make the most earnest effort to date.

The day before Obama's speech, I received an e-mail from Adam Horowitz, the editor of a progressive Jewish American blog called Mondoweiss, asking me to record a man-on-the-street video interview segment about the Obama speech. I told Joseph I was too exhausted to do any more filming, but he insisted. I relented and slapped a new battery pack into the back of my camera.

Our first interview took place on the Ben Yehuda Pedestrian Mall. There, we filmed an ultra-nationalist hippie settler from the United States ranting, "Obama doesn't have any place here. This is our land. I'm a Jew. I'm a Yid. *Am Yisrael!*" Then, we found ourselves in a nearby gathering place known by Jerusalem youth as "Crack Square." Israeli and American teenagers were sprawled out along concrete benches in front of a social services center decorated with stickers that read "Kahane Was Right." Some were yeshiva students treating their time away from their conservative families as a chance to party into oblivion. Others were rejected, runaway children of settlers, who had fled domestic abuse and religious fanaticism for a life of narcotics, alcohol, and the constant specter of police violence.

A drunk fifteen-year-old with an acne-scarred face lamented to me, "It was so much better being back in the States. The police beat so much harder here and treat us like fucking animals. I wish my parents had never brought me to this hellhole." Next to him, a kid who could not have been any older than thirteen lifted himself from a bench, staggered in our direction for a few seconds, then crashed on the ground with a face-first flop. His friends broke out in uproarious laughter.

A skinny Israeli-American guy with a knit *kippah* who might have been around twenty introduced himself to us. He said he lived in "Judea and Samaria" with his Israeli-American family and was actively involved in setting up hilltop settlement outposts. "Obama needs to know that this is *our land*," he declared.

Leading toward a warren of seedy bars packed with American Jews, he told me wanted to introduce us to a few of his friends. It was there that we stumbled upon a group of Jewish-American college students from the Five Towns area of suburban Long Island, New York. The young men were smoking a nargileh and drinking heavily at an outdoor bar overflowing with international Jewish tourists. I approached and innocently asked what flavor of sheesha they were smoking. "Your mom's pussy!" one barked at me. Then I simply asked what they thought of Obama. With the mention of Obama's name, they surrounded me, jostling one another out of the way to take a turn at ranting against the president.

"White power! Fuck the niggers!" one of them shouted. "He deserves to get shot."

"My grandma was in Auschwitz, Obama! We're not gonna take any Nazi bullshit," said another, before reciting the number supposedly tattooed on his grandmother's arm.

A beefy frat boy type stood up and bellowed, "Netanyahu told Obama to go fuck himself, and that's how we do it in Israel, baby!"

At a nearby table, a young woman from Florida in a revealing tank top said Obama "was like a terrorist." She wondered if he was even an American citizen. When I challenged her, she assured me, "I'm a political science major, so I know my shit." But when I asked if she knew who the prime minister of Israel was she could not tell me, nor could any of her friends. "I don't know. Benjamin Yahoo?" she said with befuddlement.

The mere mention of Obama's name had stirred up a hornet's nest. "Fuck Obama, fuck him! You like Obama? Fuck Obama!" an excited young American shouted into my camera. "I know where the White House is, Obama," said a beefy jock wearing a gold *Chai* necklace, "and I'm gonna teabag your ass and put it on YouTube, faggot. I'm comin' for you, Obama."

The next day, Joseph and I posted a four-minute video of our experience online. We called it, "Feeling the Hate in Jerusalem."

Within twelve hours, the video was ricocheting across cyberspace, generating half a million hits and counting. "The video has gone viral," wrote a young *Ha'aretz* correspondent named Ben Hartman, "linked from a hundred political blogs, and is circling the Internet at a critical velocity on a mission to humiliate the Jewish people." Another young Israeli scribe, Lahav Harkov of the *Jerusalem Post*, wrote, "One of Israel's biggest problems today is *hasbara* and young Jews like Dana and Blumenthal are only aggravating the problem. Too many Jewish people have forgotten what Israel has done for their people. Instead, they try to fit in with the American liberal intelligentsia." (Soon after, Hartman and Harkov were promoted to top correspondent positions at the *Jerusalem Post*).

Ron Kampeas, a dual Israeli-American citizen who wrote for the Jewish Telegraphic Agency, joined the chorus of outrage, declaring, "Blumenthal needs to grow up and put his talents to good use." Meanwhile, the liberal Zionist Israeli author and columnist Gershom Gorenberg, another dual American-Israeli citizen, asserted that because some of the people who appeared in our video were American, their racist opinions had no little or no connection to the reality of Israeli society. He concluded that the video was "an argument for old media," claiming that traditional mainstream media editors would have immediately spiked it.

Coverage from the Israeli national news and New York City's Channel 5 local news followed, with death threats and angry, insulting letters pouring into my e-mail.

After receiving nearly half a million hits on YouTube, our video was censored by YouTube administrators and formally banned from the site for "explicit content." The video-sharing site, Vimeo, did the same.

On February 11, 2011, on Jerusalem's King George Street, just blocks from the warren of seedy bars where Joseph and I filmed *Feeling the Hate*, two drunk Jewish Israeli youths approached Hsam Rwidy, a twenty-four-year-old Palestinian from East Jerusalem, and asked him and his friend, Murad Khader Joulani, if they were Arabs or not. When Rwidy and Joulani ignored them, they suddenly found themselves under assault. "More guys came, about four, and everyone was hitting us and my friend ran away and slipped in the middle of the road. I started to run after [Rwidy] and I saw that his shirt was all bloody in the front," Joulani recalled. During the attack, one of the youths stabbed Rwidy in the face, reportedly shouting "Death to Arabs!" and leaving him bleeding badly. While waiting for an ambulance to arrive, Rwidy slipped into unconsciousness and then died.

What happened next was eerily familiar. After a media blackout imposed by the Shin Bet, the Israeli media produced a series of articles dismissing the gravity of the murder. "A drunken brawl gone bad" was how several reports described the killing of Rwidy, parroting statements by the Jerusalem police that his death was the result of a fight. The violent behavior of Jewish nationalists was downplayed as a product of intoxication, while the incident was portrayed as an aberration.

Almost a month after Rwidy's killing, the mother of the teenage stabber revealed her son's motives to the Jerusalem police: "He doesn't like Arabs, he says he hates them. He has a lot of anger and hate, he hates them. He told me, 'I feel like killing them.' But I told him, 'To kill an Arab, is that worth your life?'"

After being indicted for manslaughter, not murder, the teen killer was sentenced to eight years in prison, a punishment that highlighted the double standard in Israel's criminal justice system. Rwidy's father, Hussein, told *Ha'aretz*: "This is not worth anything, that he serves eight years for what he did. . . . Those are the courts, I can't do anything. He murdered my son just because he is an Arab." The two accomplices to the murder, meanwhile, received no more than six months of community service.

Isaac "Boujie" Herzog, at the time the minister of Social Affairs and the face of Israel's enlightened Ashkenazi elite, demanded that Israeli president Shimon Peres speak out against the plague of racism and hate crimes sweeping the country. "Israel today feels like Alabama in the 1940s," Herzog reportedly complained. But Peres kept silent.

The Israeli Experience

very year, thousands gather at the Western Wall Plaza in Jerusalem's Old City to celebrate Yom Yerushalayim, or Jerusalem Day, the commemoration of the Israeli army's conquest of East Jerusalem in the 1967 Six Days War. It was also here, on June 10, 1967, that Israeli forces ethnically cleansed the Old City's Moroccan Quarter, a neighborhood of 650 people whose homes abutted the Western Wall, and whose presence there dated back to the eleventh century.

Once the soldiers entered the Moroccan Quarter, residents were informed they had two hours to gather their belongings and leave. Those who refused were violently evicted. While the new class of refugees marched off to what would become Shuafat Refugee Camp on the outskirts of Jerusalem, Israeli bulldozers rumbled in, destroying every home in their path. Just days after the last indigenous Arabs were expelled from the former Moroccan Quarter, the first among the anticipated wave of Jewish visitors flocked to the Western Wall, literally walking over the rubble of Arab homes to arrive at the site.

The Israeli government placed a private company in charge of renovating the new Jewish Quarter. One of the company's first acts was the introduction of a rule banning non-Jews from living inside the neighborhood. The Israeli Supreme Court later ruled the stipulation was "good law," rejecting the appeal of a former resident of the Moroccan Quarter to return to his home, which had been seized by the state. In turn, the law provided a basis for the expulsionist and discriminatory agenda Israel would implement over the coming decades throughout the "united" city of Jerusalem.

In short order, the Western Wall was renovated into a spacious plaza that provided a postcard-perfect image of the rapturous Holy Land that existed in the minds of Western tourists, and especially among American Jews. A giant sculpture of six candles representing the six million Jews who perished in the Holocaust and an Israeli flag sprung up in the center of the plaza. Along with the wall, one of the holiest sites in the Jewish religion, the candles and the flag symbolized the three pillars of Jewish identity. The Israeli Army promptly relocated its swearing-in ceremonies for new soldiers from Masada to the Western Wall, linking its military mission to the messianic narrative of exile and return.

The 2011 Jerusalem Day celebrations on June 4 organized by the Jerusalem Municipality and endorsed by Prime Minister Benjamin Netanyahu and a host of top cabinet ministers, brought thousands of Israeli youth out of their settlement homes and the fundamentalist *yeshivas* around the country into East Jerusalem's Palestinian neighborhoods, where they harassed and taunted local residents. "Jerusalem is the capital of the Jewish people and the capital of the State of Israel," Yitzhak Ze'ev Pindrus, the senior deputy mayor of Jerusalem, told a flag-waving crowd of Jewish youth in the Palestinian neighborhood of Sheikh Jarrah, where forced evictions had already replaced several Arab families with Jewish settlers. "And I'm telling you today, on this joyous day, in the name of the Municipality of Jerusalem, the municipality will continue to settle the Sheikh Jarrah neighborhood."

To the sound of marching drums, hundreds of young men surrounded the mosque in Sheikh Jarrah and chanted, "Muhammad is dead!" "May your village burn!" and "Death to leftists!" Shouting that Arabs were "sons of whores," the marchers celebrated Baruch Goldstein, the Jewish fanatic who massacred twenty-nine Muslim worshippers in Hebron in 1994 during the Purim holiday. The night before the march, groups of settler youth had gathered in Sheikh Jarrah to flaunt their sense of ethnic and religious supremacy. The youth waved flags and bellowed, "This country is ours forever and we won't give it up for anyone!"

Sleeping in a tent next to the house he had lived in since 1956 was Nabil Al Kurd. A white-haired Palestinian man expelled from his property in "Israel proper" in 1948, Al Kurd joined thousands of other Palestinian refugees in Sheikh Jarrah, the East Jerusalem neighborhood established by the United Nations and the International Red Cross to house them. In the dead of night on November 3, 2009, Al Kurd and his family were thrown out of their home by a squad of riot policemen on the orders of the Jerusalem Municipality, which had decided that the pre-1948 deeds to the homes presented by a group of settlers were valid. A month later, the settlers moved in, spray-painting stars of David around the front door to mark the property as officially Judaized. A banner above the doorway declared, "We are all settlers—We are Israelis."

"This march is not like in the last forty years," Al Kurd told the journalist Lia Tarachansky. "Because the government is weak, they make the march like this—to tell the Palestinians in Jerusalem, 'We are many people here and we can kill you if you do anything.'"

As Yom Yerushalayim's 2011 festivities approached their culmination, thousands of Jewish American youth poured into the Muslim Quarter of Jerusalem's Old City under the protection of the Israeli Border Police. After merging with the Israeli youth, they marched through the narrow corridors booming the Hebrew slogans "Muhammad is dead!" and "Slaughter the Arabs!" The chants reverberated across the stonewalls and seeped through the shuttered windows of Palestinian homes, signaling to local Arabs that their replacement by Jewish settlers was imminent. During the celebration that took place the next year, a group of marchers attacked journalists attempting to film the march, bludgeoning a young woman with the wooden handle of an Israeli flag.

"This parade is out of control! This is the Israel experience!" a college-aged Jewish American man from Miami, Florida, told Lia Tarachansky, who covered the march for the Real News Network.

Surrounded by a group of friends from the United States, the pumped-up American continued, "We're celebrating that in 1967, we took our city back. . . . We took it for its rightful owners. Regardless of who we took it from, it's now ours, where it belongs. And there's still a lot left to go."

Ultras

N amed for Jerusalem's first Israeli mayor, Teddy Kollek, Teddy Stadium is a favorite venue for young Israeli men seeking to ventilate their pent-up passions. They pour in from all around Israel to root for the Beitar Jerusalem football club. The soccer team was named after the world right-wing Zionist youth movement founded by Ze'ev Jabotinsky. Its matches also serve as a forum for the neo-fascist "Ultra" group known as La Familia. Beitar Jerusalem has counted Yisrael Beiteinu's Avigdor Lieberman among its greatest fans, binding him with his far right enthusiasts.

Back at Teddy Stadium, fans let out the routine "Death to Arabs!" chant after Beitar scored goals and unfurled gigantic banners displaying the symbol of Kach, the banned terrorist group founded by Rabbi Meir Kahane, who advocated the creation of a *Arabrein* theocracy in the West Bank. According to Amir Ben-Porat, a Ben Gurion University professor of behavioral sciences and leading expert on racism in Israeli society, "In the late 1990s and onwards, 'Death to the Arabs' became a common chant in almost every football stadium in Israel." Ben-Porat noted that because of the prominent role football occupied in Israeli popular culture, "This chant is heard far beyond the stadium."

When Salim Tuama, a Palestinian citizen of Israel who plays on the Israeli national football team, appeared on the pitch at Teddy Stadium, Beitar fans sang, "What is Salim doing here, I don't know. . . . Tuama, this is the Land of Israel. Tuama, this is the state of the Jews. I hate you Salim Tuama! I hate all the Arabs!" When Toto Tamuz, the Nigerian-born striker for the fierce Beitar rival Hapoel Tel Aviv, makes his way from the locker room to the field at Teddy Stadium, Beitar fans pelt him with bananas as though he's a monkey, heckle him with racist chants, and sing what has become a traditional team song: "Give Toto a banana!" During a close match in November 2012, Tamuz put his index finger up to his lips to silence the crowd after he scored a goal. Though he had weathered racists taunts throughout the entire game, the Israeli referee ejected him on the grounds of "provoking the crowd."

After Beitar won the Israeli Cup in 2009, several of its players including the young star, Amit Ben Shushan, joined in the racist chants. When, during celebrations of their cup victory a year earlier, then-minister of Sports and Culture Raleb Majadele, an Israeli Arab, attempted to congratulate the Beitar players, one by one they conspicuously refused to shake his hand. Unlike Ali Baher, the Hebrew University Arab student body chairman who refused to shake the hand of Israeli president Shimon

Peres, and who was arrested and stripped of his student ID as punishment, the players were not penalized by the Israeli Football Association.

In recent years, Arab players have emerged as a goal-scoring force in Israeli soccer, taking on starring roles for a few major clubs. But Beitar Jerusalem refuses to employ them, maintaining an Arab-free policy to the wishes of its fans and managers—and with the quiet complicity of the Israeli Football Association, Jerusalem mayor Nir Barkat, and the major Israeli corporations that sponsor the team. "Since Beitar Jerusalem was founded in 1936 there hasn't been an Arab player in the team and the fans are trying to keep it that way," boasted a leader of La Familia. "We used to be friends with the fans of Bnei Yehuda [another Israeli football club] but then they brought an Arab player, we dissed them and from there on we fight a lot."

When Aviram Baruchyan, the former captain of Beitar, volunteered his opinion at an antiviolence conference that he "would be happy" to play alongside an Arab player, he provoked the full wrath of Beitar's fans, who claimed they were outraged and emotionally wounded by his words. A day later, Baruchyam rushed to apologize for his grave transgression, promising in a meeting with La Familia's leaders that he would never make such tolerant statements again. "The most painful thing is that I unfortunately hurt Beitar's fans, and I understood that I hurt them very much," Baruchyam said afterward. "It's important for me that the players know and that everyone knows that I am with them through thick and thin, and I don't care what other people think or write."

While Beitar fans are usually content to display their hatred for Arabs in the form of chants, Beitar matches have occasionally transformed into scenes of mob violence against Arabs. In February 2012, after Beitar lost to Sakhnin, an all-Arab team from Northern Israel, bitter Beitar fans relieved their humiliation with a mass rampage against Sakhnin's players. After attacking the team's buses with stones, smashing windows, and wounding some players, the Jerusalem police belatedly arrived to drive away the rioters and make a few token arrests.

A month later, the rioting poured into the streets outside Teddy Stadium, when hundreds of teenaged Beitar fans burst into West Jerusalem's Malcha Mall, crazed and shirtless after a dramatic victory over the Tel Aviv club Bnei Yehuda. Inside the mall's food court, they attacked Arab cleaning personnel, spat on a group of Arab women workers, and chanted (what else?) "Death to Arabs!" *Ha'aretz* called the incident, "one of Jerusalem's biggest-ever ethnic clashes." Though the cleaners momentarily chased assailants away with broom handles, the security camera video revealed that the melee hardly comprised a "clash." A member of the mall's cleaning crew, Mohammed Yusuf, offered a more appropriate description: "It was a mass lynching attempt."

"I've never seen so many people," a shopkeeper commented. "They stood on chairs and tables and what have you. They made a terrible noise, screamed, 'Death to the Arabs,' waved their scarves and sang songs at the top of their voices."

Malcha Mall security and the Jerusalem police treated the riot as a mundane event. No one who witnessed the attack reported it to the police. And when two female officers arrived on the scene, they filed no report and made no arrests. After learning of the official non-response, Arab member of Knesset Ahmad Tibi called the incident "an unprecedented pogrom."

"The fact that no complaints were filed is puzzling and is part of the capitulation in the face of racism," Tibi said. "Besides, the fact that police did not carry out any arrests, even after they arrived at the scene and viewed the security footage encourages the rioters."

In early 2013, Beitar Jerusalem broke with tradition by signing two Muslim players from Chechnya in order to remain competitive. La Familia staged a massive demonstration at its training field when the new team members were introduced, spitting on them, shouting racist epithets, and demanding that they remove the sacred Beitar jerseys. Unable to practice, police escorted the players away. The team felt compelled to pay for bodyguards for them. At the first game where the Muslim players took the field, La Familia fans unfurled a large banner in the stands: "Beitar is pure forever." On February 8, the team's offices were set on fire and its historic trophies and memorabilia destroyed. Two members of La Familia were arrested and confessed to the arson. In the aftermath, Beitar's midfielder Ofir Kriaf, who had posted support for La Familia on his Facebook page, was forced by the team's management to apologize and briefly suspended.

The Best Time of Their Lives

n the summer of 2010, a chubby-cheeked twenty-year-old girl from Ashdod named Eden Abergil posted on her Facebook page. Nestled among the photos of Abergil and her friends during their army service and labeled "The army . . . best time of my life" were shocking trophy shots depicting Abergil mocking blindfolded Palestinian detainees during Operation Cast Lead in Gaza.

In one photo, a uniformed but heavily made-up and coiffed Abergil pouts for the camera while three older Palestinian men sit behind her on concrete blocks, their eyes blindfolded and their hands bound with plastic ties. One of the prisoners appears to be straining with discomfort, as his hands are tied behind his back. Abergil's best army buddy, a young woman named Shani Cohen, commented on the photo: "LOL all my loves in one picture!!! My heart is pumping hard!!!" In another shot, Abergil appears seated inches from the man whose hands were bound behind his back. He is a pathetic sight, rail thin, slumped forward, and completely unaware that Abergil was blowing mocking kisses at him. A comment thread below the photo read:

> Adi Tal: You're the sexiest like that . . .
> Eden Abergil: Yeah I know lol mummy what a day it was look how he completes my picture, I wonder if he's got Facebook! I have to tag him in the picture! lol
> Shani Cohen: LOL you psycho. . . . I wonder who's the photographerrrrr
> Shani Cohen: Eden . . . he's got a hard-on for you . . . lol for sure!!!
> Eden Abergil: Lol no honey he's got a hard-on for youuu this is why you took that picture lol you took my picture!!!!

Hours after a blogger discovered the photos, Abergil's name appeared in headlines across the Israeli and international media. The Israeli Army Spokesperson's Unit attempted to dismiss Abergil as an isolated bad apple, whose actions represented "a serious violation of our ethics and moral code." In her initial reaction, Abergil played down her behavior, claiming, "There's no violence. . . . There's no contempt." But former soldiers knew that such sadism was common across the ranks of the military. After all, what did anyone expect heavily armed teenagers to do when placed in control of a largely defenseless population that had been presented to them throughout their lives as a murderous enemy?

Abergil's photos prompted the editor-in-chief of *Ha'aretz*, Aluf Benn, to detail his own military experience for the first time. "The photographs of the female soldier Eden Abergil on Facebook with the young, bound Palestinians did not 'shock' me, as did the automatic responses of people on the left who complained, as usual, about the corrupting occupation and our moral deterioration," Benn wrote. "Instead, the photos brought back memories from my military service. Once, I was also Eden Abergil: I served in a Military Police unit in Lebanon whose mission was to take prisoners from the Shin Bet's interrogation rooms to the large holding camp of Ansar. I covered many eyes with pieces of cloth, I bound many wrists with plastic cuffs."

Despite having knowingly shuttled men from Shin Bet torture chambers to a prison notorious for its brutal conditions, Benn insisted that he and members of his unit emerged with their liberal, democratic values intact: "The occupation did not 'corrupt' me or any of my colleagues in the unit. We didn't return home and run wild in the streets and abuse helpless people. Coming-of-age problems preoccupied us a lot more than our prisoners' discomfort. Our political views were also not affected."

The editor-in-chief's remarkable claim shocked his colleague, Gideon Levy, who many Israeli leftists regarded as the conscience of *Ha'aretz*. In an editorial response, Levy accused Benn of having lost his moral bearings as soon as he joined the invasion of Lebanon. "You didn't return home to riot in the streets and abuse innocent people, you write, and that's all very well. But you were silent," he wrote. "You were a complete accomplice to the crime, and you don't even have a guilty conscience."

Breaking the Silence, the Israeli veterans' organization that published harrowing testimonies from the soldiers who maintained Israel's occupation, echoed Levy, insisting that army culture had corrupted an entire generation. "This norm is wide-ranging and was created as result of the occupation and the daily control over the civilian population," Breaking the Silence cofounder Yehuda Shaul remarked. "Every soldier becomes used to seeing cuffed and blindfolded Palestinians as a matter of routine, and by seeing it so often, these troops become blind to the fact these are human beings."

In 2007, well before Israeli society was forced to reckon with the phenomenon of trophy photos, Breaking the Silence collaborated with filmmaker Tamar Yarom in the production of a documentary film about the experiences of six female Israeli soldiers who served in the occupation. Entitled *To See If I'm Smiling*, the film opened with one of the ex-soldiers, Meytal Sandler, peering into an album of photos she took during her service in the West Bank during the Second Intifada. The contents of the album are not revealed until the documentary's final scene, when Sandler returns to find a photo she had avoided gazing at for years, drowning her memories of the army in alcohol abuse, and chain smoking. In the photo, she is seen posing next to the nude corpse of a Palestinian man with an erection brought on by rigor mortis. And she is smiling from ear to ear. "How the hell did I think I'd ever be able to forget about it?" Sandler muttered in horror.

In the days after the Abergil scandal, Breaking the Silence and a handful of Israeli bloggers released dozens of Facebook photos that depicted scenarios at least as shocking as anything that appeared on Abergil's page. Among the disturbing shots culled from Facebook pages belonging to young Israelis was a photo of four smiling troops towering over a blindfolded preadolescent Palestinian girl kneeling at the point of their machine guns; a pretty female soldier smiling winsomely beside a blindfolded Palestinian man cuffed to a plastic chair; two soldiers posing triumphantly above a disheveled corpse lying in the street like a piece of discarded trash; a soldier pumping his rifle in the air directly behind an older Palestinian woman tending to pots on her kitchen stove; a soldier defacing the walls of a home in Gaza by spray-painting a star of David and the phrase, "Be Right Back"; troops in the Gaza Strip playing with and posing beside corpses stripped half nude in acts of post-mortem humiliation; a young soldier mockingly applying makeup from a Palestinian woman's dresser. The Facebook pages were so replete with documents of humiliation, domination, and violence it seemed that army basic training had been led by Marquis de Sade.

Graphic trophy photos are, of course, a common feature of modern military conflict. But the images of fresh-faced Israeli kids smiling beside corpses reflected much more than the dehumanization of the enemy in the "fog of war." These photos were documents of a colonial culture in which Jewish Israeli youth became conditioned to act as sadistic overlords toward their Palestinian neighbors, and of a perpetual conquest that demanded indoctrination begin at an early age and continue perpetually throughout their lives. The young soldiers provided a perfect example of cognitive dissonance, in which chants of "*Am Yisrael Chai!*" ("The People of Israel Live!") alternated easily with "Death to Arabs!"

In March 2011, months after her photos drew international attention and widespread condemnation, Abergil began uploading other soldiers' trophy shots to her Facebook page. She captioned one upload with the increasingly common refrain: "DDDEATHHH to ARABSSSSSS."

Beside the next photo, Abergil wrote: "Fuck you, stinking Arabs!!!"

And then: "C'MON LET'S MAKE AN ARAB SHOAH NOWWWWW!!!!!!!!"

Later, Abergil mustered a few thoughts about her role in the scandal, though she was incapable of recognizing the moral conundrum. "I can't allow Arab lovers to ruin the perfect life I lead. I am not sorry and I don't regret it." She added, "I am in favor of a Jewish-Zionist State. I defend what has been rightfully mine for ages."

Not only was Abergil unable to recognize any wrong in her actions, she also believed with all her heart, and with apparently considerable peer encouragement, that she had acted heroically in the name of the Jewish state and its mythical claim to "Eretz Yisrael." And she would do it again.

"I would gladly kill Arabs—even slaughter them," she declared.

Abergil never got the chance to fulfill her fantasies. Having generated international headlines that embarrassed the army, she was promptly dismissed from reserve duty. But there were others aching to kill Arabs for sport. Maxim Vinogradov, an immigrant from Russia who joined the Border Police, was one of them. On a social media site, the young Vinogradov described himself as follows:

Favorite food: Arabs
Things that you love to do: To hit, violence
Hobbies: Hitting and destroying things
Favorite sports: Beating Palestinian wetbacks
What turns me on: Violence
I belong to: Extreme Right
Things I am looking for: Red Headed Arabs

Vinogradov's friend and fellow soldier, Avi Yakobov, was of a similar mindset. In December 2007, Yakobov arrested Ihsan Dababseh, a thirty-five-year-old woman accused of belonging to the militant group Islamic Jihad. After binding Dababseh and blindfolding her at an Israeli prison near Bethlehem, Yakobov decided to stage what he believed was a jocular prank. Gathering his army buddies around, he turned the veiled woman against a wall, blasted some Arab pop music, and performed a parodic belly dance just inches away from her backside, mocking her with gyrating, overtly sexual hip motions. His friends laughed hysterically, filming as they reveled in the humiliation. The video of the incident lingered on YouTube until it surfaced on a Hebrew blog in October 2010, leading to more international media attention and embarrassment for the army. "A disgusting picture of the diseased mentality of the occupier," is how a spokesman from the Palestinian Authority described the video.

While the new scandal gathered momentum, Yakobov was away on a rowdy beer bust at Berlin's Oktoberfest. On his Facebook page, he posted a photo of himself in Berlin affectionately wrapping his arms around a huge, inflatable Jagermeister bottle. In the comment thread that followed, he and Vinogradov joked about killing prostitutes, screwing MILF's (Mothers I'd Like to Fuck), and drinking to the point that they were sick from alcohol poisoning.

In an earlier comment provoked apparently by the massacre by Israeli commandos of activists on the *Mavi Marmara* ship, Yakobov proclaimed, "Destroy Turkey and all the Arabs from the world."

Vinogradov replied, "I'm with you, bro, and with God's help I'll start it"

"Haha and you are capable of it, with no intervention from the evil eye," Yakobov posted.

Less than two weeks after that exchange, Vinogradov and his Border Police unit barreled into the East Jerusalem neighborhood of Wadi Joz for a routine Friday deployment. There, they encountered a forty-one-year-old Palestinian man named Ziad Jilani returning from Friday prayers to his home in nearby Shufat, where he lived with his American wife, Moira, and their three daughters. Jilani owned a profitable business importing massage chairs from Switzerland and had no record of political activity. That afternoon, he and his family planned on taking an excursion to the beach. But he never made it home. Instead, as he drove through the winding and crowded streets of Wadi Joz, a group of boys allegedly rained down a hail of rocks on his car, apparently aiming at the Border Policemen stationed nearby. Jilani swerved suddenly, accidentally striking three members of Vinogradov's unit and badly wounding two. Chaos immediately ensued.

As the Border Policemen fired wildly around the streets, riddling parked cars, shattering windows, and wounding a little girl, Jilani took off running down an alley toward a family member's house. Vinogradov's commander, a Druze police super-intendent named Shad Hir al Din, fired a volley of bullets at Jilani, striking him in the back and immobilizing him. With the wounded Jilani lying on the ground, Vinogradov approached and fired a short burst into the back of his head. It was, by all accounts, an execution-style killing.

An eyewitness described the scene: "The policeman was yelling at Ziad [Jilani] and talking to him in Hebrew . . . and he was holding his rifle and aiming at Ziad with his foot on Ziad's neck. . . . Suddenly he shot Ziad two or three times. . . . Then he kicked Ziad in the face with his foot." For his part, Vinogradov claimed Jilani was in fact a "terrorist" who "lay there scaring me," so he executed him in self-defense. But the young tough who described Arabs as his "favorite food" had never expressed such fears before.

Jilani joined the more than sixty-four hundred Palestinians killed by Israeli forces since the beginning of the Second Intifada. And like all who had killed Palestinians while in army uniform, Vinogradov was immune from prosecution. Indeed, since 2000, not one member of the Israeli army has been charged with a capital offense. "I just want the two men that shot him, with the bullets that my friends and my family's taxpayer dollars paid for, behind bars," Jilani's widow, Moira, told journalist Jillian Kestler D'Amours. "I'm an American, and they shot him with [American] taxpayers' money."

In interviews after the shooting became news, Vinogradov sought to downplay the racist diatribes he posted on various social media sites by claiming his perspective was typical of the culture of frontline Border Police units. His defense was that everybody was guilty and therefore he was innocent. "Go to any Border Police-man's Facebook profile and you will see more or less what I wrote," Vinogradov said. Instead of punishing him or his belly dancing friend, Yakobov, or even publicly chastising them for what they had done wrong, the army initiated a new program instructing soldiers on how to best avoid embarrassing the State of Israel when using social media.

While the abuses piled up and the army stifled efforts at accountability, the mili-tary occasionally invited a few trained human rights facilitators onto its bases to lead seminars for the young Border Policemen. By accompanying one of those trainers, I managed to gain entry to Beit Horon, an army base in the West Bank that serves as a key staging point for raids on Palestinian villages and cities. There, I got to know the members of a frontline Border Police unit while they were led through an exercise in human rights education. Over the course of the day, I gained an intimate look at a group of young men who yearned to be unfettered from all legal and moral limita-tions so they could, as one said, "finish the job" once and for all.

The Base

Known popularly as the *Magav*, the Israeli Border Police evolved in part from an army division created in the wake of the state's foundation for the explicit purpose of capturing and deporting Palestinian refugees who have slipped into their former villages to reunite with family and spouses. Named the Minorities Unit, the division was comprised mostly of deeply impoverished young men recruited from Druze villages in the north and Bedouin Arab enclaves in the south. Their recruitment of non-Palestinian Arab subgroups served David Ben Gurion's divide-and-conquer strategy, which he dubbed, "fragmentation." As one Israeli official said, the Minorities Unit formed "the sharp blade of a knife to stab in the back of Arab unity."

Today, a disproportionate percentage of Border Police commanders are Druze seeking to consolidate their citizenship rights through service to the Jewish state. Their units are supplemented with Jews from the lower rungs of Israeli society, from Ethiopians to Russians to Jews from the Arab world, all seeking status in a society that treats them as second class. Denigrated by the Ashkenazi elite as *arsim*, or Israeli rednecks, and regarded as the least prestigious arm of the country's armed forces, many *Magav* members project their resentment against the only groups more poorly regarded than they: Palestinians, leftists, and African migrants. As Israel's frontline occupation maintenance force, the Border Police exceeded the rest of the army in documented abuses committed in the West Bank between 2000 and 2011. Of the 244 reported abuse cases—most abuses are not documented—only 12 were prosecuted.

My friend Rona (name changed to protect identity) was an academically credentialed expert on human rights who supplemented her modest teaching income by leading sessions for Border Police units as a facilitator. By the time we met, she had grown disillusioned with the human rights work, concluding it was a fruitless exercise that allowed the army to wash its hands of the abuses its soldiers committed by letting them vent it all to a token leftist. In August 2010, Rona led a session at an army base in Jericho in which members of a Border Police unit bragged to her about executing an African migrant they had captured in the southern Israeli city of Eilat. They told her how he had fiercely resisted his arrest and cursed them—*chutzpon*, they called him, claiming he did not "respect them adequately." As punishment for his impudence, the policemen beat the migrant half to death, and then finished him off with a bullet to the head. The crime went undocumented and unprosecuted. For her, it was the final straw.

Before she quit, Rona insisted on taking me to a session at the West Bank army base Beit Horon so I could document the disturbing proceedings. All I needed to do to secure entry, she said, was declare that I was one of the human rights facilitators and keep my mouth shut. A week later, Rona and I were standing at the train station in Modiin, a mega-settlement located in a no man's land between Israel and the Occupied Territories, baking under a cloudless sky as we waited for our ride. After fifteen minutes, a Border Police truck arrived to escort us to the base, with a gruff, middle-aged officer curtly welcoming us in. Hoping to avoid eliciting his suspicion, Rona introduced me as "the new guy." He nodded affirmatively, grunting, "B'seder," or "okay." I had worried the officer might address me in Hebrew, but luckily, he did not seem to have much interest in chit-chatting with lefty do-gooders.

On our way to Beit Horon, we cruised unhindered through a checkpoint, turning onto Highway 443, an Israelis-only freeway that sliced through Palestinian towns, relegating their residents to a network of crumbling roads and tunnels while concealing them from view with miles of concrete dividing walls. At the gates of the Beit Horon base was a Jewish settlement with the same name that housed about six hundred Orthodox and secular Israelis in modest subdivision homes. Just a few hundred meters down the road was Ofer military prison, a gargantuan complex of kangaroo courts and jail cells holding Palestinians from age eleven to eighty, including many who were imprisoned without charges. At Beit Horon, I found all the key components of the settler-colonial project in one area: an apartheid highway, an army base, a military-run prison full of Arabs, and a settlement that resembled a heavily fortified shtetl.

Inside a small, one-story office building, Rona and I met the base commander, Lt. Amar, a short and friendly Druze man (the names of all who appear in this chapter have been changed for legal reasons). He welcomed Rona warmly, remarking with admiration that she was the first and only person he had ever met who possessed a PhD. The Border Police high command was filled with Druze like Amar who believed, as he told Rona, that the only way to secure their rights in the Jewish state was to serve in the armed forces. Army service has become so central to Druze life in Israel that nearly 40 percent of Druze citizens subsisted on income from the military. Despite their service, Druze communities still suffer from official neglect. At a protest outside Prime Minister Benjamin Netanyahu's office a year before, Druze demonstrators accused the state of discrimination, holding placards reading, "Our soldiers serve at the front but there's no state support at home."

On our way to Beit Horon's education center, where the human rights seminar was to take place, Rona and I strolled around the base. With its wide patches of grassy lawns, single-story office buildings, and paved paths, it resembled a community college campus. But instead of passing processions of commuter students, I gazed at a constant stream of young cadets sprinting from the barracks to training sessions in heavy olive garb, gasping for breath in the oppressive midday heat.

We stopped at a field to watch young men fire single M-16 rounds at human torso-shaped targets about a hundred meters away. Rona told me that until two years ago, the targets were adorned with Palestinian keffiyehs. In the hills beyond the base, we could see homes belonging to residents of the Palestinian Authority's Ramallah district. It was from here that the Border Police set out on raids in East Jerusalem, Ramallah, and Bethlehem, or embarked to nearby Palestinian villages to crush non-violent demonstrations against the occupation.

The education center consisted of a series of classrooms and a large lecture hall. Inside one classroom, a group of about a dozen young men stomped into the room in full battle dress uniform, joking and bantering with one another. They formed a circle with Rona and me on one end, and placed their M-16's under their chairs, as schoolchildren would do with backpacks. Rona seemed uncomfortable, complaining that the gun barrels all seemed to be pointed at her. She asked them to stack them in a corner of a room. The young soldiers were confused by her request. "Don't these guns make you feel safe?" one asked her. "They are here for security, not to harm you," another said reassuringly. Rona let out a sigh of resignation. For the rest of the seminar, the guns remained on the floor.

As she began the session, Rona asked each Border Policeman to introduce himself and describe an incident in his life when he felt that he had been discriminated against. None of them struggled for material. They were all, in one way or another, relegated by the Ashkenazi upper class to the lower levels of Israel's ethnic totem pole, which made their enlistment in the *Magav* virtually inevitable.

First was Oleg, a Russian immigrant with close-cropped blonde hair and a face ruddied by the sun: "When I go out to the clubs in Tel Aviv, I can never get in. They always say I look like trouble or they make up some excuse. It's because I ride a motorcycle and, you know, they call me an *arsim*."

Next was Shai, a tall, brown-skinned Mizrahi kid: "When I was in high school I wanted to study literature but beginning in ninth grade my teachers told me that I was going to learn a trade and that was it."

Yasha, a gawky Russian immigrant with a pimply face, echoed Shai: "They wouldn't let us study anything in my school outside of technical stuff or matriculation [intermediary courses]."

A short, pudgy Mizrahi officer named Tzvi took his turn: "During basic training it was so hot and they made us run so much I became dehydrated. No one would believe I needed water no matter what I said. I fainted and had to be taken to the hospital. They let me stay on an IV for four hours before they came to threaten me with a loss of prestige if I did not return right away to the course."

Ismail, a stocky Druze member of the unit wearing a walkie talkie, told of how during Yom Kippur, all the Jewish members of the Border Police were given the day off while the Druze officers were forced to remain on duty at the base. He said some of the Druze officers resented the favorable treatment so much they vandalized the walls of the base with anti-Jewish graffiti—"Dirty Jews," "The Jews are lazy," "Fuck the Jews." When the Jewish Border Policemen returned, the base commanders had already painted over the graffiti. "No one ever talked about the incident again," he recalled. "It was like it never happened."

Rona interjected, "Sort of like covering up abuses of human rights." Her comment was met with dead silence from the group.

There was only one member of the unit who volunteered for ideological reasons, a tall, husky twenty-year-old with tan skin and vaguely Asian eyes. His name was Alex. Born in Kazakhstan, a former republic of the Soviet Union where Muslims, Christians, and the twenty-thousand-strong Jewish community traditionally enjoyed good relations, and where anti-Semitism has generally remained at a low ebb, Alex nonetheless suffered as a child. In one of many instances of discrimination he described, he was badly beaten by a gang of kids shouting anti-Jewish slurs. They had broken his collarbone, but he said no hospital would treat him because he was Jewish, he claimed, forcing his father to jury-rig a cast. The violence continued after his family relocated to Israel, where the Jewish Agency sent them to live in the desolate development city of Ashdod. Like many of his neighbors, Alex fell in with a gang of juvenile delinquents. By age fifteen, he had grown accustomed to routine beatings, arrests, and humiliation at the hands of the police.

"One time, the cops lined me and my friends up along the side of the road," Alex recalled, "and one by one, they went '*kef, kef, kef*,' slapping us in the head. Then they arrested us, took back to the station and ordered us to strip naked. As soon as we took our clothes off they just started beating us with clubs. We were tortured. I can feel my adrenaline pumping just by talking about it—it makes me so angry to remember. . . . When I got older, I decided I wanted to be on the other side of the violence; I wanted to be on the side of power."

And so Alex joined the Border Police.

Rona trained teachers in Alex's hometown of Ashdod and in development towns like it. In order to enroll in an Israeli university, she explained, students needed to obtain a score of four points on their matriculation exams. But in the development towns where she worked, there were no matriculation teachers, so students rarely received a score above three, rendering them ineligible for college. Rona remarked to me, "With the soldiers I work with, this is the main theme: they're denied education and only some are literate. They didn't drop out officially but they stopped learning in seventh or eighth grade; you stop going except for a day a week but the teachers are afraid of you and you're not part of the system. They cannot see how the government takes advantage of them by preventing them from progressing in society as a result of the same policies that it uses against Arabs, so they compartmentalize the situation of the Palestinians from that of themselves."

Rona redirected the session to a debate on the responsibilities of power. She asked the group if they thought the Border Police should have total discretion in how they conducted their job. The reply was a unanimous "yes." Should they have discretion in who is allowed to enter Israel? she asked. "Of course!" came the response from several members of the unit. Only when Rona asked if they agreed that the rule of law should apply to how they conduct themselves on the job did anyone protest.

Yasha recounted the operation at Havat Gilad, a fanatical Jewish settlement outpost that his unit was ordered to evacuate. They arrived with paintball guns and rubber bullets, withstanding ferocious resistance from the settlers, who pelted them with stones, danced on the roofs of their jeeps and even threw a Molotov cocktail at his jeep. "When we're in Hebron," he said, "the settlers want to kill us and the Palestinians want to kill us. We're caught in the middle and the state never backs up our force. The courts only want to listen to the leftists who follow us around at every demonstration with cameras."

"Why do we spend so much time defending ourselves in the courts?" complained Yitzhak, the only member of the unit wearing a *kippah*. "We see the crime and we should be able to punish people for it. Period." He said he was more afraid of the settlers than of the Palestinians because the settlers had a massive lobby inside the government to protect them. "They should be folded," he said adamantly. "Their bodies need to be collapsed."

During a break, I followed Alex outside and introduced myself. Before long, we fell into conversation. Alex was eager to share his experiences with me, and to do so in fairly good English, thus relieving me from bothering Rona for constant translations. We sat down at a picnic bench with a few of the guys from the unit. I could tell they admired Alex, even if they considered him slightly volatile. He was taller and seemed more virile than the rest of them and expressed himself with total conviction. When he held forth on the foreign migrants slipping into Israel with increasing frequency, they listened intently.

Alex said that his father used to run a ceramics business until the Chinese began importing cheap ceramics into the country. "They ruined my father's business. We need to stop letting the migrants in because we need to solve our own problems here. And the biggest problem in Israel is terror. I want to walk the streets without a suicide bomber killing my family. So we've got to do *something*," he said, pounding his fist on the table for emphasis. "I want to make a war. I know it sounds really childish but it's the only way. The talking is going nowhere."

"This could mean a lot of blood," I responded.

"But someone has to do it, otherwise it will go on more slowly like now, just slow bleeding."

"So, like, push the button?" I asked.

"Yeah, something like this!" Alex replied excitedly. "Maybe with a prime minister who is strong, like [Avigdor] Lieberman, it could happen."

After the break, all the units involved in the day's human rights seminars gathered in a large lecture hall to listen to a talk by Abdullah, a neatly dressed, twenty-eight-year-old Sudanese migrant Rona had invited to speak for the Border Policemen. He described being terrorized by the government-backed Janjaweed in his native Darfur, and how he was forced to flee the country with his life. Now that he was in Israel, he was consumed with panic about being deported. Even though he risked being killed if he returned to Sudan, because he was not Jewish, he was unable to receive asylum in Israel.

I could tell many of the guys in the unit were affected by Abdullah's lecture. Whether or not they sympathized with his plight, they felt respected, as though for the first time someone actually bothered to offer them some context on the situation they had been thrust into. Back in the meeting room, members of the unit debated the African migrant situation, peppering Rona with issues: "There is no clear policy on migrants so we don't know what do when we catch them," said Yitzhak. "That's why many of us feel the need to beat them—because they have to release them soon after." There are too many gray areas, said a few others. We are basically good people, they insisted, so we should be able to make the ultimate decision on policy. "We've let people cross checkpoints when they look totally miserable and harmless," said Tzvi.

Joining the debate on the rule of law, Yasha recalled a Border Patrol unit that captured an African migrant in Eilat and executed him without reason. It was the same unit that Rona had encountered during training in Jericho. According to Yasha, members of the unit bragged openly about running a protection racket in which Palestinians were forced to pay them to defend their communities against rampaging settlers. They also claimed to escort Palestinians through checkpoints in army vehicles, and then demand exorbitant taxi fees. Oleg said he loathed the *Magav*'s internal investigation unit, Machash, claiming leftists who only wanted to harass soldiers ran it. But in the case of this unit, he believed they should be investigated for murder.

Alex protested: "Why do we need to be more humanist? So everyone will come here from Turkey and from Africa and park themselves on our head? If we want people to stop encouraging people to come into our country, we should not be so humane." A few of the guys nodded their heads in agreement. As it was throughout the day, the most confidently bellicose opinion won out.

On the wall of the lecture hall was a brightly painted quote containing the wisdom of a Jewish intellectual icon renowned for his wisdom and moral bearing. "Do not confuse a successful person with a person of values," it read. "The successful person takes from life more than he gives to it, while a man of values gives to life more than he takes."

The quote was by Yeshayahu Leibowitz, a polymath genius, a scientist, and a philosopher, who might have been the greatest mind in the history of the Zionist movement. Leibowitz also happened to be one of the country's most ferocious opponents of the Israeli army, and was a fierce critic of the state institutions that orchestrated the occupation. But this was not a legacy the state wanted to see linger after his death. And so it enshrined him with an anodyne quote inside Beit Horon.

PART VIII

INDOCTRINATION MILLS

The Prophets

I n the days after Israel's conquest of the West Bank, the Gaza Strip, East Jerusalem, the Sinai Peninsula, and the Golan Heights in 1967, as the whole of Israeli society erupted in celebration, a group of Israel's most renowned writers gathered in smoky cafés in Tel Aviv to compose a manifesto channeling the mood of the nation's intelligentsia. Led by Labor Zionist literary icon Nathan Alterman, the so-called poet of the establishment, the group included the legendary Hebrew novelist S. Y. Agnon; Isser Harel, the spy who oversaw the operation to capture Adolph Eichmann; revisionist Zionist intellectual Uri Zvi Greenberg; the famed Tel Aviv poet Haim Gouri; and Mapai cofounder Yitzhak Tabenkin—in all, around 150 cultural and political luminaries representing Zionist factions from the left, right, and center. The best and brightest of Israel pored over the minute details of their manifesto, editing it meticulously until they were satisfied. Entitled "For a Greater Israel" and published in full-page ads in the country's major newspapers, the manifesto demanded that the state treat its newly acquired lands as the foundation of its national glory and that it never, ever give them up.

"Just as we have no right to give up the State of Israel, so we are commanded to realize what it has given us: the Land of Israel," the manifesto read. Its authors declared that no democratically elected government had the authority to negotiate over the lands: "We are bound to loyalty to the integrity of our land—to the past and to the future, and no government in Israel has the right to give up this integrity." The manifesto inspired enthusiastic reactions from across the whole spectrum of Jewish Israeli opinion. Hoping to seize on the momentum they had generated, its authors founded the "Greater Israel Movement," a political party that would eventually merge into Likud. Alterman, the movement's most influential member and a figure previously seen as a moderate, humanistic voice inside Labor's inner circle, dubbed the West Bank, "the Cradle of the Nation."

Yeshayahu Leibowitz stood almost alone against the tide of messianism and jingoistic euphoria. A slight man with a thin, severe face, a black *kippah* invariably balanced atop his bare skull, and a distinctively tinny voice that rose suddenly with indignant passion, but then fell to a whisper during pensive ruminations, Yeshayahu Leibowitz earned his keep as a neurophysiology professor who headed Hebrew University's Biological Chemistry Department. With eight doctorates, he taught everything from philosophy to quantum mechanics, though his employers at Hebrew University never allowed him to teach political science. He authored the

Encyclopedia Hebraica and published countless works on Judaism, philosophy, and Zionism, yet still found time to counsel thousands of Israelis who beseeched him with letters and late night phone calls seeking advice on everything from existential personal crises to whether they could smoke on Shabbos. The liberal philosopher Isaiah Berlin once said of Leibowitz, "He is the conscience of Israel."

Leibowitz's opinions on the Jewish religion and Israeli society instilled fear and loathing in the reactionary court rabbis he routinely targeted. He reviled their fetishization of ancient Jewish sites, mocking the Western Wall captured in the 1967 war, known in Hebrew as the Kotel, as the "Discotel." He argued vehemently for the separation of church and state, warning that failing to do so would give rise to a corrupt rabbinate that would warp Judaism into a fascistic cult. "Religious nationalism is to religion what National Socialism was to socialism," Leibowitz famously declared. The state-funded religious nationalist camp, however, shied from public confrontations with Leibowitz, fearing his reputation as the only man who was said to know more about Maimonides than Maimonides.

After 1967, when Israel captured the West Bank and the Gaza Strip, Leibowitz witnessed the euphoric celebrations of the army's conquest of East Jerusalem with disdain, and shuddered at the sudden veneration of military commanders as demigods, warning without hesitation that the occupation would warp Jewish society beyond recognition and, ultimately, bring about the self-destruction of the state. In an essay published in 1968, he wrote that Israeli society lacked the means or desire to constrain the state's expansionist impulses; without limits imposed by outside powers, Leibowitz predicted, "Our situation will deteriorate to that of a second Vietnam, to a war in constant escalation without prospect of ultimate resolution."

He continued with a harrowing forecast of the storm looming on Israel's horizon: "The Arabs would be the working people and the Jews the administrators, inspectors, officials, and police—mainly secret police. A state ruling a hostile population of 1.5 to 2 million foreigners would necessarily become a secret-police state, with all that this implies for education, free speech and democratic institutions. The corruption characteristic of every colonial regime would also prevail in the State of Israel. The administration would have to suppress Arab insurgency on the one hand and acquire Arab Quislings on the other. There is also good reason to fear that the Israel Defense Force, which has been until now a people's army, would, as a result of being transformed into an army of occupation, degenerate, and its commanders, who will have become military governors, resemble their colleagues in other nations."

Leibowitz likened the "unpartitioned Eretz Israel" to the apartheid states lording over indigenous blacks in southern Africa, warning that a culture of racism would consume Jewish society. Israel's "problems, needs, and functions will no longer be those of the Jewish people in Israel and abroad, but those arising from the specific tasks of government and administration of this strange system of political domination," he wrote. "To the intense national antagonism between them will be added the passionate hatred evoked by the rule of one people by the other. There would also be a deep social strife, similar to the one that existed in Rhodesia-Zimbabwe, with its constant fear and insecurity caused by the strained relations between whites and blacks. All that country's resources were consequently channeled into the one endeavor of maintaining white dominance over the blacks."

In a separate essay published two years after Israel's conquest of the Occupied Territories, Leibowitz predicted that the occupation would descend into a malignant phase in which "concentration camps would be erected by the Israeli rulers" and "Israel would not deserve to exist, and it will not be worthwhile to preserve it."

There were a few others who dared to voice their opposition to the occupation, but they existed on the margins and often under the watchful eye of the Shin Bet. They were a ragtag band of artists and blue-collar intellectuals born into Israel's founding generation, mostly products of social Zionist youth movements, who wound up convening around the organization Matzpen. Founded in 1962, Matzpen represented the first organized iteration of anti-Zionism inside Israel. "We rejected what Ben Gurion always said, that Arab opposition to Israel was based on anti-Semitism, on irrational hatred of Jews," Akiva Orr, one of Matzpen's founding members, told me. "We saw Zionism as a colonial movement, and saw colonialism at the root of the conflict with the Arab world." Though most of its members were Jewish, Matzpen also included Palestinians like Ghada Karmi, the exiled daughter of an elite Palestinian family expelled from Jerusalem; Palestinian Israeli student activists Azmi Bishara and Jamal Zehalka joined Matzpen in demonstrations outside the Ministry of Defense, where they were often confronted by right-wing mobs that included a young ultra-nationalist named Avigdor Lieberman.

Shimon Tzabar, a widely read political cartoonist and journalist who helped found Matzpen, decided to place a full-page ad in *Ha'aretz* that would serve as the answer to "For a Greater Israel." In stark contrast to the flowery, messianic style that characterized the Greater Israel manifesto, Tzabar's ad achieved its power through blunt simplicity. It read:

> *Our right to defend ourselves against extermination does not give us the right*
> *to oppress others*
> *Occupation leads to foreign rule*
> *Foreign rule leads to resistance*
> Resistance leads to oppression
> *Oppression leads to terror and counter-terror*
> *The victims of terror are mostly innocent people*
> *Keeping the occupied territories will turn us into a nation of murderers and*
> *murder victims*
> *LET US GET OUT OF THE OCCUPIED TERRITORIES IMMEDIATELY*

Next, Tzabar scrambled back and forth between Tel Aviv and Jerusalem searching for signers. He imagined his artist friends would be eager to sign—they always spoke to him of their desire for peace with the Arabs, after all—and that they would pass the document on to their friends until a sizable movement developed against the occupation. But almost everyone Tzabar approached reacted with shock as soon as they saw what he had handed them. "Are you crazy signing this thing? You know what will happen to you if you sign it?" one of his friends, the sculptor Yigal Tumarkin, said to another famous sculptor Yitzhak Dantzinger. In the end, most seemed more opposed to the way the occupation was being handled than the occupation itself.

Tzabar had learned about Leibowitz, the fierce foe of Ben Gurion and critic of the army, and wondered if he would lend his name to the open letter. But when he met Leibowitz at his office, accompanied by Uri Davis, one of the first Israeli army refusers, the professor turned him away. Leibowitz refused to sign the letter not because he disagreed with its contents, but out of fear that he would be linked to figures he viewed as communist agitators, making him unable to influence the Jewish Israeli mainstream. More important to Leibowitz's decision, perhaps, was his unwillingness to ally himself with any organized political movement. When Tzabar's letter appeared in *Ha'aretz*, it contained signatures from exactly twelve citizens of Israel, all virtually unknown to the Israeli public and most connected to Matzpen.

As expected, *Ha'aretz* readers bombarded the paper with letters of protest, including one that read, "Do they really desire us to continue to live in the tragic circumstances in which we lived until the war? How long should we go on with this fake democracy that undermines the foundation of our lives?" Public officials and major pundits lashed out at Matzpen, denouncing them as traitors and a Fifth Column. "An orgy of hatred and threats began," Haim Hanegbi, a Matzpen founding member, told the documentarian Eran Torbiner. "We didn't even understand how the media and influential people were so intensely occupied with a group of our size. I think we were less than twenty."

"When I realized that I could do nothing more in Israel, I decided to go to Europe and try to mobilize world opinion against the occupation," Tzabar wrote. He sought sanctuary in London, where he joined fellow Israeli dissident Akiva Orr in the midst of a radical counterculture that was transforming the Western world, and where they successfully infused anti-Zionism into the New Left's broader struggle against colonialism. From exile, they published unflinching, first-person accounts of hideous abuses by Israeli soldiers and satirized the triumphalistic culture that had overtaken the country, infuriating members of the Zionist intelligentsia in Tel Aviv. But back in the Holy Land, as Israelis discovered the West Bank and Gaza for the first time, new frontiers for activism suddenly opened up. "A barrier was broken down in the Six Day War," said Hanegbi, whose family was among the original Jewish clans of the West Bank city of Hebron. "As a result of the occupation, after only a few weeks, we were in Hebron, and we met people who had the same ideas as us, and the relationship took off from there. Here we people who had an international outlook that crosses cultures and frontiers found each other. And that meant, to a certain extent, that our international dream had backing in reality."

Leibowitz, on the other hand, was determined to maintain his cachet among Jewish Israeli society. Akiva Orr, who would sometimes drive Leibowitz home after his weekly lectures, remarked to me, "He was capable of shaking the entire country with one sentence." Orr recalled a broadcast reporter beseeching Leibowitz for his opinion on a national Bible trivia contest that had captivated the country's attention.

"One does not need to know the address of the prostitute Rahab to be an intelligent person," Leibowitz snapped at the reporter. Orr said his comments enraged Ben Gurion, his nemesis, who had personally promoted the trivia contest as a means of encouraging a popular connection to "Eretz Israel." Leibowitz might have dismissed the stock justifications for the establishment of the Jewish state, insisting that Jews could practice their religion without also worshipping "Jewish peoplehood," and he may have mocked the unremitting Zionist demand for complete security as a product of a "nineteenth-century outlook," but he somehow claimed to be a committed Zionist all along.

His rationale was simple: "Perhaps life for a Jew in the State of Israel is more dangerous than in Brooklyn or New York, but I want to be a Jew in Israel and not in Brooklyn." Like his hero, Maimonides, Leibowitz was a strict religious exclusivist. He emphasized that his concern was not for the welfare of Palestinians or anyone else who existed in the realm of the *goyim*, but for how Jewish society's relationship with them determined its moral health and physical survival. "I am concerned with nothing else than Jewish people and Jewish man," he said.

Many found his religious and political views paradoxical, but Leibowitz did not believe he had strayed from his understanding of Judaism. Recalling an incident in the West Bank in which soldiers forced a Palestinian woman to give birth while she was handcuffed and shackled, Leibowitz said, "For that the Jewish people is responsible." (According to Fabrizia Falcione, a women's human rights officer for the United Nations Development Fund for Women, Palestinian women in Israeli prisons have been known to be shackled during childbirth). Hoping to mobilize opposition to the violence and repression in the occupied territories, he turned not to his peers in the intelligentsia, but to high school students, urging them to rebel, to rise up not just against the occupation, but against the state itself. He told them that in the Passover Haggadah, the opposite of the wise son was not the wicked son who turned against his community, but the simple son who did not know how to question.

When Israel's first invasion of Lebanon transformed into the "second Vietnam" Leibowitz had predicted over a decade before, he found a steady stream of army refusers lining up at his office door. Over time, as the occupation of Gaza and the West Bank deepened, Leibowitz said he became "overwhelmed" by requests for advice. "They come to open up their hearts to me," he said of his young visitors. "They come to me because they know that twenty years ago, I predicted what would happen if we opted for military occupation of the territories and prevented independence for the Palestinian people. It was inevitable." To the high school students who asked Leibowitz if they should serve in the occupied territories, he had a simply reply, "I tell them they are sent there as assassins."

"I'm not interested in the position of the Israeli government," Leibowitz remarked to the Israeli filmmaker Eyal Sivan in 1991. "I'm interested in the position of these young people. . . . I tell them, you come individually; you are many but isolated. Organize mass insubordination. I encourage them to revolt. . . . I want to put an end to the regime that is in power in the State of Israel. To shake this regime. A regime whose only meaning is to impose an apparatus of state power on another people."

"Why do you want to shake this regime?" Sivan asked him.

"Because humanity comes first," the professor responded, seeming to contradict statements he had made expressing exclusive concern for Jews.

By this time, Leibowitz was near the end of his life. He saw no point in withholding his true opinions of the state or its leadership. Instead, he gave voice to what he considered a painfully obvious truth: the country had become what he warned would be "Rhodesia under a Jewish authority." "The state willfully deprives two million people of their political and civil rights," the professor declared in a public lecture. "South Africa was not a democracy either. But the people were governed by a great statesman whose name shall go down in history: DeKlerk. In stages but quite rapidly he is indeed giving the population including the blacks all the civil and, it would seem, political rights. That is happening throughout the world today in all the enlightened countries. But Israel is the only dictatorship that exists today in the enlightened world."

When a state commission led by former Supreme Court chief justice Moshe Landau authorized the Shin Bet to apply methods of torture to extract confessions from Palestinian detainees, Leibowitz introduced his most incendiary condemnation. "A Nazi-like mentality also exists in our country," he declared before a packed auditorium in Haifa in 1991. "That is a fact. In the Israeli legal system neither the judges nor the lawyers challenged [Landau]. That says a great deal about the Nazi mentality that is dominant here."

In the eyes of even some of his liberal allies, Leibowitz had crossed the line. Landau, after all, was the judge who sentenced Adolf Eichmann to death. How could anyone compare him to a Nazi? Loud jeers and howls of protest emanated from throughout the crowd, but Leibowitz refused to back down. "There *are* Judeo-Nazis. Judeo-Nazis exist!" he shouted.

In 1993, Shulamit Aloni, an Israeli parliamentarian and social justice activist who founded the Meretz Party, nominated Leibowitz for the Israel Prize, the country's most prestigious civilian award. Just before the ceremony, Leibowitz stopped to speak at Uri Avnery's Israeli Council for Israeli-Palestinian peace, a group that established some of Israel's earliest contacts with the Palestine Liberation Organization. There, he echoed his call for Israeli youth to refuse army service, to organize mass revolt or risk becoming assassins. He went on to compare the Israeli army's elite Sayeret Makhtal unit to the Nazi SS—"Judeo-Nazis" who were "just following orders."

The professor's speech inspired widespread outrage, with Prime Minister Yitzhak Rabin vowing to boycott the Israel Prize ceremony if it did not rescind its award. Knesset members took to the floor the following day with breathless denunciations, branding Leibowitz a traitor. As the national temper tantrum built to a fever pitch, Leibowitz announced he would not accept the prize. He said he did not want to cause further rancor. A year later, Leibowitz died in his sleep at age ninety-one.

Change from Within

Many members of the Zionist left still claim to revere Yeshayahu Leibowitz, but few are willing to heed his most consequential advice. Indeed, almost twenty years after his death, Israeli society only produces a handful of youth willing to pay the price of prison and outcast status for refusing army service. In the culture of the Zionist left, which centers around the notion that Israel "must be saved from itself," the best and brightest young men and women are seldom encouraged to directly confront the occupation, but are instead called on to serve as an internal check on its most abusive aspects. This is the practice Israelis call "change from inside," in which well-educated Ashkenazi teens insert themselves into frontline combat units to civilize their less cultivated, lower-class peers from Mizrahi and Russian backgrounds.

During the height of the Eden Abergil's trophy photo scandal, the American wing of the Meretz Party, Meretz USA, posted an essay entitled, "Why recent events make me want to serve in the IDF." Authored by a young American Jew named Mimi Micner, the piece perfectly reflected the notion of "change from inside." Micner claimed that "the IDF needs to detoxify its ranks . . . transforming the institutional culture so that it is categorically humane toward the Palestinians." To accomplish the goal, she urged a massive influx of patriotic left-wing Israelis into the army, declaring that they "should have long military careers, ascending the ranks of the military so that they gain influence and decision-making power. If this were to become the status quo, then I think we would notice a markedly better culture and better conduct within the IDF."

In Hebron's occupied H2 zone, a home to Israel's most violent, fanatical settlers, I met a twenty-year-old soldier named Ben, who embodied the concept of "change from inside." He was a member of the Nahal Brigade, an elite infantry force partly comprised of rigorously trained kibbutzim required to perform community service before entering the field. They were the "leftists" of the army. He was standing on a corner of Shuhadah Street with another young soldier, guarding the residents of a small Jewish settlement that ruled over thousands of Palestinians trapped in the heart of H2's "sterilized zone."

"Sterile means that all the shops on this street, that were once shops, nearly all of them, except for one or two, are shut down," a soldier who served in Hebron explained. "It means that all the houses that were once inhabited, now stand empty. They've been blocked and no one can go on living in them. No Palestinian may enter this street." In 2006, the Israeli attorney general revealed that the army established

Hebron's "sterilized zone" without any official legal authorization. But Israeli civilian authorities did nothing to challenge the order, giving the army carte blanche to abrogate laws according to its whims.

Short and wiry with a sandy brown crew cut and deep-set eyes and a face made ruddy by the sun, Ben described himself as a Meretz supporter who had spent his adolescence in a leftist youth movement that revered the teachings of Yeshayahu Leibowitz. Like most of his friends, he was dismayed by the direction of his society. "If you want to know who the most dangerous man in Israel is," he told me, "look at Gideon Sa'ar, the education minister. He seems very reasonable, very slick. But what he is doing is turning the education system into an indoctrination factory for the right wing. The next thing he wants to do is bring Jewish youth here, to Hebron, to teach them about Zionism."

"It sounds crazy," I responded. "This place is like a theater of apartheid. I mean, it's all out in the open here." As we spoke, a bearded settler with an M-16 slung over his shoulder pushed a baby stroller down the eerily empty street.

The soldier patrolling alongside Ben protested my choice of terms. "Are you here to make a provocation?" he asked. In recent years, the word "provocation"—*provocatzia* in Hebrew—had become a choice term in the Israeli lexicon. It was a favorite among government officials denouncing the Gaza Freedom Flotilla, soldiers complaining about unarmed popular protests in the West Bank, and common citizens confronted with "leftist" arguments. To them, everything done in the name of upsetting the status quo was a provocation.

Ben argued against his friend: "It *is* apartheid. It is also fascism. It is not just here, but across the West Bank—I've seen it. One people controlling another."

"So, like, what the hell are you doing in the army, guarding a bunch of settlers, if you know that you are involved in a system of apartheid?" I asked Ben.

"I can tell you that out of my friends from youth group who entered the army, almost all of them wanted to be in combat units," he responded. "Not to make war or because they like combat so much, but because they wanted to make change from the inside. So if I can spread humanistic values in my unit, why not?" Ben added that he had recently stopped settlers from dumping a batch of eggs on the shopkeepers in the Old City.

I told him I had just visited the market. The shopkeepers were forced to cover the entire marketplace with a metal screen to prevent the settlers of Avraham Avinu from dropping bricks, soiled diapers, eggs, and urine on their stores. I told Ben one shopkeeper showed me a rack of silk shawls stained with egg yolks a group of settler children dumped on him earlier in the day.

"Look, I can't be everywhere all the time," Ben said. "What do you want me to do? Nothing?"

"So are you going to go to Breaking the Silence after your service is over to talk about all the stuff you regretted doing here?"

Breaking the Silence was an NGO founded by combat soldiers just like Ben. Founded during the Second Intifada, the organization became a means of shattering the mood of complacency that prevailed over Israeli society, where the occupation was seen as a normal phenomenon that hardly corrupted civilian life behind the Green Line. Relying often on the testimony of sons and daughters of Ashkenazi elite—youth like Ben—who had served on the frontlines of occupation, Breaking the Silence produced regular booklets of anonymous confessionals exposing the abuses of occupation in sometimes shockingly clinical language. Since Prime Minister Benjamin Netanyahu's election in 2009, the organization had become the target of a sustained assault from both his office and the Knesset to deprive it of its foreign sources of funding, and by extension, to paint it as Fifth Column for anti-Semitic European interests. In an op-ed for *Yedioth Ahronoth*, Anne Herzberg and Naftali Balanson, staffers for the organization NGO Monitor and close allies of Netanyahu's government, called Breaking the Silence, "Mouthpieces for Europe." "Europe" in their lexicon is shorthand for "anti-Semitism." Meanwhile, member of Knesset David Rotem questioned whether groups like Breaking the Silence were "being backed by terrorists or al-Qaeda."

Every few years, Breaking the Silence has published a booklet containing the harrowing testimonies of the latest class of veterans emerging from the nightmarish world of Hebron's H2. Soldiers who served between 2005 and 2007 described a litany of atrocities to Breaking the Silence, from witnessing a soldier wrap a Palestinian man with wire until his limb had to be amputated, to beating children and random storeowners with axe handles and steel clubs before looting their shops, to watching Border Policemen smash random passersby in the face with their helmets, to using children as human shields during riots. Many of the Hebron testimonies were delivered by members of Nahal, including a self-described "lefty *kibbutznik*" who did nothing as members of his unit punished a Palestinian man for supposedly beating his donkey by whipping him as they rode him like a saddled animal.

"I am not going to Breaking the Silence. No way," Ben insisted to me. "When I'm done I'm going to be part of a commune. I want to be engaged in a communal, natural lifestyle and go back to my studies." He told me with conviction that he wanted to become a teacher, and that he would put his experience here behind him.

I noticed Ben's friend squinting to focus in the distance. Ben looked in the same direction, and then shouted with exasperation, "That gate is not supposed to be open!" A fat Palestinian boy was pedaling across an empty intersection on an absurdly oversized bicycle. The two soldiers grabbed their rifles and bolted after him, leaving me alone on the corner with their half-empty ration tins.

The Insiders

n 1987, the editors of the Israeli news magazine *Koteret Rashit* sent David Grossman, then a thirty-three-year-old Israeli writer fluent in Arabic, to produce a long dispatch from the West Bank on the twentieth anniversary of the occupation. Grossman toured Palestinian refugee camps, schools, villages, and cities, painting a picture of a besieged society seething with anger and ready to explode in a massive rebellion. His portrayal of the settlers was unforgiving, depicting armed fanatics exploiting all those around them, while army commanders lorded over Palestinians with impunity. Grossman's editor, Tom Segev, now an internationally renowned historian, said of his reports, "It was a real shock. We did not know then how much [occupied Palestinians] hated us."

A year after *Koteret Rashit* published Grossman's report in a full issue, the First Intifada erupted, earning him his reputation as a prophetic figure. The same year, Grossman's report appeared in English, as a book entitled *The Yellow Wind*. Just as Grossman's reporting played a seminal role in galvanizing the peace camp inside Israel, his book informed an international audience about the mood in the Occupied Territories. With his command of Arabic and ground-level knowledge with the West Bank, Grossman became the unofficial chronicler of the Palestinian situation for both his own society and a Western elite that trusted the voices of Israeli liberals more than those of the Arabs intellectuals who had already produced volumes of work on the conflict. But as a committed liberal Zionist, Grossman was more than a journalist; he was a human filter who presented a narrative of the conflict that stripped it of its colonial origins.

According to the philosophy of liberal Zionism, Israel was an enlightened, European-style democracy before the rise of the settlement movement. The era before the post-1967 occupation began was, in the words of peace camp icon Yossi Beilin, "the most beautiful and peaceful decade of our existence." Yossi Sarid, another liberal Zionist stalwart of Israeli politics, claimed, "The second decade of the state was a decade of normality . . . who would believe in 1965 that soon, in less than two years, the country would lose its mind."

Through *The Yellow Wind*, Grossman helped popularize what the Israeli sociologist and critical theorist Yehouda Shenhav called "the new nostalgia," or "the nostalgia of a political group which is identified with the left but advances the nationalistic ideas anchored in the time of the Green Line." In the narrative of the new nostalgia, Israel's crisis began in 1967 with its conquest of new Arab land, and not in 1948, when it defined its settler-colonial character. To liberal Zionists, 1967 represented the beginning of the crisis. Israel entered the West Bank with messianic zeal, and "afterward, everything happened," Grossman claimed.

"I could not understand how an entire nation like mine, an enlightened nation by all accounts, is able to train itself to live as a conqueror without making its own life wretched," Grossman pined in *The Yellow Wind*. "What happened to us?" he wondered.

Despite his outrage at the misdeeds committed after 1967, Grossman excised the Nakba from his frame of analysis. Of course, he knew the story of Israel's foundation, warts and all. But the Nakba was the legacy also of the Zionist left, as were the mass expulsions committed in its wake, and the suite of discriminatory laws passed through the Knesset to legalize the confiscation of Palestinian property. Were these the acts of an "enlightened nation?" By singling out the settlement movement as the source of Israel's crisis, Grossman and liberal Zionists elided the question altogether, starting the history at 1967.

Though the Zionist left kept the past tucked behind the narrative of the Green Line, veterans of the Jabotinskyite right-wing were unashamed. In September 2010, when sixty actors and artists staged a boycott of a new cultural center in the West Bank–based mega-settlement of Ariel, earning a public endorsement from Grossman, who cast the boycott as a desperate measure to save the Zionist future from the settlers, they were angrily rebuked by Knesset chairman Reuven Rivlin.

A supporter of Greater Israel from the Likud Party, Rivlin was also a fluent Arabic speaker who rejected the Labor Zionist vision of total separation from the Palestinians of the West Bank and Gaza. (He appeared earlier in this book to defend Hanin Zoabi's right to denounce Israel's lethal raid of the *Mavi Marmara* against dozens of frothing members of Knesset.) Contradicting the official Israeli Foreign Ministry version of the Nakba, which falsely asserted that Palestinians "abandoned their homes . . . at the request of Arab leaders," Rivlin reminded the liberal Zionists boycotting Ariel of their own history. Those who bore the legacy of the Nakba, Rivlin claimed, had stolen more than the settlers ever intended to take.

"I say to those who want to boycott—*Deer Balkum* ["beware" in Arabic]. Those who expelled Arabs from En-Karem, from Jaffa, and from Katamon [in 1948] lost the moral right to boycott Ariel," Rivlin told *Maariv*. Assailing the boycotters for a "lack of intellectual honesty," Rivlin reminded them that the economic settlers of Ariel were sent across the Green Line "due to the orders of society, and some might say—due to the orders of Zionism."

Greater Israel had become the reality while the Green Line Israel had become the fantasy. But with the election of Barack Obama, a figure the Zionist left considered their great hope, figures like David Grossman believed that they would soon be released from their despair.

I met Grossman in June 2009 at a shade-covered outdoor café near Jerusalem's Givat Ram neighborhood. He had not yet emerged from the semi-solitary confinement he imposed on himself since his son, Uri, had been killed in a tank that became trapped in a wadi during Israel's invasion of southern Lebanon in 2006. After the war, which Grossman had initially supported alongside his "peace camp" partners, the writers A. B. Yehoshua and Amos Oz, he emerged as the voice of national tragedy.

Through a touching eulogy for his son, whom he lauded for making change from inside—"the leftist of [his] battalion," Grossman called him—and with a major address lacerating Israel's leaders for their military and political incompetence, Grossman provided Israeli society with a vocabulary for expressing its sense of mourning and frustration. A year after lashing out at Prime Minister Ehud Olmert, the bungling scapegoat of Lebanon II, Grossman nevertheless accepted the prime minister's Emet Prize for Science, Arts and Culture. "Emet," of course, is Hebrew for "truth." Rather than sit out the spectacle, Grossman announced beforehand that he would only refuse to shake Olmert's hand.

Ari Shavit, the influential columnist for *Ha'aretz*, dubbed Grossman, the "Israeli Martin Luther King," while Shlomo Avineri, the liberal Zionist academic luminary, declared that Grossman was "above criticism." Following the dramatic episode, the scribe retreated from public view to work on his next book, *To the End of the Land*, an intimate novel of an Israeli mother who embarks on a hike around Israel, having convinced herself that as long as the army cannot find her to notify her of her son's death, he will be safe. Like Amos Oz and A. B. Yehoshua, Grossman specialized in tales of Israelis desperately seeking an escape from lives wracked with tragedy and loss, but who simply couldn't manage to find their way out.

Grossman had told me in advance that he would agree to speak only off the record. But when I arrived at our meeting famished and soaked in sweat after a journey from Tel Aviv, he suddenly changed his mind. "Since you have come such a long way, I will offer you an interview," he said. But he issued two conditions. First, "You must order some food. I cannot sit here and watch you starve." And second, "No questions about my son, okay?"

Grossman was a small man with a shock of sandy brown hair and intense eyes. He spoke in a soft, low tone tinged with indignation, choosing his words carefully as though he were constructing prose. Though his Hebrew accent was strongly pronounced, his English was superior to most American writers I had interviewed, enabling him to reduce complex insights into impressively economical soundbites.

At the time, Grossman was brimming with optimism about Barack Obama's presidency. Though the Israeli right loathed Obama, joining extreme rightists in the campaign to demonize him as a crypto-Muslim, a foreigner, and a black radical, liberal Zionists believed they had one of their own in the White House. Indulging their speculation, some looked to Obama's friendship in Chicago with Arnold Jacob Wolf, a left-wing Reform rabbi who had crusaded for a two state solution during the 1970s before it was a mainstream position. If only Obama could apply appropriate pressure on Benjamin Netanyahu, still widely regarded as a blustering pushover, Israel could embark again on the march to the Promised Land, with the peace camp leading the tribe.

"This is the moment when Israel needs to see Likud come into contact with reality," Grossman told me. "For years they have played the role of this hallucinating child who wants everything and asks for more and more. Now they are confronted with a harsh counterpoint by Mr. Obama, and they have to decide if they cooperate with what Obama says—a two-state solution—or continue to ask for everything."

Grossman seemed confident that Obama was willing to confront Netanyahu, and that he would emerge victorious. "A clash with a strong and popular president is not possible for Israel. Israel can never, ever subjugate an American president," he claimed. "I see Netanyahu reluctantly accepting the demands of Obama to enter into a two-state solution. [Netanyahu] will pretend to be serious about it, but he will do everything he can to keep the negotiations from becoming concrete. He will drag his feet, blame the Palestinians, and rely on the most extreme elements among the Palestinians to lash out in order to stop negotiations. My hope is that there is a regime in America that recognizes immediately the manipulation of the Likud government and that they won't be misled."

I asked Grossman if Obama should threaten Netanyahu with the withholding of loan guarantees in order to loosen his intransigent stance, as President George H. W. Bush had done to force Prime Minister Yitzhak Shamir (Netanyahu's former boss) to the negotiating table. He rejected this idea out of hand. "I hope it shall be settled between friends," Grossman responded. "The pressure Obama applies should be put in a sensitive way because of Israeli anxieties and our feeling that we're living on the edge of an abyss. The reactions of Israelis are very unpredictable. It will take simple and delicate pressure for the United States to produce the results they are looking for. But whenever American presidents even hinted they were going to pressure Israel, they got what they wanted. Netanyahu is very ideological, but he is also realistic and he is intelligent, after all. He will recognize the reality he is in."

Like the millions of liberals and leftists who had experienced Obama as a blank screen for their own projections, Grossman and other Israeli Obama supporters had not factored the tightly conscribed limitations of America's political system into their equation. At first, President Obama demanded that Netanyahu freeze all settlements as a basis for reengaging in the peace process. The building of settlements went on. When Vice President Biden visited Israel in March 2010 to pursue the peace process, Netanyahu announced the building of sixteen hundred illegal houses in East Jerusalem. Upon landing, Biden declared, "The decision by the Israeli government to advance planning for new housing units in East Jerusalem undermines that very trust, the trust that we need right now in order to begin . . . profitable negotiations." Netanyahu ignored him. By the time of the midterm congressional elections in 2010, concrete American pressure on Israel was politically out of the question, with Obama facing attacks from Republicans and pro-Israeli lobbyists as "anti-Israel" for merely reaffirming the American position of negotiations based on 1967 armistice lines. And by the time Obama embarked on his bid for reelection, it was the Israeli prime minister pressuring the American president, leveraging threats to bomb Iran to put him on the defensive. Thus Obama became the one forced to "recognize the reality he is in," not Netanyahu.

With the last glimmer of hope of the US-led "peace process" for a two-state solution sputtering into oblivion, Israel's one-state reality stood exposed.

For liberal Zionists who sought to remove the occupation of the West Bank from Israeli life in order to preserve their country's Jewish demographic majority, these were frightening times. "This option that terrifies us all the time [is] that there might be an end to this country, which really freaks me out to think that after sixty-two years of independence, sovereignty, having [an] enormous strong army," Grossman said when asked by TV host Charlie Rose in October 2010 about the possibility of a dissolution of the whole Zionist project.

For Grossman and liberal Zionists like him, the transformation of Israel from an ethnically exclusive Jewish state into a multiethnic democracy was not an option. "For two thousand years," Grossman told me when I asked why he believed the preservation of Zionism was necessary, "we have been kept out, we have been excluded. And so for our whole history we were outsiders. Because of Zionism, we finally have the chance to be insiders."

I told Grossman that my father had been a kind of insider. He had served as a senior aide to Bill Clinton, the president of the United States, the leader of the free world, working alongside other proud Jews like Rahm Emanuel and Sandy Berger. I told him that I was a kind of insider, and that my ambitions had never been obstructed by anti-Semitism. "Honestly, I have a hard time taking this kind of justification seriously," I told him. "I mean, Jews are enjoying a golden age in the United States."

It was here that Grossman, the quintessential man of words, found himself at a loss. He looked at me with a quizzical look. Very few Israelis understand American Jews as Americans but instead as belonging to the Diaspora. But very few American Jews think of themselves that way, especially in my generation, and that, too, is something very few Israelis grasp. Grossman's silence made me uncomfortable, as though I had behaved with impudence, and I quickly shifted the subject from philosophy to politics. Before long, we said goodbye, parting cordially, but not warmly. On my way out of the café, Grossman, apparently wishing to preserve his privacy, requested that I throw my record of his phone number away.

On October 10, 2010, the remnant of the original Zionist left gathered on the grassy median of Tel Aviv's Rothschild Boulevard, at the base of a statue honoring the city's founder, Meir Dizengoff. On one end of Rothschild Boulevard was Dizengoff House, the stately townhouse where David Ben Gurion publicly declared the establishment of the "Jewish and democratic" state. On the other end was the recently refurbished Ha'Bima Theater, the symbol of the Zionist resuscitation of the Hebrew language. Among the sea of silver-and-gray heads assembled for the occasion was Uri Avnery, the eighty-eight-year-old ex-publisher of *Haolam Hazeh*, Israel's first opposition newspaper, and leader of Gush Shalom, a Jewish-Arab group that campaigned for two states; Shulamit Aloni, a former Palmach fighter who founded the Meretz Party; and Yoram Kaniuk, another Palmach veteran and artist who was fighting to define his nationality as Israeli, rather than Jewish, as the state mandated.

Many of those assembled had played a critical role in the foundation of the Jewish state, either by fighting in the 1948 war or injecting its early institutions with cultural energy. They represented the core of Israel's founding generation, the enlightened

Ashkenazi elite that bore the legacy of the kibbutz movement and also the Nakba. Now that their society demanded strong leaders to maintain the occupation by any means necessary, they claimed their country was gone.

Before the crowd stood Hannah Marom, a famed actress who starred in productions during the 1940s at the Ha'Bima Theater. At the steps of the Dizengoff House, which now served as a museum called Independence Hall, Marom read a manifesto. It was entitled, "A Declaration of Independence From Fascism."

"Behind these stairs where we stand, the State of Israel was proclaimed," Marom intoned. "The state which increasingly takes Israel's place—a state which fills the country with a variety of racist legislation, promoted by the Knesset and the cabinet—is excluding itself from the family of democratic nations. Therefore we, citizens of the Israel envisaged in the Declaration of Independence, hereby declare that we will not be citizens of a country purporting to be Israel and which violates its basic commitment to the principles of equality, civil liberty, and sincere aspiration for peace—principles upon which the State of Israel was founded."

But "A Declaration of Independence From Fascism" was purely rhetorical, delivered without any binding consequences. And so it was a requiem for a movement that now found its identity in nostalgia for a past that never was, and in despair about a fascist future its members seemed to view as inescapable.

The Hunted

Not all among the old Israeli left were content with displays of anguish and hand-wringing. Among the old Ashkenazi elite of Tel Aviv that pined for the glory days, a group of middle-class, mostly middle-aged feminists—academics, activists, and mothers—broke the consensus, banding together to challenge the central institutions of Israeli militarism. Calling themselves New Profile, they set up a national network to counsel Israeli youth considering refusing army service. To complement their efforts, they set about exposing the militaristic imperatives that dictated Israel's educational curriculum, and challenged popular culture that reinforced the archetype of the warrior as the ideal Israeli male. Almost as soon as Israel's rightist government took power in 2009, New Profile felt the full wrath of the state.

In April 2009, the Shin Bet called in five leading New Profile members for interrogations, raided their homes, and seized their computers. Following the interrogations, in which they were accused of "incitement for draft evasion," a crime in Israel punishable by up to five years in jail, the women were ordered not to contact other members from the organization for thirty days.

Among those interrogated was Analeen Kish, a seventy-year-old grandmother who converted to Judaism after her marriage to a Dutch Holocaust survivor, and whose family was enshrined among the "Righteous of the Nations" for saving Jews during the Holocaust. Outside the Ramat Hachiyal police station, where the women were being interrogated, a police riot squad waded into a crowd of New Profile members protesting the arrests and dragged a few inside.

"It's very clear by the way they've run this investigation, by the questions they ask, they are trying to stop the activities we are doing," said one of the demonstrators, Tali Lerner, an educator and member of New Profile. "They're saying that to be a citizen in Israel, you have to be a soldier. And if you are not, then you're not really a part of this society—and we will hunt you."

More than one year after the arrests, I became acquainted with a few of the New Profile leaders targeted by the state. Over coffee at quaint cafés in pleasant neighborhoods around Tel Aviv, they described to me a suffocating climate where everything was tinged with violence. Miriam Hadar, a fifty-two-year-old translator and editor married to an Israeli psychology professor, was one of the first called in for questioning. Hadar lived in Ramat HaSharon, an affluent suburb of Tel Aviv, where in the wake of the Free Gaza Flotilla crisis, she said the mayor authorized students to wear patriotic armbands to school. Two purportedly left-wing professors protested the armbands, but only after stating their reverence for the flag and the Jewish state. Across the street from Hadar's home stood a nondescript house with unknown occupants. Every day, men in dark glasses and dark suits carried bags in and out. The blinds were always drawn. Her neighbors knew the men were Shin Bet agents, but no one ever discussed them. "It could be trouble to talk about it," they told one another.

Most of Hadar's friends from the Zionist left instinctively accepted the official line after the army attacked the *Mavi Marmara*. "There is a total haze between civil society and the military," she said. "Even at these social functions filled with Meretz people I saw how they were driven to see their soldiers as their boys. The distinction between military and ordinary life is no longer observed, so they can no longer distinguish between your husband or your son and a complete killing machine."

Hadar's son, Micha, sat down at our table to chat with me for a few minutes. He was tall and slender and despite his shaggy blond locks, looked like he would have made a good soldier. But instead of following in the steps of his cousins, who graduated from the left-wing Zionist youth group Habonim Dror to the Israeli army—"We're joining for adventure," most of them told him—he had just completed a prison term for refusing. While in jail, he was forced to wear a surplus army uniform and ordered to do menial tasks, as though he were on an army base. He spent much of his time watching over a Bedouin prisoner placed in solitary confinement after having been sentenced for trafficking Eastern European women into the country for sex work. "I was having nightmares that I was actually enlisting my friends into the army by telling them to refuse," Micha remarked. "Because there I was, wearing an army uniform and doing a different kind of service."

Like Hadar, New Profile founder Ruth Hiller raised a son who refused army service. During the 1980s, Hiller moved from California to a kibbutz near the Jordanian border. "As a parent I wanted to be part of this collective, especially coming from California, and if you do it for something you were raised to revere like Zionism, coming to a kibbutz is really easy," she reflected. At the time, the First Intifada was just beginning. With her proximity to Jordan, where Queen Noor had just modernized the national news services, Hiller consumed a version of events largely unseen by other Israelis. "We saw the First Intifada unlike Israelis who never even knew there was a First Intifada because it was completely censored on their networks," she recalled. "Israelis were told that the Palestinians wanted to push us into the sea, that kind of thing. My youngest son already understood by watching these scenes that he couldn't be an Israeli soldier."

When her son discovered the writings of Yeshayahu Leibowitz, he was able to formulate a vocabulary for articulating his refusal to participate in the occupation. "Any material he had to read about peace movements and pacifist movements was in English. Now there's some in Hebrew, but pacifism was not part of the Israeli reality at all," Hiller said.

In recent years, according to Hiller, army enlistment has fallen from around 90 percent to 75 percent, with around a quarter more dropping out during their service. She said New Profile was bombarded with requests for counseling from young people without any clear political views. Hiller explained, "The kids from today's generation are thinking about when they're gonna get laid next. So they tend to say it doesn't feel right for them, which is an indication that it's not right at all. To have the courage to say 'I oppose occupation' or 'I'm a pacifist' is great, but I don't really care; I have just as much respect for someone who says it doesn't feel right, I don't want to be there. It's all about not cooperating with the establishment whether it's about ideology or that it just doesn't feel right."

The wave of apolitical draft evasion sent shock waves through the army, with the high command ordering a crackdown. In 2008, Israeli attorney general Menachem Mazuz approved an investigation of New Profile after receiving a demand from army military advocate general Avichai Mandelblit for swift action. Joining the calls for a crackdown was a group of army reservists calling themselves the Forum for Sharing the Burden, which advocated increased army service from Arabs and the ultra-Orthodox along with harsher penalties for refusers. A year after Mazuz authorized the investigation, the Shin Bet acted, sending its agents after the women of New Profile.

Since then, the hunts have continued unabated; in May 2012, the military police set up a temporary detention facility to incarcerate the more than forty-five hundred young draft dodgers and deserters—those popularly referred to as "service shirkers"—that it planned to arrest that month. Six months later, Israeli police arrested a thirty-year-old citizen named Yana Gorelik as soon as she landed at Ben Gurion International Airport. At age seventeen, Gorelik left Israel to live in Canada and had lived there ever since. Upon returning thirteen years later to attend a cousin's wedding, Gorelik was taken from the airport in handcuffs and locked in a prison. "I am being held under very harsh conditions," she told the Israel paper *Maariv*. "I am dying of heat here. They are treating me like a criminal." Though she pleaded to be able to give up her Israeli citizenship, the state prosecuted her anyway, hoping to secure a five-month prison term for draft dodging. In the courtroom where her trial was to take place, Gorelik was chained and forced to wear an olive drab army uniform. In the end, she was sentenced to three months in prison. Gorelik went on: "They treated us like we were dogs. That's it—I am finished with Israel. I don't want to be a citizen anymore."

Even though a military committee recommended transforming the military into a professional army, the high command would not even consider implementing its findings. The Israel army was not only an instrument for war, but it was also the most important institution of socialization and indoctrination.

While Hiller pointed to the escalating crackdown as proof of the popularity of refusal, the educator and Israeli anti-militarism pacifist activist Hagith Gur saw a deeper crisis playing out. "When we started our work of raising questions and education during the 1980s and 1990s, people would tell us, 'How can you talk about us as a militaristic society? You're self-hating Jews.' Then we confronted them with the question: When is it okay to give guns to kids? People started to agree with me that we're a militaristic country but they said we needed it—we have to survive and the whole world is against us, or we'll be thrown to the sea. So I told them, 'Okay, let's go with your assumption. Then the question is: When do you start preparing children to go the military? Do you start at age six? At five? At diapers? When? And this was a question that troubled them. They could not answer it."

The state had supplied the answer where many parents could not. "The zero sum game begins around kindergarten," Gur said. "The games of opposites—night is opposite of day—the concept of opposites are emphasized in early stages. That reinforces the simple labels of left and right. So when I speak before Jewish audiences in America, I can build my credibility by explaining that my father was a Holocaust survivor, he helped build the state, et cetera, and then they are receptive to my criticisms of my country. Here, with the black-and-white understanding of reality, I'm either pro- or anti-Israel. There is no nuance."

Gal Harmat, a peace education professor at Kibbutzim College, recalled how her elementary school imprinted the slogan, "It is good to die for your country" over the blackboards in the classroom. By 2010, her son, Or, who was not yet two years old, was being assimilated into the military culture. "Or's teachers just told me he should be a commando in the military because he is so good at weasel-walking," she said. "The kid is just a little more than a year and half old and they are telling me what unit he should be in!"

Harmat showed me a worksheet her son was given in preschool. It required students to draw lines between matching objects lined up on opposite sides of the page. There was nothing remarkable about the exercise except that the objects it depicted were pieces of military hardware: tanks, attack jets, missiles, and assault rifles. In other schools, Gal told me, her friends' children were given coloring activities with military gear specially tailored to their social class: "The upper-class kids get to color helicopters because they are supposed to go into the Air Force," she said.

The spring season of the Israeli education system is dictated by an intensely observed, heavily condensed suite of holidays intended to evoke a mood of perpetual siege against the "Jewish people." Beginning with Passover, the Jewish festival of liberation from slavery in Egypt, in which observers ritually proclaim, "In each generation, they have risen to destroy us," the holiday season moves swiftly through Yom Ha'Shoah, the Holocaust Memorial Day requiring all Israelis to stand at attention for two minutes while air raid sirens ring out across the country; then onto Memorial Day, a period of deep mourning and grief for the soldiers who have fallen in war. The martial heroics of the dead are recalled in elaborate detail, while the suicides and fratricides that now comprise the leading cause of death for Israeli soldiers are not mentioned.

"It's shocking that at these ceremonies, the public is invited to observe the heroism of our military at army cemeteries when almost half the soldiers in our cemeteries were not killed by our enemies, but through accidents and by their own hands," said Diana Dolev, a New Profile director and leading academic expert on the connections between Israeli national identity and architecture.

The nation erupts in joy on Independence Day, a climactic festival highlighted by fireworks and picnics, often held at Jewish National Fund–owned parks built over the ruins of Palestinian villages destroyed during the Nakba. Scheduled at the end of the holiday season, Independence Day reinforces the notion of Jewish statehood as a form of deliverance from the history of two thousand years of exile and persecution.

"The holidays are used as a tool to teach children from kindergarten on that we are always under siege and people are out to kill us, to finish us," Dolev explained. "In each holiday it's a different group that was out to kill us."

"At five years old the teachers start to say that Independence Day commemorates a military victory over the Arabs," said Gur. "They decorate the kindergartens with symbols of the military units. It's not just a celebration of the birthday of the state, it's the story of how the state was established. Then the Jewish holidays here become holidays of war: Purim is against the Persians, Passover is against the Egyptians. Then we have the Nazis and then the Arabs. So as kids, they get all the enemies mixed up but the message is the same."

During the 2012 holiday season, preschoolers in the Tel Aviv satellite city of Holon were seated before a poster and forced to contemplate their precarious existence in a world of enemies.

The poster read:

> Who wants to kill us?
> Pharaoh | Greeks | Haman | Nazis | Arabs
> !   !ì   !ì   !ì   !ì
> What do we need?
> WE NEED A STATE

That year, on Independence Day, the Israeli satirist and filmmaker Itamar Rose traveled to Yad La-Shiryon, the Armored Corps Memorial Site and Museum, to interview the Israeli children shepherded to the site by their families. Built on the former site of Imwas, Yalu, and Beit Nuba, three Palestinian towns bulldozed by Israeli forces in 1967, the museum serves as an annual destination for Israeli families seeking to instill army values in the next generation. As on every other Independence Day, the museum's tanks and armored vehicles transformed into virtual playgrounds for bands of Israeli kids as young as four years old.

"Here is the Merkava, the glory of our nation," a female soldier told an excited group of Israeli children, encouraging them to clamber onto the tank's grill.

A girl who looked to be about ten years old sat on the 120 mm cannon of a Merkava IV, dangling in the air. "I think I will serve in a combat unit," she told Rose with a broad smile.

"What could you imagine yourself doing in that tank?" he asked her.

"I think I would be killing lots of people," she responded.

"Who?"

"The Arabs who continue to want to kill us."

"And how will you feel when you shoot them from the tank?" Rose wondered.

"I think I will feel happy."

"I imagine that each time I see a dead Arab it will relieve me greatly," remarked a boy who appeared to be twelve years old, informing Rose that he dreamed of piloting a Merkava IV—"the finest tank in the world." He added, "I definitely want to serve in Lebanon. . . . We need to have another war there."

Next, a boy who could not have been older than five informed Rose, "I want to be in the air force so I can shoot missiles in the sky." The little boy said he was eager to fight in Gaza.

"Do you feel afraid to fight in Gaza?" Rose inquired.

"No, because when I shoot, my friends will come to help me," he responded with an angelic smile.

The indoctrination of small Israeli children relied as much on the fetishization of offensive military weaponry as it did on insidious techniques designed to hardwire them with the impression of the army as a safe surrogate family. Israeli kindergarten classrooms are invariably filled with uniformed female soldiers filling in for teachers who have taken leave, or who require additional support in neglected school districts in Israel's impoverished development towns. "The idea is to make the military seem cuddly and user-friendly," Hiller said of the soldier-teachers. "What the young ladies are doing in the schools as uniformed babysitters is replacing legitimate teaching jobs and sending the wrong message of the sense of duty. It's an obvious type of moral corruption, but then again, the military can get away with anything."

In high school, indoctrination takes on a more overt quality when students prepare to join the army and by extension are readied for direct participation in the national project of controlling the Palestinians. In April 2011, in an incident that was not atypical of state-sanctioned "IDF preparation," the Israeli Ministry of Education herded students from Havoyel High School in the affluent coastal city of Herzliya to an army base in the Negev Desert. There, they heard lectures by soldiers who told them that those who do serve in the army "do not perform meaningful service." Then, the students took part in an "electronic shooting range," firing on computer-simulated targets that wore Palestinian *keffiyehs*. Afterward, one person involved in the event complained that the state was "educating toward hatred of Arabs." "Some citizens of the State of Israel wear *keffiyehs*," the anonymous source told *Ha'aretz*. "Now they are viewed as legitimate targets for a shooting simulation."

Israeli university life is also heavily structured to support the culture of militarism, with army veterans receiving steeply discounted housing in new developments, reduced tuition fees, and even government-subsidized training to become sushi chefs in a program designed to reduce the number of non-Jewish Asians working in the country. At Ariel University, a secular Israeli college in the occupied West Bank, the dean, Yigal Orgad, has forbidden insufficiently loyal citizens from enrolling. "One whose actions or behavior do not fit with the Declaration of Independence cannot study at the Centre or work here, whether he is Jewish or an Arab," Orgad declared. "In every classroom or in every laboratory a flag of Israel is hung and there is a clear message in this decision," he added, explaining that every student is required to take at least one Judaism, Zionism, or "Land of Israel" course.

At the Western Galilee College, an institution in Northern Israel with a high level of Arab enrollment, the administration has gone to great lengths to compel student compliance. In May 2012, when students were asked to stand and observe a moment of silence for the fallen Israeli soldiers during Memorial Day, a dozen Arab students remained seated on a bench. Panic ensued, with a cleaning crew dispatched to hose down the bench to prevent them from remaining seated. The students finally rose for the moment of silence, but only because a security guard threatened to spray them with water if they remained seated.

"You begin with a Zionist narrative, and it goes on and on and on through the ceremonies, through the media, and then through the army, with intense indoctrination," Daniel Bar-Tal, the professor of political psychology at Tel Aviv University, told me. "Think about an American kid who is taught from a very young age that America is great, and then add to this context where the Israeli kids live, that they have to serve in the army, and you can see why they need so much preparation, legitimization, and justification for the acts they have to participate in. How do you go to the checkpoints? How do you go to Gaza? You have to form a particular framework or prism of thought. That's why the army goes into the high schools. So when you take into account all this information, it's not surprising that there is a right wing consensus in Israel today."

Canceling the Other Narrative

I n the campaign to indoctrinate Jewish children into the culture of militarism, no tool has proven more effective than schoolbooks. Nurit Peled-Elhanan, a professor of language and education at Hebrew University, has conducted the most comprehensive academic survey of Israeli public school textbooks in history, "Palestine in Israeli School Books: Ideology and Propaganda in Education."

I traveled to Peled-Elhanan's home in the Jerusalem suburb of Mevezeret Zion at twilight, just as the cool mountain air began to gust in for the evening. I was the last fare for a tired taxi driver who happened to live on her street. During the course of the conversation with the driver, which began with the usual questions about my profession and what I'm doing in the country, and proceeded with the usual, deliberately vague answers I gave to avoid the rancorous exchanges that often occurred when I volunteered my political opinions to Jewish Israelis, he asked if I was on my way to interview Peled-Elhanan.

"Well, I don't agree with her views, to be honest," the driver said, "but she has the right to whatever she wants, as far as I am concerned."

"Why's that?" I asked.

"You know about her daughter, right?"

During my conversation with Peled-Elhanan, she did not mention or even allude to the topic, leading me to assume it was off limits. But the fate of her only daughter, Smadar, seemed to have ignited her passion as an academic and activist. At age two, Smadar appeared on Labor Party billboards that appeared across Israel during the national elections in 1986. "Our children deserve a better future," they declared. Eleven years later, as the Oslo era began to unravel, Smadar was killed in a suicide bombing while she was shopping in central Jerusalem.

The thirteen-year-old child was buried next to her grandfather, Mati Peled, a former member of the Hebrew Canaanite movement, the ex-military governor of Gaza in 1956, and later, an outspoken dissident who attempted to organize talks with the PLO while condemning Israel's military conquest in 1967 as a disastrous war of choice. Smadar's funeral was attended by Labor Party chairman Shimon Peres and by officials from the Palestinian Authority, who offered condolences to Peled-Elhanan and her husband, Rami. Smadar's suicide attackers were three young Palestinian men from a village near Nablus. In retaliation for the lethal attack, the Israeli government ordered their families' homes demolished and refused to return their bodies for a proper burial.

A reporter asked Peled-Elhanan after the attack how she could have accepted condolences from the "other side," referring to the Palestinian Authority. She replied that
in fact, she had not: she refused to accept condolences from then–prime minister
Benjamin Netanyahu and rejected an offer to sit with him and his top advisers. "For
me, the other side, the enemy, is not the Palestinian people," she said at the time. "For
me, the struggle is not between Palestinians and Israelis, between Jews and Arabs.
The struggle is between those who seek peace and those who seek war. My people
are those who seek peace."

Unlike many of their peers from the Israeli peace camp, who reflexively closed
ranks with the Likudnik right-wing during the most violent period of the Second
Intifada, Nurit and Rami Peled-Elhanan thrust themselves into anti-occupation
activism. By joining the group Combatants for Peace, they became close friends
with Salwa and Bassam Aramin, Palestinian parents of Abir Aramin, a murdered
ten-year-old girl shot in the head by Border Policemen on her way to school. As they
followed the Aramins throughout their futile quest for justice, the Peled-Elhanans
gained an intimate perspective on the Israeli legal system's role in sustaining an illegal
occupation.

After initially accepting the Border Police's false claim that the little girl was killed
by a stray rock, an Israeli district court eventually ruled that the State of Israel was
responsible for her death, ordering a payment of $430,000 to the Aramin family.
Although the officers who killed Aramin lied under oath, the Israeli Supreme Court
rejected a petition to put them on trial, instead ruling that they should pay a fine
amounting to the price of an old used car—about $2,000.

Following a frustrating day inside the Supreme Court, where Chief Justice Dorit
Beinisch, a standard bearer of the Zionist left, told the Aramins' attorney that because
soldiers were so seldom indicted, he should save his energy, Peled-Elhanan published
a scathing editorial. "Those who have murdered our Israeli children, the Palestinian
suicide bombers, have at least said 'let me die with the Philistines' (Judges 16:30) and
spared any questions about their presence in the world," she wrote. "The murderer
of Abir Aramin no doubt spent that very evening in a bar (Shit! What a nasty day! A
little girl walked right into my crosshairs!), and will continue to spend many more
evenings in many more bars, while Abir's parents seek justice from the occupier,
from the oppressor."

Rami Elhanan took the experience to heart as well, opening a 2008 address before
an audience in Poland that included the Israeli ambassador and the country's Chief
Rabbi, "I am Bassam Aramin!" In September 2010, Rami Elhanan joined Yonatan and
Itamar Shapira, and a small group of Jewish activists, including two Holocaust survivors, in an attempt to sail a catamaran packed with aid into the besieged Gaza Strip.

On September 28, the Israel navy dispatched a destroyer and a group of heavily
armed frigates to intercept the little boat on the high seas. "All I could think of is
why are these warships coming to board our little catamaran with nine Jews mostly
in their sixties, seventies, and eighties?" Lillian Rosengarten, a seventy-six-year-old
Holocaust survivor from the United States, wrote afterward. "What insanity brought
these soldiers dressed to the gill with high boots, tasers, guns, helmets, and gloves
with their fingers uncovered to take over our boat, in essence to kidnap?" As soon as

they stormed the ship, the commandoes charged straight toward Yonatan Shapira, ripping off his life jacket and knocking him to the ground. He let out a guttural groan as they tazed him in the heart until he was unconscious, an assault that might have killed a less fit person. After dragging Shapira onto a frigate, the navy towed the rickety boat back to Ashdod, and then transferred the gray-haired activists to prison cells around the country.

In a statement to the Israeli media, a Foreign Ministry spokesman named Yoni Levy cast the dingy and its mostly gray-haired crew as a grave threat to Israeli security, describing them as Holocaust-denying terrorists: "This former pilot, who has joined the ranks of Hamas and sprays hateful graffiti on the walls of the Warsaw Ghetto, is not a pilot but an astronaut," Levy said, referring to Shapira. He then lashed out at the two Holocaust survivors aboard the boat: "A Holocaust survivor who sanctifies the name of the Jews' murderers and takes time to justify those who don't accept Israel's right for sovereignty has probably not learned anything from the terrible past."

When I set up my laptop in the living room of Peled-Elhanan, Rami was just beginning to prepare for the fateful sail, while Nurit was busy completing her most consequential academic work to date. Both joined me in their spacious salon, while their son, Elik, prepared to travel to New York City, where he had accepted a faculty position to teach in the Jewish Studies department at Columbia University. "My sons have each reacted to the situation here in his own way," Peled-Elhanan told me with a proud grin. "One has immersed himself in Palestinian history and identity, and the other is a Yiddish specialist."

Outside of their academic work, Peled-Elhanan described her family's experience with the militarism and racism in the Israeli school system. During pre-army training at her youngest son's high school, an officer from the Givati Brigade attempted to impress the class with tales of glory from Operation Cast Lead. He boasted that he shot a pregnant woman, justifying his act to the students on the grounds that he killed a future terrorist. "My son stormed out of the room in protest," Peled-Elhanan said, "and the administrators told him he was right to do so and that such things will never happen again. But the rest of the children just stayed there, accepting the officer's words."

Peled-Elhanan told me she spent many of her days volunteering as a teachers' assistant at a nearby absorption center for Jewish immigrants from Ethiopia. The center is a vast residential compound run by the Jewish Agency. Besides providing the new immigrants with basic social services, it served as a key destination for American politicians and celebrities on state-sponsored tours of Israel. Most schools in affluent Mevezeret Zion refused to accept the center's black students, according to Peled-Elhanan, so they were often bused to the only institutions that would accept them: religious nationalist schools in the settlements.

"They get up at six in the morning, go to religious schools and learn nothing but dogmatic Judaism and racism," Peled Elhanan said of the children at the center. "All they know is they have to hate Arabs and go into the army." She recounted a conversation with an eight-year-old Ethiopian child who told her how happy she was that the army had massacred activists on the *Mavi Marmara*: "She said that Israel is only for the Israeli people. She can't read or write, but this is what she knows."

Peled-Elhanan's work on Israeli textbooks, published in English in the United States and Europe in 2012—but never released in Hebrew—bore out her conclusions in clinical detail. In her study, Peled-Elhanan analyzed seventeen school texts on history, geography, and civic studies. She found that "none of the textbooks studied here includes, whether verbally or visually, any positive cultural or social aspect of Palestinian life-world: neither literature nor poetry, neither history nor agriculture, neither art nor architecture, neither customs nor traditions are mentioned." Instead, she writes, Palestinians are represented almost invariably as "terrorists, refugees, and primitive farmers—the three 'problems' they constitute for Israel." In one recent history textbook, *50 Years*, the only image of a Palestinian was a single photo of a group of armed men clad in *keffiyehs*.

Peled-Elhanan found that Israeli massacres were usually explained away in history textbooks as inventions of the "Palestinian narrative." If they were ever deemed deplorable, it was only because of the damage they did to the perception of Jewish moral superiority. A supposedly progressive 2009 textbook contained a prime example, informing students that the 1948 massacre in "Deir Yassin became a myth in the Palestinian narrative . . . and created a horrifying negative image of the Jewish conquerer in the eyes of Israel's Arabs."

Peled-Elhanan explained, "Israeli actions are usually presented in history books as right morally, according to universal and Jewish norms, while Palestinian actions are presented as whimsical and vicious. Israel 'reacts to Arab hostility,' performs 'operations' in their midst, and executes 'punitive deterring actions' against Palestinian terror, while the 'Arabs' murder Israelis, commit terror actions against Israel, take revenge, and use what they call their suffering in anti-Israel propaganda."

The geography textbooks she studied were no less infused with nationalism. According the Peled-Elhanan, "geography curricula in Israel are meant first and foremost to inculcate, as the national curriculum defines it, 'Love and Knowledge of Our Homeland.' Thus the presence of Palestinian Arabs and other non-Jews in the area during the past two thousand years is either glossed over or not mentioned. Instead, a textbook informs students, "The Land of Israel is the land of the Jews. During the many years the Jews were away from their country . . . they yearned to come back and resettle it. . . . When the Jewish people came back and the State of Israel was founded, Jerusalem, our capital, became once again the most important Jewish center of the Jewish people."

The transmission of nationalist attitudes through Israel school textbooks, both through implicit and explicit messaging, was systematic and comprehensive. "This is a clear socialization process," Peled-Elhanan said. "The state has to enforce some kind of narrative that will cancel out the other narrative and make it disappear. In this way, they can create a situation where Palestinian life is dispensable with impunity. Their goal is to make good soldiers."

Even outside the classroom, Israeli children could expect to be consumed in a sea of media bombarding them with anti-Arab imagery. One of the most popular children's books series in Israeli history, *Hasamba*, was identified to me by several interviewees and friends as a key vehicle for instilling anti-Arab attitudes in Jewish Israeli youth. Authored by Yigal Mossinson, a Tel Aviv bohemian type, and adapted into a feature-length cartoon film, *Hasamba* stories portrayed a group of children operating in a secret intelligence unit dedicated to Israel's defense. In almost every book, Arabs were depicted at once as buffoonish and sinister.

"I grew up reading *Hasamba,* in which all the Arabs are ridiculed and stupid and vicious," Diana Dolev, the New Profile director and expert on Israeli architecture and nationalism, recalled. "Everybody read these books and you prided yourself on memorizing the plots. Among kids my age, it was a competition of how knowledgeable you were about the different plots. So we learned that Arabs were okay as long as they were nice, as long as they look like us and act like us. As I grew up I lived through this paradox—the Arabs I knew were not stupid and they were nothing like the characters in the books."

Noam Sheizaf, a journalist for the online Israel news site, 972Mag.com, remembered enjoying *Danni Din,* a children's book series tailored for the consumption of second graders. In a *Danni Din* tale published in 1997, for example, a group of Israeli children were kidnapped by aliens. After a violent battle, the kids wrested control of the alien spaceship just in time to stop Hamas from sending an aerial suicide bomber crashing into President Bill Clinton's Air Force One as he junketed to Israel. The back cover of the book read: "Will our invisible heroes succeed in saving the beloved president and the plane's passengers from death?"

"*Danni Din*'s war on Arab terrorists is not unique," Sheizaf wrote. "Almost every adventure book I remember from my childhood featured at least a handful of evil Arabs (never mention the P word), if not full Egyptian military divisions. Some of the Arabs in those books were thieves and kidnappers, but most of them were terrorists."

Popular children's books also contained depictions of blacks that ended up reinforcing racial stereotypes. A perfect example was a book called, *Yeled Shel Shokolad,* or *The Little Chocolate Boy.* The book told the story of Moshe, a little black boy who was shunned and insulted by his white classmates. In the end, the children's teacher explains all the delightful things that are the same color as Moshe, from sweet chocolate to cuddly teddy bears, and finally, the children agreed to accept him.

Well before *The Litle Chocolate Boy* appeared on Israeli library shelves, there was *Alikama,* an acclaimed toddler-oriented book drawn in a striking, primitivistic woodcut style by the German-born Jewish illustrator Miriam Bartov.

Alikama began:

> *See children, here stands Alikama*
> *Happy and joyful, can you guess why?*
> *First he's a little nigger [kushon]*
> *Second he's a little blackie [sharcharon]*
> *Third he knows how to ride a little elephant*
> *This is his mother Sambina [play on the word "Sambo"]*
> *She smiles to her child, "You need to walk to the city.*

Here's a basket, diligent sharchari [my little blackie]
Buy everything we need in the store."

With criticism mounting from groups advocating on behalf of the recently arrived Ethiopian Jews, some Israeli scholars stepped forward to defend the book and its author's casual use of the word "nigger." "You can't say that Bartov isn't obsessed with blacks," said Yael Dar, an Israeli children's literature expert. "At the same time, she really handles the characters well, and it would be superficial to call it racism." Dar called *Alikama,* "one of the best books in Hebrew for toddlers." Orna Granot, the associate curator of illustrated children's books at the Israel Museum, suggested that "children's books reflect the concept of childhood of its time. I believe that this childhood as reflected in *Alikama* is playful and mischievous, somewhat naïve. I believe that innocence."

Rather than allow the book to fade away in the dustbin of history, it was republished on the fiftieth anniversary of its publication and awarded the Israel Prize for illustration. A comment was inscribed inside the new edition justifying the author's use of the word "nigger." It read, "Remember that fifty years ago, when *Alikama* was 'born,' the word kushon [nigger] was not considered an insult; it was a term used for a person who was born in Kush (Ethiopia)."

Through an array of afterschool television programs, cuddly puppets and goofy actors dressed as generic children helped prepare Israeli kids for military service. In a typical episode of the Israeli TV show *Songs and Games,* a Hebrew Sesame Street–style program targeted to Israeli children under eight years old, a new recruit returns home on leave in full army uniform, with a rucksack slung over his shoulder. Upon his arrival, the soldier, Uzi, who bears the same name as the Israeli-made machine gun, encounters two friends from the old neighborhood. One of them, a pig-tailed girl (played by an adult actor) is naïve to an exaggerated degree, peppering Uzi with questions about army life, thus allowing the soldier to educate small children on the process of induction.

> Girl with pigtails: Wow, Uzi! You've changed. What happened to your beautiful long curls?
> Uzi, the new recruit: They cut them at the BAKUM . . .
> Girl with pigtails: But what's BAKUM?
> Uzi: Oh, BAKUM is the name of the new recruits' base.
> Girl with pigtails to male actor dressed in a little farm-boy costume, with overalls and a striped shirt: He's a soldier now! One week exactly.
> Farm-boy: Wow, you're so lucky. Congratulations!
> Uzi, the soldier: Thanks!

Later in the show, inside a bakery owned by Uzi's doting grandfather, the naïve girl is belittled for her childish pacifism:

> Pigtailed girl: I don't really understand. What's so great about the army?

Male friend named "Guy": What do you mean? The army is the most fun! What, you don't want to join?

Pigtailed girl: I hope by the time I'm eighteen there won't be an army. Because there will be peace.

Guy: No, no, anything but that.

Pigtailed girl: What, you don't want peace?

Guy: Of course, I want peace, but I don't want the army to be cancelled.

If the naïve, pigtailed girl chooses to follow Guy into the army, her experience is likely to be drastically different than his, and not necessarily "the most fun." Though the state of Israel markets its conscription of female citizens to the outside world as an equalizing, inherently feminist measure, many women soldiers find that they are expected to serve as "mattresses" for their male counterparts as soon as they exchange their civilian clothes for olive garb.

The Beauty Brigade

Other than Eritrea, a country ruled by a despotic military regime trapped in a perpetual border war with Ethiopia, Israel is the only country in the world that requires women to serve in the military. Though the State of Israel touts female conscription as a feminist achievement that guarantees women equal citizenship rights after their service—a system supported by many liberal feminists—women are rarely able to attain a sense of equality inside the army's hierarchical structure, where they are sandwiched between randy generals and stir-crazy conscripts desperate to relieve their pent-up frustration.

Instead of earning respect by displaying military élan, as their male counterparts do, women soldiers are often induced into the role of "mattresses," realizing their value to the state through sexual availability and by maintaining an impeccably prim, alluring appearance. In the words of Ezer Weizman, a former Israeli president and commander of the country's Air Force, "The best men to the cockpit, the best women to the pilots." (Weizman resigned as president in 2000 amid allegations of bribery that were not legally investigated because the statute of limitations had passed.)

When the process of military indoctrination begins around age five, Jewish Israeli boys are encouraged to play with guns or dress up in mock military uniforms while chanting texts about serving as warriors. Young girls, on the other hand, are trained to fear violence and, in turn, to seek protection from male soldiers. In a research paper titled "Fresh Meat, Fresh Sweets—Militarism and Sexism in Israel," Gal Harmat of Kibbutzim College argued, "Girls are not part of the main game of soldiers and guns; they are indoctrinated to play a supportive role rather than a central role—they are part of the game, but only as protected and do not take part in the focal occurrence and events."

The Jewish holiday of Purim has become an annual celebration for reinforcing Israeli gender roles. The holiday commemorates the deliverance of the Jewish people living in the Persian Empire from a plot to destroy them. According to the Book of Esther, the drunken King Ahasuerus orders his wife Vashti to perform a striptease for the Persian nobility. When she refuses, he casts her away, ordering a parade of nubile young women to have sex with him until he finds a suitable replacement queen. He settles on the orphan Esther, a Jew who eventually uses her wiles to convince the king to spare her people from the genocidal plot of his evil prime minister, Haman.

In modern-day secular Israeli society, Purim is the occasion for a giant bacchanal—a cross between Halloween and Mardi Gras—in which young people dress up in gaudy costumes and party the night away. For the very young, the holiday outlines the gender roles they are expected to play, preparing them for the duties they will assume in the army later in life. "Purim is a very sexist holiday," the academic Hagith Gur remarked. "These days, the costumes are getting more and more gendered. Boys have macho costumes, dressing as soldiers, Batmen, Spidermen, ninjas. The girls are Barbies, queens, fairies, et cetera. This is the story of what you'll grow up to be. The boys have to define their sexual identity through power, so they play heroes, and the girls learn how to be beautiful. When they get to the army the women serve the coffee, they are little more than ornaments. It puts the lie to the myth of equality in the army."

Upon their induction into the army, female soldiers are designated as members of a women's corps called *Chen,* which means "beauty" and "grace" in Hebrew—the Beauty Brigade. While male soldiers focus on maximizing their physical prowess, many women are provided with beauty tips and help on custom tailoring their uniforms for maximum sex appeal. In turn, they are used as props in pro-army propaganda, with comely female soldiers in full makeup appearing frequently on the covers of Israeli newspapers, presenting the military as a heavily armed Ibiza. A May 2012 *Ha'aretz* article about a bikini-clad woman photographed with an M-16 slung over her shoulder on a Tel Aviv was headlined "Hot Israeli chick with gun occupies internet."

With big guns in their hands, female soldiers appear capable of eliminating the thing they are told to fear the most: the Arab male. Indeed, the concept of an Arab man raping a Jewish woman represents perhaps the greatest attack on the Israeli nation's honor. The army instructs female soldiers to guard themselves against Arab predations, providing them with "kidnapping kits" while forbidding them from hitchhiking without a male soldier present. The men of army combat units are thus posited as their protectors, as noble centurions who would exact immediate revenge on any Arab who dared violate their sexual purity.

But cases of Arabs raping female Israeli soldiers have always been extremely rare and are now virtually unheard of. In reality, young Israeli women are far more likely to be raped or abused by the male soldier assigned to them as their protector. A survey provided to the Knesset Committee for the Advancement of the Status of Women in the Israeli army in 2003 found that one out of three female soldiers had been sexually attacked during her service, and that at least 80 percent had suffered from sexual harassment. Over a quarter had been offered rewards in exchange for sex, while almost 70 percent said they had encountered an unwanted sexual proposition. The survey exposed a terrifying culture of rape that demanded the sexual servitude of young Israeli women while training them to view their attackers as guardians.

"Israel is so small you don't need prostitution," Gur commented. "The soldiers just go to their wives and girlfriends, or inside the army on the weekend. The women are so available there—they are part of the militarization by serving the army with sex. The woman who is usually the clerk of a medium-size unit automatically becomes a sex object. She will be known as 'the mattress of the unit.'"

Shlomo Benizri, a former member of Knesset from the right-wing Shas Party, echoed Gur, but from an alternately opposed viewpoint: "It is common knowledge that new male recruits are called 'fresh beef' or 'meat' and new female recruits, 'fresh mattresses,'" he remarked casually. (Benazri has previously blamed homosexual activity for an earthquake that shook Israel in 2008.)

According to Harmat, one of the many rewards offered to the winner of the Miss Israel competition is the opportunity to serve in the office of the Israeli army's chief of staff, who is one of the most revered men in the country. The Israeli media heavily covers Miss Israel's recruitment process, Harmat wrote, with photos of her in full makeup and tightly fitting olive drab splashed out in full-page newspaper spreads.

In recent years, top Israeli military and political figures have been placed on trial for raping and sexually attacking their female subordinates. Among those disgraced by charges of sexual misconduct was Haim Ramon, accused of forcing himself on a twenty-one-year-old woman in his office while serving as Minister of Justice. Yitzhak Mordechai, a former army chief of staff, was convicted of sexual assault two female soldiers working in his office. Then, in 2010, after years of legal wrangling, former Israeli president Moshe Katsav was convicted of rape, indecent assault, and the sexual harassment of several female subordinates.

A study by Avigail Moor, a clinical psychologist and head of the women's studies program at Tel-Hai College in northern Israel, demonstrated how the army culture of harassment extended into general Israeli culture, with one of four women reporting that they have been sexually assaulted—and only a few even bothering to seek legal recourse against their abuser.

Neomi, a former female soldier whose experience transformed her into a radical feminist activist, reflected to Harmat, "I still cannot believe how I was treated during my military service—like a whore, like a piece of meat—with chauvinist songs and jokes. I feel that the education system, and for sure the military, tried to educate me to be a small, obeying, lovely wife that gives birth to many new soldiers. Fuck them! It took me years to overcome this, but I will do anything to assist other women not to fall for it."

Lifelong Draftees

At the head of the Israel's educational system between 2009 and early 2013 was Minister of Education Gideon Sa'ar, a clean-cut forty-five-year-old Likud ideologue who doubled by night as a hard-partying techno deejay at raucous Tel Aviv clubs. With his wire-rimmed glasses, nicely tailored suits, and soft-spoken style, Sa'ar appeared to be the mirror opposite of gruff warrior-politicians like Ariel Sharon and Moshe Dayan. Yet under Sa'ar's direction, the Education Ministry became a virtual auxiliary of the army, partnering with the Ministry of Defense and the army to establish the "Path of Values," a program designed to "strengthen a teenager's commitment to having a meaningful service in the [army]."

At a June 2012 meeting at a high school in Pisgat Ze'ev, a large Jewish settlement in East Jerusalem, inside a room decorated with posters of heroic-looking soldiers and nationalistic paraphernalia, Sa'ar introduced dozens of teachers to the program. By Sa'ar's side sat Lt. Gen. Benny Gantz, the chief of staff of the army, and hence, the most respected man in Israel. "Our meeting today is for those who charge ahead," Sa'ar told the teachers. "Encouraging service in the [army] is not a favor that we are doing for the [army], but a moral issue."

Sa'ar continued, "Teachers are lifelong draftees. This project is one of the best things taking place in high schools."

According to a reporter from *Ha'aretz,* teachers were handed pamphlets outlining the values they were expected to instill in students. "The army for me is a question of national survival; it's the essence of the Jewish people," the pamphlet read. "The army is the soul of the Jewish people; it's a part of my soul." Under the guidelines of the "Path of Values" program, local municipalities were expected to fund the creation of a position called "army preparation coordinator" who would monitor each student's "readiness to serve and preparation for the army."

When Zeev Dagani, the principal of one of Tel Aviv's most prestigious high schools, Gymnasia Herzliya, refused to enlist in a similar program that brought army officers to schools to instruct teachers on how to encourage military values, he was flooded with death threats and widespread condemnation, including from then-army chief of staff Gabi Ashkenazi. "The idea that the army will educate teachers casts major doubt on the work teachers do, all day all the time," Dagani remarked. "It damages one of the most basic foundations of our profession." At Aleph High School for the Arts, a school attended mostly by the children of North Tel Aviv's liberal elite, principal Ram Cohen invited a firestorm of controversy by merely attempting to instill a different set of values in his students than those proscribed by the military. In January 2010, Cohen gathered his eleventh-graders to a meeting on their upcoming army service. Instead of feeding them clichés about the glory of army life or stoking their fears with the looming specter of Arab evildoers, he told them about the unsettling scenes he had witnessed during a tour of the occupied West Bank with the Israeli human rights group Ir Amin.

Cohen challenged the students to explain whether they could live the rest of their lives under occupation. He told them he understood why Palestinians felt compelled to resort to terror, even if he did not accept their actions as legitimate. Finally, he told them to protest against the occupation. "Talk to each other, talk to your parents, go out and demonstrate," Cohen reportedly said. But he added an important caveat: The students should demonstrate only *after* completing their military service, during which they should serve as agents of change from inside the army, mitigating the cruelty of the occupation with their enlightened values.

As punishment for the civics lesson, Cohen was heatedly denounced by Shimshon Shoshani, the director general of the Education Ministry. "A principal who thinks he can preach has no place in the education system," he said, equating Cohen's speech with the right-wing incitement that inspired the murder of Prime Minister Yitzhak Rabin. At the heart of Shoshani's accusation against Cohen and grounds for his dismissal was that he had said that the occupation existed: "Are we looking at what's happening in the West Bank as occupation?"

Next, the Tel Aviv municipality and Education Ministry summoned Cohen for "clarifications." Finally, after being forbidden by the state from giving interviews to the media, Cohen was brought before the Knesset to be interrogated about his actions.

I visited Cohen in July 2010 inside his office at Aleph High School for the Arts. He sat inside a spacious, dimly lit room at a simple, well-worn wooden desk upholding a clunky PC and a stack of manila files. Nearly bald, dressed in a short-sleeved polo shirt, and still possessed with a youthful look though well into his forties, Cohen spoke in a soft, measured tone, even when describing events that sounded remarkably stressful. I suddenly realized that this was the first time in my life I had been seated across a desk from a principal without having to brace myself for a stern lecture about my own mischief making.

Cohen began by explaining what motivated him to engage his eleventh-grade class on a contentious topic like the occupation. He told me, "After seeing the occupation for myself, I wondered, what does it mean for me as an educator to be pushing kids into the army? What does it mean to send students to be at the checkpoints? When you fight for a budget for education or for the poor on the one hand, and on the other hand you put a lot of money for the army and developing the settlements, it's a mistake. It made me irritated. I decided something here is not right. It goes against my basic morality."

Cohen stopped himself to qualify his indignant commentary about the occupation with reminders of his commitment to the army—"it's the only army we've got," he said—and assurances that he would not encourage students to refuse service, even if doing such a thing was legal. The point he emphasized most was that the creation of a Palestinian state was necessary to preserve the Jewish demographic majority inside "Israel proper." His views should not have been considered threatening or traiterous by a rational government or a society.

Cohen told me that after engaging his students about the occupation, he organized a trip for teachers across Tel Aviv to see the checkpoints in the West Bank. The night before the trip, he received a call from an Education Ministry official ordering him to cancel it. "It would be dangerous for you to continue with these tricks," the official said. Though he protested, Cohen ultimately acceded to the ministry's demand. But by then, it was too late; news of the trip had already leaked out to the Israeli public. Before long, right-wing members of Knesset were calling for his firing and filing requests with the attorney general to oust him. When they failed to establish sufficient grounds for his termination, the lawmakers invited him to appear before the Knesset Committee on Education, Culture and Sports.

When Cohen arrived to testify, he was seated next to members of the Islamic Movement in Israel, a sectarian Islamist group accused of exploiting the Arab sector's educational system to promote political Islam. "Some people said it was strange and insulting that I was put next to them," Cohen said, "but what they do is legal, and what I do is legal." As soon as the hearing began, right-wing members of Knesset including Sa'ar bombarded Cohen with hostile questions, demanding to know if he had actually called for Israel to withdraw to the Green Line. "I said, no I didn't say to withdraw all the way to the Green Line," he recalled. "I said we should have two states for two nations. Then I quoted Netanyahu, who said the same thing. At this point they laughed and seemed very embarrassed. After two hours, they finally let me go."

Having weathered the wrath of demagogues in the Knesset, Cohen reflected on the silence of his peers. Were they self-censoring because of the state's intimidation, or had they simply retreated into an armored, beachside bubble where the occupation existed only in occasional news flashes? "Unfortunately, all this time I haven't seen any other educators who spoke up about the occupation," he said. "Democracy is no longer something that educators understand deeply. They are not thinking about how they should reinforce it to make it stronger and how to transfer it to the kids. The occupation is simply not an issue in the secular public and it bothers me a lot. Why don't we talk about it?"

Cohen's comments highlighted a disturbing aspect of the controversy he withstood: It was an entirely isolated affair. In most schools in Israel, principals welcomed the army into classrooms with zeal, placing open discussion of the occupation outside the frame of acceptable behavior. "As soon as the army shows up, a group of women takes off their shoes, as if on holy ground, in unwilling adoration," a teacher at Pisgat Ze'ev High School complained. Indeed, with its pool of "lifelong draftees," the state did not need to intimidate most principals into compliance with the army's agenda.

On December 31, 2010, a group of young teachers sent a petition to Education Minister Gideon Sa'ar calling on him to "speak out clearly against expressions of racism that are present everywhere."

The teachers announced, "We can not remain silent in light of the increasing presence within the walls of schoolhouses of expressions of racism wherever it is directed—against Arabs, immigrants from Ethiopia and Russia, homosexuals and migrant workers. We see ourselves as educators who must issue a warning. A series of studies and surveys reflect the everyday reality that we all experience in encounters with our students: the prevalence of racism and cruelty is growing among young people in Israel. We are witnesses to this growing racism in education."

The educators blame state-funded rabbis, Knesset members, and mayors for "offensive and racist formulations," which provided "legitimacy to these expressions" by Israeli students—"a phenomenon that makes the educators' attempts to deal with racism even more difficult."

Miriam Darmoni, a teacher-training specialist who signed the petition, explained, "These are idealistic young teachers who see their job as a mission, but they are helpless in the face of rising racism among the youth. . . . The increase in racism in recent years may cause damage to Israeli society, especially when it seems that there is a legitimacy among the general public."

"The views that students present in the classroom are a reflection of what they hear at home," said Assaf Matzkin, an Israeli high school teacher. "Instead of express-ing permissive liberal opinions, the students have become more nationalistic in recent years."

Ignoring the petition, Sa'ar began slashing the budget for civic studies, channeling the funding back into a "Jewish culture and tradition" curriculum that requires even secular junior high schoolers to memorize weekly Torah portions and sayings of the Jewish patriarchs while studying Theodore Herzl's novel, *Alteneuland*, or "Old New Land," his fantasy about his ideal Jewish state, which would among other things have no place for religious teaching. The new program also emphasized state-sponsored field trips to Jewish holy sites in the occupied city of Hebron under the protection of the military.

Thanks in part to the "Jewish revolution" Sa'ar claimed to be conducting in Israel's education system, the racist attitudes of Israeli high schoolers surged to shocking levels. A poll taken in August 2012 by Tel Aviv University statistician Camil Fuchs revealed that a majority of Israeli twelfth-graders supported the total deportation of non–Jewish African asylum seekers living in the country, and the expulsion of their Israeli-born children. While almost half of secular high schooler seniors declared their refusal to live next door to an Arab, nearly 90 percent of their religious coun-terparts endorsed the segregationist view.

Bolstering the infrastructure of racist indoctrination was an influential coterie of state-sponsored rabbis who expressed an aggressively segregationist, and even geno-cidal philosophy toward Arabs and other non-Jews. In December 2010, thirty of the state rabbis' wives issued a public letter urging Jewish girls to keep away from Arab men. A year and a half later, the letter became the basis for a question in a matricu-lation guide distributed to Israeli high school students by the thousands.

The study guide asked students for their opinion on the letter. Then it provided them with a sample answer: "If the daughters of Israel will hang around with Arabs, they are liable to have relationships and marry them. This would harm the Jewish majority of the state." The guide provided another justification: "If the daughters of Israel will hang around with Arabs, they are liable to fall victims to violence for nationalistic reasons. This would harm their right to life and security."

The rabbis' influence extended well beyond the school system, and into the core institutions of Israeli life. And the state demonstrated little interest in limiting it, a sign of the rising power of religious nationalism.

PART IX

THIS BELONGS TO THE WHITE MAN

How to Kill Goyim and Influence People

On another dry, sunny day in Jerusalem during the summer of 2010, I weaved through the crowds of tourists, baby-faced soldiers, and packs of Orthodox settlers milling around on Ben Yehuda Pedestrian Mall, and headed toward Pomeranz, a Jewish book emporium on Be'eri Street, a busy road a few blocks away. As soon as I was inside the shop, a short, mild-mannered man greeted me with American-accented English. He was the owner, Michael Pomeranz, a former undercover narcotics agent and firefighter from New Jersey who had experienced a religious awakening and immigrated to Israel. When I inquired about the availability of a widely discussed book called *Torat Ha'Melech*, or the King's Torah, a commotion immediately ensued.

"Are you sure you want it?" Pomeranz, asked me half-jokingly. A middle-aged coworker chortled from behind a shelf. "The Shabak [Israel's internal security service] is going to want a word with you if you do," he warned. When a few customers stopped browsing and began to stare in my direction, Pomeranz pointed to a security camera affixed to a wall. "See that?" he said. "It goes straight to the Shabak! [Shin Bet]"

Upon its publication in 2009, *Torat Ha'Melech* sparked a national uproar. The controversy began when the Israeli paper, *Maariv*, panned the book's contents as "230 pages on the laws concerning the killing of non-Jews, a kind of guidebook for anyone who ponders the question of if and when it is permissible to take the life of a non-Jew." The description was absolutely accurate.

According to the authors, Rabbi Yitzhak Shapira and Rabbi Yosef Elitzur, non-Jews are "uncompassionate by nature" and may have been killed in order to "curb their evil inclinations." "If we kill a gentile who has violated one of the seven commandments [of Noah] . . . there is nothing wrong with the murder," Shapira and Elitzur insisted. Citing Jewish law as his source (or at least a very selective interpretation of it) he declared, "There is justification for killing babies if it is clear that they will grow up to harm us, and in such a situation they may be harmed deliberately, and not only during combat with adults."

Torat Ha'Melech was written as a guide for soldiers and army officers seeking rabbinical guidance on the rules of engagement. Drawing from a hodgepodge of rabbinical texts that seemed to support their genocidal views, Shapira and Elitzur urged a policy of ruthlessness toward non-Jews, insisting that the commandment against murder "refers only to a Jew who kills a Jew, and not to a Jew who kills a gentile, even if that gentile is one of the righteous among the nations."

The rabbis went on to pronounce all civilians of the enemy population "rodef," or villains who chase Jews and are therefore fair game for slaughtering. Shapira and Elitzur wrote, "Every citizen in the kingdom that is against us, who encourages the warriors or expresses satisfaction about their actions, is considered rodef and his killing is permissible."

Shapira and Elitzur also justified the killing of Jewish dissidents. "A rodef is any person who weakens our kingdom by speech and so forth," they wrote.

Finally, the rabbis issued an extensive but crudely reasoned justification for the killing of innocent children, arguing that in order to defeat "the evil kingdom," the rules of war "permit intentional hurting of babies and of innocent people, if this is necessary for the war against the evil people." They added, "If hurting the children of an evil king will put great pressure on him that would prevent him from acting in an evil manner—they can be hurt."

Shapira and Elitzur justified killing babies and small children on the grounds of satiating the national thirst for revenge. "Sometimes," the rabbis wrote, "one does evil deeds that are meant to create a correct balance of fear, and a situation in which evil actions do not pay off . . . and in accordance with this calculus, the infants are not killed for their evil, but due to the fact that there is a general need of everyone to take revenge on the evil people, and the infants are the ones whose killing will satisfy this need."

In January 2010, Shapira and Elitzur were briefly detained by the Israeli police, while two leading, state-funded rabbis who endorsed the book, Dov Lior and Yaakov Yosef, were summoned to interrogations by the Shin Bet. However, the rabbis refused to appear at the interrogations, essentially thumbing their noses at the state and its laws. And the government did nothing. The episode raised grave questions about the willingness of the Israeli government to confront the ferociously racist swath of the country's rabbinate. "Something like this has never happened before, even though it seems as if everything possible has already happened," the liberal commentator Yossi Sarid remarked with astonishment. "Two rabbis [were] summoned to a police investigation, and announc[ed] that they will not go. Even settlers are kind enough to turn up."

(In 2011, British security officials prohibited Rabbi Elitzur from entering the UK in a formal letter signed by the Home Secretary for "fomenting or justifying terrorist violence . . . and seeking to provoke others to commit terrorist acts.")

Prime Minister Benjamin Netanyahu maintained an eerie silence about the rabbis' flouting of the law. Following the publication of *Torat Ha'Melech*, Netanyahu strenuously avoided criticizing its contents or the authors' leading supporters. Netanyahu's submissive posture before the country's religious far right highlighted the power religious nationalist figures wielded both in his own party and in his governing coalition. For the prime minister, a showdown with the rabbis threatened to unravel his coalition, derail his agenda, and alienate his party's hardcore base in "Judea and Samaria."

When Israel's first prime minister, David Ben Gurion, established the country's Chief Rabbinate, he pulled from a pool of religious nationalists following in the tradition of the first Ashkenazi Chief Rabbi, Abraham Isaac Kook, and his son, Zvi Yehuda Kook, the spiritual leader of the Gush Emunim who spearheaded the settlement movement in the West Bank and Gaza Strip after 1967.

"I will never agree to the separation of religion and state," Ben Gurion once told Yeshayahu Leibowitz. "I want the state to hold religion in the palm of its hand." Ben Gurion thus entered into a Faustian bargain with both the non-Zionist ultra orthodox and the still-marginal religious nationalist camp, buying their loyalty to establish the image the secular government of Israel believed it needed to appear "Jewish" in the eyes of the world. Leibowitz chastisted Ben Gurion for his fecklessness, warning that however mediocre and malleable the state rabbis might have seemed, their thirst for power was insatiable, and their reactionary impulses obvious. As usual, his prophecies were ignored, and his most dire predictions were fulfilled.

Convinced they were living in the era of redemption, Zvi Yehuda Kook and his followers exploited the tacit alliance with secular Zionism to realize the dominionist goals of religious nationalism, positing the state as an ass that the Gush Emunim would ride until "the fulfillment of the Zionist vision in its full scope." The *Torat Ha'Melech* affair demonstrated how far the Kookists had come since embarking on their heavenly mission. The dynamic that Ben Gurion had hoped to create had been entirely reversed, with the Israeli rabbinate holding the state in its palm, and molding it as it pleased.

On August 18, 2010, a pantheon of Israel's top fundamentalist rabbis convened an ad hoc congress at Jerusalem's Ramada Renaissance hotel to flaunt their power. I stood in the audience with about 250 settlers and hardline rightists, watching in astonishment as one state-sanctioned rabbi after another rose from to the podium to speak in defense of the authors of *Torat Ha'Melech*.

My roommate, Yossi David, agreed to accompany me to the *Torat Ha'Melech* congress. He was the perfect person to help me translate the seemingly arcane Hebrew religious formulations that were likely to fill discussions at the event. Yossi was raised in an ultra-Orthodox home and was forced to spend his adolescence in a stuffy *yeshiva* where sports and the study of foreign languages were forbidden. He suffered under layers of stiff religious garb in the stultifying summer heat but never turned against the faith until the extremist environment his rabbis cultivated became unbearable.

Five months after leaving his family and the ultra-Orthodox community, he had enlisted in the army, having been told by his adoptive family that it was the best way to assimilate into secular society. After basic training, Yossi was assigned to what is known in army speak as "the texile factory in Dimona," but what is actually Israel's secret nuclear reactor. His assignment was rescinded, however, when he was outed for dating a Palestinian girl, resulting in his deployment to Hatmar Etzion, a base near the settlement of Efrat. "I was still wearing a hot uniform, just like in the *yeshiva*, and still worshipping the God of Israel, but now the God was the commanders—the generals and the chief of staff—and my Torah was my gun."

By the end of his time in the army, Yossi was questioning everything, not just religious and army life, but the entire philosophy of Zionism. "The society educates you to be stupid. If you ask questions you are immediately labeled an annoying person. If you ask questions, you can't accept racism," he said. "If you ask questions, you can't accept violence. You might be able to accept it for ten, twenty years, even, but after a while, if you keep questioning, it all falls apart. Maybe our national slogan should be, 'Don't ask, don't tell.'"

In 2005, Yossi visited Jerusalem's first gay pride march out of curiosity. He arrived at the end of the event, finding himself in a scene of chaos. A young man had just lunged into a crowd of marchers and slashed three men with a knife he had just purchased. The perpetrator turned out to be a thirty-year-old ultra-Orthodox fanatic named Yishai Shlisel. "I came to murder on behalf of God. We can't have such abomination in the country," the unrepentant Shlisel said afterward. Yossi remembered Shlisel from his *yeshiva* days. "I realized then that if I had stayed, if I hadn't asked questions, that he could have been me," he said of the fanatical slasher.

Having suffered inside the two most powerful institutions in Israeli society, the army and the synagogue, Yossi finally found a measure of personal freedom studying for his graduate degree in sociology at Hebrew University. There, he explored issues of identity and his own connection to the Middle East through the radical Mizrahi discourse pioneered by academics such as Ella Shohat and Sami Shitrit. Yossi was born into a Tunisian family and saw himself as a part of the Arab world, defying the typical Israeli orientation toward Europe. He recalled the days before Oslo, before the separation, when he could take trips to Gaza with his grandfather, who spoke Arabic and employed Palestinians on his farm. One day, while standing in a market in Gaza City, his grandfather pointed back toward Israel, to the Ashkenazim, and remarked, "These are our cousins." Then, motioning to the Palestinians in the street, he declared, "These are our brothers."

"He completely reversed the dynamic we were raised on in Israel," Yossi said. "It made a big impression on me."

Before we left for the *Torat Ha'Melech* congress, Yossi showed me how to dab water on a knit *kippa* so that it would stay affixed to my head. We posed as modern Orthodox settler types out of concern that the secular media might not be particularly welcome at such a gathering, and that participants might be more open to volunteering their opinions to fellow religious Jews. On the bus ride to the Ramada Renaissance Hotel, I noticed that the young *haredi* women who normally treated me as though I were invisible were making eye contact, and holding their gaze for uncomfortably long periods.

"Do you think the *Torat Ha'Melech* authors can offer any dating tips?" I asked Yossi.

"Yeah. Make lots of Jewish babies."

Outside the conference hall, in a 1970s-era hotel lobby decked out with mirror columns, track lighting, and fake plants, a clean-cut, thirty-something man with a knit *kippa* checked our IDs, presumably to confirm that we had Jewish names, then waved us in with an approving nod. In the hall, prayers had just begun. Now I was swaying from side to side with a crowd of bearded settlers, chanting along to every prayer I could remember. Nearby stood a secular-looking young man with a red Golani Brigade T-shirt. Yossi recognized him as an Im Tirtzu activist from Hebrew University. His shirt showed a crude drawing of a ferocious-looking tank above the slogan, "Force Without Mercy."

At the conclusion of prayers, eight major state-funded rabbis ambled up to the platform above the crowd, most representing an official *yeshiva* from a settlement or major Israeli city. With their long, gray beards, black suits, black fedoras, and wizened, wizardly appearances, they looked as though they had been lifted from the imagination of some deranged anti-Semite. And here they were to defend a book that openly justified the mass slaughter of gentile babies, though to be sure, not all were willing to say that they agreed with its contents. The only point the rabbis agreed on, at least openly, was that the state should never scrutinize or punish the speech of religious authorities. With their penchant for firebreathing tirades against Arabs, homosexuals, and other evildoers, these rabbis knew they were next in line if Shapira and Elitzur were officially prosecuted.

Yaakov Yosef was escorted into the gathering by Baruch Marzel, a notoriously violent leader of the Jewish terrorist group, Kach. Up at the podium, Yosef hailed Marzel as a "gever," or a great man of honor. Yosef was the son of Ovadiah Yosef, the spiritual guide of the Shas Party and former Chief Sephardic Rabbi of Israel. Despite Ovadiah Yosef's penchant for outrageous ravings ("Goyim were born only to serve. Without that, they have no place in the world," he proclaimed in a weekly sermon), he opposed the publication of *Torat Ha'Melech*, calling it "racist" and dangerous to Israel's international image. But since joining the extremist, cultic Jewish sect of Chabad, Yaakov had taken on a decidely more radical posture than his father. (Elitzur was a Chabad rabbi.)

In his speech, Yosef attempted to couch *Torat Ha'Melech* within the mainstream tradition of the Torah. Quoting from Psalms Chapter 79 in order to demonstrate the book's supposed consistency with established Halakhic teachings, Yosef declared, "Pour out your wrath on the nations that do not acknowledge you, on the kingdoms that do not call on your name; for they have devoured Jacob and destroyed his homeland." He then reminded his audience of the Passover tale. "We asked the Jewish people, 'You don't want to read from the Hagadah at the Passover table [citing the slaughter of non-Jews]? Does anyone want to change the Bible or the statements of the Torah?" Shapira and Elitzur's only crime, Yosef claimed, was remaining faithful to the oral and written statements contained in the Torah.

Next, Rabbi Haim Druckman, rose to speak. A former member of Knesset and winner of the 2012 Israel Prize for education, Druckman was a figurehead of Jewish extremism in Israel. In 1980, after a group of settlers embarked on a semi-successful terror plot to maim the leading Palestinian mayors of the West Bank (they crippled the mayors of Nablus and Ramallah), Druckman celebrated: "Thus may all of Israel's enemies perish!" Hunched over the podium, the hoarse-throated Druckman was careful to avoid endorsing the contents of *Torat Ha'Melech*, volunteering only that he "hope[d] what happened here will end soon and that we will never have to make such conferences again."

A more strident statement of support came from Rabbi Yehoshua Shapira, head of the state-sponsored yeshiva in the Tel Aviv suburb of Ramat Gan. Yehoshua Shapira bellowed, "The obligation to sacrifice your life is above all others when fighting those who wish to destroy the authority of the Torah. It is not only true against non-Jews who are trying to destroy it but against Jewish people from any side."

Outside the conference hall, where the Kahanist Knesset member Michael Ben-Ari milled around with Baruch Marzel and Itamar Ben-Gvir, another aide he pulled from the ranks of Kach, Yossi and I chatted with a twenty-two-year-old settler who spoke to us in an American accent. We demanded to know if he was willing to defend the provisions in *Torat Ha'Melech* justifying the murder of innocent children. Without hesitation or any initial shame, the young man, who refused to give his name, told us, "There is such a concept in Jewish law as an enemy population, and under very, very specific circumstances, according to various rabbinic opinions, it would be seemingly permissible to kill, uh, uh . . ."

For a moment, he trailed off, and his eyes darted around the room. But the settler managed to collect himself and complete his statement. "To kill children," he muttered uncomfortably.

The genocidal philosophy expressed in *Torat Ha'Melech* emerged from the fevered atmosphere of a settlement called Yitzhar located in the northern West Bank near the Palestinian city of Nablus. There, Shapira helps lead the settlement's Od Yosef Chai yeshiva, holding sway over a small army of fanatics eager to terrorize the Palestinians tending to their crops and livestock in the valleys below them.

Shapira was raised in an influential religious nationalist family. Like Yaakov Yosef, he took a radical turn after joining the Chabad sect under the tutelage of Rabbi Yitzchok Ginsburgh, the director of Yitzhar's Od Yosef Chai *yeshiva* who defended seven of his students who murdered an innocent Palestinian girl by asserting the superiority of Jewish blood. In 1994, when the Jewish fanatic Baruch Goldstein massacred twenty-nine Palestinian worshippers at the Cave of the Patriarchs in Hebron, Ginsburgh lionized Goldstein in a lengthy article entitled "Baruch, Hagever," or "Baruch, the Great Man." Ginsburgh cast Goldstein's murder spree as an act consistent with core Halakhic teachings, from the importance of righteous revenge to the necessity of the "eradication of the seed of Amalek."

Under the direction of Ginsburgh and Shapira, Od Yosef Chai has raked in nearly $50,000 from the Israeli Ministry of Social Affairs since 2007. The Israeli Ministry of Education has supplemented the government's support by pumping over 250 thousand dollars into the *yeshiva*'s coffers between 2006 and 2007. Od Yosef Chai has also benefited handsomely from donations from a tax-exempt American non-profit called the Central Fund of Israel. Located inside the Marc Brothers Textiles store in Midtown Manhattan, the Central Fund transferred at least $30,000 to Od Yosef Chai between 2007 and 2008. (Itamar Marcus, the brother of Central Fund founder Kenneth, is the director of Palestine Media Watch, a pro-Israel organization ironically dedicated to exposing Palestinian incitement). In April 2013, the Israeli government finally announced that it would cease funding Od Yosef Chai, citing the *yeshiva* as a threat to public safety.

Though he did not specify the identity of the non-Jewish "enemy" in the pages of his book, Rabbi Shapira's longstanding connection to terrorist attacks against Palestinian civilians exposes the true identity of his targets. In 2006, another rabbi in Shapira's *yeshiva*, Yossi Peli, was briefly held by Israeli police for urging his supporters to murder all Palestinian males over the age of thirteen. Two years later, Shapira was questioned by Shin Bet under suspicion that he helped orchestrate a homemade rocket attack against a Palestinian village near Nablus. Though he was released, Shapira's name arose in connection with another act of terror, when in January 2010 the Israeli police raided his settlement seeking the vandals who set fire to a nearby mosque. After arresting ten settlers, the Shin Bet held five of Shapira's confederates under suspicion of arson. None ever saw the inside of a prison cell.

Asked if the students at the Oded Yosef Chai *yeshiva* were taking the law into their own hands in attacking Palestinians, one of Shapira's colleagues, Rabbi David Dudkevitch, replied, "The issue is not taking the law into our hands, but rather taking the entire State into our hands."

Jewish settler violence has been a fact of life in the occupied West Bank since the 1970s. Since 2007, however, settler violence has spiked dramatically. A 2008 article in *Ha'aretz* attributed the rise in attacks to the 2005 withdrawal of settlers from the Gaza Strip, after which West Bank settlers vowed to answer each state action against them by with a "price tag" assault on Palestinians, thus establishing a deterrent "balance of terror."

But a detailed analysis of documented settler attacks that occurred during the past decade by the Washington-based research institute, the Palestine Center revealed the violence as structural, not reactive. Staged without pretext and most frequently in West Bank areas under Israeli security control, the settlers acted without restraint. The report identified northern settlements such as Yitzhar as hotbeds of violent activity, with shooting attacks and arson on the rise. According to Yesh Din, an Israeli human rights group, the Israeli police closed 91 percent of investigations into settler attacks without indicting anyone, and usually failed to locate the suspects.

According to a March 2011 Ynet-Gesher poll of 504 Israeli adults, 48 percent of Israelis supported settler violence in retaliation to Palestinian or Israeli government actions, with only 33 percent stating their belief that settler violence was "never justified." While a vast majority of Orthodox and religious nationalist respondents expressed strong support for settler attacks, 36 percent of secular Israelis did as well—a remarkably high number for a population that lives primarily inside the Green Line.

While Ginsburgh and Shapira provided the halakhic seal of approval for settler rampages in the north of the West Bank, in the south, their comrade, Dov Lior, the chief rabbi of Hebron, has cheered on the murder of anyone, Jew or non-Jew, who appeared to interfere with the redemptive cause of Greater Israel. At the funeral for Baruch Goldstein, Lior extolled the mass killer as "a righteous man" who was "holier than all the martyrs of the Holocaust." Thanks in part to Lior's efforts, a shrine to Goldstein stands inside the Jewish settlement of Kiryat Arba, where Lior presides over the *yeshiva*. At the same time, Lior pronounced Prime Minister Yitzhak Rabin a *moser* (a Jew who snitches to the goyim) and a *rodef* (a traitor worthy of elimination), helping establish the religious justification for Yigal Amir, one of Lior's admirers, to assassinate him.

Lior's penchant for overheated, fascistic tirades has not diminished with age. He has warned Jewish women not to allow in vitro fertilization with the sperm of non-Jews, claiming that "gentile sperm leads to barbaric offspring," described Arabs as "evil camel riders" and said captive Palestinian militants could be used as subjects for live human experiments. The short, gray-bearded rabbi has even held forth on the evils of "boogie woogie," declaring that rock and roll "expresses people's animalistic and lower urges." He added, "Something that belongs to the rhythms of *kushim* [Negroes] does not belong in our world."

Thanks to the growing corps of religious nationalist youth signing up for army service after studying in *hesder yeshivas*, or institutions of religious learning that train young men for the military, Lior has secured considerable influence inside the military. In 2008, when the chief rabbi of the Israeli army, Brigadier General Avichai Ronski, brought a group of military intelligence officers to Hebron for a special tour, he concluded the day with a private meeting with Lior, who was allowed to regale the officers with his views on modern warfare, which includes vehement support for the collective punishment of Palestinians. Ronski, for his part, has overseen the distribution of extremist tracts to soldiers during Operation Cast Lead, including "Baruch, Hagever," and a pamphlet stating, "When you show mercy to a cruel enemy, you are being cruel to pure and honest soldiers."

In October 2009, a group of soldiers from the army's notoriously abusive Shimshon Battalion upheld a protest banner vowing to refuse orders to evacuate settlements during a swearing-in ceremony at the Western Wall—"Shimshon does not expel." When the army punished the two soldiers who organized the display of disloyalty by ejecting them from the unit, rabbis Ginsburgh and Lior promptly planned a religious revival in Jerusalem in their honor. A source told the *Jerusalem Post* that the ceremony would include the mass distribution of the newly published *Torat Ha'Melech*. Weeks after the incident, two more major Israeli army brigades, Nahson and Kfir, decorated their training bases with banners announcing their refusal to evacuate settlements.

Less than two years later, Matanya Ofan, the cofounder of a Jewish extremist media outlet based in Yitzhar, appeared in a viral online video in full army uniform, cradling an army-issued M-16 in one hand and a copy of *Torat Ha'Melech* in the other. The book had come to represent the unofficial code of the religious nationalist soldier. Staring into the camera, Ofan declared, "When I come at the border, with God's grace, I will not listen to the nonsense that the commanders will tell me, and if I see an enemy coming towards the border I will do anything to stop him from passing and I will try and harm him—because this is how we can save the lives of the

Jews. Only this way no Sudani or Syrian will get to Tel Aviv." A caption at the end of the video read, "Jews, let's win."

By this time, the ranks of the army were overrun by religious nationalists, with more than a third of infantry officers expressing a right-wing religious point of view—a 30 percent jump since 1990. A 2010 study showed that 13 percent of company commanders lived in West Bank settlements. The army's second-in-command, Deputy Chief of Staff Yair Naveh, was the first religious officer appointed to a position on the General Staff. He was also the officer implicated in the Anat Kamm scandal for ordering the assassination of Palestinian militants in flagrant violation of a Supreme Court ruling.

Another prominent religious Zionist was Yaakov Amidror, the former director of the analysis wing of the army's military intelligence and commander of its officer academies. A settler with a puffy white beard (imagine a demographics threat-obsessed Santa-for-hire), Amidror was appointed by Prime Minister Benjamin Netanyahu to serve as the director of his National Security Council. Besides advocating the reoccupation of the Gaza Strip, Amidror stirred controversy by calling for summary executions of Israeli soldiers who refused to advance in battle, and for using disproportionate force against the enemy's civilian population. "What should be said is 'kill more of the bastards on the other side, so that we'll win.' Period," he bellowed during a panel discussion on "National Values in the Israel Defense Forces."

While Amidror's views appeared to dovetail with some of those of the authors of *Torat Ha'Melech*, he did not dare defend them. This was a job for Rabbis Lior and Yaakov Yosef, who became the most prominent apologists, if not the most enthusiastic boosters, of *Torat Ha'Melech*. In early 2011, with the controversy over the book still raging across Israel, Yosef and Lior provided the supreme rabbinical stamp of approval: a *haskama*, the kind of endorsement provided at the preface of Judaic works by scholars testifying to their halakhic value and the veracity of their contents. "I was gladdened, seeing this wonderful creation," Lior said of the book.

That February, the minister of Internal Security issued an arrest warrant for Lior after he refused to come in for questioning on suspicion of incitement to racism, a crime in Israel that is seldom punished, but which carries a penalty of as much as five years in prison. Lior rejected the state's order on the grounds that he had no obligation to abide by its rules; the Torah itself was being put on trial, he claimed. Thus the self-proclaimed voice of Judaism in its purest form placed himself above the law.

Meanwhile, the arrest order provoked calls for total resistance from right-wing members of Knesset like Yaakov Katz, who said the government was behaving like the "dark regimes" that persecuted Jews throughout history, casting the attorney general in the role of Nazis and Pharoahs. Twenty-four members of Netanyahu's coalition, including David Rotem, the chair of the Knesset's Constitution, Law and Justice Committee, joined Katz in denouncing Lior's arrest. Both chief rabbis of Israel, Yona Metzger and Shlomo Amar, issued a joint statement denouncing the arrest of a man they called "one of Israel's greatest rabbis."

The religious right's ire exploded at a boisterous protest outside the Supreme Court in July 2011, with hundreds of young settlers breaching a wall outside the courthouse and attempting to storm the building. That same month, when two right-wing activists were caught breaking into his home, Shai Nitzan, the deputy state prosecutor, was forced to travel with a special security detail.

In May 2012, the government buckled under unrelenting pressure—the right-wing caved to the far-right—with Attorney General Yehuda Weinstein ruling that he had insufficient evidence to conclude that *Torat Ha'Melech* incited racism, mainly because the book was written in a "general manner." Lior walked free along with the book's authors, Shapira and Elitzur, consolidating their political dominance while ensuring that the tract they produced would continue circulating freely within the ranks of the army. Astonished by the state's decision, Sefi Rachlevsky, a liberal columnist for *Ha'aretz*, pronounced Lior "the ruler of Israel."

Having successfully exerted its influence on the military and the justice system, the religious right set out into mixed cities across Israel to promote segregation and punish miscegenation in a campaign that spread block by block, street by street.

The Daughters of Israel

"We castrated you! We castrated you, Mohammed!" members of the Palmach strike force sang during the 1940s, celebrating an incident in which an undercover intelligence unit punished an Arab man for attempting to rape a Jewish woman living in a nearby kibbutz. Palmach founder Yitzhak Sade provided his men with courses on castration at a local hospital, training them to punish the male other who threatened the honor of the Jewish collective with calculated, clinically executed brutality.

Two of his students, Yohai Bin-Nun, who went on to found the Israeli Navy, and Amos Horev, later the president of the Technion and an original member of the Turkel Commission of Inquiry into the Gaza Flotilla Raid, hunted down the Arab suspect and dragged him into an open field. There, according to the Israeli historian Gamliel Cohen, they "deal[t] with him in accordance with the biblical principle that calls for the chopping off of a thief's hand and which, in this case, would call for attacking the organ he used to perform the crime, namely, for castrating him."

The fear of the indigenous male's sexuality struck terror in the hearts of Israelis, provoking widespread hysteria and violent countermeasures. In a purely strategic sense, castrations carried out by the Palmach under the guidance of medical professionals were designed as a deterrent against further sexual attacks, instilling terror in the Palestinian rural population while restoring the confidence of Jewish women living in adjacent *kibbutzim*. But they also contained a deeper significance that found its roots in *fin de siècle* European colonialism. Through its brazen castrations, the Palmach militia sought to symbolically neuter the Palestinian national movement, asserting Zionist dominance in a struggle between two patriarchal societies where virility and victory were intertwined.

During the early years of Zionist settlement in Palestine, the kibbutz movement tasked Jewish women with an equal role in labor and the military required her to serve in some capacity, but her most essential function was as the national womb. "Any Jewish woman who does not bring into the world at least four healthy children is comparable to a soldier who evades military service," said David Ben Gurion, the first prime minister. In order to establish the stability of its ethnocratic political structure, Israel's founders demanded policies of selective pronatalism that aimed to maximize the production of Jewish babies while keeping the Arab population to a minimum. As Ben Gurion said, "Any future pronatal policies must be administered by the Jewish Agency and not the state because its aim is to increase the number of Jews and not the total population."

In the years after Israel's establishment, the state rewarded women for giving birth to their tenth child with the "heroine mothers" award. The program was discontinued a decade later, however, when state planners discovered that most of those eligible for the prize were Arabs. Until the late 1950s, birth control was banned, as was abortion until 1976. The motives for such restrictive policies were not moral, as in the United States, but nationalistic—women's reproductive rights were seen as a threat to Jewish demography. In 1967, Prime Minister Levi Eshkol established a demographics center that inspired policies providing a range of substantial benefits to families with more than three Jewish children.

Just as the state incentivized Jewish reproduction, reducing Jewish women to human incubators, it prioritized separation from the indigenous population to protect its demographic advantage. To encourage the exclusion of Arabs from the workplace, the early Zionist left introduced the concept of *Kibush Ha'avodah,* or "the conquest of labor."

The boycott of Arab labor flowed directly into the left-wing Israeli peace camp's Oslo-era slogan, "Them over there, over here," which became the motto of Ehud Barak's 1999 campaign for reelection as prime minister. The ultimate manifestation of Zionist left ideology arrived with construction of the separation wall, a demographic Maginot Line designed to produce the virtual disappearance of Palestinians from Israeli life. Explaining his support for the wall, Barak told the liberal Israeli activist and conflict resolution specialist Gershon Baskin that his ultimate goal was to restore the values of *Kibush Ha'Avodah* by eliminating the presence of Palestinian laborers inside Israel, an aim he was already accomplishing by revoking their work permits by the thousands.

The Ashkenazi elite who guided the policy of separation enjoyed the greatest distance from Palestinians, their "villa in the jungle," as Barak said. But among the lower rungs of Jewish society, especially those deliberately planted in development cities in the "periphery," Arabs and, in more recent years, migrants from Africa were a constant presence in daily life.

Having seized the reins of the state from the old left-wing Zionist establishment, the religious right plunged into the mixed cities to stir moral panic, and to tap into their resentment against the Ashkenazi elite, hoping to extract publicity and droves of new followers from the crisis their presence inevitably stirred. Once again, the Jewish woman emerged as a symbol of purity in peril who demanded ironclad protection and, if necessary, commando-style rescue operations.

In December 2010, around fifty state-sanctioned Israeli rabbis including chief rabbis from suburbs of Tel Aviv issued a *psak din,* or a public religious edict, urging Israelis against renting to Arabs and other non-Jews. The letter was complemented with a second edict signed by twenty-seven of the rabbis' wives warning young Jewish women against dating or marrying Arabs, and urging them to avoid working in areas where Arabs might be lurking. "Your grandmothers never dreamed or prayed that one of their descendants would commit an act that would remove future generations of her family from the Jewish people," the wives wrote. Among the signatories of the letter were the spouses of leading state-sponsored rabbis including Haim Druckman and Dov Lior. The wife of Ovadiah Yosef, the spiritual guide of the Shas Party, and the wife of his son, Yaakov, also lent their names to the manifesto.

In the letters, the rabbis cited a genocidal verse from the Bible (Deuteronomy 7:2) to justify their position. The verse read:

> When your god, Yahweh, brings you to the land that you are going to inherit, he will banish other nations. . . . And your god, Yahweh, will deliver them to you, and you will strike them down. Utterly destroy them, and do not sign any pacts with them. Show them no mercy. And do not intermarry with them. Do not give your daughters to their sons, and do not take their daughters for your sons. . . . But instead do this to them: Shatter their altars, and break their monuments, and chop down their goddess figures, and burn their idols. Because you are a holy people to your god Yahweh, he chose you to be his special people from all the nations in the world.

Both rabbinical letters were initiated by Shmuel Eliyahu, the chief rabbi of the northern mixed city of Safed, and the son of Mordechai Eliyahu, the former Sephardic chief rabbi of Israel and until his death, one of the most revered figures of Israel's Orthodox community. Like many of his rabbinical peers, Eliyahu distinguished himself with a mixture of kabbalistic wisdom and naked enthusiasm for genocide.

In 2007, the rabbi called for "carpet bombing" the Gaza Strip, writing that if the Palestinians do not stop firing rockets "after [we kill] 1,000 then we must kill 10,000. If they still don't stop we must kill 100,000, even a million. Whatever it takes to make them stop." The following year, Eliyahu suggested the army lynch the children of Arab terrorists from trees as revenge.

Eliayhu also was responsible for a pamphlet whose publication he arranged by the Union of Orthodox Jewish Congregations of America that claimed Pope Benedict and the Vatican organized tours of Auschwitz for Hezbollah terrorists to train them how to wipe out Jews—a pamphlet that was distributed to elite units of the Israeli army. "The book is distributed regularly and everyone reads it and believes it," one soldier told *Ha'aretz*. "A whole company of soldiers, adults, told me: 'Read this and you'll understand who the Arabs are.'" The pamphlet quoted as its source a supposed Hezbollah spy who was on the Vatican-sponsored Auschwitz tour: "We came to the camps. We saw the trains, the platforms, the piles of eyeglasses and clothes. . . . We came to learn. . . . Our escort spoke as he was taught. We quickly explained to him: Every real Arab, deep inside, is kind of a fan of the Nazis." When *Ha'aretz* exposed the patently risible conspiracy mongering, the IDF Spokesperson's Unit released a statement: "The book was received as a donation and distributed in good faith to the soldiers. After we were alerted to the sensitivity of its content, distribution was immediately halted."

With the two edicts he organized, Eliyahu emerged as a nationally significant figure. Prime Minister Benjamin Netanyahu denounced the rabbinical letters as undemocratic and un-Jewish, while the Likud Party's grand old man, Knesset

Speaker Reuven Rivlin, called them "another nail in the coffin of Israeli democracy." But the Israeli public came down less decisively, with only a narrow plurality—48 to 44 percent—expressing opposition to the segregationist manifestoes.

With outrage over Eliyahu's proclamations building among the secular Israeli intelligentsia, and within establishment political circles concerned over Israel's worsening international image, the Israeli police ordered him to appear for questioning over suspicion that he had committed the crime of inciting racial hatred. Eliyahu followed in the footsteps of his comrade Rabbi Dov Lior and refused to honor the order, declaring that he too was above the unholy law of the secular state. Amid calls for Netanyahu to strip the rabbi of his publicly funded position, the government did nothing. And the racism Eliyahu inspired spread into synagogues and cities across the country.

An article in the family-oriented Orthodox magazine *Fountains of Salvation*, a popular religious nationalist publication distributed to synagogues around Israel, lambasted the rabbis who opposed Eliyahu's letter. The author of the article swiftly descended into an apparent endorsement of Arab genocide. "It will be interesting to see whether [the rabbinical critics of the letter] leave the assembly of the Amelekites [Palestinians] in extermination camps to others, or whether they declare that wiping out Amalek is no longer [historically] relevant," he wrote. "Only time will tell." On the next page of the magazine, a manifesto by Eliayhu demanded the illegalization of abortion, a practice he cast as both evil and a grave threat to Jewish demographics.

Days after the publication of the rabbinical letters, Israel's burgeoning anti-miscegenation movement took its campaign into the streets. The first target was the Tel Aviv suburb of Bat Yam. Populated largely by the Russian-Jewish working class, the area was witnessing an increasing influx of young Palestinian couples and families denied housing in nearby Jaffa, where the Tel Aviv municipality refused to authorize new units for Arabs in order to pursue a campaign of aggressive gentrification for the nearly exclusive benefit of affluent Jews from Tel Aviv.

In a society where assimilation was officially discouraged, social friction naturally accompanied the increasing Arab presence, with the rare mixed Jewish-Muslim relationship exacerbating the situation. But there was no evidence to support wild claims like the kind leveled by Likudnik member of Knesset Danny Danon, who announced from the parliament floor that Bedouins were responsible for one thousand kidnappings of Jewish girls each year. Indeed, there was no factual basis to claim that Jewish-Arab relationships or marriages were on the rise, or that they were responsible for any of the troubles afflicting blue-collar communities. If anything, by spreading fear of widespread kidnappings, casting the daughters of Israel as prey for Arab predators, right-wing elements distracted from the real sources of the myriad economic problems facing working class Israelis, thus enabling the predations of the country's oligarchic elite.

On December 18, 2010, soon after the release of the publication of the rabbis' letters, Bat Yam was plastered with posters reading "Keep Bat Yam Jewish." Other posters read, "Hundreds of girls from Bat Yam and the center get together with Arabs, they are integrated among us, their confidence rising. Put an end to it! Lower their confidence!"

The following day, about two hundred religious nationalists marched into the town center to rally against Jewish-Arab relationships. They were joined by a substantial group of secular locals who supported the "Arabs out" theme of the protest, while a small crowd of left-wing demonstrators from Tel Aviv chanted nearby against racism. Rabbi Shlomo Ariel Malka, the rabbi of a synagogue in the city, proclaimed before the crowd, "A woman who goes to an Arab home is hated by them. God will bless when he opens our sisters' eyes." His warning was echoed by Rabbi Nissim Itah, the rabbi of a Bat Yam school. "Girls, there are plenty of Jewish youth. I am asking our Arab neighbor not to hit on our girls," Itah said. Driven into a frenzy by the rabbis, one demonstrator cried out, "Any Jewish woman who goes with an Arab should be killed! Any Jew who sells his home to an Arab should be killed!"

Behind the rally was a newly formed anti-miscegenation group called SOS Israel, or Lehava, which is the Hebrew acronym for "The Organization for Preventing Assimilation in the Holy Land." The group's founder Benzi Gopstein promoted the rabbis' letter as the opening salvo in a nationwide campaign against interreligious relationships. Like many of the figures who gathered around the banner of Lehava, Gopstein was an open admirer of Rabbi Meir Kahane, the Jewish fascist leader who advocated the forced expulsion of all non-Jews from Greater Israel. In 1990, Gopstein was arrested on suspicion of murdering a random Palestinian couple in the West Bank as revenge for Kahane's assassination by an Arab Muslim in New York City. The crime was never solved. Four years later, Gopstein hailed the fanatic Baruch Goldstein as a "hero" after his shooting spree claimed the lives of twenty-nine Palestinians in Hebron.

With the publication of the rabbis' letters, Gopstein took on the role of street-level enforcer, ensuring that businesses that employed Arabs were boycotted and landlords who rented to non-Jews were sufficiently punished. A supermarket in the settlement of Gush Etzion that employed Arab men and Jewish women was the first target of a Lehava boycott. Then Lehava opened a hotline that encouraged Israelis to report landlords who rented to Arabs and African migrants. Mock kosher certificates issued by Lehava began appearing in storefronts from Jerusalem to Safed, signifying the enforcement of the Jews-only business environment. In 2011, Gopstein formed an "anti-assimilation Coast Guard," dispatching bands of vigilantes onto Israeli beaches to warn Jewish women against dating Arab men. "Organizers hope this campaign will stop the phenomenon of mixed marriages," a Lehava press release read, "and restore 'the values needed to preserve Israel.'"

One of the first victims of a Lehava-inspired boycott was Eli Tzvieli, an eighty-nine-year-old Holocaust survivor and ex-social worker living in Safed. Tzvieli supplemented his pension by renting rooms in his house to three Arabs studying at a local college. "They are nice boys," he said of his tenants. But in December 2010, following a conference held in town called "Quiet War: Combating Assimilation in the Holy City of Safed," and then the notorious rabbis' letter, Tzvieli was bombarded with death threats. Notices denouncing him as a traitor to Judaism were regularly posted on his door. Even a young, secular neighbor who rented a café out of one of Tzvieli's properties told a reporter he thought his landlord was "wrong" and should "listen to what people say."

"We feel threatened, we feel helpless. They don't want us here. We came to learn in peace, not to make war," said one of Tzvieli's renters, a nineteen-year-old Palestinian citizen of Israel named Nimran Grefat.

Presented by a reporter with criticism that Lehava's segregationist crusades seethed with racism, Baruch Marzel, a Kahanist settler and leading supremacist activist, fired back with a deft retort. Like many figures of Israel's religious right, Marzel justified his activities as the natural progression of a cause inaugurated by Israel's founding generation. "If this is racism," the bearded Marzel bellowed in thickly accented English, "then the Jewish state is racism, the Torah is racism, the Jewish National Fund that only sells land to Jews is racism, and everything is racism!"

While Lehava relied on intimidation and public relations stunts to enforce religious and sexual segregation, a closely affiliated organization called Hemla, or "Mercy," dedicated itself to the salvation of Orthodox Jewish women supposedly corrupted by unholy relationships with Arab men. On a leafy street in a residential neighborhood in Jerusalem sits Hemla's hostel, a home that claims to provide shelter and therapy to Jewish women "rescued" from hyper-possessive, predatory Palestinian men. Hemla claimed to be tending to at least twenty women in 2011, however, when two reporters from *Ha'aretz* arrived at the home, they found it completely empty except for a single staffer. Under orders from Hemla's director, Rachel Baranes, the staffer ordered the journalists to leave the premises.

Baranes had joined avowed supporters of the late Meir Kahane to operate Hemla. She was also a signatory of the rabbis' wives letter urging Jewish women to avoid Arab men. "Hemla was established for the purpose of building a warm home in order to help girls—saving Jewish girls from assimilation, whether it's foreign workers, Arabs, [or] people with no connection to our religion," Baranes said in an interview with an Orthodox cable channel. Assisting Baranes as Hemla's director of public relations was Benzi Gopstein, the director of Lehava and veteran Kahanist, and Rabbi Yehuda Kroizer, who ran the *yeshiva* Kahane established in Jerusalem and receives mail for Hemla at the same address. (Kroizer delivers regular, army-sanctioned lectures for religious combat soldiers). The network of characters behind Hemla revealed the organization as a wing of Lehava and both groups as comprised largely of figures who have been associated with Kahane's outlawed Kach organization.

In fact, the roots of Hemla lay in a hostel for "rescued" Jewish women personally established by Kahane in the settlement of Kiryat Arba in 1984. Among those who volunteered to help at the home was Baruch Goldstein, the man who later massacred twenty-nine Palestinians at the Cave of Patriarchs. During the brief period the hostel operated, it housed no more than four women, all victims of domestic abuse who left almost as soon as they arrived.

When the organization reconstituted in 2005 as Hemla, it gained a material advantage Kahane never had: direct government funding. According to documents revealed by *Ha'aretz*, the Israeli Ministry of Social Affairs has supported Hemla's operations with around $250,000 in taxpayer money every year—about half the organization's annual budget. "We can't say that we won't fund the association because the director wrote a racist letter or disseminates hatred," a Social Affairs Ministry spokesman claimed, "because we're not the ones who decide on that—our hands are tied and I can't intervene, it's the job of the Attorney General."

Hemla was rivaled by another outfit of the Jewish far-right called Yad L'Achim, which boasted of commando-style raids to rescue Jewish girls and young women supposedly trapped in Palestinian villages. Based in the Orthodox Jewish Tel Aviv suburb of Bnei Barak, Yad L'Achim once relied on the volunteer service of Jack Teitel, an immigrant from the United States who was eventually convicted of serial killing. According to reports in the religious nationalist media, Yad L'Achim conducted its rescue missions with close army coordination. A January 2012 raid that allegedly delivered an abused Jewish woman from her Palestinian husband in the West Bank city of Tulkarm required "advance permission from a senior IDF officer," according to the settler news outlet Arutz Sheva. The news site reported, "One of [the rescued Jewish woman's] first actions was to take off her Muslim garb and tell Yad L'Achim officials, 'Throw them in the trash can.'"

Rabbi Shalom Dov Lifschitz, the founder of Yad L'Achim, marketed his organization's efforts as a countermeasure against the Palestinian campaign of "non-conventional warfare." "People must understand that Jewish-Arab marriages are part of the larger Israeli-Arab conflict," Lifschitz said in a promotional article posted on Yad L'Achim's website. "These girls are in distress, they are wandering the streets and the Arabs take advantage of them. They see it as their goal to marry them and ensure that their children aren't raised as Jews. This is their revenge against the Jewish people. They feel that if they can't defeat us in war, they can wipe us out this way. We must fight this threat as well; it's a matter of national security."

Like Lehava, Yad L'Achim has focused its propaganda efforts on the Jewish residents of mixed cities in Israel, distributing videos and pamphlets warning of the sexual danger supposedly presented by Arab males. A lurid, Yad L'Achim–produced video distributed by the thousands, opened with graphic scenes of Palestinian violence against Israelis, then segued into recorded testimonies by Jewish women describing how Arab men courted them with gifts and lofty promises before holding them as virtual captives in their villages.

In an anonymous testimony of captivity, a Jewish woman recalled how her Palestinian ex-boyfriend "portrayed [his village] quite like living in a kibbutz or an Israeli cooperative agricultural village. Just as I entered, the abuse began. I was already pregnant. . . . Even though I converted into Islam, they reminded me that I was always Jewish, and there was nothing I could do about it. And every time there was a terror attack, you should see their happiness. Our people died, and they held celebrations all night long. And when somebody of theirs died from the fire of our soldiers, I was beaten with hard blows."

Next a baritone voiced narrator appeals to viewers: "We are surrounded with Arabs that hate us in any direction we look, and the Arabs that live among us and suck on our honey, become stronger, and there is not much time until they control the country. And when it will happen, we will be in a crisis, because their hate is something we can't even imagine! We are only left with helping each other, we're only left with strengthening one another."

Finally, an animated sequence depicts the righteous hand of Yahweh striking down the Dome of the Rock with thunderous fury, revealing the foundation of the Temple Mount. As the gloomy skies over Jerusalem rapidly clear, signaling the removal of the Islamic occupation of Eretz Israel, a flock of doves floats blithely across the horizon. The video closes with plea for donations: "If you have fallen into such a situation and you need help, call free now. Lev L'Achim . . . Yad L'Achim. This movie is for the rescue of the daughters of Israel from the captivity of the Enemy."

Children Whose Hearts Were Unmoved

Since I first arrived in Israeli-controlled territory, hardly a week passed without a few incidents of unprovoked violence against the Arab outclass, particularly in the occupied West Bank, where settlers were afforded carte blanche to rampage across Palestinian land. But the final eleven days of 2010 seemed to bear a special quality.

The violence centered at first in southern Tel Aviv, a working-class area inhabited by Mizrahi Jews who had grown irate with the presence of thousands of African asylum seekers and migrant workers increasingly residing in their neighborhood, and taking the place of the Palestinian laborers blocked from entering Israel by the new regime of demographic separation. On December 17, 2010, three teenage girls born to African refugee parents were assaulted and badly beaten by a mob of Jewish youth while walking to their homes in Tel Aviv's Hatikvah neighborhood, an impoverished Mizrahi area. "Israel is facing a wave of hate crimes, crimes whose main motive is the hatred of foreigners," the Hotline for Migrant Workers declared.

The same day, in the development city of Ashdod, an apartment inhabited by seven refugees from Sudan was torched. The assailants left a burning tire outside the front door of the residence, forcing all those inside to break through the burglar bars on their window in order to escape the blaze.

Also that day, in the village of Aqraba in the occupied West Bank, armed settlers from the Ma'ale Efraim settlement, located just south of the Palestinian city of Nablus, arrived on the farmland of Sameer Mohammed Khader Bani Fadel, a forty-year-old shepherd, daring him to walk in their direction. When he refused and attempted to flee, the settlers gathered his goats and burned them alive on a wooden pyre, killing all twelve in his flock. Bani Fadel, a father of six, said the goats were his only source of income. The Israeli army promised an investigation but never made any arrests. According to the Israeli human rights group Yesh Din, 91 percent of investigations into crimes committed by Israelis against Palestinians and their property are closed without indictments being served.

Three days later, hundreds of local residents gathered near the marketplace of Shapira and Hatikvah neighborhoods in southern Tel Aviv to rally against the presence of African refugees in their neighborhood. "When I walk in the neighborhood today, I see that we have become the foreigners," Knesset member Michael Ben-Ari boomed through a megaphone, proposing that the government pay each African

$200 to leave Israel. Also at the protest was Yoel Hasson, a member of the supposedly moderate Kadima Party. "This struggle isn't one of extremists or racists," Hasson said. "It is a struggle of people who want to protect Israel as a Jewish state, and a state for its citizens."

Just hours after the anti-African rally in Tel Aviv, nine Jewish youths were arrested in connection with a wave of hate crime assaults on young Arab men in Jerusalem. At the head of the gang was a fourteen-year-old boy who allegedly used a girl to lure Arab victims to a meeting point in Jerusalem's Independence Park. There, in the darkness of the park, the rest of the gang savaged its victims with rocks, glass bottles, and pepper spray.

"This is not new to us. Almost everyday there's an incident in which settlers attack Arabs," said Hussam Tamimi, a Palestinian resident of East Jerusalem. Jafar Farah, director of the Mossawa Center, an NGO dedicated to Arab legal rights in Israel, said of the youth gang, "These are [Avigdor] Lieberman and [Interior Minister] Eli Yishai's boys." The violence, Farah said, was "a result of the education and legal system, as well as the political environment that does nothing to stop the incitement across the country."

While the mob attacks multiplied across Israel, Christmas approached in Nazareth, the home of Jesus Christ. On December 23, just days before the city's Palestinian residents planned to celebrate the holiday, Shimon Gaspo, the mayor of Nazareth Illit, a mostly Jewish *mitzpe* community adjacent to Nazareth proper, announced a literal War on Christmas, declaring his refusal to tolerate the display of a single Christmas tree within city limits. "Nazareth Illit is a Jewish city and it will not happen—not this year and not next year, so long as I am a mayor," Gaspo proclaimed. Aziz Dahdal, a thirty-five-year-old Palestinian Christian resident of Nazareth Illit, put the ban into context, explaining, "The racism of not putting a tree up is nothing compared to the real racism that we experience here."

The hostile official attitude toward indigenous Christians living inside Israel gradually escalated into a series of vandalism attacks by hardline Jewish nationalists. In September 2012, in the most shocking instance of anti-Christian bigotry in years, a group of nationalist vandals set fire to the door of an ancient Franciscan monastery at Latrun, the only remnant of the Palestinian communities ethnically cleansed from the area in 1967. "Jesus is a monkey," read graffiti spray-painted beside the door, along with the names of two extremist West Bank settlements. A month later, graffiti was scrawled on the door of Jerusalem's Church of the Dormition, a sanctuary built on Mount Zion at the site of the Last Supper: "Jesus, son of a bitch, price tag."

In an official statement, the Assembly of Catholic Ordinaries in the Holy Land pointed blame not at an isolated group of extremists, but at the very structure of Israeli society. "More than anything, the Assembly again asks, that radical changes be made in the educational system, otherwise the same causes will produce the same effects over and over," the statement read.

Reverend Pierbattista Pizzaballa, the top Vatican official in the Holy Land, echoed the Assembly of Catholic Ordinaries, remarking, "When you say 'Christianity' to

Israelis they immediately think of the Holocaust and the [Spanish] Inquisition. People don't know that we are here and have roots here." Though Israeli government officials condemned the attacks on Christian property, none of the vandals were prosecuted or even arrested.

The mounting wave of mob violence culminated in Jerusalem, in the middle of Zion Square, the site of Joseph Dana's and my widely condemned and censored "Feeling the Hate in Jerusalem" video. There, on August 16, 2012, dozens of Jewish teenagers set themselves on three Palestinians innocently strolling through the Ben Yehuda Street pedestrian mall, just feet from the apartment Joseph and I stayed in. After the Jewish youths fled, one of the victims lay unconscious in a pool of blood. Hundreds of bystanders witnessed the attack, but no one had attempted to intercede.

One eyewitness wrote on her Facebook page, "Today I saw a lynch with my own eyes, in Zion Square, the center of the city of Jerusalem . . . and shouts of 'A Jew is a soul and Arab is a son of a bitch,' were shouted loudly and dozens (!!) of youths ran and gathered and started to really beat to death three Arab youths who were walking quietly in the Ben Yehuda street." ("A Jew is a soul" was a popular chant by both settlers and fans of the football club Beitar Jerusalem).

The witness continued: "When two volunteers [from local charities] went into the circle, they tried to perform CPR, and the mass of youths standing around started to say resentfully that we are resuscitating an Arab, and when they passed near and saw that the rest of the volunteers were shocked, they asked why we were so in shock, he is an Arab. When we returned to the area after some time had passed, and the site was marked as a murder scene, and police were there with the cousin of the victim who tried to reenact what happened, two youths stood there who did not understand why we wanted to give a bottle of water to the cousin of the victim who was transferred to hospital in critical condition, he is an Arab, and they don't need to walk around in the center of the city, and they deserve it, because this way they will finally be afraid."

"Children aged fifteen to eighteen are killing a child their own age with their own hands," the eyewitness concluded. "Really with their own hands. Children whose hearts were unmoved when they beat to death a boy their age who lay writhing on the floor."

Less than a week after the mob assault, the Israeli police arrested seven of the approximately fifty teenaged perpetrators, including a thirteen-year-boy and two girls. Inside a Jerusalem courthouse, the main suspect, a fifteen-year-old boy, stood before a gaggle of reporters and boasted of his violent exploits. "For my part, he can die," he said of Jamal Joulani, the seventeen-year-old Palestinian still on a life support machine in a local hospital. "If it was up to me, I'd have murdered him," he added. "Everyone hit him, there were some forty people there and all of them hit him."

According to the Jerusalem police, the Jewish teens began searching for a Palestinian to pulverize when a girl complained to them that she had been raped by an Arab. Later on, under police questioning, the girl admitted that the allegation was false. She had invented it knowing that rumors of sexual advances by young males of the racial out-group against the officially sanctified females of the "white" overclass were enough to provoke a lynching. Decades and continents away, the incident had an underlying dynamic reminiscent of Alabama circa 1931. Outside the courthouse where Joulani's attackers were to stand trial, Lehava's Benzi Gopstein vigorously defended the assailants. "It seems that here the youth raised Jewish pride off the floor," Gopstein told a reporter from Arutz Sheva, "and did what the police should have done. They did justice with the Arab criminals harassing Jewish girls. It is too bad teenagers are given this job instead of the police having to deal with it."

A week after the attack, the Israeli online edition of *Yedioth Ahronoth* dispatched a reporter to the scene of the crime to produce a viral video that looked remarkably similar to "Feeling the Hate." At Zion Square, *Yedioth*'s reporter stumbled onto large groups of drunken Israeli youths celebrating the racial violence they had witnessed. "I saw the whole beating," one teenager exclaimed as though he had witnessed his favorite football team win a league championship, "and it's a good thing they beat the Arabs. [Death] to the Arabs," he said, repeating La Familia's Beitar chant. "They should all die!"

The reporter also encountered Palestinians working in the area who described routine assaults that were never reported or punished. "The truth is that it's dangerous to go around here because . . . there are problems almost every weekend," said one local Palestinian worker, recalling a recent incident in which thirty-four Jewish youths jumped him with glass bottles and screwdrivers, forcing him to rush to the hospital for stitches. In the final scene of the video, dozens of Jewish youths gathered spontaneously before the camera, chanting, "I hate all the Arabs!" until an embarrassed police officer dispersed them.

The young idlers who gather spontaneously at the squares of central Jerusalem each night were probably unaware of the existence of Lehava, but they knew they wanted Arabs removed from their world, and by all means necessary. With an army of teens ready to rampage against Arabs at a moment's notice, Lehava stepped up its threats.

Days after the mob beating in Zion Square, leaflets appeared on streets around occupied East Jerusalem. Written in Hebrew on one side and Arabic on the other, the letters were addressed, "Dear Arab Guy." They read, "We don't want you to get hurt! . . . If you are thinking of visiting Jerusalem malls or the [Ben Yehuda] pedestrian street with the intention of dating Jewish girls—this isn't the place for you. You may walk around in your own village freely and find girlfriends there, not here! Last week an Arab who thought he might find Jewish girls got hurt. We don't wish for you to get hurt, so respect our daughters' honor. As we mind it dearly!—Lehava organization."

Shocking as they might have seemed, the leaflets resembled a Haganah militia note left at the dawn of Israel's foundation on the bleeding body of a Palestinian rape suspect its members castrated on direct orders from David Ben Gurion—"This is what will happen to anyone who rapes Jewish girls." Echoes of the submerged violent past, the leaflets also stood as harbingers of wild, racial violence in the future.

When Kahane Won

A mid the angriest ultra-nationalist gatherings and the displays of their street theater, from protests against Arab-Jewish relationships to demonstrations against the presence of African asylum seekers, there was one man—Michael Ben-Ari—who invariably took hold of the microphone to whip up the crowd. His outrageous stunts ranged from tearing up a New Testament on the Knesset floor to leaping atop an army truck in protest of the arrest of settlers blocking roads in the northern West Bank, provoking Border Policemen to drag him to the ground. He has earned international headlines and embarrassment from the established, buttoned-down right wing, which attempted to distance itself from his histrionics while simultaneously advancing his agenda.

When state-funded rabbis gathered to defend the publication of *Torat Ha'Melech*, the guide to killing non-Jews, Ben-Ari was seated in the front row of the audience with two of his young sons by his side. When he was not racing between far-right confabs to the fever swamps of "Judea and Samaria," Ben-Ari could be found seated on Knesset committees, denouncing Arab colleagues like Hanin Zoabi as treacherous criminals, or cheering on the passage of the latest legal assault on Palestinian citizens of Israel and human rights NGOs, whom he called "traitors who must be persecuted at any cost." Everywhere he went, reporters and camerapeople seemed to be in tow, eager to document his colorful hysterics.

In October 2010, when the cabinet of Prime Minister Benjamin Netanyahu's governing coalition approved a Knesset-authored amendment to the country's Citizenship Law requiring new citizens to take an oath of loyalty to the "Jewish and democratic state," Ben-Ari erupted with rapturous joy. His political and spiritual mentor, the late rabbi Meir Kahane, who was banned from running for a Knesset seat in part for advocating loyalty oaths for non-Jews, had been vindicated. "Twenty years after Rabbi Kahane's murder," Ben-Ari said, "the Likud has admitted that Rabbi Kahane was right."

Referring to former prime minister Yitzhak Shamir and his deputy chief of staff Benjamin Netanyahu, who approved Kahane's electoral ban in part because they viewed him as a dangerous competitor, Ben-Ari proclaimed, "It's refreshing to hear the Likud government that haunted Rabbi Kahane wants the Arabs to sign a loyalty oath. It was admitted today that what Rabbi Kahane stated twenty years ago was correct and proper."

Writing from the opposite perspective, *Ha'aretz* columnist Chaim Levinson came to the same conclusion as Ben-Ari. Levinson dredged up a 1984 campaign manifesto of Kahane's Kach Party called, "The Arabs." According to the manifesto, any Arab who refused to immediately evacuate the land of Greater Israel would "be asked to sign an oath of allegiance to the Jewish state. In this declaration, he will recognize Israel as the homeland of the Jewish people and its sole sovereignty over the land and will receive the rights of a resident alien. Any Arab who acts in this way will remain a resident of Israel without national rights, but with full individual, cultural, and minority rights forever."

Twenty-six years later, the Israeli government approved a law almost identical to the kind Kahane proposed, and with the support of the then-chairman of the Labor Party, Defense Minister Ehud Barak, a figure portrayed in Western media as a pragmatic centrist. "Kahane's vision for [a] loyalty oath was not so different from Barak's," Levinson concluded.

The Israeli political establishment drove Kahane out of the Knesset without ever bothering to confront him directly—even the Israel Broadcast Authority refused to cover his activities. Though he was ousted on the grounds that he had committed racial incitement, Likud leaders like Shamir were privately concerned about polling showing that Kahane's Kach Party was set to win three to five Knesset seats in the 1988 elections, eating into Likud's base. By vanquishing him without attempting to discredit his vision, the Israeli governing establishment ensured that Kahane's ghost would haunt the country long after his assassination in 1994 by a lone gunman with no connection to any Palestinian faction.

The late rabbi loomed large over the 2009 elections, and not only because Yisrael Beiteinu chairman Avigdor Lieberman was implicated in various media reports for once belonging to Kach, or because many among the Likud Party's next generation of politicians sounded remarkably like him. Running on the fourth slot of the National Union Party list was Ben-Ari, who proudly campaigned as Kahane's student and follower.

"I'm not the only one who represents Kahane," Ben-Ari said at the time. "He's represented by a great many people today, within the Knesset and outside it. [Foreign Minister Avigdor] Lieberman masquerades as Kahane to win more mandates, [Minister of Sports and Culture] Limor Livnat also sounds like Kahane, and everybody realizes the need for a solution to the problem of Israeli Arabs—a subject which was once taboo."

Ben-Ari continued, "The saying, 'Kahane was right,' has already been used up. You can practically see how what Rabbi Kahane brought up twenty-four years ago has now become the central issue of this election campaign."

As a candidate, Ben-Ari pledged to forge a new path for Kahane's agenda, promising to create a "humanitarian corridor" for the mass expulsion of Palestinians to far-away countries like Venezuela and Turkey. Even more important, he said, was packing the Supreme Court with right-wing ideologues who "act in favor of the Jews and the IDF soldiers, whose lives are more valuable than those of others."

Once Ben-Ari secured a seat, he appointed Baruch Marzel and Itamar Ben-Gvir, two veteran members of Kahane's outlawed Kach Party, as his parliamentary aides. Then he watched from his seat on the Knesset's Constitution, Law and Justice Committee as bills remarkably similar to those authored by his mentor were passed by sweeping majorities.

At the helm of the Knesset committee was David Rotem from Lieberman's Yisrael Beiteinu Party, perhaps the parliament's most zealous advocate of stripping away Israel's already threadbare democratic provisions. And seated by his side was Ben-Ari. "It's bad enough that Rotem is the chair of the Constitution committee," said Orna Kohn, a lawyer for the Adalah, the legal center dedicated to defending the rights of Israel's Arab sector told me. "But when Rotem gets up to go to the bathroom, Ben-Ari actually sits in his chair, grabs the gavel, and takes over for a few minutes. It is truly shocking and I think if a situation arises where Ben-Ari takes control of a committee, it might be time to move outside of politics and find other means of activism."

Ben-Ari's aides and allies who ran the Lehava anti-miscegenation organization had refused to speak to David Sheen and me, calling us agents of the Enemy. But when Sheen requested an interview with Ben-Ari, he obliged without any reservations. When we arrived at his small office in the Knesset in August 2010, Ben-Ari was seated at a desk littered with pro-settler propaganda DVDs and pamphlets. On his wall was a sketched portrait of Kahane, his patron saint and longtime teacher.

Clad in a tight-fitting, short-sleeved white shirt, and with a full but neatly groomed salt-and-pepper beard, Ben-Ari's wild, darting eyes were his most distinctive feature, brimming with intensity each time he launched into an extended diatribe. When I asked him to pose for a photo beneath his portrait of Kahane, he said, "So you want to make me out to be the big Kahanist?"

"Well, isn't that what you are?" I said. He shrugged and nodded sheepishly.

At the time, Ben-Ari was attempting to generate publicity for a bill he had introduced that would have banned "disloyal" Israeli filmmakers from receiving state funding. Sheen seated himself across from Ben-Ari's desk and asked him why he had introduced a proposal that even a few of his colleagues in Likud had described as anti-democratic.

"We need to request from people that are going to represent the state, or who are receiving prizes from the state, to say in advance, are we loyal to the state or are we disloyal to the state," Ben-Ari declared, citing the Oscar-nominated joint Israeli-Palestinian production, *Ajami*, a crime drama about a mixed, working-class neighborhood in Jaffa, as an example of traitorous cinema. "We won't jail someone who says they're not loyal to the state. He can walk around freely and create. He can curse, he can dump garbage on himself and others freely! But the state will not pay for him to do that. You want to spit on me? I don't have to pay you for that. That's the whole law."

Ben-Ari stressed that *Ajami*'s director, Scandar Copti, had refused to appear at the Academy Awards, claiming that as a Palestinian citizen whose family had endured gratuitous abuse at the hands of the Israeli police, he could not represent the State of Israel. "You say it's not your state, so why do I have to pay you? I want one person to explain to me the logic in that," Ben-Ari exclaimed, punching his desk with an index finger. But he was just warming up.

"It angers me," he went on. "I believe the occupation in the territories is the Arabs conquering our territories. This is our home, and the people who conquered are Arabs. They were the regents here. And they were the invaders, Philistines. Even their name proves they are invaders. This is my home for all time. This was your father's father's land, and they kicked us out of here. And we just returned home. They are the invaders. Not us. It angers me. But it's something else. If someone would come up to the Knesset and say, 'I'm not a representative of the State of Israel'—what is that? You were sent by Israel, you were funded by Israel!"

Throughout the interview, Ben-Ari, like Kahane before him, went to pains to distinguish himself from more established right-wingers. Avigdor Lieberman's Yisrael Beiteinu, "is a scarecrow" that supports quasi-autonomy for Palestinians in the West Bank—"not a real, values-driven right that speaks like me." "Today the Likud party is carrying out the party platform of Meretz, two states for two peoples," he added. "It's not even the platform of Meretz, it's the platform of [the defunct Arab communist party] Rakach."

Even most of the pro-settler representatives who advocated transferring Palestinians to Jordan were too soft for Ben-Ari: "I would never allow these words to leave my lips: Jordan is Palestine. God forbid! Jordan is part of the land of Israel, it belongs to the people of Israel, it's not Palestine, it was never Palestine."

Borrowing from Kahane, Ben-Ari presented his devout, messianic Judaism not just as an article of faith, but as a secret weapon in the struggle against the Palestinians—a characteristic he claimed none of the enlightened figures of Likud and the secular liberal politicians possessed. "I am still not encouraged," he said. "The process of cutting off the Jewish people's roots is very deep. The people who did it were very sneaky, over several years. So all the people have in the world is *American Idol*, fallen idol; that's all they have in the world, it's unbelievable. Our culture is completely empty, *Big Brother*, little brother, a bunch of *Survivor* foolishness."

Leaning close, Ben-Ari asked in a plaintive tone, "Tell me, what chances does a man of the world at large have standing up to a Palestinian with an agenda? What does he have? He's got nothing. He's empty."

This was the same sort of pitch that brought droves of followers to Kahane's side: Secular Zionists had established the foundation for a Jewish state—"they once sailed here in ships and were willing to drown," as Ben-Ari said—but they had exhausted themselves of messianic energy. Meanwhile, the Palestinians maintained their sense of *sumud*, or steadfastness, no matter what hardships they endured. They knew who they were and what they wanted, and no one could deter them from resisting Zionism. What Israelis needed, according to Kahane and disciples like Ben-Ari, was not clever *hasbara* or military sophistication, but a rearmed identity.

But the gradual mainstreaming of Kahane's agenda presented a quandary for the apostles who bore his legacy. As Ben-Ari freely acknowledged, younger members of

Likud struck a remarkably similar tone to Kahane, and the kind of segregationist legislation the late rabbi advocated was flying through the Knesset with wide majorities of support. Ben-Ari reminded me of American white supremacists like David Duke who struggled to retain popular influence after elected national representatives of the Republican Party coopted the anti-immigrant agenda they pioneered in the 1970s. His only hope for prolonged relevance was in out-demagoguing the greatest demagogues of the right.

So, where the enemy was once Palestinians, Ben-Ari found a new social menace: asylum seekers fleeing war and genocide in Africa. As the only industrialized country directly bordering Africa, Israel had become home to some seventy thousand non-Jewish migrants and asylum seekers from countries like Sudan, Eritrea, the Ivory Coast, and Cameroon. Others had come from the Philippines and Thailand to fill low-wage jobs as domestic workers and custodians—those which used to be occupied by Palestinians before they were blockaded in Gaza or tucked behind the separation wall. Many of the African and Asian migrants were concentrated in a single, low-wage district in southern Tel Aviv inhabited for decades by Mizrahi Jews who traditionally supported hardline rightist parties like Likud and Shas. With tension smoldering, Ben-Ari did what he did best: he doused it with gasoline.

Now, even liberal Tel Aviv was feeling the hate. And while the street-level incitement against African asylum seekers mounted, the Knesset and Israeli government accelerated plans to construct the world's largest prison, illegalize the presence of non-Jewish migrants and build a wall on the African border—all in the name of preserving Israel's Jewish demographic majority. The anti-immigrant movement would build over the next year, culminating where it began, in southern Tel Aviv, with several nights of violence that left sidewalks littered with the shattered windows of non-Jewish homes and storefronts.

This Belongs to the White Man

The village of Salama had stood against the Mediterranean coast, just north of Jaffa, since the sixteenth century, providing generations of residents with an easy-going lifestyle of farming and fishing. But with the arrival of Zionist settlers, the town and its four thousand or so Palestinian Arab inhabitants were gradually encircled by the rapidly growing, all-Jewish neighborhoods of Tel Aviv, Neve Tzedek, and Neve Sha'anan. The Zionists had built to conquer, and in April 1948, after declaring the birth of Israel, David Ben Gurion's commanders delivered soldiers from the Palmach strike force with instructions to finish the job. Despite having mounted little to no resistance, the villagers of Salma were deemed hostile to the new Jewish state.

The Palmach's instructions read, "The villagers do not express opposition to the actions of the [Arab Liberation Army] gangs and a great many of the youth even provide [the ALA irregulars with] active cooperation. . . . The aim is . . . to attack the northern part of the village . . . to cause deaths, to blow up houses, and to burn everything possible."

Despite a cable from Israeli forces informing the military command that the people of Salama "have no stomach for war and . . . would willingly return to their villages and accept Jewish protection," they were not allowed to return to their property. Instead, they were marched to refugee camps, while gangs of "hooligans" from Tel Aviv's lower-class Hatikvah Quarter vandalized and looted their homes. Weeks later, the Israeli government and Jewish Agency arranged for the settlement of hundreds of new Jewish immigrants, mostly from Arab countries, in the homes seized from the Palestinians expelled from Salama, or in new developments on those which were destroyed.

The newcomers—impoverished Mizrahim subject to the whimsy and abuse of Israel's Ashkenazi founders—were deployed as placeholders, ensuring that Palestinian refugees would have nowhere to return. Thanks to a law passed by the Knesset in 1954, the Prevention of Infiltration Act, Palestinian refugees who did attempt to re-enter Salama or other areas conquered by Israeli forces would be punished with automatic jail time and immediate expulsion. Under the new legal provision, refugees and absentees whose property was confiscated were officially criminalized as "infiltrators," enabling the authorization of brutal army raids and round-ups to rid the country of their presence.

What was once the village of Salama became Kfar Shalem, a rough, blue-collar neighborhood in Tel Aviv next to the working-class districts of Shapira and Hatikvah, and just west of the increasingly gentrified hipster mecca known as Florentin—the geographical embodiment of the Tel Aviv "bubble," where trendy, young bohemians maintained a studious apathy toward the myriad injustices taking place all around them. Over the years, the area's Mizrahi population was supplemented with Jewish immigrants from Russia and *Bukharin* Jews from Central Europe who arrived with less education and democratic immersion than the Askhenazi middle and upper class to their North.

For decades, the neighborhoods of south Tel Aviv remained underserviced and poor, rendering their residents powerless to resist the machinations of wealthy developers. In the early 1980s, the Tel Aviv Municipality began demolishing homes in the area to make room for more profitable ventures, from luxury condos to more affordable office space. The families that had been essentially installed as a human wall against Palestinian repatriation now faced an ironic fate, as they were evicted without any legal recourse or compensation. In 1982, a local activist named Shimon Yehoshua was killed by Israeli police when he attempted to defend his property against demolition.

The evictions accelerated on the watch of Ron Huldai, the Tel Aviv mayor whose electoral campaigns depended on handsome financial backing from real estate developers and bankers practically drooling at the prospect of gentrifying south Tel Aviv. In 2007, Israeli police expelled thirty families from Kfar Shalem before a bulldozer was brought in to destroy their homes, which stood on the future site of an upscale housing development. Avi Harayti, a thirty-two-year-old father of three, protested as he watched the bulldozer trundle toward what had once been his home. "Ben Gurion put my wife's grandfather and grandmother here," he protested. But unlike his grandparents, whose presence helped prevent the return of Palestinian refugees, Harayti had become superfluous.

One of the few Israelis able to make the connection between the Nakba and the present-day struggles of south Tel Aviv was Mya Guarnieri, a freelance journalist much of whose work focused on the working-class areas of the city. The area's current problems were "about 1948," Guarnieri wrote. "It's about internal class struggle and divisions and inequalities between Mizrachim and Ashkenazim. For some activists on the far-left, it can open up the difficult question of supporting people who live in the homes of dispossessed Palestinians. For the Zionist left, a place like Kfar Shalem forces consideration of ethnic cleansing in Israel's history. It might make those of us who live within the Green Line wonder if we aren't another kind of settler."

In 2005, the crisis in South Tel Aviv deepened when African asylum seekers fleeing violence and genocide in Sudan's Darfur region and other war-ravaged areas began crossing into Israel through Egypt's Sinai Desert. Among them was Jacob Berry, a refugee in his late twenties who fled the genocide in Darfur, traveling through the Sinai to Israel. After crossing the border, Berry was captured by the Israeli army. He recalled in an interview with David Sheen, "One day they released me [from a detention center] and took us to Beersheva, a city in the south, then told us, 'Go home now.

I was saying, where is home? I knew nothing about Israel and where I came from there was no television. . . . So we came to Tel Aviv, and also we didn't know where Tel Aviv was."

By 2007, as the southern Tel Aviv neighborhood of Shapira filled up with African asylum seekers like Berry, right-wing activists began holding meetings at the local community center about "kicking out the *kushim* [blacks]." David Sheen, my journalistic associate, attended one meeting where he was shouted down for protesting the disturbing implications of expelling Africans on the basis of their ethnicity. He told me, "Respectable looking people, grown adults in suits and ties in the middle of a community meeting—not riff-raff—would get up and shout at me and others, 'Dirty leftist, you fuck Arabs!' But at that point it wasn't that scary to be in the room. Leftists could shout back. You didn't feel like you would get your throat slit afterwards. But that day was coming."

The number of African refugees in south Tel Aviv had swelled to around twenty thousand by 2010, with most settling around the Central Bus Station, while others wound up in southern development towns like Ashkelon and Eilat, a resort city on the Red Sea. Convinced that the government had deliberately burdened them with the refugees, and not without some justification, impoverished Mizrahi Jews already struggling against evictions in neglected neighborhoods had an additional cause for indignation. Compounding the problem were the longtime residents' attitude toward Arabs and other non-Jewish "enemies," an entrenched bigotry cultivated under the political leadership of Likud and Shas—right-wing factions that pumped state welfare into the West Bank settlements while neglecting impoverished areas in Israel's cities.

While African asylum seekers slept by the hundreds in South Tel Aviv's Levinsky Park, seeking out low-paying jobs that often placed them in competition with the Jewish underclass, the Israeli government refused to honor its obligation under the 1951 United Nations Refugee Convention to provide them with work permits. If the migrants had the ability to work, they would have been able to integrate into Israeli society and out of the neglected neighborhoods near the bus station.

Jacob Berry, the asylum seeker from Darfur, explained, "If the government was capable of addressing the issues at the right time when it had the momentum at that time, it could have done it. We presented the government with a number of proposals and we said, 'We don't want the accumulation of people in one place, this is not our interest and it's not your interest and it's not the interest of the people in South Tel Aviv.' You can spread people in different cities . . . and then there is no one making problems. But no one listens to what you say."

The refugees were not afforded asylum, nor were they allowed to integrate into the mainstream of Israeli society, even as temporary workers. As non-Jews, the African migrants posed a threat to the demographic majority. The only options an ethnocracy could exercise in this case were internment and mass expulsion, two practices with which the State of Israel happened to boast unparalleled expertise and experience.

Arnon Sofer, the most influential demographer in Israel, who consults to the security agencies and the prime minister, lashed out at the human rights NGOs that urged the government to adopt policies to absorb the migrants. "They do not want a Jewish state but a state of 'human beings.'" Sofer said. "They do not understand that this is not the reason why we are here and that if their vision becomes a reality the Jews will become a minority that will be slaughtered by the majority."

Echoing Sofer, Prime Minister Benjamin Netanyahu called the African asylum seekers a "concrete threat to the Jewish and democratic character of the country."

Eli Yishai, the Israeli Interior minister and leader of the religious Shas Party, whose job it was to determine who was allowed to enter the country and who received citizenship, distilled the concept of the Jewish majority into crude racialist terms. Warning that the migrants "will quickly bring us to the end of the Zionist dream," Yishai declared, "Most of those people arriving here are Muslims who think the country doesn't belong to us, the white man."

This might have seemed like an ironic formulation by a son of Tunisian immigrants like Yishai, but for him and many of his constituents, being classified Jewish was a superior racial category of "the white man." By contrast, he cast the African migrants as a diseased subclass of people that should be expelled to preserve the racial purity of the country. They were, he claimed, infected with "a range of diseases such as hepatitis, measles, tuberculosis, and AIDS," and refused to back down after the Ministry of Health released data, prompted by press inquiries after Yishai's statement, disproving it. Physicians for Human Rights, an NGO, also refuted Yishai's claim. "We have 24,000 patient files and we keep records of every visit," said Dr. Ido Lurie, medical director of its clinic. "If there was pervasive evidence that infiltrators and asylum seekers bring in diseases, we would be able to tell, but there is nothing that I know of that confirms the fear."

Inciting against Africans promised additional political benefits for demagogues like Yishai, enabling them to divert from social problems in south Tel Aviv and cities like Ashkelon, drowning out any protests of economic grievances with the all-unifying rhetoric of Jewish hyper-nationalism. Many in the neighborhood were keenly aware of the political scheme. "The government has an interest in inflaming the [south Tel Aviv] Shapira neighborhood," one local resident told journalist Lia Tarachansky, "because that way the public will talk about the refugees instead of talking about all the social problems." Another local remarked, "People like [Michael] Ben-Ari come here and they incite all this anger not against the government or its planning, but against the refugees, and they are already suffering."

But others in the area were easily susceptible to the backlash populism of Yishai, who now competed with other rightist ministers for the title of the most forceful advocate for expelling Africans. "Given a choice between being called 'an enlightened liberal' without a Jewish and Zionist state, and being called a 'benighted racist' but a proud citizen, I choose the latter," Yishai proclaimed. "The era of slogans is over, the era of action has begun."

The crisis in south Tel Aviv propelled Michael Ben-Ari into action, and his bearded visage had become a ubiquitous sight at anti-African rallies throughout 2011. Unlike Yishai, a slight figure who rarely appeared in public without an entourage and security detail, Ben-Ari appeared to be a genuine man of the street. He spoke charismatically, with the rhetorical skill of a veteran rabble-rouser, and was known to mingle into crowds of commoners alone without a phalanx of burly guards. In his style and strategy, Ben-Ari followed in the footsteps of his mentor, Meir Kahane. "I go into the neighborhoods," Kahane explained, "to the poor, to the people who have nothing and are not interested in anything, and I offer them action. There is drama here, it is interesting because it opens new vistas for a bitter, frustrated people full of problems."

David Sheen documented the anti-African demonstrations closely—perhaps more closely than any other reporter in Israel—following Ben-Ari and his cadres as they hounded African asylum seekers with Kahane-inspired vigilante squads and spread the toxin of ethnic resentment throughout the cities of Israel. By April 2011, Ben-Ari and his minions had established a regular presence in the Shapira neighborhood of Tel Aviv, where thousands of African asylum seekers lived among longtime, mostly Mizrahi residents. At a rally that month covered by Sheen, Ben-Ari addressed a crowd of a few hundred ultra-nationalist activists and disgruntled local Jewish residents. He boasted to them of his pivotal role in influencing the government's decision to construct a massive detention center for non-Jewish Africans:

"I want to tell you how Netanyahu awoke," Ben-Ari said. "It was two weeks ago in the Defense Committee meeting. The committee asked Netanyahu, 'What about the detention centers for African infiltrators?' He answers, 'We priced it out, we don't have the budget.' In other words, nothing! I told him, 'Mr. Prime Minister, members of your political party are crossing over to mine!' I saw from his facial expression that he got it. The next day, he was with the mayor of Eilat, who is doing a great job with the Africans there. I only wish we did the same here in Tel Aviv! He doesn't allow them to attend schools, he restricts their movements, he knows what to do. But there's still a lot of work to do."

Ben-Ari positioned himself to the right of Yishai, mocking the Interior minister as a faux populist who talked tough but did little. He said, "On Thursday, Interior Minister Eli Yishai told the Knesset that the detention center will be built. I asked him, 'Is there a start date?' He wouldn't answer me. I put the pressure on! Two days later, I saw Yishai and he told me, 'Netanyahu screamed at the Finance Minister to come up with the money.' It's all because of one thing: We have awoken!"

Following a raucous ovation from a street crowd, he led it on a provocative march through the neighborhood, beside the dwellings of African asylum seekers and through Levinsky Park, the grassy field abutting Tel Aviv's Central Bus Station, where the migrants picnicked and often slept. "Tel Aviv for the Jews! Sudan for the Sudanese!" the marchers chanted. "We have come to expel the darkness!"

When a small group of Africans and Jewish leftists gathered nearby, chanting, "Enough with the racism!" they were set on by furious local residents. "Disgusting! Why should my son go to school with thirty Sudanese in a class?" a middle-aged woman shrieked at the counterdemonstrators. "And he won't speak Hebrew! He'll speak English! Right?! Let's see you take them [Africans] home to your neighborhood and we'll see you complain that your property values are dropping!"

Another Shapira resident, a balding, middle-aged man, addressed the leftists: "Go fuck yourselves, you sons of bitches! You are the cancer of this country! You're two percent of the population, you sons of bitches. Leave the fucking country!"

And another: "Their place is in Sudan, not here! This is a Jewish state!"

And finally, a long-haired, twenty-something man: "You celebrate May Day along with Hitler! Damn you! You Holocaust deniers! Have you no shame? You kill the Jewish people! You're a murderer! You represent the worst of the human race!"

The Concentration Camp

At 1 a.m. on January 10, 2012, the Knesset passed an amendment to the 1954 Prevention of Infiltration Law, a bill originally authorized to consolidate the ethnic cleansing of Palestinians that began in 1947. The new law authorized the government to arrest and hold anyone the government deemed an "infiltrator"—namely, non-Jewish asylum seekers and migrants—in internment camps for a period as long as three years and without being charged or receiving trial. Even the handful of Africans who managed to garner refugee status or permanent residency from the Israel government would now be labeled criminal "infiltrators." The bill passed by a whopping majority of 37–8, with Dov Khenin from the communist Hadash Party leading the marginal opposition, filibustering the bill until late into the night. Many supposedly moderate members of Labor and Kadima headed home well before the debate concluded, abstaining from registering their votes.

The anti-migrant bill included substantial funding for the expansion of the Saharonim facility at Ketziot, a Negev Desert mega-prison that once held thousands of Palestinians detained during the First Intifada, and which was due to be renovated to hold around eight thousand Africans fleeing persecution—"infiltrators"—for an indefinite period. Suggesting preparations to hold the asylum seekers for the long run, the plan outlined the construction of sports facilities and medical centers. *The Independent*, a British newspaper, wrote that Ketziot would amount to "the world's biggest detention center." Reuven Rivlin, the speaker of the Knesset, described the planned center in much starker terms. "As a democrat and a Jew, I have a hard time with concentration camps where people are warehoused," he remarked. But Netanyahu countered the critics by arguing that the desert prison was a "humanitarian solution" that would prevent non–Jewish Africans from "chang[ing] the character of the state."

In 1969, Yeshayahu Leibowitz predicted, "Concentration camps would be erected by the Israeli rulers." Two decades later, he reiterated his warning, predicting that if the status quo remained, "the growing savagery of Israeli society will be as inevitable as the severance of the state from the Jews of the world." Leibowitz's darkest prophesy had been fulfilled, though under conditions he never could have imagined.

His prediction that the international community would conclude that "Israel would not deserve to exist, and it will not be worthwhile to preserve it" was still a long way off, but that did not mean the government was not terribly worried about how the new camp might stain its image. In a bid to ward off outside condemnation without upsetting the present order, the National Planning and Building Council appointed Tomer Gotheft, an MIT graduate in urban planning serving as a senior adviser to the Interior Ministry, and Shlomit Dotan-Gissen, another planning specialist, to prepare an outline presenting the facility not as an internment camp, but euphemistically as a "closed accommodation center."

In a leaked government document, the planners wrote, "The difference between the two terms is not as great as it may seem. By 'closed accommodation centre' we mean an accommodation centre which prevents the residents from leaving without the permission of those in charge of the facility, but with a possibility of different degrees of openness within different sections of the prison, and between the living quarters and the public areas. The degree of openness within the facility will be determined through accumulated experience of its operation."

The Orwellian language of the document suggested a harrowing fate awaiting the thousands of asylum seekers whose presence in the Jewish state had been suddenly criminalized. Indeed, if the state did not wish to obscure the true nature of the camp at Ketziot, it would not have needed to rely on such sophistry. In the end, the popular demand to expedite construction of the camp forced the government to abandon the original master plan altogether, erecting a massive tent city with no sewage or health facilities in its place. Bikrom, an Israeli group of architects advocating "responsible" planning, said the new proposal would create "a huge concentration camp with harsh conditions. The changes would enable the imprisonment of thousands of people in tents for three years or more, in difficult physical conditions and extreme climate conditions."

The anti-migrant law authorized by the Knesset hinted at another draconian measure that would soon be enacted. With funding in the bill for the construction of a massive wall stretching 241 kilometers across Israel's border with Egypt, Israel was planning to erect another demographic Maginot Line, this time to halt the migrant menace. "If we don't stop the problem, 60,000 infiltrators are liable to become 600,000, and cause the negation of the State of Israel as a Jewish and democratic state." Netanyahu declared at a cabinet meeting. He added that it was also imperative "to physically remove the infiltrators. We must crack down and mete out tougher punishments."

For Sofer, Israel's demographics guru and longtime adviser to Netanyahu, the wall must be only the beginning of a much broader plan to guard the state against a future wave of non-Jews fleeing environmental catastrophe in Africa. "We are an island," the professor said. "We don't belong to this region, and we have to defend Israel from waves of migration from Egypt, from Jordan and maybe from Syria. If we want to keep Israel a Jewish state, we will have to defend ourselves from what I call 'climate refugees,' exactly as Europe is doing now." In a two-hundred-page paper presented to Israel's minister of Environmental Protection, Sofer and a team of one hundred academics from the Israel Climate Change Knowledge Center argued for completing the ongoing project of transforming Israel into a gigantic fortress encircled by walls "all around Israeli borders," including "sea fences."

While the government prepared for a massive round-up of "infiltrators," a small group of Israelis gathered on a busy Tel Aviv boulevard to protest the newly passed anti-migrant legislation. Numbering only a few dozen scraggly leftists, the protesters represented the only iteration of internal resistance to the expulsion policy, to the internment camp in the desert, to its poisonous climate of scapegoating and race-baiting. While the demonstrators blocked traffic by lying prone in the middle of the intersection, prompting the arrival of a squadron of riot police, a young woman took hold of a small megaphone and calmly addressed the cops.

"We have no choice," she said, explaining why they had halted traffic. "In our names, they are opening concentration camps, and if we get up and leave, it is as if we are consenting to it. Seventy years ago, we would have been happy if people would have stood up for our rights in Europe, and if they would have blocked streets for and for our grandfathers and grandmothers. We have no choice but to do this. We request that you wait patiently, Mister Police Officer, sir."

But the police ignored the appeal to conscience. They were, after all, just cops. Wading into the crowd with batons drawn, they peeled the few dozen protesters off the pavement and dragged their limp bodies away. With the path cleared, a long line of cars proceeded freely down the boulevard.

Emboldened by the government's new legislation, officials across the country offered their own proposals, each more grotesque than the next. In February 2012, a Tel Aviv council member named Benjamin Babayof delivered a letter to the city's mayor and Israel's Transportation minister proposing separate buses for Sudanese migrants. "A bad smell wafts from them and may, god forbid, lead to all kinds of diseases," Babayof said of the Africans.

Though the councilman's idea went nowhere, the Tel Aviv Municipality agreed to entertain a separate proposal from Benny Tal, a former Israeli army colonel and elite bodyguard operating a private security firm. Tal told Tel Aviv municipal representatives he would gather intelligence on the African migrant population, send in hundreds of security guards to cuff them, and ship them away on buses or trucks. "This should be a very violent action," Tal insisted. The municipality ultimately rejected Tal's proposal, though a local official raised the plan again in a meeting of the Israeli Knesset's Special Committee regarding Foreign Workers, claiming he intended only to highlight the severity of the situation in southern Tel Aviv.

On April 15, 2012, a few days after the Knesset heard from Tal, a group of Israeli politicians and activists gathered in the city of Ramle to discuss strategies for expelling the African menace. At the conference, which is normally convened each year to rally support for the forced transfer of Palestinians from Israel, a lobbyist named Ilan Tsion from a group called Fence for Life was seated next to Interior Minister Eli Yishai, and beneath a banner featuring an illustration of six white figures standing against a dark-colored human wave. Tsion opened his remarks by plugging his organization's role in rallying public support for the West Bank separation wall and was cheered for describing his efforts to "prevent Palestinian families from living in Israel."

But now there was a new threat: "The migration from Africa and from the Palestinian Authority and the Arab states is about to sentence us to death," he warned.

Invoking the traditional Zionist imperative for expulsion, Tsion continued, "If Israel loses its Jewish character, they'll slaughter every one of us here! . . . Therefore, I say, enough with this about refugees. This isn't Sweden or England, we are a special case. We cannot accept even one of them!" He described the encircling separation wall—and who could and could not pass through it. "The separation fence must be closed and sealed," he said. "The Egyptian border fence must be closed and sealed. We must build a fence on the Jordanian border immediately, no one gets in or out! Jews who live in Judea and Samaria [West Bank] may come in and out—Arabs may not come in and out."

Yishai built onto Tsion's jeremiad, declaring that a wall was not enough—the government needed to round up all fifty thousand Africans in the country and deport them as soon as possible. They were all, he said, "a criminal element." A week earlier Yishai had appeared on Israel army radio to stir demographic panic, declaring, "The migrants are giving birth to hundreds of thousands, and the Zionist dream is dying."

While the government rushed construction of the new border wall, residents of Tel Aviv's southern Shapira and Hatikvah neighborhoods took measures into their own hands. Woody, my former roommate in Jaffa, had relocated to Shapira just as the troubles began in April 2012, on Israel's Independence Day. While standing on a corner of the Neve Sha'anan pedestrian mall, a walkway that serves as a flea market and gathering place for Tel Aviv's migrant community, Woody noticed a phalanx of Border Policemen marching down the path with truncheons drawn. The police ordered everyone out of the street, menacing crowds of migrants until they dispersed, and demanding that he leave the area, too. Though he did not understand what motivated the operation, he soon learned of rumors filtering through the neighborhood that an African migrant had attempted to sexually assault a teenage Jewish girl. A frightening scene was beginning to take shape.

That night, following a string of arson attacks on the residences of foreign workers in Jerusalem, a series of coordinated firebomb attacks damaged African property in Tel Aviv's Shapira neighborhood. The assault began at 1:30 a.m., with three Molotov cocktails thrown through the window of an African apartment, then attacks on three more houses. Finally, an hour later, vandals torched a local kindergarten operated by a Nigerian couple. Though children arrived at the school the following day to find their modest playground reduced to ashes, no one was hurt by the firebombings.

"When I have experiences in Darfur, like watching Janjaweed taking kids and throwing them into the fire, it reminds me of the same trauma, because when you see people burning down people's property, it's horrific," Jacob Berry, the Darfuri refugee, said of the firebombings. "And second of all, it's like you see someone is insulting you because you are black, and you are *kushi*, and you are not a human being, and you don't deserve to be in this state—this is really an underestimation of the dignity of human beings."

Haggai Matar, a left-wing Israeli journalist, interviewed a Jewish resident of the neighborhood the day after the arson attacks. "Whoever did this is right, but he's doing it the wrong way," the neighbor complained. "This fire almost burned my car, and also—there is a small girl in that house. He should have waited until nobody was home, and then blown the place up to send them a message." (Haim Moula, the twenty-one-year-old charged with firebombing the African properties, was set free after the prosecutor mysteriously altered his indictment, allowing him to strike a plea bargain.)

The violence in April was only a prelude to a great release of pent-up resentment, a harrowing vision of what was possible when the government chose to tap into the public's unfathomably deep wellspring of prejudice.

As the disgruntled denizens of south Tel Aviv summoned their rage for another round of violence, the governmental incitement continued, as senior members of the Israeli police presented the government with false statistics asserting that African asylum seekers were responsible for 40 percent of the crime in Tel Aviv. In fact, the crime rate of foreigners living in Israel was half that of the overall population, which stood at around 5 percent.

This inconvenient fact did not deter Israel's minister of Public Security, Yitzhak Aharonovitch, from indulging public hysteria about a nonexistent "crime wave." Following a tour of south Tel Aviv, Aharonovitch returned to the Knesset with a grim report for the Internal Affair and Environment Committee: "We are fighting for the face of Israeli society," the minister declared. "This is a strategic issue, no less so than the Iranian threat." Demanding a round-up to fill the thousands of new prison cells built for the non–Jewish Africans, Aharonovitch proposed enticing the migrants to leave with payments of around $300 and a plane ticket home.

In May 2012, as the government's demagogy peaked, the Israeli media filled with panicked accounts like Avi Shoshan's "fifteen minutes of terror in south Tel Aviv." In the *Yediot Ahronoth* editorial, Shoshan described the moments of sheer hell a friend suffered through as she was forced to wait for him to pick her up at the Central Bus Station while dark-skinned Africans stood nearby, doing nothing in particular. "It is not Iran, Hamas and Hezbollah that scare me," Shoshan wrote. "What is it? The transformation of Tel Aviv." The Africans were a terrifying sight, indeed. After all, they resembled blacks in the United States. "I feel sorry for the residents of south Tel Aviv," he continued, "because they live in the Israeli version of Harlem in the '80s. I feel sorry for them because they do not have the [strong-armed former New York City Mayor Rudy] Giuliani to come and impose order."

But Shoshan's nightmare could not compare to that of Seth Franztman, a former itinerant worker and low-level Republican activist who emigrated from the United States to Israel, where he reinvented himself as a scholarly "critiquer of modernity." The conservative *Jerusalem Post* saw fit to publish Franztman's column—a horror story about the insidious Africans. According to Frantzman (who announced in a bio he posted on his personal Amazon.com account that he "only date[s] non-white women"), an African migrant dared to tell his Jewish Ethiopian girlfriend "hello" in Amharik, a Semitic language spoken in Ethiopia. "Why is it that when some of these men see a mixed couple they decide that it is their prerogative to say 'hello?'" Frantzman wondered. "They don't say hello to white women on the streets in their language. They don't greet white women walking with their husbands." Saying "hello" was the hostile act that confirmed the Africans as the real racists.

As they assembled their rap sheet of African transgressions, it seemed that staring, saying "hello," and having the audacity to stand near Israelis at the Central Bus Station were among the worst offenses the proponents of mass expulsion could conjure. Of course, the asylum seekers' greatest transgression was not being Jewish and white. For this, many were doomed to weather a maelstrom of xenophobic hatred and violence. "My feeling is that when I walk down the street everyone is looking at me as though I am a big disaster," said Viktoria James, a ninth-grade Tel Aviv resident from Sudan. "They say that they are afraid of me but I am afraid of them. I am afraid they will do something to me on the way, or they will hurt me because I am a black African."

Left-wing social justice activists had volunteered in the past to walk Palestinian children to school in occupied Hebron, shielding them from attacks by extremist Jewish settlers. Now they found themselves back at home in Tel Aviv, the supposed liberal cultural bubble, guarding young African children from locals incited into a violent frenzy by settlers from Hebron. Rotem Ilan, an Israeli volunteer chaperone, told journalist Lia Tarachansky, "I think more than one hundred [African] people called me to tell me that they're very scared for themselves and especially their children. They asked me to escort them to their homes just to make sure that they wouldn't be attacked in the street."

Even the journalists who covered the anti-African demonstrations became targets. Sheen told me that when a few protest leaders had begun to recognize him, they sometimes sicced crowds on him as soon as he appeared. Sheen's wife, Anne, a black woman whose family had emigrated to Canada from Jamaica, said she avoided going near south Tel Aviv for her own safety. Sheen explained, "When they see me, one guy might approach me, shouting, "You should get raped by an African! Then another says it. Then another, and they are laughing. Then someone spits at you or slaps you. They have crossed the line and dehumanized you too. Your security is gone and anything can happen. It's completely terrifying."

The Night of Broken Glass

Throughout May 2012, a gang of about a dozen youths terrorized Africans in Tel Aviv, attacking them with clubs and iron chains, while robbing their stores of thousands of shekels. Their motive, the youths confessed after they were finally arrested at the end of the month, was to exact revenge for the horrible crimes the Israeli media claimed the foreigners had committed against the Jewish public. On May 22, following weeks of high-level government incitement, Michael Ben-Ari and his minions returned to south Tel Aviv to arouse the angry, left-behind community with the message that the time for action had begun.

The demonstrations began with Ben-Ari standing before a crowd of fifty at the front door of a small community center that provided services to asylum seekers, claiming without any evidence that Sudanese migrants had urinated on synagogues, desecrating the holiest sites of the "Jewish people." Another speaker declared that the greatest threat to Israel was African refugees, claiming they had been shepherded into Israel by the Arab states in a devious plot to upend the Jewish demographic majority. A young woman in the crowd sported a gold Star of David necklace and a white T-shirt emblazoned with the hand-scrawled phrase, "Death to Sudanese."

With Ben-Ari standing a few meters away, a middle-aged man in the crowd took the megaphone and addressed a small group of leftists staging a counterprotest nearby: "We want to remind you of the new protocol regarding women. If you are pretty, don't leave your home! You'll get fucked in the ass at night by a Sudanese man."

A woman in her thirties who was well known in the neighborhood for her activism against Africans charged across the street with a young girl who appeared to be her daughter. There, they confronted two leftists sitting at the door of the community center. "May you all get cancer! May the cancer spread!" the woman screamed at the two young women, who silently endured the abuse with a look of resignation. "May your entire family die in a car accident tomorrow! With the help of God, you piece of garbage! You spawn of Amalek!"

When the demonstration ended, the protesters set themelves on Yossi Gurvitz, a widely read, left-wing Israeli blogger, and his girlfriend, Galina, who had dared to shout back at Ben-Ari. Comprised mostly of women, the crowd hectored Galina with graphic sexual and racial slurs while David Sheen filmed their shocking antics. With Border Police officers standing by and doing absolutely nothing, an elderly man barked at Galina, "Who are you married to? You're married to a nigger!"

"A Sudanese man will rape you and then you'll cry," said a bald man wearing aviator sunglasses who appeared to be in his late thirties. "A Sudanese man will rape you in the ass! May your mother be raped! A Sudanese man will fuck you! Then you will cry out in pain!

"She wants some nigger dick. She's not getting any from her husband," said an old woman with bright yellow hair, gesticulating wildly just inches from Galina's face. "You know why she wants them here?" the old woman continued. "She wants a man!"

A young woman from the neighborhood added, "What Israeli would want her? She wants a nigger!"

In modern day Israel, the African refugee occupied a similar role as the devious Jew in Weimar-era Nazi propaganda and the criminal "nigra" constantly invoked by racist Dixiecrats such as Strom Thurmond in the Jim Crow South. According to opinion writers in center-right papers like *Yedioth Ahronoth*, the country's burgeoning anti-miscegenation movement, and elements in Netanyahu's governing coalition, the African male's crimes were legion, but his greatest danger was his propensity for violating the sexual dignity of Jewish women, and by extension, of the Jewish nation. While the state constructed a vast internment camp in the desert for the refugees, the Jewish man on the street assumed the role of the aggrieved victim and avenger. In projecting sexual anxiety onto the Africans—"A Sudanese man will fuck you!"—the time-tested language of genocide was updated.

"I am as afraid to live in the Israel of 2012 as any right-minded German should have been in 1938, or as any right-minded American should have been in the 1960s," confessed Aliyana Traison, the normally subdued deputy editor of *Ha'aretz*.

On May 23, the night after the rally at the community center, a crowd of at least one thousand demonstrators gathered in south Tel Aviv for the largest protest ever held against the presence of Africans in Israel. Besides Ben-Ari, the crowd heard from Danny Danon, the right-wing Knesset member who served as chairman of World Likud, who proclaimed, "The infiltrators have to be expelled. We shouldn't be afraid to say that word—expulsion, now!" Next up was Miri Regev, a Likud Knesset member who previously served as the chief spokesperson of the Israeli army.

"The Sudanese are a cancer in our body!" Regev railed from the dais, echoing the tirade Meir Kahane delivered against Palestinians over decades before. "We will do everything in our power to return them to their countries of origin."

"All they do is reproduce! Deport them!" a man in the crowd answered back.

Following Regev's comparison of Africans to a terminal disease, a chant erupted from the crowd: "Nigger, nigger, you're a son of a bitch!"

When a woman in the audience spotted the journalist Haggai Matar, shouting that she had seen him at West Bank protests "throwing stones at soldiers and calling them Nazis"—a baseless slander—a mob formed almost immediately to chase him and Ilan Lior, a reporter from *Ha'aretz*, with the apparent intention of beating them to a pulp. Matar managed to slip behind a police detail dispatched to the neighborhood ostensibly to protect its residents from migrant crime, but an old woman charged through the line of cops and began battering him with her fists. Lior was sucked back into the crowd, but was saved from possible death by a police officer who threw him in a squad car. Mattar was able to flee to safety. As he bolted down the street, he heard a speaker from the stage announce, "Haggai Matar is here, and he and his mother are traitors who should be kicked out of the country."

The mob that chased Matar and Lior swelled to several hundred enraged locals of all ages. They sprinted directly toward Levinsky Park, the center of African refugee life, chanting "Sudanese to Sudan!" But their advance was halted by a detachment of Border Policemen, forcing the mob to disperse into small groups. The rioters spent the next few hours in the Hatikvah neighborhood attacking any African targets they could find.

Among the businesses they vandalized was a local Eritrean bar. "They said 'Bitch! You black son of a bitch!' in Arabic," the bar's owner, Amine, recalled. "After that they started to hit me. . . . They took the legs of a table and hit me, all of them: They all came together at once. What can I do?" Amine added, "After a week or ten days later, they came and broke the windows again." It was the fifth time in a year his bar had been attacked.

Gathered around a burning pyre and waving Israeli flags while riot police stood by passively, the mob chanted, "The people want the Africans to be burned!" mocking a popular slogan from the Arab Spring—"The people want to overthrow the regime"—for their spree of racial violence.

Next, the rioters attacked a Sudanese woman holding a small baby. She dropped the child in shock, leaving the sidewalk spattered with blood. After smashing the windows of an African-owned grocery shop and looting it, members of the mob spotted a man from the Ivory Coast driving up the street with his Israeli girlfriend in the passenger seat. Rami Gudovitch, an Israeli community activist who lived in the area, witnessed the scene. "They smashed all his car windows, and then they tried to pull him out of the car, through the broken window. They would have killed him. Now, it's important to emphasize that when I say they would have killed him, that's not speculation. There were pieces of broken glass that would have got stuck inside him. They tried to pull him out . . . through the broken glass. And then the police arrived, and the police did move the crowd back. But it was a lynch, pure and simple."

Gudovitch, a veteran south Tel Aviv resident, reflected, "In the past few months I've seen things that are impossible to imagine. I don't know if I can go on living with the things I've seen."

The next morning, shards of broken glass glimmered across the soot-stained sidewalks of Hatikvah. For the Africans still bunkered inside their homes, including some who had escaped Janjaweed massacres in Sudan's Darfur region, the scene summoned the worst demons of history. "When I saw what they did in the Hatikva neighborhood, I remembered Kristallnacht," a twelfth-grade asylum seeker educated in Israeli schools said of the night of attacks. "The next morning I came [to school] wearing a shirt with the date of Kristallnacht on it and the date of the demonstration."

Such impressions were common among Israel's refugee population, according to Gudovitch. "One of the things that moved me the most when I started working with the children of refugees," he said. "I was just overwhelmed with how much these children are obsessed with the Holocaust. With their history and experiences, suddenly they felt that finally, they had come to the right place; finally, people will understand them."

On June 6, on a primetime Israeli news talk show called *London and Kirschenbaum*, Channel 10 military correspondent Or Heller made the connection between Israel's treatment of Africans and the treatment of Jews in 1940s Europe as clearly as any major personality in Israel would. "I think everyone should be asking themselves what's next," Heller warned. "Because if you change their skin color and add numbers, you'll get my own grandmother sixty years ago."

A week after the attacks, the Knesset Interior Committee held a discussion on the situation in south Tel Aviv. Among the few members who issued any reservations about the violence that transpired in south Tel Aviv was Benjamin Fuad Ben-Eliezer, the grand old man of the Labor Party. The eighty-two-year-old former Defense minister had arrived in Israel in 1950 with his parents after fleeing a spate of anti-Jewish mob attacks in their hometown of Basra, Iraq. Before the Knesset committee, Eliezer declared that he had heard the same rhetoric about Jews in Iraq as he heard in the past several days from his colleague, Miri Regev, who had taken to calling the Africans a "cancer." "Jews cannot speak like that. The Jewish state is a humane state," he vainly protested.

His protests were immediately drowned out by Regev's allies. Mocking Eliezer, Limor Livnat, the Likud minister of Sports and Culture, said, "If a strange person entered the plenum, he would not be able to guess that you were a member of this government." Danny Danon, another face of Likud's next generation, slammed "bleeding hearts" who opposed the mass deportation of Africans. While Ben-Eliezer proposed nothing beyond a softening of anti-African rhetoric, a chorus of lawmakers from the supposedly centrist Kadima Party echoed the rightists from Likud.

Marina Solodkin, a Kadima representative who immigrated to Israel from Soviet Russia, equated expelling refugees to Africa to her immigration to Israel, a place she and her family had never lived in before her arrival. "Returning someone to their homeland *is* repatriation," she claimed. "I was repatriated to Israel."

Joining her Kadima comrades, Yulia Shamalov-Berkovich demanded the construction of more internment camps on Israel's border with Egypt. Then Shamalov-Berkovich lashed out at the leftists who had protested the right-wing demonstrations in south Tel Aviv. She proclaimed, "All human rights activists should be imprisoned and transported to camps we are building."

Regev, for her part, had issued a formal apology on her Facebook page for her controversial comments equating Africans with "cancer." But she addressed her apology to cancer patients, not African asylum seekers, doubling down on her incendiary rhetoric. Next, she posted a video clarifying her view of non–Jewish Africans: "Heaven forbid, I did not talk about human beings, and I did not compare them to human beings."

Regev's sentiments were widely shared. According to a May 2012 poll by the Israel Democracy Institute, 52 percent of Israeli Jews agreed with Regev that Africans were "a 'cancer' in the body of the nation." A poll by Yediot Tel Aviv corroborated the findings, showing that 63 percent of Tel Aviv's residents supported the expulsion of all non–Jewish Africans from Israel.

In the months after the rioting in south Tel Aviv, the stories of racist incidents piled up with depressing frequency. In Ashkelon, when residents scrambled to bomb shelters during a rocket attack from Gaza, Russians occupying one facility refused to allow any black-skinned residents inside. "I cannot be with them in the shelter, it's too unpleasant," said one Russian resident. "I'd rather be outside." In Jerusalem, the state arrested and deported an eight-year-old Filipino child adopted by a Palestinian family that found her left outside a monastery by her mother, who had also been arrested. "'I'd die before having her taken from me," pleaded the child's adoptive Palestinian mother. Meanwhile, African diplomats stationed in Israel protested to the Foreign Ministry that they no longer felt safe walking in public, and that their spouses were "picked on" almost anywhere they went.

As soon as South Sudan declared independence from Sudan, pledging to enter into a special alliance with Israel and the United States that undermined the strategic deterrence of the anti-Western government in Khartoum, the Israeli government seized on the news just to justify sending asylum seekers from the region back home. "They are going from house to house and rounding up people. They tell us, 'Get your things and go,'" one South Sudanese asylum seeker said. "The (people) are willing to go home, but not in this manner. We are tired of this. We've only had independence for ten months. You can't build a state in ten months." Another Sudanese refugee told an Israeli reporter, "They treat us like animals so we have no choice but to go back."

In September, as the state rushed to complete construction on its refugee internment camp, twenty-one Eritrean refugees became trapped behind Israel's new border fence after completing a harrowing trek through the Sinai Desert. Denied entry through the gates of the Jewish state, the group was then denied food by the Israeli army, which limited them to eight ounces of water a day as they roasted in the scorching sun. After nearly a week of exposure and dehydration, a pregnant female member of the group suffered a miscarriage. Israel "must act with a heavy hand," said Interior Minister Yishai. "We cannot let them enter."

Conditions in Israel had become so desperate for asylum seekers, and their future appeared to be so bleak, scores of Africans began appearing at the prime minister's office to beseech government officials to allow them to convert to Judaism. Having been accused by Israeli officials of seeking to subvert the fundamental character of the state, the refugees now demonstrated their sincere desire to join it as Jewish citizens. But no matter how earnest the Africans, their conversion applications were rejected in absolutely every case. "We cannot just allow anyone who wants to, to convert to Judaism!" Israel's Minister of Justice, Yaakov Neeman exclaimed. "Because then it permits anyone to enter the State of Israel and receive citizenship, or if someone is in the country illegally, he can convert and become legal."

The race to complete the electrified, sixteen-foot-high, refugee-repelling wall on the 165-mile stretch running from the city of Eilat to the tip of the besieged Gaza

Strip would cost the Israeli government more than $200 million to complete, forcing across-the-board cuts in social spending. But the new wall represented only the latest attempt by the State of Israel to seal itself off from the surrounding region. It had already built a massive fence sealing off the frontier it conquered in 1967 connecting the Sea of Galilee to the Dead Sea. That fence connected to the barriers constructed along the 1973 ceasefire line with Syria in the occupied Golan Heights—built inside Syrian territory—which were liberally mined with explosive charges.

Then there was the fence built along Israel's fifty-mile border with Lebanon in the 1970s. Following a May 2011 march by hundreds of unarmed Palestinian refugees symbolically demanding their right of return, an incident that left fifteen dead and many more wounded by Israeli gunfire, Israel elected to build a new, 16-foot-high wall on the Lebanese border. To Israel's south, a 30-foot-high wall surrounded the Gaza Strip, complementing the wall separating Gaza from Egypt, and all designed to keep the mostly refugee population from escaping its overcrowded, embargoed coastal enclave.

The only area controlled by Israel that had not been walled off was the southern border with Jordan that ran between the Gulf of Aqaba and the Dead Sea. But that would soon change. "When the security barrier along the Egyptian border is finished," Netanyahu said at a cabinet meeting, "one will be built along the border with Jordan." At a cost of $360 million, the wall would guarantee the total encirclement of the Jewish state by concrete, electrified fencing, steel, and barbed wire.

Intended as an aggressive security measure to keep indigenous enemies out, the walls had instead established a suffocating climate that locked its inhabitants into a hermetically sealed ghetto ravaged by Jewish extremism. What was prophesied in the Book of Numbers was being fulfilled: The people of Israel dwelled alone and were not reckoned among the nations.

"You could argue that this is a Zionist, incredibly important defense venture," wrote *Yedioth Ahronoth*'s Alex Fishman, one of Israel's few independent-minded military affairs correspondents. "Yet one must admit that this fence is the mirror we look into. This is our face. In the past twenty years we've turned into porcupines; we've become a frightened nation that imprisons itself behind fences and retreats into defensive walls."

Fishman concluded, "In the past twenty years, we were completely overcome by the national mental illness. . . . Such a society, which loses its self-confidence, does not convey deterrence. With all the bombs and advanced aircraft, this is not a society that conveys a sense of strength."

Of all of Israel's walls, its most ambitious, visually jarring, and legally dubious endeavor was the 180-mile-long, twenty-five-foot-high separation wall it constructed inside and along the border with the West Bank. Promoted to the world as a temporary "security fence," the wall was in fact designed to serve two major purposes: preserving the Jewish demographic majority by effectively annexing the main settlement blocs into "Israel proper"; and fragmenting the Palestinian population in order to shatter their struggle for independence once and for all. Ironically, it was in the West Bank, as I lived among occupied Palestinians, that I was able to glean the clearest image of the kind of future that awaited the architects of the walls.

PART X

THE BIG QUIET

The Big Quiet

The men and women who set out to build a Jewish state in historic Palestine began with a dream of escaping from the crippling confines of European anti-Semitism into an imagined utopia in which Jews would be a normal people like the English or Germans and whose normality, even socialism, included a version of nineteenth-century Western colonialism, an uplifting "*mission civilisatrice*," as the French put it. Those who invented modern Zionism had little knowledge of, and no regard for, the actual people living in Palestine, then a province of the Ottoman Empire. And if they had any regard for them, it was expressed in typically colonialist terms. Zionism's intellectual author, Theodor Herzl, a Viennese playwright and journalist, described the country "as a portion of a rampart of Europe against Asia, an outpost of civilization as opposed to barbarism." "All the means we need, we ourselves must create them, like Robinson Crusoe on his island," the literary-minded Herzl told an interviewer in 1898. The Labor Zionist movement's chief ideologue, Berl Katznelson, blunter than the dreamy Herzl, declared in 1929, "The Zionist enterprise is an enterprise of conquest." More recently, and perhaps most crudely, former prime minister and Defense minister Ehud Barak described the goal of Zionism as maintaining "a villa in the jungle."

Those who dedicated themselves to the formation of the Jewish state may have formulated their national identity through an idealized vision of European enlightenment, but they also recognized that their lofty aims would not be realized without force. As Katznelson said, "It is not by chance that I speak of settlement in military terms." Thus the Zionist socialists gradually embraced the ideas of radical right-wing ideologue Ze'ev Jabotinsky, who outlined an utterly unromantic strategy in his 1923 essay, "The Iron Wall," for fulfilling their utopian ambitions.

"Zionist colonization, even the most restricted, must either be terminated or carried out in defiance of the will of the native population," Jabotinsky wrote. "This colonization can, therefore, continue and develop only under the protection of a force independent of the local population—an iron wall which the native population cannot break through. This is, in toto, our policy towards the Arabs." According to Jabotinsky, residents of the Zionist *yishuv* (community) could not hope to enjoy a European standard of life in the heart of the Arab world without physically separating themselves from the natives. This would require tireless planning, immense sacrifice and no shortage of bloodshed. And all who comprised the Zionist movement, whether left, right, or center, would carry the plan towards fulfillment. As

Jabotinsky wrote, "All of us, without exception, are constantly demanding that this power strictly fulfill its obligations. In this sense, there are no meaningful differences between our 'militarists' and our 'vegetarians.'"

One of the greatest misperceptions of Israeli politics has been that the right-wing politicians who claimed Jabotinsky's writings as their lodestar were responsible for the most egregious violence against the Palestinians. While brimming with anti-Arab resentment and surging in influence, the Israeli right's real legacy has consisted mostly of producing durable strategies and demagogic rhetoric. Until very recently, it was the Labor Zionists who bore the real responsibility for turning the right's ideas into actionable policies. The dynamic was best illuminated by the way in which successive Labor Party governments implemented the precepts outlined in Jabotinsky's "Iron Wall" under the cover of negotiations with the Palestinians.

As early as 1992, the peace camp icon Yitzhak Rabin advocated the construction of a concrete wall to "take Gaza out of Tel Aviv," closing off the Gaza Strip and West Bank to pave the way. But it was not until the violence of the Second Intifada accelerated that the process of what Rabin and Barak called "hard separation" became a plausible strategy. Suicide bombing confirmed to even liberal-minded Israelis the stereotype of the Arab native as inherently violent, incurable, and culturally retrograde. By extension, the wave of terrorism ratified Jabotinsky's original thesis. "Something like a cage has to be built for [the Palestinians]," the famed Israeli historian Benny Morris declared in a 2002 interview. "There is a wild animal that has to be locked up in one way or another."

Thus while Israeli forces set about in tanks and combat jets to crush the Intifada, 709 kilometers of steel and concrete immediately began to spring up around Jewish demographic enclaves, detaching Israel from the occupied population to its West while gobbling up over 180,000 dunams of Palestinian land. For the residents of Israel's coastal center, and especially its more affluent members who had suffered through a wave of suicide bombings targeting cafés and nightclubs, the wall promised a return to normal life. "We can no longer keep fooling ourselves," read a 2002 Ha'aretz editorial. "This is a war about the morning's coffee and croissant. About the beer in the evening. About our very lives."

Channeling the mood of Israel's Enlightened Public, Ha'aretz published a separate editorial that same year endorsing the wall as a possible stepping-stone toward the two-state solution. The editors wrote, "A new, tangible reality of separation between two national, geographic entities, will ensue. This reality will gradually become part of the consciousness of both peoples. . . . The change could be revolutionary: A physical change that leads to a psychological change, with which it may be possible to rehabilitate the much longed-for political change."

But as usual, the devil was in the details. The plan for the wall had been years in the making, and its designs were unlikely to produce the kind of political change that many liberal Zionists longed for. Indeed, the wall was intended primarily as a means to consolidate Israel's Jewish demographic majority without risking the removal of the major settlement blocs that encircled Palestinian East Jerusalem, and severed it from the West Bank. Rather than delivering a viable country to the Palestinians, it became the backbone of a policy of forced ghettoization that would guarantee a one-way peace while limiting the Palestinian Authority to a realm of disjointed Bantustans. The process of drafting a blueprint for the wall began beneath the media's radar, under the first government of Benjamin Netanyahu.

During the late 1990s, when Ariel Sharon, the so-called "Bulldozer," served as foreign minister in the government of Netanyahu, he became acquainted with a professor with a long basset hound-like face who claimed he could tell his future. "You don't look like a gypsy," Sharon told the professor. The professor elaborated on his prophecy: Sharon, the patron saint of the settlers, would soon see the error of his ways. He would begin removing some settlements, recognize a Palestinian state, and erect a wall between Israel and the Palestinians, separating the two peoples forever. He handed Sharon a copy of his new book, *The Need for Separation: Israel and the Palestinian Entity*.

The professor was Dan Schueftan, a professor of political science at Haifa University and deputy director of the school's National Security Studies Center. Under Sharon, Schueftan's book became the blueprint for Israel's policy doctrine toward the Palestinians living in the Occupied Territories. And Sharon committed himself to implement Schueftan's concept of separation, or *hafrada*, to resolve Israel's demographic crisis. Schueftan, a committed Zionist and hardheaded realist, saw no other option. If the state followed his guidelines, it could remain "Jewish and democratic." If not, it would be recognized worldwide as an apartheid regime.

As the separation plan took effect under the government of the Labor Party's Ehud Barak in 1998, Barak began distributing copies of Schueftan's book to his cabinet ministers. Next, he appointed Schueftan to his National Security Council. The prime minister treated the professor's work like the gospel, promoting it to anyone who would listen, in hopes that it would become a blueprint for redefining Israel's relationship with the Palestinians.

In the book, which journalist Gershom Baskin, who negotiated the release of captive Israeli soldier Gilad Shalit, called "one of the most explicit exposés of modern Zionism," Schueftan wrote that the main reason for separation was to prevent Israel from becoming a Middle Eastern country—from being "Levantinized," as the old generation of Zionists liked to say. Israel had to separate itself from the Arab world, he said, to preserve its cultural superiority, economic prosperity and very identity. Arabs were anti-democratic, corrupt, violent, and generally retrograde people, Schueftan claimed, cherry-picking quotes from Palestinian Authority leaders to illustrate his points. To negate the danger of the surrounding Arab culture, the professor called for *hafrada*, or the physical segregation of Jews and the Palestinians of the West Bank and Gaza on a demographic basis.

Shueftan focused his *hafrada* strategy around the construction of a literal iron wall constructed along lines that excluded as many Palestinians as possible from inside its borders, especially in Jerusalem. This would mean annexing major settlement blocs into "Israel proper," drawing an armored border that would swallow up large portions of the West Bank and Jordan Valley. Ultimately, Shueftan said, his wall would lower the curtain on the Palestinian refugees' demand for a right of return, demoralizing them over time through a permanent regime of exclusion. Schueftan viewed factors related to Israeli security as added value that could be exploited to generate political support for separation. But in essence the wall was little more than a demographic barrier. "The idea that just delineating a border on a map will stop people coming is becoming more and more unrealistic," Shueftan told *Time* magazine. "[Openness] is actually a calamity. Immigration is changing demographics in places like Europe, and I can't think of anything in the next century that is more important than dealing with that."

Behind Schueftan's logic lay a brazen racism that he made no attempt to conceal. While teaching at Tel Aviv University's master's program on Diplomacy and Security, the professor delighted in unleashing vitriolic, anti-Arab outbursts before his students. On the policy of *hafrada*, he once declared, "The Palestinians are a repulsive part of the Middle East, let's leave those ratbags." In another class, Schueftan exclaimed, "While Israel sends a satellite into space, the Arabs come up with a new kind of hummus." He went on: "The best thing that has happened to the Arabs is that they agreed to be occupied." And finally: "If you want to be a hero in the Arab world, you have to get blown up. I am prepared to make a personal contribution." According to the Israeli paper *Maariv*, "some of the students burst out loud laughing and applauded" at this line.

Schueftan's racism never denied him entry into the halls of power. As he revealed to *Maariv*: "A senior official told me that he does not call me for consultation because I sit in his head and every time, before he makes a decision, he hears me telling him: 'You idiot, what are you doing?' And then he answers me and decides. Many people in the military and political establishments have taken my courses. My level of contact with that group is very high. A large proportion of Israel's decision makers were students of mine or have listened to my lectures. I gave a lecture to all the division and brigade commanders of the ground forces and some of them invited me afterwards to talk to their units. Sometimes they contact me afterwards to consult with me. Nearly all the political-military establishment has some kind of relationship with me. I would not want them to be alienated from the important people who are outside the establishment. Access to decision-makers here is among the easiest in the world."

Once Sharon was elected prime minister, Schueftan enjoyed unfettered access to him and his advisers. The professor impressed upon Sharon the practicality of *hafrada* while Schueftan's colleague, the self-styled "Arab Demographic Threat" specialist Arnon Sofer, sold him on the strategy's demographic benefits. Sofer, who directed the National Security Studies Center at the University of Haifa, where Schueftan served as his deputy, had spent decades focusing on the escalating danger that the Palestinian birthrate posed to the "Jewish and democratic state."

In 2001 Sofer produced a monograph, *Israel and Demography: 2000–2020*, that spelled out the dire consequences of not enacting a policy of separation. With an unprecedented level of Israeli Jews citing the country's Jewish character as more important than its democratic system, Sofer suddenly had the ear of everyone from backbenchers in the Knesset to the prime minister. In a presentation before a Knesset committee in 2001, Sofer warned his rapt audience that Jews would comprise a mere 42 percent of the population between the Jordan River and the Mediterranean Sea by 2020. At the same time, he said, the population of Palestinians inside Israel would exceed 50 percent, meaning they could end Zionism simply by exercising their democratic right to vote. "If this is the process, and the problem is not dealt with, our country is finished in seventeen years, and there will be a collapse," Sofer warned.

Seated in the audience and hanging on to Sofer's every word was Sharon. Days later, according to René Backmann, the foreign affairs columnist for *Le Nouvel Observateur* and author of the essential history of the separation wall, *A Wall in Palestine*, Sharon invited the professor to a private meeting where he explained his plan in detail. Sofer recommended that Israel absorb 80 percent of the West Bank's Jewish settlers and all the settlers in East Jerusalem by evacuating fifty distant settlements while engulfing the major Jewish population blocs with the wall or fenced extensions of it—a unilateral redrawing of borders. With more than three hundred thousand Jews absorbed into the new "Israel proper," the threat posed by gestating Arab fetuses would be severely diluted.

Then the Palestinians of the West Bank would be crammed into what Sofer called "three sausages," or population clusters, which would comprise only half of the West Bank's land. Electrified fencing and army checkpoints would serve as the casing for these "sausages," indefinitely confining the Palestinians to heavily militarized ghettoes. Finally, Israel needed to maintain a constant military presence in the Jordan Valley in order to sever the Palestinians from the broader Arab world while maintaining the vast Israeli agricultural enterprises in the occupied area, including profitable date farms, wineries, and mineral extraction projects. To accomplish this, Sofer urged Sharon to build the separation wall along demographic lines.

Sharon initially opposed the wall out of concern that it would disconnect central Israel from the settlement enterprise he claimed as his legacy, thus ending a long love affair symbolized by his purchase of a confiscated Arab home in the heart of Jerusalem's Muslim Quarter. During a series of meetings and correspondences, Sofer battered Sharon with statistics highlighting the existential nature of the Arab "demographic threat," including studies from Israeli think tanks and universities reinforcing his own findings. "In the absence of separation, the meaning of such a majority [of Palestinians]—is the end of the Jewish State of Israel," he wrote Sharon in March 2002. "You should remember that on the same day as the Israel Defense Forces is investing efforts and succeeding in eliminating one terrorist or another, on that very same day, as on every day of the year, within the territories of western Israel, about 400 children are being born, some of whom will become new suicide terrorists! Do you realize this?"

While Sofer lobbied Sharon, a working group of academics met at a think tank in Jerusalem called the Van Leer Institute to plot the separation step by step. "Had the Jewish underground operated with the same degree of secrecy as the team that meets at Van Leer, it is doubtful that it would ever have been exposed," reporter Lily Galili wrote in 2002. Yiftah Spector, a famous former Air Force pilot who joined the Van

Leer group, warned that if the Palestinians ever came to outnumber Israeli Jews, "the new majority could, through democratic means, eliminate the Jewish state."

At the Inter Disciplinary Center (IDC), a privately funded university in the affluent coastal city of Herziliya, a team of academics and intelligence figures were also hard at work on a plan to counter the "demographic threat." They concluded that some form of transfer was necessary, though they believed it could be accomplished through redrawing the borders of Israel to exclude the Arab city of Umm al-Fahm, which lies just on the Israeli side of the Green Line, forcing tens of thousands of Palestinian citizens of Israel and their property into the hands of the Palestinian Authority simply because they were not Jewish. Sofer cheered the plan, remarking, "This is not expulsion, it's irredentism."

Sofer took his apocalyptic presentation to the general public at the 2002 Herziliya Conference, an annual affair held at the IDC that American journalists nicknamed "the neocon Woodstock." His data on the looming threat to Jewish political dominance in Israel riveted the audience. Shlomo Gazit, the former director of Israeli Military Intelligence and longtime president of Ben Gurion University, came to a startling conclusion after listening to Sofer: "Democracy has to be subordinated to demography."

Sofer echoed Gazit's view. "If you endanger the Jewishness of my country, we will have to compromise democracy. You will see long nails," the professor told a documentary filmmaker, flicking out his fingers for effect. Benjamin Netanyahu, who served at the time as Finance Minister in Sharon's government, sounded a similar note when he spoke at Herziliya the following year, positing democracy as a potential threat to the Jewish state. "The [Israeli] Declaration of Independence depicts Israel as both Jewish and democratic," Netanyahu said. "To stop democracy from wiping out the Jewish nature of the country we must ensure the Jewish majority."

Like Sharon, Netanyahu was a lifelong proponent of Greater Israel. But he heartily endorsed the separation wall, describing it a necessary barrier against "demographic spillover" from the West Bank. By 2001, Sharon pledged to implement separation, vowing to "make *hafrada* across the land." Thanks to Sofer, Schueftan, and military intelligence confidants like Avi Dichter, he had come to accept the importance of a giant concrete wall that established demographic lines while voiding Palestinian national aspirations. Yet he recognized that in style and in substance, Israeli separation was remarkably similar to South African apartheid—the Afrikaans term translated literally to "separateness." Thus Sharon consciously replaced the term "separation" with "withdrawal," whitewashing the racist undertones of his policy by co-opting the conciliatory language of the Zionist left.

The stylistic alteration was apparent when Sharon addressed a 2003 Likud Party meeting. "You might not like the word, but what's happening is occupation," he told his stunned audience. "Holding 3.5 million Palestinians under occupation is bad thing for Israel, for the Palestinians, and for the Israeli economy. We have to end this subject without risking our security." The remark seemed so out of character that it convinced influential liberal Washington columnists and leaders of Israel's Zionist left that the patron saint of Greater Israel was undergoing a change of heart.

The Sharon government went to pains to present the wall as a temporary measure that would not affect any negotiations on permanent borders. It was officially designated as a "fence" and a "barrier," not a wall, giving the impression that it could be removed as soon as the Palestinians gave up their bloodthirsty campaign to conquer Israel. For Israeli Jews, the language encouraged the widespread belief that the occupation was an ephemeral phenomenon resulting entirely from urgent security needs. As long as they believed the occupation was fleeting, Israelis were psychologically freed to participate in its maintenance as conscripted soldiers, military desk jockeys, and as the Tel Aviv mortgage brokers who financed homes in "Judea and Samaria."

Sharon was aware that the reaction from international allies could be harsh if the wall was seen as a permanent border. After all, the wall had not been drawn along legally recognized 1949 armistice lines, but along demographic lines instead, absorbing major Jewish settlement blocs on the Palestinian side of the Green Line into Israel just as Sofer and Schueftan advised. The result was the unilateral confiscation of 184,868 dunams (more than 34,000 acres) of privately owned Palestinian land, an act the International Court of Justice of the United Nations called "de facto annexation," but which the Israeli Supreme Court would eventually approve. Eighty percent of Israeli settlers now lived within areas annexed by the wall while Palestinian villages like Bilin and sizable towns like Ni'lin were due to be severed in half by the wall, with much of their land effectively annexed to nearby settlements. Towns like al-Walajeh would be literally encircled, with residents required to pass through army-administered tunnels just to tend their fields.

Thanks to the wall and the overall regime of *hafrada*, Israeli contact with Palestinians was reduced to a minimum. For those living inside the Tel Aviv cultural bubble, the occupation existed only in the media, and even there, it was not always scrutinized in a particularly critical manner. Meanwhile, just thirty minutes away, a giant zone of exclusion had been established, with a new regime of checkpoints surrounding Palestinian population centers, forcing the urban population into micro-zones. Passing through the checkpoints was a daily exercise in humiliation that reminded the non-people of the dominant force controlling their every move.

"Animals. Animals. Like the Discovery Channel," an Israeli soldier posted outside Ramallah commented to the documentary filmmaker Yoav Shamir, pointing at a line of Palestinians shivering in a snowstorm while they waited to pass through a checkpoint. "All of Ramallah is a jungle. There are monkeys, dogs, gorillas. The problem is that the animals are locked in, they can't come out. We're humans. They're animals. They aren't human. We are." Though delivered in a crude manner, the soldier's diatribe presented a neat distillation of the logic behind *hafrada*.

Back in Tel Aviv, where suicide attacks faded from memory, in large part because Palestinian factions had scrapped the tactic, the "war over the morning coffee and croissant" appeared to have been won. By 2010, Prime Minister Netanyahu was celebrating what he called "the Big Quiet," a phrase he had coined to describe his strategy of "neither war nor peace" and that he amplified to highlight Israel's position as despotic Arab regimes collapsed in popular uprising. Under Netanyahu's direction, the occupation would be carefully managed—but never ended—to guarantee tranquility for Israeli Jews and harsh consequences for any Palestinian who dared resist Israeli control. As long as the one-way peace held, Israelis would support the status quo, and by extension, Netanyahu.

"We have gotten used to the idea that every problem has a solution," said Netanyahu's vice prime minister and confidant Moshe Ya'alon. "We are so patronizing and feel so powerful that we feel that we can solve everything. . . . Mankind arrived on the moon so why can't we solve the Israeli-Palestinian conflict?"

Distilling Netanyahu's Big Quiet philosophy into a single sentence, Ya'alon explained, "There are some things that we can't solve, it has to be managed."

Although most major Palestinian factions in the West Bank increasingly had concluded that the tactic of suicide bombing had been a tactical mistake, and that a continual armed struggle was futile, at least for the moment, they could not seem to agree on a new strategy to resist Israeli domination. How could they challenge Israel's occupation and disrupt the Big Quiet without a military strategy? This question vexed many Palestinians during the lull that followed the Second Intifada. In the rural villages that lay in the path of the separation wall, however, an unarmed protest movement arose in almost spontaneous fashion, filling the void with new energy and a sense of creativity that attracted a generation of Israeli and international social justice activists to the Palestinians' side. It was there, in the teargas-choked olive fields of villages like Ni'ilin, Bil'in, and Nabi Saleh, that Palestinian nonviolence would be tested, and where questions about its efficacy would be resolved.

The Joint Struggle

With the rise of *hafrada*, a sense of urgency spread throughout the Palestinian villages in the path of the separation wall. In March 2003, the bulldozers and earthmoving machines arrived at Mas'ha, town of about two thousand in the northern West Bank, near the city of Nablus. The separation wall was going to annex 97 percent of Mas'ha's land to Elkana, an adjacent Jews-only settlement, forcing the residents of the town to pass through a special gate at army-approved hours to reach their fields, or visit the outside world. A group from the village immediately formed a popular committee to begin coordinating resistance. Elsewhere in the West Bank, particularly in the refugee camps around Nablus, the armed struggle still raged. But Mas'ha decided to try a different approach.

On March 29, 2003, Mas'ha's popular committee staged its first demonstration against the wall. Joining the local residents were Israeli and international activists invited to the village for the protest. A week later, the Israelis and internationals returned, mobilizing a protest of five hundred people that generated global media attention. At the end of the demonstration, someone pitched a tent on the plot of land confiscated by the State of Israel for the construction of the wall. The tent became the center of Mas'ha Camp, a spontaneous community that Israelis and Palestinians made into their home for four months, nurturing an unprecedented sense of binational solidarity while developing the tactics for a joint struggle against occupation.

From Mas'ha, activists set out to other villages to build the movement, helping to organize protests in places like Qalqilya, a city of forty-five thousand that would be completely surrounded by the twenty-five-foot-high wall. Those who convened at Mas'ha Camp were not waiting for a government-led process of negotiations to deliver peace; they were embarking on a process of decolonization on their own terms. "At Mas'ha Camp we lived together, ate together and talked together twenty-four hours a day for four months," a Palestinian participant, Nazeez Sha'alabi, reflected. "Our fear was never from each other, but only from the Israeli soldiers and settlers."

The camp produced the first joint act of civil disobedience against the wall, with Israeli activists rushing a section of the fencing installed inside Mas'ha and literally tearing it down—a symbolic rejection of *hafrada*. On other side of the fence stood a platoon of Israeli soldiers with live ammunition in their magazines. They opened fire on the protesters, wounding one in the thigh and nearly killing him. The incident generated a firestorm of media coverage, prompting Israeli society to evaluate the human cost of the wall for the first time. "The military had difficulty dealing with us because they weren't allowed to use the same means of repression if it were a Palestinian-only demonstration," said Uri Gordon, an Israeli anarchist, lecturer at Loughborough University in the United Kingdom, and veteran of the Mas'ha Camp. "So there was an initial feeling that the group was able to catch the state off guard but that rapidly changed."

The original protest tent moved wherever the bulldozers were, eventually winding up in front of the home of Hani Amer, a Palestinian farmer whose home would be surrounded on all sides by the wall and a fence separating the settlement of Elkana. Finally, under the auspices of Order 101, a military order forbidding anyone from gathering in groups of more than ten in the Occupied Territories, effectively banning any form of protest in the West Bank, the army evicted the activists from Mas'ha Camp. The veterans of Mas'ha formed a new protest faction called Anarchists Against the Wall. Despite the name, its members explicitly eschewed any concrete political framework. "The name didn't carry strong ideological implications but was chosen more for the provocative impact," Gordon explained. "We could have named it 'Satanists Against the Wall.' The aim was just to use the transgressive value of that word, although the form of that initiative has taken on some anarchist characteristics."

Indeed, the Anarchists were dedicated to little more than the informal principles of direct action and civil disobedience. In one of its few communiqués, the protest camp veterans declared: "We forced open the gate at Mas'ha to open a gap in the wall of hatred and to provide without actions a living, kicking alternative to the apartheid policy of the Israeli government. . . . The Berlin Wall was not dismantled by rulers and agreements, but by the citizens who felled it with their own hands. . . . The ethnic cleansing is occurring before our eyes and we have only one option: to use the few rights we still have from the remnants of Israeli democracy and break the racist, immoral laws."

Following the success at Mas'ha, the struggle graduated to Budrus, a town set to lose three thousand trees, three hundred acres, and its residents' livelihood to the wall. The village's weekly popular protests spread across the West Bank to as many as twenty more towns, eventually becoming the subject of the award winning 2009 Palestinian-Israeli documentary film, *Budrus*. Nearby, in Bil'in, residents injected the popular struggle with a sense of theatrical flair that attracted attention from an international media that had dismissed unarmed Palestinian resistance for what seemed like generations. At a typical Bil'in protest that captured international attention, Israeli and Palestinian demonstrators painted themselves blue and dressed up as the Nawi, the aliens from James Cameron's blockbuster film *Avatar* that depicted an indigenous race battling marauding colonialists seeking to usurp their land and natural resources. In another Bil'in demonstration, protesters wheeled a cardboard model of the *Mavi Marmara* toward Israeli troops, provoking the surreal but revealing scene of soldiers destroying a miniature replica of the ship their navy had assaulted just days before.

Almost as soon as they began, many of the popular protests ground to a halt. Repressive measures, from night arrests to permit revocations, were too overwhelming for most villages to withstand. But in a select few other villages, the struggle persisted, thriving on a rare sense of factional unity in the face of dispossession. Indeed, in towns from Bil'in to Beit Ommar to al-Walajeh, and in Ni'lin, members of rival groups like Hamas, Islamic Jihad, and Fatah, along with Palestinian independents and leftists, put aside their disputes to challenge the occupation with tactics agreed on through consensus in village popular committees.

As the resistance mounted, the Israeli army ratcheted up the violence. In Bil'in, a soldier fired a high velocity teargas projectile—"The Rocket"—directly into the chest of Bassem Abu Rahme as he shouted, "Stop firing! Stop firing!" from across the separation fence. He happened to be standing on land recently handed over to the residents of Bil'in by the Israeli Supreme Court, but the army simply ignored the ruling. A beloved local protest leader known for his jovial attitude and generosity to the protesters who poured into Bil'in each Friday, Abu Rahme, died as his friends, both Israeli and Palestinian, laid their hands on his chest, applying pressure in a futile attempt to stop the bleeding. (Footage of Abu Rahme's death is featured in the Oscar-nominated documentary about Bil'in's protest struggle, *Five Broken Cameras*). Months earlier, Abu Rahme's brother, Ashraf, was bound and shot in the foot by an Israeli soldier after being arrested while delivering medicine to nearby Ni'lin. Abu Rahme's sister, Jawaher, was killed months later when she was overcome by teargas fired by Israeli soldiers. Israeli army spokespeople initially claimed Jawaher Abu Rahme had been murdered in an "honor killing" until medical evidence forced them to admit responsibility for her death.

In Ni'lin in July 2008, a Border Policeman fired a single shot into the head of ten-year-old Ahmed Mousa. "I ran toward the ambulance with Ahmad in my hands," recalled Saeed Amireh, a twenty-four-year-old member of the Ni'lin popular committee. "But when his insides started falling out I couldn't bear it anymore." (After a haphazard police investigation into the killing, an Israeli court found Mousa's killer, Omri Abu, innocent of all major charges, accepting his explanation that he felt "immediate danger and alarm.") Just hours after Mousa's emotionally charged funeral, a Border Police officer fired a rubber bullet at close range into the head of seventeen-year-old Youssef Amireh, mortally wounding him in his front yard with his family, observing the demonstration that had just begun—"They've exploded his head," a friend remarked.

The same night, in Tel Aviv, the Anarchists Against the Wall protested Mousa's death by attempting to block the road outside the home of Defense Minister Ehud Barak. At the time, they were unaware that Amireh had been killed as well. "We're here to ask, 'What about accountability?'" Pollack said of the protest. "[Barak] is directly in charge of the army. He is the head commander of the army. He is accountable." A few days later, Alex Cohn, a twenty-one-year-old army refuser and activist, spotted the Israeli Army spokesman Avi Benayahu noshing at a Tel Aviv restaurant. Benayahu had denied that Israeli soldiers were responsible for Mousa's death. Cohn quickly printed out a photo of the ten-year-old child, rushed back to the restaurant, and stood next to Benayahu's table, silently holding the photo aloft while the portly military flack nervously licked an ice cream cone a few feet away.

In Ni'lin, the casualties continued to pile up, from Tristan Anderson, an American social justice activist struck in the head by a high-velocity Israeli teargas canister and left half-paralyzed and half-blind, to Yousef Srur, a thirty-six-year-old village resident killed by a single shot from a soldier's .22 Ruger rifle (among those who rushed Srur's body into a Red Crescent ambulance was Pollack). The use of .22 rifles, deployed by the army to shatter the bones and maim the limbs of protesters, had been explicitly banned by Israel's Supreme Court, but the army continued to use them anyway without any restraint. In the face of the escalating violence, however, the village obstructed the completion of a section of the separation wall that would transform what had been one of Palestine's most prosperous municipalities into an encircled ghetto, an economic dead zone.

Bekah Wolf, a Jewish-American activist who had lived in the West Bank since marrying one of the Palestinian leaders of the popular struggle in Beit Ommar, said at the time of the demonstrations, "What I think has been happening is that Ni'lin has become not only a symbol of Palestinian resistance, but a rebirth of the kind of popular resistance that has been successful in the past. And so it has become incredibly dangerous in some ways to the Israeli military and the Israeli government as a whole."

Abdullah Abu Rahme, the head of the popular committee in Bil'in, agreed. In his village, the protests eventually forced the army to reroute the path of the wall, a partial victory that at least guaranteed less land would be annexed. "We know that what worries the Israelis more is that this style of a non-violent struggle might spread from Bil'in, Ni'lin and other numbered centers and become a wide model," Abdullah Abu Rahme said. "So they are seeking to suppress this model before it spreads even more, because they know our struggle is justified and that they are losing."

On May 15 2009, a Jewish-Canadian independent journalist named Jesse Rosenfeld took me to my first protest in Ni'lin. With a full beard and a thick mane of hair glinted with gray streaks that made him look much older than twenty-six, Rosenfeld had apparently made little attempt to insulate himself from the stress of life under occupation. He was brimming with nervous energy but showed no sign of trepidation as we navigated around army checkpoints to enter into the occupied village. Jesse had moved to Ramallah three months after graduating from McGill University in Montreal, where he helped lead student Palestine solidarity groups in rancorous battles with the Canadian pro-Israel lobby. Jesse arrived at the end of the Second Intifada.

"The major cities like Ramallah were pacified and most Palestinians were politically coping with the ramifications of the Intifada when I moved to Palestine," Jesse told me. "Because of the wall, that was one of the major points for Israel to colonize land around the Green Line, so one of the only centers of popular action was centered on those villages. The popular struggle against the wall provided an interesting model for them to link together. These were farming villages not really involved in the intifada now thrusting themselves to the center of Palestinian resistance without a hell of a lot of people, and what I found compelling was the way they tried to force Palestinian debate about resistance. And it was really the only thing going on at the time. So the villages were the place to go, watching them play out to the cameras of the West to keep resistance alive."

We entered the center of Ni'lin on the sixty-first anniversary of Nakba Day, a commemoration of the process of ethnic cleansing that stripped the village of vast stretches of farmland extending all the way to the Israeli city now known as Lod (with the completion of the wall, the village would be reduced to 56 percent of its original size). Jesse charged up a hill, asking a group of local boys where the protest was. Trying to conceal their amusement at Jesse's mangled Arabic, they pointed up the road toward the wall to an open field where we arrived at the friction point between a long procession of protesters and a phalanx of soldiers bristling with weapons and determined to prevent the marchers from reaching the wall.

In the parched hills above the village, Israeli soldiers took positions behind rows of cacti, preparing to launch a fusillade of percussion grenades. Suddenly, a deep, unbearably loud explosion reverberated through the crowd of protesters, sending everyone barreling downhill, through the narrow lanes of the town center, then into a dilapidated lot that seemed to provide adequate cover. A hundred meters away, the local *shabab*—teenage and preadolescent boys who formed the frontlines of the protest—wound up their slingshots, sending a volley of rocks in the soldiers' direction. Then, seemingly from out of nowhere, teargas canisters rained down on us. They were the high-velocity kind that had killed Bassem Abu Rahme and severely wounded Tristan Anderson. I followed a dozen protesters up a ladder, over a cinder-block wall, scurrying frantically through a warren of yards, and then I watched them reassemble for another futile push toward the wall.

As the army chased the protesters around the village, the march dispersed and fanned out across town. On several corners, masked *shabab* continued to launch stones toward the soldiers, who had begun moving in to make arrests. An older man shouted at me not to photograph those who did not conceal their faces; the Shin Bet would use any photos posted online to identify stone throwers, arrest them in night raids, then subject them to harsh interrogations at a nearby military prison. By three p.m., a cloud of teargas hung over the entire village, searing my eyes with a stinging pain. The army eventually scored a direct hit on me and Jesse, blanketing us in a cloud of gas that sent us staggering into a nearby grocery store, where Jesse collapsed on the ground, requiring three mildly amused clerks to revive him. When he came to, he asked me if I wanted to stay in the village any longer.

"Why wouldn't I?" I replied. "I haven't breathed this well since my last aromatherapy session."

"Well, the army usually gets more violent as the day goes on and the journalists and Israelis start to leave," Jesse warned. "They will probably move into town soon with the .22's out."

The prospect of ducking live bullets was enough to persuade me to leave. With my head throbbing with a dull pain, my eyes still stinging, and my clothes soaked in teargas residue, we drove past a flying Israeli checkpoint blocking Ni'lin's main entrance and out of town on Highway 446. The highway connected three settlements, providing their residents an easy path to Israeli urban centers, and generally without having to endure the sight of Arabs. (As a promotional pamphlet distributed in Brooklyn by the ultra-Orthodox settlement of Emmanuel promised, "A motored system is being developed that will make it possible to travel quickly and safely to the Tel Aviv area and to Jerusalem on modern throughways, bypassing Arab towns.") In order to limit Palestinian contact with the settlers—*hafrada* on a micro level—Israel's military administrators planned to close the entrance that connected Ni'lin to

Highway 446, officially segregating the road. The plan would sever the town in two, forcing Palestinians to travel between upper and lower Ni'lin in a tunnel, reducing them to the status of Morlocks.

Just moments ago, Jesse and I were dodging teargas canisters in a high-intensity riot. Now, after being waved through a checkpoint and an easy twenty-five-minute drive uninterrupted by traffic, we were back in Tel Aviv.

That night, I met some Israeli activist friends at Hudna, a trendy outdoor bar on a bleak, industrial street in Florentine. The bar was originally established as a gathering place for Israeli leftists and young Palestinians who lived in nearby Jaffa. Having fallen under the ownership of an Israeli army reservist who appeared out of uniform as a dreadlocked bohemian, the place quickly became a virtually Jews-only mecca for local hipsters. Jesse arrived at the table with a round of beers and news from Ni'lin. Soldiers had lightly wounded a twelve-year-old girl, Summer Amireh, in the arm with a shot from a Ruger .22 caliber rifle.

Rising over Florentine was the brightly lit "ghost tower" in Neve Sha'nan where wealthy Jewish foreigners spent their vacations, but which remained empty for most of the year. It was essentially a luxurious glass-and-steel mausoleum. Among the tower's most famous residents was Marty Peretz, the former *New Republic* magazine owner who had abandoned his East Coast intellectual environs. "I've made Tel Aviv my locale now because in Jerusalem you wake up in the morning with the Jewish problem, and you go to sleep with the Palestinian problem," Peretz told a reporter, invoking the cliché of the Tel Aviv bubble.

I turned to Jesse to complain about the sense of cognitive dissonance, of hanging out at a hipster bar that could have been anywhere in the West, in Berlin or Brooklyn, with the residue of teargas still on my shirt. "Yeah, I know," he said. "It's always incredibly jarring to be in these rural Palestinian villages and experience army raids and repression at demos, and then you get back into this bright urban metropolis where you're living in the cultural equivalent of Brooklyn, except it's completely segregated. Most of the people at this bar not only have no idea what's going on but no capacity to deal with the proximity of Palestinians. You talk to them and it's like this distant thing—they talk about Palestine with less familiarity than Kuala Lumpur."

As we talked, the pulsing sound of a fusion jazz band jamming in an adjacent bar wafted our way. The guitarist was soloing over a driving bass vamp, working to a furious climax with a keyboardist who urged him forward with emphatic, attacking chord stabs. These were top players; I had met a few Israelis like them in jazz clubs in New York City, and in the cities of Europe. Most of them hated the occupation, the militancy of Jewish nationalism, the whole suffocating climate of an enclosed Israeli life. Soon these musicians would be overseas again, cutting sessions and touring clubs. But as they thrilled fans with their chops, Palestinians were confined *over there*; behind concrete cordons, in underground tunnels, out of sight and out of mind, in "something like a cage," as Benny Morris said. The Tel Aviv bubble required the Iron Wall.

My Mother Before Justice

On a late Friday morning in August 2010, beneath a blistering hot sun, Joseph Dana and I set out on foot from central Jerusalem to the East Jerusalem neighborhood of Sheikh Jarrah. There, we followed directions provided beforehand until we located an old Ford hatchback parked on a hill. A few hundred meters below was the Shimon Ha'Tzadek compound that fundamentalist settlers had recently established in the homes of Palestinians forcibly expelled on orders by the Jerusalem municipality. Later that day, a protest of mostly Jewish Israeli leftists known as the Sheikh Jarrah Solidarity Movement would take place outside the compound.

Our destination was Ni'lin. A wave of arrests and harsh Israeli raids had whittled the weekly protests down from several hundred protesters to about twenty locals who could afford to risk arrest and the revocation of their work permits, and whoever was able to join them from the outside.

Joining for our excursion to Ni'lin was Uri Agnon, a twenty-year-old music teacher with long, sandy locks. A lifelong Jerusalemite, Uri had experienced his first taste of the joint struggle in the demonstrations that took place each week in Sheikh Jarrah, joining them soon after they began in the summer of 2009 against the government-approved expulsions of Palestinian families. With families thrown out in the street with their belongings, Orthodox settlers who claimed they held pre-1948 certificates proving the homes in the neighborhood were rightfully theirs moved in under police guard. Joseph was among the first on the scene to videotape the expulsions as they took place.

Initially led by radical leftists who emphasized solidarity with the dispossessed local families, the Sheikh Jarrah movement quickly attracted liberal Zionist luminaries of Israel's Enlightened Public, from the writer David Grossman to former Knesset Speaker Avraham Burg to members of the Meretz Party. For them, the protests represented a chance to reassert the values of "Israeli democracy" against fundamentalist settlers, and to struggle for the "soul" of the Jewish state against a right-wing government that had little interest in the two-state solution.

And yet, some of Jerusalem's liberal Zionist activists lived in Arab homes confiscated from their original owners in 1948. Ethan Bronner, who at the time served as the chief of the *New York Times*' Jerusalem Bureau, said in May 2010, "One of the things that is most worrying not just the left but a lot of people in Israel about this decision [regarding the Sheikh Jarrah evictions] is if the courts in Israel are going to start recognizing property ownership from before the State [of Israel was founded]."

He added, "I think the Palestinians are going to have a fairly big case. I for example live in West Jerusalem. My entire neighborhood was Palestinian before 1948." In fact, Bronner operated out of the former home of exiled former BBC Arabic broadcaster and scholar Hasan Karmi, one of ten thousand properties seized by Israeli authorities in West Jerusalem. The house was purchased by Thomas Friedman in 1984 just as he began his four-year stint as the *Times*' Jerusalem bureau chief.

As mainstream liberals poured into Sheikh Jarrah, seizing the opportunity to inject the moribund peace camp with new energy, the joint struggle risked mutating into a Jews-only affair, with Palestinians deployed primarily for moral ornamentation. Budour Hassan, a twenty-two-year-old Palestinian activist and law student at Hebrew University, wrote of the Sheikh Jarrah movement, "For all their activism, they have failed to fully embrace the Palestinian public and get it involved. Their demonstrations are dominated by white, secular liberal Zionists and the Palestinian voice, which they supposedly want to make heard, is inaudible amid a chorus of Hebrew-language chants about peace and coexistence."

Nestled within the Sheikh Jarrah movement, behind the high-profile figures who increasingly dominated its ranks, a new generation of Israelis was experiencing the demonstrations. From Jerusalem, they moved their protests into the Palestinian-Israeli ghetto of Lod to challenge home demolitions, and into the West Bank, to join up with the Palestinian-led popular struggle. Among them was Uri, who led the Sheikh Jarrah "Joy Resistance" drummers who had become the movement's trademark (and whom I nicknamed the Ashkenazi Rhythm Disaster for the excessively regimented, martial-sounding, and frustratingly grooveless beats they banged out at protests). He had brought his snare drum for the protest in Ni'lin, provoking uncomfortable looks between Joseph and me.

"Uh, I hope you can run with that thing on," Joseph told him.

"What do you mean?" Uri said with confusion. Only then did it occur to us that he might not have been to a popular struggle demonstration before.

On the way to Ni'lin, as we puttered toward Highway 446 in our little Ford Fiesta, passing the gated outskirts of the city of Modi'in, where a dozen young settlers were waiting to hitch a ride deeper into the West Bank, Uri peppered us with questions about the demonstrations. He seemed especially concerned about the throwing of stones by Palestinians. "They're just sending a message," I told him. "And it's not like some soldier who's outfitted to resist live rounds and shrapnel is worried about getting hurt by a twelve-year-old with a rock."

But Uri was not satisfied. He told me he was a pacifist, and therefore opposed all forms of violence. When I asked him how he reconciled his pacifism with a situation in which violence was disproportionately on one side, Uri quoted a famous line by the French existentialist Albert Camus: "I believe in justice, but I will defend my mother before justice."

Camus delivered the remark in 1957, a day after having received the Nobel Prize for Literature, during a heated debate with a group of students at the University of Stockholm over the question of Algeria. Camus had rejected the Algerian National Liberation Front's demand for an independent state, arguing that the French *pied noirs* should be allowed to remain in the country in a confederation arrangement. When an Algerian student questioned his commitment to democracy and equality, a flustered Camus replied, "I have said and repeated that we have to bring justice to the Algerian people and grant them a fully democratic regime. . . . I have always condemned terror. I must also condemn a terrorism that is practiced blindly, in the streets of Algiers, for example, and which one day could strike my mother or my family. I believe in justice, but I will defend my mother before justice."

Camus was a *pied noir* who had no intention of leaving the country of his birth, even though France was a short ferry ride away. The rise of the Algerian liberation movement, with its demand for a land free of any French presence and its use of terrorism to achieve that goal, forced him to walk the tightrope between his self-interest and the universal values he had espoused throughout his career. In the end, Camus came down on the former side, alienating himself from left-wing European intellectuals who identified with the Algerian anti-colonial struggle. His experience foreshadowed the quandary of Israelis who sought to unite their liberalism with their Zionism.

Uri had deeper roots in Jerusalem than most Israelis. His great-grandfather was Shmuel Yosef "S. Y." Agnon, the most famous writer of the early Zionist movement, and the recipient of the 1966 Nobel Prize for Literature. Agnon's 1943 short story, "The Lady and the Peddler," was required reading for many Israeli high-schoolers. Written from Mandate Palestine while he watched his native Germany devour its Jewish population, the story portrays a hapless Jewish man welcomed into the home of a generous but mysterious gentile who turns out to be a cannibalistic vampire. The fairytale's lesson was clear: don't trust the *goyim*.

Though his grandfather joined the Movement for a Greater Israel that celebrated Israel's conquest of Arab territory in 1967, Uri's parents reacted to the entrenchment of the occupation by joining up with the earliest inceptions of the peace camp. When Uri came of age, his indignation at the ethnic cleansing of Jerusalem propelled him into the founding ranks of the Sheikh Jarrah movement. In March 2010, he was at the front of what might have been the largest joint Israeli-Palestinian (though overwhelmingly Israeli) demonstration since Mas'ha, leading the Joy Resistance through East Jerusalem. But now that he was branching out, experiencing the struggle beyond the wall, he was forced, as Camus was, to confront his status with his professed ideals. Could he live beside Palestinians without occupation? Or would they devour him like vampires?

We entered the village after midday, barreling down a craggy road full of potholes, and past a butcher shop where a freshly slaughtered cow lay on its side, with blood still drizzling from its throat. Ni'lin's pockmarked, cinder block homes might have been dilapidated and its streets badly underserviced, but the town of five thousand boasted a reputation as one the most prosperous in the West Bank—"the village of entrepreneurs" was its nickname. As the British journalist Jonathan Cook reported, the town had even produced a few millionaires, beneficiaries of what had once been a roaring agricultural business and factories providing soda and gas to Palestinians who lived in and around Ramallah.

But in the year since my first visit to Ni'lin, Israel had completed the section of the wall the protests had attempted to obstruct, consolidating the first stage in the process of ghettoization. The next phase would come with the tunnels, which would drive Ni'lin's factories into ruin by blocking access to Highway 446, turning the town into a replica of Qalqilya, which had seen an exodus of thousands of residents since being surrounded on all sides by the wall. And that was the point. In the long term, the Israeli administrators of the West Bank aimed to coerce much of the Palestinian population out of Area C, the vast area placed by the Oslo Accords under full Israeli control. They would be relocated to Area A, the population clusters overseen by the Palestinian Authority, thereby establishing an encircled, disjointed quasi-state that left the majority of the West Bank's land for the use of Jewish settlers. Through home demolitions, the denial of building and work permits, and general repression in Area C, Israel implemented a strategy Palestinians called "the silent transfer."

The protest in Ni'lin began in a rocky field of olive trees that had been classified as Area C. Men lounged in small groups—women were usually absent from Ni'lin's protests—in the shade of the trees. There we met Saeed Amireh, then a twenty-two-year-old protest leader, with his passable English and Internet savvy, making him the town's de facto emissary to the international activist community. We settled at the base of the tree reserved for international and Israeli activists, joined by two veteran members of Anarchists Against the Wall: Efrata, a rail-thin, olive-skinned young woman with close-cropped hair and striking, angular features who offset her model-like looks by dressing in drab, sweat-stained secondhand work uniforms; and Shai, a curly-haired bassoonist in the Tel Aviv Symphony Orchestra with an intense, penetrating gaze. After spending hours with these two, they never said more than a few sentences to me. Their stoicism might have stemmed from their austere punk rock ethos or perhaps from the stress they had absorbed from spending several days each week in the crosshairs of Israeli soldiers. Actually, I never mustered up the nerve to ask them what made them tick.

It was Ramadan, and the village was fasting; the men rose slowly for a prayer and then assembled for a march down a rocky path toward the wall. "Thank you for coming! Thank you!" Muhammad Amireh, a heavy-set, thirty-something protest leader who taught elementary school by day, told the activists through a megaphone. "You are welcome here in Ni'lin, for helping in our struggle for freedom. You are all a credit to humanity." A year ago, the march to the wall would have comprised hundreds of activists and local residents. But Israel had turned the screws on Ni'lin, arresting key protest leaders and revoking scores of work permits, making participation untenable. Only a few dozen were able to join at this point.

"If you have a family and they send you to jail, who will feed them? How can you work?" Saeed Amireh explained to me. "So you can see very few people in this town—and it's a pretty big town—are willing to join us anymore on Fridays. For me, it's possible because I don't have a family to feed." Saeed had just completed a four-month sentence in Ofer Military Prison after a conviction for stone throwing. "The food was shit," he recalled. "Everything was terrible." At the time, Saeed's father,

Ibrahim, was detained without charges in a cell in Ofer, forcing Saeed to drop out of college so he could help support his mother and siblings.

I stood back from the crowd and watched as Muhammad Amireh taunted a small platoon of soldiers posted in a tower behind the wall. "Gilad Shalit is in Gaza, and Netanyahu is sitting in a leather chair, in an air-conditioned office, eating Bomba [a popular Israeli snack food]!" Muhammad shouted in Hebrew. "Netanyahu doesn't give a shit about you! Who are you fighting for? You are little pawns. You occupy and get nothing!" But the soldiers wouldn't budge. A year ago, I thought, they would not have even allowed the demonstration to reach the wall without violently dispersing it.

Another demonstrator threw a live teargas shell recovered from a past protest toward the soldiers. It exploded in mid-air, sending a gust of gas toward the troops and provoking excited cries of "Aywa! Aywa! Aywa!" from the *shabab*. "Tom and Jerry," a local man grumbled to me as he passed by. "Cat and mouse time." The soldiers let loose a volley of teargas on the demonstrators, filling the skies with large, rubber-coated projectiles designed to bounce after hitting the ground, scattering the gas in all directions. I fell back a hundred meters and met a slightly built Israeli with a fuzzy beard observing the demonstration with an impassive gaze. He introduced himself as Limor Goldstein, a lawyer who represented Palestinian demonstrators arrested and put on trial in Israel's military court system. Most of his clients were children.

"They arrest them at night," he told me while a few teargas rounds tumbled from the sky, landing two hundred yards away. "Then they take them to Ofer [Military Prison], usually into a dark cell. It's about 4 a.m. by then. The kids are twelve, thirteen years old. They don't know where they are, and they were just asleep in bed at home. Now a scary soldier is threatening them. Because the kids are so scared, they will confess to anything. And that usually means making something up about the older protest leaders so the army can get long sentences for them and break down the structure of the popular committees."

Limor told me his advocacy work had suffered since he was shot in the head with a rubber bullet by a Border Policeman during a protest in Bil'in in 2008. After several life-saving operations, he said he still suffered from bouts of memory loss and impaired vision. I had become so engrossed in our conversation I nearly forgot about the protest. When I finally retrained my attention on the fields, I spied a dozen men sprinting away from the wall a hundred yards behind us, whooping like Sioux Indians, but I did not think to follow them. Then, when I turned to my left, I saw a uniformed man clasping an M-16, charging furiously toward Limor and me.

"Soldier!" I shouted.

Limor took off, and I sprinted after him, struggling not to fall or twist my ankle on the sharp rocks that lined our path back to the safety of the village. As I sprinted frantically toward the town, the sound of the soldier's boots clomping behind me grew fainter until it disappeared. Having narrowly escaped arrest, I retreated to the edge of town and watched as the soldiers seized a hilltop over the village, firing teargas shells at the *shabab* who had reassembled in the fields to launch rocks from their slingshots. Efrata and Shai waded back into the fields, establishing positions in between the adolescent boys in the fields, deploying human shielding tactics to limit the soldiers' lethal capacity. But the troops seemed unfazed, sending a volley of high-velocity shells directly at the *shabab*. Joseph was wearing one of the gas masks that had been distributed to Israelis virtually for free to prepare them for a chemical weapons attack—or to at least help convince them of its looming danger—and had managed to remain among the gassy clouds hovering over the wall. Uri, for his part, had followed me back into the village. He sidled up beside me and watched the drama unfold.

"I wonder," he said, pointing at a Red Crescent volunteer treating one of the *shabab* who had cut his arm in a fall, "would they care for a soldier if they wounded him? Like, would they take him to the hospital?"

My heart had been pumping from sprinting through the fields and I felt anger swell up in my chest at Uri's question. As my heart rate lowered and I was able to contain my outrage, I considered explaining to him the dire consequences Ni'lin residents would face if one of them harmed a soldier. Then I reminded myself that despite his mature demeanor, Uri was a twenty-year-old kid. I told him, "Maybe you should ask them what they think, instead of relying on me." He nodded and said nothing.

Over the next months, Uri and his snare drum became a frequent presence at West Bank demonstrations, including in Hebron, where I watched soldiers tackle him during a protest on Shuhada Street and drag him away to prison. The following year, he and a handful of activists from the Sheikh Jarrah Solidarity movement would interrupt an appearance at a Jerusalem literary festival by the British author Ian McEwan, hoisting a banner reading, "Don't Shake Hands With Apartheid." McEwan had just accepted the million-dollar Jerusalem Prize from Nir Barkat, the mayor of Jerusalem who orchestrated the mass demolition of Palestinian homes and the forced evictions of Palestinian families to make room for Jewish settlers. After McEwan sought atonement by attending the weekly Sheikh Jarrah demonstration at the invitation of David Grossman, Uri and the young activists delivered him with a stinging rebuke.

In the meantime, Uri and I retreated from a cloud of teargas that wafted in our direction from the fields below. Choking and gasping for air, we staggered toward the center of town to collect ourselves. By the time we returned to the fields, the demo had drawn to an uneventful conclusion. The soldiers retreated behind the wall and the protesters marched back to the village. Muhammad Amireh thanked everyone for coming in a short but effusive megaphone address, as he probably had week after week, and then Efrata and Shai rushed into their car to catch the next protest in nearby Nabi Saleh, a routine they repeated each Friday. I thought about the first time I was in Ni'lin, how the demonstration lasted until nightfall and required live fire to suppress. This time they only needed a small platoon and about an hour's worth of teargas. The Israelis were grinding down the popular struggle village by village, starting with Ni'lin.

I returned to Ni'lin on several occasions, and instead of depending on the Anarchists for a ride back to Tel Aviv, making me a prisoner to the grueling schedule they observed with military precision, I sometimes stayed behind to socialize with the local guys afterward. After one protest in January 2011, Saeed Amirah guided me through the village's olive fields, which were stunningly verdant from the seasonal rains. "I have so many stories from these fields," he said wistfully. "I can't even begin to tell you. He pointed to the settlement of Hashmonaim that lay directly across the wall. Above the neat lines of suburban style subdivision homes with red, mission-style roofs was a tower lined with antennae. Saeed said, "That's how they watch every day. It is the army's camera, and they can see our every move right now."

Then he pointed to the olive fields on the other side of the wall. "My grandfather goes out every morning to see those trees," he explained. "Those were his trees and now he can only look at them over an annexation wall to see how they are doing. You know why we still struggle here when they are killing us, shooting us, arresting us all the time? These fields mean everything. And so resistance has become our way of life."

To experience the world beyond the wall, Saeed had to apply to the Israeli military administration for a permit, a process that could take months, and which the army could manipulate in order to punish him for his role in the protests. "When we are arrested," he said, "they take us to a little prison. But when we are out here, we are in the big prison." As I followed Saeed through the grassy fields, I collected a few expended teargas shells labeled, "Made in the USA." In the distance, over the concrete wall that formed a cordon around the village, we could see the skyline of Tel Aviv. From the clouds above the city, I watched a plane make its final approach to the runway at Ben Gurion International Airport.

The Crazy Village

By early 2011, the West Bank villages were reeling from a wave of arrests that not only targeted protest leaders, but also children as young as eleven years old. Israeli forces tested new and unusual "less lethal" weapons on the demonstrators, seeking to market its elaborate matrix of control as a model for the Western world. The draconian measures reflected growing frustration among the army's high command with its inability to decisively crush the demonstrations. As Defense Ministry official Amos Gilad complained to diplomats in a private meeting, "We don't do Gandhi very well."

Avi Mizrahi, the former Israeli Army Central Command chief in charge of the West Bank, visited a demonstration in the village of Nabi Saleh in early 2010. During a briefing at the US embassy in Tel Aviv a few weeks later, he told then-ambassador James Cunningham he had no idea what motivated the protesters. They were many kilometers from the separation wall, he claimed, and in his mind, they enjoyed unrestricted movement. He was infuriated by the impudence of the Palestinians, who staged weekly marches to a freshwater spring that had been recently seized from them by Jewish settlers.

Cunningham reported back to Washington, informing them that the Israeli army "will start to be more assertive in how it deals with these demonstrations, even demonstrations that appear peaceful." Among the measures he said Mizrahi had authorized was the introduction of "dirty water" trucks, or what demonstrators referred to as "the Skunk"—a vehicle-mounted cannon that sprayed protesters with chemicals that smelled like a rotted corpse and were nearly impossible to wash out. Another weapon introduced into the field was "the Scream," a Long Range Acoustic Device (LRAD) that blasted demonstrators with focused, high-intensity beams of sound, leaving them nauseous and dazed. Having perfected the weapons on demonstrators in the West Bank, Israeli weapons firms were able to market them to American law enforcement departments as "field-tested."

On December 27, 2010, an Israeli court sentenced one of the most respected and prolific Israeli activists, Anarchist Against the Wall veteran Jonathan Pollak, to three months in prison. The twenty-eight-year-old was the key Israeli link to the West Bank villages, and as the Popular Struggle Coordination Committee's media director, a liaison between the movement, the international press corps and Western diplomats, Pollak had taken dozens of European officials into Israeli military prisons to witness the trials of Palestinian demonstrators. Having monitored Pollak for years, the Israeli authorities managed to convict him for participating in a 2009 mass bike ride in Tel Aviv that blocked traffic in protest of Operation Cast Lead, a direct action he had played no role in organizing.

Pollak issued no appeal for leniency. Instead, he appeared in court wearing a shirt emblazoned with the image of Steve Biko, the martyred South African anti-apartheid activist. He addressed the judge: "I will go to prison wholeheartedly and with my head held high. It will be the justice system itself, I believe, that will need to lower its eyes in the face of the suffering inflicted on Gaza's inhabitants, just like it lowers its eyes and averts its vision each and every day when faced with the realities of the occupation."

With his media skills and fluency in English and Hebrew, Joseph Dana was delegated as Pollak's replacement. On a routine basis throughout the week, I watched as Joseph was interrupted with phone calls from Palestinians reporting settler attacks and Israeli raids. He would deliver the news to the list of reporters compiled by Pollak. Joseph's new role required him to observe the full gamut of protests across the West Bank, a grueling task that took him from two or three villages on Friday to two more during the weekend. Though he was unfazed by the harsh conditions he had to endure, Joseph was noticeably uncomfortable in his designated role as spokesman for a protest network that ran on a shoestring budget and had little to no formal organization.

On a cool afternoon in the middle of the week in January 2011, Joseph and I piled into a tiny hatchback on a leafy residential street off Tel Aviv's Allenby Street. At the wheel was Shai, the Anarchists Against the Wall veteran and Tel Aviv Symphony Orchestra musician. On the short drive into the West Bank, Shai popped in a tape of Rachmaninoff and lost himself in the sonata. We were not heading to a protest today, but rather to collect information from the popular committee members of Nabi Saleh, where the army was arresting children during night raids, preparing the legal groundwork for mass detention of the protest leaders. On the way, right before we turned off Highway 443, an Israelis-only bypass road, and onto Highway 446, we parked at a rest stop so Joseph and Shai could compose a press release.

A fourteen-year-old boy, Islam Tamimi, had just been arrested at gunpoint during a night raid in Nabi Saleh and locked inside Ofer Military Prison. Under an intense interrogation from the Shin Bet punctuated by beatings, a frightened and sleep-deprived Islam Tamimi gave the army the confession it wanted, telling them that two of the village protest leaders, Bassem and Naji Tamimi, had organized the equivalent of militant stone throwing brigades, and commanded them by cellphone from rooftops around the town. "It's the first stage in breaking down the village's resistance structure," Shai said.

Joseph wondered if Bassem and Naji were next.

The forced confession eventually formed the basis of a mock expose in *Yedioth Ahronoth* stoking fears of an "organized army of boys" in Nabi Saleh commanded by a "man who organizes violence with military precision"—Naji Tamimi—and the commander of a "group of under fifteen-year-olds"—Bassem Tamimi. Israel's most influential newspaper had once again volunteered its services to the military-intelligence

apparatus, publishing an article that relied on the confession of a frightened, imprisoned boy, exploiting it to offer the army increased political space to intensify its
campaign of repression in the West Bank. Through their press release to the Jerusalem press corps, Joseph and Shai hoped to counter what appeared to be a concerted campaign by Israel's military-media complex to fracture Nabi Saleh's popular
committee.

Arresting and interrogating small children had become a routine task for the
soldiers who maintained Israel's system of control over the Palestinians of the West
Bank. One soldier who served in Hebron in 2010 testified to the reservists' group
Breaking the Silence, "You never know their names, you never talk with them, they
always cry, shit in their pants. . . . There are those annoying moments when you're
on an arrest mission, and there's no room in the police station, so you just take the
kid back with you, blindfold him, put him in a room and wait for the police to come
and pick him up in the morning. He sits there like a dog."

Another soldier who served near Qalqilya in 2007 described arresting a boy for
throwing stones and holding a gun to his head until he begged for mercy: "That
specific kid who actually lay there on the ground, begging for his life, was actually
nine years old. I mean, a kid has to beg for his life? A loaded gun is pointed at him
and he has to plead for mercy? This is something that scars him for life. But I think
if we hadn't entered the village at that point, then stones would be thrown the next
day and perhaps the next time someone would be wounded or killed as a result."

But few children in the West Bank were as well acquainted with the Israeli army
as those who inhabited Nabi Saleh. Many went to bed in fear, knowing that on any
given night, they could be ripped from sleep and taken to a dark cell.

It was midday when we reached Nabi Saleh. The village of 530 lay on a rolling hill
that had turned a lush green from the winter rains. Once inside, we gained a sweeping view of the grassy hills and of the neat rows of red-roofed, suburban-style homes
that comprised the settlement of Halamish—it looked as though a neighborhood in
Gaithersburg, Maryland, had been airdropped into Palestine. Established in 1977
on land privately owned by Palestinians from Nabi Saleh, the settlement of fifteen
hundred stood directly across Route 465, a winding, two-lane road that abutted a
small freshwater spring. No wall separated the settlers from Nabi Saleh, and since
Nabi Saleh's outskirts had been designated as Area C, its residents grew suspicious
that the spring and their outlying farmland would soon be annexed to Halamish.

For generations, the farmers had used the spring that they called Ein al-Quos to
irrigate their fields. But when fundamentalist youth from Halamish turned the spring
into a swimming hole in 2008, then began attacking and intimidating the farmers,
the Tamimi clan that comprised the majority of Nabi Saleh's residents organized a
popular committee. The following year, the demonstrations began, prompting arson
attacks from the settlers and a harsh army crackdown. In turn, Jonathan Pollak and
the Anarchists Against the Wall arrived to bolster the ranks of the local protesters.

The Tamimis were notable among the people of the West Bank, and not only for
their striking appearance. Nearly everyone in the village bore a pale complexion, like

Northern Europeans, with hair colored bright blonde or sandy brown, light-colored eyes, and high, sharply angled cheekbones. Their features reflected a lineage drawn directly from the Crusaders, offering a reminder of the many invaders and occupiers whose blood became intertwined with the heritage of Palestine. Because the village consisted mainly of a single clan, it proved nearly immune to the kind of collaborator networks and permit manipulation Israel had used to fracture other village networks. When the occupation began in 1967, Nabi Saleh became an exceptionally active node of resistance, losing nearly twenty of its residents in both armed and unarmed actions while almost the same number served long sentences in Israeli prisons.

I was accustomed to entering Nabi Saleh on Friday afternoons, during the heat of the protest, after soldiers had entered the village and begun firing teargas shells and rubber bullets in all directions, especially at the *shabab* who lobbed rocks from behind the dumpsters they wheeled down a narrow road for cover. The soldiers routinely tackled the most unruly international activists, sometimes beating or pepper-spraying them, dragging them into army jeeps and off to prison. In recent months, the troops had begun spraying "the Skunk" at anything in their way, including inside the open windows of local homes. The protests went on until nightfall, provoking some of the harshest measures I had seen. Unlike in Ni'lin, women took on a central role in Nabi Saleh, both in the popular committee and in the field, while children stood on the frontlines of the protest, frustrating soldiers who risked humiliation for brutalizing small kids in front of the countless camera-wielding activists on the scene.

Without any demonstration planned, the village was calm, allowing me to appreciate its bucolic setting for the first time. Joseph and I approached the home of Bassem Tamimi, a large, stone structure constructed before the occupation began. Because Bassem built a second floor onto the home without a permit—Israeli authorities almost never granted building permits to Palestinians in Area C—he was threatened by a demolition order. The demolition of structures in Area C threatened to force Palestinians like Bassem to move to one of the urbanized Bantustans in Area A, where he would languish on a Palestinian Authority salary, while the next generation of Nabi Saleh would be relegated to the center of the village designated as Area B, in a kind of bedroom community shorn from its traditional connection to agriculture and the surrounding land.

The dispossession witnessed in Nabi Saleh mirrored the colonial processes Israel had set into motion across the West Bank, from water and land theft to permit denials to home demolitions. But only a few villages located near the Green Line seemed interested in the kind of unarmed protest tactics witnessed in Nabi Saleh. The structure of *hafrada* was not just designed to separate Israelis and Palestinians, but to sever Palestinian communities from one another, preventing new modes of organizing from spreading.

Bassem was waiting for us on his porch. His house was a large stone villa perched on a grass hill lined with little rows of gardens. A slender man with a neatly trimmed moustache, light brown hair, and blue eyes that betrayed an unusual tranquility, he spoke carefully but with occasional rhetorical flourishes that reflected an exceptional command of English. Bassem had been arrested twelve times by Israeli forces, once spending more than three years in prison without ever seeing a judge or being charged. In 1993, he was arrested on suspicion of having murdered an Israeli settler in Beit El. He said he was severely tortured for weeks by the Israeli Shin Bet officers seeking to extract a confession to violent crimes he had never committed. During the torture he described, he was dropped from a high ceiling onto a concrete floor, waking up only a week later in an Israeli hospital. In the end, he was cleared of all charges.

When I entered Bassem's linoleum-tiled, dimly lit salon, he seated himself cross-legged in a chair across from the sofa where Joseph and I sat, proceeding to turn what I thought would be an informal visit into an hour-long seminar on the recent history of the town. On another sofa sat some *shabab* from Qurawa, one of the nearby towns in the Ramallah district. "We come here because this is where the Palestinian struggle is alive," one of them told me. The boys listened intently as Bassem spoke. His eyes were bloodshot and sunken from fatigue. He told us he had slept little since the false confession of Islam Tamimi; he was anticipating the moment when the army would arrive at his door at three in the morning to take him away to Ofer.

Bassem emphasized that unlike other villages involved in the protests, Nabi Saleh's goals extended beyond immediate, localized concerns. "Our problem is not just with the settlement of Halamish," Bassem explained. "Our problem is the whole occupation. The settlement is merely a face of the occupation. In Bil'in and Ni'lin they set specific goals like moving the separation fence to the Green Line. That is a problem. Our only goal is to end the occupation. So if the American consul came to us and said, 'I am Superwoman; I can immediately remove Halamish,' I would say, 'Fine, but we want to end the whole occupation.'"

Echoing the disgruntlement quietly expressed by many participants in the popular struggle, but especially in Nabi Saleh, Bassem lashed into the Palestinian Authority as he saw it, the foreign-backed rulers of the Bantustan fiefdom that comprised the West Bank's Area A, and its technocratic, unelected prime minister, the former World Bank official Salaam Fayyad. "We had an intifada based on popular struggle, but the Oslo Accords crushed it," Bassem told me. "Now the people are tired since the Second Intifada was crushed. So Fatah [the party controlling the Palestinian Authority] talks and talks, but they can't manage to bring the popular struggle across the West Bank. Fayyad wants to come here and be seen and use our struggle as a theater to have his picture taken. We know that Fatah could bring thousands of people here, but they don't want to. They don't order their members to join the struggle. We want to ask them to make popular struggle everywhere. We do all that we can, but without them we can only do so much."

Bassem said he and other popular struggle leaders wanted to resuscitate the model of unarmed resistance that produced the First Intifada, but the two-pronged force of the Palestinian Authority and the Israeli army had flouted their attempts so far. He explained, "We have experience in military resistance but we decided the best way to resist was nonviolent. We want to build a model that looks like the First Intifada, an alternative to military resistance. Our village knows exactly what to do because we were involved in the Intifada. And the reason the army wants to break our model is because we are offering the basis for the Third Intifada."

While we spoke, Bassem's wife, Nariman passed through the salon, pausing to shake our hands before rushing after one of her daughters, a blonde-haired girl with green eyes who looked to be about eight years old. Nariman was an active figure in Nabi Saleh's popular struggle, following in the tradition of the First Intifada, when women's organizations assumed a central role in organizing the cooperatives that served as the basis of resistance. "From the beginning of our struggle the Israelis targeted the women of our village," Bassem said. "My wife was arrested and jailed for ten days. The army targets the women here because they know our culture; they know that we see women as fifty percent of our struggle and no less. Women raise our children; women can convince people more easily than men. When our men see the women being brave, they want to be more brave. Women are in the center of our struggle because we believe women are more important than men. It's that simple."

The army's repression had been increasing at such a dramatic rate, Bassem said, because the unarmed model of popular struggle threatened Israel's deterrence strategy, which depended on casting all resistance to its occupation in terms of "terrorism." If it became a model, spreading into the West Bank's urban centers, he believed the consequences for the occupation could be calamitous. "The army is determined to push us toward violent resistance," he stated. "They realize that the popular resistance we are waging with Israelis and internationals from the outside, they can't use their tanks and bombs. And this way of struggling gives a good reputation. Suicide bombing was a big mistake because it allowed Israel to say we are terrorists and then to use that label to force from our land. We know they want a land without people—they only want the land and the water—so our destiny is to resist. They give us no other choice."

Night

What was the cost of unarmed resistance, of "doing Gandhi," as the Israeli general Amos Gilad called it? Was it worth the price? And would it spread across the West Bank, as Bassem hoped, reviving the steadfast spirit and solidarity of the First Intifada? Or would it sputter out under the jackboot of Israeli repression, with villages overwhelmed, families shattered, and lives destroyed?

During the early months of 2011, I watched the army intensify its repression of Nabi Saleh's protest movement. Homes across the village were subjected to regular night raids, with soldiers bursting into children's bedrooms early in the morning, lining the boys against the wall to photograph them or dragging them away into waiting jeeps for interrogation and extended time in military prison, where they were detained alongside adult men. To deter the arrests, or at least to ensure that they were properly documented and exposed, Nabi Saleh's popular committee requested that Israeli and international activists spend the night with families expecting raids.

Early in the evening in the middle of the week in late January, my cellphone rang with a call from Yonathan Shapira. He told me Nabi Saleh needed volunteers to stay with a family expecting a night raid. "If the soldiers see Israelis or internationals in the houses when they come to arrest the kids, they are usually less aggressive, they get kind of shaken by seeing us," Yonathan explained. "The army came last night looking for one of the local guys, and they are coming back, because for some reason, they didn't get him."

Three hours later, I pushed through the crowds outside Tel Aviv's Central Bus Station and found Yonathan's car waiting on a corner on Levinsky Street. In the passenger seat was an eighteen-year-old guy with spiky, jet-black hair named Yuval. He was new but deeply committed; he represented the next generation of Anarchists Against the Wall. Yonatan and Yuval had met in Neve Shalom, a Jewish-Arab intentional community where Israelis and Palestinians engage in dialogue seminars, though not the kind familiar to peace industry NGOs like the Peres Center. "We were forced to acknowledge the power imbalance," Yonathan said, "by speaking not as individuals, but as part of a group. It really helped everyone understand the dynamics of occupation and the privilege of being born a Jewish Israeli."

Yonatan seemed agitated for the first leg of the ride. He said he had just learned that his brother-in-law had received an assignment as the Israeli commanding officer at Bil'in and would now direct the army's repression of the village protests each Friday. "I can't understand people sometimes," Yonatan said. "I mean, the guy is this vegan hippy type who refuses to touch meat at our family's Seders. He comes off as a gentle, sensitive guy, but when he got the assignment in Bil'in, he was proud. Like, he didn't see anything wrong with it!"

"Cognitive dissonance is a term that keeps coming up in this place. In my life I've never met so many hippies who wanted to expel people," I said. "Actually, I don't think I ever met one before I got here."

"Yeah, well, that's what keeps the occupation going," Yonatan explained. "The idea that we can be one person on one side of the wall and be a monster on the other, and neither will ever come together."

I thought of the psychologist Robert Jay Lifton's description of the process of socialization that led ordinary people to participate in evil. He called it "doubling." Having studied participants in some of history's greatest crimes, from the doctors in Auschwitz to the members of the murderous Japanese Aum Shinrikyo cult, Lifton found people who had managed to establish an impenetrable psychological barrier between their lives as ordinary parents and husbands and their assignments as killers. "Each of these selves functioned as though it were a separate, autonomous self. And that's why I called it 'doubling,'" Lifton said, "even though, of course, they were part of the same overall self.

"The socialization to evil, I discovered, is all too easy to accomplish," Lifton concluded. "So it can be used by anyone."

As we crossed over the Green Line without even noticing, making the familiar turn onto Highway 446, Lifton's concept took on a larger meaning. The binary of a "Jewish and democratic" state and an undemocratic land of settlers was a geographic form of doubling. Both realms were part of the whole, artificially divided by a separation wall and increasingly rigid psychological barriers.

Yuval had turned against the state at a much younger age than most leftists I knew, freeing him from the internal conflicts they often grappled with. "When I was sixteen, I started watching these videos on the Internet from Ni'lin, from Nabi Saleh, from Bil'in," he said, "just seeing people directly taking on the occupation. I had never seen anything like this. I was like, 'Wow, how do I become a part of these demos?' So I noticed that the videos were all posted by a guy named Yisrael Puterman, and I looked this Puterman guy up in the phone book, called him and said, 'Can you take me to a demo?' So he took me to Nabi Saleh. And here I am."

The previous evening, another group of Israeli activists was blocked from entering Nabi Saleh by an army patrol. When they attempted to hike through the hills to enter the village, one noticed that another in the group had a bright red bead on her forehead—an army sniper had trained his sights on her. "Don't shoot! We are unarmed!" they shouted in Hebrew until the bead disappeared. They quickly retreated, slipping back into the darkness of the hills until they reached the village through another route. The same night, a bus full of Israeli regulars arrived to capture Mustafa Tamimi, a twenty-eight-year-old wanted for arrest for his participation in the popular protests.

Route 465, the winding, two-lane road that led into Nabi Saleh, was wide open when we rolled in. The army watchtower installed just outside the village, on the land annexed by Halamish, was dark. It was a few minutes past eleven p.m. and our path was clear. Just inside town, we parked at the home of Abdel Razzaq and Ikhlas Tamimi, the parents of Mustafa and his four siblings. Mustafa's sister, Ola, a slender, boisterous eighteen-year-old with a big laugh and a ruddy face framed with a tight *hijab*, led us to a wide salon in the back of the house where her father sat with Bashir Tamimi, the town's mayor.

The two men were huddled over a small coal-burning grill that fed the drafty room with its only source of warmth. We crowded in with them, each of us wearing a winter jacket to insulate us from the penetrating cold that set in over the hills of the West Bank at this time of year. Ikhlas brought plastic cups filled with tea saturated with sugar on a silver tray. She smiled at us, lit up a cigarette, and waved goodnight as she retired to her room. We would spend the night in the salon with Abdel Razzaq and Bashir, who both feared being arrested, or at least having to fend off another raid.

Abdel Razzaq told us in Hebrew about the frightening episode of the night before, and Yonatan translated back to me in English. He was a taxi driver who worked around Ramallah by day. Like his cousin, Bashir, he was fifty-four years old, but his kidney disease and years of exposure to Israeli violence made him look at least ten years older. After midnight, Abdel Razzaq said, about sixty soldiers arrived in a large bus and took positions all around his home. "They were just a bunch of kids who were told there was a terrorist on the loose," he said. "They were ready to shoot when they arrived."

With the soldiers positioned hard against the wall of the house, ready to burst in through the backdoor, Mustafa rushed onto a balcony that hung off the roof. In a daring move, he leapt from the balcony, directly over the heads of the soldiers, sprinting through a phalanx of confused troops. From inside, Abdel Razzaq heard the piercing crackle of gunfire. He rushed into the yard and screamed at the soldiers, "Why are you shooting at us? Why don't you go fight Hezbollah? You cowards!" When a soldier forced him back into the house to calm him, he became convinced that his son had been shot. Then he heard another soldier in the yard exclaim, "Just let him get away. He's *meshugat!* (crazy)" Mustafa's daring escape had succeeded, but the army would be back, if not tonight, then soon.

While we waited nervously for the humming sound of army jeeps to shake the windowpanes followed by a hard knock at the door, Abdel Razzaq and Bashir told us their stories about the time they spent in Israel's prisons. Their first encounter with the system of occupation jails began in July 1987, when the two cousins bought an old rifle from a local Palestinian who turned out to be an Israeli collaborator. Though the rifle was nonfunctional, Israeli troops swept up the two in a raid and jailed them without charges. In prison, they shared the experience of the tens of thousands of other Palestinian men who had been detained by Israel, and who would propel the intifada from inside a vast network of concrete cellblocks.

Sentenced to three years at the military jail in Tulkarm, Abdel Razzaq and Bashir organized a prison-wide hunger strike to protest what they said was routine torture and the deprival of water and bathrooms. To break the strike, the two were transferred to a jail in Hebron, where they organized another hunger strike. Their resistance earned them another transfer to a notoriously harsh prison in Dahariya, where they said they were ruthlessly tortured by a duo of officers named Doron and Weizman who bound them in chairs and beat them with batons, sometimes three times a day. Almost as soon as the beatings stopped, they were transferred to another prison near Nablus filled with Palestinians captured during Israel's invasion of Lebanon.

The frequent transfers, designed to break the cohesion of the prisoners' struggle just as the regime of checkpoints and walls aimed to fracture resistance on the outside, instead resulted in a wider network of contacts between Palestinians from across the occupied areas of the map. During the First Intifada, when tens of thousands of Palestinian males experienced arrest by the time they reached thirty, though many were never charged with crimes, the Israeli prisons became known as "The University," an institution of informal learning where the nationalist cause attained coherence, and where the seeds of the next intifada grew up. At the jail in Nablus, Bashir said the prisoners maintained a strict schedule: after breakfast, they would exercise, study literature and read history; after lunch, they studied politics and taught one another other languages from Hebrew to English to French.

Bashir reflected, "It was the university of the revolution. You go in raw and come out with concrete political theory and ideology."

"This is how our life is," Abdel Razzaq said, raking the coals with a stick. "They made sure we all went to jail. And now they're starting with our kids."

When the unarmed demonstrations began in the villages of the West Bank, Nabi Saleh was already experienced in the tactics of the struggle. In 2001, when the Israeli military attempted to seize a home in the village and transform it into a military outpost, Bashir said the entire village rushed to the site, surrounding the house and refusing to leave. "They had to bring in tanks to try to move away," he recalled, laughing heartily. "They were totally immobilized. They brought in the Border Police and shot with rubber bullets, but they couldn't move us. For two weeks we stayed there, and when a few members of Knesset came into to see what was happening, I heard one of them call us 'the crazy village' because no one cared—the old, the kids, the women, everyone would resist to the end."

"Here we are a big family," added Abdel Razzaq. "I will care for a boy here who needs help, and he will care for an elder there in return. We are a small village and everyone breathes the gas whether they are in or out of the house, so on Fridays, when the demonstrations start, we all go out."

We slept on foam mattresses on the floor of the salon, beneath heavy blankets. Along with the symphony of snoring from Yonatan, Abdel Razzaq, and Bashir, a sound that reminded me of Sunday morning lawnmowers, my lingering fear of an army raid kept me in a shallow, uneasy slumber, slipping out occasionally to listen for the rumble of jeep engines. In the end, the raid we all expected never came.

We arose in the late morning to the smell of coffee wafting from the kitchen and the sound of jovial banter echoing from the fields around the house. Wandering out on the little cement porch, we seated ourselves on plastic chairs and took in the scene of rolling green hills still coated with a light residue of the morning mist. "We should come out here more often," Yuval said. "It's so beautiful."

"Just don't start liking it so much you move to Halamish," I joked.

Luai, Abdel Razzaq's broad-shouldered, nineteen-year-old son brought a tray of large plates heaped with scrambled eggs, potatoes, cheese, and rice, and a pot of Arabic coffee. While we ate, Ola sat in a chair next to us, asking in broken Hebrew how we slept. As a child of *hafrada*, part of the first generation that had come of age behind the separation wall, she lacked her father's command of the language. Yonatan switched to Arabic, showing off the skills he had learned during several months of courses at Al-Quds University in Jerusalem. Now, Ola, Yonatan, and Yuval were trading Hebrew and Arabic lessons on my reporter's notebook, teaching each other basic script and how to write their names, and giggling at each other's mistakes.

As we pulled away from the family's house in Yonatan's car, I turned back and watched Abdel Razzaq and Ola walk back into the house. Ola stopped on her way in, turned back, and waved joyfully to us. It was the last time I would see them. And soon, the occupation would deliver their family an indelible scar.

During a protest in Nabi Saleh that November 2011, a soldier thrust open the door of an army jeep and fired a single teargas canister at point blank range into the face of Mustafa Tamimi. He was killed instantly; as he crumpled to the ground, a slingshot fell from his hand. His sister, Ola, attempted to break through the line of soldiers who had assembled to prevent protesters from reaching his body. "I want to see him! I want to see him!" she screamed. But the soldiers would not let her through.

In March, the army came for Naji Tamimi, locking him in Ofer Military Prison for three months before charging him with incitement, "solicitation to stone throwing," and organizing "unauthorized processions." His conviction was based entirely on the confession of Islam Tamimi, the fourteen-year-old who had been coerced into implicating his elders.

Then, as expected, the army arrested Bassem Tamimi. After being sentenced to thirteen months in prison in a military court for "solicitation to stone throwing," Bassem rose and delivered a lengthy, stirring address explaining why he protested, even when he knew it meant imprisonment.

"The military prosecutor accuses me of inciting the protesters to throw stones at the soldiers. This is not true," Bassem declared. "What incites protesters to throw stones is the sound of bullets, the occupation's bulldozers as they destroy the land, the smell of teargas, and the smoke coming from burnt houses. I did not incite anyone to throw stones, but I am not responsible for the security of your soldiers who invade my village and attack my people with all the weapons of death and the equipment of terror.

"These demonstrations that I organize have had a positive influence over my beliefs; they allowed me to see people from the other side who believe in peace and share my struggle for freedom. Those freedom fighters have rid their conscience from the occupation and put their hands in ours in peaceful demonstrations against our common enemy, the occupation. They have become friends, sisters, and brothers. We fight together for a better future for our children and theirs.

"If released by the judge, will I be convinced thereby that justice still prevails in your courts? Regardless of how just or unjust this ruling will be, and despite all your racist and inhumane practices and occupation, we will continue to believe in peace, justice and human values."

Months after Bassem's conviction, Israeli forces arrested his wife, Nariman, prying away her distraught young daughters who had attempted to clasp themselves onto her body while the soldiers hauled their mother into an army jeep. Then they arrested Luai Tamimi, the brother of Ola. For her part, Ola dropped out of high school right after the arrests and left Palestine to stay with family members in Jordan. In the army's campaign to fracture Nabi Saleh's resistance, the Tamimi clan was slowly torn apart, with mothers physically torn from their daughters, and sons separated from fathers through imprisonment and death.

"Sometimes my wife and I can't go to sleep, and we stay awake the whole night crying and comforting one another," Abdel Razzaq Tamimi told the Palestinian journalist and activist Linah Alsaafin. "It's not good to keep crying and mourning our son the martyr. I keep telling my wife we must be strong; this is a blessing, an honor to have a martyred son, but sometimes I feel like I don't believe what I'm saying and my heart feels so heavy with grief."

"Thank God for everything," he said in a weary tone. In October 2012, Abdel Razzaq succumbed to kidney disease, dying at age fifty-six.

The Children's Court

At a demo in Nabi Saleh in November 2010, two Border Police officers tackled two Israelis to the ground and dragged them into a jeep, a mundane instance of repression witnessed almost every Friday by the village. Though neither of the Israelis had done anything to merit the arrest besides being present at the demonstration, they were subsequently accused of throwing stones. The Border Policemen also grabbed Ala Tamimi, a seventeen-year-old resident of Nabi Saleh, arresting him, even though another officer told them he had not thrown any stones. The Border Police took Tamimi and the Israelis to a prison near the Sha'ar Binyamin industrial zone. According to one of the Israelis, who spoke to me on condition of anonymity, a stocky officer named Yaniv and a thin officer named Nadav cuffed him and Ala, then proceeded to beat them, kicking them in the stomach and slamming them repeatedly on the ground.

When the commander arrived at Sha'ar Binyamin, he asked the arresting officers, "Which ones are the Jews?" He ordered the release of the Israelis and gave them a tin of food. But Ala remained cuffed. "You're out of here," the commander told the Israelis, "but the Palestinian is in deep shit. And you ever come back here," he added, "we will beat you way worse than before." Before uncuffing them, Yaniv smashed one of their heads against the ground one last time.

More than two months later, Ala was locked in Ofer Military Prison, awaiting a trial that would inevitably end with a conviction.

It was late January 2011 and I was driving into the West Bank with Joseph and Shai, on our way to the trial of Ala Tamimi. We traveled through a hard, bone-chilling rain on Highway 443, the Israelis-only bypass route that sliced through the West Bank on the way from Tel Aviv to Jerusalem. I stared out the window at the miles of concrete wall Israel had installed to conceal the view of Palestinian villages, and to block the Palestinians from accessing the road. Schubert hummed through a single speaker behind my head while windshield wipers slapped and squeaked in a hypnotic rhythm. As usual, Shai faced the road with silence. Just after passing Modi'in, we stopped at a bus station that appeared to be empty. From behind the bus stop, Efrata emerged. She walked slowly toward the car, clad in all black, and impervious to the pouring rain, then settled in the back seat beside me. Like Shai, she sat with a stone face, saying nothing.

A few kilometers down the highway lay an imposing structure of fifty-foot-high concrete blast walls and sentry towers. Bolted onto the tower facing an intersection was a giant steel Israeli flag. This was Ofer Military Prison, a vast complex of cell-blocks and kangaroo courtrooms that thousands of Palestinians caught in the occupation's dragnet called home. We pulled into a little dirt parking lot behind the jail and rushed through the rain toward an outdoor waiting area, splashing mud all over ourselves as we ran. Dozens of Palestinians of all ages huddled inside with us. They were the family members of prisoners locked inside. Waiting for hours on benches surrounded by cages and concrete walls, but covered with nothing but a corrugated tin board, had become a routine activity, like waiting at a bus stop.

A leak had sprung in the tin roof over the shelter, forcing the waiting families to huddle in a corner. After fifteen minutes, a tall, olive-skinned prison guard—a Mizrahi guy who looked as Arab as any of the Palestinians—called us over to the gate and took our IDs, including my passport. We had arranged in advance to observe the military trials through the Israeli Prison Service, taking advantage of one of the ornamental features the occupation employed to project a sense of democratic transparency. While we stood at the gate, inside what amounted to a cage, in a puddle of mud while sheets of rain poured down on us, a female guard appeared from inside the jail.

"Youuuu, you will haaaave to wait, you will haaaaave to wait," she sang in Hebrew, mangling a pop song at the top of her voice while shaking her hips, and flashing an occasional winsome smile at the tall guard.

She was young, nineteen or twenty perhaps. The moment I saw the young guard, I thought of Eden Abergil, the girl soldier who reveled in the notoriety she gained by posting photos of herself mocking bound Palestinian prisoners. Dancing in our direction now, she continued her singing, taunting us as we soaked in the rain.

"Are you trying to impress your boyfriend?" Efrata shouted at her sternly. "Why don't you do your job and give our fucking IDs back?"

The girl looked embarrassed. She flipped a hand mirror open and began applying a bright red shade of lipstick. "Sorry, I don't talk to *smolinim* [leftists]," she said with exaggerated contempt, staring at herself in the mirror.

Finally, after fifteen minutes, the warden appeared, unlocking the gate to allow us inside and out of the rain. He was a notorious figure among Palestinians of the West Bank and the few Israeli activists who made the trip to Ofer. A gruff ogre with a large paunch, thick arms like slabs of pork, and a baldhead with fat bunched at the back of his neck, he looked as though he were lifted from the pages of a Dickens novel. The warden led us through a security check with a few grumbled commands, ordering us to leave everything in our pockets with him. Then his underlings took us into closed rooms where they patted us down (activists were sometimes subjected to strip searches here). For the first time, thanks to pressure from European Union diplomats, as a journalist I was allowed to take my reporter's notebook inside, allowing me to document the proceedings with more precision than in the past. With a pad and a pen in my hand, I rushed behind the others through the rain in a long, narrow cage that led into a yard filled with trailers and toward the waiting room.

Inside the brightly lit room, we stood around a heating vent, our clothes saturated with rain, and did our best to dry off. I was shivering uncontrollably but tried not to appear too demonstrative in front of the wives, parents, and children of prisoners seated impassively on metal chairs lining the walls and draped with prayer rugs, where they sat fiddling with tasbih beads and chatting softly. In the corner of the room was a small café that flooded the area with the smell of cooking grease. On the other side of the counter stood three young guards crowded over a computer, checking their Facebook pages and giggling about their friends' photos. A Hebrew bumper sticker slapped on a wall above the café read, "Observe the Sabbath."

Over the past summer, I had grown familiar with Ofer, traveling to and from the prison with the anarchists on regular occasions. The jail was the central node of Israel's military justice system, where soldiers dressed in judicial garb and prosecutors dressed as soldiers played a game with a predestined result, with the Shin Bet making up the rules as it went along. According to the military courts' annual 2011 report, Palestinians were convicted at a rate of 99.74 percent, with only twenty-five full acquittals out of thousands of cases. Between 2005 and 2010, Israeli military courts had convicted 835 minors for the crime of stone throwing, coercing many into confessions through harsh interrogations and promising them more lenient sentences for pleading guilty. Among those convicted were dozens of children as young as twelve years old.

In the past, I had attended trials of local Palestinian leaders placed under administrative detention, a code phrase the Israeli military administration used to denote imprisonment without charges. In July, I witnessed the sentencing of Ibrahim Amireh, a key organizer of Ni'lin's unarmed protest movement and the father of Saeed. Charged with "organizing illegal and violent demonstrations," "being present in a declared closed military zone," and other Orwellian-sounding crimes, Amireh was ultimately pressured into pleading guilty after waiting to be charged for months.

Before accepting a sentence of eleven months, Amireh stood before the court and spoke without permission. "I live between a rock and a wall," he declared in Hebrew. "When I go to farm my land, the army blocks me. And when I protest to reach my land again, I am attacked and arrested. What do you want me to do? What choice have you given us?"

On this visit, I would witness the trial of a minor for the first time.

In 2009, the Israeli military administration established a Youth Court in the West Bank, assigning it the mission of trying and convicting children under the age of sixteen. (Israel regards Palestinian children over sixteen as adults, while Jewish children must turn eighteen before losing their status as minors.) Though a few judges demanded that the court observe international conventions on the protection of children and conform to Israeli regulations that mandate that a child's parents must be present during their interrogation, these suggestions were dismissed as soon as the children's court came into being. Of twenty-nine child prisoners interviewed by the Israeli human rights group B'tselem, only one was allowed to receive regular visits by family members. Classified as "security prisoners," none was allowed access to a telephone.

A chubby man with curly black locks soaked with rain staggered into the waiting room and summoned outside toward the courtroom. He was Neri Ramati, a Jewish

Israeli lawyer who worked under Gabi Lasky, a renowned human rights attorney who emerged from the left-wing of the Israeli peace camp, once running for a Knesset seat on the Meretz list. Lasky and Ramati had defended most of the major leaders placed under administrative detention, from Ibrahim Amireh to Bil'in's popular committee director Abdallah Abu Rahme. We followed Ramati into a tan trailer, where he hastily slipped a black robe over his wet clothes and seated himself at a folding table beside Lasky and Limor Goldstein, the lawyer who had been shot in the face by Border Policemen in Bil'in, and had battled back from brain damage to advocate on behalf of Palestinians at Ofer.

All the courtrooms at Ofer lay inside trailers. Like the sections of concrete that comprised the separation wall, they stood as symbols of temporality, reinforcing the illusion of the occupation as a passing phase.

At a witness stand in the middle of the room stood Yaniv and Nadav, the two officers who had arrested and abused the Israeli leftists and Ala Tamimi. They kept their M-16's slung over their shoulders throughout the hearing. Tamimi sat in a booth to the side of the court, dressed in a baggy surplus American uniform. His hands and legs were shackled. He looked back at us, smiled broadly, and gave a nod of acknowledgment. With his parents unable to attend, we were his only witnesses. Joseph and Efrata had gone to a separate trailer to attend the trial of one of the *shabab* from Bil'in, leaving me with Shai, who provided me with diligent translations of the proceedings.

Leaning on the witness stand, Yaniv joked around with the court officers, a group of young women who looked, like him, to be about twenty years old. The prosecutor, a woman in her early thirties, stood nearby wearing a military uniform. Like the prosecutor and the witness, the judge was clad in the olive drab of the Israeli army. A stout woman of about forty who also wore a military uniform, she sat before a wall emblazoned with the symbol of the State of Israel, a menorah framed by dual lictors. Like so many in the Israeli military court system, the judge and prosecutor were gaining the experience necessary to move into civilian positions in the Israeli legal world across the Green Line.

In Israel's military courts, judge, prosecutors, Shin Bet interrogators, and soldiers felt united in this mission. As Col. Oded Pessenson, a former judge in the military courts, told Ra'anan Alexandrowicz, the director of *The Law in These Parts*, a 2012 documentary about Israel's martial justice system, "These are people [the soldiers and Shin Bet agents] whose job is to protect me so I can go to a movie theater and not get blown up. . . . To begin with, I believe the agent of the authorities because his job is to protect me."

Before Yaniv, the Border Police officer, delivered his testimony, he swore before the judge to tell the whole truth. Then he began, claiming to the prosecutor that Ala had thrown stones and attempted to hide among a group of village elders.

"He had the residue of stones on his hands [when we captured him] so we arrested him in the village and transferred him to the police," Yaniv declared. "I maintained visual contact with him at all times, from about thirty meters away. He was wearing a grey sweater so he was easy to recognize."

"How are you able to remember this?" the military lawyer asked.

"From testimony I gave to police that day, after the arrests," Yaniv claimed.

Ramati looked back at with a wry grin. Yaniv was reconstructing events based on a video of the arrests posted on YouTube. He had not been close enough to Tamimi at any point to have seen him throwing stones. Thus his testimony contradicted his initial police report, in which he was unable to offer any of the details the video provided, and which he was now recapitulating before the court.

As Ramati stood before the judge to cross-examine Yaniv, water dripped from his robe, forming little puddles on the floor. A soldier who was either Druze or Mizrahi sat in the center of the courtroom translating tidbits of the proceedings back to Tamimi. Chomping on a bag of potato chips, the translator cracked jokes to the female court officers, who, like him, appeared to be about twenty years old. There was very little order in this court.

"Why did you offer different testimony just now from your report to the police?" Ramati asked Yaniv. "You appear to be relying on a YouTube video that shows a different version than one you originally offered."

Yaniv paused before answering, "My report to the police was given at 8 p.m., after a very long day at work, so I watched the YouTube video to help me focus on a point or two."

The military lawyer stood and protested hyperbolically, "He is exposing military secrets!"

But the judge allowed Ramati to proceed. "According to the defendant, you were told to release him by one of the officers under your command. Doesn't it seem odd that he told you that? And that the only people who identified him throwing stones were you and Nadav [the other Border Police officer]?"

"As an officer I have the authority to arrest a man, and when Nadav arrived I added his testimony to the report. Maybe another cop saw him [Tamimi] throwing stones. I don't know," Yaniv said, trailing off at the end of this answer. He appeared to be cracking under cross-examination.

When Nadav, Yaniv's lanky, baby-faced counterpart, stood to testify, he was unable to name any of the officers who were with him when he arrested Tamimi and the two Israelis. "I remember some of those with me, but it isn't very clear," he told Ramati. He then contradicted Yaniv's claim to have arrested Tamimi on his own, testifying that they arrested them together. The case against Tamimi was shabby at best, but this was just another show trial. The kid's conviction was a sure thing, no matter how valiantly his lawyers performed.

At the end of the proceeding, the judge ordered another hearing, prolonging Tamimi's time in prison. He lifted his manacles and waved sheepishly as a guard led him out of the trailer to his cell. Like the other prisoners at Ofer, he would have to wait in detention for a long arbitrary period before finally receiving his sentence, which would almost certainly mandate more jail time. Meanwhile, the two Israelis arrested with him awaited hearings of their own, but from the comfort of their homes in Tel Aviv. "One of the army's new methods of prosecuting Israeli activists is to accuse them of stone throwing," Ramati told me afterward. "We are getting more and more of these cases, but none of them come with any evidence."

"They are now claiming the Palestinians pay us four hundred shekels per demo," Shai interjected, flashing a rare smile. "I could live pretty well off that!"

Back in the waiting room, I flipped open my reporter's notebook to jot down a few more notes from the hearing. But two Palestinian women in their late twenties interrupted me with a string of questions in English. "Do you know how long it takes before the trials start?" one asked me. She was tall, with shoulder length curly hair and dark eye shadow. Though heavily accented, her English was fluent. "Where do they take you? Are the courtrooms out there?" asked the other. Short and stout, with a colorful *hijab* that matched her light green jacket, she spoke in a voice that rippled with anxiety.

It was clear to me that these two women were simply seeking to talk to someone who appeared to be a Western reporter. I had wanted to interview the people in the waiting room, and now it seemed like I had a good chance. "Whose trial are you waiting for? Like, one of your husbands?" I asked.

"Mine," said the woman in the *hijab*, introducing herself as Diyala. She told me she had met her husband while they both studied at Bir Zeit University near Ramallah. During his college years, he was a member of Jabah, a wing of the secular socialist Popular Front for the Liberation of Palestine (PFLP), but he quit the group soon after he graduated. "The Israelis arrested him for his political activities at Bir Zeit, but he had graduated already and wasn't involved any more in anything."

Diyala said they swept her husband up in a mass arrest of PFLP members on the anniversary of the Israeli assassination of Abu Ali Mustafa, then the group's secretary general. After Apache helicopters killed him with a missile strike at his Ramallah office, fifty thousand mourners attended Abu Ali's funeral. His assassination triggered the revenge killing of Rehavam Ze'evi, the Israeli Transportation minister who had gained notoriety among Palestinians, and support from many Israelis, for his unabashed call for the forced transfer of Palestinians to Jordan. Diyala assumed that unfounded Israeli fears of more reprisals on the anniversary of Abu Ali's death triggered the arrest of her husband and many of his college friends.

Now, after almost four months, she was waiting to attend her husband's trial. She was pregnant with what would be their second child, and had been repeatedly prevented from visiting him at Ofer. "Prisoners are supposed to have the right to see their family or their lawyer, but they keep delaying our requests, and the judge refused to allow us to be present at his last hearing," Diyala said. With her new pregnancy, she had demanded to be patted down rather than pass through the metal detectors at the entrance to Ofer, but the soldiers refused to consent. "Today I agreed to pass through the metal detector because I miss my husband so much. I just wanted to see him so bad, you know."

Diyala added, "Because of all the checkpoints, women have to pass through metal detectors every day just to get out of their villages. I work in the refugee camps and keep seeing women giving birth to defective babies. We are trying to make women from the villages more aware, to tell them to demand to be checked by hand. But so far, no one talks about this issue."

I asked Diyala's friend if she was also at Ofer to see a spouse. "No, I'm just here to support my friend," she said. A Palestinian Catholic originally from Ramallah, the woman said her name was Rawan.

"How do you speak English so well?" I asked her. "Did you spend time in the States?"

It turned out Rawan had studied at North Park Theological Seminary in Chicago. Two years earlier, Don Wagner, the director of the school's Center on Middle Eastern Studies, had invited me to deliver a lecture on Christian Zionism, the apocalyptic pro-Israel evangelical movement in the United States. My appearance prompted a letter of protest from Chicago's Jewish Federation chapter to the school's dean. It was another salvo in a sustained and ultimately successful campaign to defund Wagner's program and drive him out of his position.

When I asked Rawan if she knew Wagner, she said she not only knew him, but that he had been her teacher and mentor. "Every day in the US, I felt like as an Arab, my identity was under attack. But Don gave me so much support, I can't even tell you. If it was not for him maybe I would not have made it through school. But they just forced him out," she said. "They said it was for financial reasons, but everyone knows what it was really about. He spoke out too much for us Palestinians."

I was astonished that I had made such a chance connection in the soul-crushing waiting room at Ofer. But just as our conversation deepened, Shai and Efrata signaled to me that it was time to leave. They were always in a rush, traveling from flashpoint to flashpoint around the West Bank with the punctuality of stereotypical Germans. I had no idea where they were headed next but had no choice but to follow them. "Come on!" Joseph urged me. "These guys will just leave you here if you don't go right now."

As we passed through an iron turnstile into the Ofer parking lot, I noticed that Rawan and Diyala were following closely behind us. I stopped and waited for them in a puddle of mud while the rest of my group ran toward the car. "What happened? Weren't you supposed to go to the trial?" I asked Diyala, shouting over the sound of rain pounding on the tin roof of the outdoor shelter.

"Security reasons," she said angrily, making air quotes with her hands. "They say I can't see my husband for *security reasons!* You can't go there, you can't do this, just say the magic word: 'Security!'"

I asked Diyala if I could meet her sometime for an interview. The rain had soaked through my shoes, and I was beginning to shiver again. She looked uneasy about the idea. But her friend, Rawan, passed me her e-mail. After a series of e-mail exchanges over the next two weeks, Rawan finally convinced Diyala to trust me enough to tell me about her experience with the military prisons and, if possible, to show me around her neighborhood as well. Diyala had moved to the only area in all of Israel-Palestine where the laws of Israeli occupation allowed her and her husband to live together.

The Lovers' Camp

On another cold, damp night in early February 2011, I rode a crowded service bus from Jerusalem through East Jerusalem, easing through the Qalandia checkpoint into the Ramallah district. Getting into the West Bank was substantially smoother than getting out. As we neared Manara Square in the center of town, a crush of pedestrian shoppers and taxis honking furiously at what seemed like nothing ground traffic to a standstill. I exited the bus and walked to the roundabout that surrounded the square and waited for Rawan and Diyala. Across the street was Stars and Bucks, a coffee shop modeled after the American corporate chain that had taken full advantage of the absence of copyright law in the West Bank. At eight a.m. on the dot, they sped around the bend and picked me up.

After a short drive through the winding roads of Ramallah's hilly central neighborhoods, we were at a table at the Eiffel Café, one of the many French-style cafés and restaurants that had sprouted up in the city since the Second Intifada was diffused. The waiter brought me an English menu, while Diyala chided a group of glamorously dressed young women for blowing smoke in our direction, demanding they open a window. We were in the heart of the Ramallah bubble, the shining example of the "economic peace" Netanyahu sought to forge with the Palestinian Authority in place of an actual two-state solution.

"The Palestinian Authority says they gave us our independence," Rawan said to me, "so what we got was an Independence Day celebration. We all laugh at the whole thing now."

While Rawan, a Palestinian Christian, worked for the International Bible Society, Diyala spent her days working in the West Bank refugee camps run by the United Nations Relief Works Agency (UNRWA). She was a social worker who specialized in psychological counseling. "I work for Palestine, not for any faction," she said. "To fight Israel, we need to fight the problems in Palestine, and we have so many of them." She pointed to domestic abuse and rampant psychological problems in the camps, where UNRWA budget limitations caused by pressure from the Congress and Israel prevented the distribution of antidepressant drugs. Diyala concluded, "We need to gather as a community and that's why I decided to study community psychology."

Even as she began to open up, Diyala was still slightly uncomfortable about the interview. "It's not easy for me to trust you," she reminded me, "but if you want to know the truth, I have to tell you. You know, it wasn't easy for me to get out tonight because of my daughter."

I told her, "I'm sorry, I mean, I hope I didn't . . ."

"No, no, no," she interrupted. "To be honest, I actually am very glad to meet with you. I have hardly gone out since my husband was in jail—I have to be with Zeina all the time—so I was happy for the excuse."

Diyala told me she honed her English skills during a stay in California, but that she suffered from culture shock: "When I came to the US I couldn't handle the freedom. I was used to having someone ask me where I was going all the time, being searched and suspected everywhere I went. I couldn't handle being able to go wherever I want, to just drive on a highway with no one stopping me. You have to know that the occupation isn't just checkpoints, it's about making our lives impossible and convincing us we have no options."

"It is a psychological war," Rawan added. "They are trying to demolish our attitudes as Palestinians and build us up into what they want."

Diyala was raised in the Sheikh Jarrah neighborhood of East Jerusalem, a wealthy area until the Jerusalem Municipality began evicting its Palestinian residents and replacing them with ultra-Orthodox settlers. With her status as a Palestinian resident of Jerusalem, she was granted automatic Jordanian citizenship, entitling her to more freedom of movement than West Bank Palestinians, but few of the rights enjoyed by Jewish Israeli citizens. In order to keep her residency status, she had to abide by the Israeli Interior Ministry's discriminatory "center of life" policy, which required her to maintain a constant presence within the borders of the Jerusalem municipality. Any Palestinian who left their address in the city for a prolonged period of time to pursue studies at a foreign university, for example, risked losing their permanent residency.

Though Palestinians represented the indigenous population of Jerusalem, the State of Israel treated them essentially as though they were tourists in a foreign land. "I am always running around making sure my ID card is in order, spending hours on my national insurance paperwork, proving where I live, always to make sure they don't expel me," Diyala explained.

Since the occupation began in 1967, Israel has used the "center of life" policy to strip more than fourteen thousand Palestinians of their right to live anywhere inside the borders of Israel-Palestine. To advance its stated policy of preventing Jerusalem's Arab population from growing beyond the 28.8 percent it represented in 1967, the state has ramped up its efforts to strip Palestinians of permanent residency. Thanks to the policy, Palestinians like twenty-one-year-old Amir Salima exist without any official identity. After being stripped of his residency on the grounds that he was born in a hospital in Ramallah, not Jerusalem, Salima was officially barred from holding a passport, registering to study, or opening a bank account. According to *Ha'aretz*'s Nir Hasson, he was not allowed to live anywhere, even in his own room, where he spent almost all of his time. When a police officer attempted to expel Salima from his own house, he declared him "illegally present."

The "center of life" policy dictates every aspect of Palestinian life in Jerusalem—even romance. Diyala met her husband while they studied at Bir Zeit University in 2004. At first, they were friends who spent long hours discussing literature and reading together. But soon enough their friendship blossomed into love. "He was the kind of man who built his own future," she told me. "He got his high school degree in prison, then by age twenty he built his own house with the salary he earned. And unlike so many of the men around here who only care about their own business, he put Palestine and his family first."

In October 2004, Diyala's husband was arrested for his membership in the PFLP and jailed at Al Nakab prison, where he spent the next twenty-seven months. While he and Diyala stayed in touch through letters—"He is a really nice writer," she commented—she tried to convince her family to allow her to marry him.

Thanks to the "center of life" policy, his status as a West Bank Palestinian and hers as a Jerusalem resident cast their future together in doubt. "I couldn't leave him because I loved him so much," Diyala explained. "But my family kept telling me that I will never see him again. He was not allowed to enter Jerusalem, and I was not allowed to live with him in the West Bank. He was out of work, just out of prison; we seemed to have no future. Everything was working against us."

Finally, she put her foot down. "I told my family, 'Look, we are all Palestinians. The Israelis want us to be apart from each other, to be separated, but we can't let them define us. Let make our own choices. So we got married. And like I expected, it was a happy marriage."

Unfortunately for Diyala, her husband's friends were arrested in a raid on their wedding night. "That's when we realized they wouldn't leave us alone," she recalled, "even though he was no longer involved in politics."

During their first year of marriage, her husband was arrested again. "I was six months pregnant at the time, with our first daughter, Zeina, and it was the anniversary of Abu Ali [Mustafa]'s assassination. I thought they might decide to arrest him so I said let's sleep somewhere else. He said, 'I'm so sick of running away. We are not going anywhere.' So they came, took him away, and I had the baby without him."

Because Diyala's daughter was born in the West Bank but resided within the borders of the Jerusalem Municipality, she had not been granted permanent residency. "According to Israel, my daughter does not exist," Diyala declared. "She is not registered anywhere."

Like many Palestinian children growing up under Israeli occupation and siege, Diyala's daughter began to develop symptoms of continuous traumatic stress disorder. "Zeina keeps asking me, 'Where's Daddy?' When she sees a soldier she gets so afraid and begins to cry. She wakes up with nightmares shouting, '*Jaish! Jaish!*' ("Army!"). But what scares her most is if one of my cousins knocks on the door at three a.m. She thinks it's the army."

The stress on Diyala's marriage became so unbearable she sometimes thought about seeking a divorce. "For a while I hated my husband," she confessed. "For being in prison and leaving me all alone, I began to blame him. I mean, here I am, holding ten balls with one hand. But I realized I can't blame him when we are living under occupation. Sometimes it so hard, though."

She threw up her hands despairingly, prompting looks from a few of the women puffing cigarettes in the corner of the café. "Ofer [Military Prison] is twenty minutes from my home and he's *in there*! I want to tell you how I feel, but I can't put my feelings into words."

We left Ramallah in Diyala's car, dropping Rawan off along the way. Now, Diyala set out to show me her neighborhood. We took a winding route through the hills of Ramallah and back toward Jerusalem, driving along the separation wall for most of the ride. "Me and my husband loved living in Bir Zeit," Diyala said of the town outside Ramallah where they met. "We had a lot of space there, a lot of sun came in our house, and we kept a garden. He loved to grow vegetables. But now we are stuck here."

"Here" meant Kufr Aqab, a depressing, densely populated neighborhood that lay on the furthest outskirts of the Jerusalem Municipality. Traveling through narrow streets lined with drab, dilapidated apartment blocs and steep piles of garbage, I noticed a complete absence of traffic lights. Diyala swerved carefully through the streets, jerking the steering wheel rapidly from side to side to avoid potholes the size of miniature canyons. The car rocked up and down as we turned a corner toward her apartment. "We pay 3,200 shekels [about $1,000] a month in taxes to the city and get no services," she explained. "No garbage pickup, no street repairs, nothing."

Though Kufr Aqab lies within the administration of the Jerusalem Municipality, it has been severed from the rest of the city by the thirty-six-foot-high separation wall. The neighborhood of twenty thousand was once a prosperous enclave that provided its residents with comfortable access to both Ramallah and Jerusalem. Now, thanks to the wall, it is an impoverished ghetto severed from the outside world. Elementary school students who once crossed the street to get to class now must travel kilometers away to the Qaladia checkpoint to traverse the wall. During Israeli army curfews and the closures frequently imposed on the West Bank during Jewish holidays, the students must stay home. Although its inhabitants pay taxes, Kufr Aqab has no mail service and a sole traffic light that has stopped functioning, a signpost serving as a perverse reminder of the time before the separation.

Firefighters routinely refuse to enter Kufr Aqab from Jerusalem without army protection, and firefighters from the Palestinian Authority are forbidden from entering. With no police officers, crime is rampant, forcing residents to rely on a coalition of local elders and family patriarchs to maintain a semblance of order. In 2010, the Israeli police refused pleas to help resolve a standoff when an armed local gang took hundreds of students hostage at a school belonging to the Jerusalem Education Administration. The situation was resolved only when residents assembled enough manpower to chase the gang away. That same year, when flooding in the neighborhood caused widespread electricity outages, the Jerusalem municipality refused to restore power.

Since Kufr Aqab was classified as Area C under the Oslo Accords, placing it under full Israeli control, its residents have been unable to receive building permits from the authorities. And with city building inspectors from Jerusalem refusing to visit anyway, most of the new construction in the area is illegal under Israeli law. Israel has demolished over twenty-five thousand Palestinian homes since 1967, some on the basis of collective punishment for terrorist attacks but most destroyed on the grounds that they were "illegally constructed." Like the majority of Kufr Aqab's residents, Diyala lived in constant fear of homelessness.

"Jews can build anywhere, but we have no way to get permission to build here, so the only solution to having a family was to build anyway," she said. "The place I'm renting could be demolished any day now. This is all part of them trying to push [Arabs] out of Jerusalem by refusing to allow our population to grow."

In recent years, Jerusalem Municipality officials openly revealed what Kufr Aqab residents knew all along: they had been placed on the other side of the wall for demographic reasons. As Jerusalem city councilmember Yakir Segev said in 2010, the "separation fence . . . was built for political and demographic reasons—not just security concerns." A year later, Jerusalem Mayor Nir Barkat announced his desire to remove Kufr Aqab from the city's administrative control, stripping its residents of their permanent residency and effectively transferring them into the hands of the Palestinian Authority. A city official justified the move to the *Jerusalem Post* on the grounds that "the exchange would result in a very small territorial gain for Jerusalem, with a loss of approximately forty thousand Arab residents."

"They want to transfer us, I am sure of it," Diyala said. "They don't want to live with Palestinians, and I think one day they will force all to go to Jordan."

We arrived at the base of Diyala's apartment on a craggy side street littered with trash. She pointed up at her balcony, which stood on the third floor, only a few meters across from another tall apartment bloc. "There is no sun in my house and you can see, three buildings are surrounding it," Diyala said. I noticed that she lined her balcony with little boxes of flowers. She told me, "I put those there to remind us of when we were in Bir Zeit, when we had our garden."

So why did she live here, of all places? I asked. Wasn't there another option? Diyala explained that because Kufr Aqab lay inside the borders of the Jerusalem Municipality, she could reside there without being stripped of her residency status. And because it existed on the other side of the separation wall, her husband, a Palestinian with only a West Bank ID, could live with her without being arrested. If Barkat's plan went through, however, they could legally live together anywhere in Israel-Palestine.

"Almost everyone living in my building are couples forced into Kufr Aqab because, like me, you have one person from Jerusalem and the other one is a West Banker," she said.

"This place has become a big refugee camp. We are refugees because of who we fell in love with."

Diyala gave me a lift to Qalandia, the mega-checkpoint separating Jerusalem from the Ramallah District. "Tell people about us, what we are going through," Diyala called to me from her car window as I walked into the blinding glow beaming from floodlights hanging over the separation wall. I navigated through the long, chaotic line of traffic backed-up outside the checkpoint, where soldiers blaring orders through a megaphone competed with the angry din of drivers honking their horns in frustration. Inside, I squeezed through a long, metal cage and stood quietly in a crush of mostly middle-aged Palestinian men waiting to pass through a turnstile while Israeli teenagers in army dress examined our ID cards from behind a thick wall of bulletproof glass. I listened intently for the buzzing sound to signal me through the gate then flashed my ID to a bored girl soldier. After carefully examining my visa stamp, she waved me through. I exited the wall on a dark, barren street in East Jerusalem, somewhere between Israel and Palestine, wondering where one ended and the other began.

A Wet Dream

Three and a half years had passed since Israel elected Prime Minister Benjamin Netanyahu and the most right-wing government in its history. Dozens of laws proposing to strip away whatever was left of the country's democratic patina had been brought up in the Knesset, and many had passed. The siege of the Gaza Strip was still in place, and the Israeli air force was conducting periodic raids it referred to as "mowing the lawn." The Palestinian cities of the West Bank remained under the administration of a Palestinian Authority sapped of funding from the international donors tightening its strings and teetering on the brink of a major crisis, its legitimacy constantly undermined by its inexorable role as Israel's occupation subcontractor. Meanwhile, the settlement enterprise expanded without even a word of public protest from a cowed Obama administration in Washington that had once demanded it be frozen.

In the dying hours of 2012, I was following a mob of about twenty right-wing Jewish nationalists as they marched through South Tel Aviv chanting, "Sudanese to Sudan!" and menacing every black person they encountered. The only thing that prevented the mob from physically assaulting African asylum seekers in the street, or me, or the handful of journalists shadowing them, was the presence of a small police detail. When the nationalists reached a corner store staffed by Africans, they lunged inside.

"This is my country here! This is my home!" a freckle-faced teenager barked at a pregnant African woman who was shaking nervously beside a counter piled with snack food. An Israeli journalist told me the kid was a well-known rightist street thug whose family had immigrated to Israel from post–Soviet Russia. "Get the hell out of here! Get out of our country! Criminals!" the kid shouted.

"The Sudanese should be raped in the ass with a dick this big," an old woman yelled, pointing to her forearm. On her forehead, she had pasted a bumper sticker that read "Strong Israel," and she seemed incapable of breathing without uttering some kind of graphically sexualized or scatological imprecation against non-Jewish Africans living in Israel. "Whores! Sudanese are whores!" she shrieked at two young African men strolling along the sidewalk.

Strong Israel was the name of a new, openly fascistic political party formed by Knesset members Michael Ben-Ari and Aryeh Eldad to leverage the rising tide of anti-African bile into votes. Since the last national elections, the kind of outrageously bigoted rhetoric Strong Israel's leaders traded on had become an increasingly common feature of Israeli political language. The mood of Israeli voters was exacerbated by a brutal, sustained aerial assault on the Gaza Strip that took place just as elections were announced in November 2012. According to a report from the Coalition Against Racism in Israel, instances of racist incitement by Israeli public figures doubled in 2012.

The Strong Israel march through South Tel Aviv ended at Ben Ari's campaign office, which was strategically planted on a street heavily populated by non-Jewish Africans. On the wall inside hung a portrait of the party's patron saint, Rabbi Meir Kahane, alongside posters of Ben Ari and Eldad. The party activists milled around outside, snacking on little packages of vanilla pudding—sweet rewards after a satisfying rampage. The men were a colorful mixture of right-wing rabble, from veteran settler militants to local derelicts to wayward young men who had become entranced by the adventurous world of Israeli proto-fascism. As I stood near a small group of journalists that included Sheen, who was still filming the marchers, I noticed that the police had conveniently disappeared from the area. It was then that the Strong Israel activists turned violent.

A heavily built, clean-shaven twenty-something man whose appearance recalled a generic army reservist rushed forward at Sheen. "Get the hell out of here, you ass fucker!" he said, throwing a shirt over Sheen's camera lens. "Get the hell out of here or I'll break your camera." As the young tough's violent threats turned to slaps and fierce shoving—tactics familiar to the settlers of the South Hebron Hills—I obstructed his path, hoping to allow Sheen to retreat before the rest of the mob could join in the attack. When five more Strong Israel activists began swarming Sheen, I chased after a lone police commander for one block and demanded to know if he intended to stand aside while a journalist was assaulted. He shrugged his shoulders and casually exclaimed, "Sure." Luckily for Sheen, the mob eventually allowed him to retreat once he reached a busy intersection a few blocks away, safe from what looked likely to be another ugly scene of right-wing street violence.

Two hours later, we were celebrating New Year's Eve with arak and a mezze of Middle Eastern hors d'oeuvres at a trendy loft-style apartment filled with Jewish and Palestinian-Israeli leftists. I leaned out of the window and stared at fireworks sparkling brightly over the Mediterranean Sea, still dazed from what I had just witnessed.

The New Year would not bring any change in the status quo that prevailed on both sides of the illusory Green Line. And from the perspective of Prime Minister Benjamin Netanyahu and his inner circle, there was no reason to rock the boat. Even while he reassured Israel's guarantors in Washington of his commitment to "two states," Netanyahu authorized the construction of new housing units in the E1 corridor, a swath of settlements that would complete the encirclement of occupied East Jerusalem, severing it permanently from the West Bank and slicing the West Bank itself in half. "E1 is not just another settlement," said Danny Seidemann, a liberal Israeli attorney and expert on settlement construction around Jerusalem. "E1 is the fatal heart attack of the two-state solution."

By the time of the new elections, the status quo had become so entrenched, and the occupation seemed so manageable, that the next generation of rightists no longer felt compelled to mask their agenda with disingenuous appeals to Western opinion. The popularity of Naftali Bennett, the new leader of the religious nationalist Jewish Home party, was dramatic evidence of the trend.

The forty-year-old son of American immigrants from California, Bennett took the reins of the far-right Jewish Home after leading the Yesha Council, the political lobby of the settlement movement. With the millions he earned from running a start-up technology firm, Bennett purchased a home in Ra'anana, a bedroom community near Tel Aviv populated by the denizens of Israel's knowledge economy. Doing his best to conceal his religious nationalist edge, Bennett campaigned as the start-up success, the savvy impresario reaping the fruits of the modern Israeli dream.

Bennett's attempt to cultivate a moderate image did not stop him from promoting his so-called stability plan at every opportunity. Intended to supplant the unrealized proposals for establishing a Palestinian state that emerged throughout the peace process, Bennett's blueprint called for Israel to annex Area C, the 60 percent of the West Bank where most of the Jewish settlements lay. The area's Palestinian population would be placed under full Israeli control and would be granted national rights only in Jordan. The major Palestinian population centers would enjoy the status of Bantustans under direct Israeli police control, while the Gaza Strip would somehow be forced into a confederation with Egypt. After decades of US-guaranteed impunity for settlement expansion, annexing the West Bank had finally entered the mainstream.

"It's less than a state, I acknowledge that," Bennett told reporters at an English language quasi-debate at Hebrew University, which I attended. "Israel would retain the security umbrella on 100 percent of the area. But if we vacate our responsibility, they're just gonna shoot missiles at us!"

He continued in a pleading tone, "There is no perfect solution for living here, but there are imperfect ways to live together on the ground. When you bash your head against the wall a hundred times trying to make a solution and don't get it, it's time to take a fresh look."

Bennett's forthright style and unvarnished Greater Israel agenda captivated a new breed of Jewish Israelis who were increasingly dictating the direction of their society. Among them was Jeremy Gimpel, a thirty-two-year-old Israeli transplant from Atlanta who lived in the settlement of Efrat and was running near the bottom of the Jewish Home election list. I met Gimpel after another English language "debate" in Jerusalem, while he was in deep conversation with an old woman from the United States. "When was Palestine called Palestine? We're from Judea . . . we are the indigenous people of the land of Israel!" I heard him proclaim in a suburban American accent. "How dare they try to kick us out of our homeland!"

Gimpel was a devotee of Avichai Rontski, the former chief rabbi of the Israeli army who helped convince Bennett to enter politics, and who provided Israeli troops with a pamphlet that read, "When you show mercy to a cruel enemy, you are being cruel to pure and honest soldiers." An ordained rabbi, Gimpel had cultivated close political and financial ties with Christian Zionist groups in the United States. Before an audience of evangelical End Timers at a Florida church in 2011, Gimpel openly fantasized about blowing up Jerusalem's Al Aqsa Mosque, the third-holiest site in Islam. "It would be incredible!" he exclaimed.

I spoke with Gimpel for a half-hour in a darkened hallway in Jerusalem's Great Synagogue, outside the cavernous auditorium where the debate was held. This fresh-faced son of Atlanta, who could have passed for a frat boy at any American university, was adamant that the United States get out of Israel's backyard. "We may have to try to stop this political, Western dialogue that doesn't relate to [Palestinian] culture, doesn't relate to our culture. It doesn't work in the Middle East," Gimpel told me, waving his hands effusively like a Bible Belt televangelist. "It's time to realize that the right-wing are the only ones who can bring any stability to the area."

Though Gimpel expected to ride Bennett's surge of popularity into the Knesset, he and other right-wingers including Ben Ari missed out on a seat, thanks to the unexpected rise of a previously unknown politician named Yair Lapid. Lapid was an Israeli broadcast media personality and former head of the TV division at New Regency Films, a Hollywood studio founded by the Israeli producer and former weapons dealer, Arnon Milchan, who became one of Lapid's main political donors. Handsome, suave, and articulate, Lapid was the perfect picture of the post-Oslo Ashkenazi, the secular representative of Tel Aviv fed up with the ultra-Orthodox haredim of Jerusalem's Mea Shearim neighborhood, who shirked military service and drew state welfare—the longtime cause of his father, Tommy Lapid, who had founded an aggressively secular party that focused almost as much resentment against Palestinian citizens of Israel and the Mizrahim as it did against the haredim.

"[I am concerned because] we reside in the corrupt, lazy, retarded environment of the Middle East," the elder Lapid declared in 2002, six years before his death. "What holds us above the water is our cultural difference. The fact [that] we are a forepost of Western civilization. But if our Westernness is eroded, we don't have a chance. . . . We will merge into the Semitic region and will be lost in a horrific Levantine mire."

Picking up where his father left off, Yair Lapid named his party Yesh Atid, or "There Is a Future," expressing the rising frustration with the whole political class, left and right, and Israel's dead-end politics. On his appeal of vague uplift and particular distaste for the presence of both the ultra-Orthodox and the Palestinians, Lapid managed to secure nineteen seats in the next Knesset, suddenly making the newly formed party the second largest in Israel behind Likud. It was not known during the campaign that he had forged a backdoor alliance with Naftali Bennett.

Though Lapid's economic vision seemed scarcely different from Netanyahu, whose proposals mirrored those of his old friend and former colleague at the Boston Consulting Group, Mitt Romney, he aimed to capitalize on energy left over from the tent protests that brought hundreds of thousands of protesters into the streets of Israel during the summer of 2011. Frustrated by a declining standard of living and dwindling social benefits, the tent protesters raged against the neoliberal policies that had concentrated much of the country's wealth into the hands of about twenty politically connected, oligarchic families. As in the tent protests, where student union leaders and other self-styled "social justice" crusaders studiously avoided any mention of the occupation, and even held rallies in the settlement of Ariel and in the occupied Golan Heights, Lapid campaigned with the Palestinians out of sight, and out of mind.

When Lapid unveiled his foreign policy platform, he chose to do so at a university inside the illegal mega-settlement of Ariel. Israel "must at last get rid of the Palestinians and put a fence between us," he declared, explaining that he chose to launch his campaign at the settlement because "there is no map on which Ariel isn't a part of the state of Israel." Like Netanyahu, Lapid strongly supported Israel's annexation of Palestinian East Jerusalem, an implicit rejection of the international consensus for a Palestinian state.

The Labor Party, which sought to rebrand itself as the party of social justice—a term that in Israel had come to mean improving the economic lot of the Jewish middle class—placed some of the tent protests' most prominent leaders at the top of its election list. Shelly Yachimovich, the new leader of the Labor Party and like Lapid, a former broadcast journalist, seemed to have accepted Netanyahu's formula of "peace without peace," or managing the occupation. Indeed, she had all but dropped support for a Palestinian state from her party's plank, focusing almost exclusively on kitchen table economic issues. Seeking to woo residents of the major settlement blocs, Yachimovich boasted in an interview, "It was the Labor Party that founded the settlement enterprise in the [occupied] territories," and supported officially accrediting the university in the settlement of Ariel. When a reporter referred in passing to the perception that Labor represented the left of the Israeli political spectrum, Yachimovich snapped back, "Calling Labor 'left-wing' is a historic injustice!"

After securing a surprising nineteen seats in the elections, making his party the second largest in Israel, Lapid immediately rejected forming a left-of-center bloc to prevent Netanyahu from returning to office. His primary objection was that such a maneuver would have required him to invite an Arab party into the coalition. "We will not do that with Haneen Zoabiz—it is not going to happen," he told reporters, adding a "z" to the end of the parliamentarian Zoabi's name to denigrate all Arab parties as a single, homogenous Fifth Column.

Lapid instead formed a pact with Bennett, the settlement movement hero whose previously marginal party earned twelve Knesset seats, ensuring them prominent roles in the government and control over key ministries. They eventually entered into a coalition with Likud and Yisrael Beiteinu, consolidating the right-wing's political dominance until at least the next election. During coalition negotiations, the parties agreed to advance a law subjugating Israel's democratic charter to its Jewish character and subject any future deal with the Palestinian Authority to a public referendum, a clause that virtually guaranteed it would never be ratified.

Netanyahu emerged from the elections weakened but still dominant. Besides Bennett and Lapid, the prime minister's greatest challenge emerged from inside his own party, where a generation of extremists had taken the reigns of Likud. Gone were relatively tolerant figures such as Reuven Rivlin, the Likud elder who defended Zoabi's right to condemn Israel's raid on the *Mavi Marmara* before the Knesset. In his place stood zealots like Tzipi Hotovely, the thirty-four-year-old former Im Tirtzu member who appeared earlier in this book to lead Knesset hearings on the danger of Jewish-Arab relationships. She was appointed Deputy Transportation Minister, a stepping-stone to long-term influence.

With Avigdor Lieberman forced to temporarily abandon his post as Foreign Minister to stand trial for fraud and breach of trust—the charges of his brazen corruption and proximity to organized crime was beginning to hinder his ambitions—the ministry fell under the control of one of the Likud's most draconian figures, Ze'ev Elkin. An immigrant from the Soviet Union whose appointment as Deputy Foreign Minister was endorsed by Lieberman, Elkin earned acclaim as the author of the law designed to impose financial penalties on any Israeli citizen who boycotted settlement products.

The Education Ministry was handed over to Shai Piron, a settler rabbi who ran on the ticket of Lapid's "centrist" party, and who had previously advised residents of Haifa that renting houses to Arabs violated Jewish law. Miri Regev, the notoriously unhinged Likud parliamentarian who called African asylum seekers "a cancer" at a rally that devolved into a full-scale race riot, was granted the Internal Affairs and Environment Committee. She thus attained control over Israel's population registry and the Knesset Interior Committee. Moshe Feiglin, an open theocrat banned from entering the United Kingdom for "inciting racial hatred," was appointed deputy Knesset speaker. Yuli Edelstein, the annexationist settler who previously directed Israel's international *hasbara* efforts, became the speaker of Knesset.

Assessing the results, a settlement movement leader named Gershon Mesika remarked, "On the face of it, it does look like a wet dream."

The Shadows and Mirrors Game

The protesters of Ni'lin, Bil'in, and Nabi Saleh still arose each Friday to confront their occupiers, and fell back under a fog of teargas and a hail of rubber bullets, but as 2013 began, the Palestinian popular struggle was transforming against a dire scenario. The protests spilled out of the villages and onto Israelis-only roads, catching settlers and the army by surprise with human roadblocks; and appeared at the gates of Ofer Military Prison, where Palestinians were held without trial for months, drawing international attention to the practice of administrative detention. When Prime Minister Benjamin Netanyahu announced the construction of hundreds of new settlement units in the E1 corridor, the popular struggle responded with a brand new tactic.

Early in the morning on January 11, a caravan of vehicles filled with Palestinian activists from across the West Bank snaked through the hills above East Jerusalem. Within a few hours, they had established Bab Al Shams, a protest village named for the epic novel about the Palestinian struggle, *Gate of the Sun*, by the Lebanese author Elias Khoury. Erected entirely on privately owned Palestinian land, the tent village stood directly in the way of what would be the capstone of Israel's settler-colonial enterprise in the West Bank.

Abir Kopty, a thirty-eight-year-old Palestinian feminist and human rights activist handling media for the Popular Struggle Coordination Commitee, remarked to me about Bab Al Shams, "Israel has been imposing facts on the ground, and we are doing exactly the same. We want to impose facts on our land. So, yes, it might seem that we have taken a model from them, but the difference is that we are building on our land and we are not taking others' land and building on it."

Netanyahu reacted to news of the Palestinian protest village with extreme consternation. He was not going to let a bunch of scraggled Arabs stand in the way of what would be the most enduring symbol of his legacy in "Judea and Samaria." And so, on January 12, Netanyahu dispatched a lawyer from the Ministry of Justice to the Supreme Court to argue for the immediate eviction of the protesters. To the government's chagrin, the Supreme Court rejected its arguments, issuing a temporary injunction that prevented the camp's eviction for six days pending further deliberations. Meanwhile, the row of generator-powered media trucks at the base of Bab Al Shams was growing.

As the clock struck midnight on January 13, Netanyahu directed his lawyers to issue a statement overriding the Supreme Court. Treating the court's ruling as a mere suggestion, the Israeli Ministry of Justice concocted a justification that was as ludicrous as it was predictable: "There is an urgent security need to evacuate the area of the people and tents," it claimed, suggesting without evidence that a few hundred unarmed activists presented a grave threat to public safety.

I arrived at the site of Bab Al Shams with journalists Lia Tarachansky, Jesse Rosenfeld, and my former roommate from Jaffa, Woody, about two hours before Netanyahu ordered its eviction. The main entrances to the tent encampment were sealed off by squads of Israeli police. A police commander told me and other journalists that no reporters were allowed inside the area. Though he claimed to hold a formal order from the military, he failed to produce any kind of documentation. An Israeli journalist told me he had been told earlier in the evening by Israeli army GOC Central Commander Nitzan Alon that he was free to travel anywhere in the West Bank—but that "this [Bab Al Shams] was something different."

In order to enter Bab Al Shams, we had to navigate the narrow, pothole-scarred roads of al-Zaim, an impoverished Palestinian town severed from the rest of the Jerusalem municipality by Israel's separation wall and a checkpoint. Though al-Zaim was already an overcrowded, under-serviced ghetto prevented from expanding to meet the needs of a growing population, the construction of the E-1 corridor threatened to enclose it on all sides, completing that process of isolation that drove its immiseration. At a muddy field strewn with trash at the outskirts of al-Zaim, we climbed out of a small car and hiked toward Bab Al Shams, walking for 3 kilometers along a craggy path through the hills in the bone-chilling cold. There were no signs of any army presence on our way, only vehicle caravans heading out of the village to gather more supplies for the next day.

At the entrance of the village, I found about a dozen residents of Bil'in village huddled around a campfire, sipping coffee and smoking cigarettes. "Forget about the food," Bil'in popular committee leader Abdallah Abu Rahme joked. "If we don't have cigarettes and coffee, we won't survive a night here."

After visiting with the protesters for a few hours—many were weary or sick from two nights in the cold with little sleep—I took a ride out of the village in the back of a pickup truck loaded to the gills with journalists and activists. We had no idea whether the army was set to raid tonight, or if it might wait another day. With the news that the high court had issued a temporary injunction against the eviction, we assumed the government would wait to secure formal permission. We were wrong.

Toward the end of the rocky path leading into Bab Al Shams, and just outside al-Zaim, we barreled by a detachment of Israeli Border Police officers milling around a group of jeeps. It was clear now that the raid was imminent, and that even if we wanted to re-enter Bab Al Shams, there was no way back inside. Woody grumbled to me that he felt like one of the white Western aid workers conveniently airlifted out of some Third World disaster zone before a catastrophe ravaged the entrapped locals.

Within two hours, five hundred Border Police in full riot gear were storming the village, carrying its inhabitants away by force. By this time, I was back at my flat in Ramallah, watching the police push cameramen away from the scene through an Al Jazeera livestream of the eviction. Days later, the police tore what was left of the village to pieces, clearing the path for new settlements that would complete the systematic negation of what peace process negotiators liked to call "a viable Palestinian state."

This seemingly small incident was about much more than another Palestinian eviction. Under pressure from right-wing upstarts in his own party amid a heated election contest, Netanyahu's order was in flagrant contempt of the Supreme Court's injunction. And not one of the judges said a word of protest. They were silent as their authority was shoved aside. Once again, the rule of law was trampled by an illegal occupation.

As the new year of 2013 began, the struggle for Palestinian rights increasingly found its energy inside Israel's vast network of prisons, where hundreds of Palestinians languished without charges and thousands of others were doomed to spend their adult lives, separated from family and friends for interminable periods. By April 2013, a prisoner named Samer Issawi had carried on a hunger strike for over 250 days to protest his detention for visiting family members in the West Bank, violating the terms of his previous release from prison, which confined him to the Jerusalem Municipality—an Israeli official claimed he left Jerusalem to establish "terror cells."

Summoning his last stores of energy, Issawi wrote a desperate letter from his hospital bed. Appealing to the elements of Israeli society that fashioned themselves as its most humanistic and enlightened—"intellectuals, academics, writers, lawyers, journalists, and activists"—Issawi wrote, "Israelis, I'm looking for an educated one among you who has passed the stage of the shadows and mirrors game." The prisoner urged his audience, "Hear my voice, the voice of remaining time—mine and yours. . . . Don't forget those you have incarcerated in prison and camps, between the iron doors that imprison your consciousness. I'm not waiting for a prison guard to free me, I'm waiting for the one who frees you of my memory."

A few Israeli women kept a vigil at Issawi's bedside, but the cultural luminaries addressed in the letter had done and said nothing for more than two hundred days. At last, a group of Israeli intellectuals, including the two writers hailed by Western liberals as the conscience of their society—A. B. Yehoshua and Amos Oz—answered Issawi. But they did not call for the prisoner's freedom or for an end to the Israeli policy of administrative detention, where Palestinians are routinely held for many months without being charged. Instead, they chided Issawi for his hunger strike, accusing him of engaging in a "suicidal act" that would "pile more despair on the despair already in existence." Finally, they accused him of eroding hope in the US-led peace process, which by this time existed in name only.

After 277 days and numerous Israeli attempts to have him deported to Europe, and then to Gaza, where other West Bank hunger strikers had been sent and would be confined indefinitely—"This calls to mind the operations of forced expulsion that befell the Palestinians in 1948 and 1967," Issawi commented—the State finally agreed to Issawi's terms, mandating his release to his family's home inside the Jerusalem Municipality. Pushed to the brink of his existence, Issawi won back his freedom, but without the help of the partners he had sought out on the other side.

In 2000, in one of his last interviews, Edward Said remarked to the Israeli journalist Ari Shavit, "I never use terms like 'balance of power.' But I think that even the person doing the kicking has to ask himself how long he can go on kicking. At some point your leg is going to get tired. One day you'll wake up and ask, 'What the fuck am I doing?'"

Thirteen years later, Israel's system of institutional discrimination and occupation had only grown more entrenched, with its administrators, ambassadors, and arbiters confronting every challenge thrown in their way with unsentimental determination. From the gun-toting zealots of the South Hebron Hills to the mediagenic politicians and poets of Tel Aviv, Israeli society was less anguished than ever about its control over the lives of Palestinians. In the absence of consequences from the United States, which under Barack Obama had doubled US taxpayer funding of Israel's military, it was easy to understand why Said's warning had not yet come to bear.

There were, of course, many Israelis who had dared to reflect, to engage the hard questions about occupation, militarization, and apartheid, and who ultimately refused their designated roles in the project of controlling the Palestinians. Their sense of fatigue and demoralization was palpable during my time inside Israel-Palestine. Many Israeli human rights activists had resolved to stay and struggle, but there were others who decided to extricate themselves from despair by leaving Israel for good. And so in a steady stream they escaped for a better life in places such as Germany, seeking the free air of Berlin, where a rapidly growing community of Israeli exiles gathered.

The Exodus Party

The sonorous voice of the Egyptian classical *tarab* singer Farid El Atrache drifted from inside a low lit bar into the alleyway of the Jaffa market. "I'll write on the wings of the bird my letter, words written with tears, and oh bird, if you see my beloved, promise to send them my greetings," he sang in Arabic. The single-story storefronts and cobblestone lanes of the old Palestinian market area had been transformed into a conglomeration of trendy bars and upscale apartments under the direction of Tel Aviv Mayor Ron Huldai and the commercial developers who backed him. The market was ground zero of Jaffa's gentrification project, where the more cultivated denizens of Tel Aviv's knowledge economy came for arak and spacious new Arabesque condos. With the romantic sound of El Atrache in the air, the sultry feeling of life in the Orient persisted, but without the Arabs who had made it so uncomfortable.

Deep inside the market, I arrived at a table at a bar called Pua to find a small international group at a long table. At the head of the table was Edo M., a twenty-eight-year-old Tel Avivian computer expert on his way out of the country. He wore a black-and-white Palestinian *keffiyeh* around his neck. Tali Shapira, the activist helping lead the Boycott From Within movement, was the only other Israeli at the table. Filling out the group was Edo's friend, the Swedish photojournalist Linda Forsell, and her Dutch assistant.

It was Edo's going-away party, and he was not in the mood to mince words. "Well, as you can see," he told me, "I don't have too many friends left in Israel. Over time, I realized I couldn't really talk to anyone anymore. There is no place left for me in this country. It has turned fascist and that's it. So I've decided that the best way to carry on the struggle was from outside. From there," he continued, "I'll have to wait until Israel goes so crazy, and commits a massacre so big that the world will finally see what it really is."

Edo was in a military intelligence unit during Israel's second invasion of Lebanon, the war that began with a massive aerial assault leaving Southern Lebanon littered with four million cluster munitions. During the war, Edo was assigned with targeting. "By the end, the Air Force had run out of targets, so they just told us to make them up, to invent new ones," he said.

As his military service drew to a close, Edo began tearing his wisdom teeth out, one by one. He explained, "For every tooth I lost I got a week off, and this kept me out of the army." Next, he asked his friend to break his leg with a wooden plank to get more time off. His friend smashed his leg as hard as he could, but could not manage to break it. Finally, Edo gave up on his future in Israel. Like thousands of young Israelis, he decided to move to Germany.

With easy access to second passports (a luxury most Mizrahi Israeli citizens who emigrated from Arab countries do not enjoy) Israel's Ashkenazi middle and upper classes have escaped the claustrophobic atmosphere of the country of their birth in droves. According to current Israeli government estimates, as many as one million Israelis—a full 13 percent of the population—now live outside Israel, an increase of almost seven hundred thousand since 1980. While similarly high proportions of the population from deeply impoverished, war-torn states like Mexico and Sri Lanka lived in foreign countries, few, if any, industrialized nations shared Israel's emigration problem. And in contrast to immigrants from developing nations, Israel's expatriate population was disproportionately affluent, educated, secular, and liberal. The exodus of Israelis is the greatest and most immediate demographic threat the Jewish state faces.

Tapuz, a website for Israelis living abroad, hosted a 2005 forum on the topic of leaving Israel. According to the site's administrator, Limor Abis, the most frequently cited explanation for why they left was, "The question is not why we left, but why it took so long to do so." A 2007 poll of Israeli youth between the ages of fourteen and eighteen found that more than half would prefer to live abroad and would do so if they had the chance. Their greatest grievance was not terrorism or the occupation but the miserable social situation in Israel, with 84 percent claiming the government had failed to ameliorate the deepening economic and social problems plaguing Israel.

Most Israelis who lived abroad had settled in the United States, and many more wanted to join them. Israelis seeking forged or illegal work visas to get jobs selling beauty products and trinkets at mall kiosks in the United States had become such an epidemic the US Embassy in Tel Aviv delegated a special investigator, Charles Shannon, to lead the crackdown. Shannon appeared in a 2011 informational film called *The Price Is Too High*, which the US embassy produced to deter Israelis from seeking the visas. The video featured young Israelis telling their sob stories of being conned by shady Israeli businessmen into entering the United States with the wrong visa, then getting caught and punished with lifetime bans from America. "It's too bad you hear about the great job, the money, and the good life, and they don't tell you it's illegal," said one of the failed Israeli jobseekers.

The Israeli government also disseminated propaganda films to sway Israelis against the lure of life in the United States. A 2011 video produced by the Israeli Ministry for Immigration and Absorption showed a gray-haired Israeli couple speaking to their granddaughter, who had moved to America and married a gentile. "Do you know what holiday it is today?" they asked, with a menorah in the background. "Christmas!" she responded. Finally, a Hebrew narrator intones, "They will always remain Israelis, but their children won't. Help them return to Israel." The video sparked outrage among Jewish American communal leaders who rarely complained about Israel's policies toward the Palestinians. In a rare act of dissent, they lashed out against Prime Minister Benjamin Netanyahu. Ultimately, Netanyahu, who was raised in the Philadelphia suburbs and whose second wife was American, gave in to the pressure and ordered the videos removed.

Though the United States remained the favorite country for Israeli émigrés, Germany had emerged as the choice destination for the younger, artsier set, and for committed leftists like Edo. As many as 50,000 Israelis have applied for German citizenship and some 100,000 already held a second German passport. "For [young Israelis]," the German newspaper *Der Spiegel* reported, "Germany is not just a country like any other—it also happens to be one of their favorites." And Berlin, with an Israeli population of 15,000, was their utopia, the *Alteneuland* they could not find in Tel Aviv. As *Der Spiegel* put it, "The city from which the Final Solution was once managed now lures Israelis with its cheap rents and the promise of life in an exciting city that never sleeps."

Nati Ornan, an Israeli musician who made the move to Berlin, told *Ha'aretz*, "I don't look for a caring attitude here, but I get it here more than in Israel. Berlin is no utopia, but it is sensitive toward the 'other' because of the Holocaust. In Israel there was no such catastrophe to make people realize an individual's life has great value."

He explained, "When I go running in the street, people over ninety, about whom I can surmise where they were during the Holocaust, applaud me. In Israel, in contrast, I see how Holocaust survivors are treated. . . . There is respect for the old and weak here. They are treated properly. Society cares about them."

For his part, Edo found fulfillment in Freiburg, getting engaged to an attractive blonde woman and settling comfortably into the atmosphere of the southwestern German city that boasted a reputation as the most eco-friendly city in the world. Another Israeli who had settled in Germany, Yossi Bar-Tal, told me Berlin had become a hotbed of Israeli-led radical left-wing activism. Whenever a major Israeli government official arrived, Bar-Tal told me, left-wing Israeli expats staged raucous demos. They had even published anti-occupation journals in Hebrew and German, he said.

Inside Israel, many of my friends have made preparations to leave for good. After relocating to Ramallah for two years, Joseph Dana made plans to move to Istanbul, Turkey, telling me he was burned out by the years of conflict. Meanwhile, nearly everywhere I go in the Western world, I encounter young Israelis who made the exodus long ago. In Barcelona, I met Moshe, a thirty-five-year-old Israeli living in one of the city's many anarchist squats. He told me he decided to leave Israel after a harrowing experience in the army, during which he manned a checkpoint and was ordered to harass Palestinian commuters day after day. In the Red Hook section of Brooklyn, I met Rafi Magnes, the grandson of Rabbi Judah Magnes, and his wife, Liz. They had left Israel for good, purchased a house in the chic, formerly industrial neighborhood, and painted a giant mural on the wall that faced the street reading, "NY Loves Obama." "I call ourselves luxury refugees," Liz Magnes told me. "We could have stayed, of course, but the fascism had gotten to be too overwhelming. Thank God we left."

At a party in Brooklyn in 2011, I encountered Maya Wind, the twenty-two-year-old Israeli army refuser, who had become a member of Columbia University's Students for Justice in Palestine Chapter. Later in the year, she would dress up at an

Israeli soldier manning a checkpoint at the mock separation wall the students' group constructed at the center of Columbia campus, generating headlines back in Israel, and outrage from many of her Israeli classmates. She was with at the party with her boyfriend, Eran, a former soldier who had given testimony to Breaking the Silence about his service on the Egyptian border, and scenes of misery and abuse of African migrants he witnessed there. They told me they were relieved to be out of Israel and in the multicultural atmosphere of New York City. It was then that I noticed that Yonatan Shapira, the Israeli pilot-turned-Palestine solidarity activist, chatting in Hebrew in the next room with Elik Elhanan, the son of Nurit Peled-Elhanan, and now a professor of Yiddish literature at Columbia. The sound of Hebrew chatter was pouring from the room, and there was also English in a smattering of foreign accents. Everyone here seemed to feel at home.

ACKNOWLEDGMENTS

This book was dedicated to Akiva Orr, who died on February 9, 2013, at age eighty-one. Orr was a founding member of the anti-Zionist Israeli group, Matzpen, an author and blue-collar historian, a pioneering activist for equality in Israel-Palestine, a rare role model and teacher to many, and most importantly, a friend. I will sorely miss visiting him at Mikhmoret Beach.

As with my last book, this one depended on the editorial judgment, vision, and patience of Carl Bromley. Brendan O'Connor, Keenan Duffy, Daniel LoPreto, Chris Granville, and Lori Hobkirk provided important research and editorial help. Thanks to Anna Stein, Taya Kitman, Hamilton Fish, and the Lannan Foundation for their steady support, and to John Sherer for his confidence in this project. Phil Weiss, Adam Horowitz, and Scott Roth from *Mondoweiss*; Ali Abunimah, Maureen Murphy, and Nora Barrows-Friedman of *Electronic Intifada*; and Jan Frel of *Alternet* provided essential outlets for much of the reporting contained on these pages—material that less courageous publications have shied away from. Thanks also to Roane Carey and Betsy Reed of *The Nation* and to Hicham Safieddine.

Throughout this project I was lucky to have the unwavering support of my parents, my indefatigable grandmother, Claire, and my brother, Paul. Eman Morsi offered encouragement and kept me sane while trying to see a challenging endeavor to its completion. I am especially grateful to those in Israel-Palestine who extended me their assistance and hospitality. While not all can be named, some who can be include Shai Haddad, Yossi David, Nitzan Menagem, Tomer Lavie, Masha Averbuch, Saeed Amireh, David Jacobus, Netta Mishly, Karla Green, Emilie Baujard, Randa May Wahbe, Ala Milbes, Gal Harmat, Eran Torbiner, Gaby Rubin, Alex Cohn, Abir Kopty, Yonatan Shapira, Michael Solsbery, Dimi Reider, Ayed Fadel, Jonathan Pollak, and Noam Sheizaf. I have relied heavily on Linda Forsell, Joseph Dana, George Hale, Lia Tarachansky, David Sheen, and Jesse Rosenfeld as journalistic colleagues and as friends. This book would not have been possible without them.

NOTES

CHAPTER 1: TO THE SLAUGHTER

3 **to the brink of collapse**: Wikileaks, "Cashless in Gaza," Reuters, January 5, 2011, http://www.haaretz.com/news/diplomacy-defense/wikileaks-israel-aimed-to-keep-gaza-economy-on-brink-of-collapse-1.335354. According to US officials at the US Embassy in Tel Aviv, Israeli officials wanted Gaza's economy "functioning at the lowest level possible consistent with avoiding a humanitarian crisis."

3 **It's like an appointment**: Steven Erlanger, "Hamas Leader Faults Israeli Sanction Plan," *New York Times*, February 18, 2006, http://www.nytimes.com/2006/02/18/international/middleeast/18mideast.html?ex=1297918800&en=5b778e6679d-ba2cf&ei=5090&partner=rssuserland&emc=rss.

3 **During the time of the siege**: Yousef M. Aljamal, "During the Time of the Siege," *Mondoweiss*, July 20, 2010, http://mondoweiss.net/2010/07/during-the-time-of-the-siege.html.

3 **free and fair election**: Aaron D. Pina, "Fatah and Hamas: The New Palestinian Factional Reality," CRS Report for Congress, March 3, 2006, http://www.fas.org/sgp/crs/mideast/RS22395.pdf.

3 **faithfully observing a ceasefire**: Rory McCarthy, "Gaza Truce Broken as Israeli Raid Kills 6 Hamas Gunmen," *Guardian*, November 5, 2008, http://www.guardian.co.uk/world/2008/nov/05/israelandthepalestinians See also Rick Sanchez, "CNN Confirms Israel Broke Ceasefire First," CNN, January 5, 2009, http://www.youtube.com/watch?v=Kntmp0RXFX4.

4 **will bring upon themselves**: "Israeli Minister Warns of Palestinian 'Holocaust,'" *Guardian*, February 29, 2008, http://www.guardian.co.uk/world/2008/feb/29/israelandthepalestinians1.

5 **massacre and act of criminal aggression**: Julia Fitzpatrick, "Gaza on Their Minds: The Effect of 'Operation Cast Lead' in Mobilizing Palestinian Action," *Al Nakhlah, Online Journal of Southwest Asia and Islamic Civilization*, Spring 2011, p. 6, http://fletcher.tufts.edu/Al-Nakhlah/~/media/6F1D365405694E1B88142EB94DB5D443.pdf.

5 **Palestinian Authority forces swarmed**: Ibid.

5 **Though Abbas refused**: Barak Ravid, "WikiLeaks Exposé: Israel Tried to Coordinate Gaza War with Abbas," *Ha'aretz*, November 28, 2010, http://www.haaretz

.com/news/diplomacy-defense/wikileaks-expose-israel-tried-to-coordinate-gaza
-war-with-abbas-1.327487.

CHAPTER 2: THE PEACE CAMP

6 **the sound of knocking**: Gidi Weitz, "No Hard Feelings," *Ha'aretz*, March 18, 2011, http://www.haaretz.com/weekend/magazine/no-hard-feelings-1.350004.

6 **I am living with the constant tension**: Ibid.

6 **The time has come to act**: Cited in Roni Singer-Heruti, "New Meretz Leftist Party Launches Campaign against IDF Operation in Gaza," *Ha'aretz*, January 11, 2009, http://www.haaretz.com/print-edition/news/new-meretz-leftist-party-launches -campaign-against-idf-operation-in-gaza-1.267869.

6 **understandable and acceptable**: Johann Hari, "Israel's Voice of Reason: Amoz Oz on War, Peace, and Life as an Outsider," *Independent*, March 19, 2009, http://www .independent.co.uk/news/world/middle-east/israels-voice-of-reason-amos-oz -on-war-peace-and-life-as-an-outsider-1648254.html.

6 **not a word about civilian casualties**: David Grossman, "Fight Fire with a Cease-fire," *New York Times,* December 30, 2008, http://www.nytimes.com/2008/12/31 /opinion/31grossman.html?_r=0.

6 **Even though we supported initiating**: Gil Hoffman, "Peace Now, Meretz Hold Left's First Anti-War Protest," *Jerusalem Post*, January 10, 2009, http://www.jpost .com/Israel/Article.aspx?id=128676.

7 **Meretz and Peace Now**: Ibid.

7 **You are bad Arabs!**: Jared Malsin, "Go Back unto Death: Life in Postwar Gaza," *Ma'an News Agency*, posted December 17, 2009; updated July 7, 2010, http://www .maannews.net/eng/ViewDetails.aspx?ID=247109.

7 **Go back unto death**: Ibid.

8 **There was no resistance in this area**: Ibid.

8 **forty-eight corpses**: Tim Butcher, "Gaza: Palestinian Family Mourns 48 Dead," *Daily Telegraph*, January 19, 2009, http://www.telegraph.co.uk/news/worldnews/ middleeast/palestinianauthority/4290553/Gaza-Palestinian-family-mourns-48 -dead.html.

8 **1 is DOWN 999,999 TO GO**: Ibid.

CHAPTER 3: BLOOD FOR VOTES

9 **who could believe a woman**: Liel Leibovitz, "Say Anything," Tablet, February 3, 2009, http://www.tabletmag.com/jewish-news-and-politics/1452/say-anything.

9 **Hamas now understands**: Kim Sengupta and Donald MacIntyre, "Israeli Cabinet Divided over Fresh Gaza Surge," *Independent*, January 13, 2009, http://www.inde-pendent.co.uk/news/world/middle-east/israeli-cabinet-divided-over-fresh-gaza -surge-1332024.html.

9 **Iranian missiles that would fire**: Peter Beaumont, "Courting Settled Opinion," *Guardian*, February 9, 2009, http://www.guardian.co.uk/world/2009/feb/09/ israeli-settlements-peace.

9 **whacked when they're on the toilet**: Lily Galili, "Did Barak Quote Putin or Did Putin Quote Barak?" *Ha'aretz*, January 28, 2009, http://www.haaretz.com/news /did-barak-quote-putin-or-did-putin-quote-barak-1.269057

9 **Russian speakers' eyes**: Lily Galili, "Barak Seeking to 'Putinize' Image to Attract Russian Vote," *Ha'aretz*, January 27, 2009, http://www.haaretz.com/news/elec-tions/barak-seeking-to-putinize-image-to-attract-russian-vote-1.268930.

10 **The present negotiations**: Dana DePietro and Rachel Dodd, "The 2013 Israeli Elections: Consequences for the Palestinian Arab Citizens in Israel," Mossawa Center, December 2012, http://www.mossawacenter.org/my_Documents/pic001 /2013_Israeli_Elections.pdf.

10 **future Palestinian state**: Lisa Goldman, "Lieberman, Arabs and Cannabis: Pick of the Israeli Election Campaign Clips," *Guardian*, February 10, 2009, http://www .guardian.co.uk/world/blog/2009/feb/10/israel-election-campaign-clips.

CHAPTER 4: THE HILL OF SHAME

11 **Of course I'm happy:** Martin Fletcher and Yonit Farago, "Hill of Shame Where Gaza Bombing Is Spectator Sport," Times (London), January 13, 2009, http://www .timesonline.co.uk/tol/news/world/middle_east/article5505390.ece.

11 **Yeah, I'm a little bit fascist**: TV report by Ulla Terkelsen, [Danish TV] Nyhederne TV2 [uploaded on YouTube January 10, 2009] http://www.youtube.com /watch?v=Tjw8UoAcH4Q[.

11 **People in Israel are addicted to violence**: Fletcher and Farago, "Hill of Shame."

11 **support for the bombing**: Yehuda Ben Meir, "Operation Cast Lead: Political Dimensions and Public Opinion," *Strategic Assessment*, Volume 11, No. 4, 30. Eighty-one percent of the Israeli public supported the operation on its first day, with only 12 percent opposed; subtracting Palestinian citizens of Israel from the poll respondents, support was 90 percent.

12 **We are very violent**: Jonathan Cook, "'We Are Very Violent': Israeli War Crimes Mount," *AlterNet*, January 9, 2009, http://www.alternet.org/story/118686/%27we _are_very_violent%27%3A_israeli_war_crimes_mount.

12 **deterring the protesters with force**: Akiva Eldar "How Israel Silenced Its Gaza War Protesters," *Ha'arez*, September 22, 2009, http://www.haaretz.com/print-edition /features/how-israel-silenced-its-gaza-war-protesters-1.7477.

12 **great appreciation for the residents**: Ibid.

13 **torn to pieces with flechette darts**: Human Rights Council, Twelfth Session "Human Rights in Palestine and Other Occupied Arab Territories: Report of the United Nations Fact-Finding Mission on the Gaza Conflict," United Nations General Assembly, pp. 196–197, http://www2.ohchr.org/english/bodies/hrcouncil /docs/12session/A-HRC-12-48.pdf.

13 **covered in burns**: Ibid.

13 **found dead with bizarre wounds**: Adam Horowitz, Lizzy Ratner, and Philip Weiss, eds., *The Goldstone Report* (New York: Nation Books, 2011), 143; Raymond Whitaker, "'Tungsten Bombs' Leave Israel's Victims with Mystery Wounds," *Independent*, January 18, 2009, http://www.independent.co.uk/news/world/middle -east/tungsten-bombs-leave-israels-victims-with-mystery-wounds-1418910.html.

13 **while waving a white flag**: Human Rights Watch, "Israel: 2009 Killings of Mother and Daughter Unresolved," August 22, 2012 http://www.hrw.org/news/2012/08 /22/israel-2009-killings-mother-and-daughter-unresolved. According to Human Rights Watch, "The two women were killed when an Israeli soldier opened fire on a group of civilians holding white flags to demonstrate their civilian status."

13 **destroyed by a missile**: Horowitz, Ratner, and Weiss, *The Goldstone Report*, 99.

13 **Israeli soldiers killed**: Jen Marlowe, *One Family in Gaza*, Donkeysaddle Projects, http://vimeo.com/18384109.

13 **I feel good**: *Cleansing Gaza: Brutal Truth of Operation Cast Lead Revealed*, directed by Nurit Kedar, (2011, Journeyman Pictures), http://www.journeyman.tv

/?lid=61426&tmpl=transcript. See also Channel 4 UK, "Israeli Filmmaker Receives Death Threats over Gaza Report," January 27, 2011, http://www.channel4 .com/news/israeli-filmmaker-receives-death-threats-over-gaza-report.

13 **Levy reflected**: Gideon Levy, "Twilight Zone / Baron of Manipulation," *Ha'aretz*, October 22, 2010, http://www.haaretz.com/weekend/magazine/twilight-zone -baron-of-manipulation-1.320636.

13 **My daughters! Oh God!**: "Israeli TV Airs Gaza Doctor's Pleas after Children Killed," YouTube video, 4:18, January 16, 2009, http://www.youtube.com/watch ?v=OLUJ4fF2HN4.

14 **They only want to see one side**: Dudi Cohen, "Soldiers' Mother: Stop Gaza Doctor's Propaganda" *Ynetnews*, January 17, 2009, http://www.ynetnews.com/articles /0,7340,L-3657587,00.html.

CHAPTER 5: HOOLIGANS

15 **This country has needed**: Yotam Feldman, "Lieberman's Anti-Arab Ideology Wins Over Israel's Teens" Ha'aretz, February 5, 2009, http://www.haaretz.com /news/elections/lieberman-s-anti-arab-ideology-wins-over-israel-s-teens-1 .269489.

15 **Someone who doesn't declare**: Ibid.

15 **Bibi [Benjamin Netanyahu] doesn't want**: Ibid.

16 **youngest person ever to serve**: Ibid.

16 **Slansky moaned**: Ibid.

16 **old Ashkenazi establishment**: Israel was founded largely by European Jewish (Ashkenazi) immigrants who developed their political sensibility in quasi-socialist, Jews-only communes known as kibbutzim. Though commonly regarded as leftist, the kibbutzim were largely responsible for the greatest wave of ethnic cleansing in Israel's history.

16 **I thought it was idiotic**: *Cleansing Gaza: Brutal Truth of Operation Cast Lead Revealed*, directed by Nurit Kedar, (2011, Journeyman Pictures), http://www .journeyman.tv/?lid=61426&tmpl=transcript.

16 **Israel suffered 15 casualties**: B'Tselem —The Israeli Information Center for Human Rights in the Occupied Territories, "B'Tselem's Investigation of Fatalities in Operation Cast Lead," September 9, 2009, http://www.btselem.org/download /20090909_cast_lead_fatalities_eng.pdf.

CHAPTER 6: PAWNS IN THE GAME

17 **never to sit with Yisrael Beiteinu**: Oren Yiftachel, "Voting for Apartheid: The 2009 Israeli Elections," Journal of Palestine Studies, Vol. 38, no. 3 (Spring 2009) http://www.geog.bgu.ac.il/members/yiftachel/new_papers_2009/JPS%20 Yiftachel%202009.pdf.

17 **No loyalty, no citizenship**: Ibid.

17 **apartheid-like measures as popular**: Ibid.

18 **Israeli Jews' consciousness**: Akiva Eldar, "Is an Israeli Jewish Sense of Victimization Perpetuating the Conflict with Palestinians?" *Ha'aretz*, January 29, 2009, http://www.haaretz.com/is-an-israeli-jewish-sense-of-victimization-perpetuating -the-conflict-with-palestinians-1.269152.

18 **Arabs are a security and demographic**: Jack Khoury, Eli Ashkenazi, and *Ha'aretz* correspondents, "Poll: 68% of Jews Would Refuse to Live in Same Building as an Arab," March 22, 2006, http://www.haaretz.com/news/poll-68-of-jews-would -refuse-to-live-in-same-building-as-an-arab-1.183429.

18 **Tammany Hall-style wheeler**: Asher Schechter, "The Return of the King: Aryeh Deri's Unlikely Redemption," *Ha'aretz,* November 11, 2012, http://www.haaretz .com/news/israeli-elections-2013/israeli-elections-news-features/the-return-of -the-king-aryeh-deri-s-unlikely-redemption.premium-1.476627.

19 **They are evil and damnable**: "Rabbi Calls for Annihilation of Arabs," *BBC News,* April 10, 2001, http://news.bbc.co.uk/2/hi/middle_east/1270038.stm.

CHAPTER 7: THIS MAN IS CLEAN

20 **The man was hunting for:** "Avigdor Lieberman Was Convicted of Assaulting a 13-Year-Old," Ha'aretz [Hebrew], September 25, 2001, http://www.haaretz.co.il /opinions/today-before/1.1482454; See also Richard Silverstein, "Avigdor Lieberman, Convicted Child Beater to Be Israeli Foreign Minister," Tikun Olam, March 7, 2009, http://www.richardsilverstein.com/2009/03/07/avigdor-lieberman-convicted -child-beater-to-be-israeli-foreign-minister.

20 **well connected legal fixer**: *Ha'aretz,* Ibid; Silverstein, Ibid.

20 **from the famous Eugene Ionesco play**: "Netanyahu Defends Likud 'Feinshmekers,'" *Arutz Sheva,* January 11, 2011, http://www.israelnationalnews.com/News /News.aspx/141661#.UV5wNVb8dzE.

20 **Any American notions of political**: Lily Galili, "All Is Heaven with Avigdor Lieberman," *Patheos,* June 28, 2010, http://www.patheos.com/Resources/Additional -Resources/All-Is-Heaven-with-Avigdor-Lieberman?offset=4&max=1.

21 **favors inside Israel**: Ofra Edelman, "Everything You Need to Know: Lieberman Graft Case 101," *Ha'aretz,* December 13, 2012, http://www.haaretz.com/news/ national/everything-you-need-to-know-lieberman-graft-case-101.premium-1 .484688.

21 **Accused of paying Lieberman**: Gidi Weitz, "Draft Charges: Lieberman Made Millions in Illegal Business Deals," *Ha'aretz,* May 31, 2011, http://www.haaretz .com/print-edition/news/draft-charges-lieberman-made-millions-in-illegal -business-deals-1.365032.

21 **US officials described Cherney**: Tom Peck, "From Russia with Hate: Aluminum Wars Spill Over into London Court," *Independent,* December 15, 2011, http://www .independent.co.uk/news/uk/home-news/from-russia-with-hate-aluminium -wars-spill-over-into-london-court-6277152.html.

21 **Russia's "aluminum war"**: Ibid.

21 **you are responsible for murder**: Gidi Weitz, "Michael Cherney: On Deripaska, the Russian Mafia and the Israeli Police," *Novinite.com,* December 12, 2009, http:// www.novinite.com/view_news.php?id=111687.

21 **This man is clean**: Ibid.

21 **Another prolific financial angel**: Gidi Weitz, "The Schlaff Saga / Laundered Funds & 'Business' Ties to the Stasi," *Ha'aretz,* September 7, 2010, http://www .haaretz.com/weekend/2.283/the-schlaff-saga-laundered-funds-business-ties-to -the-stasi-1.312799.

22 **run by his twenty-one-year-old daughter**: Uri Blau, "*Ha'aretz* Probe: Company Owned by MK Lieberman's Daughter Made Millions of Shekels," *Ha'aretz,* April 4, 2007, http://www.haaretz.com/print-edition/news/haaretz-probe-company -owned-by-mk-lieberman-s-daughter-made-millions-of-shekels-1.217383 See also Guy Rolnik, "How Did Avigdor Lieberman's 20-Something Daughter Become a Millionaire?" *Ha'aretz,* June 9, 2009, http://www.haaretz.com/print-edi-tion/business/how-did-avigdor-lieberman-s-20-something-daughter-become-a -millionaire-1.277601.

22 **wrote Azmi Bishara**: Azmi Bishara, "Ministry of Strategic Threats," *Al-Ahram Weekly*, November 1-7, 2006, Issue 818, http://weekly.ahram.org.eg/2006/818/op22.htm.

22 **faked her master's degree**: Gideon Alon, "Tartman Withdraws Candidacy for Tourism Ministry amid Scandal," *Ha'aretz*, February 28, 2007, http://www.haaretz.com/news/tartman-withdraws-candidacy-for-tourism-ministry-amid-scandal-1.214256.

22 **Disability payments**: Frimet Roth, "Disabilities Are Not Just Willed Away" *Ha'aretz*, March 7, 2007, http://www.haaretz.com/print-edition/opinion/disabilities-are-not-just-willed-away-1.214846. See also John O'Neil, "Esterina Tartman: A Controversial Minister," *L'Humanitie*, March 16, 2007, http://www.humaniteinenglish.com/spip.php?article523.

22 **Russian model crowned**: A mother of seven children who was the first pregnant woman to serve in the Knesset, Michaeli held forth during an interview on the role of good wives: "A man remains a man, at least in terms of his sexual needs, even in Judaism. A man can go to another city and can sleep with another woman and go back to his wife. A woman has no such privileges. A woman must be a mother and clean." She was not so permissive towards men who wished to sleep with other men, calling homosexuals "miserable" and claiming that, "in the end they commit suicide by 40," See Netty C. Gross, "Israel's Politician as Super Woman," *Jewish Daily Forward*, July 15, 2009, http://forward.com/articles/109592/israel-s-politician-as-super-woman/#ixzz1mR4nfJ6C"; Nathan Jeffay, "Anastasia Michaeli: Gay People Are Miserable," The Shmooze in *Jewish Daily Forward*, June 14, 2012, http://blogs.forward.com/the-shmooze/157800/anastasia-michaeli-gay-people-are-miserable.

23 **I am looking at this competition**: Netty C. Gross. "Israel's Politician as Super Woman" *Jewish Daily Forward*, July 15, 2009, http://forward.com/articles/109592/israel-s-politician-as-super-woman/#ixzz1mR4nfJ6C.

23 **You take steps against the country!**: translated by *Ha'aretz* as "You are marching against the state," Jonathan Lis and Talila Nesher, VIDEO / "Israeli Knesset Member Throws Cup of Water on Colleague at Height of Heated Argument," *Ha'aretz*, January 9, 2012, http://www.haaretz.com/news/national/video-israeli-knesset-member-throws-cup-of-water-on-colleague-at-height-of-heated-argument-1.406298.

23 **more than 300,000 of the new immigrants**: NPR, "On Multiple Fronts, Russian Jews Reshape Israel," January 2, 2013, http://www.npr.org/templates/transcript/transcript.php?storyId=168457444.

23 **A 2009 poll taken by**: "Poll: 77 Percent of Soviet Olim Support Transfer," *Ynetnews*, August 3, 2009, http://www.ynetnews.com/articles/0,7340,L-3756355,00.html000

24 **talk of trenches and enemies**: Liel Leibovitz, "Left for Dead," *Tablet*, July 26, 2011, http://www.tabletmag.com/jewish-news-and-politics/72834/left-for-dead.

24 **They began with graffiti**: "Israel's Nightmare: Homegrown Neo-Nazis in the Holy Land," *Independent*, October 9, 2007, http://www.independent.co.uk/news/world/middle-east/israels-nightmare-homegrown-neonazis-in-the-holy-land-396392.html.

25 **Haider is far from being**: Akiva Eldar, "Let's Hear It for the Haiders," *Ha'aretz*, October 30, 2006, http://www.haaretz.com/print-edition/opinion/let-s-hear-it-for-the-haiders-1.203725.

25 **a concern with 'the demographic issue**: Bishara, "Ministry of Strategic Threats."

26 **I took a deep breath**: Condoleezza Rice, *No Higher Honor: A Memoir of My Years in Washington* (New York: Random House, 2011), 282–283.

26 **You need to look forward**: Condoleezza Rice, "Meeting Minutes: US-Palestinian Bilateral Session," Al Jazeera Transparency Unit: The Palestine Papers, July 16, 2008, http://transparency.aljazeera.net/en/projects/thepalestinepapers/201218 2334190274.html.

26 **Far from enabling**: Ziyad Clot, "Why I Blew the Whistle About Palestine," *Guardian,* May 13, 2011, http://www.guardian.co.uk/commentisfree/2011/may/14/blew -the-whistle-about-palestine.

26 **We will be happy to hear:** "Yisrael Beiteinu: Livni Progam Sounds Like Ours," *Arutz Sheva*, January 25, 2011, http://www.israelnationalnews.com/News/Flash .aspx/202743#.UVRnc47Wd8g.

26 **Thanks to Al Jazeera**: "Kadima Rejects Israel Beiteinu's Meeting Invite Quip," *Jerusalem Post*, January 25, 2011, http://www.jpost.com/DiplomacyAndPolitics /Article.aspx?id=205147.

CHAPTER 8: THE SALESMAN

28 **self-hating Jews:** Leon T. Hadar, "Benjamin Netanyahu: The Joe Isuzu of the Middle East Media Wars," Washington Report on Middle East Affairs, July 1991, http://www.wrmea.org/wrmea-archives/132-washington-report-archives-1988 -1993/july-1991/1732-benjamin-netanyahu-the-joe-isuzu-of-the-middle-east -media-wars.html.

28 **a propagandist for the Israelis**: Ibid.

28 **Joe Isuzu of the Middle East Wars**: Ibid.

29 **It doesn't matter if justice**: Akiva Eldar, "Why Should Anyone Believe Netanyahu?" *Ha'aretz*, November 14, 2011, http://www.haaretz.com/print-edition /opinion/why-should-anyone-believe-netanyahu-1.395439.

29 **the trap into which it has**: Benjamin Netanyahu, *A Durable Peace: Israel and Its Place Among the Nations* (New York: Warner Books, 2000), 383.

29 **a display case in Netanyahu's office**: George Will, "Netanyahu, the Anti-Obama," *Washington Post*, August 12, 2010, http://www.washingtonpost.com/wp-dyn /content/article/2010/08/11/AR2010081104747_pf.html.

30 *Time* **magazine managing editor**: Noam Sheizaf, "Déjà Vu: Netanyahu on *Time* Cover – Will He Make Peace?" *972 Magazine*, May 18, 2012, http://972mag.com /deja-vu-netanyahu-on-time-cover-will-he-make-peace/46197.

30 **every opportunity to explain**: Barak Ravid, "Quality Time with King Bibi," *Ha'aretz*, May 17, 2012, http://www.haaretz.com/blogs/diplomania/quality-time -with-king-bibi.premium-1.431154.

30 **I know what America is**: "Netanyahu: 'America Is a Thing You Can Move Very Easily,'" *Washington Post*, July 16, 2010, http://voices.washingtonpost.com/check point-washington/2010/07/netanyahu_america_is_a_thing_y.html.

30 **one of Israel's "main enemies"**: Barak Ravid, "Netanyahu Denies Calling *Ha'aretz* and *New York Times* Israel's 'Main Enemies,'" *Ha'aretz*, January 19, 2012, http:// www.haaretz.com/news/national/netanyahu-denies-calling-haaretz-and-new -york-times-israel-s-main-enemies-1.408167.

31 **Oren was flustered**: Adam Horowitz, "*60 Minutes* Profiles Palestinian Christians, Michael Oren Falls on His Face," *Mondoweiss*, April 22, 2012, http://mondoweiss .net/2012/04/60-minutes-profiles-palestinian-christians-michael-oren-falls-on -his-face-defending-israel.html.

31   **the insatiable crocodile**: Benjamin Netanyahu, "Full Transcript of Netanyahu Speech at UN General Assembly," *Ha'aretz*, September 24, 2011, http://www .haaretz.com/news/diplomacy-defense/full-transcript-of-netanyahu-speech-at -un-general-assembly-1.386464.

31   **the Iranian "nuclear duck"**: Benjamin Netanyahu, "Full Text of Netanyahu Speech to AIPAC 2012," *Algemeiner*, March 5, 2012, http://www.algemeiner.com /2012/03/05/full-text-of-netanyahu-speech-to-aipac-2012.

32   **mass expulsions among**: Yaakov Lazar, "On the One Hand and on the Other," Hotam supplement, *Al Hamishmar*, November 28, 1989, http://cosmos.ucc.ie /cs1064/jabowen/IPSC/articles/article00134874.html.

33   **the relentless Jewish desire**: Netanyahu, *A Durable Peace,* 370.

33   **an ongoing national exertion**: Ibid.

CHAPTER 9: NUMBER 1

37   **account by Rabin:** David Shipler, "Israel Bars Rabin from Relating '48 Eviction of Arabs; Sympathy for Palestinians 'I Can't Violate the Law' Survivors' Reports Confirmed," New York Times, October 23, 1979.

37   **forced to dig a grave**: Amos Kenan, "The Legacy of Lydda: Four Decades of Blood Vengeance," *Nation*, 154–156, February 6, 1989, http://cosmos.ucc.ie/cs1064 /jabowen/IPSC/articles/article0059831.html. A celebrated Hebrew artist, anti-establishment columnist, and bon vivant, Amos Kenan was not only present during the ethnic cleansing of Lydda, but also participated in the massacre at Deir Yassin. Though he claimed that he never took part in the Deir Yassin killings, Kenan later confessed to his wife, the film scholar Nurit Gertz, that he murdered an innocent woman. Kenan spent the 1950s in Paris cultivating bohemian affectations while on assignment for Uri Avnery's newspaper, *Haolam Hazeh*. His girlfriend, the wealthy Parisian socialite Christiane Roquefort, wrote her first book about her notoriously churlish but compelling Israeli beau. It was later adapted into a feature film in which Roquefort was played by Brigitte Bardot. In 1967, Kenan served as regiment commander of the division that ethnically cleansed three Palestinian villages in the Latrun Valley—Beit Nuba, Yalu, and Imwas. "They said every place they went they were turned away, and they are not allowed to enter anywhere," he wrote of those he expelled in a letter to Israeli prime minister Levi Eshkol that was later leaked to the public. "That they had been walking for four days, without food, without water, and that a few of them had died. They asked to return to the village and said it would be better if we killed them."

37   **Riding into Lydda**: Michael Palumbo, *The Palestinian Catastrophe: The 1948 Expulsion of a People from Their Homeland* (London: Quartet Books, 1989), 126–138. See also Ilan Pappe, *The Ethnic Cleansing of Palestine* (Oxford: Oneworld Publications, 2006) 168.

37   **reporter from the *New York Herald Tribune***: Ibid. See also Pappe, *The Ethnic Cleansing of Palestine,* 168.

37   **Operation Dani**: Pappe, *The Ethnic Cleansing of Palestine*, 166–170.

37   **About twenty to fifty more**: Arieh Vitzhaqi, originally in *Yediot Aharonot,* April 14, 1972, translated in "From the Hebrew Press," *Journal of Palestine Studies*, vol. 1, no. 4 (Summer 1972), 145. See also Sami Hadawi, *Bitter Harvest* (New York: Olive Branch Press, 1989 & 1991), 88. According to Hadawi, citing official Palmach claims, "250 Arabs were killed."

38   **took further liberties**: Kenan, "The Legacy of Lydda." In his article, addressed to George Habash, Kenan continued, "Once, only once, did an Arab

woman—perhaps a distant relative of George Habash—dare complain [about being raped]. There was a court-martial. The complainant didn't even get to testify. The accused, who was sitting behind the judges, ran the back of his hand across his throat, as a signal to the woman. She understood. The rapist was not acquitted, he simply was not accused, because there was no one who would dare accuse him. Two years later, he was killed while plowing the fields of an Arab village, one no longer on the map because its inhabitants scattered and left it empty."

38   **As Rabin later recalled**: Shipler, "Israel Bars Rabin." See also Simha Falpan, *The Birth of Israel: Myths and Realities* (NY: Pantheon Books, 1987), 101.

39   **who has not experienced**: "Suspected Citizens: Racial Profiling against Arab Passengers by Israeli Airports and Airlines," *Electronic Intifada*, January 12, 2007, http://electronicintifada.net/content/suspected-citizens-racial-profiling-against -arab-passengers-israeli-airports-and-airlines.

39   **allowing Mossad officers**: Lionel Slier, "S. African Alleges El Al a Mossad Front," *Jerusalem Post*, October 22, 2009, http://www.jpost.com/International/S-African -alleges-El-Al-a-Mossad-front.

39   **EL AL was forced to pay**: "Israeli Arab Brothers Win Payout for El Al 'Abuse' in New York," *National*, April 20, 2010, http://www.thenational.ae/news/world/middle -east/israeli-arab-brothers-win-payout-for-el-al-abuse-in-new-york#full.

39   **I felt like they were**: Jack Khoury, "Israeli Arab Journalist Switches Airline after 'Humiliating' El Al Security Check," *Ha'aretz*, February 16, 2012, http://www .haaretz.com/print-edition/news/israeli-arab-journalist-switches-airline-after -humiliating-el-al-security-check-1.413176.

39   **banned from flying to Egypt**: "Olmert Promises to Investigate Incident Involving *Ynet* Reporter," *Arutz Sheva*, June 9, 2004, http://www.israelnationalnews.com /News/Flash.aspx/63804#.UTd-f9EjrxY.

40   **Shalala was born to Lebanese**: Itamar Eichner, "American VIP Humiliated at Airport," *Ynetnews*, August 6, 2010, http://www.ynetnews.com/articles/0,7340,L -3931210,00.html.

41   **Ethnic Minorities Form**: Dimi Reider, "A Special Form for Arab Passengers to Warn Airport of Their Arrival," *972 Magazine*, July 9, 2011, http://972mag.com /airport3/18301.

41   **a clear and stark example**: Ibid.

41   **an authentic expression**: Larry Derfner, "Mobocracy at Ben-Gurion Airport," *972 Magazine*, July 8, 2011, http://972mag.com/derfner-2017-872011/18252.

41   **We must prevent the disruption**: "Police Deployed at B-G Airport Anticipating Gaza Activists," *Jerusalem Post*, July 6, 2011, http://www.jpost.com/Defense/Article .aspx?id=228162.

42   **I'm sorry but we had**: Lily Sussman, "I'm Sorry But We Blew Up Your Laptop (Welcome to Israel)," Lilysussman's Blog, November 30, 2009, http://lilysussman .wordpress.com/2009/11/30/im-sorry-but-we-blew-up-your-laptop-welcome-to -israel.

CHAPTER 10: SETTLING IN THE HEARTS

43   **the road was named for**: "Al-Dajani Private Hospital which had 50 beds & served 2,221 patients in 1944, was built in 1933 by Dr. Fouad Ismail Bakr Dajani," PalestineRemembered.com, uploaded on September 3, 2000, http://www.palestine remembered.com/Jaffa/Jaffa/Picture1225.html. See also Raja Shehadeh, "A Roundabout Named Dajani," New York Times, February 29, 2012, http://www

.nytimes.com/2012/03/01/opinion/a-roundabout-named-dajani.html?_
r=2&ref=global-home&.

43 **We lived among the Arabs**: *Jaffa: The Orange's Clockwork*, directed by Eyal Sivan, (2010, Trabelsi Productions).

44 **We were considered**: Ibid.

44 **I wasn't happy about it**: David Hacohen, "Speech to the Secretariat of the Mapai," Palestine: Information with Provenance (PIWP database), November 1969, http://cosmos.ucc.ie/cs1064/jabowen/IPSC/php/quotation.php?qid=2197.

44 **The destruction of Jaffa**: Tom Segev, *One Palestine, Complete: Jews and Arabs Under the British Mandate*, (Macmillan, 2001), 383.

44 **5,000 troops**: Ilan Pappe, *The Ethnic Cleansing of Palestine* (Oxford: Oneworld Publications, 2006), 102.

45 **weep like a helpless child**: Ghassan Kanafani, "Jaffa: Land of Oranges," *Al-Ahram Weekly*, http://weekly.ahram.org.eg/1998/1948/kanafani.htm.

45 **Absentee Property Law**: Israeli Knesset, March 14, 1950, full text: http://unispal.un.org/UNISPAL.NSF/0/E0B719E95E3B494885256F9A005AB90A

45 **Land Acquisition Law**: Israeli Knesset, 1953, full text: http://www.israellawresourcecenter.org/israellaws/fulltext/landacquisitionlaw.htm.

45 **wholesale robbery**: Sami Hadawi. *Bitter Harvest: A Modern History of Palestine*, (Interlink Books, 1991), 153.

45 **They are Arabs and you are a Jew**: Sami Hadawi, "Israel and the Arab Minority," 1959, http://archive.org/details/IsraelAndTheArabMinority.

45 **We had to create a Jewish state**: Ben White, "Happy Palestine Land Day: Israel Earmarks 10% of West Bank for Settlement," Informed Comment, March 30, 2012, http://www.juancole.com/2012/03/happy-palestine-land-day-israel-earmarks-10-of-west-bank-for-settlements-white.html.

45 **two hundred thousand dunams**: *Jaffa: The Orange's Clockwork*.

45 **expropriated orange groves**: Ibid.

45 **we didn't even know what a ghetto was**: Interview with Sami Shehadeh, Jaffa, Israel, July 14, 2010.

46 **fragile Jewish demographic majority**: To implement the emergency laws, the Israeli government simply repackaged the Defense Regulations of 1945 that the British had imposed on the residents of Mandate Palestine, both Jewish and Arab. Zionist founding father Chaim Weizmann had harshly denounced the British emergency laws, proclaiming, "Martial law is a sort of automatic machine which gradually and relentlessly strangles life out of a community….Military law will not only not produce security, but will have the opposite effect." Yaakov Shimson Shapira, who later became Israel's Minister of Justice, called the British laws worse than those that existed in countries occupied by Nazi Germany. But now that the tables had turned, martial law was a cornerstone of Israeli policy, allowing the state to banish legal Arab residents, confiscate their property, erect barbed wire fences around Arab neighborhoods to restrict their residents' movement, and wipe entire villages off the map.

46 **Prevention of Infiltration Law**: Israeli Knesset, August 16, 1954; full text: http://www.israellawresourcecenter.org/emergencyregs/fulltext/preventioninfiltrationlaw.htm.

46 **we must do nothing to foreclose**: Benny Morris, *Israel's Border Wars, 1949-1956: Arab Infiltration, Israeli Retaliation, and the Countdown to the Suez War* (Clarendon Press, 1997).

46 **destroyed three thousand**: Interview with Sami Shehadeh, July 14, 2010.

46 **497 Jaffan houses**: Shehadeh and Shbayatah, "Jaffa: From Eminence."

47 **the "new hedonist representative"**: Ronnie Tzach, "Israeli Architectural Diva Introduces Designer Homes to the Masses," *Ynetnews*, December 12, 2004, http://www.ynetnews.com/articles/1,7340,L-3017249,00.html.

47 **Outside everything is abnormal**: Simon Trainor, "Israeli S&M Turns Three," *Ha'aretz*, November 23, 2005, http://www.haaretz.com/news/israeli-s-m-turns-three-1.174860.

47 **We don't need to be more liberal**: Larry Derfner, "Bibi Backs Law to Ban Loudspeakers at Mosques (!!!)," *972 Magazine*, December 12, 2011, http://972mag.com/bibi-wants-to-outlaw-loudspeakers-at-mosques/29605.

48 **a 15 percent discount**: Yoav Zitun, "Arabs: Jaffa Housing Benefits for Reservists 'Discriminatory,'" *Ynetnews*, October 26, 2010, http://www.ynetnews.com/articles/0,7340,L-3975377,00.html.

48 **I cannot represent a country**: "Ajami Director: I Don't Represent Israel," *Jerusalem Post*, March 7, 2010, http://www.jpost.com/ArtsAndCulture/Entertainment/Article.aspx?id=170393.

49 **This is a completely minor foreignness**: "Aesthetic Dispossession in Jaffa," *Alternative News*, July 22, 2009, http://www.alternativenews.org/english/index.php/component/content/article/28-news/2020-aesthetic-dispossession-in-jaffa-.

49 **a different reality than we**: Baruch Gordon, "New Yeshiva to Strengthen Jewish Presence in Yafo," *Arutz Sheva*, February 12, 2008, http://www.israelnationalnews.com/News/News.aspx/125230#.UTe4tNEjrxY.

49 **This is our land**: Mya Guarnieri, "Settlers Target 'Shared Cities,'" *Al Jazeera*, June 21, 2010, http://www.aljazeera.com/focus/2010/06/201062193950686530.html.

50 **Death to Arabs**: "Dozens of Jewish Settlers Attack Mosque in Jaffa," *Middle East Monitor*, January 17, 2011, http://www.middleeastmonitor.com/news/middle-east/1958-dozens-of-jewish-settlers-attack-mosque-in-jaffa.

50 **to go to Jaffa in order**: Max Blumenthal, "Why the Israeli Elections Were a Victory for the Right," *Nation*, January 23, 2013, http://www.thenation.com/article/172398/why-israeli-elections-were-victory-right#.

51 **I expect the hands of those who**: Robert Mackey, "Angered by Shalit Deal, Israeli Defaces Rabin Memorial," The Lede, *New York Times*, October 14, 2011, http://thelede.blogs.nytimes.com/2011/10/14/angered-by-shalit-deal-israeli-defaced-rabin-memorial.

52 **Tel Aviv had far fewer**: Central Bureau of Statistics, Prime Minister's Office, *The Arab Population in Israel*, Statistitlite No. 27, 3.

52 **The city has an overwhelming**: Gilad Morag, "Tel Aviv Council Rejects Arabic Caption in City Logo," *Ynetnews*, August 7, 2012, http://www.ynetnews.com/articles/0,7340,L-4265546,00.html.

52 **the ruins of Manshiyya**: The Israeli NGO Zochrot has produced a wealth of resources on Manshiyya, including a 2010 film featuring testimony from Saleh Masri and Iftikhar Turk, two internally displaced former residents of the destroyed Palestinian neighborhood: http://www.youtube.com/watch?v=KGUjQE68_vI.

CHAPTER 11: BANNING BOOKS

53 **a frenzy of fear**: Walid Khalidi, "Plan Dalet: Master Plan for the Conquest of Palestine," Journal of Palestine Studies, Vol. 18, No. 1, Special Issue: Palestine 1948, (Autumn 1988), 4–33.

53 **Excalibur of ethnic cleansing**: The Commission of Experts established in 1992 pursuant to the United Nations Security Council Resolution 780 expressed "grave

alarm" at the international law violations in the former Yugoslavian territory, including acts of "ethnic cleansing." In its May 27, 1994 report, the Commission of Experts defined ethnic cleansing as "the planned deliberate removal from a specific territory, persons of a particular ethnic group, by force or intimidation, in order to render that area ethnically homogenous." References to ethnic cleansing in this book rely on the 1994 UN definition.

53 **Each year, on Independence Day**: Max Blumenthal, "In a Fear Society, Where Some Facts Are Crimes," MaxBlumenthal.com, April 26, 2012, http://maxblumenthal .com/2012/04/in-a-fear-society-where-some-facts-are-crimes.

55 **The Arab public deserves**: Isabel Kershner, "Israeli Textbook to Add Mention of Arab 'Catastrophe,'" *New York Times*, July 22, 2007, http://www.nytimes.com/2007 /07/22/world/africa/22iht-mideast.4.6770284.html.

55 **their villages were destroyed**: Mati Wagner, "'Nakba' Debate Shows Israel's Divisions," *JTA*, July 31, 2007, http://www.jta.org/news/article/2007/07/31/103346 /nakbabook.

55 **I can't remember a greater**: Ibid.

55 **we would not tolerate a Palestinian**: Ibid.

55 **Nakba day of the Israeli education system**: Ibid.

55 **the establishment of the state**: "Israeli Textbooks to Drop 'Nakba,'" *BBC News*, July 22, 2009, http://news.bbc.co.uk/2/hi/8163959.stm.

CHAPTER 12: THE FORTRESS OF DEMOCRACY

56 **to steal and torch**: Benny Morris, The Birth of the Palestinian Refugee Problem Revisited (Cambridge University Press, 2004), 122.

56 **A Jewish home in Palestine**: Laurence Zuckerman, "A Pacifist Leader Who Was More Prophet Than Politician," *Jewish Daily Forward*, January 5, 2011, http:// forward.com/articles/134451/a-pacifist-leader-who-was-more-prophet-than -politi/#ixzz1r8e9FglV.

56 **Friends, stop the bloodshed**: Ofri Ilani, "1948 Diaries: Saving the Jews from Themselves," *Ha'aretz*, May 5, 2008, http://www.haaretz.com/print-edition/news /1948-diaries-saving-the-jews-from-themselves-1.245287.

57 **such a huge and acute**: Judah Leon Magnes, *Dissenter in Zion* (Harvard University Press, 1982), 520.

57 **national unity will increase**: "This Week in Ha'aretz 1966 / The Knesset Is Inaugurated in Jerusalem," *Ha'aretz*, September 2, 2010, http://www.haaretz.com/print -edition/features/this-week-in-haaretz-1966-the-knesset-is-inaugurated-in -jerusalem-1.311642.

57 **in revenge for the Holocaust**: Tom Segev, *The Seventh Million: The Israelis and the Holocaust* (Macmillan, 2000), 140.

58 **denounce our very existence**: "MK Miller Calls for Ban of 'Nakba' Events," *Ynetnews*, May 15, 2008, http://www.ynetnews.com/articles/0,7340,L-3543979,00 .html.

60 **Friedrich Ebert Foundation poll**: Or Kashti, "Poll: Young Israelis Moving Much Farther to the Right Politically," *Ha'aretz*, March 31, 2011, http://www.haaretz.com /print-edition/news/poll-young-israelis-moving-much-farther-to-the-right -politically-1.353187.

60 **only Israel's Arab citizens**: Benjamin Netanyahu, "Speech by PM Netanyahu to a Joint Meeting of the U.S. Congress," Israel Ministry of Foreign Affairs, May 24, 2011, http://www.mfa.gov.il/MFA/Government/Speeches+by+Israeli+leaders /2011/Speech_PM_Netanyahu_US_Congress_24-May-2011.htm.

61 **all rights over the Land**: Jonathan Cook, "Israeli Palestinians: The Unwanted Who Stayed," October 30, 2008, http://www.jonathan-cook.net/2008-10-30/israeli -palestinians-the-unwanted-who-stayed.

61 **refused entry to a club**: Nir Yahav, "Arab Youth Expelled from Club for Carrying Tibi Image," Walla [Hebrew], July 30, 2012, http://news.walla.co.il/?w=/90 /2554247.

61 **disconnect the radical trends**: Roni Shaked, "Israel's Arabs: The Enemy from Within?" *Ynetnews*, April 21, 2011, http://www.ynetnews.com/articles/0,7340,L -4059570,00.html.

61 **I'll be delighted**: Ben Hartman, "The 'Radical Agenda' of Israel's Arab Elite," *Jerusalem Post*, April 25, 2011, http://www.jpost.com/Features/InThespotlight/Article .aspx?id=222228.

62 **You will die soon**: "MK Ahmad Tibi Receives Death Threats on Facebook," *Ma'an News Agency*, January 15, 2012, http://www.maannews.net/eng/ViewDetails.aspx ?ID=452569.

63 **Livni cannot say that her**: Editorial, "Kadima and McCarthyism," *Ha'aretz*, May 4, 2010, http://www.haaretz.com/print-edition/opinion/kadima-and-mccarthyism-1 .288242.

CHAPTER 13: CUT OFF FROM THE TRIBE

65 **unironic admiration:** David Sheen, "Will Israel Turn Into the Fascist State of Judea by 2022?" Ha'aretz, July 23, 2010, http://www.haaretz.com/culture/will -israel-turn-into-the-fascist-state-of-judea-by-2022-1.303585.

65 **overwhelming the country's**: Liel Kyzer, and Oran Koren, "Netanyahu: Migrant Workers Risk Israel's Jewish Character," *Ha'aretz*, January 21, 2010, http://www .haaretz.com/news/netanyahu-migrant-workers-risk-israel-s-jewish-character-1 .261840.

65 **neo-Nazi expressions in the Knesset**: Richard Silverstein, "Amnon Dankner: 'I'm Ashamed of Being Israeli,'" *Tikun Olam*, January 11, 2011, http://www.richardsil-verstein.com/2011/01/11/amnon-dankner-im-ashamed-of-being-israeli.

65 **engulfed the Zionist project**: David Landau, "Boycott the Knesset," *Ha'aretz*, July 16, 2010, http://www.haaretz.com/print-edition/opinion/boycott-the-knesset-1 .302259.

65 **threatened by fascism**: Uri Avnery, "Weimar in Jerusalem," *Gush Shalom*, October 23, 2010, http://zope.gush-shalom.org/home/en/channels/avnery/1287833121.

67 **the army had killed at least 202**: "UN: 202 Palestinians Killed Since 'Operation Summer Rain,'" *Ha'aretz*, August 27, 2006, http://www.haaretz.com/news/un-202 -palestinians-killed-since-operation-summer-rain-1.195904.

67 **800,000 Lebanese citizens**: "Report of the Commission of Inquiry on Lebanon pursuant to Human Rights Council Resolution S-2/1," Human Rights Council: Third Session, November 23, 2006, 3, http://www2.ohchr.org/english/bodies/hrcouncil /docs/specialsession/A.HRC.3.2.pdf.

67 **killing more than 1,100**: Ibid.

67 **There is no longer any need**: Yaron London, "The Dahiya Strategy," *Ynetnews*, October 6, 2008, http://www.ynetnews.com/articles/0,7340,L-3605863,00.html.

CHAPTER 14: THE ROBBED COSSACK

69 **establishment of the state:** Idith Zertal and Akiva Eldar, Lords of the Land: The War Over Israel's Settlements in the Occupied Territories, 1967-2007 (Nation Books, 2007), 53.

70 **pastrami sandwich**: Foundation for Middle East Peace, "Sharon's New Map," Settlement Report, Vol. 12, No. 3, May–June 2002, http://www.fmep.org/reports /archive/vol.-12/no.-3/sharons-new-map.

70 **There is no meaning**: Zertal and Eldar, *Lords of the Land,* 172.

70 **I am closer to these people**: Ibid.

70 **Arab members of Knesset**: "MK David Rotem: 'Arab MKs Represent Terror Organization,'" *Jerusalem Post*, June 2, 2010, http://www.jpost.com/Headlines /Article.aspx?id=177268.

70 **cause damage to the State of Israel**: "MK Rotem: Leftist groups lie, tattle," July 20, 2011, http://www.ynetnews.com/articles/0,7340,L-4098107,00.html.

72 **revoked the citizenship of anyone**: "Israel Begins Revoking Arabs' Citizenship," *Ynetnews,* May 5, 2009, http://www.ynetnews.com/articles/0,7340,L-3711185,00 .html. See also Jonathan Lis, "Knesset Passes Law to Strip Terrorists of Israeli Citizenship," *Ha'aretz*, March 28, 2011, http://www.haaretz.com/news/national /knesset-passes-law-to-strip-terrorists-of-israeli-citizenship-1.352412.

72 **a potential Fifth Column**: Ari Shavit, "Survival of the Fittest," *Ha'aretz*, January 8, 2004.

73 **Such a law does not exist**: "The Citizenship Law, Adalah," YouTube, March 12, 2009, http://youtu.be/BmC_11HK6Ho.

73 **The government must be**: "Demographic Self-Defense," *Jerusalem Post*, April 5, 2005, http://www.israeldemography.com/Jerusalem%20Post%20demographic %20self-defense.htm.

73 **'talked security'**: Yoram Rabin, "Talking Security, Thinking Demographics," *Ha'aretz*, January 15, 2012, http://www.haaretz.com/print-edition/opinion/talking -security-thinking-demographics-1.407368.

73 **I want a decisive Jewish majority**: Tikva Honig-Parnass, *False Prophets of Peace: Liberal Zionism and the Struggle for Palestine* (Chicago: Haymarket Books, 2011), 43.

74 **If this country is not**: Daniel Treiman, "Former Jewish Agency Chief Avraham Burg Rejects Idea of a 'Jewish State,'" Bintel Blog, *Jewish Daily Forward*, June 7, 2007, http://blogs.forward.com/bintel-blog/tags/yossi-beilin.

74 **You're not even an animal**: Lahav Harkov, "Rivlin Orders Probe of Legislation of 'Sohlberg Law,'" *Jerusalem Post*, November 16, 2011, http://www.jpost.com/ DiplomacyAndPolitics/Article.aspx?id=245776.

74 **He is their favorite son**: Dalia Karpel and Tomer Zarchin, "The Quiet Man Who's Making a Storm in Israel's Supreme Court Scene: Justice Asher Grunis," *Ha'aretz*, December 17, 2011, http://www.haaretz.com/weekend/magazine/the-quiet-man -who-s-making-a-storm-in-israel-s-supreme-court-scene-justice-asher-grunis-1 .401911.

75 **even if it's a three-year-old**: Chris McGreal, "Not Guilty. The Israeli Captain Who Emptied His Rifle into a Palestinian Schoolgirl," *Guardian*, November 15, 2005, http://www.guardian.co.uk/world/2005/nov/16/israel2.

75 **like the robbed Cossack**: Tomer Zarchin, "Beinisch Blasts Ministers, MKs for 'Poisonous' Campaign against Judiciary," *Ha'aretz*, December 2, 2011, http://www .haaretz.com/print-edition/news/beinisch-blasts-ministers-mks-for-poisonous -campaign-against-judiciary-1.399060.

75 **defend the judges with her own body**: Ibid.

77 **every Jewish town needs**: Jonathan Lis and Jack Khoury, "Knesset Panel Approves Controversial Bill Allowing Towns to Reject Residents," *Ha'aretz*, October 27,

2010, http://www.haaretz.com/news/national/knesset-panel-approves-controversial
-bill-allowing-towns-to-reject-residents-1.321433.

CHAPTER 15: JUDAIZATION

78 **Jewish settlement inside:** Though the Jewish National Fund (JNF) technically controls 13 percent of Israeli state land, it is legally mandated to control over half of the seats on the board of the Israeli Land Authority (ILA), which controls the rest of the land. Thus, according to the JNF's stated policy of leasing land exclusively to members of "the Jewish people," ILA land is transferred to Jews only. As Professor Amnon Rubinstein wrote in Ha'aretz on October 13, 1991, "These transfers present a grave problem, because lands that were intended for use by all Israeli citizens were handed over to an agency that sells and leases land only to Jews," Nur Masalha, Catastrophe Remembered: Palestine, Israel and the Internal Refugees (London: Zed Books, 2005), 35.

79 **"Here We Shall Stay":** Tawfiq Zayyad, "Here We Shall Stay," in *Anthology of Modern Palestinian Literature*, ed. Salma Khadra Jayyusi (Columbia University Press, 1992), 327–328.

80 **whose imagination tends:** Israel Koenig, "The Koenig Report," SWASIA, Vol. III, No. 41 (October 15, 1976), 1–8, http://issuu.com/joeexample1/docs/koenig
_report?mode=embed&documentId=080506204439-216255f2c4b346bc921ee
88643ce527b&layout=grey.

80 **Special teams should:** Ibid.

80 **this policy is apt to:** Ibid.

80 **preferential treatment:** Ibid.

81 **two young villagers:** Hatim Kanaaneh, "Memories of the First Land Day," *Mondoweiss*, March 31, 2011, http://mondoweiss.net/2011/03/memories-of-the-first
-land-day.html.

81 **Your children will never:** Yossi Klein, "The Other Israelis," *Ha'aretz*, July 3, 2002, http://www.haaretz.com/the-other-israelis-1.40685.

81 **Seven Stars plan:** David Kretzmer, *The Occupation of Justice* (Albany, NY: SUNY Press, 2002), 76.

81 **Misgav's real reasoning:** Jonathan Cook, "Apartheid Targets Palestinian Home-Owners inside Israel," *Electronic Intifada*, March 10, 2005, http://electronic intifada.net/content/apartheid-targets-palestinian-home-owners-inside-israel
/5505.

82 **best advanced the values:** Sheryl Gay Stolberg, "Praise for an Israeli Judge Drives Criticism of Kagan," *New York Times*, June 24, 2010, http://www.nytimes.com
/2010/06/25/us/politics/25kagan.html?_r=0.

82 **the problem which arises:** Tikva Honig-Parnass, *False Prophets of Peace: Liberal Zionism and the Struggle for Palestine* (Chicago: Haymarket Books, 2011), 61.

83 **the very essence of:** Joel Golovensky and Ariel Gilboa. "Is This Land Still Our Land?" p. 23, http://izsvideo.org/papers/kkleng.pdf.

83 **separate communities for Jews:** Ruth Gavison, "The Jews' Right to Statehood: A Defense," *AzureOnline*. Summer 5763 / 2003, No. 15, http://azure.org.il/article
.php?id=239&page=all.

83 **The demographic clock:** Arnon Soffer and Evgenia Bystrov, "Israel: Demography and Density: 2007-2010," 15, http://web.hevra.haifa.ac.il/~ch-strategy/images
/publications/demography_2007_en.pdf.

84 **doomsday scenario:** Ibid., 17.

84 **part of the implementation:** Ibid.,14.

84 **an isolated island:** Ibid., 5.

84 **We don't see this as racism:** Jonathan Cook, "Israeli Towns Adopt 'Loyalty Oaths' to Bar Arab Residents," *Electronic Intifada*, June 8, 2009, http://electronicintifada .net/content/israeli-towns-adopt-loyalty-oaths-bar-arab-residents/8280.

CHAPTER 16: HOMOGENEITY

85 **dependent on the social make-up:** David Sheen, "Can't We All Just Get Along— Separately?" Ha'aretz, February 24, 2011, http://www.haaretz.com/news/national/ can-t-we-all-just-get-along-separately-1.345450.

85 **the Zionist dream:** Jonathan Lis, "Knesset to Water Down Bill Barring Arabs from Jewish Towns," *Ha'aretz*, December 21, 2010, http://www.haaretz.com/news/ national/knesset-to-water-down-bill-barring-arabs-from-jewish-towns-1 .331707.

85 **This is not about homogeneity:** Interview with Israel Hasson, August 4, 2010.

CHAPTER 17: AT THE HEAVY GATES OF GAZA

89 **My heart is singing:** Avihai Bekker, "I Came to Ask Forgiveness, Ha'aretz [Hebrew], April 23, 2004.

89 **The Jews want them:** Benny Morris, *Israel's Border Wars, 1949-1956* (Clarendon Press, 1997), 160–161.

90 **Who are we that we:** Mordechai Bar On, *Moshe Dayan: Israel's Controversial Hero* (Yale University Press, 2012), 75–76.

90 **have we forgotten this?:** Ibid.

90 **In order that the hope:** Ibid.

91 **275 unarmed civilians:** "Special Report of the Director of the United Nations Relief and Works Agency for Palestine Refugees in the Near East: Covering the Period 1 November 1956 to Mid-December 1956," http://domino.un.org/unispal .nsf/0/6558f61d3db6bd4505256593006b06be?OpenDocument.

91 **the army massacred 111 more:** Ibid.

91 **They planted hatred:** Patrick Cockburn, "'They Planted Hatred in Our Hearts,'" *New York Times*, December 24, 2009, http://www.nytimes.com/2009/12/27/books /review/Cockburn-t.html.

91 **Unilateral separation doesn't:** Ruthie Blum, "It's the Demography, Stupid," *Jerusalem Post*, May 21, 2004; reprinted in Rabbi Brant Rosen, "Israel and Gaza: One Geographer's Prediction," Shalom Rav blog, January 6, 2009, http://rabbibrant.com /2009/01/06/israel-and-gaza-one-geographers-prediction.

91 **If we don't kill, we will cease to exist:** Ibid.

CHAPTER 18: BEETHOVEN FOR GAZA

92 **bombarded picnicking families:** Chris McGreal, "Who Really Killed Huda Ghalia's Family?" Guardian, June 16, 2006, http://www.guardian.co.uk/world/2006/ jun/16/israel.

93 **Salam Ruzian:** "Concert for Gilad Shalit in Front of Gaza," NTD Television, July 7, 2010, http://ntdtv.org/en/news/world/middle-east-africa/2010-07-08/299546987 637.html.

CHAPTER 19: THE ZIONIST

95 **runway was cut to pieces:** Alan Johnston, "Years of Delays at Gaza Airport," BBC News, April 15, 2005, http://news.bbc.co.uk/2/hi/middle_east/4449461.stm.

95 **Palestinian scavengers**: Nicole Johnston, "Gaza Airport Destroyed by Scavengers," *Al Jazeera English*, August 15, 2010, http://www.youtube.com/watch?v=g5 a3x3l93t8.

96 **it's a kill zone**: Mercedes Melon, "Shifting Paradigm—Israel's Enforcement of the Buffer Zone in the Gaza Strip," Al Haq Organization, June 2011, http://www.alhaq .org/publications/publications-index/item/shifting-paradigms-israel-s-enforcement -of-the-buffer-zone-in-the-gaza-strip.

96 **determines the borders**: Yanir Yagna, "Kibbutz Kerem Shalom Looking for a Few Good Zionists Willing to Settle Right Next to the Gaza Strip," *Ha'aretz*, May 31, 2011, http://www.haaretz.com/print-edition/news/kibbutz-kerem-shalom-looking -for-a-few-good-zionists-willing-to-settle-right-next-to-the-gaza-strip-1.365049.

97 **Only when a tragic incident**: Gil Sedan, "Bedouin 'Pathfinders,' Arabs Find Little to Like in IDF," *JWeekly*, January 18, 2002, http://www.jweekly.com/article/full /17092/bedouin-pathfinders-arabs-find-little-to-like-in-idf.

98 **talking peace but**: Kevin Flower, "Protestors Rally to End Economic Blockade of Gaza," CNN, December 31, 2009, http://edition.cnn.com/2009/WORLD/meast /12/31/gaza.march.

CHAPTER 20: DARK FORCES

101 **May 26, 2010, began:** "Israel Mounts Air Strike on Gaza Tunnels Overnight," News Agencies, May 26, 2010, http://www.haaretz.com/news/diplomacy-defense/ israel-mounts-air-strike-on-gaza-tunnels-overnight-1.292305.

101 **We have been told the beef stroganoff:** Lisa Goldman, "Move to Gaza, Where the Living Is Easy," LisaGoldman.net, May 26, 2010, http://lisagoldman.net/2010/05 /26/move-to-gaza-where-the-living-is-easy.

102 **We are afraid that there will be**: Max Blumenthal, "The Flotilla Raid Was Not 'Bungled.' The IDF Detailed Its Violent Strategy in Advance," MaxBlumenthal. com, June 3, 2010, http://maxblumenthal.com/2010/06/the-flotilla-raid-was-not -bungled-the-idf-detailed-its-violent-strategy-in-advance.

102 **members of the German Bundestag**: John Goetz, "Aftermath of the Israel Flotilla Raid: German Activists File War Crimes Complaints," *Der Spiegel*, June 11, 2010, http://www.spiegel.de/international/world/aftermath-of-the-israel-flotilla-raid -german-activists-file-war-crimes-complaints-a-700127.html. See also Chaim Levinson, "Israel Denies Entry for Swedish MP and Ex-Israel Who Sailed on Gaza Flotilla," *Ha'aretz*, November 7, 2010, http://www.haaretz.com/news/diplomacy -defense/israel-denies-entry-to-sweden-mp-and-ex-israeli-who-sailed-on-gaza -flotilla-1.323419.

103 **immediately killing two men**: Report of the Secretary-General's Panel of Inquiry, on the May 31, 2010, Flotilla Incident, September 2011, http://www.un.org/News /dh/infocus/middle_east/Gaza_Flotilla_Panel_Report.pdf.

104 **I have never seen anything**: Furkan Dogan, Official Website, http://www.sehit furkandogan.com/gunluk.html. Many translations of Dogan's final diary entry are available; the most accurate version appears to be a translation that appears on the above website. The Israeli government–linked Meir Amit Intelligence and Terrorism Information Center claimed Dogan "wrote a diary entry attesting to his desire to become a shaheed [martyr]," http://www.terrorism-info.org.il/en/article /18068. However, Dogan's father countered to *Ha'aretz*, "As far as I know, his last entry was written that night, when it was feared that something bad was about to happen. Under normal circumstances, he never would have written anything like that. If my son had planned to become a martyr, he would not have gone out of

his way to ask me to submit his university application forms in the event that he got held up in Gaza. He had big plans, he was very ambitious. You think he all of a sudden forgot about all of his plans for the future and decided to die?" http:// mondoweiss.net/2013/02/documents-execution-american.html.

104   **It was a bloodbath**: Sumeyye Ertekin, "First, They Appeared as Shadows" in *Midnight on the Mavi Marmara*, ed. Moustafa Bayoumi (O/R Books, 2010), 55.

104   **gunshot wounds to the head**: Robert Booth, "Gaza Flotilla Activists Were Shot in Head at Close Range, *Guardian*, June 4, 2010, http://www.guardian.co.uk/world /2010/jun/04/gaza-flotilla-activists-autopsy-results.

104   **Blood was pouring**: Lubna Masarwa, "From '48 to Gaza" in *Midnight on the Mavi Marmara*, 42.

104   **We have surrendered**: Jamal Elshayyal, "Kidnapped by Israel, Forsaken by Britain" in *Midnight on the Mavi Marmara*, 49.

105   **being punished**: Henning Mankell, "Flotilla Raid Diary: 'A Man Is Shot. I Am Seeing It Happen'" in *Midnight on the Mavi Marmara*, 24.

105   **gathered up all of the knives**: Israel Defense Forces, Pictures of Weapons Found on the *Mavi Marmara* Flotilla Ship, IDFBlog, May 31, 2010, http://www.idfblog .com/2010/05/31/pictures-of-weapons-found-on-the-mavi-marmara-flotilla -ship-31-may-2010.

105   **they had just killed innocent**: Masarwa, *Midnight on the Mavi Marmara*, 43.

105   **We are taken ashore**: Mankell, *Midnight on the Mavi Marmara*, 24.

105   **robbing passengers**: "Framing the Narrative: Israeli Commandos Seize Videotape and Equipment from Journalists After Deadly Raid," *Democracy Now!*, June 9, 2010, http://www.democracynow.org/2010/6/9/framing_the_narrative_israeli _commandos_seize. Australian journalist and flotilla passenger Paul McGeough remarked on *Democracy Now!* "The systematic attempt and very deliberate first priority for the Israeli soldiers as they came on the ships was to shut down the story, to confiscate all cameras, to shut down satellites, to smash the CCTV cameras that were on the *Mavi Marmara*, to make sure that nothing was going out. They were hellbent on controlling the story."

105   **what their uniforms represent**: "Israel Probing Claims of Flotilla Ship Thefts," CNN, August 19, 2010, http://articles.cnn.com/2010-08-19/world/israel.flotilla .investigation_1_mavi-marmara-israeli-army-belongings?_s=PM:WORLD.

105   **arbitrary and summary executions**: Human Rights Council, United Nations. "Report of the International Fact-Finding Mission to Investigate Violations of International Law, Including International Humanitarian and Human Rights Law, Resulting from the Israeli Attacks on the Flotilla of Ships Carrying Humanitarian Assistance," September 27, 2010, p. 37, http://www2.ohchr.org/english/bodies /hrcouncil/docs/15session/A.HRC.15.21_en.PDF.

106   **cooling off period**: Jonathan Lis, "Legal Official Slams Bill That Would Expel Israeli's Foreign Partners with Undetermined Residency Status," *Ha'aretz*, January 3, 2011, http://www.haaretz.com/news/national/legal-official-slams-bill-that-would -expel-israelis-foreign-partners-with-undetermined-residency-status-1.334995.

107   **Our refusal comes first**: Members of the Shministim, "The Shministim Letter 2008," http://www.refusingtokill.net/Israel/ShministimLetter2008.htm.

107   **deprive it of funding**: Gabe Kahn, "Bibi Races to Back Foreign NGO Funding Bill," *Arutz Sheva*, December 2, 2011, http://www.israelnationalnews.com/News /News.aspx/150337#.UWX6qnx4a8V.

108   **knack for manipulation**: Yossi Klein, "No News Is Good News," *Ha'aretz*, July 23, 2010, http://www.haaretz.com/weekend/magazine/no-news-is-good-news-1 .303600.

110 **The first official retraction**: Max Blumenthal, "Under Scrutiny, IDF Retracts Claims about Flotilla's Al Qaeda Links," MaxBlumenthal.com, June 3, 2010, http://maxblumenthal.com/2010/06/under-scrutiny-idf-retracts-claims-about-flotillas-al-qaeda-links.

111 **ties with World Jihad**: Max Blumenthal, "The Israeli Media's Flotilla Fail," in *Midnight on the Mavi Marmara*, 187. Also see the same article at MaxBlumenthal.com, June 22, 2010, http://maxblumenthal.com/2010/06/the-israeli-medias-flotilla-fail.

111 **Go back to Auschwitz!**: Max Blumenthal, "IDF Releases Apparently Doctored Flotilla Audio; Press Reports as Fact," MaxBlumenthal.com, June 4, 2010, http://maxblumenthal.com/2010/06/idf-releases-apparently-doctored-audio-press-reports-as-fact.

111 **releasing a "clarification"**: Max Blumenthal, "IDF Admits It Doctored Flotilla Audio; *Washington Post's* Kessler Must Retract," MaxBlumenthal.com, June 5, 2010, http://maxblumenthal.com/2010/06/idf-admits-it-doctored-flotilla-audio-clip-washington-posts-kessler-must-retract.

111 **five flotilla passengers**: Blumenthal, *Midnight on the Mavi Marmara*.

112 **daytime deception**: Ibid.

112 **Ha'aretz quietly altered the caption**: Max Blumenthal, "(Updated) Nailed Again: IDF Description of Suspicious Photo It Distributed Is Retracted," MaxBlumenthal.com, June 8, 2010, http://maxblumenthal.com/2010/06/nailed-again-under-pressure-idf-and-haaretz-retract-description-of-suspicious-idf-distributed-photo%22.

113 **competition is for the diligent**: Klein, "No News Is Good News."

113 **it's important to me to see the IDF win**: Ibid.

113 **an Iranian port in the Mediterranean**: Benjamin Netanyahu, "Statement by Prime Minister Netanyahu: 'No Love Boat,'" Israel Ministry of Foreign Affairs, June 2, 2010, http://www.mfa.gov.il/MFA/Government/Speeches+by+Israeli+leaders/2010/Statement_PM_Netanyahu_2-Jun-2010.htm.

113 **the tapes that have been released**: Ibid.

113 **violent supporters of terrorism**: Ibid.

114 **Israel cannot clean**: Ian Traynor, "Gaza Flotilla Raid Draws Furious Response from Turkey's Prime Minister," *Guardian*, June 1, 2010, http://www.guardian.co.uk/world/2010/jun/01/gaza-flotilla-raid-turkey-prime-minister-israel.

114 **reversing decades of official**: Vita Bekker, "Israel May Recognize Ottoman Armenian Genocide," *National*, June 2, 2011, http://www.thenational.ae/news/world/middle-east/israel-may-recognise-ottoman-armenian-genocide.

115 **the low chair**: Deputy Foreign Minister Danny Ayalon was forced to apologize to Turkish ambassador Ahmet Oguz Celikkol after a January 2010 incident in which he summoned Celikkol to his office and berated him about an anti-Israel television program in Turkey while Celikkol was photographed sitting in a chair positioned beneath Ayalon, specially designed to present an image of humiliation. See Barak Ravid, "Deputy FM Ayalon Apologizes to Turkish Ambassador," *Ha'aretz*, January 13, 2010, http://www.haaretz.com/print-edition/news/deputy-fm-ayalon-apologizes-to-turkish-ambassador-1.261346.

115 **Now we'll show them**: Yossi Sarid, "Too Late, Too Ugly," *Ha'aretz*, May 27, 2011, http://www.haaretz.com/opinion/too-late-too-ugly-1.364328.

115 **Dark forces from the Middle Ages**: Attila Somfalvi, "Netanyahu Warns: Dark Days Ahead," *Ynetnews*, June 14, 2010, http://www.ynetnews.com/articles/0,7340,L-3905022,00.html.

115 **apologize for the lethal raid**: Charles Levinson, Joe Parkinson, and Colleen McCain, "Israel's Apology Resets Alliance with Turkey," *Wall Street Journal*, March

22, 2013, http://online.wsj.com/article/SB10001424127887323419104578376352
205848268.html.

CHAPTER 21: THE PEOPLE, UNITED

117 **he was stabbed and assaulted:** "Biographical Note" Avnery-News.com, http://
www.avnery-news.co.il/english/uri2.html.

117 **The violence of the rightists:** "The Violence of the Government Is Drowning Us
All," *Gush Shalom,* http://zope.gush-shalom.org/home/en/events/1275859507.

117 **Jew against Jew:** Yoav Zitun, "Rightists Slam 'Stinking Tel Avivians,'" *Ynetnews,*
June 5, 2010, http://www.ynetnews.com/articles/0,7340,L-3899404,00.html

117 **46 percent of Jewish Israelis believe:** David Pollack, "Israelis Agree with Bibi,"
Foreign Policy, June 11, 2010, http://www.foreignpolicy.com/articles/2010/06/11
/israelis_agree_with_bibi.

117 **39 percent felt that the commandos did not use enough force:** Ibid.

117 **his disapproval rating among Israelis rose:** Ibid.

117 **The rally was organized:** Footage of the rally, and my and Lia Tarachansky's
interviews with participants can be viewed on YouTube.com at Max Blumenthal
and Lia Tarachansky, "Israelis Celebrate Flotilla Attack," June 6, 2010, http://www
.youtube.com/watch?v=ZWhaoaMGIlQ.

CHAPTER 22: THE ENEMIES

122 **Zoabi approached the Knesset podium:** A translated video and transcript of
Knesset members heckling Zoabi can be viewed on YouTube.com at "Knesset
Members Attack Haneen Zoabi after Gaza Flotilla," posted by user LSRochon,
June 7, 2010, http://www.youtube.com/watch?v=VsrHmsoRhSc.

122 **an inseparable part:** Zvi Zrahiya, "Israel Official: Accepting Palestinians into
Israel Better Than Two States," *Ha'aretz,* April 29, 2010, http://www.haaretz.com
/news/national/israel-official-accepting-palestinians-into-israel-better-than-two
-states-1.287421.

122 **the ethic of liberty:** Leonard Fein, "Anti-Liberal Cloud Hangs Over Israel," *Jewish
Daily Forward,* November 27, 2011, http://forward.com/articles/146835/anti-liberal
-cloud-hangs-over-israel.

123 **Zoabi must be punished:** LSRochon video on YouTube.

123 **the last person capable of preaching:** Ibid.

123 **They left only nine floating voters:** Ibid.

123 **What do you care?:** Ibid.

124 **terrorist:** Ibid.

CHAPTER 23: BY RIGHT AND NOT GRACE

125 **psychological war against the Arab public:** Shira Robinson, "Occupied Citizens
in a Liberal State: Palestinians Under Military Rule and the Colonial Formation
of Israeli Society, 1948-1966." PhD diss., Stanford University, 2005, 129.

125 **Operation Hafarferet:** Ilan Pappe, *The Forgotten Palestinians: A History of Palestinians in Israel* (Yale University Press, 2011), 58–59.

125 **massacring 47 innocent people:** David Hirst, *The Gun and the Olive Branch*
(Nation Books, 1977, 1984, 2003), 312.

125 **I don't want any sentimentality:** Ibid.

125 **Dahan was appointed:** Ibid., 314.

125 **ordered a media blackout:** Tom Segev, "If the Eye Is Not Blind Nor the Heart
Closed," *Ha'aretz,* October 26, 2006, http://www.haaretz.com/if-the-eye-is-not
-blind-nor-the-heart-closed-1.203445.

125 **because of Latif Dori**: Ibid.

126 **sneaking into Kafr Kassem**: Pappe, *The Forgotten Palestinians*, 57–58.

126 **suspicion that was confirmed**: See Nur Masalha, "Operation Hafarfaret and the Massacre of Kafr Qassem, October 1956," *Arab Review*, Summer 1994.

126 **What we wanted to escape in Vilna**: Lawrence Joffe, "Meir Vilner," *Guardian*, June 20, 2003, http://www.guardian.co.uk/news/2003/jun/21/guardianobituaries.israel.

126 **stricken from the Knesset record**: Segev, "If the Eye Is Not Blind."

126 **will be permitted and go unpunished**: Giora Goldberg, *Ben-Gurion Against the Knesset* (London: Routledge, 2004), 272.

126 **A fascist movement has emerged in Israel**: Ibid.

126 **by right and not by grace**, Zaki Shalom, "Ben-Gurion and Tewfik Toubi Finally Meet (October 28, 1966)," Israel Studies, June 22, 2003, http://www.accessmy library.com/article-1G1-111063890/ben-gurion-and-tewfik.html.

127 **some of my struggles are because**: Elana Maryles Sztokman, "The Knesset's Feminist Awakening," *Jewish Daily Forward*, March 16, 2011, http://forward .com/articles/136235/the-knesset-s-feminist-awakening.

CHAPTER 24: THE SILENCE OF THE LAMBS

128 **you will be able to have their homes:** Nur Masalha, "Towards the Palestinian Refugees," 1948, 16, http://www.robat.scl.net/content/NAD/pdfs/refugees_7full .pdf.

128 **settle in their houses**: Ibid, 17.

130 **I can't stand MK Zoabi's opinions**: Amnon Meranda, "Knesset Committee: Revoke Zoabi's Rights," *Ynetnews*, June 7, 2010, http://www.ynetnews.com/articles /0,7340,L-3900899,00.html.

130 **You have no place**: Tania Kepler, "MK Zoabi Loses Knesset Privilege," *Alternative News*, July 15, 2010, http://www.alternativenews.org/english/index.php/news /news/2739-mk-zoabi-loses-knesset-privileges.html.

130 **Ms. Zuabi, I take your loyalty**: Jonathan Lis, "Knesset Revokes Arab MK Zuabi's Privileges over Gaza Flotilla," *Ha'aretz*, July 13, 2010, http://www.haaretz.com/news/ national/knesset-revokes-arab-mk-zuabi-s-privileges-over-gaza-flotilla-1.301750.

130 **for a full parliamentary season**: Jonathan Lis, "Arab MK Stripped of Further Parliamentary Privileges for Role in Gaza Flotilla," *Ha'aretz*, July 18, 2011, http:// www.haaretz.com/news/national/arab-mk-stripped-of-further-parliamentary -privileges-for-role-in-gaza-flotilla-1.373859.

130   **twenty-one had been enacted**: David Sheen, "Israel's Champion of Lawmakers," *Open Democracy*, November 8, 2012, http://www.opendemocracy.net/david -sheen/israels-champion-of-lawmakers.

131 **free groceries for life**: Rebecca Ann Stoil, "Facebook User Calls for MK Zoabi's Death," *Jerusalem Post*, June 6, 2010, http://www.jpost.com/Israel/Facebook-user -calls-for-MK-Zoabis-death.

131 **Execute Zoabi**: Hagai El-Ad, "Israel's Sad Slide from Democracy," *Jewish Chronicle*, August 26, 2010, http://www.thejc.com/comment-and-debate/comment /37238/israels-sad-slide-democracy.

CHAPTER 25: DEFENSIVE DEMOCRACY

132 **a Canadian named Benjamin Dunkelman:** Peretz Kidron, "Truth Whereby Nations Live," in Blaming the Victims: Spurious Scholarship and the Palestinian Question, ed. Edward Said and Christopher Hitchens (Verso, 2001), 87. Also see Benjamin Dunkelman, Dual Allegiance: An Autobiography (Crown Publishers, 1976), 266–267.

132 **Ben Gurion was forced to refuse**: Kidron, Ibid.

132 **first Arab to serve on Israel's**: Hillel Cohen, *Good Arabs: The Israeli Security Agencies and the Israeli Arabs, 1948–1967,* (University of California Press, 2010), 22–23.

133 **Israeli police immediately arrested**: Ibid, 157–158.

133 **a natural home for most**: Leena Dallasheh, "Political Mobilization of Palestinians in Israel," in *Displaced at Home: Ethnicity and Gender among Palestinians in Israel,* ed. Rhoda Ann Kanaaneh and Isis Nusair, (State University of New York Press, 2010) 21–38.

134 **a poisonous nationalist character**: Ibid.

134 **I did what the people wanted**: Ibid.

134 **I say that a nation should**: Azmi Bishara in *I Also Dwell Among Your Own People,* documentary by Ariella Azoulay, (2005, Alma Films).

135 **I can't take anymore**: Ibid.

135 **The curriculum drove us crazy**: Ibid.

135 **Imagine if Arabs had attacked the house**: Ibid.

136 **take [their] bundles**: Jonathan Cook, "Israel's Minister of Strategic Threats," *Counterpunch*, October 25, 2006, http://www.counterpunch.org/2006/10/25/israel-s-minister-of-strategic-threats.

136 **has independently gathered**: Azmi Bishara, "Why Israel Is After Me," *Los Angeles Times*, May 3, 2007, http://www.latimes.com/news/opinion/commentary/la-oe-bishara3may03,0,5123721.story.

136 **conducting subversive activity**: Jack Khoury and Yuval Yoaz, "Shin Bet: Citizens Subverting Israel Key Values to Be Probed," *Ha'aretz*, May 20, 2007, http://www.haaretz.com/news/shin-bet-citizens-subverting-israel-key-values-to-be-probed-1.220965.

136 **take their rights too far**: Ofer Aderet, "Shin Bet Chief, an Unlikely Advocate for Israel's Arabs," *Ha'aretz*, April 8, 2011, http://www.haaretz.com/weekend/haaretz-wikileaks-exclusive-shin-bet-chief-an-unlikely-advocate-for-israel-s-arabs-1.354802.

137 **Balad just went a bit too far**: Nathan Jeffay, "Citing Disloyalty, Knesset Bans Main Arab Parties From Elections," *Jewish Daily Forward*, January 15, 2009, http://forward.com/articles/14954/citing-disloyalty-knesset-bans-main-arab-parties-.

138 **there will be two countries**: Isabel Kershner, "Israeli Cabinet Approves Citizenship Amendment," *New York Times*, October 10, 2010, http://www.nytimes.com/2010/10/11/world/middleeast/11mideast.html.

138 **Expel Zoabi from the Knesset**: "Report: Police Sanction Protest against Zoabi in Nazareth," *Ma'an News Agency*, February 28, 2012, http://www.maannews.net/eng/ViewDetails.aspx?ID=463557.

138 **maintain the Jewish character**: Ben White, "Initiative in Upper Nazareth: $10,000 to Every Arab Family That Leaves," *Electronic Intifada*, June 13, 2012, http://electronicintifada.net/blogs/ben-white/initiative-upper-nazareth-10000-every-arab-family-leaves.

139 **put the brakes on the demographic**: Ibid.

139 **the end of democracy**: My interview with Haneen Zoabi is published as "Haneen Zoabi: The Largest Threat to Zionism Is Democracy," *Electronic Intifada*, July 22, 2010, http://electronicintifada.net/content/haneen-zoabi-largest-threat-zionism-democracy/8937.

CHAPTER 26: CALIBER 3: "THE VALUES OF ZIONISM"

141 **makes the activity**: "Remarks," Caliber 3 Range website, http://www.caliber3range.com/tourist2hour-en.php.

141 **I do not know if this is:** Amira Hass. "Don't Shoot Till You Can See They're over the Age of 12," *Ha'aretz*, November 20, 2000, http://www.mafhoum.com/press /childtsahal.htm

142 **Are you ready to take out a terrorist?:** Akiva Novick, "Tourists Venture to West Bank to 'Shoot Terrorists,'" *Ynetnews*, June 18, 2012, http://www.ynetnews.com /articles/0,7340,L-4243882,00.html.

142 **They should know where:** Ibid.

CHAPTER 27: A LESSON IN ISRAELI DEMOCRACY

145 **Kill any Arab you encounter:** Ilan Pappe, The Ethnic Cleansing of Palestine. (Oxford: Oneworld Publications, 2006), 95.

145 **Men stepped on their friends:** Ibid., 96.

146 **an international symbol:** Amir Buhbut, "Cruiseship Marmara," *Maariv*, July 8, 2010, translated by Didi Remez: "Haifa Mayor Wants to Turn *Mavi Marmara* into 'Floating Hotel' So It Can Become a 'Symbol of Reconciliation and Hope.'" *Coteret*, July 9, 2010, http://coteret.com/2010/07/09/haifa-mayor-wants-to-turn-mavi-marmara -into-floating-hotel-so-it-can-turn-into-symbol-of-reconciliation-and-hope.

146 **Who is the man of the house?:** Interview with Janan Abdu, Haifa, Israel, July 29, 2010.

147 **went public with Israel's worst-kept secret:** Makhoul's speech translated by Foundation for Middle East Peace, "Knesset Presses Nuclear Issue," *Settlement Report*, Vol. 10. No. 7, Spring 2000, http://www.fmep.org/reports/special-reports /the-uncertainties-of-peace-regional-implications-of-israeli-arab-rapproche- ment/knesset-addresses-nuclear-issue.

148 **People like you shouldn't:** Jonathan Cook, "Hush, Hush about Israel's Bomb," *Al-Ahram*, November 27–December 3, 2003, Issue No. 666, http://weekly.ahram .org.eg/2003/666/re2.htm.

148 **the Shin Bet's all-purpose "Hezbollah agent":** Richard Silverstein, "Hassan Jaja, Shin Bet's All-Purpose 'Hezbollah Spy,'" *Tikun Olam*, May 14, 2010, http://www.rich- ardsilverstein.com/2010/05/14/hassan-geagea-shin-bets-all-purpose-hezbollah -spy.

149 **Israel is a normal country:** Joanna Paraszczuk, "High Court Upholds State of Emergency," *Jerusalem Post*, May 8, 2012, http://www.jpost.com/NationalNews /Article.aspx?id=269156.

150 **steps reminiscent of dark:** Richard Silverstein, "Latest on Ameer Makhoul, Secret Arrest, Gag Order, and Silence of Israeli Press," *Tikun Olam*, May 10, 2010, http:// www.richardsilverstein.com/2010/05/10/latest-on-ameer-makhoul-secret-arrest -gag-order-and-thundering-silence-of-israeli-press.

151 **the State of Israel has detained:** Adri Nieuwhof, "Justice Upside Down: A New Study on Israel's Military Courts," *Electronic Intifada*, June 9, 2012, http://electronic intifada.net/blogs/adri-nieuwhof/justice-upside-down-new-study-israels-military -courts.

151 **lie to human rights groups:** Chris McGreal, "'I Can't Imagine Anyone Who Considers Himself a Human Being Can Do This,'" *Guardian*, July 27, 2003, http://www .guardian.co.uk/world/2003/jul/28/israel.

151 **four and a half years in jail:** Naama Cohen-Friedman, "Anat Kam Sentenced to 4.5 Years in Prison," *Ynetnews*, October 30, 2011, http://www.ynetnews.com/articles /0,7340,L-4141015,00.html.

151 **for possession of classified:** Naama Cohen-Friedman, "Uri Blau Convicted in Anat Kam Affair," *Ynetnews*, July 24, 2012, http://www.ynetnews.com/articles /0,7340,L-4259704,00.html.

152 **landmark hunger strikes**: Ameer Makhoul, "How Hunger Strikers 'Tied the Hands of the Occupation': A View from Israeli Prison," *Electronic Intifada*, June 9, 2012, http://electronicintifada.net/content/how-hunger-strikers-tied-hands -occupation-view-israeli-prison/11379.

CHAPTER 28: JUST BEING A GUY

153 **a positive image of Israel:** David Hazony. "The Hasbara Test," Commentary, January 21, 2010, http://www.commentarymagazine.com/2010/01/21/the-hasbara -test.

154 **Technion was a key idea factory**: Max Blumenthal, "New York to Host Israel's Top Drone Lab," *Al Akhbar* English, December 24, 2011, http://english.al-akhbar.com /node/2798.

154 **the military has invested heavily**: Tobias Buck, "Israel's Army of Tech Start-Ups," *Financial Times*, November 30, 2011, http://www.ft.com/cms/s/0/d45b0c5c-1a83 -11e1-ae4e-00144feabdc0.html.

154 **I told them that you have**: Marwan Dalal, "Law and Politics before the Or Commission of Inquiry," Adalah: The Legal Center for Arab Minority Rights in Israel, July 2003, p. 20.

154 **work to wipe out the stain**: "The Official Summation of the Or Commission Report," Jewish Virtual Library, September 2, 2003, http://www.jewishvirtual library.org/jsource/Society_&_Culture/OrCommissionReport.html.

155 **The Interior Ministry plans**: Yoav Stern, "Interior Ministry: Israel to Okay New Arab City This Year," *Ha'aretz*, February 13, 2008, http://www.haaretz.com/print -edition/news/interior-ministry-israel-to-okay-new-arab-city-this-year-1 .239220.

155 **The government has lost its Zionism entirely**: Ibid.

CHAPTER 29: LEAVING HAIFA

159 **I didn't break any laws:** Ben Hartman, "ACRI: Eatery Broke No Laws by Banning Soldiers in Uniform," Jerusalem Post, March 3, 2010 http://www.jpost.com/Israel /ACRI-Eatery-broke-no-laws-by-banning-soldiers-in-uniform.

159 **Boycott Azad**: Maayana Miskin, "Haifa Restaurant Bans Soldiers in Uniform," *Arutz Sheva*, March 4, 2010, http://www.israelnationalnews.com/News/News .aspx/136339#.UWec5iv71D4.

159 **a mob of Israeli students**: Video of Im Tirtzu orchestrated protest outside Azad can be viewed on YouTube.com at "azad.avi" posted by user mourice sahoury on March 8, 2010, http://www.youtube.com/watch?feature=player_embedded&v=et LHQGlNg2Q.

160 **The alleged discrimination**: "Haifa Municipality's Request to Close Arab-Owned Azad Restaurant for Refusing to Serve Uniformed Soldiers Rejected by Court," News Release, Adalah Legal Center for Minority Rights in Israel, April 8, 2010, http://www.old-adalah.org/eng/pressreleases/pr.php?file=08_04_10.

160 **The action taken by the restaurant**: Ron Friedman, "Sailor Refused Entry to Restaurant to Be Compensated," *Jerusalem Post*, July 1, 2011, http://www.jpost.com /NationalNews/Article.aspx?id=227442; Ahiya Raved, "Haifa Cafe to Compensate Soldier tor Discrimination," *Ynetnews*, June 30, 2011, http://www.ynetnews.com /articles/0,7340,L-4089544,00.html.

CHAPTER 30: THE DAYS OF '48 HAVE COME AGAIN

165 **left [Jenin's] residents**: "Razing Rafah: Mass Home Demolitions in the Gaza Strip," Human Rights Watch, October 17, 2004. Also see Tsadok Yeheskeli, "I Made

Them a Stadium in the Middle of the Camp," *Yedioth Ahronoth*, May 31, 2002, translated by Electronic Intifada: http://electronicintifada.net/content/i-made -them-stadium-middle-camp/4459.

166 **They are poor in culture**: Anne Usher, "Family Takes Stock after Mass Lod Demolition," *Ma'an News*, December 16, 2010, http://www.maannews.net/eng/View Details.aspx?ID=342478.

166 **42,000 such orders had been**: Ibid.

166 **I arrived at the Abu Eid camp**: Max Blumenthal, "The Days of '48 Have Come Again, 15 Minutes from Tel Aviv, Israel Creates a New Refugee Camp," MaxBlumenthal.com, January 26, 2011, http://maxblumenthal.com/2011/01/the-days-of -48-have-come-again-15-minutes-from-tel-aviv-israel-creates-a-new-refugee -camp.

167 **If there is a democracy**: Max Blumenthal, "The Village of Dahmash Fights to Survive Inside Israel," YouTube.com, July 28, 2010, http://www.youtube.com /watch?v=w2R2JAqo63A.

167 **Go to Gaza!**: Max Blumenthal, "MK Dov Khenin: Video of Cops Beating Dahmash Family, Shouting "Go to Gaza," Exists and Must Prompt Investigation," MaxBlumenthal.com, January 30, 2011, http://maxblumenthal.com/2011/01/mk -dov-khenin-video-of-cops-beating-dahmash-family-shouting-go-to-gaza-exists -and-must-prompt-investigation.

168 **I broke the law?**: DAM, "Born Here," August 22, 2006, http://www.youtube.com /watch?v=zIo6lyP9tTE.

168 **Who's the terrorist?**: DAM, "Min Erhabi – Who's the Terrorist?" Full video and translation: "Palestinian Hip-Hop: 'Who's The Terrorist?!'" posted on YouTube. com by user youboob83, April 3, 2006, http://www.youtube.com/watch?v=OgSVX jNLFgo.

168 **while they were holding a Shabbat dinner**: Nir Hasson, "Jerusalem Police Arrest Sheikh Jarrah Activist," *Ha'aretz*, March 27, 2010, http://www.haaretz.com/news /jerusalem-police-arrest-sheikh-jarrah-activist-1.266768.

CHAPTER 31: THE BLUEPRINT

171 **criminal act of discrimination**: Neve Gordon. "'Algorithm of Expropriation': Plan to Uproot 30,000 Bedouin," 972 Magazine, April 4, 2012, http://972mag .com/algorithm-of-expropriation-the-plan-to-uproot-30000-bedouin/40202/

171 **This phenomenon of the Bedouins**: Donald MacIntyre, "The Arab Bedouin Are Israeli Citizens and Many Fight in the Israeli Army. But an Attempt to Force Them off Their Land Has Led to Violent Clashes with the Police," *Independent*, November 29, 2005, http://www.independent.co.uk/news/world/middle-east/end-of-the -road-for-the-bedouin-517396.html.

171 **concentrate the Bedouin population**: Or Movement, Negev Information Center. "Northern Negev/Rahat—About the City," http://eng.negev-net.org.il/HTMLs /article.aspx?C2004=12605&BSP=12580.

172 **self-described messianist**: David Ben-Gurion, *Memoirs* (Cleveland, OH: The World Publishing Company, 1970), 120–121; Ben Gurion's collected memoirs contain an entire section distilling his secular messianic perspective. While describing himself as an atheist, Ben Gurion wrote, "As to the Jews, I can only point to the Bible and to its sequence in the many Jewish initiatives to regain Israel stretching across the centuries since Masada and say: This is our Mandate. Come see for yourselves.".

172 **five million Jews**: Ibid.,147.

172 **reproach to mankind**: Ibid., 146.

172　**occupied territory**: Ibid., 137.

172　**When I look out of my window**: Ibid., 149.

172　**our force will enable**: David Ben-Gurion, "Letter from David Ben-Gurion to His Son Amos," October 5, 1937, http://www.docstoc.com/docs/117343519/B-G -Letter-translation.

172　**If we don't work fast**: Tim Whewell, "Israeli Push to Fulfill Desert Dream Unsettles Negev Bedouin," *BBC News*, January 16, 2013, http://www.bbc.co.uk/news/world -middle-east-20945253.

173　**The trouble with the Bedouin**: Chris McGreal, "Bedouin Feel the Squeeze as Israel Resettles the Negev Desert," *Guardian*, February 26, 2003, http://www .guardian.co.uk/world/2003/feb/27/israel.

173　**forever show concern for the rights**: Evgenia Bystrov and Arnon Soffer, "Israel: Demography and Density: 2007-2020," May 2008, p. 74, http://web.hevra.haifa.ac .il/~ch-strategy/images/publications/demography_2007_en.pdf.

173　**The United States had its**: Ronald S. Lauder, "The Negev-Israel's Manifest Destiny," http://support.jnf.org/site/PageServer?pagename=PR_Negev.

173　**This land is ours**: Rebecca Manski, "Blueprint Negev," *Mondoweiss*, November 9, 2010, http://mondoweiss.net/2010/11/blueprint-negev.html.

173　**it can be taken from us**: Ibid.

173　**who want to make aliyah**: Zvi Alush, " New Town for Rich US Immigrants," *Ynetnews*, May 2, 2006, http://www.ynetnews.com/articles/0,7340,L-3246513,00.html.

174　**Central Israel is already developed**: Uriel Heilman, "The Negev's 21st-Century Pioneers," *B'Nai B'Rith* , Winter 2008–09, http://www.urielheilman.com /0101negev.html.

174　**Pure Zionism**: Raphael Ahren, "U.S. Rabbi Envisions Pluralistic Utopia in Planned Negev Town," *Ha'aretz*, July 10, 2009, http://www.haaretz.com/u-s-rabbi -envisions-pluralistic-utopia-in-planned-negev-town-1.279739.

174　**less a concrete development**: Rebecca Manski, "Blueprint Negev," *Mondoweiss*, November 9, 2010, http://mondoweiss.net/2010/11/blueprint-negev.html.

175　**As the bulldozers trundled**: Video of the demolitions: Max Blumenthal, "In The Wasteland of Democracy, Israel Destroys Al-Arakib…Again," MaxBlumenthal.com, August 11, 2010, http://maxblumenthal.com/2010/08/israels-third-destruction-of -al-arakib.

175　**permanent solution**: Lilly Rivlin, "Bedouin Village Razed for 9th Time," Partners for Progressive Israel, January 20, 2011, http://meretzusa.blogspot.com/2011/01 /final-solution-for-bedouin-village.html.

CHAPTER 32: THE SUMMER CAMP OF DESTRUCTION

176　**busloads of cheering civilians**: "Bedouins Evicted from Village in Southern Israel," CNN, July 27, 2010, http://edition.cnn.com/2010/WORLD/meast/07/27 /israel.bedouins.demolitions/index.html?hpt=T2#fbid=K3vLQYhbZ8q.

177　**the people of Israel live**: Max Blumenthal. "The 'Summer Camp of Destruction:' Israeli High Schoolers Assist the Razing of a Bedouin Town," July 31, 2010, http:// maxblumenthal.com/2010/07/the-summer-camp-of-destruction-israeli-high -schoolers-join-in-the-destruction-of-a-bedouin-town.

177　**funded by Christian Zionists**: The International Fellowship of Christians and Jews Facebook group, Fellowship house in Kiryat Gat, https://www.facebook.com /media/set/?set=a.10150301932009896.414692.30914589895&type=3 More on IFCJ: Max Blumenthal, "Born Agains For Sharon," Salon.com, November 1, 2004, http://www.salon.com/2004/11/01/christian_zionism.

177 **The girls, in their innocence**: Jonathan Cook, "Israel's Fear of Jewish Girls Dating Arabs; Team of Psychologists to 'Rescue' Women," *AlterNet*, September 25, 2009, http://www.alternet.org/story/142900/israel's_fear_of_jewish_girls_dating _arabs;_team_of_psychologists_to_%22rescue%22_women.

178 **There is no element of love**: Matan Tzuri, "Kiryat Gat Teens Warned Against Dating Bedouins," *Ynetnews*, July 16, 2007, http://www.ynetnews.com/articles /0,7340,L-3425981,00.html.

CHAPTER 33: PREPARING THE LAND FOR JESUS

179 **New World Order:** Rachel Tabachnick, "Part Two: The Prophecy/Conspiracy Genre," Talk to Action, December 8, 2010, http://www.talk2action.org/story/2010 /12/8/185728/155.

179 **first exposed by activists**: Alternative Information Center, "JNF Establishes Bulldozer Camp Near Demolished Bedouin Village for Planting of 'God-TV Forest,'" *Alternative News*, November 24, 2010, http://www.alternativenews.org/ english/index.php/component/content/article/28-news/3032-jnf-establishes -bulldozer-camp-near-demolished-bedouin-village-for-planting-of-god-tv-forest -.html.

179 **GOD TV is planting**: "Preparing the Land for the Return of the King," GOD TV, http://www.god.tv/israeltrees.

180 **twenty-first-century pioneers**: Max Blumenthal, "GOD TV and Jewish Nation Fund's Forest of Hate," http://vimeo.com/17795451.

180 **bodies bursting open**: Tim LaHaye and Jerry B. Jenkins, *Left Behind* (Tyndale House, 1996), 226, 286.

180 **a private jet supplied**: Craig Unger, *The Fall of the House of Bush* (New York: Simon and Schuster, 2007), 109.

180 **Half-Jewish, as was Adolf Hitler**: Max Blumenthal, "Pastor Hagee: The Antichrist Is Gay, 'Partially Jewish, as Was Adolph Hitler' (Paging Joe Lieberman!)," *Huffington Post*, June 2, 2008, http://www.huffingtonpost.com/max-blumenthal/pastor -hagee-the-antichri_b_104608.html.

180 **Israel loves you**: Max Blumenthal, " Netanyahu and Pastor Hagee's Lovefest on Eve of Biden's Arrival in Israel," MaxBlumenthal.com, March 9, 2010, http://max-blumenthal.com/2010/03/pastor-hagee-and-netanyahus-lovefest-on-eve-of -bidens-arrival-in-israel.

181 **These claims are false**: GOD-TV, "Tree Planting in the Negev," http://www.god .tv/negev.

181 **I can tell you one**: Adam Horowitz, "JNF Feeling the Heat over Al Araqib," *Mondoweiss*, March 28, 2011, http://mondoweiss.net/2011/03/jnf-feeling-the-heat -over-al-araqib.html.

181 **the State of Israel filed**: Jack Khoury. "Israel Sues 34 Bedouin for Costs of Repeated Demolition of Their Homes," *Ha'aretz*, July 27, 2011, http://www.haaretz.com /print-edition/news/israel-sues-34-bedouin-for-costs-of-repeated-demolitions-of -their-homes-1.375439.

181 **We had been sitting**: Interview with Nuri El Okbi, Elizabeth Freed, February 5, 2010, YouTube, http://www.youtube.com/watch?v=lA09-3RDzKY Also see Australia's *Dateline SBS* April 11, 2011 report, "Israel's Mabo," http://www.youtube .com/watch?v=lA09-3RDzKY.

182 **We're not going to let**: Max Blumenthal, "On Land Day, the Jewish National Fund's Racist Legacy Is Exposed," March 30, 2011, http://maxblumenthal.com /2011/03/on-land-day-the-jewish-national-funds-racist-legacy-is-exposed.

182 **vindictive designs of the state**: "Israel: Human Rights Defender Mr. Nuri Al-Okbi Sentenced to Seven Months Imprisonment," Frontline Defenders, January 6, 2011, http://www.frontlinedefenders.org/node/14154.

182 **There are no two states of Israel**: Max Blumenthal, "All 'Are Equal in the Eyes of the Law?' Al-Arakib Activist Hit with 7 Month Jail Sentence for…Operating Garage Without License," MaxBlumenthal.com, December 31, 2010, http://maxblumenthal.com/2010/12/all-are-equal-in-the-eyes-of-the-law-al-arakib-activist-hit-with-7-month-jail-sentence-for-operating-garage-without-license.

CHAPTER 34: THERE ARE NO FACTS

183 **the worst jail ever**: "Palestinian Female Inmates Appeal to the Red Cross to Close Al-Damon Prison," Middle East Monitor, August 9, 2010, http://www.middleeastmonitor.com/news/middle-east/1397-palestinian-female-inmates-appeal-to-the-red-cross-to-close-al-damon-prison.

183 **a catastrophe the likes of which**: "PM on fire: Catastrophe the Likes of Which We've Never Known," *Ynetnews*, December 2, 2010, http://www.ynetnews.com/articles/1,7340,L-3993344,00.html.

183 **It's worse than a terrorist**: Ahiya Raved, "Israel's Deadliest Fire Leaves 40 Dead," *Ynetnews*, December 2, 2010, http://www.ynetnews.com/articles/0,7340,L-3993206,00.html.

183 **We do not have what it takes**: Max Blumenthal, "The Carmel Wildfire Is Burning All Illusions in Israel," *Electronic Intifada*, December 6, 2010, http://electronicintifada.net/content/carmel-wildfire-burning-all-illusions-israel/9130.

184 **the normative lordly attitude**: Jack Khoury, "Israel Refuses Entry to Palestinian Firefighters Being Honored for Carmel Fire Assistance," *Ha'aretz*, December 14, 2010, http://www.haaretz.com/news/diplomacy-defense/israel-refuses-entry-to-palestinian-firefighters-being-honored-for-carmel-fire-assistance-1.330580.

184 **for the good of expanding**: John Lyons, "Jerusalem's Bulldozer Diplomacy," *Australian*, March 18, 2010, http://www.theaustralian.com.au/news/features/jerusalems-bulldozer-diplomacy/story-e6frg6z6-1225842053277.

184 **here is a lynching**: Yair Ettinger, " Yishai: I'm Being Lynched Because I Am Ultra-Orthodox, Right-Wing and Mizrahi," *Ha'aretz*, December 6, 2010, http://www.haaretz.com/print-edition/news/yishai-i-m-being-lynched-because-i-am-ultra-orthodox-right-wing-and-mizrahi-1.329065.

184 **It is all divine providence**: Jonah Mandel, "Ovadia Yosef: Fires Only Happen Where Shabbat Is Desecrated," *Jerusalem Post*, December 4, 2010, http://www.jpost.com/Headlines/Article.aspx?id=197988.

184 **That was how we lost**: Tom Segev, *1967: Israel, the War, and the Year that Transformed the Middle East* (Macmillan, 2007), 410.

185 **with Zionist intentions**: Ibid.

185 **petitioned the Supreme Court**: Racheli Shor, "JNF's Response to Zochrot's Canada Park Petition," Zochrot, May 2006, http://zochrot.org/en/content/jnfs-response-zochrots-canada-park-petition.

185 **Not one village must be left**: Benny Morris, *The Birth of the Palestinian Refugee Problem Revisited* (Cambridge University Press, 2004), 54.

186 **die soon after taking root**: Deborah Sontag, "Arboreal Scandal in Israel: Not All of the Trees Planted There Stay Planted," *New York Times*, July 3, 2000, http://www.nytimes.com/2000/07/03/world/arboreal-scandal-in-israel-not-all-of-the-trees-planted-there-stay-planted.html?src=pm.

186 **Thanks to Janco**: Ilan Pappe, *The Ethnic Cleansing of Palestine* (Oxford: One-world Publications, 2006), 163–164.

187 **welcoming committee**: Ben White explains the exclusionary purpose of welcoming committees, alternately referred to as admissions committees in "Land, Citizenship and Exclusion in Israel," *Open Democracy*, March 30, 2011, http://www.opendemocracy.net/ben-white/land-citizenship-and-exclusion-in-israel.

188 **more dangerous than**: Rami G. Khouri, "Disgraced Palestinians Want to Lay Their Nakba Ghosts to Rest," *Daily Star*, May 19, 1998, http://www.dailystar.com.lb/Opinion/Commentary/May/19/Displaced-Palestinians-want-to-lay-their-nakba-ghosts-to-rest.ashx#axzz2N57053tY.

189 **Hezbollah overjoyed**: Roee Nachmass, "Hezbollah Overjoyed by Fire," *Ynetnews*, December 3, 2010, http://www.ynetnews.com/articles/0,7340,L-3993898,00.html Also see Richard Silverstein, "Israel's Carmel Fire: Racism Rears Its Ugly Head Even in Tragedy," December 4, 2010, http://www.richardsilverstein.com/2010/12/04/israels-carmel-fire-racism-rears-its-ugly-head-even-in-tragedy.

189 **may turn out to be the worst**: Max Blumenthal, "The Carmel Wildfire Is Burning All Illusions in Israel," *Electronic Intifada*, December 6, 2010, http://electronicintifada.net/content/carmel-wildfire-burning-all-illusions-israel/9130.

CHAPTER 35: THESE THINGS THAT WERE DONE TO US

193 **We never talk like this:** Max Blumenthal, "Never Again? Elderly Palestinian Women Called 'Whores' on Yad Vashem Tour, While Racism Explodes across Israel," Mondoweiss, December 30, 2010, http://mondoweiss.net/2010/12/never-again-elderly-palestinian-women-called-%E2%80%9Cwhores%E2%80%9D-on-yad-vashem-tour-while-racism-explodes-across-israel.html.

194 **The alternative [to war] is Treblinka**: Tim Cole, *Selling the Holocaust* (Routledge, 1999), 138.

194 **In every generation**: Daniel Bar-Tal, *Shared Beliefs in a Society: Social Psychological Analysis* (Sage Publications, 2000), 111.

194 **Uriel Abulof showed**: Ian Lustick, "Israel Needs a New Map," Remarks at the Carnegie Foundation for International Peace, February 26, 2013, http://www.mepc.org/articles-commentary/commentary/israel-needs-new-map

194 **Swastika ribbons were torn**: Shimon Tzabar, "What Really Happened in Deir-Yassin 54 Years Ago?" Deir Yassin Remembered, http://www.deiryassin.org/shimontzabar.html.

194 **Because of the Holocaust**: Giulio Meotti, "Will West Help the Jews?" *Ynetnews*, January 2, 2012, http://www.ynetnews.com/articles/0,7340,L-4183238,00.html.

195 **thrashing of limbs**: James Brooks, "The Israeli Poison Gas Attacks," *Media Monitors*, January 8, 2003, http://www.mediamonitors.net/jamesbrooks2.html. Footage of Gazan victims suffering effects from mysterious Israeli chemical weapons and testimony from Dr. Mohammed Salawa, director of the Palestinian Health Ministry, appears in BBC's March 11, 2003 documentary, "Israel's Secret Weapon," and in this YouTube excerpt: https://www.youtube.com/watch?feature=player_embedded&v=buB8QiBuHmo.

195 **the kind of anti-Arab outlook**: Daniel Bar-Tal, "Why Does Fear Override Hope in Societies Engulfed by Intractable Conflict, as It Does in the Israeli Society?" *Political Psychology*, Vol. 22, No. 3, 2001, 17.

196 **Israel was founded**: Yoav Shamir, *Defamation,* (2009, First Run Features).

197 **the researchers found a drop**: Chaim Levinson, "Study: IDF Officers Less Committed to Jewish Values after Visits to Nazi Death Camps," *Ha'aretz*, January 20, 2012,

http://www.haaretz.com/print-edition/news/study-idf-officers-less-committed-to
-jewish-values-after-visits-to-nazi-death-camps-1.408237.

198   **Yes. I think that at some point**: "Testimony 63," "Breaking the Silence: Women
Soldiers' Testimonies," p. 93, http://www.breakingthesilence.org.il/wp-content
/uploads/2011/02/Women_Soldiers_Testimonies_2009_Eng.pdf

198   **it conflicts with the desire**: Steve Weizman, "Israeli Army Criticized for Writing
I.D. Numbers on Detainees," Associated Press, March 12, 2002, http://www.belief
net.com/Faiths/Judaism/2002/03/Israeli-Army-Criticized-For-Writing-I-D
-Numbers-On-Detainees.aspx.

198   **not for abusing Arabs**: Chris McGreal, "Israel Shocked by Image of Soldiers Forcing Violinists to Play at Roadblock," *Guardian*, November 28, 2004, http://www
.guardian.co.uk/world/2004/nov/29/israel.

CHAPTER 36: THE FORBIDDEN TOUR

200   **Yad Vashem would have acted:** Yoav Stern, "Yad Vashem Fires Employee Who
Compared Holocaust to Nakba," Ha'aretz, April 23, 2009, http://www.haaretz.com
/print-edition/news/yad-vashem-fires-employee-who-compared-holocaust-to
-nakba-1.274624.

CHAPTER 37: BLEEDING OVER THE PARTY

201   **whether they have been committed:** "The Warsaw Ghetto Re-liberated," Jews sans
frontieres, July 3, 2010, http://jewssansfrontieres.blogspot.com/2010/07/warsaw
-ghetto-re-liberated_9226.html.

202   **This vile act demonstrates**: Itamar Eichner, "'FreePalestine' Sprayed on Warsaw
Ghetto Wall," *Ynetnews*, July 5, 2010, http://www.ynetnews.com/articles/0,7340,L
-3915181,00.html.

203   **If you nevertheless want**: Vered Levy-Barzilai, "Halutz: the High and the Mighty,"
Ha'aretz, August 21, 2002.

204   **We refuse to continue**: Cornal Uruquhart, "Israeli Pilots Refuse to Fly Assassination Missions," *Guardian*, September 24, 2003, http://www.guardian.co.uk/world
/2003/sep/25/israel.

204   **a propaganda weapon**: Bernard Avishai, "Flight School," *Slate*, October 17, 2003,
http://www.slate.com/articles/news_and_politics/foreigners/2003/10/flight
_school.html.

204   **the IDF issues only legal orders**: Gideon Alon and Amos Harel, "Mofaz: IAF
Pilots' Letter of Refusal Benefits Terror Groups," *Ha'aretz*, September 24, 2003,
http://www.haaretz.com/news/mofaz-iaf-pilots-letter-of-refusal-benefits-terror
-groups-1.101072.

204   **Aya Korem's "Yonatan Shapira":** with English subtitles, uploaded to YouTube on
December 30, 2008 by user Israelisongs, http://www.youtube.com/watch?v=Ghy
RLHjl4xg.

CHAPTER 38: A DATE WITH THE DEVIL

206   **fall into some other reporter's hands:** Amira Hass was the first reporter to cover
Yonatan Shapira's interrogation; as a Jewish Israeli citizen she enjoyed legal protections I did not. See Hass, "Conscientious Objector Yonatan Shapira Questioned by Shin Bet," Ha'aretz, July 20, 2010, http://www.haaretz.com/print-edition
/news/conscientious-objector-yonatan-shapira-questioned-by-shin-bet-1
.302896.

CHAPTER 39: DELEGITIMIZATION

208 **The BDS movement:** "Palestinian BDS National Committee," http://www.bds movement.net/BNC.

208 **three key obligations:** "Palestinian Civil Society Call for BDS," July 9, 2005, http:// www.bdsmovement.net/call#top.

208 **fourteen hundred Palestinians:** "B'Tselem Publishes Complete Fatality Figures from Operation Cast Lead," B'Tselem, September 9, 2009, http://www.btselem.org /press_releases/20090909.

209 **They kept me for six hours:** Sarah Smith, "PennBDS Activists Fight for Their Cause," *Daily Pennsylvanian*, February 7, 2012, http://www.thedp.com/article /2012/02/pennbds_activists_fight_for_their_cause I participated in two panels at the Penn BDS conference; video is available at http://pennbds.org.

209 **the Jewish Federation of Philadelphia:** Glenn Shrum and Irene Rivera-Calderon, "Alan Dershowitz Advocates Support for Israel," *Daily Pennsylvanian*, February 3, 2012, http://www.thedp.com/article/2012/02/alan_dershowitz_advocates _support_for_israel.

209 **David L. Cohen:** Ibid.

209 **Size Doesn't Matter:** "Israel: Small Country Big Paradise," YouTube, February 18, 2010, http://youtu.be/pjwRXicA9Gs.

210 **a $6 million fund:** "Israeli, US Jews disrupt Netanyahu speech," Maan News, August 11, 2010, http://www.maannews.net/eng/ViewDetails.aspx?ID=332088.

211 **diamond baron whose:** "Leviev's Africa-Israel Continues Settlement-Building, Contradicting 2010 Pledge," Adalah-NY, June 18, 2012, http://adalahny.org/press -release/937/leviev-africa-israel-continues-settlement-building-contradicting -2010-pledge.

211 **Halle Berry and Drew Barrymore:** Trans. Sonia Farid, "Hollywood Stars Shun Pro-Israel Diamond Store," *Al Arabiya News*, November 2, 2010, http://www .alarabiya.net/articles/2008/12/30/63111.html.

211 **quit building settlements:** Adam Horowitz, "Is Lev Leviev Out of the Settlement Building Business?" *Mondoweiss*, November 3, 2010, http://mondoweiss.net/2010 /11/is-lev-leviev-out-of-the-settlement-building-business.html. Note: Africa-Israel may have started building new settlements in 2013.

211 **Anti-Israel boycotters:** Giulio Meotti. "Is BDS Campaign Working?" YNetnews. com, August 31, 2011, http://www.ynetnews.com/articles/0,7340,L-4115718,00 .html.

211 **dignity that they all deserve:** Roger Waters, "Tear Down This Israeli Wall," *Guardian*, March 11, 2011, http://www.guardian.co.uk/commentisfree/2011/mar/11 /cultural-boycott-west-bank-wall.

211 **cultural terrorism:** Hazel Ward, "Israel Slams 'Cultural Terrorism' as Pixies Cancel Gig," Google News / AFP, June 6, 2010, http://www.google.com/hostednews/afp /article/ALeqM5jnuiLTovjxjwSwo415F9qITUTsZA.

211 **The state must intervene:** Max Blumenthal, "News from Chelm: Knesset Discusses Ways to Pressure Performers Not to Cancel Concerts in Israel," February 1, 2011, http://maxblumenthal.com/2011/02/news-from-chelm-knesset-discusses -ways-to-pressure-performers-not-to-cancel-concerts-in-israel.

211 **government insurance or state compensation:** Ibid.

212 **in practice promoting delegitimization:** "The BDS Movement Promotes Delegitimization Against Israel," The Reut Institute, June 13, 2010, http://reut-institute .org/en/Publication.aspx?PublicationId=3868.

212 **Reut's recommendations**: Ali Abuminah, "Israel's New Strategy: 'Sabotage' and 'Attack' the Global Justice Movement," *Electronic Intifada*, February 16, 2010, http://electronicintifada.net/content/israels-new-strategy-sabotage-and-attack -global-justice-movement/8683.

212 **The problem is not hasbara**: Anshel Pfeffer, "British Envoy Tells Israelis Some Un-Diplomatic Truths, and U.K. Jews Should Also Listen In," *Ha'aretz*, February 8, 2012, http://www.haaretz.com/news/diplomacy-defense/british-envoy-tells -israelis-some-un-diplomatic-truths-and-u-k-jews-should-also-listen-in-1 .455643?block=true.

CHAPTER 40: THE EXPLAINERS

213 **despicable nation:** Noam Sheizaf, "Rightist Propaganda Min. Looking for Arabs, Gays to Represent Israel," 972 Magazine, January 4, 2012, http://972mag.com /ultra-right-propaganda-minister-looking-for-arabs-gays-to-represent-israel /32106.

213 **from the comfort of home**: Ali Abunimah, "Israeli Students to Get $2,000 to Spread State Propaganda on Facebook," *Electronic Intifada*, January 4, 2012, http:// electronicintifada.net/blogs/ali-abunimah/israeli-students-get-2000-spread-state -propaganda-facebook.

214 **EL AL Airlines**: Mairav Zonszein, "WATCH: ELAL, Israel's National Airline, Now Part of State PR Efforts," *972 Magazine*, June 28, 2012, http://972mag.com/watch -elal-israels-national-airline-now-part-of-state-pr/49627.

214 *The Ambassador*: Israel At Heart, "The Ambassador Reality TV Show," December 9, 2010, http://www.israelatheart.org/wp/2010/12/the-ambassador-reality-tv-show.

215 **pinkwashing**: Sarah Schulman, "Israel and Pinkwashing," *New York Times*, November 22, 2011, http://www.nytimes.com/2011/11/23/opinion/pinkwashing-and -israels-use-of-gays-as-a-messaging-tool.html?_r=0 Also see Sarah Schulman, "A Documentary Guide to Pinkwashing," *Huffington Post*, December 6, 2011, http:// www.huffingtonpost.com/sarah-schulman/israel-pinkwashing_b_1132369.html, and Asa Winstanley, "In New Pinkwashing Recruitment Campaign, Israel Offers Free Travel for Propaganda Services," *Electronic Intifada*, November 24, 2011, http://electronicintifada.net/blogs/asa-winstanley/new-pinkwashing-recruit -ment-campaign-israel-offers-free-travel-propaganda#.Ts9OKJOqTCQ.twitter.

215 **Mahmoud Ahmadinejad being**: Benjamin Doherty, "Israel Lobby Group Iran180 'Sodomizes' Ahmadinejad Effigy with Nuke at San Francisco Pride," *Electronic Intifada*, June 11, 2012, http://electronicintifada.net/blogs/benjamin-doherty/ israel-lobby-group-iran180-sodomizes-ahmadinejad-effigy-nuke-san-francisco.

215 **I find it absolutely maddening**: Jamie Glazov, " Michael Lucas: A Gay Man for Israel," *FrontPageMag*, May 13, 2011, http://frontpagemag.com/2011/jamie-glazov /michael-lucas-a-gay-man-for-israel.

215 **these men shot their seeds**: Max Blumenthal, "Money Talks, Desecration Walks: Nakba Porn Kingpin Michael Lucas Bullies LGBT Center Against Anti-Apartheid Party," February 24, 2011, http://maxblumenthal.com/2011/02/money-talks -nakba-porn-kingpin-michael-lucas-bullies-the-lgbt-center.

215 **Marc3Pax**: Ali Abunimah, " What Does Fraudulent "Anti-Gay Flotilla" Video Tells Us About Israeli Hasbara Strategy?" *Electronic Intifada*, June 28, 2011, http:// electronicintifada.net/blogs/ali-abunimah/what-does-fraudulent-anti-gay-flotilla -video-tells-us-about-israeli-hasbara.

216 **Guy Seeman**: Max Blumenthal, "Anti-Flotilla Video Fraud Linked to PM Net-anyahu's Office, Official Israeli Hasbara Agents (Updated)," MaxBlumenthal.com,

June 24, 2011 http://maxblumenthal.com/2011/06/anti-flotilla-video-fraud-has
-links-to-pm-netanyahus-office-official-government-hasbara-agents.

216 **All you want to do**: Benjamin Doherty, "Firm That Produced Anti-Flotilla Video
Works for Israeli Government," *Electronic Intifada*, July 7, 2011, http://electronic
intifada.net/blogs/benjamin-doherty/firm-produced-anti-flotilla-video-works
-israeli-government.

216 **Language: A Key Mechanism of Control**: Text of Frank Luntz's 1996 memo for
Gingrich's GOPAC appears at Information Clearing House: http://www.information
clearinghouse.info/article4443.htm.

216 **Luntz was contracted by**: Richard Silverstein, "The Israel Project's Secret Hasbara
Handbook Exposed," Tikun Olam, July 10, 2009, http://www.richardsilverstein
.com/2009/07/10/the-israel-projects-secret-hasbara-handbook-exposed.

216 **undermine the Occupy Wall Street**: Chris Moody, "How Republicans Are Being
Taught to Talk About Occupy Wall Street," Yahoo! News, December 1, 2011,
http://news.yahoo.com/blogs/ticket/republicans-being-taught-talk-occupy-wall
-street-133707949.html.

217   **Palestinian activist Mohammad Othman**: Human Rights Watch, "Israel: End
Arbitrary Detention of Rights Activist," December 4, 2009, http://www.hrw.org
/news/2009/12/04/israel-end-arbitrary-detention-rights-activist.

217 **detained Jamal Juma**: Front Line Defenders, "Israel / OPT: Arrest and Extended
Detention of Human Rights Defender, Mr Jamal Juma," December 23, 2009,
http://www.frontlinedefenders.org/node/2310.

217 **I could be held responsible for**: Leehee Rothschild, "Israeli Interrogated En
Route Home for Activism in Palestinian Cause," *972 Magazine*, March 28, 2012,
http://972mag.com/israeli-interrogated-en-route-back-to-israel-for-her-activism
-in-palestinian-cause/39570.

218 **It is forbidden to initiate**: Avirama Golan, "Protecting Israel from Its Citizens,"
Ha'aretz, February 14, 2011, http://www.haaretz.com/print-edition/opinion
/protecting-israel-from-its-citizens-1.343274.

218 **Alan Dershowitz accused**: Max Blumenthal, "Dershowitz Goes to Tel Aviv," Max-
Blumenthal.com, May 14, 2010, http://maxblumenthal.com/2010/05/dershowitz
-goes-to-tel-aviv.

CHAPTER 41: THE REAL GOVERNMENT

220 **Ramle conference:** Footage from 2012 Ramle Conference by David Sheen can be
viewed at bluepilgrimage's YouTube page under "Racist Ramle Conference:" http://
www.youtube.com/playlist?list=PL84C61219C00A874E.

220 **Application of Israeli Sovereignty**: Tovah Lazaroff, "Likud Politicians Call on
Israel to Annex Area C," *Jerusalem Post*, January 1, 2013, http://www.jpost.com/
Diplomacy-and-Politics/Likud-politicians-call-on-Israel-to-annex-Area-C.

220 **While he casually labeled**: Chaim Levinson, "Right-Wing Extremists Cite Israeli
MK as Source on IDF Movements in West Bank," *Ha'aretz*, January 8, 2012, http://
www.haaretz.com/news/national/right-wing-extremists-cite-israeli-mk-as
-source-on-idf-movements-in-west-bank-1.406158.

220 **this is a battle between**: Harriet Sherwood, "Israel Prepares to Pass Law Banning
Citizens from Calling for Boycotts," *Guardian*, July 11, 2011, http://www.guardian
.co.uk/world/2011/jul/11/israel-law-banning-citizens-boycotts.

222 **The settlers are the real**: Yossi Verter, "The settlers Are the Real Government of
Israel," *Ha'aretz*, July 15, 2011, http://www.haaretz.com/weekend/week-s-end/the
-settlers-are-the-real-government-of-israel-1.373415.

222 **admirable objectives**: Einat Wilf floor speech at Knesset [Hebrew], http://www
.youtube.com/watch?v=SAvwomw_tBQ.

222 **she remembered she was**: Verter, "The settlers are the real government"

223 **I approved the law**: Jonathan Lis, "Netanyahu: Boycott Law Reflects Democracy
in Israel," *Ha'aretz*, July 13, 2011, http://www.haaretz.com/news/diplomacy
-defense/netanyahu-boycott-law-reflects-democracy-in-israel-1.373058.

223 **leading Israel into an abyss**: Leslie Susser, "Livni Sticks to Her Guns," *Jerusalem
Post*, June 30, 2011, http://www.jpost.com/JerusalemReport/Israel/Article.aspx
?id=227306.

223 **you gave in to that pressure**: Lahav Harkov, "Netanyahu at Knesset: I Approved
'Boycott Bill' into Law," *Jerusalem Post*, July 13, 2011, http://www.jpost.com/Diplo
macyAndPolitics/Article.aspx?id=229221.

CHAPTER 42: IT IS NO DREAM

224 **hundreds of young Israeli**: Gil Ronen, "Faux Hamas Demonstration Outside
Home of New Israel Fund Head," Arutz Sheva, January 31, 2010, http://www
.israelnationalnews.com/News/News.aspx/135786#.UW3IqSvwIgI.

225 **Israel would not be facing**: "New Israel Fund Opens Australia Branch," JTA.org,
May 11, 2011, http://www.jta.org/news/article/2011/05/11/3087653/new-israel
-fund-opening-australian-branch.

225 **a leading documenter**: Esti Ahronovitz, "Fighting for Israel's Soul," *Ha'aretz*, July
22, 2011, http://www.haaretz.com/weekend/magazine/fighting-for-israel-s-soul
-1.374700.

225 **a state of all its citizens**: Chemi Shalev, "New NIF Head Brian Luri: 'The Occupation Is a Cancer That Is Eating Us,'" *Ha'aretz*, February 8, 2012, http://www
.haaretz.com/weekend/magazine/new-nif-head-brian-lurie-the-occupation-is-a
-cancer-that-is-eating-us-1.455599?block=true.

225 **foreign agents**: Andrey Ostroukh. "Russia's Putin Signs NGO 'Foreign Agents'
Law," Reuters, July 21, 2012, http://www.reuters.com/article/2012/07/21/us-russia
-putin-ngos-idUSBRE86K05M20120721.

225 **right in every word**: "Israeli Lawmaker Says McCarthy Was Right," JTA, December
5, 2011, http://www.jta.org/news/article/2011/12/05/3090569/israeli-lawmaker
-says-mccarthy-was-right.

226 **the Israeli government's extreme**: Barak Ravid, "U.S., EU Pressure Netanyahu to
Scrap Proposed Bill against Israeli NGOs," *Ha'aretz*, November 13, 2011, http://
www.haaretz.com/print-edition/news/u-s-eu-pressure-netanyahu-to-scrap
-proposed-bill-against-israeli-ngos-1.395220.

226 **the Knesset rushed through**: Jack Khoury and Jonathan Lis, "Knesset Passes Two
Bills Slammed as Discriminatory by Rights Groups," *Ha'aretz*, March 24, 2011,
http://www.haaretz.com/print-edition/news/knesset-passes-two-bills-slammed
-as-discriminatory-by-rights-groups-1.351462.

226 **The year of democracy**: Ronen Shoval, "Probing Israel's Leftist NGOs Is Democracy at Its Best," *Ha'aretz*, January 10, 2011, http://www.haaretz.com/print-edition
/opinion/the-year-of-democracy-1.336142.

CHAPTER 43: RIDING THE ASS

229 **Before founding Im Tirtzu**: Jonathan Lis, "Amid Controversy over New Israel
Fund, Jerusalem Post Drops Group's Head as Columnist," Ha'aretz, February 5,

2010, http://forward.com/articles/125085/amid-controversy-over-new-israel
-fund-jerusalem-po/#ixzz2Qfe2oyg1.

229 **We will burn**: Max Blumenthal, "Revenge of the Nerds: Partying with the Boys of
Im Tirtzu," MaxBlumenthal.com, August 20, 2010, http://maxblumenthal.com
/2010/08/revenge-of-the-nerds-partying-with-the-boys-of-im-tirtzu.

229 **stripped of his rank**: Ibid.

230 **Gush Emunim adopted**: Israel Harel, "Not Gush Emunim, but Zionism," *Ha'aretz*,
December 2, 2011, http://www.haaretz.com/weekend/week-s-end/not-gush
-emunim-but-zionism-1.399141.

230 **Rabbi Zvi Yehuda Kook**: David Hirst, *The Gun and the Olive Branch* (Nation
Books, 1977, 1984, 2003), 83–84.

230 **to be holy, not moral**: Ibid., 84.

230 **death camps**: Yair Ettinger, "Editorial Calling for Death Camps for 'Amalekites'
Raises Storm among Religious," *Ha'aretz*, January 23, 2011, http://www.haaretz
.com/print-edition/news/editorial-calling-for-death-camps-for-amalekites-raises
-storm-among-religious-1.338588.

230 **I will always want**: Shalom Boguslavsky, "The Israeli Right's Secret Strategy to
Promote 'Greater Israel,'" *Mondoweiss*, August 25, 2010, http://mondoweiss.net
/2010/08/the-israeli-rights-secret-strategy-to-promote-greater-israel.html.

231 **you still don't understand**: Richard Silverstein, "Israeli Pop Star Joins Im Tirtzu,
Accusing Peace Activists of 'Knifing' Israel in Back," *Tikun Olam*, April 19, 2010,
http://www.richardsilverstein.com/2010/04/19/israeli-pop-star-joins-im-tirtzu
-accusing-peace-activists-of-knifing-israel-in-back.

231 **The second Zionist revolution**: Ronen Shoval, *Im Tirtzu: A Manifesto For A
Renewed Zionism* (Simania, 2010) [Hebrew].

232 **Everyone can choose to be Jewish**: Ibid.

232 **our connection and commitment**: Coby Ben-Simhon, "Neo-Zionism 101,"
Ha'aretz, June 5, 2009, http://www.haaretz.com/neo-zionism-101-1.277397.

232 **struggle against assimilation**: Rebecca Anna Stoil, "MKs Told More Education
Is Needed to Combat Intermarriage," *Jerusalem Post*, February 11, 2011, http://
www.jpost.com/DiplomacyAndPolitics/Article.aspx?id=207772.

232 **We can change**: Israel National TV, July 28, 2011, http://www.youtube.com/watch
?v=nlzyp8jJMO8.

232 **we can finally denote**: Jonathan Lis, "Kadima Lawmakers Retract Support for Bill
Scrapping Arabic as Official Language in Israel," *Ha'aretz*, August 5, 2011, http://
www.haaretz.com/print-edition/news/kadima-lawmakers-retract-support-for
-bill-scrapping-arabic-as-official-language-in-israel-1.377031.

232 **a $100,000 cash infusion**: Gil Shefler, "John Hagee to Cut Im Tirtzu Funding,"
Jerusalem Post, August 23, 2010, http://www.jpost.com/JewishWorld/JewishNews
/Article.aspx?id=185721.

233 **Nakba Bullshit**: Yossi Gurvitz, "Rightwing Group Publishes Nakba Denial Booklet," *972 Magazine*, May 14, 2011, http://972mag.com/rightwing-group-publishes
-nakba-denial-booklet.

233 **investigate and punish**: Yaakov Katz, "Im Tirtzu Calls for Criminal Investigation
of Machsom Watch," *Jerusalem Post*, May 2, 2011, http://www.jpost.com/Defense
/Im-Tirtzu-calls-for-criminal-investigation-of-Machsom-Watch.

233 **early and troubling signs**: Nir Hasson, "Jerusalem Court Starts Debating Meaning of Fascism as Im Tirtzu Sues Activists," *Ha'aretz*, February 12, 2012, http://

www.haaretz.com/print-edition/news/jerusalem-court-starts-debating-meaning
-of-fascism-as-im-tirtzu-sues-activists-1.412357.

CHAPTER 44: THE REVOLUTIONARIES

234 **gathered for a night:** Blumenthal, "Revenge of the Nerds: Partying With The Boys
of Im Tirtzu," MaxBlumenthal.com.

CHAPTER 45: ZION SQUARE

237 **Oz Unit had appeared:** Nir Hasson, "Report: Israel Cops Nab Czech Peace Activist in Ramallah Raid," Ha'aretz, January 21, 2010, http://www.haaretz.com/print
-edition/news/report-israel-cops-nab-czech-peace-activist-in-ramallah-raid-1
.261798.

237 **planned demolition:** "Controversy in Jerusalem: The City of David," *CBS News*,
October 18, 2010, http://www.cbsnews.com/8301-18560_162-6958082.html.

239 **Death to Arabs!:** Max Blumenthal, "Inside the Occupation, Part Two," May 30,
2009, http://www.youtube.com/watch?v=E1q8yfdpmv4.

239 **a 150 percent rate:** Harriet Sherwood, "Jewish Settler Attacks on Palestinians
Listed as 'Terrorist Incidents' by US," *Guardian*, August 19, 2012, http://www
.guardian.co.uk/world/2012/aug/19/jewish-settler-attack-terrorist-us-palestin
ian.

239 **trumped-up charges:** Unedited video of the incident Nawi was charged for can
be seen on YouTube.com at "Support Israeli Human Rights Activist Ezra Nawi,"
uploaded on April 29, 2009, http://www.youtube.com/watch?v=ysIaQUJWBdk.

240 **shot by a settler:** Tovah Lazaroff, "Settlers Fire at Palestinian and Israeli Olive Pick-
ers," *Jerusalem Post*, October 19, 2002, http://www.taayush.org/new/harvest4.htm.

240 **torched the farmers' fields:** "Settlers Destroy over 120 Fruit Trees Belonging to
Farmers from Khirbet Safa," Taayush, June 22, 2009, http://www.taayush.org
/?p=173.

240 **self-hating Jew:** Barak Ravid, "Netanyahu's Paranoia Extends to 'Self-Hating Jews'
Emanuel and Axelrod," *Ha'aretz*, July 9, 2009, http://www.haaretz.com/print-edition
/news/netanyahu-s-paranoia-extends-to-self-hating-jews-emanuel-and-axelrod
-1.279611.

240 **Our first interview:** Max Blumenthal and Joseph Dana, "Feeling the Hate in Jerusalem," MaxBlumenthal.com, http://maxblumenthal.com/feeling-the-hate-in
-jerusalem.

240 **Crack Square:** Erica Chernofsky, "Falling Through the Cracks," *Jerusalem Post*,
March 9, 2006, http://www.jpost.com/Local-Israel/In-Jerusalem/Falling-through
-the-cracks.

242 **on a mission:** Benjamin Hartman, "Jews Gone Wild: Why Camcorders and Booze
Don't Mix," *Ha'aretz*, June 11, 2009, http://www.haaretz.com/news/opinion-jews
-gone-wild-why-camcorders-and-booze-don-t-mix-1.277739.

242 **they try to fit in:** Lahav Harkov, "Jewish Americans Bash Obama in Jerusalem
Beer Fest," *France 24*, June 16, 2009, http://observers.france24.com/content/2009
0615-jewish-americans-bash-obama-tel-aviv-beer-fest-israel-racism-muslims.

242 **Blumenthal needs to grow up:** Ron Kampeas, "Best Take So Far on Blumen-Jour-
nalism," *JTA*, June 6, 2009, http://blogs.jta.org/politics/article/2009/06/05
/1005678/best-take-so-far-on-blumen-journalism.

242 **I saw that his shirt:** Aviad Glickman. "Alleged Stabber 'Hated Arabs,'" *Ynetnews*,
March 4, 2011, http://www.ynetnews.com/articles/0,7340,L-4037569,00.html.
Also see Max Blumenthal and Joseph Dana, "Facing Up to Jewish Nationalism

and Racist Violence," *Electronic Intifada*, March 3, 2011, http://electronicintifada .net/content/facing-jewish-nationalism-and-racist-violence/9254.

242 **To kill an Arab**: Ibid.

243 **This is not worth anything**: Ira Glunts, "Light Sentence in Brutal Murder Shows Double Standard for Jews, Palestinians," *Mondoweiss*, July 15, 2012, http://mondoweiss.net/2012/07/light-sentence-in-brutal-murder-shows-double-standard -for-jews-palestinians.html.

243 **Israel today feels like**: "Social Affairs Minister: Israel Today Feels Like Alabama in the 1940s," *Ha'aretz*, January 13, 2011, http://www.haaretz.com/news/ national/social-affairs-minister-israel-today-feels-like-alabama-in-the-1940s-1 .336802.

CHAPTER 46: THE ISRAELI EXPERIENCE

244 **whose presence there dated**: Tom Abowd, "The Moroccan Quarter: A History of the Present," Jerusalem Quarterly, Winter 2000, 7, http://www.jerusalemquarterly .org/images/ArticlesPdf/7_the%20moroccan.pdf.

245 **the municipality will continue**: Lia Tarachansky, "Thousands of Israeli Youth Chant 'Mohammed Is Dead,'" *TheRealNews*, June 5, 2011, http://therealnews.com /t2/index.php?option=com_content&task=view&id=31&Itemid=74&jumival =6886#.UT35cdEjpz1.

245 **we can kill you**: Ibid.

245 **in the dead of night**: Video of the al-Kurd family being thrown out of their home to make way for Jewish settlers can be viewed on Youtube at "Israeli Police evicts Palestinian Family, Sheikh Jarrah, 3 November 2009," uploaded by user 1969scooter, November 3, 2009, http://www.youtube.com/watch?v=GryF_GoZ4iw.

246 **there's still a lot left to go**: Tarachansky, "Thousands of Israeli Youth"

CHAPTER 47: ULTRAS

247 **a common chant in almost**: Ali Abunimah, "Anti-Arab Racism and Incitement in Israel," Palestine Center Information Brief No. 161 (March 25, 2008), http:// www.thejerusalemfund.org/ht/display/ContentDetails/i/2242/pid/v.

247 **provoking the crowd**: Larry Derfner, "When an Israeli Soccer Game Looks Like a Klan Rally," *972 Magazine*, November 2, 2012, http://972mag.com/when-an -israeli-soccer-game-looks-like-a-klan-rally/58818.

248 **arrested and stripped**: Ofri Ilani and Yoav Stern, "Arab Student Chair Apprehended for Refusing to Shake Peres' Hand," *Ha'aretz*, November 2, 2008, http:// www.haaretz.com/news/arab-student-chair-apprehended-for-refusing-to-shake -peres-hand-1.256482.

248 **the players were not**: Todd Warnick, "Israel's Arab-Free Soccer Team," *Tablet*, May 14, 2012, http://www.tabletmag.com/jewish-news-and-politics/99407/israels -arab-free-soccer-team.

248 **from there on we fight**: "Interview with La Familia (Beitar Jerusalem-Israel)," Ultras-Tifo.net, January 6, 2008, http://www.ultras-tifo.net/interviews/36-interview -with-la-familia-beitar-jerUSalem-israel.html.

248 **I don't care what**: Izzy Ein Dor. "Beitar Jerusalem Captain: Sorry for Wanting Arab Player," *Ynetnews*, November 20, 2009, http://www.ynetnews.com/articles /0,7340,L-3808080,00.html.

248 **scenes of mob violence**: Gabe Fisher, "Soccer Fans Riot after J'lem Loss to Arab Team," *Times of Israel*, February 5, 2012, http://www.timesofisrael.com/soccer -fans-riot-after-jlem-loss-to-arab-team.

248 **It was a mass lynching**: Oz Rosenberg, "Hundreds of Beitar Jerusalem Fans Beat
     Up Arab Workers in Mall; No Arrests," *Ha'aretz*, March 23, 2012, http://www
     .haaretz.com/print-edition/news/hundreds-of-beitar-jerusalem-fans-beat-up
     -arab-workers-in-mall-no-arrests-1.420270.

249 **an unprecedented pogrom**: Gilad Schubert, "Tibi: Beitar Riots—Unprecedented
     Pogrom," *Ynetnews*, March 25, 2012, http://www.ynetnews.com/articles/0,7340,L
     -4207555,00.html.

249 **two Muslim players**: Moshe Boker. "Muslim Soccer Players at Beitar Jerusalem
     Met with Spitting and Insults," *Ha'aretz*, January 2, 2013, http://www.haaretz.com
     /news/national/muslim-soccer-players-at-beitar-jerusalem-met-with-spitting
     -and-insults.premium-1.500881.

249 **Beitar is pure forever**: Orly Halpern, "Are Beitar Jerusalem's Racist Fans Ruining
     Israeli Soccer?" *Daily Beast*, February 21, 2013, http://www.thedailybeast.com
     /articles/2013/02/21/are-beitar-jerusalem-s-racist-fans-ruining-israeli-soccer
     .html.

249 **Two members of La Familia**: Moshe Boker, "Israel Arrests Beitar Jerusalem Fans
     Suspected of Torching Soccer Club's Office," *Ha'aretz*, February 19, 2013, http://
     www.haaretz.com/news/national/israel-arrests-beitar-jerusalem-fans-suspected
     -of-torching-soccer-club-s-office.premium-1.504555.

CHAPTER 48: THE BEST TIME OF THEIR LIVES

250 **The army:** Dimi Reider, "The Best Years of Her Life: Fond Memories of Blind-
     folded Prisoners," August 16, 2010, http://reider.wordpress.com/2010/08/16/the
     -best-years-of-her-life-fond-memories-of-blindfolded-prisoners.

251 **I bound many wrists**: Aluf Benn, "When I Was Eden Abergil," *Ha'aretz*, Septem-
     ber 1, 2010, http://www.haaretz.com/print-edition/opinion/when-i-was-eden
     -abergil-1.311390.

251 **Our political views**: Ibid.

251 **you don't even have**: Gideon Levy, "A Response to Pfc. Benn," *Ha'aretz*, September
     2, 2010, http://www.haaretz.com/print-edition/opinion/a-response-to-pfc-benn
     -1.311650.

251 **blind to the fact**: Boaz Fyler. "Facebook Scandal: More Soldiers' Photos Pub-
     lished," *Ynetnews*, August 17, 2010, http://www.ynetnews.com/articles/0,7340,L
     -3938324,00.html.

251 *To See If I'm Smiling*: Tamar Yarom, *To See If I'm Smiling*, (2007, First Hand
     Films); also see Dalia Karpel, "My God, What Did We Do?" *Ha'aretz*, November 8,
     2007, http://www.haaretz.com/weekend/magazine/my-god-what-did-we-do-1
     .232798.

251 **at least as shocking**: "'Facebook Photos of Soldiers Posing with Bound Palestinians
     Are the Norm,'" *Ha'aretz*, August 17, 2010, http://www.haaretz.com/news/diplo
     macy-defense/facebook-photos-of-soldiers-posing-with-bound-palestinians-are
     -the-norm-1.308582.

252 **I am not sorry**: "'I Would Gladly Kill Arabs— Even Slaughter Them,'" *Ha'aretz*,
     August 19, 2010, http://www.haaretz.com/news/national/i-would-gladly-kill
     -arabs-even-slaughter-them-1.309031.

253 **Favorite food**: Richard Silverstein,"Ziad Jilani's Israeli Police Murderer Exposed for
     First Time," RichardSilverstein.com, April 12, 2012, http://www.richardsilverstein
     .com/2012/04/19/ziad-jilanis-israeli-police-murderer-exposed-for-first-time.

253 **A disgusting picture**: Richard Silverstein, "AFP Identifies Palestinian Abuse Vic-
     tim in YouTube Video, Twitter Does the Rest," *Tikun Olam*, October 7, 2010,

http://www.richardsilverstein.com/2010/10/07/afp-identifies-palestinian-abuse-victim-in-youtube-video.

253 **Destroy Turkey and all**: Ibid.

254 **It was, by all accounts**: Amira Hass, "Israel Police Shoots First and Asks Questions Later," *Ha'aretz*, April 27, 2012, http://www.haaretz.com/weekend/week-s-end/israel-police-shoots-first-and-asks-questions-later-1.426844.

254 **I just want the two men**: Jillian Kestler-D'Amours, "American Demands Justice for Her Husband, Murdered by Israel in Broad Daylight," *Electronic Intifada*, May 24, 2012, http://electronicintifada.net/content/american-demands-justice-her-husband-murdered-israel-broad-daylight/11325.

254 **how to best avoid**: Richard Silverstein. "Aftermath of IDF Belly-Dancing Sex Abuse Video: New Courses on How to Avoid Cyber-Emarrassment [sic.]," *Tikun Olam*, October 7, 2010, http://www.richardsilverstein.com/2010/10/07/aftermath-of-idf-belly-dancing-sex-abuse-video-new-courses-on-how-to-avoid-cyber-emarrassment.

CHAPTER 49: THE BASE

255 **the sharp blade of a knife:** Shira Robinson, Occupied Citizens in a Liberal State: Palestinians Under Military Rule and the Colonial Formation of Israeli Society, 1948-1966, PhD diss., Stanford University 2005, p. 118.

255 **only 12 were prosecuted:** B'Tselem, "Human Rights in the Occupied Territories: 2011 Annual Report," March 10, 2011, p. 14.

256 **Our soldiers serve:** "Druze Rally Against 'State Discrimination' near Netanyahu Office," *Ha'aretz*, June 21, 2009, http://www.haaretz.com/news/druze-rally-against-state-discrimination-near-netanyahu-office-1.278517.

CHAPTER 50: THE PROPHETS

263 **For a Greater Israel:** Tom Segev, 1967: Israel, the War, and the Year that Transformed the Middle East (Metropolitan Books, 2005), 545.

264 **the conscience of Israel:** Isaiah Berlin, *Isaiah Berlin: Volume 1: Letters, 1928-1946* (Cambridge University Press, 2004), 18.

264 **Religious nationalism is:** Eyal Sivan, *Yeshayahu Leibowitz: He Will Overcome*, 1993, http://www.eyalsivan.info/index.php?p=fichefilm&id=23#&panel1-2.

264 **war in constant:** Yeshayahu Leibowitz, *Judaism, Human Values, and the Jewish State,* (Harvard University Press, 1992), 224.

264 **The Arabs would be:** Ibid., 225–226.

264 **unpartitioned Eretz Israel:** Ibid., 233.

264 **this strange system:** Sivan, *Yeshayahu Leibowitz.*

265 **concentration camps:** Tanya Reubnhardt. *Road Map to Nowhere: Israel/Palestine Since 2003* (Verso, 2006), 173.

265 **Matzpen represented:** Eran Torbiner, *Matzpen: Anti-Zionists in Israel,* (2003, Alma Films).

265 **right-wing mobs:** from interview with Akiva Orr, August 20, 2010; also "The Return of Kahane," *Palestine Monitor*, October 19, 2010, http://www.uruknet.info/?p=70942. According to the article, Jamal Zahalka was a student at the same time in Hebrew University; he studied pharmacology while Lieberman studied International Relations. Zahalka remembers Lieberman's guttural Hebrew "calling to throw Arabs from the university," and his discrimination as a bouncer for the student club Kastel. "He tried all the time to make a selection between Arabs and Jews," Zahalka said, adding Lieberman was never on the front lines of

violence. "Because he's a coward, when there was physical violence, he just escaped."

265 **Shimon Tzabar**: Shimon Tzabar, "The Aftermath of the 6 Days' War," ShimonTzabar.com, http://www.shimontzabar.com/about/shimons-own-words-politics/the -aftermath-of-the-six-days-war.html.

265 **Occupation leads to**: Ibid.

266 **Do they really desire**: Ibid.

266 **When I realized**: Shimon Tzabar, "Israel Imperial News and Beyond," ShimonTzabar.com, http://www.shimontzabar.com/about/shimons-own-words-politics /israel-imperial-news-1968-and-beyond.html.

267 **nineteenth-century outlook**: Leibowitz. *Judaism, Human Values*, 196.

267 **I want to be a Jew**: Ibid.

267 **I am concerned with**: Sivan, *Yeshayahu Leibowitz*.

267 **For that the Jewish people**: Ibid.

267 **I tell them they are**: Ibid.

267 **I'm not interested**: Ibid.

268 **Israel is the only dictatorship**: Ibid.

268 **cause further rancor**: Ibid.

CHAPTER 51: CHANGE FROM WITHIN

269 **better culture and better conduct**: Mimi Micner, "Why Recent Events Make Me Want to Serve in IDF," Partners for Progressive Israel, August 18, 2010, http:// meretzusa.blogspot.com/2010/08/why-recent-events-make-me-want-to-serve .html.

269 **No Palestinian may enter**: "Definition of Sterile," Breaking the Silence, http:// www.breakingthesilence.org.il/testimonies/database/54145.

271 **Mouthpieces for Europe**: Anne Herzberg and Naftali Balanson, "Mouthpieces for Europe," *Ynetnews*, November 20, 2011, http://www.ynetnews.com/articles /0,7340,L-4150695,00.html.

271 **backed by terrorists**: Nathan Jeffay and Nathan Guttman, "Knesset to Investigate Funding of Left-Wing Israeli NGOs for Terror Ties," *Jewish Daily Forward*, January 21, 2011, http://forward.com/articles/134637/knesset-to-investigate-funding -of-left-wing-israel.

271 **a litany of atrocities**: "Soldiers' Testimonies from Hebron: 2005-2007," published in 2008, http://www.breakingthesilence.org.il/wp-content/uploads/2011/02/Soldiers _Testimonies_from_Hebron_2005_2007_Eng.pdf.

CHAPTER 52: THE INSIDERS

272 **We did not know then**: Jonathan Shainin, "David Grossman, The Art of Fiction No. 194," The Paris Review, Fall 2007, No. 182, http://www.theparisreview.org /interviews/5794/the-art-of-fiction-no-194-david-grossman.

272 **The most beautiful**: Yehouda Shenhav, *Beyond The Two-State Solution: A Jewish Political Essay* (Polity Press, 2012), 23.

272 **The second decade**: Ibid., 42.

272 **advances the nationalistic ideas**: Ibid., 25.

273 **afterward, everything happened**: David Grossman, *The Yellow Wind* (Macmillan, 2002), 212.

273 **What happened to us?**: Ibid.

273 **boycott of a new cultural center**: Boaz Fyler, "Yehoshua, Oz, Grossman Back Boycott of Ariel," *Ynetnews*, August 30, 2010, http://www.ynetnews.com/articles /0,7340,L-3946485,00.html.

273 **abandoned their homes**: "FAQ: Israel, the Conflict and Peace," Israel Ministry of Foreign Affairs, November 1, 2007, http://www.mfa.gov.il/MFA/MFAArchive /2000_2009/2003/11/Israel-%20the%20Conflict%20and%20Peace-%20 Answers%20to%20Frequen.

273 **due to the orders of Zionism**: Max Blumenthal, "Knesset Speaker Reuven Rivlin's Admission: Israel 'Expelled Arabs' from Palestine in 1948," September 9, 2010, http://maxblumenthal.com/2010/09/knesset-speaker-reuven-rivlins-admission -israel-expelled-arabs-across-palestine-in-1948.

274 **the leftist of**: David Grossman, "Uri, My Dear Son," eulogy translated and published in *The Observer*, August 19, 2006, http://www.guardian.co.uk/world/2006 /aug/20/syria.comment.

274 **Israeli Martin Luther King**: George Packer. "The Unconsoled," *New Yorker*, September 27, 2010, http://www.newyorker.com/reporting/2010/09/27/100927fa_fact _packer?currentPage=all.

276 **This option that terrifies**: Philip Weiss, "I Don't Think Zionism Will Be Redeemed by David Grossman," *Mondoweiss*, October 17, 2010, http://mondo weiss.net/2010/10/i-dont-think-zionism-will-be-redeemed-by-david-grossman .html.

277 **A Declaration of Independence from Fascism**: "We Will Not Be Citizens of a Fascist State Purporting to Be Israel," *Gush Shalom*, October 10, 2010, http://zope .gush-shalom.org/home/ar/events/1286745470.

CHAPTER 53: THE HUNTED

278 **we will hunt you**: Max Blumenthal, David Jacobus, and Jesse Rosenfeld, "Israel's Terror Inside—Documentary Trailer," http://www.youtube.com/watch?v=9Qt 38NoPqrU.

280 **Menachem Mazuz approved**: Amos Harel, Tomer Zarchin, and Yuval Goren, "Police Arrest Seven Suspected of Inciting IDF Draft-Dodging," *Ha'aretz*, April 27, 2009, http://www.haaretz.com/print-edition/news/police-arrest-seven-suspected -of-inciting-idf-draft-dodging-1.274862 Also see Aviad Glickman, "Case against 'New Profile' Closed," *Ynetnews*, http://www.ynetnews.com/articles/0,7340,L -3798368,00.html.

280 **more than forty-five hundred**: Sahar Vardi, "IDF on 'Hunt' for Draft Dodgers, Deserters," *972 Magazine*, May 22, 2012, http://972mag.com/idf-on-hunt-for -draft-dodgers-deserters/46443.

280 **I am being held**: "IDF Imprisons Canadian Israeli Who Arrived for a Chasunah," *Yeshiva World News*, September 5, 2012, http://www.theyeshivaworld.com/article .php?p=139343000

280 **They treated us like we were dogs:** Philip Podolsky, "Canadian-Israeli 'Deserter' Sentenced to 3 Months In Prison," *Times of Israel*, September 27, 2012, http://www .timesofisrael.com/canadian-israeli-deserter-sentenced-to-3-months-in-prison.

281 **intensely observed, heavily condensed**: For a critical exploration of the effect of the spring holiday season on the Israeli psyche, and of the militaristic undertones that course through the national ceremonies, see Eyal Sivan's 1991 documentary, *"Yizkor: Slaves of Memory."*

282 **Who wants to kill us?**: Dimi Reider. "Israeli Preschool Activity: Who Wants to Kill Us?" *972 Magazine*, May 5, 2011, http://972mag.com/fear.

283 **when I shoot, my friends**: Itamar Rose, " Israeli Kids in the Army Museum," September 20, 2012, http://www.youtube.com/watch?v=Qp67KehlVGU.

283 **they are viewed**: Or Kashti, "Students on Trip to IDF Base Simulated Shooting Targets with Arab Headdress," *Ha'aretz*, April 3, 2011, http://www.haaretz.com/print

-edition/news/students-on-trip-to-idf-base-simulated-shooting-targets-with
-arab-headdress-1.353728.

283 **reduced tuition fees**: From the Mahal "lone soldiers" recruitment website: "Opt-
ing for an upgraded status in Israel after discharge from the IDF (from A1 or A2
to "immigrant") makes you eligible for assistance from the Student Authority
including exemption from Israeli university tuition fees," http://www.mahal-idf
-volunteers.org/about/stepbystep.htm

283 **training to become sushi chefs**: Gili Cohen, " Israel Allocates Funds to Help Former IDF Soldiers Become Sushi Chefs," *Ha'aretz*, January 2, 2012, http://www
.haaretz.com/print-edition/news/israel-allocates-funds-to-help-former-idf-soldiers
-become-sushi-chefs-1.404985.

283 **there is a clear message**: "Deal of Ariel University Centre: No Loyalty, No Studies," *Alternative News*, August 20, 2012, http://www.alternativenews.org/english
/index.php/news/news-updates/5090-dean-of-ariel-university-centre-no-loyalty
-no-studies-html.

284 **threatened to spray them**: Annie Robbins, " Palestinian Students at Israeli College Say They Were Forced to Stand to Honor War Dead," *Mondoweiss*, May 6,
2012, http://mondoweiss.net/2012/05/palestinian-students-at-israeli-college-say
-they-were-forced-to-stand-to-honor-war-dead.html.

CHAPTER 54: CANCELING THE OTHER NARRATIVE

285 **Smadar was killed:** Harriet Sherwood, "Academic Claims Israeli School Textbooks Contain Bias," Guardian, August 6, 2011, http://www.guardian.co.uk/world
/2011/aug/07/israeli-school-racism-claim.

286 **My people are those**: Munib A. Younan, *Witnessing for Peace: In Jerusalem and
the World* (Fortress Press, 2003), 105.

286 **ordering a payment**: Sami Kishawi, "Abir Aramin, Age 10, Killed and 'Bought' by
the State of Israel," *Sixteen Minutes to Palestine*, September 26, 2011, http://smpal-
estine.com/2011/09/26/abir-aramin-age-10-killed-and-bought-by-the-state-of
-israel.

286 **a fine amounting to**: Ibid.

286 **Abir's parents seek justice**: Nurit Peled Elhanan, "No Sympathy from the Court,"
Ma'an News Agency, October 19, 2009, http://www.maannews.net/eng/ViewDetails
.aspx?ID=233359.

286 **I am Bassam Aramin**: Rami Elhanan, "I Am Bassam Aramin," *Ha'aretz*, April 4,
2008, http://www.haaretz.com/print-edition/opinion/i-am-bassam-aramin-1
.243374.

286 **What insanity**: Lillian Rosengarten, "Rosengarten Reflects on the 'Insanity' of the
Response to the Jewish Boat to Gaza," *Mondoweiss*, November 21, 2010, http://
mondoweiss.net/2010/11/rosengarten-reflects-on-the-insanity-of-the-response
-to-the-jewish-boat-to-gaza.html.

287 **has probably not learned**: Aviel Magnezi, "Navy Stops Gaza-Bound 'Jewish Ves-
sel,'" *Ynetnews*, September 28, 2010, http://www.ynetnews.com/articles/0,7340,L
-3961280,00.html.

287 **a key destination:** "Mevasseret Zion Absorption Center," The Jewish Agency for Israel,
http://www.jewishagency.org/JewishAgency/English/Aliyah/Contact+Addresses
/delegations/EthiopianAliyah/AbsorptionCenters/Mevasseret.htm.

288 **neither customs nor traditions**: Nurit Peled-Elhanan, *Palestine in Israeli School
Books: Ideology and Propaganda in Education* (I.B. Tauris, 2012), 49.

288 **a group of armed men**: Ibid., 54.

288 **use what they call**: Ibid., 51.

288 **geography curricula in Israel**: Ibid., 102.

288 **the Land of Israel is**: Ibid., 104.

289 *Danni Din*'s **war on Arab**: Noam Sheizaf, "The Israeli Incitement Problem: A Look at a Children's Book," *972 Magazine*, March 29, 2011, http://972mag.com /the-israeli-incitement-problem.

290 **it would be superficial**: Tamar Rotem, "From a More Innocent Time: The Little Black Boy of Our Childhood Books," *Ha'aretz*, July 18, 2012, http://www.haaretz .com/news/features/from-a-more-innocent-time-the-little-black-boy-of-our -childhood-books-1.451826.

290 **I believe that innocence**: Ibid.

290 **awarded the Israel Prize**: Ibid.

290 **it was a term used**: Ibid.

290 **Wow Uzi!**: Lia Tarachansky, "Selling Israeli Militarism Like Toothpaste," *TheReal-News*, June 23, 2011, http://therealnews.com/t2/index.php?option=com_content &task=view&id=31&Itemid=74&jumival=6942#.UT9ZSNEjpzo.

CHAPTER 55: THE BEAUTY BRIGADE

292 **best women to the pilots**: Maryann Bird, "Pilot Scheme Has Chauvinist Overtones," *Independent*, November 17, 1995, http://www.independent.co.uk/news/world/pilot -scheme-has-chauvinist-overtones-1582309.html.

292 **Weizman resigned**: Jonathan Lis, Ran Reznick and David Ratner, "Former President Ezer Weizman, an Architect of Peace with Egypt, Dies at 80," *Ha'aretz*, April 25, 2005, http://www.haaretz.com/print-edition/news/former-president-ezer -weizman-an-architect-of-peace-with-egypt-dies-at-80-1.156846.

292 **Girls are not part**: Gal Harmat, "Fresh Meat, Fresh Sweets–Militarism and Sexism in Israel," United Nations University for Peace, 2004.

293 **Hot Israeli chick**: Alison Kaplan Sommer, "Hot Israeli Chick with Gun Occupies Internet," *Ha'aretz*, May 31, 2012, http://www.haaretz.com/blogs/routine-emer gencies/hot-israeli-chick-with-gun-occupies-internet-1.433693.

293 **kidnapping kits**: "IDF Hands Out 'Anti-Kidnapping Kits,'" *Arutz Sheva*, September 14, 2012, http://www.israelnationalnews.com/wap/Item.aspx?type=0&item=159998.

293 **at least 80 percent had suffered**: "80% of IDF Women Claim Harassment," *JWeekly*, June 6, 2003, http://www.jweekly.com/article/full/20046/80-of-idf -women-claim-harassment.

293 **It is common knowledge**: Harmat, "Fresh Meat."

294 **Homosexual activity**: Amnon Meranda, "Homosexual Activity Cause of Earthquake, Shas MK Says," *Ynetnews*, February 20, 2008, http://www.ynetnews.com /articles/0,7340,L-3509263,00.html.

294 **Haim Ramon, accused of**: Aron Heller, "Former Israeli President Convicted of Rape," Associated Press, December 30, 2010, http://www.nbcnews.com/id /40849923/ns/world_news-mideastn_africa/#.UT9HVtEjpzo.

294 **Yitzhak Mordechai, a former**: Joel Greenberg, "Ex-Israeli President Convicted of Rape, Other Sexual Offenses," *Washington Post*, December 31, 2010, http://www .washingtonpost.com/wp-dyn/content/article/2010/12/30/AR2010123004292 .html.

294 **Moshe Katsav was convicted**: Ibid.

294 **one of four women**: Richard Boudreaux, "Israeli Women Battle a Culture of Harassment," *Los Angeles Times*, December 24, 2006, http://articles.latimes.com /2006/dec/24/world/fg-harass24.

CHAPTER 56: LIFELONG DRAFTEES

295 **meaningful service:** Talila Nesher, "IDF Launches Educational Offensive on Israel's Schools," Ha'aretz, June 12, 2012, http://www.haaretz.com/news/national/idf-launches-educational-offensive-on-israel-s-schools.premium-1.435940.

295 **a moral issue:** Ibid.

295 **Teachers are lifelong draftees:** Ibid.

295 **it's a part of my soul:** Ibid.

295 **damages one of the most:** Or Kashti, "Tel Aviv Principal Defends Banning IDF Program from His School," Ha'aretz, February 8, 2010, http://www.haaretz.com/print-edition/news/tel-aviv-principal-defends-banning-idf-program-from-his-school-1.262934.

296 **Talk to each other:** Gideon Levy, "Teacher of a Lifetime," Ha'aretz, January 7, 2010, http://www.haaretz.com/print-edition/opinion/teacher-of-a-lifetime-1.260947.

296 **A principal who thinks he can preach:** Ibid.

297 **as if on holy ground:** Nesher, "IDF Launches Educational Offensive"

297 **expressions of racism:** Max Blumenthal, "Israeli Teachers: 'Racism . . . Is Growing among Young People in Israel. We Are Witnesses to This Growing Racism in Education," December 31, 2010, http://maxblumenthal.com/2010/12/israeli-teachers-racism-is-growing-among-young-people-in-israel-we-are-witnesses-to-this-growing-racism-in-education.

298 **more nationalistic in recent years:** Ibid.

298 **Jewish culture and tradition:** Or Kashti, "Israel to Introduce Revamped Jewish Studies Curriculum in State Schools," Ha'aretz, June 24, 2010, http://www.haaretz.com/news/national/israel-to-introduce-revamped-jewish-studies-curriculum-in-state-schools-1.297957.

298 **the total deportation:** Talila Nesher. "Most Israeli 12th-Graders Support Deportation of African Refugees," Ha'aretz, August 22, 2012, http://www.haaretz.com/news/national/most-israeli-12th-graders-support-deportation-of-african-refugees-1.459813.

299 **This would harm:** "Israeli Civics Exam: Explain Why Jewish Girls Shouldn't Hang Around with Arabs," Alternative News, June 11, 2012, http://alternativenews.org/english/index.php/news/israeli-society/4500-israeli-civics-exam-explain-why-jewish-girls-shouldnt-hang-around-with-arabs.html.

299 **harm their right to life:** Ibid.

CHAPTER 57: HOW TO KILL GOYIM AND INFLUENCE PEOPLE

303 **230 pages on the laws:** Max Blumenthal, "How to Kill Goyim and Influence People," Alternet, August 29, 2010, http://www.alternet.org/story/148016/how_to_kill_goyim_and_influence_people%3A_israeli_rabbis_defend_book's_shocking_religious_defense_of_killing_non-jews_(with_video).

303 **uncompassionate by nature:** Ibid.

303 **not only during combat with adults:** Ibid.

304 **even if that gentile:** Max Blumenthal, "Inside Torat Hamelech, the Jewish Extremist Terror Tract Endorsed bby State-Employed Rabbis," July 7, 2011, http://maxblumenthal.com/2011/07/inside-torat-hamelech-the-jewish-extremist-terror-tract.

304 **his killing is permissible:** Ibid.

304 **any person who weakens:** Ibid.

304 **they can be hurt:** Ibid.

304 **the infants are the ones:** Ibid.

304 **Something like this**: Yossi Sarid, "Any Bastard Can Be a Rabbi," *Ha'aretz*, August 27, 2010, http://www.haaretz.com/print-edition/opinion/any-bastard-can-be-a-rabbi-1.310463.

304 **fomenting or justifying**: Chaim Levinson, "Britain Denies Entry to Israeli Rabbi Who Advocated Killing of Non-Jews," *Ha'aretz*, August 11, 2011, http://www.haaretz.com/print-edition/news/britain-denies-entry-to-israeli-rabbi-who-advocated-killing-of-non-jews-1.378065.

305 **I want the State to hold**: Stuart Schoffman, "Raw Deal," *Tablet*, October 28, 2011, http://www.tabletmag.com/jewish-news-and-politics/81660/raw-deal.

305 **the fulfillment of the Zionist**: Joseph E. Davis, *Stories of Change: Narrative and Social Movements* (SUNY Press, 2002), 139.

307 **Goyim were born only to serve**: Natasha Mozgovaya, "ADL Slams Shas Spiritual Leader for Saying Non-Jews 'Were Born to Serve Jews.'" *Ha'aretz*, October 20, 2010, http://www.haaretz.com/jewish-world/adl-slams-shas-spiritual-leader-for-saying-non-jews-were-born-to-serve-jews-1.320235.

307 **Does anyone want to change**: Max Blumenthal, "Inside Torat Hamelech, the Jewish Extremist Terror Tract Endorsed by State-Employed Rabbis," July 7, 2011, http://maxblumenthal.com/2011/07/inside-torat-hamelech-the-jewish-extremist-terror-tract.

307 **Thus may all of Israel's**: Ehud Sprinzak, *The Ascendance of Israel's Radical Right* (Oxford University Press, 1991), 97.

308 **against Jewish people**: Blumenthal, "How to Kill Goyim"

308 **Jewish fanatic Baruch Goldstein**: Avi Issacharoff and Chaim Levinson, "Settlers Remember Gunman Goldstein; Hebron Riots Continue," *Ha'aretz*, February 28, 2010, http://www.haaretz.com/print-edition/news/settlers-remember-gunman-goldstein-hebron-riots-continue-1.263834.

308 **Od Yosef Chai has raked**: Akiva Eldar, "Who Is Funding the Rabbi Who Endorses Killing Gentile Babies," *Ha'aretz*, November 17, 2009, http://www.haaretz.com/print-edition/features/who-is-funding-the-rabbi-who-endorses-killing-gentile-babies-1.4005.

308 **the Central Fund transferred**: Akiva Eldar, "U.S. Tax Dollars Fund Rabbi Who Excused Killing Gentile Babies," *Ha'aretz*, December 15, 2009, http://www.haaretz.com/print-edition/features/akiva-eldar-u-s-tax-dollars-fund-rabbi-who-excused-killing-gentile-babies-1.2137.

309 **In April 2013, the Israeli government**: Yonah Jeremy Bob, "State: No Funds for Yeshiva that Incites Violence," *Jerusalem Post*, April 10, 2013, http://www.jpost.com/Diplomacy-and-Politics/State-No-funds-for-yeshiva-that-incites-violence-309396.

309 **Yossi Peli, was briefly held**: Matthew Wagner, " West Bank Rabbi, Activist Arrested," *Jerusalem Post*, September 12, 2006, http://www.jpost.com/Israel/West-Bank-rabbi-activist-arrested.

309 **homemade rocket**: Hillel Fendel, "Homemade Rocket Fired from Jewish Hilltop at Arab Village," *Arutz Sheva*, June 20, 2008, http://www.israelnationalnews.com/News/News.aspx/126569#.UXYafyv71D4.

309 **Shapira's name arose**: "Rabbi Suspected in West Bank Mosque Arson Released," *BBC News*, January 28, 2010, http://news.bbc.co.uk/2/hi/middle_east/8482700.stm.

309 **taking the entire State**: Fendel, "Homemade Rocket Fired"

309 **balance of terror**: Amos Harel, "The Extreme Right Has Sought to Establish a 'Balance Of Terror.'" *Ha'aretz*, November 3, 2008, http://www.haaretz.com/print-edition/news/analysis-the-extreme-right-has-sought-to-establish-a-balance-of-terror-1.256501.

309 **the Israeli police closed 91 percent**: Yousef Munayyer, "When Settlers Attack," The Palestine Center, 2012, http://www.thejerusalemfund.org/ht/a/GetDocument Action/i/32678.

309 **a population that lives**: Max Blumenthal. "46% of Jewish Israelis Support Settler 'Price Tag' Terror," March 22, 2011, http://maxblumenthal.com/2011/03/48-of -jewish-israelis-support-settler-price-tag-terror-congress-blames-palestinians -for-incitement.

310 **expresses people's animalistic**: "Those Noisy Barbarians," *Ha'aretz*, August 23, 2010, http://www.haaretz.com/culture/arts-leisure/those-noisy-barbarians-1 .309629.

310 **you are being cruel**: Amos Harel, "IDF Rabbinate Publication during Gaza War: We Will Show No Mercy on the Cruel," *Ha'aretz*, January 26, 2009, http://www .haaretz.com/print-edition/news/idf-rabbinate-publication-during-gaza-war-we -will-show-no-mercy-on-the-cruel-1.268849.

310 **a religious revival**: Matthew Wagner, "Shimson Soldiers to Be Hailed at 'Farbren-gen.'" November 12, 2009, http://www.jpost.com/Israel/Article.aspx?id=160303.

311 **Jews, let's win**: "Matan Ofan— in Israeli Military Uniform—Threatens Mutiny, Indiscriminate Shooting," *Mondoweiss*, June 16, 2011, http://mondoweiss.net/2011 /06/matan-ofan-in-israeli-military-uniform-threatens-mutiny-indiscriminate -shooting-to-prevent-sudanis-or-syrians-from-getting-to-tel-aviv.html.

311 **a 30 percent jump since 1990**: Dan Williams, "In Israeli Military, A Growing Orthodoxy," Reuters, March 5, 2012, http://www.reuters.com/article/2012/03/05 /us-israel-religion-idf-idUSTRE8240G720120305.

311 **13 percent of company commanders**: Ibid.

311 **kill more of the bastards**: Chaim Levinson and Mazal Mualem, "IDF Soldiers Who Won't Fight Should Be Shot,' Says National Security Advisor Candidate," *Ha'aretz*, March 2, 2011, http://www.haaretz.com/print-edition/news/idf-soldiers-who-won -t-fight-should-be-shot-says-national-security-adviser-candidate-1.346557.

311 **I was gladdened**: "The Rav Dov Lior Affair," *Arutz Sheva*, June 28, 2011, http:// www.israelnationalnews.com/Blogs/Message.aspx/4656.

311 **one of Israel's greatest rabbis**: Nir Hasson, Yaniv Kubovich, Chaim Levinson and Tomer Zarchin, "Israel's Chief Clergy Decries Arrest of Top Rabbi Who Called for Killing Gentiles," *Ha'aretz*, June 28, 2011, http://www.haaretz.com/print-edition /news/israel-s-chief-clergy-decries-arrest-of-top-rabbi-who-called-for-killing -gentiles-1.369935.

312 **the ruler of Israel**: Sefi Rachlevsky, "A Racist, Messianic Rabbi Is the Ruler of Israel," *Ha'aretz*, July 1, 2011, http://www.haaretz.com/print-edition/opinion/a -racist-messianic-rabbi-is-the-ruler-of-israel-1.370554.

CHAPTER 58: THE DAUGHTERS OF ISRAEL

313 **We castrated you, Mohammed!**: Tom Segev, "Eye of the Beholder / Yasser Arafat Revisited," Ha'aretz, October 11, 2002, http://www.haaretz.com/misc/article-print -page/eye-of-the-beholder-yasser-arafat-revisited-1.31850?trailingPath=2 .169%2C.

313 **attacking the organ**: Ibid.

313 **comparable to a soldier**: Jacqueline Portugese, *Fertility Policy in Israel: The Poli-tics of Religion, Gender, and Nation* (Greenwood, 1998), 83.

314 **women's reproductive rights**: Rhoda Ann Kanaaneh, *Birthing the Nation: Strat-egies of Palestinian Women in Israel* (University of California Press, 2002), 35–37.

314 **Barak told the liberal**: Gershon Baskin, "Proposals for Walls and Fences and their Consequences," *Palestine-Israel Journal*, Vol. 9, No. 3, 2002, http://www.pij.org /details.php?id=119.

314 **an act that would remove**: Chaim Levinson, "Rabbis' Wives Urge Girls Not to Date or Work with Arabs," *Ha'aretz*, December 29, 2010, http://www.haaretz.com /print-edition/news/rabbis-wives-urge-girls-not-to-date-or-work-with-arabs-1 .333910.

315 **Whatever it takes**: Ilan Pappe, Noam Chomsky, Frank Barat. *Gaza in Crisis* (Haymarket Books, 2010), 100.

315 **Every real Arab, deep inside**: Ofri Ilani, "Vatican Teaching Hezbollah How to Kill Jews, Says Pamphlet for IDF Troops," *Ha'aretz*, July 19, 2009, http://www.haaretz .com/print-edition/news/vatican-teaching-hezbollah-how-to-kill-jews-says -pamphlet-for-idf-troops-1.280219.

315 **distribution was immediately halted**: Ibid.

316 **opposition to the segregationist**: Assaf Shtull-Trauring, "Report: 44% of Israeli Jews Support Rabbis' Edict Forbidding Rentals to Arabs in Safed," *Ha'aretz*, December 28, 2010, http://www.haaretz.com/news/national/report-44-of-israeli -jews-support-rabbis-edict-forbidding-rentals-to-arabs-in-safed-1.333825.

316 **Only time will tell**: Udi Aloni, "The Next Phase of the Rabbis: Concentration Camps?" *Ynetnews* [Hebrew], January 11, 2011, http://www.ynet.co.il/articles /0,7340,L-4011912,00.html; also see Richard Silverstein, "Israel's Orthodox Rabbis: 'Palestinians to the Ovens!'" RichardSilverstein.com, January 12, 2011, http:// www.richardsilverstein.com/2011/01/12/israels-orthodox-rabbis-palestinians-to -the-ovens.

316 **no evidence to support**: Yossi Gurvitz. "Israeli Government Willingly Lays Foundations for Jewish Terrorism," *972 Magazine*, August 22, 2012, http://972mag.com /israeli-government-willingly-lays-foundations-for-jewish-terrorism/54318.

317 **God will bless**: Ilan Lior. "Bat Yam residents, rightists rally to protect city from Arab suitors," *Ha'aretz*, December 21, 2010, http://www.haaretz.com/print-edition /news/bat-yam-residents-rightists-rally-to-protect-city-from-arab-suitors-1 .331718.

317 **I am asking our Arab neighbor**: Ibid.

317 **Any Jewish woman who goes**: Yoav Zitun, "Bat Yam rally: Death to Jewish Women to Date Arabs," *Ynetnews*, December 21, 2010, http://www.ynetnews.com /articles/0,7340,L-4002085,00.html.

317 **Gopstein was arrested on suspicion**: Uri Blau and Shai Greenberg, "A Strange Kind of Mercy," *Ha'aretz*, May 27, 2011, http://www.haaretz.com/weekend/magazine /a-strange-kind-of-mercy-1.364417.

317 **anti-assimiliation Coast Guard**: Yair Altman, "Jewish Group Fights Beach Harassment," *Ynetnews*, July 17, 2011, http://www.ynetnews.com/articles/0,7340,L -4096350,00.html.

317 **They are nice boys**: Harriet Sherwood, "Denounced as a Traitor," *Guardian*, December 2, 2010, http://www.guardian.co.uk/world/2010/dec/02/rabbi-land lord-jewish-arab-students-safed.

318 **We feel threatened, we feel helpless**: Ibid.

318 **everything is racism!**: "Bat Yam: Hundreds Protest 'Arab Takeover'" Israel National TV, December 23, 2010, http://www.youtube.com/watch?v=LObeQetWs6w (Marzel quote appears at 2:00).

318 **saving Jewish girls**: Uri Blau and Shai Greenberg, "A Strange Kind of Mercy," *Ha'aretz*, May 27, 2011, http://www.haaretz.com/weekend/magazine/a-strange -kind-of-mercy-1.364417.

319 **it's the job of the Attorney General**: Ibid.

319 **Throw them in the trash can**: Tzvi Ben Gedalyahu, "Jewish Woman Rescued from Arab Village—after 28 Years," *Arutz Sheva*, July 11, 2012, http://www.israel nationalnews.com/News/News.aspx/157744#.UT-VpNEjpz0.

319 **We must fight this threat**: "Non-Conventional Warfare," Yad L'Achim, http://www.yadlachimusa.org.il/?CategoryID=201&ArticleID=572.

319 **I was beaten**: "Video about Jewish Girls Who Date Arabs, Part Two," Yad L'Achim, uploaded on December 14, 2010 http://youtu.be/SWQNk97M4bI, translated from Hebrew for the author by Eyal Clyne.

320 **with strengthening each other**: Ibid.

320 **rescue of the daughters of Israel**: Ibid.

CHAPTER 59: CHILDREN WHOSE HEARTS WERE UNMOVED

321 **Israel is facing a wave**: Ben Hartman, "South TA Residents Demand African Migrants Leave Area," Jerusalem Post, December 21, 2010, http://www.jpost.com/NationalNews/Article.aspx?id=200469.

321 **an apartment inhabited**: Ibid.

321 **armed settlers from the Ma'ale Efraim**: "Israeli Settlers Violence Report: Nov/December 2010," Alternative Information Center, January 18, 2011, http://www.alternativenews.org/english/index.php/component/content/article/5-settlers-violence/3196-israeli-settlers-violence-report-november-december-2010-.

322 **a state for its citizens**: Hartman, "South TA Residents"

322 **This is not new to us**: Hassan Shaalan, "Arabs: Political Environment to Blame for Attacks," *Ynetnews*, December 21, 2010, http://www.ynetnews.com/articles/0,7340,L-4002704,00.html.

322 **nothing compared to the real**: Max Fisher, "Nazareth Suburb's Mayor: Christmas Trees 'Provocative,' Agence France Press, republished by Ma'an News Agency, December 23, 2010, http://www.maannews.net/eng/ViewDetails.aspx?ID=344641.

322 **the same effects**: Jillian Kestler-D'Amours, "Israeli Settlers Increase Their Attacks on Palestinian Christian Sites," *Electronic Intifada*, October 11, 2012, http://electronicintifada.net/content/israeli-settlers-increase-their-attacks-palestinian-christian-sites/11756.

323 **we are here**: Nir Hasson, "Senior Catholic Cleric: 'If Jews Want Respect, They Must Respect Others,'" *Ha'aretz*, September 7, 2012, http://www.haaretz.com/news/national/senior-catholic-cleric-if-jews-want-respect-they-must-respect-others-1.463320.

323 **A Jew is a soul**: Nir Hasson, "In Suspected Jerusalem Lynch, Dozens of Jewish Youths Attack 3 Palestinians," *Ha'aretz*, August 17, 2012, http://www.haaretz.com/news/national/in-suspected-jerusalem-lynch-dozens-of-jewish-youths-attack-3-palestinians-1.459002.

323 **they will finally be afraid**: Ibid.

323 **a boy their age who lay writhing**: Ibid.

323 **all of them hit him**: Oz Rosenberg, "Suspect involved in Jerusalem 'lynch' of Palestinian: 'Let him die, he's an Arab,'" *Ha'aretz*, August 20, 2012, http://www.haaretz.com/news/diplomacy-defense/suspect-involved-in-jerusalem-lynch-of-palestinian-let-him-die-he-s-an-arab-1.459490.

324 **the youth raised**: *Arutz Sheva* interview of Gopstein uploaded to YouTube as "Benzi Gopstein of Lehava Glorifying Terror and Racism Against Non-Jews," August 22, 2012, http://www.youtube.com/watch?v=FnR9EYDjRXc.

324 **I saw the whole beating**: *Ynetnews* video posted at *Mondoweiss* by Adam Horowitz as "VIDEO: Reaction to Jerusalem lynching – 'I saw the whole beating, it's a good thing that they beat the Arabs,'" August 27, 2012, http://mondoweiss.net/2012/08/video-reaction-to-jerusalem-lynching-i-saw-the-whole-beating-its-a-good-thing-that-they-beat-the-arabs.html.

324 **problems almost every weekend**: Ibid.

324 **Dear Arab Guy**: Haggai Mattar, "Poster Calls On Arab Men to Keep Out of Jerusalem, Away from Jewish Girls," *972 Magazine*, August 22, 2012, http://972mag.com/campaign-calls-on-arab-men-to-keep-out-of-jlem-away-from-jewish-girls/54263.

CHAPTER 60: WHEN KAHANE WON

325 **Traitors who must**: Roni Sofer and Yair Altman, "MK Ben-Ari: Eradicate Treacherous Leftists," Ynetnews, January 5, 2011, http://www.ynetnews.com/articles/0,7340,L-4009642,00.html.

325 **the Likud has admitted**: "Tibi: Israel Is Democratic for Jews But Jewish for Arabs," JPost.com, October 10, 2010, http://www.jpost.com/LandedPages/PrintArticle.aspx?id=190865.

325 **It's refreshing to hear**: Ibid.

326 **full individual, cultural**: Chaim Levinson, "Kahane's Vision for Loyalty Oaths Was Not So Different Than Barak's," *Ha'aretz*, October 15, 2010, http://www.haaretz.com/print-edition/news/kahane-s-vision-for-loyalty-oath-was-not-so-different-than-barak-s-1.319174.

326 **I'm not the only one**: Kobi Nahshoni, "National Union Candidate: Kahane Was Right," *Ynetnews*, February 2, 2009, http://www.ynetnews.com/articles/0,7340,L-3665554,00.html.

326 **whose lives are more valuable**: Ibid.

CHAPTER 61: THIS BELONGS TO THE WHITE MAN

330 **to blow up houses**: Benny Morris, The Birth of the Palestinian Refugee Problem Revisited (Cambridge University Press, 2004), 343–344.

330 **no stomach for war**: Ibid., 217.

330 **hooligans**: Ibid.

331 **Ben Gurion put my wife's**: Meron Rapoport, "Police Finish Evacuation of Kfar Shalem Residents in South T.A," *Ha'aretz*, December 25, 2007, http://www.haaretz.com/news/police-finish-evacuation-of-kfar-shalem-residents-in-south-t-a-1.235892.

331 **It's about internal class struggle**: Mya Guarnieri, "Housing Struggle You Didn't Hear About: The Case of Kfar Shalem," *972 Magazine*, July 28, 2011, http://972mag.com/struggles-that-dont-get-israeli-media-attention-the-case-of-kfar-shalem/19633.

331 **Berry was captured**: David Sheen interview with Jacob Berry reported at African Refugee Development Center, "WATCH: Sudanese Refugee Jacob Tells of Israeli Abuse; Hannukah in South Tel Aviv Marred by Racism," December 18, 2012, http://ardc-israel.org/en/blog/2012/12/watch-sudanese-refugee-jacob-tells-israeli-abuse-hannukah-south-tel-aviv-marred-racism.

332 **obligation under the 1951**: UN Refugee Agency, "2013 UNHCR Regional Operations Profile—Middle East," http://www.unhcr.org/pages/49e4864b6.html.

333 **a minority that will be slaughtered**: Gil Ronen, "IDF Prof.: Extreme Left Wants African Workers to Destroy Israel," *Arutz Sheva*, October 16, 2009, http://www.israelnationalnews.com/News/News.aspx/133885#.UUCaGtEjpzo.

333 **concrete threat to the Jewish**: Barak Ravid. "Netanyahu: Illegal African Immigrants a Threat to Israel's Jewish Character," *Ha'aretz*, July 18, 2010, http://www.haaretz.com/news/national/netanyahu-illegal-african-immigrants-a-threat-to-israel-s-jewish-character-1.302653.

333 **the end of the Zionist dream**: Isabel Kershner, "Israeli Leader Pledges Hard Line on Migrants," *New York Times*, June 4, 2012, http://www.nytimes.com/2012/06/05

/world/middleeast/netanyahu-vows-crackdown-on-african-asylum-seekers.html?
_r=0.

333 **there is nothing that I know**: Ron Friedman, "Health Ministry Data Refutes Yishai's Claims That African Refugees Bring In Disease," *Jerusalem Post*, June 11, 2009, http://www.phr.org.il/default.asp?PageID=184&ItemID=274.

333 **they are already suffering**: Lia Tarachansky, "Incitement Against Refugees Leads to Racist Attacks in Israel," *Real News*, June 6, 2012, http://therealnews.com/t2/index.php?option=com_content&task=view&id=31&Itemid=74&jumival=8424.

333 **The era of slogans is over**: Roxanne Horesh, "Israel Turns Up the Heat on African Migrants," *Al Jazeera*, June 14, 2012, http://www.aljazeera.com/indepth/features/2012/06/201261411491620572.html.

334 **frustrated people**: Ehud Sprinzak, *The Ascendance of Israel's Radical Right* (Oxford University Press, 1991), 241.

334 **I want to tell you**: David Sheen, "Anti African Rally in Tel Aviv," December 12, 2012, http://www.youtube.com/watch?v=7Sv14Kwuk-8.

335 **You represent the worst**: Ibid.

CHAPTER 62: THE CONCENTRATION CAMP

336 **Prevention of Infiltration Law:** Israel Law Resource Center, "Prevention of Infiltration (Offences and Jurisdiction) Law, 5714–1954," http://www.israellaw resourcecenter.org/emergencyregs/fulltext/preventioninfiltrationlaw.htm.

336 **a whopping majority**: Elad Benari, "Knesset Approves Infiltration Law," *Arutz Sheva*, January 10, 2012, http://www.israelnationalnews.com/News/News.aspx/151580#.UUCePtEjpz1.

336 **world's biggest detention**: Catrina Stewart, "Israelis Build the World's Biggest Detention Centre," *Independent*, March 10, 2012, http://www.independent.co.uk/news/world/middle-east/israelis-build-the-worlds-biggest-detention-centre-7547401.html.

336 **I have a hard time**: Merav Michaeli, "Knesset Speaker: Racist Rabbi's Letter Shames the Jewish People," *Ha'aretz*, December 9, 2010, http://www.haaretz.com/print-edition/features/knesset-speaker-racist-rabbi-s-letter-shames-the-jewish-people-1.329625.

336 **chang[ing] the character**: Stewart, "Israelis Build the World's"

336 **concentration camps would be**: Tanya Reinnhardt, *Road Map to Nowhere: Israel/Palestine Since 2003* (Verso, 2006), 173.

336 **reiterated his warning**: Yeshayahu Leibowitz, *Judaism, Human Values, and the Jewish State* (Harvard University Press, 1992), 244–45.

337 **accumulated experience**: Dimi Reider, "Israel's Open Prison for Refugees, and Other Gems of Doublespeak," *972 Magazine*, January 6, 2011, http://972mag.com/israels-open-prison-for-refugees-and-other-gems-of-doublespeak/8100.

337 **huge concentration camp**: Gili Cohen, "Israel Seeks to Build Tent Camp for African Migrants with No Sewage or Proper Facilities," *Ha'aretz*, June 19, 2012, http://www.haaretz.com/news/national/israel-seeks-to-build-tent-camp-for-african-migrants-with-no-sewage-or-proper-facilities.premium-1.437205.

337 **We must crack down**: Talila Nesher, "Netanyahu: Israel Could Be Overrun by African Infiltrators," *Ha'aretz*, May 21, 2012, http://www.haaretz.com/news/diplomacy-defense/netanyahu-israel-could-be-overrun-by-african-infiltrators-1.431589.

337 **sea fences**: Sharon Udasin, "Defending Israel's Borders from 'Climate Refugees,'" *Jerusalem Post*, May 14, 2012, http://www.jpost.com/NationalNews/Article.aspx?id=269948.

338 **We request that you wait**: David Sheen, "Racism Report: Africans in Israel," Report for the African Refugee Development Center (ARDC) to the United Nations Committee on the Elimination of Racial Discrimination (CERD) - submitted January 30, 2012, http://www.youtube.com/watch?v=cUivyO5T_34.

338 **A bad smell wafts**: Yoav Malka, "Suggestion: Separate Buses for Sudanese Refugees," MyNet, http://www.mynet.co.il/articles/0,7340,L-4190334,00.html.

338 **This should be a very violent action**: Max Blumenthal, "Israeli Mercenary Firm Proposes 'Violent Action' against African Refugees," April 11, 2012, http://maxblumenthal.com/2012/04/israeli-mercenary-firm-proposes-violent-action-to-deport-tel-avivs-african-population.

339 **Arabs may not come in and out**: Ali Abunimah, "Israel Will Collapse Unless Africans And Palestinians Are Expelled, Fenced, Says Legal Advocate," *Electronic Intifada*, May 23, 2012, http://electronicintifada.net/blogs/ali-abunimah/israel-will-collapse-unless-africans-and-palestinians-are-expelled-fenced-says.

339 **the Zionist dream is dying**: Harriet Sherwood, "Israel PM: Illegal African Immigrants Threaten Identity of Jewish State," *Guardian*, May 20, 2012, http://www.guardian.co.uk/world/2012/may/20/israel-netanyahu-african-immigrants-jewish?newsfeed=true.

339 **I have experiences in Darfur**: David Sheen interview with Jacob Berry reported at African Refugee Development Center, "WATCH: Sudanese Refugee Jacob Tells of Israeli Abuse; Hannukah in South Tel Aviv Marred by Racism," December 18, 2012, http://ardc-israel.org/en/blog/2012/12/watch-sudanese-refugee-jacob-tells-israeli-abuse-hannukah-south-tel-aviv-marred-racism.

339 **Whoever did this is right**: Haggai Matar, "Community Shaken after Night of Arson Attacks on African Refugees," *972 Magazine*, April 27, 2012, http://972mag.com/community-shaken-after-coordinated-attacks-on-african-refugees/43727.

340 **Haim Moula**: Or Kashti, "Israeli Suspect in Attack on African Migrants' Property Gets Off with Light Plea Bargain," *Ha'aretz*, December 27, 2012, http://www.haaretz.com/news/national/israeli-suspect-in-attack-on-african-migrants-property-gets-off-with-light-plea-bargain.premium-1.490354.

340 **40 percent of the crime**: Sigal Rozen, "Police Distort Crime Data, Inciting Violence against Refugees," *972 Magazine*, May 19, 2012, http://972mag.com/police-distortion-of-crime-data-encourages-rising-violence-against-refugees/46236.

340 **We are fighting for the face**: Yaakov Lappin, "Aharonovitch: Forget Stats, Public Feels Unsafe," *Jerusalem Post*, May 16, 2012, http://www.jpost.com/NationalNews/Article.aspx?id=270238.

340 **Mayor Rudy] Giuliani**: Avi Shoshan, "15 Minutes of Terror in South Tel Aviv," *Ynetnews* [Hebrew], May 18, 2012, http://www.ynet.co.il/articles/0,7340,L-4230869,00.html.

340 **only date[s] non-white women**: Amazon.com profile for Seth J. Frantzman, "In My Own Words," http://www.amazon.com/gp/pdp/profile/A2Z4KA3EFQWZOX.

341 **They don't greet white women**: Seth J. Frantzman, "Terra Incognita: How Racism Crept into My Neighborhood," *Jerusalem Post*, http://www.jpost.com/Opinion/Columnists/Terra-Incognita-How-racism-crept-into-my-neighborhood.

341 **because I am a black African**: Tamar Rotem, "Living in Dread in South Tel Aviv, Young African Migrants Feel the Hate," *Ha'aretz*, May 6, 2012, http://www.haaretz.com/news/features/living-in-dread-in-south-tel-aviv-young-african-migrants-feel-the-hate.premium-1.434423.

341 **Rotem Ilan**: Lia Tarachansky, "Incitement Against Refugees Leads to Racist Attacks in Israel," *Real News*, June 6, 2012, http://therealnews.com/t2/index.php?option=com_content&task=view&id=31&Itemid=74&jumival=8424.

CHAPTER 63: THE NIGHT OF BROKEN GLASS

342 **Death to Sudanese:** Maath Musleh, Twitter: @MaathMusleh, May 23, 2012, https://twitter.com/MaathMusleh/status/205416248090173443.

342 **May you all get cancer!:** David Sheen, "Rape Culture in Israel," http://www.youtube.com/watch?v=dKIiDeKRGQU.

343 **She wants a nigger!:** Yossi Gurvitz, "Thoughts on an Attack by a Jewish Mob," *972 Magazine*, May 24, 2012, http://972mag.com/thoughts-on-an-attack-by-a-jewish-mob/46684.

343 **I am as afraid to live:** Aliyana Traison, "Israelis Must Shun Racism, Not African Migrants," *Ha'aretz*, May 25, 2012, http://www.haaretz.com/opinion/israelis-must-shun-racism-not-african-migrants.premium-1.432591.

343 **cancer in our body:** Lia Tarachansky, "Incitement against Refugees Leads to Racist Attacks in Israel," June 6, 2012, http://therealnews.com/t2/index.php?option=com_content&task=view&id=31&Itemid=74&jumival=8424.

344 **he and his mother:** Haggai Matar, "How I Survived a Tel Aviv Mob Attack," *972 Magazine*, May 24, 2012, http://972mag.com/how-i-survived-a-tel-aviv-mob-attack/46587.

344 **they came and broke:** Kady Buchanan, "Businesses of African Refugees under Attack in Israel," Uploaded on August 25, 2012, http://www.youtube.com/watch?v=AL_h4fHVg8o&noredirect=1.

344 **The people want the Africans:** Oren Ziv, "Night of Attacks against African Refugees, Tel Aviv, Israel, 23," *Activestills*, May 23, 2012, http://www.activestills.org/content/night-attacks-against-african-refugees-tel-aviv-israel-23-49; The photo featured on the cover of this book is the image captured by Ziv as the crowd chanted this slogan.

344 **I don't know if I can:** David Sheen interview with community activist Rami Gudovitch, "How Israel Abuses Africans," September 26, 2012, http://www.youtube.com/watch?v=QPms_GLEq1E.

344 **shirt with the date:** Tamar Rotem. "Living in Dread in South Tel Aviv, Young African Migrants Feel the Hate," *Ha'aretz*, May 6, 2012, http://www.haaretz.com/news/features/living-in-dread-in-south-tel-aviv-young-african-migrants-feel-the-hate.premium-1.434423.

345 **finally, people will:** "How Israel Abuses Africans," Sheen interview with Gudovitch.

345 **everyone should be asking:** Or Heller on "London and Kirschenbaum," Channel 10 [Hebrew], September 6, 2012, http://lnk.nana10.co.il/Article/?ArticleID=923901&sid=182.

345 **The Jewish state:** Lahav Harkov, "Likud MK Warns 'South Tel Aviv under Siege,'" *Jerusalem Post*, May 29, 2012, http://www.jpost.com/DiplomacyAndPolitics/Article.aspx?id=271868.

345 **you were a member of this government:** Ibid.

345 **I was repatriated to Israel:** Ibid.

345 **All human rights activists:** Omri Efraim, "Kadima MK: Send Human Rights Activists to Prison Camps," *Ynetnews*, May 29, 2012, http://www.ynetnews.com/articles/0,7340,L-4235732,00.html.

345 **I did not compare them:** Ali Abunimah, "Israeli Lawmaker Miri Regev: 'Heaven Forbid' We Compare Africans to Human Beings," *Electronic Intifada*, May 31, 2012, http://electronicintifada.net/blogs/ali-abunimah/israeli-lawmaker-miri-regev-heaven-forbid-we-compare-africans-human-beings.

345 **Regev's sentiments:** "The Peace Index: May 2012," The Israel Democracy Institute, http://www.peaceindex.org/indexMonthEng.aspx?num=242.

346 **I'd die before**: Omri Efraim, "Filipino Girl Adopted by Palestinians Awaits Miracle," *Ynetnews*, September 4, 2012, http://www.ynetnews.com/articles/0,7340,L -4277074,00.html.

346 **They treat us like animals**: Ilana Curiel, "Illegal Migrants 'Treated Like Animals,'" *Ynetnews*, June 12, 2012, http://www.ynetnews.com/articles/0,7340,L-4241088,00 .html.

346 **We cannot let them enter**: Harriet Sherwood, "Eritrean Refugees Trapped by Security Fence at Israeli-Egyptian Border," *Guardian*, September 5, 2012, http:// www.guardian.co.uk/world/2012/sep/05/eritrean-refugees-at-israeli-egyptian -border.

346 **he can convert**: Yair Ettinger. "Dozens of African Migrants Denied Request to Convert to Judaism," *Ha'aretz*, June 18, 2012, http://www.haaretz.com/news/national /dozens-of-african-migrants-denied-request-to-convert-to-judaism.premium-1 .436992.

346 **refugee-repelling wall**: "Israel Fences Itself In with Barriers," *UPI.com*, May 1, 2012, http://www.upi.com/Business_News/Security-Indtry/2012/05/01/Israel-fences -itself-in-with-barriers/UPI-87121335904303.

347 **one will be built**: Tzvi Ben Gedalayhu, "Israel Will Build Fence at Jordanian Border," *Arutz Sheva*, January 1, 2012, http://www.israelnationalnews.com/News/News .aspx/151281.

347 **retreats into defensive walls**: Alex Fishman, "Israel Overcome by Paranoia," *Ynetnews*, February 8, 2012, http://www.ynetnews.com/articles/0,7340,L-4187120,00 .html.

CHAPTER 64: THE BIG QUIET

351 **an outpost of civilization**: Theodore Herzl, Der Judenstaat (The Jewish State), 1896, Adapted from the 1946 edition published by the American Zionist Emergency Council and published online by MidEastWeb at mideastweb.org/jewish-state.pdf.

351 **All the means**: Herzl in an interview to the London Zionist journal, *Young Israel*, July 1898, in Gabriel Piterberg, *The Returns of Zionism: Myths, Politics and Scholarship in Israel* ((New York: Verso, 2008), 36.

351 **The Zionist enterprise**: Zeev Sternhell, *The Founding Myths of Zionism* (Princeton University Press, 1998), 151.

351 **a villa in the jungle**: Ian Black, "Ehud Barak: The Military Mastermind Israel Loves to Hate," *Guardian*, November 26, 2012, http://www.guardian.co.uk/world /2012/nov/26/ehud-barak-quits-politics-israel.

351 **It is not by chance**: Sternhell, *The Founding Myths of Zionism*, Ibid.

351 **This is, in toto**: Vladimir Jabotinsky, "The Iron Wall: We and the Arabs, (1923)", http://www.marxists.de/middleast/ironwall/ironwall.htm.

352 **take Gaza out**: Daniel Byman, *A High Price: The Triumphs and Failures of Israeli Counterterrorism* (Oxford University Press, 2011), 76.

352 **Something like a cage**: Ari Shavit, "Survival of the Fittest," *Ha'aretz*, January 8, 2004, http://www.haaretz.com/survival-of-the-fittest-cont-1.61341.

352 **We can no longer keep**: Ari Shavit, "The War for a Moment's Peace," *Ha'aretz*, March 11, 2002, http://www.haaretz.com/print-edition/opinion/the-war-for-a -moment-s-peace-1.50779.

352 **it may be possible to rehabilitate**: Editorial, "In Support of the Separation Fence," *Ha'aretz*, June 18, 2002, http://www.ceps.eu/files/book/1037.pdf.

353 **one of the most explicit**: Gershon Baskin with Sharon Rosenberg, "The New Walls and Fences: Consequences for Israel and Palestine," Centre for European

Policy Studies. Working Paper No. 9, June 2003, https://www.google.com/url
?sa=t&rct=j&q=&esrc=s&source=web&cd=2&ved=0CDcQFjAB&url=http%3
A%2F%2Fwww.ceps.eu%2Fceps%2Fdld%2F889%2Fpdf&ei=DuJAUc-GOquzo
QH2u4C4Bw&usg=AFQjCNEBq43RZaBHnYTRgxLvgXlGXOwqpQ&bvm=bv
.43287494,d.dmQ.

354   **[Openness] is actually**: Simon Robinson, "A World Divided," *Time*, April 26, 2007,
       http://www.time.com/time/magazine/article/0,9171,1614903,00.html.

354   **let's leave those**: Richard Silverstein, "Dan Schueftan: Senior Israeli Arab Analyst,
       Confidant of Generals and Prime Ministers, and Arab Hater," *Tikun Olam*,
       November 6, 2009, http://www.richardsilverstein.com/2009/11/06/dan-schueftan
       -senior-israeli-arab-analyst-advisor-to-generals-and-prime-ministers-and-racist.

354   **Access to decision-makers**: Ibid.

355   **there will be a collapse**: Brian Whitaker, "Israel 'Faces Existential Crisis,'" *Guard-
       ian*, July 23, 2001, http://www.guardian.co.uk/world/2001/jul/23/israel1.

355   **Days later**: Renee Backmann, *A Wall In Palestine* (Picador, 2006), 35–36.

355   **Do you realize this?**: Lily Galili, "A Jewish Demographic State," *Ha'aretz*, June 27,
       2002, http://www.haaretz.com/print-edition/features/a-jewish-demographic
       -state-1.41134.

356   **the new majority could**: Ibid.

356   **This is not expulsion**: Ibid.

356   **Democracy has to be subordinated**: Ibid.

356   **You will see long nails**: Eliyahu Ungar-Sargon, "People Without a Land," Extended
       Trailer, September 8, 2010, http://www.youtube.com/watch?v=TUKLB9r7KW8.

356   **we must ensure**: "Mr. Benjamin Netanyahu's Speech at the Herzliya Conference,"
       Gamla, December 26, 2003, http://www.israpost.com/Community/articles/show
       .php?articleID=984.

356   **demographic spillover**: Gideon Alon and Aluf Benn, "Netanyahu: Israel's Arabs
       Are the Real Demographic Threat," *Ha'aretz*, December 18, 2003, http://www
       .haaretz.com/print-edition/news/netanyahu-israel-s-arabs-are-the-real-demo
       graphic-threat-1.109045.

356   **You might not like the word**: Greg Myre, "Sharon Defends Peace Plan Against
       Critics in Likud," *New York Times*, May 27, 2003, http://www.nytimes.com/2003
       /05/27/world/sharon-defends-peace-plan-against-critics-in-likud.html.

357   **184,868 dunams**: Amira Hass, "Supreme Court Is on Wrong Side of West Bank
       Separation Fence," *Ha'aretz*, April 11, 2011, http://www.haaretz.com/print-edition
       /features/supreme-court-is-on-wrong-side-of-west-bank-separation-fence-1
       .355251.

357   **de facto annexation**: "In Day-Long UN SC Meeting, Palestine Observer Says
       Israeli Security Wall Involves De Facto Annexation of Occupied Land," *Electronic
       Intifada*, October 14, 2003, http://electronicintifada.net/content/day-long-un-sc
       -meeting-palestine-observer-says-israeli-security-wall-involves-de-facto.

357   **They aren't human**: Yoav Shamir, *Checkpoint*, (2003 Yoav Shamir Films), entire
       film can be viewed online at http://topdocumentaryfilms.com/checkpoint.

358   **We have gotten**: Chana Ya'ar, "Ya'alon Cites Western Naivete: Not All Elections
       Bring Democracy," *Arutz Sheva*, February 2, 2012, http://www.israelnationalnews
       .com/News/News.aspx/152371#.UUDzd9Ejpzo.

358   **it has to be managed**: Ibid.

CHAPTER 65: THE JOINT STRUGGLE

359   **At Mas'ha Camp**: Uri Gordon, "Against the Wall: Anarchist Mobilization in the
       Israeli-Palestinian Conflict," Peace & Change, July 2010, http://www.academia.edu

/964089/Against_the_Wall_Anarchist_Mobilization_in_the_Israeli_Palestinian _Conflict.

359 **The military had difficulty**: "Uri Gordon: Anarchists Against the Wall" uploaded to Vimeo by Jonathan Shockley, http://vimeo.com/6804617.

360 **Order 101**: "Military order 101," B'Tselem, September 8, 2011, http://www.btselem .org/demonstrations/military_order_101; according to B'Tselem, "Order No. 101 prohibits any assembly, vigil, procession, or publication relating to 'a political matter or one liable to be interpreted as political.' The order does not include a precise definition of what is to be considered such content. This vague and sweeping phrasing is open to interpretation, and, accordingly, could be used to restrict a broad range of subjects on which people wish to express their opinions. Such restriction is not compatible with freedom of expression.

360 **We forced open**: Gordon, "Against The Wall"

360 **dressed up as the Navi**: Haitham Al Katib, "Bilin Reenacts *Avatar*," December 2, 2010, http://www.youtube.com/watch?v=Chw32qG-M7E&noredirect=1.

361 **Stop firing!**: Haggai Matar, "Testimony: Soldier Fired Directly at Bil'in Demonstrator Killed in 2009," *972 Magazine*, December 19, 2012, http://972mag.com /testimony-soldier-fired-directly-at-bilin-demonstrator-killed-in-2009/62306.

361 **bound and shot**: "Ashraf Abu Rahme Shot by Israeli Army While Handcuffed and Blindfolded," International Solidarity Movement, July 20, 2008, http://palsolidarity.org/2008/07/ashraf-abu-rahme-shot-by-israeli-army-while-handcuffed-and -blindfolded.

361 **overcome by teargas**: Ana Carbajosa, "Palestinian Mother Tells of a Family Tragedy During Protest Against Separation Barrier," *Guardian*, January 8, 2011, http:// www.guardian.co.uk/world/2011/jan/09/palestinians-ramallah-israeli-barrier.

361 **ten-year-old Ahmed Mousa**: Flashpoints Radio, "Israeli forces Mortally Wound Nilin Teenager after Funeral," *Electronic Intifada*, July 31, 2008, http://electronicintifada.net/content/israeli-forces-mortally-wound-nilin-teenager-after-funeral /7646.

361 **with Ahmad in my hands**: "Ahmad Mousa's Killer Walks Free," Ni'lin Sons, November 9, 2012, http://www.nilin-village.org/2012/11/09/ahmad-mousas -killer-walks-free.

361 **Omri Abu, innocent**: Chaim Levinson, "Israeli Officer Acquitted of Shooting Death of Palestinian Child," *Ha'aretz*, October 30, 2012, http://www.haaretz.com /news/diplomacy-defense/israeli-border-police-officer-acquitted-of-shooting -death-of-palestinian-child.premium-1.473295.

361 **seventeen-year-old Youssef Amireh**: Flashpoints Radio, "Israeli Forces Mortally Wound Nilin Teenager after Funeral," *Electronic Intifada*, July 31, 2008, http:// electronicintifada.net/content/israeli-forces-mortally-wound-nilin-teenager -after-funeral/7646.

361 **What about accountability?**: Flashpoints Radio Transcript, "Israeli Military Kills 10-Year-Old in Nilin," *Electronic Intifada*, July 30, 2008, http://electronicintifada .net/content/transcript-israeli-military-kills-10-year-old-nilin/7643.

361 **half-paralyzed and half-blind**: Charlotte Silver, "Tristan Anderson Civil Suit Delayed as New Evidence Emerges," *Electronic Intifada*, December 3, 2011, http:// electronicintifada.net/content/tristan-anderson-civil-suit-delayed-new-evidence -emerges/10649.

361 **Yousef Srur**: Yisrael Puterman, "Yusuf Aqel Srur Was Killed by Sniper Shooting Him," June 5, 2009, http://www.youtube.com/watch?v=ZL6C3DzqlsU.

362 **the army continued**: Chaim Levinson, "IDF Still Using Banned Weapon Against Civilian Protesters," *Ha'aretz*, September 19, 2010, http://www.haaretz.com/print

-edition/news/idf-still-using-banned-weapon-against-civilian-protestors-1
.314521.

362 **the Israeli government as a whole**: Flashpoints Radio Transcript, "Israeli Military Kills 10-Year-Old in Nilin."

362 **our struggle is justified**: Ali Waked, "Relatives: Bilin Protester Was Persistent in His Struggle," *Ynetnews*, April 19, 2009, http://www.ynetnews.com/Ext/Comp/ArticleLayout/CdaArticlePrintPreview/1,2506,L-3702943,00.html.

363 **bypassing Arab towns**: Rafi Segal and Eyal Weizman, *Civilian Occupation: The Politics of Israeli Architecture* (Babel, 2003).

364 **The plan would sever**: Jonathan Cook, "Palestinian Village Turning into 'Ghetto,'" *National*, November 2008, http://www.jonathan-cook.net/2008-11-11/palestinian
-village-turning-into-ghetto.

364 **Summer Amireh**: "Israeli Forces Shoot Young Palestinian Girl in Ni'lin," International Solidarity Movement, May 15, 2009, http://palsolidarity.org/2009/05/israeli
-forces-shoot-young-palestinian-girl-in-nilin.

364 **you go to sleep**: Ben Hartman, "Marty Peretz, Down by the School Yard," *Jerusalem Post*, January 27, 2011, http://www.jpost.com/Features/InThespotlight/Article
.aspx?id=205567.

CHAPTER 66: MY MOTHER BEFORE JUSTICE

365 **One of the things that:** Alu Abunimah, "NY Times' Jerusalem Property Makes It Protagonist in Palestine Conflict," Electronic Intifada, March 2, 2010, http://
electronicintifada.net/content/ny-times-jerusalem-property-makes-it-protagonist
-palestine-conflict/8705.

366 **My entire neighborhood**: Ibid.

366 **Hebrew-language chants**: Budour Youssef Hassan, "The Sham Solidarity of Israel's Zionist Left," *Electronic Intifada*, July 28, 2011, http://electronicintifada.net
/content/sham-solidarity-israels-zionist-left/10213.

366 **my mother before justice**: David Carroll, *Albert Camus, the Algerian* (Columbia University Press, 2007), 209.

367 **village of entrepreneurs**: Jonathan Cook, "Palestinian Village Turning into 'Ghetto,'" *National*, November 10, 2008, http://www.thenational.ae/news/world
/middle-east/palestinian-village-turning-into-ghetto.

369 **shot in the head**: Yael Levy, "Protestor Shot by Border Guard Officer in Bil'in Awarded Damages," *Ynetnews*, July 29, 2009, http://www.ynetnews.com/articles
/0,7340,L-3753766,00.html; video of Goldstein being shot by Border Police: "Bilin
– The Shooting of Lymor Goldstein by Israeli Military Border Police," May 21, 2009, uploaded by communichaoz, http://www.youtube.com/watch?v=S3r6VxD
kvjw.

370 **Don't Shake Hands with Apartheid**: Joseph Dana, "Great-Grandson of S.Y. Agnon Tells Ian McEwan Not to Shake Hands with Apartheid," *Mondoweiss*, February 23, 2011, http://mondoweiss.net/2011/02/life-under-the-occupation.html.

CHAPTER 67: THE CRAZY VILLAGE

372 **We don't do Gandhi**: "WikiLeaks: Israel Irked by West Bank Protests," Ynetnews, September 3, 2011, http://www.ynetnews.com/articles/0,7340,L-4117301,00.html.

372 **recently seized**: James Cunningham, Wikileaks cable reference ID: 10TELA-VIV344, http://www.cablegatesearch.net/cable.php?id=10TELAVIV344.

372 **even demonstrations**: Ibid.

372 **The Scream**: Adam Rawnsley, "'The Scream': Israel Blasts Protestors with Sonic Gun," *Wired*, September 23, 2011, http://www.wired.com/dangerroom/2011/09 /the-scream-israel-blasts-rioters-with-sonic-gun.

373 **the realities of the occupation**: Max Blumenthal, "In Israel, Non-Violent Solidarity Activist Goes to Prison, Anti-Gay Terrorist Gets Community Service," MaxBlumenthal.com, December 28, 2010, http://maxblumenthal.com/2010/12/in-israel -non-violent-solidarity-activist-gets-prison-anti-gay-terrorist-gets-community -service.

373 **organized army of boys**: Yair Altman, "Secrets of Nabi Saleh Protests," *Ynetnews*, March 26, 2011, http://www.ynetnews.com/articles/0,7340,L-4047503,00.html.

374 **You never know their names**: Harriet Sherwood, "Former Israeli Soldiers Disclose Routine Mistreatment of Palestinian Children," *Guardian*, August 26, 2012, http://www.guardian.co.uk/world/2012/aug/26/israeli-soldiers-mistreatment -palestinian-children.

374 **That specific kid**: Ibid.

375 **armed and unarmed**: Nabi Saleh resident Ahlam Tamimi escorted a suicide bomber to a pizza parlor in Jerusalem, serving as an accomplice in an attack in which 15 people were killed; see Ben Ehrenreich, "Is This Where the Third Intifada Will Start?" *New York Times Magazine*, March 15, 2013, http://www.nytimes .com/2013/03/17/magazine/is-this-where-the-third-intifada-will-start.html ?pagewanted=all&_r=0.

375 **inside the open windows**: video of Israeli forces deliberately spraying Skunk into homes in Nabi Saleh: Middle East Monitor, "Israeli Security Forces Spray 'Skunk' at Palestinian Homes," March 14, 2013, http://www.youtube.com/watch?v= -njv7RJqtRM.

376 **we want to end**: Max Blumenthal, "Bassem Tamimi: 'Our Destiny Is to Resist,'" *Electronic Intifada*, May 2, 2011, http://electronicintifada.net/content/bassem -tamimi-our-destiny-resist/9894.

CHAPTER 68: NIGHT

379 **part of the same:** Harry Kriesler, "Robert Jay Lifton Interview," Institute of International Studies, UC Berkley, http://globetrotter.berkeley.edu/people/Lifton/lifton -cono.html.

379 **It can be used by anyone**: Ibid.

382 **point blank range**: "Mustafa Tamimi Has Died," *Mondoweiss*, December 10, 2011, http://mondoweiss.net/2011/12/mustafa-tamimi-had-died.html.

382 **Naji Tamimi**: Isabel Kershner, "Palestinian's Trail Shines Light on Military Justice," *New York Times*, February 18, 2012, http://www.nytimes.com/2012/02/19 /world/middleeast/palestinians-trial-shines-light-on-justice-system.html?page wanted=all&_r=0.

382 **Bassem Tamimi**: Ibid.

382 **What incites protestors**: "Bassem Tamimi to Judge: 'Land Theft and Tree Burning Are Not Just. Your Military Laws Are Not Legitimate. Our Peaceful Protest Is Just,'" *Mondoweiss*, June 6, 2011, http://mondoweiss.net/2011/06/bassem-tamimi -to-judge-land-theft-and-tree-burning-are-not-just-your-military-laws-are-not -legitimate-our-peaceful-protest-is-just.html.

383 **the Tamimi clan**: Rana Baker. "Video: Ola Tamimi reacts to shooting of her brother," Electronic Intifada, December 10, 2011, http://electronicintifada.net/blogs /rana-baker/video-ola-tamimi-reacts-shooting-her-brother.

383 **Thank God for everything**: Linah Alsaafin, "Mustafa Tamimi's Father Passed Away," *Electronic Intifada*, October 15, 2012, http://electronicintifada.net/blogs /linah-alsaafin/mustafa-tamimis-father-passed-away.

CHAPTER 69: THE CHILDREN'S COURT

386 **Palestinians were convicted**: Chaim Levinson, "Nearly 100% of All Military Court Cases in West Bank End in Conviction," Ha'aretz, November 29, 2011, http://www.haaretz.com/print-edition/news/nearly-100-of-all-military-court -cases-in-west-bank-end-in-conviction-haaretz-learns-1.398369.

386 **835 minors**: "No Minor Matter," B'Tselem, July 2011, http://www.btselem.org/pub lications/summaries/2011-no-minor-matter.

386 **illegal and violent**: Saaed Amireh. "Israel Imprisoned My Father for Nonviolently Resisting the Occupation," *Electronic Intifada*, July 16, 2010, http://electronicintifada .net/content/israel-imprisoned-my-father-nonviolently-resisting-occupation /8926.

386 **security prisoners**: "No Minor Matter,"

390 **Don Wagner, the director**: Sara Peck, "An Assault on Academic Freedom?" *In These Times*, May 14, 2010, http://inthesetimes.com/article/5983/an_assault_on _academic_freedom.

CHAPTER 70: THE LOVERS' CAMP

392 **center of life:** Danielle C. Jefferis, "The 'Center of Life' Policy: Institutionalizing Statelessness in East Jerusalem," Jerusalem Quarterly, Summer 2012, http://www .jerusalemquarterly.org/ViewArticle.aspx?id=416, also see Jeff Halper, "Obstacles to Peace," Israeli Committee Against House Demolition, April 2005. Third Edition, http://webcache.googleusercontent.com/search?q=cache:s5WsTJ9U _1sJ:https://www.umhltf.org/uploads/ObstaclesToPeace_JeffHalper .doc+%22center+of+life%22+Jerusalem+jeff+halper&hl=en&gl=.

392 **illegally present**: Nir Hasson, "East Jerusalem Man, Denied Residency by Israel, Effectively Prisoner in Own Home," *Ha'aretz*, April 24, 2012, http://www.haaretz .com/news/national/east-jerusalem-man-denied-residency-by-israel-effectively -prisoner-in-own-home-1.426249.

392 **the Jerusalem municipality**: "Behind the Wall—Kufr Aqab," Ir Amim, http://eng .ir-amim.org.il/?CategoryID=331.

394 **Palestinian homes since 1967**: "Infographic: Palestinian homes Demolished," *Al Jazeera English*, August 30, 2012, http://www.aljazeera.com/indepth/interactive /2012/08/2012830754014332.html, also see Itay Epshatin, "Beit Arabiya Demolished for the Sixth Time, ICAHD Names Those Responsible," ICAHD, November 1, 2012, http://www.icahd.org/Beit_Arabiya_Demolished.

395 **not just security**: Ben White, "Israel Wall Used for Segregation, Not Just Security," *Al Jazeera*, July 31, 2012, http://www.aljazeera.com/indepth/opinion/2012/07 /201273091647695790.html.

395 **a very small territorial**: Melanie Lidman, "Barkat Proposes Changing Jerusalem's Borders," *Jerusalem Post*, December 17, 2011, http://www.jpost.com/National News/Article.aspx?id=249831.

CHAPTER 71: A WET DREAM

397 **mowing the lawn:** Yoni Dayan, "Mowing the Lawn," Ynetnews, November 27, 2012, http://www.ynetnews.com/articles/0,7340,L-4312017,00.html. Also see, Christa Case Bryant, "Israelis Ponder Alternatives to 'Mowing the Lawn' in Gaza," Christian Science Monitor, November 20, 2012, http://www.csmonitor.com/World

/Middle-East/2012/1120/Israelis-ponder-alternatives-to-mowing-the-lawn-in
-Gaza-video.

397 **This is my country here!**: Ali Abunimah, " Disturbing New Video of Israeli Jews
Assaulting Africans in Tel Aviv on New Year's Eve," *Electronic Intifada*, January 13,
2013, http://electronicintifada.net/blogs/ali-abunimah/disturbing-new-video
-israeli-jews-assaulting-africans-tel-aviv-new-years-eve.

398 **instances of racist incitement**: Jack Khoury, " Racist Incitement by Israeli Public
Figures Doubled in 2012, Study Shows," *Ha'aretz*, March 18, 2013, http://www
.haaretz.com/news/national/racist-incitement-by-israeli-public-figures-doubled
-in-2012-study-shows.premium-1.510230.

398 **fatal heart attack**: Philip Reeves, "Israeli Settlements Could Scuttle Peace Plan,"
NPR, December 3, 2012, http://www.npr.org/2012/12/03/166381970/israeli-settle
ment-plan. Also see Jodi Rudoren, "Diving the West Bank, and Deepening a Rift,"
New York Times, December 1, 2012, http://www.nytimes.com/2012/12/02/world
/middleeast/2-state-solution-at-risk-in-israeli-building-plan.html?pagewanted
=all.

399 **his so-called stability plan:** Max Blumenthal, "Why the Israeli Elections Were a
Victory for the Right," *Nation*, January 23, 2013, http://www.thenation.com/article
/172398/why-israeli-elections-were-victory-right#.

400 **TV division at New Regency Films**: Nathan Guttman, "Yair Lapid, Israel's Rising
Star, Is Still Great Unknown in Washington," *Jewish Daily Forward*, January 23,
2013 http://forward.com/articles/169830/yair-lapid-israels-rising-star-is-still
-great-unkn/?p=all#ixzz2RohN2GTs.

400 **corrupt, lazy**: Yehouda Shenhav, *Beyond The Two-State Solution* (Polity Press,
2012), 49.

400 **avoided any mention**: Max Blumenthal and Joseph Dana, " How Could the Largest Social Justice Movement in Israel's History Manage to Ignore the Country's
Biggest Moral Disaster?" *Alternet*, August 24, 2011, http://www.alternet.org/story
/152163/how_could_the_largest_social_justice_movement_in_israel's_history_
manage_to_ignore_the_country's_biggest_moral_disaster.

401 **Israel "must at last get rid of**: Blumenthal, "Why the Israeli Elections Were a
Victory for the Right."

401 **Labor Party that founded**: Gidi Weitz, "Leading Labor Party Candidate: I Don't
See Israeli Settlements as a Crime," *Ha'aretz*, August 18, 2011, http://www.haaretz
.com/print-edition/news/leading-labor-party-candidate-i-don-t-see-israeli-settle
ments-as-a-crime-1.379200.

401 **left-wing is a historic**: Jonathan Lis, "Yachimovich: 'To Call Labor 'Left-Wing' Is a
Historic Injustice," *Ha'aretz* [Hebrew], August 11, 2012, http://www.haaretz.co.il/
news/elections/1.1860121.

401 **with Haneen Zoabiz**: Mairav Zonszein, "What Yair Lapid's Anti-Zoabi Comments
Reveal about Israeli Politics," *972 Magazine*, January 26, 2013, http://972mag.com
/what-yair-lapids-anti-zoabi-comments-reveal-about-israeli-politics/64815.

401 **parties agreed**: Jonathan Lis, "Coalition Pact Calls for Bill Making Israel Jewish
First, Democratic Second," *Ha'aretz*, March 17, 2013, http://www.haaretz.com/
news/national/coalition-pact-calls-for-bill-making-israel-jewish-first-democratic
-second.premium-1.509903.

402 **Miri Regev**: Lahav Harkov, "Regev to Chair Knesset Interior Committee," *Jerusalem Post*, March 18, 2013, http://www.jpost.com/Headlines/Article.aspx
?id=306812&R=R101.

402 **advised residents of Haifa**: Lior Dattel, " Israel's New Education Minister Accused
of Past Ethnic Discrimination," *Ha'aretz*, March 20, 2013, http://www.haaretz.com

/news/national/israel-s-new-education-minister-accused-of-past-ethnic-dis
crimination.premium-1.510775.

402 **Moshe Feiglin**: Harkov, "Regev to Chair Knesset Interior Committee." Also see
Nadav Shragai, " Britain Bans Likud's Moshe Feiglin from Entering Country,"
Ha'aretz, March 11, 2008, http://www.haaretz.com/news/britain-bans-likud-s
-moshe-feiglin-from-entering-country-1.241081.

402 **it does look like a wet dream**: Noam Sheizaf, "Settler Leader Calls New Israeli Government 'a Wet Dream,'" *972 Magazine*, March 17, 2013, http://972mag.com/settler
-leader-calls-new-israeli-government-a-wet-dream/67684.

CHAPTER 72: THE SHADOWS AND MIRRORS GAME

403 **Israel has been imposing**: Max Blumenthal, " Eviction of Bab Al Shams Exposes
Israel as a Lawless State," Electronic Intifada, January 14, 2013, http://electronic
intifada.net/content/eviction-bab-al-shams-exposes-israel-lawless-state/12090.

403 **Netanyahu dispatched a lawyer**: Ibid.

404 **There is an urgent security need**: Ibid.

404 **push cameramen away**: "Israel Forcibly Evacuates 'Tent City,'" *Al Jazeera English*,
January 13, 2013, http://www.aljazeera.com/news/middleeast/2013/01
/201311312243144380.html.

405 **strike for over 250 days**: Michael Omer-Man, " Report: Samer Issawi Accepts
Deal to End His Hunger Strike," *972 Magazine*, April 23, 2013, http://972mag.com
/report-samer-issawi-accepts-deal-to-end-hunger-strike/69841.

405 **Issawi wrote**: Gideon Levy, "A letter from a ghost," Ha'aretz, April 11, 2013, http://
www.haaretz.com/print-edition/opinion/a-letter-from-a-ghost.premium-1
.514849.

405 **a group of Israeli intellectuals**: Chaim Levinson, " Top Israeli Authors Plead with
Palestinian Security Prisoner: End Hunger Strike," *Ha'aretz*, April 13, 2013. Also
see, " Zionist Intellectuals Offer a Pizza to Samer Issawi," *FreeHaifa*, April 14, 2013,
http://freehaifa.wordpress.com/2013/04/14/zionist-intellectuals-offer-a-pizza-to
-samer-issawi.

405 **This calls to mind**: Samer Issawi, "Victory Letter of Samer Issawi," *Alternative
News*, April 25, 2013, http://www.alternativenews.org/english/index.php/regions
/jerusalem/6337-victory-letter-of-samer-issawi-.html.

406 **What the fuck**: Edward Said, *Power, Politics, and Culture* (Random House, 2007),
450.

406 **doubled US taxpayer**: Josh Ruebner, "$40 Billion Arms Deal for Israel: Why
Obama's Palestine Rhetoric Rings Hollow," *Alternet*, April 15, 2013, http://www
.alternet.org/world/40-billion-arms-deal-israel-why-obamas-palestine-rhetoric
-rings-hollow.

CHAPTER 73: THE EXODUS PARTY

408 **a full 13 percent**: Joseph Chamie and Barry Mirkin. "The Million Missing Israelis," Foreign Policy, July 5, 2011, http://mideast.foreignpolicy.com/posts/2011/07
/05/the_million_missing_israelis.

408 **The question is not**: "Etty Abramov.Israelis Abroad," *Ynetnews*, September 28,
2005, http://www.somethingjewish.co.uk/articles/1599_israelis_abroad.htm.

408 **more than half would prefer**: Tamar Trabelsi-Hadad, "Half of Israeli Teens Want
to Live Abroad," *Ynetnews*, July 20, 2007, http://www.ynetnews.com/articles
/0,7340,L-3427762,00.html.

408 **84 percent claiming**: Ibid.

408 **they don't tell you**: "Illegal Work in the U.S.: Price Is Too High!—Part I," http://www.youtube.com/watch?v=0LiorPHmGyY&feature=player_embedded.

408 **They will always remain**: Roee Ruttenberg, "Israel Cancels Marriage Ad after Angry Response from US Jews," *972 Magazine*, December 2, 2011, http://972mag.com/israel-cancels-marriage-adverts-following-angry-response-from-american-jews/28757.

409 **Germany is not just**: Juliane von Mittelstaedt, "The Third Generation: Young Israel's New Love Affair with Germany," *Spiegel Online*, April 20, 2012, http://www.spiegel.de/international/world/young-israelis-learning-to-love-germany-and-german-culture-a-828302.html.

409 **an individual's life**: Adi Hagin, "Why Are Israelis Moving to Germany?" *Ha'aretz*, September 16, 2011, http://www.haaretz.com/weekend/week-s-end/why-are-israelis-moving-to-germany-1.384831.

409 **Society cares about them**: Ibid.

410 **headlines back in Israel**: Itamar Eichner, "Israeli Student Joins Other Side of Conflict," *Ynetnews*, November 23, 2010, http://www.ynetnews.com/articles/0,7340,L-3988387,00.html.

INDEX